The Family Letters of
Louis D. Brandeis

The Family Letters of Louis D. Brandeis

Edited by Melvin I. Urofsky and David W. Levy

University of Oklahoma Press : Norman

Also edited by Melvin I. Urofsky and David W. Levy

Letters of Louis D. Brandeis (Albany: State University of New York Press)
  Vol. 1: *Urban Reformer, 1870–1907* (1971)
  Vol. 2: *People's Attorney, 1907–1912* (1972)
  Vol. 3: *Progressive and Zionist, 1913–1915* (1973)
  Vol. 4: *Mr. Justice Brandeis, 1916–1921* (1975)
  Vol. 5: *Elder Statesman, 1921–1941* (1978)
"Half Brother, Half Son": The Letters of Louis D. Brandeis to Felix Frank-furter (Norman: University of Oklahoma Press, 1991)

Publication of this book is made possible through the generous assistance of the National Historical Publications and Records Commission.

Library of Congress Cataloging-in-Publication Data

Brandeis, Louis Dembitz, 1856–1941.
    The family letters of Louis D. Brandeis / edited by Melvin I Urofsky and David W. Levy.
        p.   cm.
    Includes index.
    ISBN 0-8061-3404-6 (hc: alk paper)
    1. Brandeis, Louis Dembitz, 1856–1941—Correspondence.   2. States-men—United States—Correspondence.   3. Judges—United States—Correspondence.   I. Urofsky, Melvin.   II. Levy, David W.   III. Title.

E664.B819 A4 2002
347.73'2634—dc21
[B]

                                                                2002020551

The paper in this book meets the guidelines for permanence and durability of the Committee on Production Guidelines for Book Longevity of the Council on Library Resources, Inc. ∞

1   2   3   4   5   6   7   8   9   10

This book is dedicated
with love and gratitude to the
members of our own families

Contents

Illustrations

viii

Introduction

Thirty-five years have now passed since we embarked upon the work of gathering and editing the letters of Louis Dembitz Brandeis. We (mistakenly) believed that we had completed the project with the publication in the mid-1970s of the five-volume *Letters of Louis D. Brandeis* (State University of New York Press, 1971–78). While working on those volumes, we were given to understand that certain bodies of Brandeis material were not going to be available to us. These included the archive of the law firm of Nutter, McClennen & Fish, the successor firm to Warren & Brandeis; the correspondence between Brandeis and Felix Frankfurter; Brandeis's working papers from his tenure on the Supreme Court; and most of the letters that he wrote to members of his family. Since then, to our surprise and gratification, things have changed with respect to each of these collections of Brandeis material.

In the mid-1960s the senior partners of Nutter, McClennen & Fish believed that client confidentiality precluded opening their files to researchers—even though many of those files were by that time more than seven decades old. After these partners retired, however, their successors reviewed the decision and decided to allow scholarly access to the firm's archive. This occurred too late for us to use those letters, but we are pleased that the Brandeis legal papers are now available on microfilm. Similarly, the Harvard University Law School, the repository of the Court papers, decided to open that collection to researchers; those files are now also available on microfilm.

The Frankfurter letters and those written to members of the family posed different problems. After Brandeis's death in 1941, Justice Frankfurter went to Louisville (the main depository of Brandeis's papers) and removed or destroyed many of his own letters to the Justice. Fortunately, he kept the letters *from* Brandeis, which were deposited in the Library of Congress after his death. Frankfurter's gift, however, allowed his designated biographer, Max Freedman, to control and even to remove files temporarily. Freedman removed the Brandeis folders and left a handful of barely legible thermofax copies in their place. His purpose in doing so remains unknown. Shortly afterward Freedman became seriously ill, and the folders containing Brandeis's letters to Frankfurter were not returned to the Library of Congress until well after his death. The richness of that collection led the two of us to return to the project after a hiatus of more than ten years. In the end we selected, edited, and published 671 of the letters in *"Half Brother, Half Son": The Letters of Louis D. Brandeis to Felix Frankfurter* (University of Oklahoma Press, 1991).

The family letters—the materials that constitute the present volume—are yet another story. When we began gathering the letters for our initial volumes, we approached both of Justice Brandeis's daughters, Susan Brandeis Gilbert and Elizabeth Brandeis Raushenbush. Ms. Gilbert told us that she had not kept any of her father's letters. But after her death two of her children, Alice Brandeis Popkin and Frank Brandeis Gilbert, found among their mother's papers several boxes of family materials, which they deposited in the Goldfarb Library of Brandeis University. When we learned about this, we approached Ms. Popkin and Mr. Gilbert and asked their permission to edit and publish some of those letters in an effort to round out the Brandeis project. They graciously agreed to our request, and we wish to thank them heartily for their permission and for their support of our work.

Brandeis's other daughter, Professor Elizabeth Raushenbush (who was until the end of her life an ardent and generous champion of our project), informed us that she had numerous letters from her father, but that for reasons of privacy she felt unable to turn them over to us. Instead she went through her papers and allowed us to print in their entirety around two dozen letters and to utilize in our annotation fragments from many others.[1] She also told us that it was her intention to destroy the bulk of the letters from her father before her death. Unfortunately, from a scholar's point of view, she carried out her intention.[2] But, we are very glad to say, she could not quite bring herself to destroy one very special group of her father's letters.

The one body of correspondence that Elizabeth Raushenbush did not have the heart to destroy consisted of several dozen letters written by her father to her mother, Alice, during their courtship. Alice Brandeis had shown these letters to Alpheus T. Mason, who used portions of them in his pioneering 1946 biography, *Brandeis: A Free Man's Life*. We republished those excerpts from Mason's biography in volume 1 of the *Brandeis Letters*, supplemented by a few additional paragraphs provided by Ms. Raushenbush. On her death, she left those letters to her niece, Alice Popkin. When we began discussing this volume with Ms. Popkin and Mr.

1. The source of the letters that we have republished in this volume is indicated as "EBR."

2. A few letters, however, escaped and eventually found their way into the hands of Elizabeth Raushenbush's son, Professor Walter Raushenbush, then of Madison, Wisconsin. He generously permitted one of us to search through the papers in his basement and to remove, edit, and publish those letters that we judged to be historically important. The source of these letters is indicated in the pages that follow as "Raushenbush MSS."

Gilbert, Ms. Popkin suggested that for a truly complete picture of her grandfather those letters should be integrated into the other family correspondence. For this act of generosity we are especially thankful to her.

Needless to say, had it been possible to do so, we would have merged all of these collections into one seamless chronological project, so that both scholars and general readers would have been able to see simultaneously the private as well as the public man, the lawyer as well as the jurist, the citizen as well as the reformer, the man of public affairs as well as the loving husband, father, and grandfather. The image that would then have emerged might have gone far to dissipate the portrait of Brandeis as cold, aloof, and lacking in basic human emotions, a man whose letters, according to one characterization, read like legal briefs.

We were faced by similar predicaments in the volume devoted to the Frankfurter letters and in this volume. We had already published portions of the then-available correspondence in our first five volumes. If we omitted the letters we had already published, we felt that the remaining letters would present a jagged narrative and tell an incomplete story. We chose, therefore, to include certain already published letters so that this volume, like the Frankfurter collection, can tell a more complete story. Thus in addition to the great bulk of heretofore unpublished letters in this volume, readers will also find some previously published letters to Brandeis's brother Alfred, to his wife, to his daughter Elizabeth, and to other members of the family. We believe that this decision is warranted on both scholarly and narrative grounds—the need to allow the letters to tell the fullest possible story of the relationship between the man and his family.

We feel obliged to note that before the completion of this volume Ms. Popkin and Mr. Gilbert decided, upon serious reflection, to withdraw their permission to present about three dozen of the letters we had hoped to publish here. Those letters touched upon health matters, internal family finances, and other topics that, in their judgments, intruded unduly upon the private affairs of the Brandeis family. As scholars, of course, we greatly regretted that withdrawal of permission—not only for the obvious reasons, but also because it seemed to us that none of the proscribed letters showed any member of the family behaving in any but the most affectionate, honorable, and respectful way. In the end we reluctantly submitted to the stipulation. We did so partly because we acknowledge the right of Ms. Popkin and Mr. Gilbert, under the terms of the gift; partly out of deference to their standards of family privacy; and partly out of the strongest possible conviction that the letters published here—even without the omitted handful—constitute a contribution of enormous and lasting value to the scholarly community. (In philosophic moments, moreover, we had to admit that it was not entirely inappropriate that two of the grandchildren of the man whose 1890 article had done so much to define "the right to privacy"[3] should, eleven decades later, invoke the right themselves.) We make particular note of this matter because we realize that those who are most familiar with Brandeis's life are already aware of these tender areas and will almost certainly wonder why we failed to include materials on these subjects. This is especially true since the popular 1983 biography by Lewis Paper,[4] who researched the letters before the donors realized the full extent of the collection, quoted passages from some of the letters in question.

That the letters presented here do in fact represent a very substantial contribution to our understanding of Louis Brandeis and of the time in which he lived is undeniable and will be obvious, we believe, to any reader. We think that these letters are especially important for two reasons in particular. First, they reveal the extent to which Brandeis was involved in the innermost workings of the progressive movement. In the daily letters that he wrote home to Alice from Washington (quite unself-consciously recounting his busy day's activities), historians will be able to see how President Woodrow Wilson, virtually all of his cabinet officers, and a score of prominent senators and representatives resorted to Brandeis regularly for advice on almost every aspect of public affairs. We think that the letters written from 1912 through 1916 (and some during American participation in World War I) will demonstrate more clearly than any other available source the central role that Brandeis played in the formation of national policy.

Second, readers of this volume will emerge with an image of Brandeis much different from the one derived both from our own earlier volumes and from many of the published biographies. Here we see a young man head-over-heels in love, who throughout his long life maintained an unwavering devotion to his wife, a daily interest in the lives and careers of his daughters, and a touching pride in the youthful achievements of his grandchildren. We detect in these intimate letters a man who reveled in family and took with utmost seriousness the obligations of kinship. There is nothing cold or detached or aloof about the private Brandeis, but it is perfectly in keeping with his views of privacy that while he was alive he kept this part of his life and personality hidden from public view.

We have followed the same general rules of editing and annotation as in our earlier volumes. We have attempted to include a representative

3. Louis D. Brandeis and Samuel D. Warren, "The Right to Privacy," 4 *Harvard Law Review* 193 (1890).

4. Lewis Paper, *Brandeis* (Englewood Cliffs, 1983).

sampling of letters that give as full a view as possible of Brandeis within the context of family relationships. In our notes we have striven to make each letter more comprehensible than it otherwise would have been. We try to identify every name that Brandeis mentions at its first appearance, to explain some aspects of problems and events as well as the laws and judicial cases he discusses, and to call attention to other letters (both in this volume and in the others) that might shed further light on the subject. In the interest of conserving space for more letters, we have omitted most bibliographic references to previous studies of the issues and personalities to which Brandeis alludes. With only a few exceptions we have published each letter in its entirety. And once again we owe a great debt to scholars, librarians, and archivists too numerous to mention who have helped us over the years.

There are, however, some debts related to this volume in particular that we are eager to acknowledge. The National Endowment for the Humanities supported this project with a generous grant, just as it supported the earlier volumes, and we can never adequately express our gratitude to the NEH for its faith in our project and in us. Smaller but critical awards were given by the Virginia Commonwealth University Faculty Research Fund and the Research Council of the University of Oklahoma. All of the handwritten letters from the Gilbert collection were originally transcribed by Philip E. Urofsky, then a student at the University of Virginia Law School and now a senior trial attorney with the U.S. Department of Justice. Throughout this undertaking we have benefited regularly from the wise counsel and limitless knowledge of Brandeis embodied in our friend and co-worker Philippa Strum. We reiterate our warm thanks to Eric Tachau, Alice Brandeis Popkin, Frank Brandeis Gilbert, and Walter Brandeis Raushenbush for their consistent and generous support of our work. We owe a special debt to Frank Gilbert, who at the very end of our labors undertook an extremely meticulous reading of the entire manuscript; he saved us from a number of embarrassing errors and was able to elaborate and enrich several of our editorial notes. We also received valuable assistance from Helga Madland, Karin L. Schutjer, Richard Lowitt, Benjamin R. Levy, Dirk Voss, Joseph Bendersky, and Peter Schulz. Our experience with the University of Oklahoma Press has been gratifying from start to finish; while we owe many debts to the staff there, we wish to single out especially John Drayton, the director; Jean Hurtado, the able and always helpful acquisitions editor, who worked closely with us from the start; and Alice Stanton, whose editorial skills, professionalism, efficiency, and unfailing pleasantness made the production of this volume a real delight. Our copy editor, Kathy Burford Lewis, subjected the manuscript to a very thorough final reading, expertly catching a number of mistakes and greatly improving the readability of our editorial notes. Valerie Sanders, editorial assistant, provided invaluable help with the proofreading. The index was capably prepared by Robert R. Fayles.

On other occasions we have expressed—however inadequately—our gratitude to our wives, Susan and Lynne, who did not realize when they took us for better or for worse that they were also taking Louis Brandeis into their lives. Our children have grown up thinking that someone called "LDB" was a part of their families—and in many ways he was. As we bring this long project to its conclusion, we thank our families for their tolerance and support, knowing that neither words alone nor the formal dedication of this volume in their honor can ever fully express the measure of our gratitude and our debt. Back in 1978, as we wrote the acknowledgments to volume 5, we addressed some similar closing words to the members of our families: "We can now say to them, and to all those many others who helped us so generously, 'We have finished.'" It was, of course, a lie. Now, twenty-three years later, we boldly repeat the assertion. And this time we really mean it.

Melvin I. Urofsky

Richmond, Virginia

David W. Levy

Norman, Oklahoma

Chronology

1822   Father, Adoph, born

1829   Mother, Frederika born

1849   May, Brandeis, Dembitz, and Wehle families arrive in America
September 5, Adolph Brandeis weds Frederika Dembitz

1851   Sister Fannie born
Family settles in Louisville, Kentucky

1852   April 9, sister Amy born

1854   March 23, brother Alfred born

1856   November 13, LDB born in Louisville, Kentucky

1872   August 10, Brandeis family leaves for three-year stay in Europe

1873   Enrolls in Annen-Realschule in Dresden, Germany

1875   Family returns to the United States
September, enrolls in Harvard Law School

1877   Graduates first in his class

1878   September, begins practice of law in St Louis
November, first courtroom experience

1879   July, returns to Boston to open partnership with Samuel D. Warren, Jr.

1881   July, publishes first article in *American Law Review*
July, admitted to the Massachusetts bar

1882   September, teaches one-year course on evidence at Harvard Law; decides against a teaching career

1887   Helps found *Harvard Law Review*

1889   Partnership with Warren dissolved
November, argues first case before the Supreme Court

1890   March 5, sister Fannie commits suicide
March, becomes reacquainted with Alice Goldmark (AGB) and begins serious courtship
October 4, engaged to Alice Goldmark
December, publishes "Right to Privacy" with Samuel Warren in *Harvard Law Review*

1891   March 23, marries Alice Goldmark

1893   February 27, first daughter, Susan, born

1896   April 25, second daughter, Elizabeth, born

1897   Appears before House Ways and Means Committee to oppose Dingley Tariff
Law firm reorganized as Brandeis, Dunbar & Nutter
April 30, opposes charter revision of Boston Elevated line

September, hearings on advanced freight rate case

September 2, Garment Workers' Protocol agreement signed

October 12, Interstate Commerce Commission (ICC) advanced freight rate hearings begin in Washington

November 1, claims railroads might save a million dollars a day by employing scientific management

December 9, gives interview on "The Jews as a Priest People" in *Jewish Advocate*

1911   January, federal government brings suit against United Shoe Machinery Company

January 17, argument before ICC in advanced freight rate case

March 7, Secretary Ballinger resigns

March 27, delivers "The New Conception of Industrial Efficiency" to Economic Club of New York

April 22, publishes "Organized Labor and Efficiency" in *Survey*

November 28, publishes "Using Other People's Money" in *New York American*

December 14–16, antitrust testimony before the Senate Committee on Interstate Commerce

1912   January, agrees to aid Stanley Committee investigation of U S. Steel

January 26–27, antitrust testimony to House Judiciary Committee

February 2, Robert La Follette collapses during presidential campaign

July 2, Democrats nominate Woodrow Wilson

July 20, publicly endorses Wilson in *Boston American*

August 13, meets Jacob deHaas, who awakens his interest in Zionism

August 28, meets Wilson for extended conference at Sea Girt, New Jersey

Mid-September, sets out on political stump tour for Wilson

September 14, publishes "Trusts, Efficiency, and the New Party" in *Collier's*

September 28, Wilson wires asking for advice on "major economic issues"; LDB replies September 30

October, publishes "Business—the New Profession" in *System*

November 2, interviewed in *New York Times*, "Regulation of Competition against the Regulation of Monopoly"

November 5, Wilson elected president

December 13, publishes "The New England Railroad Situation" in *Boston Journal*

1913   March 1, Wilson announces cabinet selections without LDB

March 1, publication of Pujo Committee report

March 4, Wilson inaugurated

August 14, refuses Wilson's request that he serve on Mexican arbitration commission

November 7, Wilson reelected

November 13, LDB celebrates sixtieth birthday

1917   April 2, Wilson asks for declaration of war against Germany

April 23, LDB meets Balfour

May 6, long discussion with Wilson on Zionist matters, including a possible British mandate over Palestine

May 7, private talk with Balfour

October 14, receives proposed text for Balfour Declaration

November 2, Balfour Declaration issued

1918   May 25, proposes reorganization scheme for American Zionism

November 11, World War I ends

December, first American Jewish Congress meets in Philadelphia

1919   January 18, Versailles Peace Conference opens

May 7, treaty presented to Germany

June 14, sails with party for England on *Mauretania*

June 20, arrives in England and meets Chaim Weizmann

June 23, party arrives in Paris

June 25, leaves Marseilles for Egypt

July 8, party arrives in Jerusalem

July 26, leaves Port Said for return to Marseilles

August, Zionist meetings in London

August 30, sails from England for home

September 25, Wilson suffers collapse in Colorado

November 10, dissents in *Abrams v. U.S.* free speech case

November 19, Senate rejects Treaty of Versailles

1920   April 20, Palestine becomes a British mandate

June 13, leaves for London Zionist conference

July 7, delivers "The Upbuilding of Palestine" address at London conference of World Zionist Organization

August 19, sets sail for home on the *Zeeland*

1921   April 2, Weizmann arrives in New York

April 26, meets Albert Einstein in Washington

June 5–7, Zionist convention at Cleveland defeats LDB-Mack administration; with thirty-six others, resigns official positions in Zionist Organization of America (ZOA)

June 19, resigns as honorary president of World Zionist Organization

July 16–17, LDB-Mack forces reorganize after the Cleveland convention

November 8, Franklin Roosevelt defeats Herbert Hoover

1933   January 30, Adolf Hitler becomes chancellor of Germany

March 4, Roosevelt becomes president, First Hundred Days begin

1934   April 19, longtime secretary and head of Savings Bank Life Insurance (SBLI) Alice Grady dies

June 7, meets with Roosevelt on unemployment compensation bill

1935   March 6, Holmes dies

May 27, "black Monday," as Court strikes down National Recovery and Frazier-Lemke Acts

1936   January 6, Court declares Agricultural Adjustment Act unconstitutional

November 3, Roosevelt elected to second term

November 13, LDB celebrates eightieth birthday

1937   February 5, Roosevelt proposes "Court-packing" scheme

March 21, Jacob deHaas dies

September 26, E. A. Filene dies

1938   January 5, Governor Herbert Lehman proposes Savings Bank Insurance for New York

March 16, New York legislature passes SBLI law

April 25, delivers opinion in *Erie Railroad Co. v. Tompkins*

September 28, European leaders meet at Munich

November 9–10, *Kristallnacht* in Germany

1939   January 5, Roosevelt nominates Felix Frankfurter to the Supreme Court

February 13, resigns from the Supreme Court

March 20, Roosevelt nominates William O. Douglas to replace LDB on the Court

May 17, MacDonald White Paper issued

August 23, Molotov-Ribbentrop agreement

September 1, Germany invades Poland; start of World War II

1940   November 5, Roosevelt elected to third term

1941   March 23, LDB and AGB quietly celebrate their fiftieth anniversary

June 13, Harlan Fiske Stone nominated to succeed Hughes as Chief Justice

October 1, suffers heart attack

October 5, LDB dies in Washington, D.C., at age 84

1945   October 12, Alice Goldmark Brandeis dies

1966   April 8, Jacob H. Gilbert dies in New York City

1975   October 8, Susan Brandeis Gilbert dies in New York City

1980   January 17, Paul A. Raushenbush dies in Madison, Wisconsin

1984   April 30, Elizabeth Brandeis Raushenbush dies in Madison, Wisconsin

Sources

Brandeis MSS   Louis Dembitz Brandeis Papers, University of Louisville Law Library, Louisville Kentucky

EBR   Letters provided through the courtesy of the late Elizabeth Brandeis Raushenbush, Madison, Wisconsin

Fannie Brandeis   Letters provided through the courtesy of the late Fannie Brandeis of Louisville, Kentucky

Gilbert MSS   Gilbert Family Papers, Goldfarb Library of Brandeis University, Waltham, Massachusetts

Goldmark MSS   Pauline Goldmark Papers, Manuscript Division, Library of Congress, Washington, D.C.

H. Nagel   Letters provided through the courtesy of the late Hildegarde Nagel of New York city and Norwalk, Connecticut

Mason, *Brandeis*   Alpheus Thomas Mason, *Brandeis: A Free Man's Life* (New York: Viking Press, 1946)

Popkin MSS   Letters in the possession of Alice Brandeis Popkin, Chatham, Massachusetts

Raushenbush MSS   Letters provided through the courtesy of Professor Walter Brandeis Raushenbush, San Diego, California

Wehle MSS   Louis Brandeis Wehle Papers, Franklin D. Roosevelt Library, Hyde Park, New York

The Family Letters of
Louis D. Brandeis

To: Otto A. Wehle
Date: March 12, 1876
Place: Cambridge, Massachusetts
Source: Brandeis MSS

DEAR OTTO:[1] Writing to *you* after a silence of five months, it is not, I suppose necessary for me to commence my letter, as most do on similar occasions, with the usual preliminary observations, the stereotype introduction consisting of tiresome or even untrue excuses.

Indeed I am not sure whether I was not doing you a great favor by keeping silent so long & with a true feeling of charity forbearing to increase the number of your epistolary debts, which were, I believe, pressing you very hard when I left Louisville.

You have undoubtedly heard from other[s] of my work here,[2] how well I am pleased with everything that pertains to the law, yet my own inclination would prompt me to repeat the same to you, though at the risk of great reiteration. My thoughts are almost entirely occupied by the law, and you know: Wovon das Herz voll ist u.s.w.[3]

Law schools are splendid institutions. Aside from the instruction there received, being able continually to associate with young men who have the same interest and ambition, who are determined to make as great progress as possible in their studies and devote all their time to the same— must alone be of inestimable advantages. Add to this the instruction of consummate lawyers, who devote their whole time to *you*, and a complete law-library of over fifteen thousand volumes and then compare the opportunities for learning which a student of the law has at Harvard Law School and in a law-office. After one has grasped the principles which underlie the structure of the Common Law, I doubt not, that one can learn very much in an office—That first year at law is, however, surely ill-spent in an office.

I remember, a few Sundays before I left L[ouisville]—you, Al[4] and I were up in your room comfortably reclining on the bed, and talking about lectures. You thought they were of no earthly use—and I almost agree with you now. A lecture alone is little better than the reading of textbooks, but such lectures as we have here in connection with our other work are quite different things. Idem non est idem.[5]

Our law-clubs are grand institutions, a great incentive to labor and the work for them is a pleasant change.[6] Last Friday we had a very interesting case.

In an action for manslaughter the d[e]f[endan]t, by virtue of a certain statute, was allowed to testify in his own behalf and testified: "I did not strike

I.S." He was acquitted and proof of his guilt being afterwards obtained was indicted for perjury. The counsel for the dft requested the Judge at Nisi Prius[7] to instruct the Jury—that if the dft had proved that the jury at the former trial had passed on the point, that the dft did not strike I.S. then they should find for the dft in this action. Judge refused so to rule and motion is made for a new trial. According to the Old English practice, as the case presented great difficulties, the same was twice argued—the counsel not having brought out at the first argument the points, which their Honors were most in doubt about. After great consideration the rule for a new trial was made absolute on the ground of estoppel,[8] the court being of opinion that the learned judge had erred in refusing to give the instructions suggested by the counsel. The reasoning of the court was as follows:—

To establish the perjury, it must be proved that dft did not strike I.S. By the judgment in the previous case, it was conclusively settled as between the same parties (Commonwealth, v Dft) that the dft did not kill I.S. Dft offered to prove by parol evidence[9] that the particular controversy sought to be concluded, i.e., whether he struck I.S. or not, had been necessarily tried and determined by the jury in the former trial and that the verdict there given could not have been rendered without deciding that particular matter. Court was of opinion that a judgment did not create an estoppel simply to the one matter in issue e.g. whether dft had killed I.S. or not, but also as to other matters *necessarily* involved in deciding that point; that it was competent for dft to introduce parol evidence to show what was really decided if it did not appear upon the record, & that the doctrine of estoppel applies equally to civil and criminal cases. The question was a difficult one to decide, as there is not a single decision upon the point and the counsel could argue only from analogies and general principles. What do you think of our decision? I wish you would let me know. It is a very nice question on the law of estoppel.

Have you seen "Hermann on Estoppel"[?][10] It is quite a good book—though not as well arranged as Bigelow.[11] Some of our professors are trying to inculcate in us a great distrust of textbooks, and to prove to us the truth of the maxim—"Melius est petere fontes quam sectari rivulas."[12] When one sees how loosely most text-books are written and how many startling propositions are unsupported by the authorities cited to sustain them—the temptation to become a convert of Coke's is very great.

Several text-books however, some late English ones, receive almost unqualified praise—among which is Leake's admirable work on Contracts.[13] Of course no one would dare to detract from Stephen's fame,[14] but to Parsons[15] and even Story[16] the epithet of "loose" is not infrequently bestowed. The rising lights among our professors are James B. Ames[17]

4

and John C. Gray Jr.[18]—the latter the editor of the last ed[ition] of Story on "Partnership" and formerly editor of the American Law Review. The former—a graduate of Harvard College and Law School, who has never practiced law, a man of the most eminent abilities as instructor, possessing an infallibly logical mind and a thorough knowledge of the Common Law. As [*][19] C.B. would say—"He'll make his mark." But enough for today. If you have not been too much bored by this letter and would like to hear any more "legal talk"—just write—and I promise you a speedy answer. Your loving cousin

1. Otto A. Wehle (1845–1931) came to Louisville from Prague in 1867 and began practice of law there a year later. From 1870 to 1874 he was in partnership with Lewis Dembitz and then opened an office of his own. A few years later he married LDB's sister Amy and became a close friend of LDB. While never achieving either the financial success of LDB or the legal eminence of Dembitz, Wehle did a fair amount of corporate work in Louisville, especially for the tobacco companies.

2. In September 1875 LDB entered the Harvard Law School after a basic preparation in the Louisville schools and the Annen-Realschule in Dresden. He entered Harvard at a most propitious time, as the institution was then being reformed and revitalized by Christopher Columbus Langdell (1826–1906). Dean Langdell tightened entrance requirements, upgraded the faculty, and, most importantly, introduced the case method of study, through which the evolution of the law and basic principles could be examined in a scientific manner. For LDB's enthusiasm, see his article "The Harvard Law School," *Green Bag* 1 (1889): 10–25.

3. Whereof the heart is full, etc.

4. Alfred Brandeis (1854–1928) throughout his life was to remain LDB's closest friend. After a year at Washington University in St. Louis, Alfred entered into a business partnership with his father and went on to become a leading merchant and an influential citizen of Louisville. When LDB settled in Boston, he wrote almost daily to his brother. After his retirement, LDB began to destroy these letters but was stopped by his daughter Elizabeth before he had completed the task. While some of the remaining letters are included in this volume for continuity, the majority are published in Urofsky and Levy, eds., *Letters of Louis D. Brandeis*, 5 vols. (Albany, 1971–78). Hereafter these volumes are cited as BL.

5. The same is not the same.

6. Law clubs were forerunners of the current moot court system. Entirely run by students, they provided would-be lawyers a chance to practice using established cases. LDB belonged to the Pow-Wow Club.

7. *Nisi prius* courts are those for the trial of issues before a jury and one presiding judge. In the United States any forum—regardless of its technical term—in which the case is tried by jury (as distinguished from an appellate court) is a *nisi prius* court.

8. There are various forms of estoppel that are used to stop or preclude an action that is tainted by suspected fraud or illegality.

9. Oral or verbal evidence.

10. Henry M. Hermann, *The Law of Estoppel*, 2 vols. (Albany, 1871).

11. Melville Madison Bigelow, *Law of Estoppel* (Boston, 1872).

12. The maxim of the great English jurist Sir Edward Coke (1552–1634): "It is better to go to the wellsprings than to follow the rivulets downhill."

13. Stephen Martin Leake, *Law of Contracts* (London, 1867).

14. Henry John Stephen was a noted English jurist whose *New Commentaries on the Laws of England*, 4 vols. (London, 1841–45), included a volume on contracts.

15. Theophilus Parsons, *The Law of Contracts*, 6th ed., 3 vols. (Boston, 1873).

16. Joseph Story (1779–1845), famed jurist, Associate Justice of the Supreme Court, and Dane Professor of Law at the Harvard Law School, wrote many books. LDB is probably referring to Story's *Commentaries on Equity Jurisprudence*, 11th ed. (Boston, 1873).

17. James Barr Ames (1846–1910) graduated from the Harvard Law School in 1872 and would be handpicked by Langdell as his successor. A brilliant teacher, he helped spread the new case method through his students, at least nine of whom became deans in other law schools. Ames also wrote a great deal and contributed a number of texts to the study of law.

18. John Chipman Gray (1839–1915) wrote many legal texts; he served as Story Professor at the Harvard Law School from 1875 to 1883 and Royall Professor from 1883 to 1913.

19. An asterisk is used throughout this volume to indicate an indecipherable or illegible word. Each asterisk represents one word.

To:	Amy Brandeis Wehle
Date:	January 20, 1877
Place:	Cambridge, Massachusetts
Source:	Wehle MSS

DEAREST AMY:[1] Still nothing from you & I fear ill-health is the cause.

Otto's New Year's congratulation I enjoyed very much. It was a real budget of news & brought much interesting matter. I should only have wished for more law-gossip and that he had told me more about the cases with which he is now occupied. Have not the Guthrie & Engeln cases come up for argument in the Count of Appeals[?][2] I have for some time been awaiting copies of the briefs.

Otto merely mentions that law-business is dull as all other. I wish Otto would employ any leisure he may have in law-writing. I feel that his strength lies in that direction and that law-writing would be an avenue of fame & profit for him. Not only that he would become known to the legal world & get paid for his work, but the amount of knowledge acquired by the work necessarily done in preparation for writing would be of immense value to him in his practice.

I am sure he would derive a great deal of satisfaction & pleasure from this kind of work.

What a delightful occupation for leisure moments, which might otherwise be devoted to unprofitable meditation on the dullness of the times. Giving has always seemed better to me than receiving—Why always absorb—why be forever reading, reading, reading—& never produce, never give anything in return. I wish my eyes would let me do some independent work, I should revel in it.[3]

You promised me to attempt to prevail on Otto to undertake some legal labor of this kind. Have you forgotten all about it? Law seems so interesting to me in all its aspects;—it is difficult for me to understand that any of the initiated should not burn with enthusiasm.

I am anxiously looking forward to the time when I shall again be able to satisfy my desperate longing for more law.

When I began this letter I intended to talk to you of Grillparzer's "König Ottokar,"[4] which Marcou[5] has been reading to me, & of the delightful evening I spent at the Cochrane's[6] yesterday talking over Europe & taking again the incomparable trip from Silvaplana over the Helvio[7] but of this no more today.

Good-bye, much love to Otto & the others. Lovingly

Tell Clay I received his letter & postal & return my Thanks. Why don't Otto send me his photo. I *shall not* criticize it.

1. Amy Brandeis Wehle (1852–1906) was the younger of LDB's two sisters.
2. *Mueller v. Engeln*, 75 Ky. 441 (1876). The case was argued on appeal from the Louisville Chancery Court, and a decision was handed down on 6 December 1876. There is no record of a Guthrie case in the Kentucky *Reports*.
3. Throughout these years LDB suffered from eyestrain, a fairly common ailment among students of the time due to the poor lighting available. He consulted several doctors, some of whom advised him to give up the law. Finally one told him to "read less and think more." Partially as a result of his defective sight, Brandeis cultivated his already formidable powers of memory and concentration.
4. Franz Grillparzer's play *König Ottokars Glück und Ende* (1823) depicts the conflicts between Ottokar of Bohemia and Rudolph of Hapsburg.
5. Philippe Belknap Marcou (1855–1927), after graduating from Harvard and taking a doctorate at Berlin, returned to become professor of romance languages at Harvard. In 1901 he left the university after a sensational breach-of-promise scandal involving a woman of rather dubious reputation, Annie L. Manley.
6. The Cochrans were a well-known Louisville family. One daughter, Jessie, was a talented pianist who had studied with Louis H. Hast, the organizer of many musical societies in Louisville. LDB played in one of them. She later studied in Europe with Franz Liszt and, after living in Boston for a while, settled in Italy. Her cousin Helen Cochran was her frequent companion. LDB often spells the name "Cochrane."
7. In eastern Switzerland.

To:	Amy Brandeis Wehle
Date:	April 5, 1877
Place:	Cambridge, Massachusetts
Source:	Wehle MSS

DEAREST AMY: Unfortunately I am not epistolarily disposed today and you must prepare yourself for an unusually stupid letter. I should wait for a happier moment but for the fact that the 9th of April[1] is drawing nigh

At last I have received a letter from you; a nice long one, but not near long enough to compensate for your unbroken silence almost of months.

Until hearing from you last Monday I was uncertain where I should address my birth-day letter, as no one had written within the last two weeks of your movements; probably because you remain stationary, which for dear Fan's[2] sake I am very glad to see,—and for your own too.

Of Minnie Ruport's engagement I had heard from Albert[3] and Alfred, the latter, of course, bewailing my sad fate, and endeavoring to console poor me who has lost forever "two friends" this season. But never mind! You speak of a new world to conquer. Do let me know something more about it! "Bereft, as I am, of all that was dear" such information might restore me to my former self.

Last week I spent two quite pleasant evenings at the Ross'. Denman Ross[4] invited me to attend the meeting of their little "Art Club," or rather Ruskin Club which met Tuesday a week ago. They are reading and discussing Ruskin's "Seven Lamps";[5] but the greatest attraction is the collection of photographs which Denman Ross has bought for the purpose of illustrating and explaining the lectures by Ruskin. They read a part of the "Lamp of Truth"—on the decline and fall of Gothic Architecture, tracing its history through the different periods; from the round to the pointed arch; from the solid to the penetrated stone-work; from the tracery in light to the tracery in stone—ending in the horizontal period of Gothic Architecture. How wise one becomes? Two weeks ago I should not have had any idea what all this means, and now I can write so learnedly on the subject! But really the evening was a very instructive one; Denman Ross explained his pictures of which he has thousands, among which are many rare and large ones, and I feel now that I might possibly understand architecture if I devoted a few centuries to the study of it. I have since the evening at the Ross [sic] felt some little curiosity to read more of Ruskin's works something which surely I was never before tempted to do. I saw an original sketchbook of Ruskin[']s, too, which belongs to Prof Norton,[6] our art professor;—but enthusiasm for the cause which enabled others to find some beauty in his daubs & stray pencil-strokes was lacking in my case, and I think I should be obliged to put them on a par with the sketches of some of our English friends at Silvaplana. Probably Ruskin's admirers would treat me with the contempt which Swinburne has for those who fail to recognize Rossetti (& himself) as the greatest of English poets.[7] They would probably say that I was lacking in the elevated feeling and thorough art-culture which alone qualifies one for the understanding of sublime works.

For Saturday evening I was also invited to the Ross' to dinner (6 P.M.) and stayed there till near midnight. There were three or four young ladies & same number of gents invited & the time passed quite pleasantly with eating, talking, music, and "chumps", an improvement on "Yes & No" which you ought to introduce in the West if not already known there. The company divides itself into two "camps", each occupying a separate room. One emissary from each camp goes out of the room; the two choose a question and the emissary from Camp A. goes into Camp B. and vice versa. The company i.e. the soldiers of each camp, asks the enemy's emissary as many questions as possible, he answering either "yes" or "no". The camp which guesses the problem first retains the emissary as captive and receives back its own emissary in triumph. When one of the camps is broken up the game ends. It is far more exciting than "Yes & No."

The game taught me, at least, that Cambridge young ladies, who have had the advantages of a European education are not necessarily omniscient; the problem to be solved by the camps was the "Shadows of the Pyramids of Egypt" and the two young ladies who proposed it, concurred in the opinion that Egypt is in Asia. On the discovery of their error there was some slight blushing. Jessie [Cochran] was to have been at the Ross'—but did not make her appearance. She was not feeling quite well I believe. Cochrans have left the Evans House and have rooms now at No 62 Bowdoin St.

I see that it is time for me to be off to the Law-school and this letter must leave Cambridge to-day. So Good-bye, ever so much love, & ever so many kisses from your

loving brother

Tell Charlie[8] that his letter of the 19th March was duly received.

1. Amy's birthday was on 9 April.
2. Fannie Brandeis (1851–90) was LDB's eldest sister; the year before she had married Charles Nagel (see note 8 below).
3. Albert Brandeis was LDB's cousin, the son of his uncle Samuel.
4. Denman Waldo Ross (1853–1935) was an expert on the fine arts, an occasional lecturer on architecture and design at Harvard, and a renowned collector. His work on behalf of the Boston Museum made that institution's collection one of the foremost in the country. The author of several books on a number of subjects, Ross frequently hosted discussion groups in Cambridge and was a close friend of LDB during these years and after. Ross gave LDB a number of valuable works of art, and LDB supervised and managed Ross's personal economic affairs until he went onto the Supreme Court in 1916.
5. John Ruskin, *The Seven Lamps of Architecture* (London, 1849).
6. Charles Eliot Norton (1827–1908) taught art history at Harvard from 1874 to 1898 and wrote a number of books on art and literature, including a study of Ruskin.
7. Algernon Charles Swinburne (1837–1901) and Dante Gabriel Rossetti (1828–82).
8. Charles Nagel (1849–1940) married Fannie Brandeis on 4 August 1876. Nagel met Alfred Brandeis while both were students at Washington University in St. Louis. He became a prominent attorney in St. Louis and active in Republican Party affairs; in 1909 President William Howard Taft named him secretary of commerce and labor.

To: Amy Brandeis Wehle
Date: December 2, 1877
Place: Cambridge, Massachusetts
Source: Wehle MSS

DEAREST AMY: Finally you are to receive thanks for your three letters, for the bracket, photograph and so forth. As to the photograph it is poor enough for all practical purposes, e.g. building a fire; but the bracket is a beauty. Emerton[1] wants to get himself one like it. At present the bracket supports a group of Angels by Raphael which Dr. Nagel[2] sent me.

I have been quite a society man for the past week—out for breakfast, out for lunch, out for dinner, out out [sic] for teas—almost less "ins" than "outs". Tuesday evening I spent at Prof. Bradley's and talked a great part of the time to a ninny of a stepdaughter, instead of to the Judge[3] & his son[4] (rather an interesting fellow)—purely for the sake of gallantry.

Wednesday evening I went to the Richards[,] studied about two hours & a half, then talked for about three quarters of an hour to Mother & daughter, and from eleven to o'clock [sic] listened to an article from the "New Quarterly" on the "Lord Chancellors & Chief Justices since Lord Campbell."[5]

I have been so fearfully "solid" for years past that I really felt quite guilty on retiring at such a late, or rather early, hour. Of course I stayed at the Richards over night and lounged about their house the next day till half-past eleven; then made a call at the Cochrans and had hardly spent an hour in my room before it was time to dress for dinner at the Parkers. The invitation was for 4 P.M. & the company broke up at eleven o'clock. Spent a very enjoyable evening, though it must be confessed that all Cambridge people are not intellectual giants. We had quite an exciting time over "Chumps" and managed to be very jolly for this staid old Cambridge.

Last night was of course devoted to Jessie's German and to-day I dined at the Ross'. What a programme of amusements. This, however, was an unusual rush and seeing only comparitively [sic] little of "Society" I generally enjoy myself in it. Very much of society would surely bore me. I could discuss the merits of Mr. Porter's portraits or Mr. Hunt's landscapes[6] fourteen times with considerable interest—but not oftener. How many times one does make the same remark (Al would suggest that more than one do likewise).

I saw very many pretty photographs at the Ross'—most of them of Italian architecture. One picture of Lucca (the city) with the surrounding villa-clad mountains made me quite home-sick for old Italy. The old houses looked so natural, so interesting. I imagined myself rushing through the narrow streets with Baedecker in hand seeking some old church or other famous work of Art. The picture reminded me especially of our day at Salerno; the hills & mountains reminded me of the one which Pa,[7] Al & I ascended at that old university town—now destitute of Colleges and beautiful lady-professors.

This morning Marcou read "Emilia Galotti" to me—a rather poor play, it seems to me.[8] I had not read it for five years and nearly all the scenes were new to me. How *one* does forget plays! and everything else for that matter—unless the mental dusting-brush is continually kept in motion.

Good-bye dearest Amy

Much love to Otto—who might write to me again in spite of my silence. I have indulged his "schreibefaulheit"[9] in the past.

I want two copies of his brief in the Engeln lunacy case. Received Ma's[10] letter to-day.   Your brother

1. Ephraim Emerton (1851–1931) earned a doctorate at Leipzig and then joined Harvard in 1876 to teach German and ecclesiastical history. Many students, including LDB, enjoyed the Emertons' hospitality in Cambridge.

2. Dr. Hermann Nagel (1819–89), the father of Charles, was a good friend of Adolph Brandeis (see note 7 below).

3. Charles Smith Bradley (1819–88), after serving as a Rhode Island state senator and chief justice of that state's supreme court, returned to his alma mater, the Harvard Law School, to teach in 1876.

4. Bradley hired LDB to serve as tutor for his son the following summer; for an account of LDB's stay in Providence, see LDB to Alfred Brandeis, 11 August 1878, BL.

5. F. Arnold, "Lord Chancellors and Chief Justices since Lord Campbell," *New Quarterly Magazine* 9 (1877): 34–67.

6. Benjamin Curtis Porter (1845–1908) was a well-known nineteenth-century American painter; the most famous works of William Morris Hunt (1824–79) were the large murals in the state capitol at Albany, New York.

7. Adolph Brandeis (1822–1906) originally wanted to be a chemist; but having failed to pass the entrance requirements of a university, he studied agriculture and marketing at a local technical institute in Prague. His family lived across the street from Amelia Wehle, and the young man soon resolved to marry Frederika Dembitz. After the failure of the 1848 revolution, the Brandeis, Dembitz, and Wehle families designated Adolph as an emissary to go to America to scout out a good place for them to settle. He first thought of becoming a farmer but soon found a more enjoyable job working for a grocery merchant. By the time his relatives and fiancee arrived in America in May 1849, his employer had offered him a partnership in the Cincinnati firm. Adolph originally brought the family to that Ohio city; but after his marriage in September 1849, they moved to Madison, Indiana, and in 1851 to Louisville, Kentucky, where he soon established a successful grain and produce house. By the time of the Civil War, Brandeis and his partner Charles Crawford operated a flour mill, a tobacco factory, a large farm, and a river freighter. The war brought even more prosperity, but the postwar depression in the South made itself felt in the border states. In 1872 Adolph decided to close the firm before it suffered ruinous losses and in May took his family to Europe on a vacation that eventually lasted three years. He resumed business in 1875; despite some lean years, by 1880 he and his son Alfred were again prospering.

8. Gotthold Ephraim Lessing, *Emilia Galotti*, English translation (Philadelphia, 1810).

9. "Writing laziness."

10. Frederika Dembitz Brandeis (1829–1901) was born in Prague, the daughter of Dr. Sigmund Dembitz and Fanny Wehle Dembitz. She received a humanistic education, primarily from her father and her aunt, Amelia Wehle, with whom she went to live at age twelve after the death of her mother. Although the Dembitz family was not directly involved in the continental uprisings of 1848, its members were sympathetic and were also Jewish, facts that did not bode well for them after the rebellions were crushed. On 8 April 1849 more than two dozen members of the extended family set sail for America aboard the steamer *Washington* from Hamburg. Before leaving Europe, Frederika had become engaged to Adolph Brandeis. They were married on 5 September 1849 and set up housekeeping in Madison, Indiana. In 1851 the Brandeises moved to Louisville, where LDB was born in 1856. A well-read and literate woman, Frederika shared her love of culture with her four children. Later, at LDB's urging, she wrote a charming volume of privately printed *Reminiscences*, which was extensively used by Josephine Goldmark in *Pilgrims of '48* (New Haven, 1930), the best single source for how the Brandeis family lived in America after its migration.

To: Otto A. Wehle
Date: July 13, 1878
Place: Providence, Rhode Island[1]
Source: Brandeis MSS

DEAR OTTO: I hope you are bringing up little Fannie[2] on the most approved theories of baby-training. I find discoveries in this important science have been great within [the] past few years, all old methods having been superceded.

Cradles are entirely condemned. Fathers, brothers, Uncles are not to be made miserable by the "Rock Me to Sleep"—Baskets are the thing now. Babies don't cry now unless they are sick—& then not as an expression of pain but merely to call attention to their condition not yet having acquired articulate speech. The eternal cry for "Mamma" is put an end to.

"I just tell you this" for fear that these advances in science have not reached the shores of the Ohio & I hope you will investigate this matter fully.

I don't want my niece to be behind the times.

Your bro

Love to Amy

1. LDB was spending the summer with Judge Bradley and serving as a tutor to his son.
2. Fannie Brandeis Wehle, the couple's first child, was born on 10 June 1878.

To: Amy Brandeis Wehle (fragment)
Date: late January 1879
Place: St. Louis, Missouri[1]
Source: Wehle MSS

12

What do you think of the plan of putting me into tableaux? Of course you know "Ekkehart"[2] had to be given up and Chas. now proposes to put "Romeo & Juliet" on the Stage—with *me* as Romeo.—Absurdly ridiculous!—most terrible inconsistency—most palpable incongruity. I! a devoted—an inanely devoted lover! Dead gone in a girl of fourteen!—forty would be nearer the mark. Truly the extremes touch here—making me lover.

"One who might indifferently be made,
The Courting stock for all to practice on."

Have been hoping that I should be called off to Washington to argue a case before the Supreme Court—merely for the purpose of escaping this trial. Miss Wislezemus is to be my Juliet—or rather I her Romeo. Just imagine her sighing—"Romeo! Romeo! Wherefore art thou not Ritzman?"

My secret opinion, however, is that through some "unaccountable accident" the tableauxers won't be ready. Nothing but talking has been done yet and a week from to-night is the time.

Don't imagine I have become utterly frivolous & depraved. Dancing and Society occupy only my young nights' thoughts. Such an idea entering my mind by day would be terribly maltreated—indeed it should leave hope behind.[3] Have worked hard these last four weeks for James Taussig on interesting & instructive work and to-day received my compensation for the month ($50). Which will be gone Alas! too soon.—Lawyers' license is a [*] dodge here for bringing poor novices to the "Bettlerstab."[4] Next week I expect to try a case for George which we both fully expect to lose; in fact, our only chance of winning rests in the possibility of total mental aberration of the judge.[5] That, probably, is the reason why George shifts the work & responsibility onto my shoulders.

Fan read "Heyse's Letzter Centaur"[6] to us Thursday night. The introduction is criminally affected and unamiable—but the story proper is very pretty.

Fan's Quartette meets again this evening. The directrix has been very well for the past few days and little Alfred[7] is splendid; indeed, too good, for Fan seeks some deep hidden reason for the slightest outbreak of enthusiasm on his part.

Charlie was very much delighted with Otto's Brief. It has been submitted to D'Arcy[8] for his opinion.

The only other news I can tell you is that Aunt Adele[9] is still suffering from a cold. Dr. T[10] ditto. Anna their servant girl ditto.   Good-bye

---

1. After graduation from law school, LDB had to decide where to practice—Boston, Louisville, or St. Louis. His mother wanted him to return to Louisville, but his brother-in-law

Charles Nagel had been persistent in his desire to have LDB come to St. Louis, probably in the hope that it would assuage his wife's frequent bouts of depression. Nagel even offered to make room for LDB in his office. LDB turned down this proposal but did accept one that Nagel helped to secure for him from James Taussig, a distant cousin. George W. Taussig, another member of the extended family, was also in the practice. For LDB's decision to go to St. Louis and a detailed account of his practice there, see Burton C. Bernard, "Brandeis in St. Louis," 11 *St. Louis Bar Journal* 54 (1964).

2. Joseph Victor von Scheffel's *Meister Ekkehard*, a popular historical romance based on the life of a tenth-century monk, was originally written in 1857 and translated into English by Sophie Dells in 1872.

3. A play on words, alluding to the inscription on the gates of hell in Dante Alighieri's *Inferno*, canto 3.

4. Literally a "beggar's staff" (i.e., to reduce to beggary).

5. From all available evidence, this was LDB's first trial experience. In November 1878 James W. Taussig filed a petition in equity on behalf of a client attempting to secure a prior lien on the assets of a debtor, a lien that in effect would take precedence over the claims of the debtor's business partners. The case was tried on 4 February, and the decision handed down on 21 March went as expected against LDB's client (*Dieckmann v. City of St. Louis*, City of St. Louis Circuit Court, Docket 48377). An appeal entered later in the year was denied; 9 Mo. App. 9 (1880).

6. A novella of 1870 by Paul Johann Ludwig von Heyse.

7. Alfred Nagel was the couple's first child.

8. Henry I. D'Arcy was Nagel's law partner.

9. Adele Taussig was the wife of Dr. William Taussig (see the next note); their daughter Jennie would marry LDB's brother Alfred in 1884.

10. William Taussig (1826–1913), Jennie's father, was an influential citizen of St. Louis and president of the St. Louis Bridge Company.

To:	Otto A. Wehle
Date:	April 1, 1879
Place:	St. Louis, Missouri
Source:	Brandeis MSS

DEAR OTTO: I delayed answering your letter principally because I wished to examine the 2 points of law you suggested before writing again & must, nevertheless, send this without having done so. I have really not had much to do of late—and yet did not find just the opportunity to look up those questions.

My case has ultimately been decided—but alas—against us,—as right and justice demands. We have, of course, filed a motion for a re-hearing and may appeal. The defendant based his defence on two grounds, the one impregnable, the other, I think, very weak. It is possible (for we have not yet learnt the grounds of the decision) that the judge took the latter ground, as we endeavored very much to confuse him of the former, & if he did we may have some chance above.

I have for the past week devoted much of my time to the investigation & particularly meditation over the: Liability of Trust-Estates on Contracts

Made for their Benefit (i.e. By Trustee, Ex[ecu]t[o]r, Adm[inistrato]r, Guardian, Committee).

The question has often attracted my attention but until recently I have never been able to find the point referred to. As the point, to my knowledge, has never been treated in text-books & not even mentioned except in Lewin & Perry[1] in a vague way & in half of one sentence, I wrote a little essay of about 14 pages on the subject with some idea of having it published in one of our Law Journals. The investigation was provoked by one of Mr. Taussig's Cases & as I find that the result, as set forth by me, is not exactly favorable to his case, or at least might be giving weapons into the hands of the other side, I shall, of course, keep it under lock & key or rather do, as I have done, leave it in his safe.[2]

In your great lunacy practice you may have thought & found much on the subject. I wish you would give me what information you have on this very nice question. The matter is of such practical importance; I am astonished that there is so little law on it. Am very glad to hear that your practice shows signs of revival & growth. Litigation & legal business is very much depressed here. Everybody complains & most with reason. Even in our office business is poor. A hash of *old* cases, dating from better times, alone serves to keep us occupied.

Charlie has considerable to do, is far more fortunate than most young lawyers here; yet his fees come in slowly.

Socially I am having a good enough time, though there are no parties or dances now. Have found quite a number of pleasant people to call on and go out many—aye most evenings of the week—as I never read or work after supper.

On what steamer does Everett Bishop sail[?] The Ross family of Cambridge leave on the "Bothnia" April 16th from N.Y. What is the explanation of your being so crowded in the new house?

Your bro

Tell Al that Ben Taussig's[3] address is
c/o Wernse, Abeles & Brookman
Leadville, Colorado

1. Thomas Lewin, *A Practical Treatise on the Law of Trusts and Trustees* (London, 1875); and Jarius Ware Perry, *Treatise on the Law of Trusts and Trustees* (Boston, 1872).

2. The following year James Taussig had LDB's brief printed and submitted to the Missouri Court of Appeals with the aim of presenting "a view on all sides of the question." LDB sent a copy to Oliver Wendell Holmes, Jr., who published it as "Liability of Trust-Estates on Contracts Made for Their Benefit," 15 *American Law Review* 449 (1881).

3. Ben Taussig was a cousin of Jennie Taussig, who lived in St. Louis.

To: Charles Nagel
Date: July 12, 1879
Place: Boston, Massachusetts[1]
Source: Brandeis MSS

DEAR CHARLIE: Your long letter was read with much attention & not a little heartbeating. I know not what might have been the effect of a telegram from you. In my extreme doubt, I might well have been swayed by it.[2]

Still, I do not repent of my decision although I feel how much I have lost in losing you all—and to what extent I have been deprived of that which contributes so much to the calm happiness of man.

On the other hand I have much to hope for here and although the loss of the advice, support & assistance of the family is very great, I find much comfort & consolation in the feeling that whatever I have achieved, or may achieve here is my own—pure and simple—unassisted by the fortuitous circumstance of family influence or social position. There is indeed small comfort in this thought if nothing is achieved, but if anything is accomplished that thought would give me much satisfaction.

Still, your letter made me very blue & doubting for a day or two.

I find my temperament much changed during the past two years. It seemed to me peculiarly equable formerly and I was rarely exultant or depressed. Now I find myself as variable as the atmosphere—as unstable as a barometer. This morning I was boiling over with joy & such good humor that I could not keep quiet.

At present everything looks rosy here. My position with the Ch. J.[3] is pleasanter than my fondest hopes had pictured. None of the unpleasant peculiarities for which Judge Gray is noted have appeared in my intercourse with him. His arrogance and impatience are apparently the judicial wig & gown, for off the bench, there is no sign of them. On the contrary, he is the most affable of men, patiently listening to suggestions and objections & even contradiction. I have worked with him daily since Tuesday and have enjoyed most of the mornings keenly. Our mode of working is this. He takes out the record & briefs in any case, we read them over, talk about the points raised, examine the authorities' arguments—then he makes up his mind if he can, marks out the line of argument for his opinion, writes it, & then dictates it to me.

But I am treated in every respect as a person of co-ordinate position. He asks me what I think of his line of argument and I answer candidly. If I think other reasons better, I give them; if I think his language is obscure, I tell him so; if I have any doubts I express them and he is very fair in acknowledging a correct suggestion or disabusing one of an erroneous idea.

16

In these discussions & investigations I shall learn very much. Many beautiful points are raised and must be decided. The Ch. Justice has a marvellous knowledge of Mass. decision[s] & Statutes and I expect much advantage in this respect.

The only mechanical work is the dictation and of that there is precious little. We have worked about 25 hours together—& there has not been an hour's dictation.

My connection with Warren[4] promises well also. There are many fine points about the man both in mind & character and it looks to me as if he would be a success. His "push" is great—the same bulldog perseverance & obstinacy which brought me here will, I think, pave a way which he seems determined to make. He is bent now on making clients and getting business and I think he will do it.

Already he has quite a number of small claims with a prospect of some larger ones. If matters continue to come in as now, we are safe.

We have taken a room No 60 Devonshire Street (desirable location) in the 3rd story (2 flights) and shall move in soon. The room is only two hundred Dollars a year—very cheap everybody says. Whether the partnership shall be ostensible as well as actual we have not decided. A word from me would make it ostensible I think.

There is no pressure for a decision as I cannot hang out my sign yet—not having been admitted to the bar. I think I shall be admitted on motion soon.

There will be *no* examination for the bar till Fall and I should like to be a member before then. The committee here ordinarily admits attys from other states only upon proof of a few years practice there; but I think I shall be able to slide in anyhow as the Ch. J intends to submit my case to some of his associates.[5]

What you say about teaching is undoubtedly sound and I recognized that, when the time comes, I shall have to decide between that and practice.[6] I have not made up my mind yet, because it is not necessary but, as far as I can analyze my feelings, I think it was the prospect of teaching that kept me here. I recognize that my being here would make it easier to get the place should I want it—& that it would be much easier, too, to test my capability & love for such a position—without risking all.

Of course I do not know how I shall feel when an opportunity offers for taking the step—if it ever does, but it seems to me that if my eyes allow, I should make the move. The law as a logical science has very great attractions for me. I see it now again by the almost ridiculous pleasure which the discovery or invention of a legal theory gives me; and I know that such a study of the law cannot be pursued by a successful practitioner nor by a Judge (I speak now from experience). Teaching would mean for me writing as well. However, this is all talk. I may feel differently in three months and the wrangling of the Bar may have the greatest attraction for me. It surely is not distasteful to me now. It is merely a question of selection between two good things—They are both good enough for me. I question only which I am good for.

I had a kind note from Mr. Taussig in which he writes: "I may say now that a longer stay would have resulted in a closer business connection between us." This was, indeed, a surprise to me—yet queerly enough made me feel rather good than blue. I suppose this feeling is attributable to vanity—but the letter was surely fortifying and gave me courage & hope that I might rise here as well as there.

Dear Chas, I never thanked you for all your kindness to me, but I assure you I have always felt the gratitude though I did not express it. And when your letter came which made me feel so very very blue—I felt in a way glad that my decision prevented my accepting your offer—which, I feared, might be prompted rather by your kindness & generosity than my own merit.[7] I know if I were in St. Louis I should not have strength to refuse the chance though I felt that what I might give was less than what I would receive. Therefore I am glad I am not there now. Sometime things may be equalized & who knows, but that sometime we may yet fight the battle together.

At present I doubt whether you need a partner—other than Fan, and she is good enough for any man.

Living away from you all I think I shall be looking around for some such partner when my income justifies such a step. Should that come before 26 I fear even Pa's ominous "offer" would not deter me. Indeed I should become very nervous already, seeing desirable girls marrying & engaging themselves so fast were I not convinced that there are more fish in the seas than ever were caught.

—Later—

The brilliant ideas expressed in the last few lines were conceived in a moment of lonesomeness. That condition having passed away, I take this all back.

I am sorry you will have the trouble of packing up my traps & especially that the books & papers (and lamp) from the office will have to be gathered together. Don't forget the *signs* either. The study chair in my room belongs to Alfred. In one of the pigeon holes in my office desk are papers in the patent-case (Roger vs. Shultz) which you might send by mail. The rest, I suppose, ought be packed up & sent *fast freight*.

18

Please make note of all the expenses on my behalf. I also owe your Mother for half a month's board & the wash woman for half a month which please pay for me.

I don't know whether the patent-suit will be brought. I wrote to Roger that, in case he wished to bring it, you would probably take it on the same terms I had suggested. Had a very kind letter from Jennie[8] dated N.Y. for which I have wanted to thank her. How is Frank?[9]

I am very pleasantly fixed at *21 Joy Street (Mrs. Smith) where I board & lodge. Address your letters there for the present.* Three of my law school acquaintances are there. The house is about 2 squares from State House and half a dozen from Warren's.

Am anxiously awaiting the papers in the Miller (?) case from which I expect to make all our fortunes. It would be splendid if there were something in it. I have been very brilliant for two days—& if this abnormal condition continues long enough may be able to discover some fine point.

Send me the boy's picture.

Love to Fan & love & regards to the other St Louisians in proper proportion.   Yours

1. At the end of May LDB's law school friend Samuel D. Warren (see note 4 below) had written urging him to leave St. Louis and join him in a partnership in Boston. Aside from the fact that an economic recession retarded the growth of his practice, LDB did not like St. Louis. He had caught a touch of malaria there and, as noted in his letters, found the city's social life superficial compared to Cambridge. Warren had heard about editorial vacancies on both the *Law Reporter* and *Law Review* and had urged LDB that they should try for the posts. The salaries, while small, would give them sufficient money to live on while building up their practice. On 30 May LDB responded affirmatively to Warren's suggestions and in a short time moved back to Boston.

2. On 5 July Nagel had written a long and affectionate letter to LDB about his decision to relocate, in which he said: "I think you did right." LDB answered: "I had been under considerable excitement during all the time; and was prevented from writing to you, only by a conviction, that I would do injury by it—From the start I have been divided with myself in reference to the question of change: My reason spoke for Boston; my heart was for St. Louis."

3. Horace Gray (1828–1902), after nine years as an associate justice, was named chief justice of the Supreme Judicial Court of Massachusetts in 1873. He held that position until named to the U.S. Supreme Court in 1882. LDB took the job as Gray's clerk when the editorial positions failed to materialize.

4. Samuel Dennis Warren (1852–1910), a member of a prominent New England family with large paper-mill holdings, met LDB at law school, and the two became fast friends. After graduation Warren joined the Boston firm of Shattuck, Holmes & Munroe, but almost immediately began imploring LDB to leave St. Louis and to join him in a Boston partnership of their own. As subsequent letters show, he and LDB not only became a successful team but remained close friends as well. Upon the death of his father, Warren left the firm in 1888 to take charge of the family interests. For his life, see Martin Green, *The Mount Vernon Street Warrens* (New York, 1989).

5. LDB had been admitted to the Missouri bar in November 1878 and to the Kentucky bar a month earlier, although he never practiced in that state. He would be admitted to the Massachusetts bar within two weeks; see LDB to Alfred Brandeis, 31 July 1879, BL.

6. Over the next several years LDB toyed constantly with the idea of teaching. In 1882 Harvard Law School appointed him as a lecturer for one year and was willing to make the appointment permanent; but although LDB enjoyed the experience, he finally decided that he preferred the challenge of the courtroom.

7. In his letter Nagel had suggested that LDB consider joining his law firm and that if he did the two would soon become partners.

8. Jennie Taussig (1858–1943), a second cousin of the Brandeis family, had known LDB and his siblings from the frequent visits between the families. She eventually married LDB's brother Alfred.

9. Frank William Taussig (1859–1940) was at the beginning of a distinguished academic career at Harvard; he would become a prominent economist and the foremost authority on tariffs in the nation. In 1916 President Wilson named him chair of the newly created Tariff Commission. His proximity at Cambridge and the family connection, as well as the fact that LDB had worked for his uncle, led the men to become good friends.

To:	Frederika Dembitz Brandeis
Date:	July 20, 1879
Place:	Boston, Massachusetts
Source:	Mason, *Brandeis*, 59–61

DEAREST MOTHER: When I received your letter and those of the others, it seems to me as if I were a fool to have settled here so far away, instead of staying with you and enjoying you and your love. Of course one can live anywhere, but there is also ambition to be satisfied.

But man is strange, at least this one is; he does not enjoy what he has— and he always wants what he does not yet have. That probably is called ambition—the delusion, for which one is always ready to offer a sacrifice.

And so I think that I shall be happier here, in spite of being alone, and if I can write you about success, it will counterbalance all the privations. And, I believe, that you too will enjoy me more from a distance, if you know that I am happy.

We shall see each other quite often and write very often. . . .

The connection with Warren seems to become more and more desirable. He, without doubt, has connections from which something may come, has energy and (at least compared with me) a practical mind. We already have some work, have not collected much money, but we hope for some fees. I am not yet admitted to the practice, but I am expecting a favorable decision this week.

You want to know how I pass my days: then read: I get up shortly after seven o'clock, have breakfast, go for a walk usually till nine o'clock. Then (every day this week) I stayed at the C[hief]. J[ustice]. till 2 o'clock. After lunch I go to our office, talk over our business affairs with Warren, work there or in the Law-library according as business requires, and shortly after six o'clock I have dinner.

The evenings of last week I spent as follows: Monday Bullock[1] and I took a walk to Cambridge and back to fetch my laundry, which was done there tentatively. Tuesday I drove with Warren to Beverly (5 miles from Manchester), where his parents are spending the summer. We left Boston at 5:15 and intended to take a long sailing trip in order to inspect a famous yacht (which belongs to the wealthy Sears). There was no wind, however, therefore we played tennis, rowed a little, swam and enjoyed beautiful nature. Warren's house is situated directly on the lake, the view is marvelous, and it is divine to listen to the rippling of the waves. Near the shore were a few boats, which threw their long black evening shadows over the water. The day had been hot, at five o'clock we were dripping with perspiration. Two hours later we were shouting for joy in the full enjoyment of a bath in the lake.

This is, indeed, an immense advantage of Boston. One can enjoy living (*Mann kann das leben lebend geniessen*), and nature is so beautiful . . . Oh, how beautiful are heaven and earth here, hills and water, nature and art!

Because I have little or no work to do for the C. J. I shall devote myself this week to our own affairs, try to collect some debts for a client and probably examine a title for a lot.

The room which I now occupy is fully furnished. In the fall I have to give it up. But I can get a little room in the same house or can move to Warren's.

The house of Mr. Warren is on Mt. Vernon Str. and runs through to Pinckney. In earlier years there were two entirely different houses and the house on Pinckney is entirely divided from the front house. In this back building Sam Warren has his rooms. But there are some rooms still unoccupied, and he wants me to take one of them.

For 10 days I have not seen any of the Cochrans. They invited me to visit them at Manchester for a few days and I probably shall do it sometime during the summer.

If I can I would like to take a walking tour to the mountains again this fall with Philip Marcou or Richards.[2]

If only a man can stay strong and healthy—he will indeed be able to accomplish something. Marcou spends the summer in Magnolia—I would like to go there for a while. If one had nothing to do, one could really live more cheaply in the mountains or at the shore than here.

When you have read my letter to Charles, you will know everything about me that can be written.

Many thanks for having kept your part of the pact.

Good-bye.   Love from

1. Rufus Augustus Bullock (1848–1930) attended Harvard Law School from 1874 to 1876 but did not take a degree.

2. William Reuben Richards (1853–1912), a classmate of LDB's at the law school, was the scion of an old Massachusetts family; he was later instrumental in arranging construction of Boston's first subway.

To: Alfred Brandeis
Date: July 31, 1879
Place: Boston, Massachusetts
Source: EBR

DEAR ALFRED: I don't feel quite sure yet, whether I was not a d—n fool giving up St. Louis and settling here, though my doubts rarely disturb me except when a letter from Chas arives [*sic*].

Still there is nothing here which has disappointed me—which has not indeed surpassed my expectations and I suppose that should satisfy me.

Distance has not, I find, lent enchantment to the view nor even have blessings (of St. Louis) brightened as they took their flight;[1] though it must be said that after my decision the prospects in St. Louis became much better. I am surely undergoing the crucial test and I hope I will stand it.

I was admitted to the bar Tuesday without an examination and contrary to all principles and precedent. Warren & I have formed a copartnership in name as well as effect. What I have seen of him since I am here has raised my opinion in every respect and I concluded that a closer union of our interests was desirable.

I think we will work well together and that he is a good supplement to me. I like his push and obstinacy & his ambition. He is a person with a fine sense of professional & commercial honor and is smart enough to lay aside his seeming hautiness which made him enemies at Cambridge. His first appearances in Court Wednesday a week ago & Monday last earned for him many compliments. My work with the C. J. began again Tuesday and will continue with slight interruptions to the 1st of September (then Court convenes). It is as pleasant and interesting as ever, and I feel very much its instructiveness.

Saturday afternoon—in spite of the rain—I went to Manchester to spend Sunday with the Cochranes. We went up to Mrs. Fields[2] after tea and then to stop at the Hotel where we criticized the people and agreed on the stupidity of the world. It was the first time I had felt savage since the last stop at the same hotel, four weeks ago.

Sunday was beautiful. We took a ride to Magnolia, then I called on Mrs. Richards.[3] Marcou came over for Dinner. After dinner Jessie played and then we went to the Fields for tea. Mrs. F. read us a very good translation of Goethe's Panora da ella stessen.

I had actually been invited to the Fields to enjoy Longfellow who had promised to spend Sunday with them, but who did not appear on account on the rain.[4] Monday at 9 A.M. I was again in Boston.

Tuesday evening Holmes,[5] Warren & I spent at Warren's room over a glass of ——— (mixture of Champagne & Beer) telling jokes & talking Summum bonum, i.e. Warren & Holmes talked and I lay outstretched on a ship['] s chair. Tuesday evening I wandered solitarily in the moonlight out to Longwood and yesterday took a beautiful walk with Cameron[6] from 8:30 to 10 P.M. (These details for Ma's benefit).

Had a letter from Emerton last week in which he speaks much of the Brandeis family and little of himself. He is at E. Lemoine Me. near Mt. Desert. He was very busy after his return from the West and before his departure. That is the reason why I did not see him.

When are you coming East? *Don't back out of it again.* Have not seen Reed or Griffith[7] since first call, but expect to soon.

Love to All

Have some good jokes for you when you come.

1. Thomas Campbell, *The Pleasures of Hope* (Edinburgh, 1799).
2. Mrs. Annie Fields (1834–1915) was a well-known New England hostess. She wrote about many of the leading artists and writers of the period and is best remembered as the editor of *The Life and Letters of Harriet Beecher Stowe* (Boston, 1897).
3. Probably the mother of his friend and classmate William Richards.
4. Mrs. Fields had a particular fondness for the poet Henry Wadsworth Longfellow (1807–82); see her long and enthusiastic essay on him in *Authors and Friends* (Boston, 1896).
5. Oliver Wendell Holmes, Jr. (1841–1935) was one of the most impressive minds and fascinating characters ever produced by New England. His path and LDB's path would often cross, and after 1916 they served together on the Supreme Court until Holmes's retirement in 1932. At this time he was engaged in a desultory practice, spending much of his time as editor of the *American Law Review* and preparing the lectures he would give the following year at the Lowell Institute on "The Common Law." Those lectures, in which he argued that the vitality of the law lay in its response to experience and not in formal logic, made his reputation as the most original of America's legal thinkers.

   LDB arranged for a professorship for Holmes at the Harvard Law School; but less than a year after accepting, Holmes resigned to go on to the Supreme Judicial Court of Massachusetts, where he served for twenty years. In 1902 Theodore Roosevelt, at the urging of Henry Cabot Lodge, named Holmes to the Supreme Court. There he fought, first alone and then with LDB, to transform the principles he had enunciated in the Lowell lectures into the law of the land.

6. Charles John Cameron (1859–1926) attended Harvard College for a few years and then returned to his native British Columbia.
7. It is impossible to determine which Reed or Griffith LDB is referring to, since there were several men by these names who attended either Harvard College or Harvard Law School at the same time as LDB.

To: Amy and Otto A. Wehle
Date: September 16, 1880
Place: Boston, Massachusetts
Source: Brandeis MSS

DEAREST AMY & OTTO: Otto's letter reached me a few minutes ago and I need not tell you how happy it made me.

My *name* is in your hands.[1]

Lovingly

Fan & Chas are here & will write themselves.

1. The Wehles had named their second child, born 13 September, Louis Brandeis Wehle (1880–1959). Like his uncle, Louis Wehle was inspired to go into the law and public service; during the 1920s and 1930s he handled the private legal work related to republication of LDB's writings. See his autobiography, *Hidden Threads of History: Wilson through Roosevelt* (New York, 1953).

To: Amy Brandeis Wehle (fragment)
Date: January 2, 1881
Place: Boston, Massachusetts
Source: Brandeis MSS

DEAREST AMY: Oh my! this is too bad! The idea of losing two years in one; and yet this is undoubtedly what has happened. Two months ago, or less, I mourned on my birthday the loss of a year, and now Time has had a birthday too and another year is gone.

"Out upon Time"—I say with Byron.[1] I wish the Old Fellow would let well enough alone.

Thus meditates your brother on the Second Day of the New Year without having imbibed immoderately on the first. Immoderately—why I haven't had a drop of the exhilaration since Christmas Day and yesterday was spent like any other business day. Such is the Custom in the Metropolis. (a word which your husband will tell you is derived from the two Greek roots — and —)

Oh—Enough of this nonsense—because I must go soon to the Turnverein[2] and try and be captivating to the DD. and get some clients from their number.

Yesterday was a Sad Day. We buried irretrivably [sic] a half a dozen of the most beautiful and lucrative lawsuits—and all for the love of our clients. Yes we settled up the complicated New Hampshire transactions by an agreement wonderfully favorable to our clients. From love of them we did it.—But I fear "The expedition of my violent love, outran the pauser reason,"[3] no more trips to New Hampshire—no nothing. The only

24

consolation is that we get our opponent for a client.—You want to know what I am doing—Why nothing. Were I Othello, I should answer,

"Little do I know of this great world
More than pertains to feats of broil & battle."[4]

But don't take that answer for mine. It is not quite true. Like the shell fish which walks backwards & is not a crab and like our forefathers I shall begin at the end & tell you of the dissipations of the week. Well at 8:45 P.M. I called at a certain Mrs. Bush a friend of Jessie's where I was invited for Christmas and was constrained to excuse myself. Previously I had been at the Cochrane's for tea. Miss Helen Cochrane and I are great friends now and I approach he[r] without fear & trembling. On the contrary I think she is almost afraid of me now. The other day when I called I was telling her about the illustrated weekly "Puck" of which she knew nothing & in praising the tendency of the paper, I said quite innocently "The remarkable fact is that the paper is always on the right side of every question." "How do you know what is the right side?" Said she in an unmistakable tone. "Oh," said I, "The side that I like." The subjugation was complete. Sedan was not a more decisive victory.[5]

Friday evening I dined at the Emertons. Marcou was there and in his honor two Misses Page of Boston were invited. One of them, the elder, a lady I should say of 28 "summers" and quite as many winters, I found extremely interesting. She is tall, has a finely chiseled, half Southern face with black hair and sparkling jet eyes, and would be very handsome but for a total absence of freshness & health in her appearance. On the other hand her delicate look gives her the charm which people of character who have suffered always possess and the appearance of refinement which goes with it.

This very inadequate description of her appearance is given merely in order to lay some kind of foundation for her conversation, which was of unusual character & quality.

She is decidedly an excellent talker, but of a different category from most persons possessing that talent. She spoke neither of books, nor of art, nor of the theatres; nor is there a particle of humor in her conversation. I had hardly seated myself next to her when she began to talk about some people whom I slightly knew and with these uninteresting persons as a theme led into the most remarkable variations of character, soul, and mind-painting that can be imagined & that cannot be described. Most persons one meets never get beyond the preliminaries of an acquaintance. Like the legendary ant, you drag, at each meeting, your barley-corn of interest up the encircling wall of conventionality; but before you reach the top you fall exhausted to the ground. Not so with her. Like Mercury, she cleared the wall-tops with a bound and in a moment I found myself in the deepest conversation, such as George Eliot's characters indulge in.—

You, of course, are very much interested in this young lady because you think I am smitten with her. But Alas! it is not so. One mistress only claims me. The "Law" has her grip on me—and I suppose I can't escape her clutches without going on a Ranch Cattle Raising. This transition is sudden—but Warren & I have been talking about the "Beef Bonaza" [*sic*] of late owing to some friends of his who have just returned from the far west on a visit.

1. George Gordon Lord Byron, "The Siege of Corinth," stanza 18.
2. A combination athletic and social club established by local German-American communities. LDB may have belonged to one for both physical and business purposes.
3. William Shakespeare, *Macbeth*, II, 3:108–9.
4. William Shakespeare, *Othello*, I, 3:87–88; the exact wording is: "And little of this great world can I speak / More than pertains to feats of broil and battle."
5. The battle of Sedan completed the thirty-day conquest of France by the Prussians in 1870.

To:	Helen Goldmark Adler
Date:	April 29, 1881
Place:	Boston, Massachusetts
Source:	Gilbert MSS

DEAR NELLIE:[1] A letter just received from Mother brings me the sad news of your Father's death.[2]

He had for so many years lived in my mind as the embodiment of strength—of moral and mental as well as bodily power—that even his long illness has left me unable fully to realize his passing away.

I know that the consideration of the virtues and good qualities of one whom we have lost serves generally but to intensify our grief. Still I cannot help feeling that we should find mitigation of our sorrow in the remembrance of that which we have been allowed to enjoy in the past and that it ought to furnish us some consolation in our grief, that one, who was dear to us, has acted his part in life nobly and manfully—that the world has been happier and better for his having been in it.

I know how much your good husband[3] will be now to your family—especially to your Mother,[4] and I wish I might know him to thank him for it.   Your cousin

1. Helen Goldmark Adler (1859–1948) was the oldest daughter of Joseph and Regina Goldmark. After her marriage to Felix Adler (see note 3 below) she was heavily involved in his social and education programs. She started a visiting nurse service for poor families and

wrote one of the first manuals for mothers on the proper care of children. She was the sister of LDB's future wife, Alice Goldmark (hereafter AGB).

2. Dr. Joseph Goldmark (1819–81) was a distinguished Viennese scientist who fled to America due to his involvement in the political uprisings of 1848. For a history of Goldmark and his family, as well as their relationship to the Brandeis and Wehle clans, see Goldmark, *Pilgrims of '48*.

3. Felix Adler (1851–1933) was the founder of the New York Society for Ethical Culture and would be a leader of the worldwide Ethical Culture movement, which attempted to inculcate moral behavior without resort to specific theological tenets. He had married Helen Goldmark earlier in the year. In 1891 Adler would perform the wedding ceremony for LDB and AGB, who was Adler's sister-in-law.

4. Regina Wehle Goldmark (1835–1925), LDB's future mother-in-law, was a close friend of her younger cousin Frederika Dembitz before the families migrated to America; their friendship continued even though the families were separated geographically.

To: **Alfred Brandeis**
Date: July 30, 1881
Place: **Boston, Massachusetts**
Source: **EBR**

DEAR AL: Yours of 27th announcing continued trouble with Ma's finger just rec'd. Too bad. I enclose (in order that you may go to the springs) our chk for One hundred & twenty five dollars to be applied on the People's Bank subscription.

Our fiscal year ends today. It show up about $3600 gross earnings which makes $3000 (little less) net profits for the year. Last year's gross earnings were something over $3400 but $435 of that came from the Chief Justice, so that legitimate fees are considerably in excess of last year.

The outlook for next year is not good. If I were a Sec'ty of Treasury making out estimates I should prepare the country for a strong deficit in the budget.

We have only one lucrative litigation on hand, the Butterworth & Smally cases, and they will probably be settled before fall. Last year this time we had a lot of monied cases on hand. Still we have chances running stronger in our favor with each year and I suppose we will pull through—only we have yet to make some desperate effort somewhere. I don't expect my practice to amount to much for the next fifteen years but I do expect to have a high old time for the twenty five following.[1] As the traveller said of Sparta:

"Here alone it is a pleasure to grow old"

Called on Miss Crest (by request) Tuesday and "was much shocked at her carryings on." Girls who talk so deserve to be kissed without mercy.

She told me that she loves you dearly. Think James Taussig will turn up here within a few days and anticipate much pleasure from his visit.

Lovingly

1. In fact the firm became quite successful within a few years. In 1890, at the age of thirty-four, LDB was earning more than $50,000 a year, while 75 percent of the lawyers in the country made less than $5,000 annually.

To: **Alfred Brandeis**
Date: **March 20, 1886**
Place: **Boston, Massachusetts**
Source: **EBR**

MY DEAR AL: Many many good wishes my dear fellow—may the years to come bring you as much joy and cause for happiness as have the last two.[1]

With this, I feel that I have said all.

Your birthday we shall celebrate with another hearing on the rag question.[2] The fight now is against the Boston Board of Health which is sustaining the grinding monopoly & fraud entitled—the Boston Disinfecting Co.[3] We petitioned to the mayor for a change of the Quarantine regulations. The mayor referred it to the City Council and the hearing is now being had before a joint Com[mit]tee of the Aldermen & Common Council, who are to report to the City Council.

We had hearings Tuesday and Thursday of this week and shall probably have several weeks more of it before The Question is finally submitted.

We have the evidence—both practical & scientific on our side—and the chances are quite good that political influence will not be potent enough to overcome that. Popular prejudice and ignorance may make us some trouble but we are in the right and must, in the end, come out successful.[4] The more the matter is canvassed & discussed (and the papers have taken up the question now), the better for us. It is only ignorance and dark dealing that we must fear.

I send you by mail DeAmicis' "Holland & its People"[5] which I thought might refresh the memories of 1873 for you. Doubtless Pa will enjoy the book.

Goodbye dear fellow

Met Frank [Taussig] at the Symphony concert last Saturday.

1. Alfred's birthday was 23 March.

2. Boston had a health requirement that all rags imported from abroad had to be disinfected in Boston, even if they had been treated abroad. Most of the rags imported by the area's paper manufacturers had, in fact, been decontaminated before shipping, and the mill

owners objected to having to pay for the process a second time. Moreover, the only firm licensed by the city to do such work was the Boston Disinfecting Company, which charged $5 per ton. Warren & Brandeis represented the paper companies in their petition to the Common Council to repeal the law and substitute a measure that would achieve the same health ends at a lower cost. The mills were backed by rail and steamship lines who feared the loss of trade to New York, which had a more lenient law accepting overseas decontamination.

3. According to his daughter Elizabeth, LDB recalled this fight as the first time he realized how evil a monopoly could be. Yet despite the fervent language of this sentence, LDB did not raise the monopoly issue in this fight. Rather, he declared that the ordinance violated the due process of the paper manufacturers and was an unreasonable exercise of the state's police powers.

4. Unfortunately for LDB and his clients, the council refused to repeal the ordinance, and one of the paper manufacturers filed suit to force release of a load of rags from the Boston Disinfecting Co. LDB handled the case on appeal, only to have the Supreme Judicial Court decide against his clients. *Train v. Boston Disinfecting Co.*, 144 Mass. 523 (1887).

5. Edmondo de Amicis, *Holland and Its People*, trans. Caroline Tilton (New York, 1881).

To:	**Alfred Brandeis**
Date:	**March 21, 1887**
Place:	**Boston, Massachusetts**
Source:	**Brandeis MSS**

MY DEAR AL: The last twelve months have brought you so much happiness that you will scarcely regret that age has scored another year. May all coming ones do as well by you.

I saw Frank and Miss Guild[1] Friday. Miss Guild was so radiantly happy—she seemed really beautiful. All that I hear about her confirms my impression that she is a very fine girl. Uncle William[2] has, doubtless, brought you an enthusiastic report.

I met Frank and Miss Guild on Commonwealth Ave at Noon yesterday. It looked suspiciously like an after-church walk.

I was coming home from my morning tramp. In the forenoon it seemed too cold and dreary to venture upon the water, but before night the sun broke forth and I found myself in the birch.

There has been little of moment occurring in practice, though I have been quite busy, in a way, on matters large and small. Except a few cases before the Supreme Court this month[3] I have tried few causes within the last weeks, and I really long for the excitement of the contest—that is a good prolonged one covering days or weeks. There is a certain joy in the draining exhaustion and backache of a long trial, which shorter skirmishes cannot afford.

Socially, I have continued quite active. I find it interesting to meet new people—although one feels too often that the result of an evening has been simply to know new people. There has been no acquisition of a new thing. Saturday at the Salon I met an extraordinary man—Berenson, I think, is his name. A student at Harvard of great talents—particularly literary talent. A Russian Jew I surmise, a character about whom I must know more. He seemed as much of an exotic lure as the palm or the cinnamon tree. He is the most interesting character I have found for some time.[4]

Miss Helen Cochran has left for [*]. Jessie will probably start in a week.

My best wishes

I wired you for short horn[5] last night and send you the "Sentimental Journey"[6] by mail. I hope you will enjoy it.

1. Edith Thomas Guild became Mrs. Frank Taussig the following year.
2. William Taussig was Alfred's father-in-law.
3. On 1 March LDB had appeared before the Supreme Judicial Court of Massachusetts to argue *Dwyer v. Fuller*, 144 Mass. 420, and on 9 March to argue the Boston Disinfecting Co. case.
4. The Lithuanian-born Bernard Berenson (1865–1959) more than fulfilled LDB's estimate of his extraordinary abilities. Over a long lifetime Berenson wrote many works on art, and his residence in Italy became one of the most famous gathering places for intellectuals in the twentieth century. See his own *Sketch for a Self-Portrait* (New York, 1949) and Ernest Samuel, *Bernard Berenson: The Making of a Legend* (Cambridge, Mass., 1987).
5. "Short horn" was a variety of Kentucky bourbon.
6. Laurence Sterne, *A Sentimental Journey through France and Italy* (London, 1780); at this time LDB probably would have bought an illustrated edition published in New York in 1884.

To: **Alfred Brandeis**
Date: **March 20, 1888**
Place: **Boston, Massachusetts**
Source: **Brandeis MSS**

MY DEAR AL: Jennie's letter of the other day pictured so charmingly the happiness of your lives, that I can hardly wish you more for the twenty-third,[1] than a continuance of the blessings which you already enjoy—& which, my dear boy, you so fully deserve. May the years to come be full of happiness, & as free from sorrows as is possible in the life of Man.

This evening I called on Miss Guild to see her & to get a breath of the Louisville air. She brought with her quite a Western atmosphere and it seemed very good to hear her talk so familiarly about home.

Miss Guild tells me that you are suffering from smoking chimneys. Have you tried the "Rotary Ventilator?" I am told that it is quite as effective in its way as Rodway's Ready Relief when applied to other ills. Mrs. Hammond gives it a good testimonial. "After years of suffering" and "after her case had been declared hopeless by the most eminent physicians."

In coming home today I saw a translation of Karl Emil Franzos "For the Right" advertised & had a copy sent you.[2]

Mother will be shocked at our reading German in the translation; but the original was not accessible & I thought you might even prefer the English. It is more convenient for passing it on.

I am reserving my novel-reading until Mrs. Deland's "John Ward, Preacher" shall appear.[3] It is advertised for April & we expect it to be very good.

Give my love to your young ladies.[4] They are the only ones (plus their cousins) of whom I am passionately fond at present. Be careful that they lose none of their charm as they advance in years.   Your brother

1. Alfred's birthday was 23 March.
2. Karl Emil Franzos, *For the Right*, trans. Julie Sutter (New York, 1888); originally *Ein Kampf um's Recht* (New York, 1882).
3. Margaret Wade Campbell Deland (1857–1945), *John Ward, Preacher* (Boston, 1888). The book, which went through nine printings in its first year, was a plea for a more liberal Christianity than the old Calvinist view, and the author argued for a just solution of the problems of labor and poverty. Mrs. Deland and her husband Lorin (see LDB to Alice Goldmark, 12 September 1890, note 1) were among LDB's closest friends. They became next-door neighbors to the Brandeises upon LDB's marriage in 1891.
4. At the time, Alfred had two daughters, Adele (1885–1975) and Amy (1886–1973). He would have two more, Fannie (1892–1971) and Jean (1894–1978). When he bought a large farm on the outskirts of Louisville in 1912, he named it Ladless Hill.

Adele never married and made a career first as an unpaid arts supervisor for the Kentucky Works Progress Administration (WPA) and later as an editorial writer for the *Louisville Courier-Journal*. Amy married William Harold McCreary and was the only one of the four who did not pursue some career. Fannie, like Adele, never married; although she never had a salaried position, she played an important role on the Louisville music scene, running the Chamber Music Society for twenty-five years and writing the program notes for the Louisville Orchestra. Jean married Charles Tachau and was president of the Louisville and Kentucky Birth Control Leagues at a time when "nice ladies" did not support such causes; in later years she would be repeatedly honored for her pioneering work in this area.

To: **Frederika Dembitz Brandeis (fragment)**
Date: **November 12, 1888**
Place: **Boston, Massachusetts**
Source: **Mason, *Brandeis*, 93–94**

I must send you another birthday greeting and tell you how much I love you; that with each day I learn to extol your love and your worth more— and that when I look back over my life, I can find nothing in your treatment of me that I would alter. You often said, dearest mother, that I find fault—but I always told you candidly that I felt and sought to change only that little which appeared to me to be possible of improvement. I believe, most beloved mother, that the improvement of the world, reform, can

31

only arise when mothers like you are increased thousands of times and have more children.

To: **Alfred Brandeis**
Date: **March 20, 1889**
Place: **Boston, Massachusetts**
Source: **EBR**

MY DEAR AL: The year has rolled 'round, and I have to you [*sic*] tell you formally again, my dear fellow, that I hope the coming one may bring you great happiness & that Jennie and the little ones may keep well & all the other good things hold their place in your life.

Jennie wrote me that you have a stenographer & an assistant. Of the improved office I have not heard, but I trust it is on the way. Our own offices we hope to change in a couple of months.[1] We are to see our prospective landlord this week. The cost of fitting up the premises including the building of a vault rather staggered us & we are taking some days to recover from the architect's figures & still hope that the proprietor may be induced to assume some part of the expense. Whatever he decides, our decision I presume is a foregone one—as we must have rooms in the same building with S.D. Warren & Co in order that I may see something of Sam.[2]

We are having a Water fight now which is quite as warm as the rag fight was a few years ago, with the advantage however of the Community being with us, instead of prima facie against us.[3] I have been making public opinion by wholesale. The press is full of our editorials, the law reviews of our articles,[4] & before the legislative committee on Water Supply we have had two hearings & another comes Monday.

Goodbye. Much love

I hope you will like the book I send.

1. The firm of Warren & Brandeis had grown so successful that LDB moved its offices from 60–62 Devonshire Street to larger quarters at 220 Devonshire.

2. Although the firm would retain his name for several more years, Sam Warren had left the practice the preceding year upon the death of his father to take over management of the family's paper mills.

3. The growth of towns and cities in Massachusetts brought into direct conflict two vital public needs, the necessity for pure drinking water and the use of water for mill power. Growing urban areas increased their use of source waters and thus reduced the flow of rivers and streams for downstream mills. LDB was working to have the state legislature require fair compensation to mill owners by the municipalities that cut into their water power sources.

4. Warren and LDB wrote two important studies of riparian rights, examining the old common law rules of water usage and statutory revisions. See "The Watuppa Pond Cases,"

2 *Harvard Law Review* 195 (1888–89), and "The Law of Ponds," 3 *Harvard Law Review* 1 (1889–90).

To:	Alfred Brandeis
Date:	October 23, 1889
Place:	Boston, Massachusetts
Source:	Brandeis MSS

MY DEAR AL: The razors arrived. Merci. I used one of them this morning with the best results. I am sure my old one will improve by the vacations it may now hope for.

The report that trade is disgusting is not so pleasant. Perhaps that is only a momentary condition. At all events Dumas must, as you say, be a comfort at such times. Life was never disgusting to those fellows. Their prowess was great, but nothing as compared with their sagacity. Why, Becky Sharp pales before Milady Clark, and more—she was not nearly so handsome.[1]

I longed for the musketeers last evening. I had dined with the Delands, then made a short call & as I returned to my rooms at nine sought something light, but found nought but an article on the "Early History of Chancery in Massachusetts"[2] Schöne [*].[3]

This evening I spent an hour and a half at the Law Library, on a case which will probably come up in the Supreme Court of Mass. tomorrow.[4] The Washington Case is promised for the first week in November.[5]

Mrs. Deland's "Sidney" is to appear serially in the Atlantic.[6] Houghton[7] hopes to "boom" his monthly with it. Poor Mrs. Deland has been made miserable with the vistas of gold which rival publishers have caused to flitter before her eyes.

I am growing very fond of the watch.

Love to Jennie & the babes   Yrs

1. Becky Sharp is the amoral heroine of William Makepeace Thackeray's *Vanity Fair*, Milady Clark is the beautiful villainess of Alexander Dumas's *The Three Musketeers*.
2. Edwin H. Woodruff, "Chancery in Massachusetts," 5 *Law Quarterly Review* 370 (1889).
3. Lovely [*].
4. On 25 and 26 October LDB argued *Washburn v. Hammond*, 151 Mass. 132 (1890).
5. In November LDB would argue his first case before the United States Supreme Court, *Wisconsin Railroad Co. v. Price County*, 133 U.S. 496 (1889).
6. Margaret Deland's novel *Sidney* was published in several installments in the *Atlantic Monthly* in 1890 and was brought out in book form that same year.
7. Henry Oscar Houghton (1832–95) founded Riverside Press around 1850, which eventually became the Houghton Mifflin Company. In addition to his book and magazine publishing, Houghton also served a term as mayor of Cambridge.

To:	Adolph Brandeis
Date:	December 16, 1889
Place:	Boston, Massachusetts
Source:	Brandeis MSS

MY DEAR FATHER: I have yours of 14th. I hope you will conclude to let nature take its course with Fannie—whatever that course may be. Don't force her to eat—or even induce her to eat if she does not desire to do so. If there is a Providence—(& I believe there is)—he may be offering the great corrective for the suffering which she has borne. We interfered once and have had reason to regret it. I am glad she knows of Alfred's death. I cannot bear to be guilty of untruth with her any more than I would interfere with her action as to herself in regard to eating. I have heard it said that with some patients the desire to refuse food was the one sane wish.

I have no telegram from you & presume there is no change to report.[1]

Your son

1. Fannie Nagel, subject to periodic fits of depression, fell into a deep melancholia after the death of her son Alfred from typhoid fever in 1888. This news was kept from her for some time, for fear that it would increase her depression. She fell ill again after the birth of her daughter Hildegarde (1890–1985) and on 5 March 1890 killed herself.

To:	Alice Goldmark[1]
Date:	June 9, 1890
Place:	Boston, Massachusetts
Source:	Popkin MSS

MY DEAR ALICE: Jim[2] brought me a very kind invitation to Keene Valley.

It looks now as if I could be there July 5th or 7th. Will you ask your Mother whether I may come then?

I know that even country houses are of limited dimensions, and the full complement of guests for that period may have already been reached. If it has, do not let me be the one too many, for I am sure that I can find shelter in the elastic Putnam shanty, and that is so near by that I shall still feel myself a guest at your Mother's.

Jim tells me that you expect to start as early as the twentieth. It makes me long to start on my vacations too. Indeed the blue sky, the abundant green and today's heat are most demoralizing to one's working forces.

I find that with each succeeding Sunday a new demoralization sets in and a holiday "ist gar arg."[3]

I called on the Smith's yesterday and shall be prepared now to report on them when we meet. They spoke very pleasantly of Jim's visit.

Father & Mother promised to come East in August for some weeks at the sea shore.   Cordially yours

1. In March LDB went to St. Louis for the funeral of his sister Fannie. He stopped for a short visit with his uncle Samuel Brandeis and found that his second cousins Alice Goldmark (1866–1945) and her brother Henry were house guests. Although the cousins had met before, this occasion marked the beginning of a serious interest on their part. When the Goldmark family went to Keene Valley, New Hampshire, for their annual summer vacation, AGB arranged to have LDB invited to join them.

A cultivated young woman, AGB belonged to a well-educated and cultured family whose accomplishments spread across the fields of business, government, and the arts (see Goldmark, *Pilgrims of '48*). Beginning with their courtship, she would provide constant encouragement to LDB in his reform activities, and some members of the family credited her with introducing him to his role in the Zionist movement. During their life in Boston, AGB worked in a variety of reform movements herself, including labor and women's suffrage, although for the most part her own accomplishments were overshadowed by those of her husband.

After LDB went onto the Court in 1916, AGB became more outspoken, providing assistance to Nicola Sacco and Bartolomeo Vanzetti, working openly for Robert La Follette's election in 1924, and taking the unusual step of becoming vice-chair of the Progressive League for Alfred E. Smith in 1928. She also worked at improving the juvenile courts system in the nation's capital.

Although AGB suffered from periodic bouts of depression, she gained a reputation after 1916 as one of the most gracious Washington hostesses. Like her husband, she had little use for ostentation or elaborate entertainment, but she made their home a center for young intellectuals, reformers, and civil servants who came seeking LDB's advice.

2. James Goldmark (1862–1947), a wire manufacturer, was AGB's older brother. During this time he was involved in a number of "good government" reforms and also helped to set up boys' clubs affiliated with the University Settlement House in New York.

3. "Is very unpleasant."

To: Alice Goldmark
Date: July 20, 1890
Place: West Chop, Martha's Vineyard, Massachusetts
Source: Popkin MSS

MY DEAR ALICE: I have made such an ignominious failure in my attempt to reach Keene Valley in July that I dare not embarrass your Mother's summer arrangements by any promise for August.

I still hope to see the Adirondacks, and you before the Fall, but it seems best to let me take my chance of finding shelter at the Shanty or Beede's; and then, if there is a spare corner in your Mother's house, I can emigrate.

My parents, Mrs. Nagel, Faunerd and Hildegarde are here. Charlie has gone to St. Louis, but expects to return on the twenty-eighth. Isn't that quite a settlement?

This island is very attractive to the lovers of the sea and one need not fear the heat. Indeed these few days past have let one long for warmth and a cessation of the wind. My canoe is lying unused on the beach. A north-easter is giving us a choppy sea, which frowns forbiddingly.

My people seem quite happy here and I am happy to have them so near Boston. Very cordially

To:	Alice Goldmark
Date:	September 6, 1890
Place:	Boston, Massachusetts
Source:	Popkin MSS

Only a word more today.

I have been reading masses of papers, legal documents of every kind, and there [*sic*] all watermarked: Alice.

Nothing has come from you yet. Indeed no letter could come and it was a great relief to be able to talk with Charlie Nagel about you. He is such a noble fellow, and this time must be a very hard one for him.[1] He said merely: "It makes me feel lonesome."

Do you know, he had an inspiration about us.

As he walked in this morning he said, before I had spoken a word about Keene Valley, that my story seemed "suspicious"—and then he told me of a conversation which he had with his mother about us Thursday.

I wish he could know you. He thought some of starting for Keene Valley tomorrow; but does not want to remain away from West Chop so long. Now he promises to come to New York Christmas week. I wish I could tell you now of all the good there is in him; but perhaps you know of it through Felix [Adler] or Mother.

There is no delivery tomorrow, so that Monday will bring me the first word from you. That will be very long to wait, and then how many days more before I can see you!

1. Nagel's wife Fannie (LDB's sister) had taken her own life in March.

To:	Alice Goldmark
Date:	September 7, 1890
Place:	Dedham, Massachusetts
Source:	Popkin MSS

MY DEAR, SWEET ALICE: Charlie is lying by my side. He has been with me since yesterday and to him I could speak of you as I could speak to no one but you. Fannie's spirit surrounds us and their ideal love brings me so near to Charlie now. It was nearly one o'clock before we finally went to sleep last night. There was so much to say of you and of Fannie, of Fannie and of you. How she would have rejoiced in you and felt with us! When Charlie arose this morning his first thought was the joyous thought of us, and he says it had been years now since his first thought on awakening was not one of sorrow. That feeling about Fannie now makes me understand your thinking so much of your Father on Thursday.

How I long to be with you, to ask and to tell all that concerns us both. It seems almost as if I should run away from the duties which called me here; but the thought that it was the performance of a duty that brought you to me fills me with a superstitious fear at neglecting any one that may present itself.

How differently duties appear now. Formerly it appeared as if the only joy in life lay in the performance of duties as duties, and now there appears the happiness of living. If only you were near me. It was a pleasure today to feel you in refraining to smoke that after-dinner cigarette, because you do not like it. That made you almost physically present.

To think you are mine and that I should know so little of my treasure— so little except its vastness, except that it is illimitable. Alice, I am so impatient to share my thoughts with you and to demand my part of yours. All the future is opening itself before me. I see us living so beautifully together. Oh! how much I have to ask and to tell and to learn.

Charlie is lying on the bed. He has finished his cigar, and the tears show in his eyes as they have done so much since yesterday. Poor fellow—how he suffers at the thought of his loss. A man less noble would envy me.

The day is beautiful, the sky almost cloudless. In the morning we rode over two hours in this lovely country. Charlie had not seen it before, and is delighted. It looked more beautiful than ever today when I thought that you would see it with me and teach me to see what I had overlooked.

This afternoon we propose driving to Dorchester, some five to six miles, where I must see the family of a client who died during my stay at Keene Valley. This man was very kind to me in the earliest days of my practice & you may remember the telegrams Father brought to camp. They announced his death.

Percival Lowell[1] and Reginald Gray[2] are below. Otherwise there is nothing to disturb the peace of this spot.

Percy you will find entertaining and Reg. you will like. His is a fine nature. But I care not to talk to either of them today.

Goodbye. Tomorrow I shall hear from you.

Charlie sends the love of a brother.

1. Percival Lowell (1855–1916), a well-known astronomer, did pioneering work on the study of Mars. He founded the observatory that bears his name in 1894 and wrote a number of books on the Far East as well as on astronomy.

2. Reginald Gray (1853–1904) was a member of LDB's class at the Harvard Law School and now had offices opposite LDB's at 220 Devonshire Street.

To:	Alfred Brandeis
Date:	September 8, 1890
Place:	Boston, Massachusetts
Source:	Brandeis MSS

MY DEAR AL: The date tells me that your wedding day is nearly upon us and I must send my Congratulations and good wishes.[1] How much you are to be congratulated I know now better than ever before.

My dear fellow, may all go well with you and yours and may you be wise enough to grasp all the happiness which comes within reach.

Much love for Jennie and the girls. Your bro

1. Alfred Brandeis married Jennie Taussig on 10 September 1884.

To:	Alice Goldmark
Date:	September 9, 1890
Place:	Boston, Massachusetts
Source:	Popkin MSS

Three letters came from you today, dear Alice, and the world was thrice gladsome. A sky grey as theory could not subdue the sunshine. How beautiful all seems now. The work went well, and the play—no, that did not go quite so well, for I felt you should be with me and how happy we should be then.

I read those letters, and read them again. They give me more of your lovely nature than the hard photograph. Perhaps the new ones will please me better; but I long for the soft tones of the one which Cax must take for you when you return to New York. Will you let him, dear?

I fear I myself am on bad terms with pictorial art. The photographers always fail to satisfy my friends and my family will not be content with the portrait. Dear Alice, you will have to take the original and if Keene Valley were not so many miles away he would be at your side now.

I am always wondering what you will say to this and that, to him and to her, as they march before me in the grand panorama of life. This evening

I called to greet the Warrens (my partner's mother, sister & brothers)[1] who have just returned from Europe. Mrs. Warren showed me her wealths of paintings and I was thinking throughout how someday they would appeal to me when you acted as Cicerone[2] among the Corots & Rousseaus. Oh, I am so impatient to pour out to you my thoughts and to plead for yours. I feel now that the world is so full of interest. Things which were dead to me have become instinct with life, in the thought that they will interest you.

How beautiful it was as I lay in the boat and you recited poetry. My dear Alice, I begin to feel the true meaning of noblesse oblige. Your love has ennobled me, and I shall be obliged to become worthy of it.

A hearty telegram came from your brother Charlie[3] today.

I have brought Pfafner (the pony) to town and had my first ride here today. He is a good fellow, almost as good as Rex.   Good Night

1. Susan Cornelia Clarke Warren (1825–1901), the matriarch of the family, had five children with her husband, the late Samuel Dennis Warren (1817–88): Sam, the oldest, was LDB's partner; Henry Clarke Warren (1854–99) was a scholar of Sanskrit and Pali; Cornelia Lyman Warren (1857–1921), the only daughter, devoted her life to philanthropy; Edward Perry "Ned" Warren (1860–1928) collected classical antiquities; and Frederick Fiske Warren (1862–1938) was a political radical and utopian.
2. Guide.
3. Charles J. Goldmark (1867–1942), Alice's brother, would become a well-known electrical and consulting engineer specializing in transportation problems.

To:	Alice Goldmark
Date:	September 12, 1890
Place:	Boston, Massachusetts
Source:	Popkin MSS

MY DEAR, SWEET GIRL I do hope the fatigue was momentary merely, but I fear that you may have exerted yourself in writing, because of my forlorn condition Monday. You must not tire yourself in writing to me, and I promise to behave better hereafter.

I have just been sitting with Lorin Deland[1] who came down from Kennebunkport today. They are most delighted and are inclined to look upon you as my savior. You will see this from Lorin's letter which reached me this morning.

Mrs. Sam Warren[2] came to the office this morning to congratulate me and was most charming. She said she would write and ask you to make them a visit in October at Mattapoisett. I told her that you might not be able to do so, but that I hoped you would come to her sometime. Mr. Warren I love as a brother, and Mrs. Warren has always been very good to me and promises to be as good as she can be to you.[3] I do hope you will feel like coming to Boston to some of the people who are so near to me, and I should wish that you would come first to the Delands. Mrs. Deland you will love and I am sure she must love you. Lorin was most excited tonight at the thought of your making them a visit.

The Nagels left at seven this evening. It was hard to have Charlie go, and hard, too, for him to leave. Poor fellow, how noble and what capacity for happiness!

It is only a week since I saw you and it seems an age, and there is another such age before me. Lorin insists that I look five years younger than when he last saw me; but I assure you the wrinkles and gray hair are coming fast.

That was clever about "Alice in Wonderland." Whose idea was it? It sounds like Christine.[4]

I like Davidson[5] for those lines of Sappho. Did you ever read the Grillparzer "Sappho"?[6] I remember only the impression of beauty and loveliness.

Good night. Don't be tired again

1. Lorin F. Deland (1855–1917), the husband of novelist Margaret Deland, was a wealthy Bostonian interested in literature and the arts. He owned an advertising agency and used the profits to support several local charities.

2. In 1883 Sam Warren married Mabel Bayard, the daughter of Thomas Bayard, the three-term senator from Delaware.

3. According to Martin Green, relations between Sam and LDB had begun to cool in 1883, primarily because of Mabel Warren's dislike of LDB. He was not among the one hundred guests invited to the wedding; and while the Warrens entertained often and lavishly, she omitted LDB's name from the guest lists whenever possible. After her husband's death in 1910, she reportedly burned all of LDB's letters to him. *The Mount Vernon Street Warrens*, 102.

4. Christine Goldmark was one of Alice's younger sisters.

5. William James once termed Thomas Davidson (1840–1900) a "knight errant," a sort of modern Socrates devoted to a rigorous search for truth. But unlike many philosophers, Davidson insisted that knowledge should be applied to practical problems. He helped the New York Educational Alliance establish the Breadwinners' College, which provided instruction for working people at night, and he also had a camp in Keene Valley where he ran Glenmore, a "summer school of the cultural sciences."

6. Franz Grillparzer's *Sappho: A Tragedy in Five Acts* was originally published in German in 1818. LDB probably used the translation by Ellen Frothingham (Boston, 1876). Sappho, an early Greek poet, was reputedly passionately in love with a beautiful youth named Phaon. Failing to arouse any affection on his part, she threw herself off the promontory at Leucadia into the sea, under a superstition that those who took the "lover's leap," if not destroyed, would be cured of their love.

To: Alice Goldmark
Date: September 13, 1890
Place: Boston, Massachusetts
Source: Popkin MSS

Alice, my heart is bubbling over with joy today and all for you. Poor Pfafner must have suffered. In my exuberance, I rode at the top of his speed.

Just as I was starting for Dedham I spied Mrs. Glendower Evans[1] who returned today from England. With difficulty I refrained from blurting out my Vita Nuova on Mt. Vernon St. Her I must tell of it tomorrow.

She is the fourth of the Deland Quartette (which must soon become a Quintette) and has been very near to me since her husband, then my most intimate friend, died in 1886. Besides I have never known anyone with such a capacity to sympathize with the joys of her friends. Mrs. Evans knows Felix [Adler] and has met your mother and Christine.

Lorin Deland said last evening "But how I pity Young."[2] I felt shocked that it had never occurred to me that there was anyone who would not be unqualifiedly glad of our happiness. The thought of Jim Young then saddened me and I concluded that I must tell him at once. We have lived together now six years with uninterrupted harmony and a broad sympathy. I cannot remember that in all those years one irritable or irritating word was spoken by one of us to the other, or that either appeared without the other being glad.

Young could not conceal a certain sadness and I realized how sad I should have been, but for you. My dear Alice, I see the future so beautiful, so rich in the blessings which your love will bring, there is a new point of view to every trivial circumstance of life. I have found the much longed for New Dimension. It must be depth. I looked into your eyes and beheld the infinite.

1. Elizabeth Gardiner Evans (1856–1937) was taken under LDB's wing when her husband of four years, Glendower Evans (1856–86), died unexpectedly. She later recalled how LDB had told her of the many social ills she could work to alleviate and how he had helped guide her into a useful career as a public-spirited citizen. Her work as a member of the Massachusetts Minimum Wage Commission in 1911–12 led to the establishment of the first permanent organization of that kind in the country. LDB's children, as well as younger colleagues in reform work, all called her Auntie B. See her series of articles "People I Have Known: Louis Dembitz Brandeis, a Tribune of the People," *Progressive* 2 (January–February 1931).

2. James Holden Young (1850–1920), after taking his law degree at Harvard in 1875, began a long practice in the firm of Hutchins & Wheeler. He and LDB had begun sharing quarters in 1884, an arrangement that would come to an end with LDB's marriage.

To:	Alice Goldmark (fragment)
Date:	September 15, 1890
Place:	Boston, Massachusetts
Source:	Mason, *Brandeis,* 72

I wish you could have seen Mrs. Glendower Evans when I told her. She fairly bounded across the room.

To: Alice Goldmark
Date: September 23. 1890
Place: Boston, Massachusetts
Source: Popkin MSS

Alice, dear, as we walked yesterday hand in hand down the road, the future pictured itself so beautifully before me. Thus we were to travel on the journey of life, to share the joys and the sorrows, the gay and the serious. I felt very grateful for that happiness and longed to be worthy of it. Then the sense of obligation weighed heavily upon me, and I could find peace only in the thought that all I am and have is now yours, to be transformed by your noble spirit.

Your Thursday's letter was such a comfort this morning and I know you will be glad, too, of Margaret Deland's letter which I enclose.

The trip was a good one & Father & Mother seemed very happy.

Your

To: Alice Goldmark
Date: September 29, 1890
Place: Boston, Massachusetts
Source: Popkin MSS

MY DEAR, SWEET ALICE: A few hasty lines went to you at noon. Let me add a few more. It was easy to keep silent when I could look into your eyes, but now when I am so far away it seems as if I must speak, as if I must call your name and tell you how different the world is now since my life is yours.

Alice, when you were in the Adirondacks I thought I would be content once you were in the city and so accessible, but now, ungrateful wretch that I am, the lessened distance seems quite as much too great.

Will you be content to make the day of publication[1] Saturday Oct 4? Then I can announce it, flee from my pursuers to your protection and we can have Sunday together before meeting the public.

Oh, Alice, I wish I were with you. Indeed I am doing many foolish things for lack of your advice. One was telling a client he could consult me tonight, and I am sure my opinion will be of little value to him. Another was accepting that invitation for Saturday. I might have declined both "on account of a previous engagement." Your

1. Of their engagement.

Alice—The house No. 114 Mt. Vernon Street is secured. Delands' is No. 112. I hope you will not be disappointed because it is not ideal. Only of the possible it seemed the best for us.

Lorin and I are maturing the plans for alterations so that they may be humbly submitted to you and are growing impatient to have you see the house.

Dear, I was not quite sure how much you liked the house for its own sake when you said so sweetly that I should do what seemed to me best. Remember, you must exercise the prerogatives of a partner—to doubt and to criticize. But I really think you will deem the choice of house wise—all things considered—and to me the thought is pleasant that it is a house we shall want to grow out of.

I spent some of last evening collecting the photographs of my family which I promised to bring Susie.[1] There are many of Fannie and Alfred Nagel, some which I consider far better than those Mother had. Poor Susie. I think of her so much. She will enjoy coming to us, I think. The distances are short here and streets smoother. The difficulties of locomotion will be far less.

The engagement is apparently leaking out here. I was congratulated yesterday from a forbidden source. When I told Copeland[2] of it, some time ago, he said: "She must like me. Tell her to—or at least—to pretend to."

Mr. Emerton came in yesterday to present his congratulations. Alice, I wish I were in New York. Margaret says I ought to go, at least four times a week. So do I.

1. Susan Goldmark (1862–1941) was an older sister of Alice's and a partial invalid throughout her life.

2. Charles Townsend Copeland (1860–1952) was one of Harvard's greatest teachers. After a brief career as a drama critic, "Copey" joined the university and "stimulated generations of men to find color and strength and beauty in books and in the world, and to express it again" (Samuel Eliot Morison, *Three Centuries of Harvard, 1635–1935* [Cambridge, 1936], 402).

Alice, I hope you understood Sunday without my saying it in so many words, that you must not let the arrangement about the house influence you in any way in fixing the time when these weekly separations shall end.

The fear that I might appear unduly impatient made me hesitate much before acting at all in the matter, and I took the step that I did merely because I thought that you were entitled to have me exercise my best judgment.

So dear, you must not be hurried, nor set the day for our wedding earlier than you feel is best. Only remember Alice, I need you very much.

Is it not strange? For seventeen years I have stood alone, rarely asking, still less frequently caring for the advice of others. I have walked my way all these years but little influenced by any other individual. And now, Alice, all is changed. I find myself mentally turning to you for advice and approval, indeed, also for support, and I feel my incompleteness more each day. But, dear, know too that I understand you, and do not fear that I shall fail to appreciate your decision whatever it may be. I feel myself growing each day more into your soul, and I am very happy.

That second letter of yesterday was a great comfort and I have read it many times. The first was meagre, "but as a sauce to make me hunger more"[1] and I feared it was all that I should have from you today.

That leak in the dam proved to be a break and I have opened wide the flood-gates of felicity.

Mrs. Shaler's[2] and [*] letter I enclose. Much love, my love,   Fondly

1. Shakespeare, *Macbeth*, IV, 3:81.
2. Sophia Penn Shaler (1843–1918) was born in Louisville and no doubt shocked that city's society when she married Union captain Nathaniel Southgate Shaler in 1863. After the war he became a professor at Harvard, and his wife was well known for her assistance to students.

To: **Alice Goldmark**
Date: **October 8, 1890**
Place: **Boston, Massachusetts**
Source: **Popkin MSS**

MY DEAR, SWEET ALICE, I do long so to be with you tonight. It seems as if I must fly to you and sit by your side, to gaze into those eyes and see you are mine. Or perhaps, it were better to say, I am yours. Put it either way, dear, only I wish we were together that I might in silence pour out my heart to you and drink in new life.

[James] Young has gone. I hardly feel sorry; it seems as if I were much nearer to you when I am alone—and then in the diary[1] I possess a bit of your past.

Pray let me warn you about the information Mrs. Moffat is to give you. Be assured, Alice, it is apocryphal, and subject to the additional infirmity of hearsay.

Many letters came from home today. Of course much love is sent to you. Father is quite pathetic. "Tell Alice," he says, "I should like to have a word from her occasionally. It is bad enough not to be able to look into her sweet face every once in a while". Yes, it is bad enough.

From Charlie Nagel a letter came too. He is making a brave fight. So brave that he must win. I transmit obediently a letter from Mr. Chamberlayne[2] to you. He used to be in our office. Possibly Henry may have spoken of him, for he was a '78 man. Two years ago I was his best man.

A multitude of letters have come which contain greetings for you. You may not find them very interesting but, perhaps, I had better bring them to you as you will doubtless meet the authors later.

Goodbye, dear Alice

When Fannie was your age ill in Dresden she read Thomas à Kempis.[3]

1. AGB had given LDB her diary to read; while the surviving sections are few, it is easy to see why he found them so fascinating. They indicated that in nearly every important area she shared his view of public service, of living simply, and of nature. The remnants are in the possession of Alice Brandeis Popkin.

2. Charles Frederick Chamberlayne (1855–1913) practiced law first in Boston and later in Schenectady, New York, where he died following a swimming accident. Chamberlayne wrote on the law and edited several treatises on evidence.

3. Thomas à Kempis (ca. 1379–1471) was a German monk best known for his influential devotional treatise *Imitation of Christ.*

To:	Alice Goldmark
Date:	October 10, 1890
Place:	Boston, Massachusetts
Source:	Popkin MSS

It was afternoon, dear Alice, when your letter came today and the morning was quite dreary. I am sorry your afternoon yesterday was so dreary, too. Was a visit to Cox[e]s among the deadening occupations?

My friends are becoming clamorous for a view and I must confess some desire myself for a really good picture of you. But it must be very good, else I should prefer my memory and imagination.

Dear, I feel more rested tonight and the temptation to go to you grows stronger, but I know it is best to adhere to my resolution of yesterday. But I really dread Sunday.

I doubt whether I can find any photograph of myself. Surely none but poor ones exist. I will make search, but care has been taken heretofore to destroy all traces.

A very urgent invitation came today from the Democratic State Central Committee to accept the nomination for Representative to the Legislature from Ward IX. It would be very interesting, but of course I cannot do it. It is one of the many things one must postpone or leave wholly undone. This year would be a great one in politics. The Republicans must yield soon and blows will tell now.

It was very nice of Mrs. Wigglesworth to write you. I have a very warm feeling for George,[1] am always happier for having been with him, but we really see very little of one another although they live quite near.

Good night, with ever so much love

---

1. George Wigglesworth (1853–1930) was a textile manufacturer and lawyer, who would later be an ally of LDB in the drive to establish Savings Bank Life Insurance (SBLI). He married Mary Catherine Dixwell in 1878.

To:	Alice Goldmark
Date:	October 11, 1890
Place:	Boston, Massachusetts
Source:	Popkin MSS

There is not a sound save the crackling of the logs. I am alone. Even the Mastiff who long lay motionless at my feet has slipped away. The other members [of the Dedham Polo Club] are scattered to the four winds.

Blessed quiet, blissful absence of people. Oh, Alice, if you were but here, how beautiful it would be. Dear, I cannot tell you how much I long to be with you, to be with you thus alone far, far away from the bustling, babbling crowd. This week, it seemed as if I must have you. The noise, the crowd, were almost intolerable. I felt as if I should flee from this wilderness of men, flee with you to a wilderness of trees & of stones, where not even an Edith could follow us. I worried [*] & did not mean to say more than that you must not worry because I am not so very tired. Only I have learned when I must rest.

12 October

At this point, I drew the willow lounge close to the fire and was soon lost in day-dreams of you, which melted into dreams of the working day, but when evening came I wanted only you, and in default of you, solitude. Here there is calm, and the brisk ride of twelve miles brought just that suggestion of fatigue which quiets the nerves.

Don't imagine, Alice, that I am working particularly hard. I have done no more than usual, only for many weeks I have felt dragged out. Indeed I have felt so all summer, for the days at West Chop could not be restful. That loneliness of which you write and which cast me so upon people for many years makes me long to escape from them now. I cannot rest where they are. My own parents can't quite understand this, can't understand how a man in perfect health who can work, ride or paddle eight hours in a day and be fresh after it, should be fatigued by what is play to most of the world. But enough of this, Alice.

The day is bright and crisp. I awoke early and lay watching the night yield to the day. The sun peeped in through the blinds; then came the chirping of the little birds near the windows and, in the distance, the cock's arrogant crow—the dog's bark—the rumbling of the milk-cart— a shot from the early sportsman—and, then, and always, I longed for you Alice, I wished you were here, or that we were by the river, or in the camp, or at Sheldon's retreat, or in Felix's study, or anywhere, if only not separated.

Maynard[1] will be coming soon for the morning's ride. He and Mrs. Maynard are afraid you won't like them, but I assured him that you are very discriminating. Somehow or other that didn't seem to allay his perturbation.

Those photographs I sent you yesterday may interest you. I am sure Jessie's[2] and those of Ottilie Benedikt Franzos[3] and Edith Harland['s] child will. Albert Otis'[4] is horrid and the same may be said of some others.

It is one minute of nine. If this were New York, I should be seeing you now, my dear.

Your

Enclosed a review of Mrs. Deland's *Sydney*, Boston H[oughton]. M[ifflin].

---

1. Laurens Maynard (1866–1917), after brief careers in law and business, founded a publishing house in Boston in 1897; in 1914 he issued a collection of LDB's early speeches and articles entitled *Business—a Profession*. He had recently married Gertrude Cain of Weymouth.

2. Probably Jessie Cochran.

3. Ottilie Benedikt was the daughter of Frederika Dembitz Brandeis's close girlhood friend Bettie Manthner. LDB had met her in Vienna in 1872 when the Brandeis family was on its extended trip to Europe. She married the Russian-born writer Karl Emil Franzos. See LDB to Susan Brandeis Gilbert, 4 April 1928.

4. Albert Boyd Otis (1840–97) was born in Belfast, Maine. After graduation from Tufts University and the Harvard Law School in 1866, he practiced law in Boston.

To: Alice Goldmark
Date: October 12, 1890
Place: Boston, Massachusetts
Source: Popkin MSS

MY DEAR GOOD ALICE: How long it seems since I woke this morning, and I have been with you alone nearly all the day.

R[eginald] Gray and Maynard came for the ride about eleven; we had two hours across country with a half-dozen fences to warm the blood; but much time wandered quietly through the woods, the men sympathized with nature and said nice things of you, and I was glad to be with them. This was all that I saw of my fellow beings except the Cabots for a moment in the afternoon. They were out for a ride & came over to bring me their congratulations.

After lunch and a siesta, I wandered off to the Charles.

Sky and river were of intense blue[,] the sun shone brightly and the red maples were reflected in all their glory. As we glided along quietly (the canoe & I) it seemed as if we were on the voyage of eternal peace. I thought, Alice, how you will love the canoe, and how well it expresses you: the silent dignity, strong but tender, sensitive to the slightest touch, responsive to every word, listening with bended head to each whisper of nature, with a heart for all human emotions and a soul to grasp the divine. Canoeing is not a sport; that were to make it frivolous and ignoble. It is the great interpreter of nature—unarticulate poetry, dumb music.

Dear, I felt ashamed at the neglected look of the canoe. It needs of scraping and of varnish, & bands and patches to make her tight, reproached me. I recalled how long this had been so—and how before you came to me I had not the interest to put her in order. Today I was thinking of the joy of working over the canoe with you by my side.

Alice, Alfred was wrong in saying I am "very much in love." No this is not a passion, not a fever with which I have fallen. It is that I love you, for the light has come to [me], as faith and religion sometimes come to man.

At dusk I started off for town. Long ride by star light was a fitting ending for the day. The air was crisp Sunday and the darkness added to the peace.   Good night, dear

To: Alice Goldmark
Date: October 13, 1890
Place: Boston, Massachusetts
Source: Popkin MSS

48

I am very, very sorry, Alice, that I could not make yesterday pleasanter for you, but today I feel quite rested and Saturday will doubtless find me in excellent trim.

Your letter to Mrs. Wigglesworth has been forwarded. Did I answer your enquiry about the letter to Mrs. Warren? If you addressed it "Mrs. Samuel D. Warren, Mattapoisett, Mass" it no doubt reached its destination.

I saw the Delands this evening. Margaret is greatly perturbed about Sidney.[1] You have found in her poems the great cloud in her life, the fear of death; not for her self, but for Lorin. So rather it is not the fear of death, but of separation from Lorin. It is that idea she has expressed in "Sidney."

It makes me very happy to think that all of you appreciate Father and Mother so, and it was sweet of you, dear, to write Father. You can be sure that he will appreciate it.

Alice, it seems an age since we met. Margaret says you rescued me from premature senility.

Goodnight,   Your

1. Her latest novel.

To: **Alice Goldmark**
Date: **October 17, 1890**
Place: **Boston, Massachusetts**
Source: **Popkin MSS**

Friday, my dear. It seems as if a hop, step and a jump would bring me to you and it is difficult to refrain from resorting to that undignified method of locomotion. Indeed, Alice, I might just as well have "cut and run" today. My thoughts have been always with you. Only the shell was here, a very uninteresting one which can have been of little use to my clients.

I am on my way home from the Curtis Club Dinner, our law club that meets on the third Friday of each month. It is early still, but I had no patience there. My only comfort was in sitting next to Russell Reed, an inveterate Democrat, to whom I could pour out my ire against the Republicans. I am so indignant at their doings that it requires some self-command not to take the stump.[1]

Yes, Ottilie Benedikt was not without arrogance. Jessie [Cochran]'s pictures are really not so poor, only the photographic art is not a fit means of reproducing what is in her face. I will send you a letter from her sometime which will introduce her better. And to really know her, you should hear her play.   Good night, dear—and tomorrow

1. The previous day LDB had written: "Today I have been having great fun acting as counsel for one of the contesting nominees for State Senator. The air was filled with O'Brien's, Reagans, Tumultys, Gallogans, Killions and the like, a very verdant and spontaneous assembly. Between times I have tried to work on my Institute of Technology lectures. Surely if 'variety is the spice of life,' no East India cargo could furnish such an assortment. These Democrats were even more entertaining than the Emigre Marquis."

To:	Alice Goldmark
Date:	October 20, 1890
Place:	Boston, Massachusetts
Source:	Popkin MSS

Yesterday was beautiful. Those peaceful hours made you seem very near to me and brought great happiness.

Alice, let me beg you again, to be frank with me always. Do not fear that I may not understand you. I have not looked in vain into your eyes. I have learned how pure and good and noble you are. I know, too, that one often feels what one hesitates to express, because reasons to support it seem wanting—and yet the feeling is true.

Only trust in me, Alice.

People, like us, with some experience could not look into the future from this perfect present, without some apprehensions. The past of others necessitates that. But we can, we must, try to win and to retain the happiness we long for, and in that attempt we must be one.

Goodbye, my dear, dear love,   Your

To:	Alice Goldmark
Date:	October 21, 1890
Place:	Boston, Massachusetts
Source:	Popkin MSS

I have been reading and rereading your letter, dear Alice, and then looking, again and again, at the picture of you taken in 1878. How much pleasure that has given me I cannot tell you. Thank Susie for it. You really have not changed since then; you have merely grown older. I feel now as if a bit of your past had become mine, and dear, I long to possess that together with the present and the future.

I forgot to take the Kaliaweiler photograph with me. For its associations I want it; but this picture of you at twelve is the only one I have yet seen which gives me any satisfaction.

The thought of Sunday has remained with me, quite as Lowell says. No, I had not seen that before.

Alice, I feel that the next Sunday too must be omitted again. I am much less tired than before, but really to be tired at all seems not quite "decent," and I am determined to get into good trim again, if possible.

Our talk about dress has been in my mind this evening. Of course I would not have you a bit less unconscious than you are, and you know how I hate frivolous frills and over-dressing. I am convinced, too, that most women make the mistake of having many dresses. But, after all that can be said, there is a truth underlying Bunthorne's pathetic remark that he was "a trustee of beauty" and dared not be derelict to his trust. When a woman happens to be both handsome and artistic a certain obligation rests upon her. There is a call upon her thought and her taste. With a woman of mind and of taste there is the same reason why her dress should be more effective as there is that her house should be more attractive or her table better.

Lorin [Deland] and I rode together this evening and then I went in for a moment to see Miss Merrington. The poor woman looks dreadfully. Surely she needs more than a short rest. Later I saw Mrs. Evans who wanted to talk with me. Her sister, Miss [Eugenia] Gardiner, was there and begged leave to call on you.

I showed Mrs. Evans the '78 photograph and she understood it. When you spoke of Emerson's appreciation of nature[1] I intended to tell you how much Mrs. Evans loves him.

The half moon is shining in upon me. Eight weeks ago this evening we met again. It was my renaissance.　　　　　　　　　　　　　　　　Your

1. Ralph Waldo Emerson (1803–82), the eminent American philosopher and essayist, wrote frequently of the ennobling power of nature.

To:	Alice Goldmark
Date:	October 25, 1890
Place:	Boston, Massachusetts
Source:	Popkin MSS

A week ago at this hour I was a hundred miles nearer to you, Alice. How I wish I were two hundred-odd nearer now.

Your letter of yesterday filled me with infinite impatience. My dear, there is such a crescendo and accelerando in my longing for you, that the next week will surely seem endless.

Last evening I had a delightful young fellow to dine with me, Andrew Hugo Green[1] of Chicago, a '94 or '93 man at Harvard and a brother of Mary Pomeroy Green[2] of Chicago, who is much admired by our family.

Miss Green wrote me last year, asking that I should see her brother, and he proved so much more attractive than many older people that I was very glad to have him look me up again this fall. He, too, is a lover of nature and of solitude, and has a tender feeling for literature which is beautiful.

Goodbye, dear, I must return to work.   Your

1. Andrew Hugo Green (1869–1939) was then training to be an engineer; in 1901 he would move to the West Indies. See LDB to Adolph Brandeis, 23 July 1905, BL.
2. Mary Pomeroy Green (1857–1945) was the daughter of one of Chicago's pioneer families and was active in social service and a variety of philanthropic activities.

To: **Alice Goldmark**
Date: **October 27, 1890**
Place: **Boston, Massachusetts**
Source: **Popkin MSS**

Of course, you are right, Alice; at least I think so for it has been a pet opinion of mine, formed early, and often recurred to.

I remember in my Cambridge days, talking enthusiastically of Mrs. John Ward[1] of Louisville, a warm friend of our[s] who possessed the rare combination of beauty and mind, charm of manner and character. When I had finished my rhapsody, Mrs. Emerton said: "What has she done?" I answered, somewhat heatedly: "Done? Nothing. She is!" That conversation defined my idea on the subject.

And only as recently as last summer, Father and I talked over the same subject. He referred to some petty success of mine and remarked: "You must be proud of that honor." I told him that I could not recall ever having been proud of anything accomplished or to have deemed any recognition an honor. Indeed, I believe that the little successes I may have had were due wholly to the pressure from within, proceeding from a deep sense of obligation and in no respect to the allurement of a possible distinction. Our talk the other Sunday touch[ed] upon the same ground.

Of course results are not to be despised. They are evidence of what produces them. But they are not the only evidence; they are often deceptive, and their absence is by no means conclusive. It is only in the Latin sense that talents are to be "admired"; they are to be wondered at. But character only is to be "admired" as we use that word. It is the effort, the attempt that tells. Man's work is, at best, so insignificant compared with that of the Creator, it is all so Lilliputian, one cannot bow before it.

Feeling that so strongly, you can imagine, Alice, what happiness it gave me to find on the flyleaf of your diary those lines of Matthew Arnold's (which I had, of course, *not* known before):[2]

Life is not a having and a getting;
but a being and a becoming.

My dear girl, I pour out my innermost thoughts to you; indeed much which I should have hesitated to think to myself. But I have longed so for the one being to whom I should give all that I am, without reserve. You must take me for better or for worse, and do not think too ill of me. I shall be better some day when you shall have made me over.

Dear, dear Alice—yes, Saturday is near and then I may look into your eyes again.   Your

1. Eliza Clendennin Peay Ward (1842–1906), a Louisville native, married Col. John Hardin Ward III (1835–1908), a former Confederate office and prominent attorney, in 1871.

2. The English poet and literary critic Matthew Arnold (1822–88) was noted for his classical attacks on contemporary taste and manners, especially on those he called the Barbarians (the aristocracy) and the Philistines (the commercial middle class). The quotation is from Arnold's best-known work, *Culture and Anarchy* (London, 1869).

To:	Alice Goldmark
Date:	October 30, 1890
Place:	Boston, Massachusetts
Source:	Popkin MSS

MY DEAR, DEAR ALICE: I have no peace & must speak with you before I commence work this morning. Dear child, I love you very much. My heart goes out to you and I need to be with you.

I knew, Alice, you would not reproach me; but I could not feel very content with myself. Soon you will be here, then all will be well.

No, I did not send that wrapper to Susie. It must have been Jim. I sent Susie only a letter, the Schurz speech[1] and Prof. Hart's pamphlet on American History,[2] since I saw you.

My pony stumbled last night and cut his knee, how badly I do not know yet. The hostler thinks he can be used today, but I shall not believe it until I try. He recovered himself after he stumbled so that I did not go off.

Jim is to dine with me tonight, and tomorrow night I am to start for New York!!!

1. Carl Schurz (1829–1906) emigrated to the United States from Germany after the failed 1848 rebellion. He then entered both journalism and politics, serving as American minister to Spain, Civil War general, senator from Missouri, and then secretary of the interior in the Rutherford B. Hayes administration. An ardent reformer, Schurz was one of the driving forces behind civil service reform. On 20 October he had spoken before the Massachusetts Reform Club on "The Question of the Hour," predicting a dramatic jump in the cost of living as a result of the Republican insistence on high tariffs.

2. Albert Bushnell Hart (1854–1943) was professor of history at Harvard and the author, co-author, or editor of more than one hundred volumes of history. The pamphlet may have been the sources and notes he put together for American history courses at Harvard that fall, *Pamphlet for the Use of Students* . . . (Cambridge, Mass., 1890).

To:	Alice Goldmark
Date:	November 28, 1890
Place:	Boston, Massachusetts
Source:	Popkin MSS

The step backward is always hard, and this return, dear, to the habits of October is not pleasing. Alice, it seems almost as if I could not write, as if writing put you farther away instead of bringing you nearer.

I have just come from Mrs. Evans and the Delands. Mrs. Evans had taken Miss Holt to the Reform the [*sic*] School and they had but returned at eight o'clock. She spoke beautifully of you.

Margaret is greatly distressed at her domestic condition during your stay and says that her perturbed state interfered even more than in the inability to entertain you as she would have desired, that her mind was so disturbed that she could not give herself up to knowing you as she hopes to soon. I think this is true, and that you have not had an opportunity of seeing her at her best. There is in her a restfulness, and a capacity for becoming absorbed in the interests of others which was scarcely manifested during our stay. Denman Ross was at the office today and spoke of his enjoyment & his mother's in having you at their house.

I have been fairly busy today, *but have not* rushed. Indeed I am far less tired than yesterday, only very sleepy.

"Dafür giebt es ein Mittel,"[1] my Mother used to say, and I propose to drink deep of the drug.

There was a fire at the [Dedham] Polo Club last night, but no serious damage was done.

Good night, dear girl.

If your Mother is not better very soon, do take her off to the country for a few days.

1. "There's a way to do it."

To:	Alice Goldmark
Date:	November 29, 1890
Place:	Boston, Massachusetts
Source:	Popkin MSS

Your beautiful letter has bridged over the abyss that seemed to separate us yesterday and today I have felt your spirit hovering over me, and I can hardly realize that we are not to meet when I leave the office this evening. But I still can find evidence of your stay in the impression you have left upon all of those for whom I care most. Margaret spoke of you so lovingly, so appreciatively last night that I loved her more for it.

The great problem of the Deland house-hold has been settled; not the servant question, for I consider revolutions there always possible, & hence the problem never settled, but I mean the dining-room enlargement. It has been decided in the affirmative, and the workmen are well under way.

Another important announcement! Lorin said last evening: "I think I shall have to confess myself beaten on the Herald-Post controversy."[1] The week does not expire until today, but I feel greatly encouraged by this report on 5/6 of the days.

And still another piece of news desiring heavy headlines:

Miss Edith Stolt & Will Gardiner[2] went skating yesterday in Brookline. When you come, we may get some in Dedham.

The proof[s] have come of the article on "Privacy"[3] & I shall write Charlie Nagel today enclosing him a copy. I have not looked over all of it yet, but the little I read did not strike me as being as good as I had thought it was.

However, I am in very good spirits today over a victory. The best conveyancer in town, who had stood out for some time against our criticism of a title which he had passed as good, concluded today "he had better succumb." Dr. Pangloss[4] would add: "Gilbert" and Margaret would say: "I take it all back."

Then I succeeded in settling with a comparatively small loss that error made by one of my assistants, about which I spoke to you last week.

Goodbye, dear, dear girl. More soon.

1. Perhaps a friendly debate over which Boston newspaper to take.
2. Will Gardiner was Bessie Evans's younger brother.
3. Originally it was believed that Sam Warren's resentment against the penny press coverage of his and his wife's entertaining led him to consult with LDB about privacy and that out of those conversations came the ground-breaking article by the two men, "The Right to Privacy," 4 *Harvard Law Review* 193 (1890). Recent research indicates that there was relatively little newspaper coverage of the Warren parties; but whatever the origins of the article, it remains a landmark in legal history. Roscoe Pound later declared that it did "nothing less than add a chapter to our law." LDB would, of course, remain a champion of the right to privacy all his life. In the article he explored the common law basis of privacy; in his dissent in *Olmstead v. United States,* 277 U.S. 438, 471 (1928), he laid out the rationale for a constitutionally protected right to privacy, a right later recognized in *Griswold v. Connecticut,* 381 U.S. 479 (1965).
4. The overoptimistic tutor in Voltaire's *Candide.*

To: Alice Goldmark
Date: December 1, 1890
Place: Boston, Massachusetts
Source: Popkin MSS

Alice, I am very sorry you were disappointed last evening by not receiving a letter. One was written which should have reached you, but I left it at my rooms & so could not mail it until evening.

Of course, I am willing to consider March 2d as "not quite definitely settled yet," since that would make you feel happier.[1] You must not force yourself before you are ready; and I want you to feel that however much I long for you, I shall be happiest with what makes you so. Perhaps I ought to say, however, that I believe it would not be wise for us to postpone the date very far.

Since yesterday noon there has been a constant rush. I was called suddenly into a case, through the illness of another lawyer, and have had to give two evenings to work besides extra long days. The only peace has been on horseback. Jack Wade joined me at half-past six this morning and promises me his company for tomorrow's ride. Have seen no one since Monday whom you know.

Letters have come from Father & Mother. Mother appears to be gaining, but very slowly.   Good night, dear

    1. Evidently LDB wanted to fix the wedding date, and the earlier the better. It is unlikely that Alice was having second thoughts, but she seemed reluctant to settle on a date, much to LDB's distress. See LDB to Alice Goldmark, 24 December 1890.

To: Alice Goldmark
Date: December 6, 1890
Place: Boston, Massachusetts
Source: Popkin MSS

MY DEAR, SWEET GIRL—Your letter has just come, and I bow humbly before the "At Home" for next Saturday. It will not be a bore, but merely less enjoyable than an evening alone with you. Some of the people I shall surely like and I want to know all the people you do, whether you like them or not.

You must surely tell me of Felix [Adler]'[s] surprising views. I did not know that he could hold any views on that subject which had not been disclosed to you.

If you do not get a letter from me on Monday, do not be surprised or anxious. It is probable that I shall go to Maine tomorrow morning to try whether something cannot be done to quiet the waves in the conflict between Will Gardiner and his father.[1] If I go, I cannot return before Monday evening & you could probably not hear from me before Tuesday evening.

I have great doubts whether I can really help Mrs. Evans much, but I think it best to leave no stone unturned.

Lorin [Deland] and the sanitary engineer have been in today. They also seem determined to leave no stone unturned.

A few lines came from Father today. Mother seems to be really no better and I cannot help feeling somewhat anxious.[2] I believe she is anxious about herself too.

Sam Warren has begged me to come & dine with him this evening and help entertain his Mother & sister. It seems very strange that he should want that, but he appeared so concerned about it that I have given up a Reform Club dinner in order to help him out.   Goodbye, dear

1. See the next letter.
2. The nature of Mrs. Brandeis's illness is unknown; she would live another eleven years before dying of cancer. See LDB to AGB, 22 August 1901.

To: **Alice Goldmark**
Date: **December 8, 1890**
Place: **Boston, Massachusetts**
Source: **Popkin MSS**

The function of a Father Confessor is to give absolution, and as dereliction of duty is abhorrent to me, I must quickly perform mine.

Dear child, I am very sorry you felt forlorn. Perhaps it was from sympathy that I felt the same.

You see, Maine claims me no more. In the language of the diplomats "a modus vivendi has been established."[1] I trust it is more than an armistice, but the future is not cloudless & there may be other outbursts.

The trip was not bad. A railroad journey yesterday until half-past five. Then sixteen miles along the coast by starlight with a fast horse. And today, boarding the train at ten minutes of five and a journey till one. "Diana of the Crossways",[2] in the best of print, helped to shorten the hours. You would surely have agreed that the trip was not "half-bad," in spite of rising at four.

You would also have been interested in my finding the Palace Car conductor an old acquaintance, one of the jurymen in a case I tried five years ago. Only, to my shame be it said, the recognition was all on his part. I did not upbraid him; but I wanted to complain that he had not given my client a larger verdict.

There must be a letter on the way for me and I long to have it. Of course I do. Perhaps it may come by a later mail.

1. Between Will Gardiner and his father.
2. George Meredith, *Diana of the Crossways* (New York, 1885).

To:	Alice Goldmark
Date:	December 9, 1890
Place:	Boston, Massachusetts
Source:	Popkin MSS

MY DEAR ALICE, I send Mother's letter and Father's picture. The latter seems to me good, only not as refined as the original.

Your letter of Sunday came. It is good, dear, to have you tell me that your love for me grows; but I do not deserve the admiration. Someday, perhaps, when there is in me more of your handiwork, I may deserve that too. At times, I feel as if there were in me the potential of some thing, & if it is there, I am sure you will bring it out.

You speak my thoughts in what you say about right living. The value of that is surely underestimated by even the good people of the world. I mean the value as an example. We Americans particularly have been so overwhelmed with huge figures that we are apt to underestimate the value of the unit in the great mass. To me the potency of example seems very great. Most people are like the iron pyrites with which the teachers in physics perform their experiments. They lie powerless, motionless, dormant before the magnet is applied. Then they move wherever they are drawn, and it is matter of chance whether it be the positive or the negative pole to which they march.

Mrs. Evans tells me that Mrs. Holt needs her and that she may go to New York soon. Of course you will see her. This last week has been a hard one to her, and she has borne it nobly.

To:	Alice Goldmark
Date:	December 10, 1890
Place:	Boston, Massachusetts
Source:	Popkin MSS

DEAR CHILD, It is nearly two weeks since we parted. The days of the week go but slowly and Saturday evening seems very far off. There shall be a strong endeavor not to be impatient.

This evening I dined at Melvin Adams'.[1] You may remember my speaking of him. He is a lawyer of perhaps forty years, whom I like very much.

A man of charm and of great kindliness. There is in him much of the native Yankee. Born in a small town of Massachusetts, he worked his way to college & through it (Dartmouth), and has won himself a good position at this bar.

The Adams[es] are neighbors of ours, live in Pinckney St. (the street east of Mt. Vernon) just above Louisburg Square. Mrs. Adams is not his equal.[2] He married when he & she were young, when a pretty face and rosy cheeks were irresistible. Since then he has grown much & she doubtless little. You must meet Adams when you come again & that, I presume, entails meeting his wife. Really, she is not so bad as these remarks would indicate. Possibly one would not consider her bad at all, save by contrast. Only I cannot keep making an odious comparison when I meet them.

Those lines of Emerson are fine & your thought most true.

Your Uncle Max' letter is very German. Alice—but I must not be impatient.

1. Melvin Ohio Adams (1850–1920) had practiced law in Boston since 1876, including two stints in the U.S. attorney's office. He was also president of the Boston, Revere Beach & Lynn Railroad.
2. Adams had married Mary Colony of Fitchburg in 1874, immediately upon graduation from the Boston University Law School.

To:	Alice Goldmark
Date:	December 20, 1890
Place:	Boston, Massachusetts
Source:	Popkin MSS

MY DEAR CHILD, It is for your own sake that Mrs. Evans cares so much for you. I was but the accident that brought you together, or at most (to use one of those legal phrases which you are learning to like) the presumptive, which ceases to have uses where once proof is adduced.

Margaret mentioned the Mastiff to me & I told her to apply to the Supreme Authority. If you care to have him, of course I shall be glad. My doubt was whether you would want to burden yourself with him at first, when many things will be strange and have to be brought into working order. Eric is quite a care, and perhaps with the other unnecessary ones it might not be wise to add this one. Of course, a dog is always obtainable. I will not give Margaret a definite answer until I hear what you think about this.

This is another glorious day. Jack Wade failed me this morning. Perhaps his mercury reached the freezing point. But it was beautiful, though cold; perhaps I should say, beautiful because cold, or, at least, beautiful and cold.

Here is another missive from Mrs. Andrews. Do you remember my telling you about her one day in the study? Nie im Leben![1]

Father says Mother is doing quite well.

1. Never in [real] life.

To:	Alice Goldmark
Date:	December 22, 1890
Place:	Boston, Massachusetts
Source:	Popkin MSS

Your letter brings very good news, the definite statement that you are coming. You had not spoken of that since your return to New York and I thought you might want to stay there longer, but feared to ask.

It seems to me best that I should not go to New York for Christmas since it will not be to bring you back. Charlie [Goldmark] will be with you, Jim [Goldmark] thinks, only that day & it seems to me that you should have all of him that you can, & you would not have much if I were there.

There is a certain amount of work here which must be done, & if I do it before you come I should have so much more time when you are here & it is best I think to make leisure for then.

If Mrs. Evans will wait till Monday & bring you here then, I am inclined to spend Sunday as well as Christmas at work & have a good time in the "open" when you arrive. We have been training [a] pony to go in harness & I hope that by another week he will go so smoothly that I shall be willing to take you out driving daily. He goes nicely in the buggy, better really than under saddle. Yesterday I drove him to Dedham & back.

If Mrs. Evans returns before Monday would you be willing to come on Sunday afternoon, say on the three (3) o'clock train, or the four o'clock? I could then take some Saturday train for New York.

I feel very heroic, Alice, in suggesting a postponement of our meeting. Still it seems the civilized thing to do, to waive an immediate pleasure for a greater one in the future. What do you say? I am ready to stay or go whichever you think best.

Miss Gardiner told me she would write you. She is very good and I think you would not object to living in her house. Of Mrs. Hecht you need have no fear. Did I not tell you that she has gone South with Miss Hattie & her brother-in-law Louis Hecht?[1]

Lorin [Deland] and I spent much time in the house and on housekeeping matters yesterday. Most of the debris has been removed from the house and one can really see how it will look. As I go over it now, I think we might, perhaps, have gotten along comfortably without adding the fourth story, but that story is certainly a great addition to the house's value—and will be of great value to use, if you make a studio of the fourth room. It is admirably adapted for that.

Lorin & I have agreed (subject to your approval) to run partly cooperative and strongly competitive households, details to be respectfully developed and submitted to you & Margaret.

I have suggested to the editor of the Post that the question of the day for women is Domestic Service, & that he should invite suggestions for its solutions. You see this is all preparatory to the formation of the "American Domestic Service Co., Limited."

Last evening I read in Process Goldmark again.[2] I earnestly pray that our English legal jargon may not be as unintelligible as that. A few pages of the German exhausts head and eyes.

Father writes that Mother is decidedly better and adds: "I am daily more impressed with Clay's skill as a physician."

There was fine skating at Dedham yesterday. The Charles was a sheet of ice, as smooth as glass. The Elliots and Cabots were all on the ice. Mrs. Elliot (whom I chanced to take from the Club to the [*] in the buggy with *pony*) looked very beautiful.

The front room at the Polo Club (which was burned) is being beautifully remodelled, hard floor, white paint & all the glories of a new establishment.

Goodbye, dear. I really feel that I am to have you again.

Where shall you go first when you return? Do you remember those Greek lines, of the seven cities each of which claims to be the birthplace of Homer?[3] It is very apposite.

1. Louis Hecht (1840–1922) was born in Germany and came to the United States as a child. In Boston he joined with his brother Jacob to build Hecht Brothers, an important wool merchandising house in Boston. The sister-in-law with whom he was traveling was probably Mrs. Jacob Hecht, wife of his brother, the merchant and philanthropist.

2. Joseph Goldmark fled Austria following the failed revolution of 1848; at the time he had been accused not only of treason but also of complicity in the murder of the minister of war, Theodor Latour. In 1867 Emperor Franz Josef promulgated a general amnesty for political offenses, and Goldmark immediately seized upon it as a chance to clear his name. The following year he returned to Vienna, stood trial, and was acquitted of all charges. The book LDB refers to is Joseph Goldmark, *Der Prozess Goldmark . . .* (Vienna, 1868), a transcript of that trial. The story is told in Goldmark, *Pilgrims of '48,* 272–82.

3. Although Homer never mentioned his birthplace, seven cities claimed him—Cyme, Smyrna, Chios, Colophon, Pylos, Argos, and Athens.

To: Alice Goldmark
Date: December 24, 1890
Place: Boston, Massachusetts
Source: Popkin MSS

Alice, I should be glad to have you talk with Felix,[1] unless you prefer that I should write him.

As to the day in March please select, dear, the one which you prefer. Monday, March 23rd is Alfred's birthday. If that is a time which you would choose, the selection of that particular day would give Mother, and probably Jennie also, much satisfaction. But do not fix upon that day if for any reason any other seems to you preferable.[2]

I am sorry I am not to be with you tomorrow to talk this over since you would wish it, but in one way I am glad: I should rather have you uninfluenced by me in making the selection of the day.

Goodbye, dear child, a merry, merry Xmas. More later today. I send this by an early mail as you should have an immediate answer.

    1. Probably about asking Adler to perform their marriage ceremony, a request to which he gladly agreed.
    2. In fact the marriage occurred on 23 March.

To: Alice Goldmark
Date: December 24, 1890
Place: Boston, Massachusetts
Source: Popkin MSS

Alice, I feel inexpressibly doleful at the thought of not going to you tomorrow, completely lost. Indeed, I am almost coward enough to hope that you will order me to come. Heroism is very fine, but not pleasant.

Copeland has been reading me Stevenson's Father Damien;[1] that has given me a bit more courage; but I am still in a most dilapidated condition.

Dear child, I do so long for the days we may spend together again. Those mere glimpses of you which a single day permits leave but an unsatisfied longing, an accentuation of the pain of separation.

Copeland was with me two hours, and was in his best mood, witty, incomparably so, and I laughed like a sorrowful king at the court fool. If this ————— I don't know what was intended for this sentence. Young has come in and is talking Father Damien with wild attacks in the Red style.

Mother writes that Jennie and the children leave for St. Louis today. A year from now, I trust, you & I will be going to New York. I think I shall be able to care for Christmas then when once you are with me.

Good night, my dear, dear girl. There is but one comfort, the thought that I am needed here.

1. Robert Louis Stevenson, *Father Damien: An Open Letter to the Reverend Doctor Hyde of Honolulu* (London, 1890). Father Damien (1840–89) was the beloved English priest who went to Molokai and tended to the lepers living there. Charles McEwen Hyde (1832–99) was an American Protestant minister who was in the vanguard of missionaries attempting to convert Hawaiian natives. The letter, which enjoyed wide circulation (especially among anti-imperialist groups), compared the two men's missions, much to Hyde's disadvantage.

To: **Alice Goldmark**
Date: **December 26, 1890**
Place: **Dedham, Massachusetts**
Source: **Popkin MSS**

Alice, I have come out [to Dedham] for an airing and have had time to think of the Sunday four weeks ago. This seems an awful waste.

The club is absolutely deserted, only Mrs. Walley is here, who says: "If I hadn't heard you were engaged I should not have given you credit for it, because the young lady looks as if she were your sister." Strange, passing strange!

The official dinner last evening was more enjoyable than I feared and it was midnight before I reached home. The Chief Justice of the Commonwealth,[1] His Excellency the Governor,[2] the Honorable Attorney-General Elect,[3] with their respective spouses, and as many others made up the dinner party. We were at table two hours and [a] half. It seemed like a perpetual returna al segno,[4] but the theme and variations, strange to say, were not oppressive and I have survived without serious detriment to health or happiness.

Her Excellency the Governess[5] was at my right, and was not too heavy, despite the burden of precious stones which she carried; and Miss Ada Forbush, an old acquaintance and quite a nice girl, was at my left.

Miss Forbush told me that the Saturday Morning Club is to discuss the Problem of Domestic Service next week. Of course, I planted my views.

1. Walbridge Abner Field (1833–99), after serving as a congressman, was appointed to the Massachusetts Supreme Judicial Court in 1881; he became chief justice in 1890.

2. John Quincy Adams Brackett (1842–1918) served in a number of political offices, beginning with Boston councilman, and was elected governor in 1890; he would serve only one term in that office.

3. Albert Enoch Pillsbury (1849–1930) had just been elected as attorney general; LDB would have extensive dealings with Pillsbury later in the decade when the latter served as counsel to the Boston Elevated Railway Co., the object of intense reform effort by LDB and the Public Franchise League.

4. In music, a direction to the performer to go back and repeat from the place marked.
5. Brackett was married to the former Angie M. Peck of Arlington.

To: Alice Goldmark
Date: December 28, 1890
Place: Boston, Massachusetts
Source: Popkin MSS

Now, dearest, it is only two days till Monday, long ones alas, but only two. Your letter has come and is a great comfort. The sketch has just come also, but I have not seen it yet. I do not want to open it at the office where I am writing this.

Of course you are right about privacy[1] and public opinion. All law is a dead letter without public opinion behind it.[2] But law & public opinion interact—and they are both capable of being made. Most of the world is in more or less a hypnotic state, and it is comparatively easy to make people believe anything, particularly the right. Our hope is to make people see that invasions of privacy are not necessarily borne—and then make them ashamed of the pleasure they take in subjecting themselves to such invasions. Of course, many, like Poo Bah,[3] desire to be insulted—"court" the insult—as if it were an investigation.

The most, perhaps, that we can accomplish is to start a back-fire, as the woodsmen or the prairie-men do.

I send you the last H[arvard]. L[aw]. S[chool]. Assoc. circular to show you how public opinion may be made.[4]   Good night dear

1. See LDB to Alice Goldmark, 29 November 1890, note 3.
2. Sixteen years later, in writing about savings bank insurance, LDB would say: "At all events, it is even more important to educate those persons who are now savings bank trustees and the wage earners as to the inequity of the present system and the necessity of developing insurance on savings bank lines, than it is to get the necessary legislation. If we should get tomorrow the necessary legislation, without having achieved that process of education, we could not make a practical working success of the plan." LDB to Henry Morgenthau, Sr., 20 November 1906, BL.
3. Poo Bah was the Lord High Everything Else in Gilbert and Sullivan's *Mikado*.
4. LDB was one of the founders of the Harvard Law School Association and served as its secretary for many years. For a summary of LDB's long relationship with the school, see James M. Landis, "Mr. Justice Brandeis and the Harvard Law School," 55 *Harvard Law Review* 184 (1941–42). Landis gives full details on LDB's tireless efforts on behalf of the association.

To: Alice Goldmark
Date: January 17, 1891
Place: Boston, Massachusetts
Source: Popkin MSS

It was good, dear Alice, that yesterday and Thursday were comparatively calm, for today was most perturbed. The Boston end of the great Westing-house Electric Co.'s financial embarrassment was dumped into our office without warning and I have spent the day at the end of telephone & telegraph wires. Then others were in trouble also. Fortunately tomorrow is Sunday. Writs cannot be served then and lawyers can hope for some peace.

Alice, we shall not be able to escape one of those Hall Clocks. That client-bringing client of mine, Mr. Ellis,[1] insists upon presenting us one, of fabulous cost & wants me to select the kind of wood.

I settled for him yesterday a much litigated case, which had cost him much money, & I refused to receive any more pay. So this is his revenge.

I will send you a cut showing the style.

Goodbye, dear, I must try to pick up a dinner at Delands or Mrs. Evans' house.

Christine [Goldmark]'s letter came.

1. Possibly William D. Ellis, a representative of midwestern distillers and a member of the executive committee of the Massachusetts Protective Liquor Dealers' Association (see LDB to Alice Goldmark, 9 February 1891). See the next letter.

To:	Alice Goldmark
Date:	January 21, 1891
Place:	Boston, Massachusetts
Source:	Popkin MSS

Alice, Your letter brought me much happiness, and much longing. I am glad now of the passing of each day, for each day gone seems to bring me nearer to you.

The estimate for the shades has come. $25.25 for 25 shades. Please let me know which shall be hung from the bottom.

The estimate for the papering has also come:

Hall	$13.50
Reception room	13.50
Dining room	11.46
Library	11.70
Spare room	10.50
Two rooms 3rd floor	8.08 &
Preparing walls	3.50
	$72.24

You & I are very economical.

I sent you today a book containing specifications of clocks. To my surprise, Mr. Ellis has selected *No. 81* which is the simplest in style & in every way the most desirable of all.

The clock which I saw is mahogany & very handsome. Shall we take it in that wood? I rather feared the clock could be a white elephant but perhaps it would look well in the northwest corner of the reception room. What do you say?[1]

The work at the house is almost at a standstill. The carpenters are waiting for the plastering to dry before laying the floors and the painters are waiting for the carpenters. Mr. Johnson says they will begin on the floors this week.

I bought a hat today, as much as possible like the former one.

Goodbye, dear

1. This clock, now more than a century old, is a treasured possession in the Maryland home of Mr. and Mrs. Frank Brandeis Gilbert; Frank Gilbert (see LDB to Susan Brandeis Gilbert, 4 December 1930) is the grandson of LDB and AGB.

To:	Alice Goldmark
Date:	January 29, 1891
Place:	Boston, Massachusetts
Source:	Popkin MSS

MY DEAR CHILD, It needs no assurance to convince me that with you matters of moment are not determined by an "idle fancy." The 23rd of March will suit me, of course, and the selection of that day will give pleasure to Mother & to Jennie.

I will, however, defer telling them of the selection until you tell me to do so.

As for myself, I shall be glad, indeed, of the postponement, if thereby you are enabled to avoid a rush or being "busy." Pray don't assume that all things of the old life are to be closed up & settled before the day, as if one were making a "last will & testament." To me it seems more beautiful to think of our lives continuing, enlarged, enriched, ennobled, but the same. Nothing, dear Alice, which you can bring with you, outside yourself, would compensate me for the thought that you had unduly tired yourself in getting it.

It will be very pleasant if the girls become convinced that "four o'clock & the family" shall be our cry, but I would not have them settle upon that plan unless they are really convinced that it is best.

Mother has recalled to me [**]'s lines:

"Wenn Du sprichst von Anverwandten
"Wird dem Hörer Angst und bang."[1]

The house is making rapid strides. The ceilings are finished. I hope you won't think the tint too yellow. As against the whitish walls it looks somewhat intense, but the paper will doubtless make it look very differently. The yard has been cleaned out & the carpenters are finishing the coal bin today. The mantels are expected this week.

My throat would not yield to the whiskey & I had to resort to Mrs. Angell's mysterious powders, which have so often worked a miraculous cure. Margaret [Deland] says Mrs. Evans is still far from well.

I stupidly left some valuable papers on my desk last evening & had the pleasure of going back to the office & convincing myself that I can work the combination.

1. "When you speak about relatives, / the listener becomes anxious and horrified."

To:	Alice Goldmark
Date:	February 3, 1891
Place:	Boston, Massachusetts
Source:	Popkin MSS

MY DEAR ALICE: The chemist reports that paper of which sample is enclosed contains a small amount of arsenic &, of course, we don't want it. As I remember, this was selected for the spare room.

What shall we do for its successor?

The B[oston] W[all] P[aper] Co. sent enclosed moulding as sample of what they propose to put in, as the white moulding. They say it is the article customarily used. Please let me know by return mail whether it is satisfactory?

Have you rec'd the bill for the gas fixtures?

All which, my dear girl, is very business-like, & I feel like talking to you of things very unlike business.

Some day, I hope, it will be different; but seven weeks seems very long. Have you written Mother of the day?

To:	Alice Goldmark
Date:	February 7, 1891
Place:	Boston, Massachusetts
Source:	Popkin MSS

"Faithful maintenance of bodily health is as much a woman's duty as to speak the truth."

I stumbled across this passage in reading the other day and delighted to find some support for my code of ethics.

In answering your remarks about not going down to hear Mr. Chubb's[1] lecture I omitted to add this.

You said you were sorry not to go because Susie wanted you to do so. Now, can you for a moment believe that Susie would knowingly have wanted you to give her the pleasure of your company at the expense of your health? What Susie wanted was to have you there, if it was best you should be there. And what you were sorry for, was, in reality, not the fact of absence, but the necessity for your absence. And this necessity was caused proximately by your letting yourself get tired. Actually the cause was more remote, doubtless. In other words, you had not done enough to make you tired if you had really been in good condition; but spend thrift living previously had reduced your capital.

I think that this elaborate reasoning (which is really not so alarmingly complicated as it sounds) should convert every such temptation into an incentive to grow stronger. The truth of this becomes very clear when one stops to think. You are sorry you cannot go downtown for your Aunt Julia.[2] Certainly no one who loves you could wish you to sacrifice your health for her comfort or pleasure. On the other hand, anyone who loves you must wish that you should sacrifice your own comfort and pleasure for others. To sacrifice comfort and pleasure ennobles, as much as to sacrifice health degrades.

It is like borrowing from your friend (and never repaying) in order to lend or give to a beggar, or even worse, in order to give another friend an entertainment.

You may give freely of your own, but have no right to give what is not yours, & become an insolvent or a beggar.

All this of course is unnecessary, dear Alice, I become so used to reasoning out positions that it came into my head & I had to say it.

Sunday morning

I left the office shortly after three yesterday & rode around the Reservoir. Sam Cabot, Arthur's brother,[3] overtook me. He is a pleasant fellow & ordinarily I should have enjoyed his company but yesterday it was only his horse's company which inspired Pfafner & that I could be glad of.

I was tired & there can be nothing to do at eight o'clock but go to bed. This morning I was up early & worked a few hours on some preparation for tomorrow's hearing before a Legislative Committee,[4] work that would have been done much earlier but for the depressed condition of the labor market during the last fortnight. I am going to ride to Dedham. Warren & others are to be out there today.

Goodbye dear. You have left Boston very dreary.

1. Edwin Watts Chubb (1865–1959), a professor of English at Ohio University, lectured widely on literature, especially on Shakespeare.

2. AGB's Aunt Julia Wehle had married S. Oettinger in 1871.

3. Samuel Cabot (1850–1906) was a prominent chemist and a member of the Massachusetts Institute of Technology (MIT) corporation; Arthur Tracy Cabot (1852–1912) was one of Boston's most prominent surgeons and, like LDB, a member of the Dedham Polo Club.

4. See the next letter.

To: **Alice Goldmark**
Date: **February 9, 1891**
Place: **Boston, Massachusetts**
Source: **Popkin MSS**

The supply of note paper has not yet been replenished.

Your two letters came today, dear girl, and were much longed for. Think of it. I sat for two hours at my desk surrounded by men, gazing at the envelope of the second letter (which came at three). What was most tantalizing was the thought that these same gentlemen, having come from Connecticut, would be a hundred miles nearer to you than I shall this evening.

All the morning I was before a legislative Com[mit]tee fighting the errors & hypocracies [*sic*] of so-called temperance people, & carrying out my pet reform of the liquor trade by making the dealers respectable.[1] I don't think I have talked to you much about that, but there is very much that I have to say on this subject. At times I think I can accomplish much with them.

On my way home this evening I fell in with Barrett Wendell[2] who expressed grief at not having seen you.

I will give Forbes directions about the closets. Please make enquiries about the gas fixtures. I have heard nothing in reply to my letter & we are very anxious to have them now.

I well see why you should have been affected by the [*] story.

Good night dear, With ever so much love,

1. The legislature was considering extending provisions of a bill that forbade the sale of liquor except with a meal and, on the urging of so-called temperance advocates, making it even tougher for the citizenry to buy a drink. The law had led to all sorts of subterfuges and even worse, from LDB's point of view, a widespread disrespect for the law. To evade the restrictions, the liquor dealers had been bribing public officials from the legislature down to local police. LDB had agreed to represent the dealers only if they gave him a free hand and did not spend any money except with his approval. Before the legislature, he argued that "no regulation can be enforced which is not reasonable" and urged the assembly to pass reasonable laws that would be fair to all; this, he said, would remove the corruption at its source. LDB proved persuasive, and the legislature passed a moderate measure fair to the dealers. For LDB's brief in this matter, see Brandeis MSS, Scrapbook 1.

2. Barrett Wendell (1855–1921), one of America's leading literary critics, taught at Harvard from 1880 until his retirement in 1917.

To: **Alice Goldmark**
Date: **February 17, 1891**
Place: **Boston, Massachusetts**
Source: **Popkin MSS**

MY DEAR GIRL: Your criticism of Mr. Clark's paper is able & seems to me very just—indeed judicial—so I don't care whether "it is generally looked upon in this way or not" being content with the decision of the Committee of One to whom it was referred with full powers.

The rain has come here also, but between times I had my ride this morning & being somewhat late secured Jack Wade's company. He is ideal as a riding companion. The horse fills Pfafner with noble emulation & the rider leaves me to coveted silence.

Now, I come from the barbers, the hair has been cut, perhaps too short, but it has time to grow sufficiently before you are to see it—alas. And after the barber, my potation of milke [*sic*] with the accompaniment of Animal Cracker.

I was before a legislative committee for three hours this morning & talk[ed] myself (& doubtless others) near to the line of exhaustion.[1] This afternoon I spent two hours on a discussion of a bill to make users of public streets, like railroad & electric light companies, pay a rental to the city.

There is more than enough work coming in. Of late I seem to be occupying the position in part of a senior counsel, that is, one taken in to assist the lawyer already engaged. That perhaps accounts for the barber's discovery of a gray hair today. There are more than he found.

The fixture man says he shipped the gas fixtures before receipt of my telegram, but he says not when nor by what line, so I shall postpone "believing" till there [is] a "seeing."

I am writing at home, where the absence of note paper still prevails.

Goodbye dear—two days.   Your

1. On the liquor question; see the previous letter.

To: **Alice Goldmark**
Date: **February 26, 1891**
Place: **Boston, Massachusetts**
Source: **Popkin MSS**

I enclose you Mother's letter, dear, from which you will see that they propose to go to New York for the twenty-third.

I think it will be better for all that Mother and Father should go with me to the Madison Avenue Hotel. Only some one should go there in time to secure a good room. They generally give me a wretched one. Of course, Mother & Father will take their meals at your Mother's.

Your house will be full enough at that time and will not be as quiet as Mother should have it.

I don't know whether to be sorry or glad that clothes & the like seem such [a] nuisance to you now.[1]

I believe in good clothes; it is only the unreasonable accumulation of them which is objectionable, like the other heresies attending weddings. Don't let the abuse of the convention sicken you of the thing; for you know I shall be very exacting about *your* dress.

I agree fully with you about the forks & spoons.

We are having today your rain of yesterday. I could not ride this morning, but hope to get a ride this evening.

My throat is much better.

Goodbye

I hope you enjoyed Tristan.[2]

1. AGB complained about the tiresomeness of spending hours shopping and with dressmakers.
2. Gottfried von Strassburg first told the story of Tristan and Isolde in the thirteenth century, and it has been retold in many editions since.

To:	Alice Goldmark
Date:	March 13, 1891
Place:	Boston, Massachusetts
Source:	Popkin MSS

ALICE—A week from today I hope to follow this letter. "I'd jump the week to come." Work attracts me no longer and I do no good here.

From Henry [Goldmark]'s letter I judge he may be with you before the twentieth.

Mine host of the Wilder Mansion[1] writes that he will be glad to see us and he does not expect any other guests at that time. If his expectations are realized, it will be better than retiring to one's country home.

For our drives I bought a carriage robe today—about which I was rather uncertain. Of its warmth I am sure & perhaps that is the most necessary quality for the immediate present.[2] I wanted you while purchasing & mentally vowed that you must select the next one. I am always thinking how different it will be after the 23rd. Even when I was getting some of those beloved animal crackers Monday, I found myself thinking: "Well, Alice will get the next." I have not entered the house since you left, but have Murdock's promise to fix the brass-work & have sent the stuff to the chemists.

Last evening I dined at Mrs. Evans. Got very much interested & *talked too much* although there was no discussion, merely narrative. However I went home at 8:20.

Dear Alice, I am very impatient to be with you.

1. Where the couple would honeymoon.
2. A few days earlier LDB had written: "I have purchased a harness and am negotiating for a buggy for you. The one I tried this morning is low, light & comfortable, phaeton style, just the thing for Susie & for our driving tours, but Lorin [Deland] says that the make is poor . . . and that I must look further."

To:	Alice Goldmark [fragment]
Date:	March 15, 1891
Place:	Boston, Massachusetts
Source:	Mason, *Brandeis,* 75

Occasionally I am oppressed by the multitudinousness of things, and I sigh for the rest and peace which can only come in the thought of your continuous presence. If the twenty-third were not fixed immutably, I should feel like anticipating it, and like the Barons of old, break away and carry you off.

To:	Amy Brandeis Wehle
Date:	July 9, 1891
Place:	West Chop, Martha's Vineyard, Massachusetts
Source:	Wehle MSS

One of the immortal Lowells once addressed me thus: "You do not write, ergo, you do worry." This same logic, my dear Amy, would convict us both. We are joint tortfeasors[1] (If your knowledge of Norman french falls short ask your good husband for a treatise on the subject.)

Seriously, it is not proper that we should let indolence, or an undue absorption in our own affairs, bring with it such absence of direct correspondence that we must rely upon the words of others—or to them—for all knowledge of one another.

I have determined to "brace up." The convenience of a correspondent in my own family[2] has relieved me for months of the *necessity* of writing even to Mother—& I find that the temptation of silence, unresisted, was altogether too great.

Alice & I are settled here—doubtless for the summer. The immediate cause of our coming now was to get a long rest myself, but I hope that the stay here will do much for Alice. Rest is good for her and even our smoothly running household entails some motion.

As for myself, I am feeling finely here & am inclined to think that the cause of my tendency to exhaustion under hard work has been discovered. I felt it unreasonable that one so strong & healthy physically should get tired eventually. Now my doctor thinks the trouble comes from my old weakness—the eyes. The strain [is] in using them & fortunately [it is] a strain which he declares can be removed by proper glasses. His theory is that whenever I become tired, the strain upon the nerves of the eyes— whether used in the close or in the distance—caused this tired feeling, which I suppose originated in the brain. I consequently look for increased working forever—and there is plenty of work which I ought to do. I shall enjoy tranquil work again, during the last six months labor has been rather a "grind."

Alice has been reading Sir Walter Scott's Journal[3] to me here. We have covered a year, and such a period gives one a very good idea of the man. He was a fine fellow, a man of the world, not a literary man. He might as well have been a lawyer (as he was) or a politician or a business-man (which he tried to be). Everything in his make-up indicates the man of the world—and not the literary man. But he was a fine fellow, & his fight against adversity, and his struggle to pay off his heavy indebtedness was truly noble.

Alice & I have brought down very many books "all sorts & condition of" books I know not how many we shall read—but the trots are here and among others—a student lamp.

E.G. Art—	Overbeck's Pompii [*sic*]
	Waldstein's Pheidias
History—	Fiske, Critical Period of American History
	Froud's [*sic*] Caesar
Biography—	Agassiz's Life
	Sir Walter Scott
	Goethe's Aus meinem Leben
Poetry—	The Ring & Books [*sic*]
	Palgrave's Golden Treasury
Prose—	Two volumes Matthew Arnold
	Goethe

Fiction—	Les Misérables (5 vols French)
	Kingsley's Westward Ho!
	Kipling[4]

You see we are well supplied.

Alice says I have written enough. She wants to know what I have written. Women are most inquisitive—but then, dear Amy, they have some virtues. I assure you, they are not merely inquisitive, they are also talkive [*sic*] and it is impossible for me to write with all the talk that comes from my wife. So good bye, Dear Amy. I should like to have written more; but I have yielded to the inevitable.   Lovingly

1. A wrongdoer; one who commits or is guilty of a tort.
2. Apparently Alice had assumed the task of keeping up with the family correspondence.
3. *The Journal of Sir Walter Scott,* ed. David Douglas, 2 vols. (New York, 1890).
4. Johannes Adolph Overbeck, *Pompeji in Seinen Gebäuden* . . . (Leipzig, 1866); Charles Waldstein, *Essays on the Art of Pheidias* (New York, 1885); John Fiske, *The Critical Period in American History* (Boston, 1888); James Anthony Froude, *Caesar: A Sketch* (London and New York, 1879); Elizabeth C. Agassiz, *Louis Agassiz: His Life and Correspondence* (2 vols., Boston, 1885); Johann Wolfgang von Goethe, *Aus meinem leben: Dichtung und warheit,* 6 vols. (Stuttgart, 1811–22); Robert Browning, *The Ring and the Book,* 4 vols. (London, 1868–69); Francis Turner Palgrave, *The Golden Treasury of the Best Songs and Lyrical Prose in the English Language* (Cambridge, 1863); Matthew Arnold, *Essays in Criticism* (London, 1865); Victor Hugo, *Les Misérables,* 5 vols. (Boston, 1887); Charles Kingsley, *Westward Ho!* (Boston, 1855).

To:	Pauline Dorothea Goldmark
Date:	December 20, 1892
Place:	Boston, Massachusetts
Source:	Gilbert MSS

MY DEAR PAULINE:[1] Many thanks for the birthday greeting and the good news about yourself.

You are evidently getting all the good out of college life[2]—the social enjoyment as well as the learning. Your description made one wish it were possible to repeat experiences.

Christine [Goldmark] supplemented your accounts & seems to have had a delightful outing at Philadelphia. We are sorry she could not stay longer with us. Remember, that you are now in the small minority of those who have not visited us, and we shall claim your first visit *anywhere*.

Alice bids me tell you that the photograph is a Cumae Sibyl—the Domenichino which is in the Borghese Palace at Rome.[3] I think I saw the original there. Alice won't let me tell how many years ago.[4]

Alice is much impressed by your report of the English instruction and insists that she will have to betake herself diligently to her books in order not to be outdone by a younger sister. Indeed, I forsee [*sic*] numerous additions to our library which is already outgrowing the allotted book-cases.   With much love   Your brother

1. Pauline Dorothea Goldmark (1874–1962) would be an important reformer during the progressive and New Deal eras, working with the Consumers' League and in 1905 becoming director of the New York Child Labor Commission. Along with Mary D. Hopkins, she supervised a number of societal studies for the Russell Sage Foundation.

2. Pauline was then in her first year at Bryn Mawr College.

3. A sibyl was a prophetess that the ancient Greeks and Romans would consult about the future. The picture is *The Sibyl of Cumae* by Domenichino (1581–1641), an important artist of the Bolognese School.

4. LDB had visited Rome with his family on its extended tour of Europe in the early 1870s; see Mason, *Brandeis,* 28–31.

To:	Amy Brandeis Wehle
Date:	April 5, 1893
Place:	Boston, Massachusetts
Source:	Gilbert MSS

MY DEAREST AMY: My—our—very best wishes for the ninth and much love. Alice and Susan[1] must be content with me as the messenger for the present but the young woman is somewhat facile with tongue already (at least with throat & lungs) and no doubt will use her little fingers with due dexterity.

Alice had a bright day and is enjoying her Mother's visit very much. Aunt Regina seems most happy with her latest grandchild and will tomorrow write Mother one of those "Geschriebenen Briefen"[2] for which there is always such a demand. I think Aunt Regina will enjoy the quiet too. The last week was quite a restless one in New York. Pauline was home on her vacation and between Spring-shopping and college friends there seems to have been little peace for the household. In order not to disturb the quiet of our own household, I am going to leave tomorrow morning.

Alice thought you would like Symond's "Greek Poets"[3] which goes to you today.   Again much love

1. Susan Brandeis (1893–1975), the couple's first child, was born on 27 February. A few days later LDB to wrote to his friend Mrs. Evans: "Susan is pronounced a very fine child. She is certainly exemplary in her behavior." Later educated at Bryn Mawr, she took a law degree at the University of Chicago. After serving briefly as a special assistant to the U.S. attorney for the southern district of New York, she opened a practice in New York with her husband, Jacob H. Gilbert. From 1935 to 1949 she served as a member of the Board of Regents of New York, the oversight agency for all educational levels in the state. Susan was the only member of the family to share her father's interest in Zionism and served on the national board

of Hadassah from 1925 until shortly before her death. She was also interested in Brandeis University and served as the honorary president of the Women's Committee and as a fellow of the university.

2. "Written letters."

3. John Addington Symonds, *Studies of the Greek Poets,* 2 vols. (New York, 1882).

To: Amy Brandeis Wehle
Date: February 1, 1895
Place: Boston, Massachusetts
Source: Wehle MSS

MY DEAREST AMY: When your birthday letter bade me pay my debts before the New Year, I thought you had given me ample lee-way. Your good letter of the other day reminds me how many weeks have passed since then.

First the Public Institutions hearing:[1]—then a series of long trials which have occupied most of January, filled the mind, as well as days and evenings—so that I had difficulty in finding much time for aught but occasional excessive indolence. Our library sofa is showing the effects of this indolence. Alice declares it is growing bald and gray "and not from years." Today I abandoned the office soon after three and we went for a long drive—made beautiful by the snow and the Charles River ice fields. Susan had much to tell us on our return—largely "Songs Without Words."[2] She has actually accomplished "Papa"—but occasionally confuses it with "Baby-ba."

Alice doesn't wholly approve of your Peixotto.[3] He is distinctly a man of ideas—and says interesting things but there is a certain forthputtingness which he cannot suppress. We have not seen any of his work recently—but I was impressed several years ago with a sketch of his sisters. It remains in my mind, as if there were three.

We have read very little this winter—except Douglas Campbell's *Puritans*[4]—who annoy me as much as the Puritans did the good people of England some centuries ago. The theme is excellent, but the man's manner is so bad, and so voluminous that my patience suffers me [not] merely to read the book but requires occasional outbursts of indignation. If your Club ever reaches again things American you may find in this work—food for thought and discussion.

I ought to be reading on Municipal Reform in which I am credited with being interested. But my ignorance is quite dense. On the whole I warn you not to believe much about anything Alice reports me as doing. She has sometimes an idea—Here the idea was dispelled by Alice's looking over my shoulder and so you must imagine the rest.

Aunt Regina has returned to Bryn Mawr & talks of coming here March 1st. I expect to go to Washington for a few days in March and Alice says she will go with me—but it seems very improbable with Susan at home.

Louis [Wehle]'s interest in Manual Training is very fine. Modern methods ought to make life much easier for the rising generation or carry them much farther. There seem to be many new ways of learning. One finds it difficult to understand how anything was learned before. Indeed—I doubt whether much was.

I have spent much time of late before juries and am becoming quite enamored of the Common Sense of the people—and some what doubtful of the uncommon Sense of the judges.

Alice thinks I have scratched enough—and wants me merely to add that your doll—surnamed Florence—is treated with loving tenderness and is given the place of honor in the landau.

Much love to Otto & the children.   Your brother

1. At the urging of his friend Mrs. Alice N. Lincoln, LDB had involved himself in efforts to reform the laws and practices of poorhouses, mental asylums, and the various public institutions for orphans and other wards of the state, including the mentally and physically ill. Throughout most of 1894 and early 1895 the Board of Aldermen held hearings at which witnesses exposed the brutality and stupidity of the directors of these facilities. LDB's arguments reflected the latest in scientific thinking, namely, that the inmates of these institutions suffered from illness and had to be treated accordingly, rather than as moral misfits or criminals. He urged that patients be screened and different types of inmates separated from one another (women from men, children from adults, etc.) and that useful work be provided whenever possible. For a statement of his views, see *Boston Herald,* 29 December 1894. While the revelations of the hearings proved sensational, solid reform took several years to accomplish, with Mrs. Lincoln frequently calling on LDB for assistance.

2. An 1830 composition by Felix Mendelssohn.

3. Ernest Clifford Peixotto (1869–1940) was an artist and book illustrator.

4. Douglas Campbell, *The Puritan in Holland, England, and America* (New York, 1892).

To: **Alice Goldmark Brandeis**
Date: **March 9, 1896**
Place: **Washington, D.C.**
Source: **Gilbert MSS**

MY DEAREST, It is half past five. I have stopped work for the day—as usual before that hour—!!!—and I wish I might have the "[*]" with Susan and a dinner with you. At all events I hope Welch has provided the oysters and that you have company.

Possibly I may have company too. I saw on the register J.W. Alling[1] of New Haven, & I have left a note for him suggesting that we dine together and go to the play.

That miserable Asst. Atty Gen'l[2] has presented an argument which removes the case[3] many parasangs[4] from child['[s play. It was weak enough already, without having him get two months or more to make mince meat of our brief. Perhaps he will argue it less well. He didn't make a very strong argument when I heard him in December.

I got myself worked up today to present the matter very clearly— Poland Spring Water was no purer—and I wish I might have closed this chapter & returned to 114 [Mt. Vernon Street]. As it was, only 3 cases were disposed of and there were 6 before mine. That leaves 3. There is a possibility of being reached tomorrow, but Ashton[5] who thinks I ousted him out of this one is in the case now on and I suppose he will take out his spite on me by arguing endlessly.

I can put in 4 or 5 hours profitably in the library tomorrow on Dodge's Authorities, but if this waiting strings out much further than that I shall be tempted to desert. At all events, be it remembered this is the last Supreme Court Case now in sight—for me.

I left my card at Mr. Justice Grays[6] (you will remember he married at 60 odd). The Honorable Gentleman looks as blooming as ever. Brewer[7] was off Venezuelaizing which was depressing as we think he may favor us.[8]

Peckham[9] is very individual looking & Margaret [Deland] would be quite content with the size of his nose. It occupies one half of the superficial area of the face seen at front view.

I made studies in Chinese physiognomy on the Jersey City boat and conclude that no people have such individuality of countenance. The differences were far more marked than in so many Caucasians. We haven't as many varieties of ugliness. One of the Celestials looked as if he hailed from Palestine.

The day is finer than any of ours last April—better than the warm days which followed after you deserted me. But it is absolutely wasted. Well, our March in Egypt will make up for this.   Very much love

1. John Wesley Alling (1841–1927) was the senior partner in a New Haven law firm.

2. Joshua Eric Dodge (1854–1921) had been a member of the Wisconsin legislature before serving as assistant attorney general of the United States during the second Grover Cleveland administration. In 1897 he returned to Milwaukee and the following year became a justice of the Wisconsin Supreme Court, on which he served until 1910.

3. LDB was in Washington to argue *Wisconsin Central Railroad Co. v. United States,* 164 U.S. 190 (1896). The case involved claims by the railroad for carrying the mails and centered on interpretation of two mid-nineteenth-century land grant laws that fixed such rates. For LDB's initial involvement with the railroad, see Mason, *Brandeis,* 70–71.

4. An ancient Persian measure of length, somewhere between 3.25 and 6.5 miles, depending on which source is followed.

5. Joseph Hubley Ashton (1836–1907), after service in the attorney general's office during and after the Civil War, opened a successful corporate practice in Philadelphia. Ashton

was then in Washington to argue *Woodruff v. Mississippi,* 162 U.S. 291 (1896), which the Court heard on 9 and 10 March; the decision, handed down on 13 April, went against Ashton.

6. LDB had known Horace Gray since 1879, when he returned to Boston to join forces with Samuel Warren. During that first year in practice, LDB supplemented his income by clerking for Gray, then chief justice of the Supreme Judicial Court of Massachusetts; Gray went onto the U.S. Supreme Court in early 1882.

7. David Josiah Brewer (1837–1910) of Kansas possessed enormous intelligence, but during his tenure on the Court (1889–1910) he was often overshadowed by luminaries such as his uncle, Stephen J. Field, John Marshall Harlan, and Oliver Wendell Holmes, Jr. He proved one of the pillars of the conservative bloc on the bench.

8. Brewer had been appointed the preceding year to the congressional commission to oversee the disputed boundary between Venezuela and British Guiana. His colleagues elected him president, and the commission brought about a successful arbitration of the matter, which prevented a possible war. Brewer voted with the majority in this case against LDB and his clients.

9. Rufus Wheeler Peckham, Jr. (1838–1909), after a successful career as an attorney in New York, was named to the High Court in 1895 by Cleveland, whose ally he had been in the fight against Tammany Hall. Peckham would prove to be one of the most conservative justices of his time and is remembered primarily for his opinion in *Lochner v. New York* (1905). Peckham was the only justice to dissent in *Wisconsin Central,* endorsing LDB's position.

To:	Alice Goldmark Brandeis
Date:	March 11, 1896
Place:	Washington, D.C.
Source:	Gilbert MSS

Your yesterday's letter has come.[1] I am glad dear Dr. Folsom[2] appeared. He must have been a comfort, more of a comfort than our Court here is to me just now.

We did not take precedence of the textile Case—that is being argued now and the new Attorney General (Harmon)[3] unlike Olney[4] is quite long winded. Dodge promises to be short in our case,[5] so that there is still some hope of our finishing tomorrow—but fear overshadows my hope and we may have to run into Friday. Fortunately that appears to be the utmost limit.

Mr. Abbot[6] stays on in spite of all engagements in New York and is really quite companionable when I see him which is not much.

I saw Sir William today and as he had no engagement this evening suggested his dining with me, which Mr. Abbot and Mr. Alling will doubtless enjoy. I hope they will let him talk and that he will be as much in the humor of it as in Boston.

It is snowing fast, and I have secured rubbers.

Harmon is a forceful lawyer, fine looking—or rather strong looking and agreeable in appearance but guilty of much violence to what "at home" would be the Queen's English. I dare say he is quite in line with the American English of the Great Great West.   Lovingly

1. AGB had written a bright and chatty letter about her visitors, Susan, and how she missed him, concluding, "Dear heart, take good care of yourself and take a great, great deal of love."

2. Dr. Charles Follen Folsom (1842–1907) was a good friend of the Brandeis family. He served as secretary of the Massachusetts State Board of Health from 1874 to 1882 and was also secretary of the State Board of Lunacy and Charity from 1879 to 1881.

3. Judson Harmon (1846–1927) served as attorney general in the last two years of the second Cleveland administration; he would later serve two terms as governor of Ohio from 1909 to 1913.

4. Richard Olney (1835–1917), a successful Boston lawyer, was named attorney general at the start of the Cleveland administration, but in 1895 Cleveland moved him over to head the State Department. Even after he left government work, Olney remained influential in Democratic Party affairs.

5. See the previous letter, note 3.

6. Edwin Hale Abbot (1834–1927) was the president of the Wisconsin Central Railroad. A former Boston newspaper editor, Hale had gone west to make his fortune in railroad management. He then returned to Boston, where he engaged in a number of philanthropic and civil activities; he would be an ally of LDB in the effort to establish Savings Bank Life Insurance.

To:	Alice Goldmark Brandeis
Date:	May 18, 1896
Place:	Milwaukee, Wisconsin
Source:	Gilbert MSS

MY DEAR: I have been talking with the Wisconsin Central phalanx all day, and they have gotten on so far as to show that the figures they have allowed to go forth were wholly misleading to themselves, and would be to any others who took the trouble to ascertain what they mean. It is quite evident that the conclusions I reached are to be modified practically only so far as their own revised figures require modification—which is considerable.[1] In the innocence of their hearts they have let figures go out which were far worse for them than the facts.

The discussions are proceeding fast enough, but it takes time to make up figures and Benjamin is clamorous that I must go up to Manitowoc [Wisconsin] which I am very loth [sic] to do. It is bad enough to go over all these figures without engaging in railroad construction.

The most cheering sight here is the efficacy of the boycott on the Street Railway.[2] If the labor unions and their patrons have virtue enough to hold out a few weeks longer, the labor men will earn a great victory, as the community is quite largely on their side and the capitalists of the town feel deeply humiliated by the condition of things. There appears to be perfect order. The cars are running with a frequency unknown to a dependent upon Beltine and Back Bay cars, and one rarely sees a passenger. The opposition is running all kinds of vehicles which are pretty well filled.

There is talk of the political leaders insisting upon a settlement by the Railway Co. because H C Payne[3] of the railway is one of the political bosses, and they say it will hurt the Republican Party. Ah, one must needs read a bit of Lowell's Political Essays[4] to have any sympathy with that shattered moral wreck.

I feel almost ready to start in as a labor leader of Democratic proclivities. If your protege Whitney and his father-in-law Payne had only been Republicans I should be very Democratic—in spite of D.B. Hill.[5]

Love to you three[6]

1. In 1893 the Northern Pacific Railroad leased the Wisconsin Central and that fall went into receivership, carrying the smaller line with it. In the extensive restructuring that followed, LDB was called upon to develop a plan of reorganization. This he did, although the final plan would not be adopted until 1899. According to Mason, it was during this work that LDB learned about railroad accountancy in minute detail, to the extent that in 1911 he could state: "My special field of knowledge is figures." On the Court, which during the 1920s heard numerous railroad cases, only LDB and Pierce Butler, a former railroad attorney, understood the complex financial matters involved. Mason also relates that through the Wisconsin Central litigation LDB made important professional contacts with major New York firms (*Brandeis*, 71).

2. LDB had previously written: "All Milwaukee is talking of the Street Railway Strike which has developed into a boycott. The Co. supplied the place of the strikers and now the community is quite effectually boycotting the road. The Co. is probably right in this particular issue, but it has a large arrear of sins and the public are learning that these immortal creatures, who have the advantage of continuity, must be made to suffer for the sins of an earlier administration."

3. Henry C. Payne (1843–1904) emigrated to Wisconsin from Massachusetts after the Civil War and soon emerged as one of the state's leading businessmen and a power in the Republican Party. Payne was responsible for the consolidation of all the street railways in Milwaukee (which he headed) as well as the new electric power companies. In 1902 Theodore Roosevelt named him postmaster general of the United States, a position he held until his death.

4. James Russell Lowell, *Political Essays* (Boston, 1888).

5. David Bennett Hill (1843–1910) was governor of New York from 1885 to 1891 and then served one term as United States senator. In early 1896 he was being touted as a possible Democratic candidate for the presidency.

6. Elizabeth Brandeis (1896–1984), the couple's second and last child, was born on 25 April. After receiving her B.A. from Radcliffe College in 1918, she served as assistant secretary then secretary of the District of Columbia Minimum Wage Board until 1923. She then entered the University of Wisconsin and earned a doctorate in economics in 1928; she joined the Wisconsin faculty and taught there until her retirement. While a graduate student, she met and married Paul A. Raushenbush. Mrs. Raushenbush, using her professional name of Elizabeth Brandeis, wrote the second half of volume 3 of John R. Commons's *History of Labor in the United States* (New York, 1935), dealing with labor legislation from 1896 to 1932. In addition to her university work, she served on the state board of the Wisconsin League of Women Voters, was a vice-president of the National Consumers' League, and until 1969 was chair of the Wisconsin Commission on Migratory Labor. She was also deeply involved, with her husband, in the struggle for unemployment compensation legislation at both the state and the federal level.

To: Alice Goldmark Brandeis
Date: July 13, 1896
Place: Boston, Massachusetts
Source: Gilbert MSS

MY DEAREST: I enclose Bryan's winning speech.[1] It must have been the voice and the manner, and above all the general temper of the audience that carried all away.

There is general sadness in the situation, and I have not thought out yet how I feel about it, although I am clearer about what I shall do.[2]

I am going to Middle Brewster, Mr. Adams's principality for the night—the long promised visit.[3]

North Shore people sweltered at 92 degrees yesterday.

    1. William Jennings Bryan (1860–1925) had just won the first of his three Democratic Party nominations for the presidency. A champion of the free coinage of silver, Bryan electrified the convention with a speech in which he declared that mankind should not be "crucified upon a cross of gold."
    2. LDB, like many northeasterners, found the Democratic platform as well as its standard-bearer distasteful.
    3. On 14 July LDB wrote to AGB: "Last night I spent with Melvin Adams at Middle Brewster, a delightful spot after a torrid day. Adams lives there like a prince, and comes up in his able steam launch."

To: Amy Brandeis Wehle
Date: November 19, 1898
Place: Boston, Massachusetts
Source: Wehle MSS

MY DEAR AMY: We are dreadfully sorry to hear of that eternal postponement. One might use another adjective but for our growing children which makes it important for us to be very circumspect in our acts and language.

Susan is keeping a very strict watch on me, and the sense of being always under the necessity of preparedness to justify myself, is doubtless as wholesome as Puritan ancestry.

The Emertons dined with us Thursday and were as enthusiastic over Louis [Wehle] as—well one might say—the rest of the world. He was in for a while yesterday on his way to the Carpenters and to the Harvard-Yale game. What a victory![1] El Caney[2] pales before it. The Crimson will turn to red tonight. And the best of it is three inches of water in which they played. Our men must have been sand—not merely had it—to have disregarded the water so.

Alice is delighted with Kenneth Grahame[3] from which law and dinner-company had kept me so far.

I am sure you will be interested in the Cameron Egypt.[4] It is a model in style—and the story of the East is irresistible. Even Susan is moved by the tale told her at school—how they went from Italy to India—"partly by boat—partly by camel—and partly by horse."   Lovingly

1. Harvard defeated Yale in their annual football rivalry 17–0, according to the newspapers, on "a sea of mud." Young Wehle was then an undergraduate at Harvard.
2. American forces had fought a pitched battle against Spanish troops at El Caney near Santiago, Cuba, about six months earlier.
3. Kenneth Grahame, *The Golden Age* (Chicago, 1895).
4. Donald A. Cameron, *Egypt in the Nineteenth Century; or, Mehemet Ali and His Successors until the British Occupation in 1882* (London, 1898).

To: Alice Goldmark Brandeis
Date: August 5, 1899
Place: [n.p.]
Source: Gilbert MSS

It is just a fortnight since we parted, dear, and now the Frolic is at [*], a most charming spot which the owner admits is superior to Maine. We came over from Saint Anne's yesterday. There we had stayed two days, given mainly to trout fishing, at which I made very poor success in spite of my new rod bought at North East Marguire. Indeed I am quite overwhelmed by the number of things I can't do and don't know and am filled with admiration for the skill and learning White[1] has acquired in his aquatic and country pursuits. He is ready for every emergency— ever full of resources and knowledge, and has a quickness and keenness of observation and mental action which is truly remarkable. In spite of his courage there is absolutely no trace of recklessness. He has far too much experience, knowledge and sense to do anything except the prudent, but his skill and knowledge are so extensive and his resourcefulness so great that he can undertake what few could. His manner with his men and with men and women of the country whom he comes in contact with shows the same masterfulness—and an equal kindness.

No word from you yet dear. Perhaps we shall get some mail Tuesday.
                                                                    Lovingly
I am feeling very well, but have not gotten my sleep yet except occasionally.

1. Herbert Hill White (1869–1963) and his wife, Clarissa, were close friends of the Brandeis family. An older brother of Norman White, who was a frequent ally of LDB's in Boston reform work, Herbert had no inclination for public service, aside from sitting on numerous boards of trustees. LDB often went sailing with Herbert aboard his various yachts and, according to LDB's daughter, greatly enjoyed his company, probably as a

change of pace from his own austere habits as well as from the pressures of business and reform activities.

To: Alice Goldmark Brandeis
Date: November 28, 1899
Place: Lincoln, Nebraska
Source: Gilbert MSS

DEAREST: I forgive the great West its Bryanism—and all the vagaries economic and social which that broad term comprises. To have lived for years amidst the depression of a broken boom might well have robbed the sanest of reason, and of hope, within the realm of ratiocination. Only the [*] could afford relief. No regular practitioner could cure; and Christian Science was naturally resorted to, for aid.

The interesting enquiry is why the boom? Why should hard-headed men be led astray so wide from wisdom's ways? Thus have buildings been reared upon the prairies which could hardly have paid in Boston, and with them hopes raised, which it would have been a mercy to rudely shatter [with] a blow;—but which it was cruel torture to deflate slowly through a long series of years.

Prosperity here would be only tolerable. Adversity must have been indeed dreadful. Let those who believe in gratitude give deepest thanks tomorrow[1] that they live in Massachusetts.   Lovingly

1. Thanksgiving Day.

To: Alice Goldmark Brandeis
Date: September 1900
Place: Boston, Massachusetts
Source: Gilbert MSS

MY DEAREST: I trust you and the children will have a beautiful tomorrow. It was a beautiful day ten years ago, and you have more than fulfilled the promise to me which your "yes" implied.

You have had many hard days in these years,[1] and we shall hope that this may come otherwise, but we shall be indeed fortunate if another ten years of such happiness is granted us.

I dined on beefsteak and the Spectator. It is the same old story—we are hardly ripe for a new subscription. Think of reading fortnightly installments about the coming military dictatorship in France and the impossible possible French invasion of England. I feel as if it were a part of our

old year's subscription. But this number made me feel again how the war interests were all-enveloping. Every editorial was of some war or war-incident. And today's news again tells of more discord among the powers in China.[2] The new is well written and makes one realize the age of Central Asia, the transmutations of governments, and our own ephemeralness. There is a fascination about its meagre present and rich past that seems to justify the struggle for Asia.

Don't travel before you should. The club is quiet, the evening pleasantly cool; but there can be no joy until the barber does his work.

Lovingly

1. For all her love of the outdoors, AGB did not always enjoy good health during these years. The exact cause of her illness is unknown. Her symptoms of severe headaches and physical exhaustion led her doctors to recommend increased rest, sometimes away from Boston, where she could be free from the distractions of home. After occasional recurrences of this condition for about twenty years, AGB seemed to recover completely. By the 1930s, as LDB grew older and less vigorous, his wife became stronger, exercising greater management of his social schedule to ensure that he would not unduly tire himself.

2. In 1900 a group of Chinese nationalists, the Society of Righteous and Harmonious Fists, known as the Boxers, began killing Western missionaries and their Chinese converts and also laying siege to foreign embassies and their compounds in Peking. The United States joined with several European powers in dispatching troops to China to put down the so-called Boxer Rebellion and maintain the "Open Door" policy.

To:	Elizabeth Brandeis
Date:	December 29, 1900
Place:	Boston, Massachusetts
Source:	Gilbert MSS

DEAR ELIZABETH: Do you like New York? And how does your doll like to be with Grandma and all the Aunts and Uncles. I hope she has not cried much. The Christmas tree and Santa Claus are very anxious to see you and Susan again, and want to know whether they shall wait until you come back from New York. Santa Claus would like to come down from the tree and rest in Susan's bed. Do you think I should let him?

To:	Alice Goldmark Brandeis
Date:	August 11, 1901
Place:	Petersham, Massachusetts
Source:	Gilbert MSS

DEAREST: Father took his fourth ride in the saddle today, and is very proud, although Cob's constant aim at flies with his hind legs led Father to change over to Grey Boy today.

I have made Cob a great walker. He approaches five-mile-an-hour walk, and would do for an advertisement of the Waukeefast boots. Grey Boy has been under training too, and the Stones are delighted with his progress. Of course 2 or 3 hours ride is only a fair foundation for a many hours drive, for one of Father's capacity and as he demands my company, there is little peace for L.D.B.

I have nevertheless managed to read most of Gilman's Story of Rome,[1] which is well done and have excited Father to the point of declaring he will take up Roman and Greek history next. I have brought from the library a volume of Rawlinson.[2] The Plutarch here (2 editions) in unreadable, diamond type. I am writing Clarke to ascertain what other editions are in the market.

Mother is about the same.[3] The morphine dose has been increased only slightly. The net pain seems about the same. Mother was out in Mrs. Taylor's rolling chair a little today, but enjoyed the finale most.

She seems to have great satisfaction at my being here and speaks of it constantly. She said this evening that I had entertained her so much that she had gotten on without her morphine pill long beyond her time. Think of my talking as an occupation. In the absence of the children I am retailing classic lore adapted to old age instead of extreme youth.

Mother is being read to much;—in German by Amy, in English by Miss Gideon and Miss Bakewell. I don't know how much she really hears, but she is quite unwilling to allow interruptions at times, and has shown frequently real interest in the stories.

We have kept the tone of the household cheerful—Charles G.[4] came Friday and will doubtless return to N.Y. tomorrow afternoon. He seems to like to be here although the entertainment must be meagre.

I wanted Father to submit to him as my substitute for riding, but he was unwilling to trust anyone but me.

I find that my clothes supply is limited, & I long for the trunkful at Dedham.

There was a fine opportunity for my oils—Wednesday—and my London trousers would celebrate a triumph.

Much love to the children

1. Arthur Gilman, *The Story of Rome, from the Earliest Times to the End of the Republic* (New York, 1886); an updated version published in 1900 was simply called *The Story of Rome*.

2. George Rawlinson (1812–1902) was a prolific historian of ancient Greece and Rome; it is impossible to tell to which of his many works LDB is referring.

3. Frederika Brandeis was quite ill and about to die from cancer. On 7 August LDB had written to his wife: "Mother is not especially comfortable, but is very tired of the whole business. She talks much of wanting to die, but also of wanting to get well. . . . She is really

enjoying the reading aloud, listens quite a little and remembers less, but concentrates her thoughts I should think rather more than last year."

4. Charles Gabriel Tachau (1892–1955) was the son of Emil Tachau, LDB's second cousin; in 1921 he wed Jean Brandeis, Alfred's youngest daughter. Charles Tachau lived in Louisville his entire life, but the nine-year-old was probably visiting his family in New York at the time.

To: **Alice Goldmark Brandeis**
Date: **August 21, 1901**
Place: **Petersham, Massachusetts**
Source: **Gilbert MSS**

MY DEAREST: I have your letter of yesterday. Don't think of leaving Manomet[1] at present. It would not be possible to have the children in the house and there is no room to be had in the hotel or any house in the vicinity.

Mother has been failing very rapidly during the past few days. The doctor says her end must come very soon; it may be within a few days. She has been delirious much of the time since yesterday. Fortunately she is probably free from pain. Father has borne up very well. He knows Mother cannot live much longer, and has been very anxious at all times that she should be relieved from suffering. So that he is as prepared, as it were possible for him to be, for the end. Even in her delirious condition, Mother seemed at one moment to know me, and smiled at the thought of my being with her.

Herbert White has come up to spend the night with me.

Lovingly

I enclose the Plymouth return tickets which I find I carried off.

1. The Brandeises had taken a summer place at Manomet Point, a few miles below Plymouth.

To: **Alice Goldmark Brandeis**
Date: **August 22, 1901**
Place: **Petersham, Massachusetts**
Source: **Gilbert MSS**

MY DEAREST: Mother died this evening. She was unconscious all day, and passed away without a struggle. It was a great mercy, we had feared blood poisoning and convulsions. Poor Mother had suffered enough and had longed steadfastly for the end, and it came finally painlessly.

Father bears up well so far, and had been prepared long for the end. Amy and I hoped that Father would be reconciled to cremation[1] but I find that he wants her to be buried in Louisville. He is however satisfied to stay in Petersham probably until October and that Mother's remains shall be put into a vault at Athol[2] meanwhile.

I think you and the children should remain at Manomet for the present. A little later it may be wise to come here, but I feel that you ought not to come now, my dearest.

Take very good care of yourself and of the children.   Lovingly

1. Both LDB and Alice would be cremated after their deaths; their ashes are under the portico of the University of Louisville Law School.
2. Athol was a somewhat larger town about ten miles from Petersham, which as a small resort community probably lacked facilities for the temporary storage of bodies.

To: **Alice Goldmark Brandeis**
Date: **August 22, 1901**
Place: **Petersham, Massachusetts**
Source: **Gilbert MSS**

MY DEAREST: I know how hard it is for you not to be here. Mother was anxious that you should be spared the added pain. Each day, almost to the last, she asked to hear what had come from you, but she said several times she would not have you come, and how happy she would have been to have you, if only she were well enough to enjoy your visit.

I am very grateful for your thought of sending the children. That visit occupied Mother much, afterwards, and made far more real to her all you wrote and I could tell her about Susan and Elizabeth.

Mother's face showed nobler and stronger during the last weeks than I have ever known it. And there came out, toward the end, a striking likeness to your Mother. It had impressed me much, but I did not mention it. The others, however, spoke of it, and seemed to see it quite as strongly as I do.

Father bears up remarkably well so far. He realizes all the happiness which has come to him and Mother, and what is left to him, and will, I think, take up his life again as fully as is possible.

I know you will want to see Father soon, and I know it will be a great comfort to him to have you and the children with him. He is, however, very anxious that you should not come until it is best for your health, and I think it would be very trying for you to come now. Aside from all else, the house is so very full.

Amy, who is not very strong, has carried much strain. I may be able to induce her, a little later, to take a trip off with Otto, and if you could be here while they are away, that would seem best.

It occurred to me that if Caroline Emerton should not get well enough to come to Petersham, they might be glad to let us have their cottage for a short time.

I did not telegraph you or telephone you of Mother's death. Of course you understood.

I hope Miss Malloch[1] will be with you Sunday.

Father is much helped by the sympathy which is shown by his many acquaintances here, who are as friendly now as they were at the Golden Wedding. Charlie Burlingham[2] has been here since Saturday and we have taken several little walks together.

Herbert [White] touched Father much by his visit. He should not have come, and was so weak that he is down today again at home (not seriously) with a nurse. He wants to come and stay here with me, but I shall try not to let him. Hay Fever and inland life would be very wearing on him, and he should have continued rest. Lovingly

1. E. Louise Malloch was a longtime and trusted employee of LDB's law firm; eventually LDB would turn over to her the day-to-day management of his finances.

2. Charles Culp Burlingham (1858–1959) was one of the leading figures of the New York bar during his long lifetime. His friendship with Felix Frankfurter and Franklin D. Roosevelt, as well as his contacts with many other important political figures, made him one of the best-informed men in the country for more than fifty years. In addition to his law work, Burlingham involved himself in a number of civic efforts and served as president of the New York City Board of Education.

To: **Alfred Brandeis**
Date: **March 21, 1904**
Place: **Boston, Massachusetts**
Source: **Brandeis MSS**

MY DEAR AL: I have suddenly awakened to the consciousness that this is your fiftieth birthday. A semi-centennial should surely thrill us, and Alice, reveling in her lack of years, is endeavoring to impress upon me the multitude of mine. I decline, however, to be impressed, and hope you do likewise—at least on Sonn- and Feier-Tagen.[1]

In honor of your fifty years we are sending you Henry Villard's Autobiography,[2] because he came to the United States in the fifties. He has doubtless painted himself unduly white, but the book should be interesting and possibly Father, too, may care for it.

The children think you should be wished 50 happy returns of the day.
Your brother

1. Sundays and holidays.
2. *The Memoirs of Henry Villard, Journalist and Financier, 1835–1900* (Boston, 1904).

To:	Alice Goldmark Brandeis
Date:	July 4, 1904
Place:	Springfield, Massachusetts
Source:	Gilbert MSS

DEAREST: Father's and my trains were on time. So we met at 2:40. Found Father very calm and looking quite as well as last year. Of course, he isn't as well, that is as strong; but he says he has been in much better shape the past 8 days than at any time since his illness. The trip was cool and entirely enjoyable he says.

The rest of the caravan are in good shape. Amy quite herself. Miss Bakewell, perhaps a little thinner. She had a bad fright. Her mother fell in getting out of an electric[1] and broke her arm.

Massachusetts, all of it, from Boston to the State line looked more beautiful than ever. What a blessing it is to live in such a state. We peeped down upon your Dalton.

But the people of Massachusetts, in their celebration of the Fourth must have absorbed all the barbarity of their Indian predecessors. Surely my Japanese or even Bessie's Phillippinos [sic]—Yea, even the Moros or Igarrotors—could not be guilty of such hideous noises.

Lovingly

I expect to return to Boston 7:45 A.M. tomorrow.

1. Possibly an electric trolley.

To:	Alfred Brandeis
Date:	July 28, 1904
Place:	Dedham, Massachusetts
Source:	Brandeis MSS

DEAR AL: You have doubtless heard from Father[1] that he was very much pleased with the bilanz.[2] That taken in connection with 24 predecessors establishes that the business in your hands is an excellent one. The only essential is to live and enjoy it—pursuing it with the same energy & originality as hitherto.

Father also talked to me about your stock purchases. I dare say those you have made are all right, but I feel very sure that unser eins[3] ought not to buy and sell stocks. We don't know much about the business—and beware of people who think they do. Prices of stock[s] are made.—They don't grow; and their fluctuations are not due to natural causes. Altogether, I don't think John Taussig[4] knows anymore about them than most other bankers who are outsiders. And even the insiders could not be relied upon for advice.

My idea is that your situation is about like mine—namely to treat investments as a necessary evil—indulging in the operation as rarely as possible.[5] Buy only the thing you consider very good, and stick to it unless you have cause to doubt the wisdom of the purchase.

And when you buy, buy the thing which you think is safe—and will give you a fair return;—but don't try to make your money out of investments. Make it out of your business. Of that you understand as much as anybody. Take in that all the risks you think it prudent to take—but risk only there.

I suppose you agree with most of this—and I should not have written you but for Father's suggestion. He I know assents to these views—& he wanted me to express them to you. He said you were selecting stocks instead of bonds, on account of your tax laws. I don't know anything about Ky. laws, but should suppose that here is no difference between the taxability of bonds and of stocks in other than Ky. corporations.

Jessie Cochrane spent last night with us and gave us a delightful evening

Grüsse Alle[6]

1. Adolph Brandeis was still vacationing in Petersham.
2. Balance-sheet.
3. People like us.
4. Jennie's uncle, a banker.
5. LDB earned a great deal of money from his practice and by this time had amassed nearly his first million dollars. Following his own advice to Alfred, he invested in railroad, utility, municipal, or government bonds and, according to his secretary, never deviated from this policy. The only exceptions were his occasional token purchases of stock in companies that were his clients, so that he could legitimately participate in certain stockholder meetings. See LDB to Edward D. White, 29 June 1916, BL.
6. Greetings to all.

To: **Susan and Elizabeth Brandeis**
Date: **August 8, 1904**
Place: **Petersham, Massachusetts**
Source: **Gilbert MSS**

DEAR SUSAN AND ELIZABETH: Frolic arrived here safely and has already become a great favorite. He walks all about town with Aunt Amy and Uncle Otto. And a little girl named Campbell comes to the house to play with him. Frolic's favorite resting place is on Grandpa's lap. He loves to sit on the shawl with which Grandpa covers himself. He sits down in the dining-room in the corner, when Aunt Do[1] says: "Charge," and behaves very well.

Everybody wants to know his exact age. Can you tell?

1. "Do" was the family name for Josephine Clara Goldmark (1877–1950), another AGB's sisters. After graduating from Bryn Mawr in 1898, she joined Florence Kelley at th National Consumers' League as the organization's research director. From that position, she greatly influenced the course of labor legislation in the first half of the twentieth century. She provided the factual material that LDB organized into the famous brief in *Muller v. Oregon,* 208 U.S. 412 (1908). After the tragic Triangle Fire in New York City in 1911, she assisted the New York Factory Investigating Commission, in which her sister Pauline was also involved. She published the pioneering study on *Fatigue and Efficiency* (New York, 1912) and worked closely with LDB on behalf of the Consumers' League in a number of cases in which he defended protective legislation the league had sponsored. During the New Deal her contacts with Frances Perkins and Felix Frankfurter made her an influential figure in drafting the administration's labor laws.

To: Adolph Brandeis
Date: July 13, 1905
Place: Dedham, Massachusetts
Source: EBR

DEAR FATHER: The publication of the testimony on which the Hendricks report was based discloses further financial iniquities.[1] Depew[2] is blackened further, and Schiff[3] has more to explain. Fair reputations are in a fair way to be ruined, and there appears to be determination on the part of the New York World and several other papers to a less degree not to let the scandal be hushed up at any point, which is fortunate.[4]

The Ryan purchase[5] was influenced in large part by the fear of panicky consequences as a result of the people's loss of confidence, but I do not see that much progress has been made toward restoring confidence. The great N.Y. trick of getting rich on Other People's Money[6] is getting pretty well aired.

1. On 21 June New York state superintendent of insurance Francis Hendricks issued a report severely criticizing the management of the Equitable Life Assurance Society. The tone of the report surprised many people, since Hendricks and his staff had been widely considered to be little more than tools of the insurance industry.
2. Chauncey Mitchell Depew (1834–1928) exploited his influence as head of the New York Central Railroad to become a power in the Republican Party. He served as one of New York's senators from 1895 to 1911, during which time he was a champion of the Equitable and other big businesses.
3. Jacob Henry Schiff (1847–1920), a member of Kuhn, Loeb & Co., was one of the most powerful investment bankers in the country. Allied by marriage to many other important Jewish banking families, Schiff also was recognized as the head of the German-Jewish community in the United States. (See Stephen Birmingham, *Our Crowd* [New York, 1967], for a popular overview of this group.) Later LDB would challenge Schiff's leadership of American Jewry in the fight to establish an American Zionist movement.
4. In fact the scandal rocked the business community and eventually resulted in the reorganization and reform of the insurance industry. The scandal also led LDB to an intensive study of insurance and from there to what he considered his most important reform effort, the establishment of Savings Bank Life Insurance. See BL, 1:336ff.

5. Thomas Fortune Ryan (1851–1928), a longtime titan of Wall Street, had purchased majority control in the Equitable less than a week after the publication of the Hendricks report, paying $2.5 million for stock with a par value of slightly over $50,000.

6. The phrase comes from Adam Smith's *The Wealth of Nations* (1776): "The directors of [joint stock] companies . . . being the managers rather of other people's money than of their own, cannot well be expected, that they should watch over it with the same anxious vigilance with which their partners in a private copartnery frequently watch over their own" (1937 Modern Library edition, 700). LDB would later use the phrase as the title of his 1914 book attacking banks and monopolies.

To:	Alice Goldmark Brandeis
Date:	July 13, 1905
Place:	Dedham, Massachusetts
Source:	Gilbert MSS

DEAREST: Give your doctor a talking to when he returns.[1]

McElwain[2] was in yesterday. He met the doctor at Portland & rode with him to Boston. McElwain is exercising diligently, has an instructor at Golf, swims in a pool, rides and walks, but his progress in sleep seems very small. Six hours is his best & I fancy he doesn't get as much very often. The doctor said he should continue so until Aug. 1 & then come to Bethel if matters didn't change for the better.

I am extremely sorry for the Cabots' attitude.—It is the old story: "Everybody is queer—except you and me etc."[3]

There are some beautiful moonlight nights being wasted this week.

People complain of the heat, but not I. Boston and Dedham are good enough for me when properly warmed.

Lovingly

The children were interested in your tennis plans, but Susan sees several objections.

1. On 7 July LDB had written: "I wish you would tell your esteemed doctor that he must do a hurry-up job, as we don't propose to leave you with him much longer. Indeed I felt quite like carrying you off with us in his absence." Alice was under the care of Dr. Gehring in Bethel, Maine.

2. William Howe McElwain (1867–1908), a client of LDB's, owned W. H. McElwain & Co. of Bridgewater, one of the leading shoe manufacturers in the country. A pioneer both in manufacturing techniques and in labor relations, he proved a willing pupil when LDB suggested that he attempt to regularize the employment of his workers by spreading the work more evenly throughout the year. The plan proved a huge success, and LDB publicly praised McElwain as one of the nation's most progressive businessmen. See LDB's *Business—a Profession* (Boston, 1914), 5–9.

3. While it is impossible to know exactly what comments or actions LDB had in mind, the general reaction to the emerging life insurance scandal among the well-to-do was that insurance matters, somewhat like religion, ought not to be publicly discussed.

To: Alice Goldmark Brandeis
Date: July 14, 1905
Place: Dedham, Massachusetts
Source: Gilbert MSS

DEAREST: What does this mean? Robert Winsor[1] came by & sat down beside me at the Exchange Club yesterday & said most lovingly:

"You have been interested in the Cambridge Subway.[2] Dana[3] came to us shortly before the end of the session in regard to our assenting to a four track Subway.[4] We looked into it, concluded it would cost about $5,000,000 & consented. Now our engineers say it will cost $10,000,000. We have already handed the engineers' estimates to Mayor Daly.[5] We don't want to seem open to the charge of unfairness, but $10,000,000 is prohibitive. We were astounded. We want to write a letter setting out the history of the whole matter, to the Mayor, and I would like to have you look over the letter and see whether we should do so. If you are to be in town a few days" etc. etc.

Of course I told him I should be glad to do so. But I don't believe Mephisto ever became a really good Christian. Lovingly

1. Robert Winsor (1858–1930), an investment banker with Kidder, Peabody & Co., was one of the directors of the Boston Elevated and had been associated with the company since its inception in 1894.
2. LDB had been involved in traction reform in the Boston area since 1897, when he unsuccessfully opposed the Boston Elevated Railway Company's successful grab of near-permanent franchises on the city's most important thoroughfares. When the Elevated attempted to secure the right to build the new Washington Street subway, several citizens' groups, including the Public Franchise League (which LDB had helped to found) and the Massachusetts Associated Board of Trade, joined to oppose the railway. Although they lost the battle in the legislature, LDB successfully appealed to Governor Winthrop Murray Crane, who vetoed the bill. In the end the reformers secured a proposal that LDB thought fair to the city, the public, and the Boston Elevated. For details of the fight, see Mason, *Brandeis,* ch. 7.
3. Richard Henry Dana (1851–1931) was actively involved in Boston civic reform for more than three decades. In the 1880s he drafted the Massachusetts Civil Service Act and later was the leading figure in the state's adoption of the Australian ballot.
4. The Boston Elevated was then pushing for a near-perpetual franchise to connect the city's lines to Cambridge. LDB and the Public Franchise League managed to defeat this effort.
5. Augustine J. Daly (1861–1938) was twice elected mayor of Cambridge but later in 1905 announced that he would not seek a third term. A graduate of the Boston Law School, he practiced in Boston and was active in the cause of Irish Home Rule.

To: Adolph Brandeis
Date: July 15, 1905
Place: Dedham, Massachusetts
Source: EBR

DEAR FATHER: I enclose some more clippings on Depew and Schiff. It is a great thing to have a man like Depew play his hand out, and not escape to the grave in the undisturbed odor of sanctity. Perhaps you will remember, whether Cicero treats of this in De Senectate.[1]

The Englishmen have the expression "Guinea Pigs," which they apply to the dummy directors who attend board meetings to get their guinea. Depew was none of these cheap men, and I dare say, his coat would have satisfied even the Saintly McKinley as to price.

Witte's[2] selection by the Russians looks as if we should have peace, for which I am sorry.[3]   Lovingly

1. Cicero's essay on the rewards of old age for those who had lived uprightly in their youth noted that "the harvest of old age is the recollection and abundance of blessings previously secured."

2. Count Sergius Yulyevich Witte (1849–1915), although born a commoner, rose to become minister of finance in the tsar's government and was chiefly responsible for building the great Trans-Siberian Railway. In July 1905 the tsar named Witte to head the Russian delegation to the Portsmouth conference, a clear victory for the moderate elements in Russia. Witte secured rather favorable terms for Russia and in 1906 became the country's first premier under a new constitution. Within a short time, though, reactionary elements forced him out of office.

3. See LDB to Adolph Brandeis, 29 August 1905.

To:	Adolph Brandeis
Date:	July 27, 1905
Place:	Dedham, Massachusetts
Source:	EBR

DEAR FATHER: I send some more twaddle on Equitable.[1]

It is extremely fortunate that the Equitable disclosures came out so gradually. If all the "exposures" had come at one time the country would have been shocked & then have quickly forgotten the matter as it is apt to with abuses. But the deferred New York legislative investigation will carry the matter along for nine months more and other legislatures will doubtless be ready to take a hand. So we shall have life insurance activity on all hands for a year to come, and the business has a fair chance of being put upon a proper basis at the end of that time.

Lovingly

1. By this time LDB had become involved in the insurance scandals as a counsel to the Protective Committee formed by New England policyholders of the Equitable to safeguard their investments in the company. See his letter to the trustees of stock, 12 July 1905, part of his letter to the policyholders' committee of 22 July 1905, BL.

To:	Alice Goldmark Brandeis
Date:	August 10, 1905
Place:	Louisville, Kentucky
Source:	Gilbert MSS

DEAREST: 33 years ago we sailed for Europe.

Delighted with your letters of Sunday & Monday, and that you are having such satisfaction from the Plymouth air and bath.

Father had a good day yesterday and a good evening, thanks to some stimulant Florence[1] gave him. He talked with Al & me long this evening of the European trip[2] and said he had not felt so well since he came to the country. He has however lost considerable ground, as compared with last year. He can't stand the more serious conversations, although he likes allusions to the serious topics and is really greatly interested in them.

The weather in the country is not objectionable, although Susan might say at times that she is "boiling, roasting, broiling, steaming, baking, frying etc."

Was off with Amy, Fanny & Jean[3] riding this morning and again with Fan in the afternoon, & between talked with Father & read "In a Balcony."[4]

Lovingly

1. Florence Brandeis, LDB's cousin, was the first woman doctor west of the Appalachians.
2. Of 1872–75; see Mason, *Brandeis,* 28–32.
3. Alfred's daughters.
4. Robert Browning, *In a Balcony,* a drama in verse written in 1853.

To:	**Alice Goldmark Brandeis**
Date:	**August 18, 1905**
Place:	**Louisville, Kentucky**
Source:	**Gilbert MSS**

MY DEAREST: Father had a very bad day yesterday. His weakness is more pronounced & his organs generally act with difficulty. He has much nausea, so eats little and is perfectly comfortable only for a little while after the heroin, but then is his old self and we have good talks together.

Al and I concluded with Florence's assent to wire for Dr. Weidner[1] Wednesday & he is to be here (from Michigan) this morning. Father seemed relieved at the prospect, and the moral effect at least ought to be good.

Father talks often of your "lovely" letters, and I hope one is on the way. He was much pleased also with the children's.

I am delighted to hear of your sleeping so well. I can't equal that, but get on unexpect[ed]ly well. The weather is almost unprecedentedly good & the last two evenings I have even succeeded in wearing my black coat & vest.

Now it is beginning to get dusty, but till now we have had frequent showers.   With much love

1. Carl Weidner (1857–1943) was born in Germany and trained there as a druggist. He came to the United States and directly to Louisville in 1874 and practiced as a pharmacist for a few years before entering medical school in Louisville and then going to Europe for postgraduate training. After that he practiced in Louisville for the rest of his life.

To: **Alice Goldmark Brandeis**
Date: **August 19, 1905**
Place: **Louisville, Kentucky**
Source: **Gilbert MSS**

DEAREST: As you can see, it has seemed best to stay with Father. He gets some pleasure out of it, & Al also wanted me to stay. Father is fairly comfortable today, much more so than when I last wrote, but he feels deeply his lessened strength.

Jennie is playing to him now the Pathetique,[1] and before that he listened for a while to Thayer's Venice,[2] & earlier in the morning listened & talked with interest on the Russo-Japanese situation, which is now thrilling.[3] It takes faith & courage to want the war to continue. But "my voice is still for war."[4] If it lasts long the Douma[5] will be a very different thing than that now planned & the story of Friesland, Poland & Asia may be very different.   Lovingly

1. Ludwig van Beethoven's *Piano Sonata No. 8 in C minor* (1799).
2. Roscoe Thayer, *A Short History of Venice* (New York, 1905).
3. After a series of spectacular sea and land victories over the Russians, the Japanese acceded to Theodore Roosevelt's request for a peace conference. Although clearly the victor, Japan had exhausted its resources in the war, a fact Roosevelt knew and exploited to gain a settlement more favorable to Russia than some believed it deserved. The Treaty of Portsmouth allowed both sides to retire from the battle and earned Roosevelt the Nobel Peace Prize.
4. From Joseph Addison's play *Cato,* III, 1.
5. The Russian parliament. LDB hoped that, following the loss to Japan, democratic forces in Russia would take a bolder position in opposing the autocracy of the tsar.

To: **Elizabeth Brandeis**
Date: **August 19, 1905**
Place: **Louisville, Kentucky**
Source: **Gilbert MSS**

MY DEAR ELIZABETH: I was glad to get your letter and to hear of your great progress in swimming. So great a swimmer will, doubtless, want to become also a great walker, and will insist soon on walking to "Drove Street" and resting in that cellar.

Fannie, Jean and I took a ride for 1³/₄ hours this morning, and came back just before a heavy shower. The other day when Fanny and I were out, we were caught in a heavy rain and I had to take down two fences to find a short route home. One of them was a barbed-wire fence, so that it was quite a difficult job.

To: Adolph Brandeis
Date: August 29, 1905
Place: Boston, Massachusetts
Source: EBR

DEAR FATHER: The Berkshires were more beautiful than ever, but the news from Portsmouth[1] which reached me with full confirmation at Pittsfield made me sad.

It was a great personal victory for Roosevelt[2] and for Witte, and perhaps also for the Japanese nation. Such moderation in victory is not within the experience of the occidental and perhaps it was wise for the Japanese, but I still think that the world would have been better served, in the long run, by more bloodletting. On my way through Massachusetts I fell in with a member of the Russian diplomatic service, fresh from Chefoo[3] and bound for Portsmouth of which I will tell you more anon.[4]

With much love

1. Of the peace conference.
2. Theodore Roosevelt (1858–1919) first became known to the American public as the hero of the Spanish-American War and from there went on to become governor of New York and then vice-president. He succeeded to the White House upon the assassination of William McKinley in 1901. Roosevelt transformed the office of the president, showing that the presidency could be a "bully pulpit" from which one could lead the Congress and the American people. A progressive in domestic policy and a realist overseas, Roosevelt gladly abandoned the semi-isolationism that had marked American foreign policy.
3. Chefoo, in northern China, was a neutral port during the Russo-Japanese war.
4. The next day LDB wrote to his father: "My Russian of the diplomatic service. . . . has been over the Trans Siberian RR. three times, the last time in July 1904. Then he had to leave the Railroad at Mukden and go on horseback with some Cossaks as protection about 60 miles overland until he reached the Chinese RR. He says he made the journey from St. Petersburg in 15 days, and that special expresses make it in 12 days" (BL).

To: Adolph Brandeis
Date: October 10, 1905
Place: Boston, Massachusetts
Source: EBR

DEAR FATHER: I am preparing for an address on "Life Insurance—the Abuses and the Remedies" which I am to deliver before the Commercial

Club of Boston on the 26th.[1] Will send you a copy which Al must read to you.

There has been considerable doing in one way or another since Labor Day and I have been well occupied with public and private problems. Gas—Railroad—Labor Insurance—City Affairs. All in a ferment.

Lovingly

1. This speech marked the real beginning of one of LDB's most important reforms, the establishment of Savings Bank Life Insurance. For further details, see BL, 1:363ff., and Alpheus T. Mason, *The Brandeis Way: A Case Study in the Workings of Democracy* (Princeton, 1938).

To: Adolph Brandeis
Date: December 1, 1905
Place: Boston, Massachusetts
Source: EBR

DEAR FATHER: Answering your several questions:

First: I agree substantially with your views on football. Your grandson L[ouis].B.W[ehle]. heard me express them 5 or 6 years ago. My remedy has always been, Abolish the gate money. That will abolish the overtraining, the crowds & the incentives to "any thing to win."

Second: I agree that Roosevelt acted very improperly on the Whitney letter.[1] Our President is gradually reaching the kingly attitude, and assumes he can do no wrong.

Third: I enclose for Al portrait of his old friend Judah Touro.[2]

Fourth: Have enclosed clippings from Vienna read to you. Do they remind you of 1848?

Lovingly

1. Henry Melville Whitney (1839–1923), a New England transportation tycoon, after an interview with President Roosevelt issued a statement regretting that the president did not favor a reciprocity treaty with Canada. Roosevelt then publicly stated that Whitney had misquoted him, although two other people at the interview said they thought that Whitney's version of the Roosevelt statement was accurate. Whitney wrote and asked the president for another interview in order to clear the matter up, but Roosevelt refused in a rather petulant tone, practically accusing Whitney of lying. See *New York Tribune,* 21 November 1905.

2. Judah Touro (1775–1854), a shipping merchant, was the leader of the Newport, Rhode Island, Jewish community in the first half of the nineteenth century.

To: Alice Goldmark Brandeis
Date: December 29, 1905
Place: Boston, Massachusetts
Source: Gilbert MSS

DEAREST: Have just wired you that I start for Louisville 10:45.

Telegram from Al. Night Message

"Weidner says if you want to see father so that you can talk to him better come at once."[1]

I have your sweet letter and suggestion about going with me. Of course, Dearest, I want you with the children and with your Mother for this little visit. It is short enough at best, but I can't spare you and the children often.

Will wire you from Louisville, but probably may not before Sunday.

I wrote Susie last night.   Lovingly

1. Two days earlier Alfred had wired: "Think no physical discomfort but pronounced mental confusion. Do not believe end can be far off." LDB arrived in time to see his father before Adolf's death on 20 January 1906.

To: **Alfred Brandeis**
Date: **February 22, 1906**
Place: **Concord, New Hampshire**
Source: **EBR**

DEAR AL: Despite Washington's birthday, we have been in Court trying our case again. That is, I have been sitting by and letting Streeter[1] try for fear of adding to the prejudice of a N.H. jury against a Mass. defendant. As it has proven, however, we can't possibly have a worse prejudice on the part of a jury than the judge has exhibited.

The incident is extremely instructive as to General Economic Sentiment. Our client the defendant has really behaved very well, but there is evidence of a trade combination, of which the judge knows or suspects more than appeared in Court & the net result has been an attitude on his part during six days of trial which goes beyond any prejudice vs corporations & trusts, than you would expect to find in Kansas or Nebraska. And this too from a Federal judge. I think his prejudice has gone so far as to lead him into errors which the Court of Appeal will rectify, if the verdict is against us as seems probable. But his attitude is extremely instructive as being symptomatic of the prevailing and growing sentiment in the U.S.[2]

I think the tide is rising rapidly and that when people feel really pinched and business is not so brisk as to keep people fully occupied, the rising resentment at plutocratic action will make itself severely felt.

After all, we are living in a Democracy, & some way or other, the people will get back at power unduly concentrated, and there will be plenty of injustice in the process.

Alice & the children went to Dedham yesterday to stay until Saturday P.M.

1. Frank Sherwin Streeter (1835–1922) was a prominent New Hampshire lawyer with whom LDB often worked. After a term in the legislature, he had built up a profitable practice while also engaging in a number of civic enterprises. Streeter served as president of the 1902 New Hampshire constitutional convention and as a member of a joint Canadian-American arbitration commission.

2. The next day, after having returned to Dedham, LDB wrote to Alfred: "The jury gave a verdict of six hundred & twenty five (625) Dollars against us. The Judge would have soaked us ten or fifteen thousand if he had had the say. It is interesting to find protection from prejudice at the hands of a jury. That is some protection. We think the judge's rulings were grossly wrong & that clients will be disposed to try the questions out before the Court of Appeals" (BL).

To:	Alfred Brandeis
Date:	March 21, 1906
Place:	Boston, Massachusetts
Source:	Brandeis MSS

MY DEAR AL: My congratulations on the 23rd.[1]

I want to have some part in the creation of your farm which you love so much, and I want therefore to make you a birthday present, either of such part of Walter's land as you think you need to give you a scientific frontier, if you can buy it at any price you think reasonable—or to put your house into condition for winter use—or anything else for the place you want.

We gave Cleta White your "Fat of the Land"[2] to read as she has farm longings. You should work her & make a convert.

Herbert & Cleta returned yesterday A.M. & dined with us last evening.

Arrived in Trieste 33 yrs ago today

1. Alfred's fifty-second birthday.
2. John William Streeter, *The Fat of the Land: The Story of an American Farm* (New York and London, 1904).

To:	Alfred Brandeis
Date:	April 20, 1906
Place:	Dedham, Massachusetts
Source:	Brandeis MSS

MY DEAR AL: How insignificant man proves to be amidst such calamities as at San Francisco.

I have not seen the morning papers yet, but last afternoon it seemed as if little would be left of the city except the opportunity of rebuilding.[1]

I will write Mr. Cooper—What [sic] there any special cause for Huxley's act?

Your daughters left Wednesday in good shape. Amy particularly seemed much benefitted by the vacation.[2] Alice was very glad to see so much of her.

I dined Sunday with a large English merchant who tells me that he pays on the average 5 per cent for his money from the London banks, & that industrial companies of excellent standing sell their debentures on a $4\frac{1}{2}\%$ basis. Money seems to be cheaper now in America than in England.

1. On 18 April an earthquake and the resulting fires devastated 3,000 acres in the heart of San Francisco, causing hundreds of millions of dollars in property loss. Within nine years, however, the city had been almost completely reconstructed.
2. Alfred's daughter Amy had been seriously ill earlier in the year.

To: **Alfred Brandeis**
Date: **May 20, 1906**
Place: **Dedham, Massachusetts**
Source: **Brandeis MSS**

DEAR AL: Glad to hear such good reports of your live-stock. I will submit your problem in arithmetic to Susan as soon as Christine and George[1] leave. The latter is now occupying too much of the children's attention to permit of due consideration of agricultural problems.

A few warm days have launched us into June vegetation. There is however still the fresh spring green which makes all nature entrancing. We have been off a horse and a canoe today, and the day has not been without "the schoensten [*] des Nachmittags[2] for me" while Alice talked Eternal Verities with Bessie Evans and Mrs. Loring who came out for luncheon.

Our sliding-scale gas fight[3] is on in the Legislature. We have won so far, triumphantly in the house, and the prospects are good in the Senate.[4] But we have many opponents—the most active being some of our own former associates who are in my opinion fanatics, & as ready to do injustice to capital as the capitalists have been ready to do injustice to the people.[5]

Susan would like to have your version of the powder-flask episode of July 4, 1865.[6] Do you remember that when I was summoned to Louis[ville] by Fan's illness in 1881 I was stalled in Cleveland Sunday, & spent it with Cushing,[7] a law school man. He was here yesterday to see me on business. Had not seen him for just 20 years.

1. Christine Goldmark Openhym was AGB's widowed sister; George was her son.
2. "The most beautiful [*] of the afternoon."
3. In 1903 legislation had been enacted merging the eight gas companies serving Boston and Brookline into one on conditions very favorable to the new Boston Consoli-

dated Gas Company. Although the Public Franchise League had opposed the law, LDB had not been involved due to the press of other business. In 1904, however, when the question of proper valuation of the company's properties came up, LDB reasserted his leadership of the league. The valuation would be the basis for gas rates: the higher the valuation, the higher the rates. The Consolidated wanted a valuation of $24,000,000, but would settle for $20,610,000, while some members of the league demanded that a fair valuation should be no more than $15,124,000.

  After considerable research into the matter, LDB concluded that the real issue was not the valuation but the price that would be charged to the public. He suggested the idea of a sliding scale, modeled on London's sliding scale utility rates: the lower the rate charged to the public, the higher the dividend that the company could pay to its investors. By this scheme, he claimed, the company would have an incentive to become more efficient and in doing so both the public and the company stockholders would benefit. LDB convinced James L. Richards, the president of the gas company, of the merits of the scheme, and in May the legislature approved the new plan. The Consolidated, in order to continue paying its eight percent dividend, immediately reduced the price of gas from 90 cents to 85 cents per 1,000 cu. ft., and a year later the price went down to 80 cents.

  4. On 18 May, despite strenuous attacks, the House passed the bill embodying almost everything that LDB and his allies had requested.

  5. Not all the members of the Public Franchise League supported LDB's proposal for the sliding scale, and none was more vociferous than Edward R. Warren, who wanted to limit the gas company's valuation to the lowest possible figure and also restrict its earnings so that customers could get cheap gas. For LDB the issue was never cheap gas but fairness. People who invested capital had a right to a fair return on their investment; in order to keep government regulation to a minimum, public utilities had to have some incentive to give the public good service at a reasonable price. For details of the dispute, see LDB to Edward R. Warren, 13 March 1905, BL.

  6. On 4 July 1865 the career of Louis D. Brandeis almost came to an end before it even began. LDB and Alfred were making firecrackers out of gunpowder when a spark ignited the flask and burned both boys around their faces and arms.

  7. William Erastus Cushing (1853–1917) graduated from Harvard Law School in 1878; in addition to his practice Cushing served as one of Ohio's uniform law commissioners.

To: Alfred Brandeis
Date: May 27, 1906
Place: Dedham, Massachusetts
Source: Brandeis, MSS

DEAR AL: Enclosed clipping about Laura Fishers [*sic*] Reception. I was sorry I had to back out. My throat was not restored, & weather bad, & it seemed unwise to go.

The Governor[1] signed our Sliding Scale Gas Bill, after much heartrending wrestling yesterday.[2] The poor man was afraid this action might injure him politically and was sorely distressed & made me lots of work. I consider this a most important step in public economics & government—an alternative for municipal ownership, which will keep the Gas Co. out of politics. If, as I anticipate, this succeeds well in Boston, there will be many followers, also in other lines of public service.[3]

I succeeded in running this campaign mainly by putting others on the firing line: as your girls would say "the man behind."

Some of our old allies—now too radical—were our most formidable opponents.

Elizabeth wants to know the name of our black & tan, and tan terriers, also of the horses other than Nellie and Brown Dick.

It occurs to me that Emily's illness may put Aunt Minna into money straights [*sic*] in spite of my $50 a month & Amy's legacy.[4] If this is so let me know & I will increase her allowance, or what perhaps would be wiser, make an extraordinary appropriation.

The Abe Flexners[5] are expected this P.M.

1. Curtis Guild, Jr. (1860–1915) entered politics after a successful career in printing and publishing. He served as lieutenant governor of Massachusetts from 1902 to 1905 and as governor from 1906 through 1909. Guild always gave LDB easy access to his office and consulted him on a number of reform issues.

2. After rumors of a veto and following last-minute conferences with LDB and his associates, the governor had signed the bill into law the previous day. For the final text, see *Boston Evening Transcript*, 26 May 1906. In all its essentials, the bill conformed to the proposal put forth by LDB and the Public Franchise League and agreed to by the Consolidated Gas Company.

3. The sliding-scale scheme worked quite well for several years, and in fact Boston in 1914 enjoyed the lowest gas rates of any large urban area in the country. But an unforeseen difficulty was that the plan had little flexibility and worked on the assumption that costs such as gas, labor, and maintenance would all remain relatively stable. The inflation that occurred during World War I proved more than the system could absorb, and the plan was abandoned.

4. Aunt Minna was Wilhelmine Wehle Dembitz, the widow of LDB's beloved uncle Lewis; Emily was her daughter. LDB's sister Amy, who died on 17 February 1906, evidently left her aunt some money.

5. Dr. Abraham Flexner (1866–1959) was a member of a Louisville family well known to the Brandeises. Abraham was a distinguished and honored educator, whose many books and studies influenced education—particularly medical education—in the United States, Canada, and Europe. See his autobiography, *I Remember* (New York, 1940).

To: Alfred Brandeis
Date: May 29, 1906
Place: Boston, Massachusetts
Source: Brandeis MSS

DEAR AL: I have been thinking over your tired feeling and am convinced that you ought, for a while, to end your day's work at two (2) P.M. and spend the rest of the day in the open—every week day.

I have made a study of mental tire [*sic*] for a quarter of a century & know more about it than I do of law or insurance.

To: Alice Goldmark Brandeis
Date: August 8, 1906
Place: Louisville, Kentucky
Source: Gilbert MSS

MY DEAR: It was good to get your Sunday letter and to know that the trip has been doing some good. I hope for even better reports when the fatigue is well over.

A heavy rain and a strong breeze has cooled the air materially, though Susan would still remonstrate at 75°. We are planning for a ride as soon as the small girls shall have breakfasted. The house though full seems very empty without Father and Amy.

I have not tackled Al seriously yet about going off. Tom Hauis who was absent 3 weeks returned Monday, and some things require Al's attention still but I shall move cautiously upon his breastworks tomorrow when I expect to go with him to Lexington, whither business calls him.

Amy's friend Judith Boyer, from Pottsville, Pa., is really interesting. She might be taken for a Massachusetts girl, tall, thin, rather homely with a calm monotonous manner of speech. I gave her a very searching, subtle examination on life in Pottsville which she stood uncommonly well. Pottsville, you may remember, was the focus of the coal strike in 1903, with the neighboring town of Hazelton and, before that, the center of the Molly Maguire agitation.[1] She told incidentally a charming tale of the effect on Pottsville of a Massachusetts schoolmaster, Thurlow who came to Pottsville with his wife 20 years ago, first as teacher in the high school; became the principal and is now as [sic] the Superintendent of their school system. Mrs. Thurlow who has no children is the head of the private school, which is really the fitting school, in part, for the high school. As Miss Boyer talked rather unconsciously about the Thurlows one had a perfect picture of what an enthusiastic, devoted and tactful school-master can accomplish in a generation. He is an Amherst man and is probably responsible for our having Jos B. Eastman[2] as Secy of the Public Franchise League. Eastman is a Pottsville boy, son of the Presbyterian Minister & an intimate of Miss Boyer's brother. Eastman was President of his class at Amherst & is much admired in Pottsville.

Pottsville has all modern "wrinkles"—Village Improvement Societies etc.

They read The Outlook and the Literary Digest.   Lovingly

1. The Molly Maguires, a secret organization of miners in the Pennsylvania coal fields from 1865 to 1875, frustrated by the owners' control of the local government and courts, turned to violence and arson in their effort to secure relief from the terrible conditions of

mine work. In 1875 they managed to form a union, but the owners called in the Pinkertons, who infiltrated the group. The evidence uncovered destroyed the organization and led to the hanging of twenty of its members.

2. Joseph Bartlett Eastman (1882–1942), then secretary of the Public Franchise League, developed into one of the nation's most astute and dedicated public servants. He served for many years on the Interstate Commerce Commission, and Franklin Roosevelt named him coordinator of transportation during the New Deal. LDB came to rely on Eastman's judgment and administrative ability in numerous reforms and once commented that "Joe Eastman has more interest in the public service and less in his own career than any one man I have ever known" (quoted in Claude Moore Fuess, *Joseph B. Eastman: Servant of the People* [New York, 1952], 81). Similarly, Fuess shows that LDB's influence on Eastman was "decisive and continuous over many years."

To: Alice Goldmark Brandeis
Date: August 11, 1906
Place: Lexington, Kentucky
Source: Gilbert MSS

DEAREST: We had a fine day yesterday. Left Versailles [Kentucky] at 7:15 A.M. & drove to Mr. Henry L. Martin's[1] farm near Midway. One of the best farms in the Blue Grass country, and unquestionably one of the best men. Indeed an extremely fine and interesting man with whom we spent from 8:30 A.M. to 4 P.M., mostly listening to his autobiography which was a tale of American manhood of which we are justly proud. He is a native Kentuckian about 58 years old, of Blue Grass family 125 years old which lost all its money before the war & its slaves through the war. Martin was in the Confederate Army from '62 to '65, came out at 17, then went into a grocery store at Midway for a few years. Worked about 17 hours a day for nearly as many years (including his studying) but did not lose sight of what it was all for. And worked out for himself a philosophy of life to which we should readily assent.

At fifty-one or two he retired from much of his business with a fortune of about half a million. Keeps up now enough business to occupy him, but to leave him leisure enough to do anything he cares to, and has a fine sense of human obligations and of culture.

He lost his first wife early. His second is an attractive Tennessee woman, who gets much joy from her numerous chickens & ducks and flowers. Martin has about 1000 acres of what he considers the best farming land in the world. His son, a man of about 25 (who studied law at Columbia but renounced practice) is to run this farm. Martin has another about as large at Columbia Tenn[essee] where he used to live. A deformed daughter is a college girl.

Martin says that Woodford Co. & two other Blue Grass counties will hold elections on the Saloon issue this fall and will surely vote "No". Of the 119 Kentucky Counties 85 have already voted No, and the cry is "still they come." The German beer interest seems to be the main support of the saloonists.[2]

We spent the night pleasantly at the Peppers'.[3] He and his ancestors since 1770 have been whiskey distillers.

The drives yesterday were finer than those from Lexington to Versailles, more pastures and rolling country. The elevation is over 900 above the sea.

Lovingly

Mrs. Martin has already read "Helen Ritchie."[4]

1. Henry Lewis Martin (1848–19[?]) had fought as a boy in the Civil War and then returned to Midway, where he headed the Citizens Bank and also built up the horse farm he inherited from his father. As a member of the executive committee of the Cane and Beet Sugar Growers Association, Martin was involved in national politics, successfully lobbying Congress for subsidies for sugar growers.

2. Although Kentucky adopted a local option law in 1874, only a handful of counties chose to exercise the option and become dry. The state did ratify the prohibition amendment in 1919 but by a narrow margin, 208,904 for and 198,671 against.

3. Probably the farm established by Robert Perry Pepper (1830–95) near Frankfort, which had a very large number of horses and was renowned for the many champion racers bred there. The farm had been sold after the death of Pepper's only son but continued in business, perhaps under the original name, for a number of years. See the next letter.

4. There is no record of a book or short story of this title in the Library of Congress catalogue.

To:	Elizabeth Brandeis
Date:	August 11, 1906
Place:	Lexington, Kentucky
Source:	Gilbert MSS

DEAR ELIZABETH: You would have enjoyed greatly our visit yesterday at Mr. Pepper's horse farm, where we saw a wonderful collection of thoroughbred horses and colts. There were about thirty colts three or four months old with their mothers, and about as many "yearlings", that is colts that are a little more than a year old. All of these colts were so well trained that they came up to us and smelled our hands as we walked about in the pastures. The yearlings were remarkably handsome. They are all destined for racing. Those that prove not to be fast enough will be sold for carriage horses. These "yearlings" will, it is expected, be sold at an average price of nearly $500, and some of them may bring as high a price as three or four thousand dollars.

They are bred quite differently from ordinary horses. They are fed about twice as much, the idea being to make them grow large and quite heavy as soon as possible, so that most of these "yearlings" are as large as ordinary horses two years old. These thoroughbreds are put to racing when they are two years old.

There were also some nice cows on Mr. Pepper's farm. Uncle Alfred has four cows, three Jerseys and one Alderley. Uncle Alfred says that he does not want a Holstein because they give little milk.

We are going now with Mr. Pepper to see some other horse-farms.

To:	Alice Goldmark Brandeis
Date:	August 13, 1906
Place:	Louisville, Kentucky
Source:	Gilbert MSS

DEAREST: I was delighted with your Thursday and Wednesday letters which told of real enjoyment of the Mountains, and brought assurance that you were really feeling better. We returned here about nine Saturday evening. Yesterday was spent without much enterprise. Lee Calahan came in in the morning. He, Al & I poked around the country a horse & ended up at Cooper's. He was not in, but we saw the daughter, [*] and Mrs. Hewitt. The former told me we ought to know the Ass[istan]t Prof Rands[1] (Greek Dept. Harvard). She was Belle Palmer, a Louisville girl whom Al says was handsome & bright & whom Mother and Father found attractive. They have been in Cambridge about 4 years. Mrs. Hewitt (whose husband was connected with the Dominion Iron & Steel Co 5 years) says the John S. McLellans are to spend the winter in Boston.

Saturday we spent among the great thoroughbred farms, James R. Keene's[2] and the J.B. Haggins,[3] the latter the greatest in the world probably. Tell Elizabeth & Susan there are 1500 horses on the place & 500 men to take care of them & other things on this 6000 acre farm.

But I tell *you* that these stallions were a revelation to me.—6 at Keene's and 20+ at Haggins. The practice is to develop them for racing; let them race while 2 or 3 years old, come here as late as the fourth year, and then for 15 to 20 years for breeding purposes. The value runs very high. One of these cost $70,000! but no price is more than they are worth.

They entirely revolutionized my ideas of race-horses. I supposed them to be lank, thin, and to the uneducated lay mind unbeautiful. Quite the contrary is the fact. They are the most beautiful living creatures I have ever seen. The only fit comparison seems to me the marbles of Praxiteles;[4] and for the wonderful Greek marbles I know no fitter comparison than these horses.

You simply cannot form an idea of their beauty. The difference between them and the plug horse is greater by far than between the lowliest peasant and our most beautiful women. I should like to hear Gaston on the subject.

Look at Aug 11 Outlook for another (short) Boston Gas blast. I recognize it as my production, but don't know where they got it.[5]

Also note Untermyer's[6] trouble with Seymour Eaton.[7]

Breakfast calls.

1. Edward Kennard Rands (1871–1945) received his doctorate at the University of Munich in 1900 and began his distinguished academic career at his alma matter, Harvard, the following year. Before his retirement in 1942 he would be known as one of the nation's leading classical scholars. He married Belle Brent Palmer in 1901.

2. James Robert Keene (1838–1913) was born in England and emigrated to the United States in 1852. He made a fortune speculating in silver and other stocks and then went broke in the 1880s trying to manipulate railroad stocks. He eventually recouped his fortune and then retired to his horse farm in Castleton, Kentucky. He raced his horses both in Europe and in the United States and won respect and admiration for his efforts to build up racing as an honest sport.

3. James B. Haggin (1827–1914) was educated as a lawyer and practiced for a while in Mississippi before moving to California, where he made a fortune in mining. He retired to build up his farm in Kentucky and became the largest individual owner of horses in training and stud.

4. Praxiteles (ca. 390–330 B.C.) is considered the greatest of the ancient Greek sculptors; working entirely in marble, he created statues that embraced a humane rather than heroic characterization of humans and even of the gods.

5. "The Price of Gas in Boston," *Outlook* 83 (11 August 1906): 831–32, described the passage of the sliding-scale plan as "the most important event of the year in Boston relating to municipal affairs." If the article did derive from something LDB had written, it was not from a published piece; his first and only article on the sliding scale was "How Boston Solved the Gas Problem," in *American Review of Reviews,* which did not appear until November 1907. LDB did, however, write a number of lengthy letters to support the plan and also testified in its behalf; the article could have drawn upon those sources.

6. Samuel Untermyer (1858–1940), a highly successful attorney whose firm handled many corporate clients, also was heavily involved in reform work and Jewish communal affairs. In 1912 and 1913 he served as counsel to the Pujo Committee investigating the money trust, whose findings became the basis for LDB's *Other People's Money.*

7. Seymour Eaton, the secretary of the International Policy Holders' Committee (which was fighting for control of the Mutual Life Insurance Association), resigned, charging that the committee no longer represented the interests of the common policyholder but only those of the larger investors. A representative for Untermyer said that Eaton was a paid employee of the committee and not a member and had no say in policy matters; the spokesman went on to say that any insinuations in Mr. Eaton's statement were "utterly and willfully untrue" (*New York Times,* 10 August 1906).

To: **Alfred Brandeis**
Date: **April 21, 1907**
Place: **Dedham, Massachusetts**
Source: **EBR**

MY DEAR AL: My thoughts were constantly of Father and of Amy on the trip to North Adams. Up to that it was the oft-travelled road; and from Greenfield on the scene of the famous drive which Amy enjoyed so much and Father was so proud of.

As I walked out from North Adams towards Williamstown, and looked up at Greylock which I climbed with Phil Marcou 28 years ago the feeling that our generation was on the [wane] and Fred's rising was quite oppressive, but I resist such pressure.

Came back from No. Adams on freight train (1:45 A.M.) and out to Dedham early for glorious winter sunshine. We had ice yesterday morning.

At No. Adams had quite a talk with an intelligent RR man. He says the Fitchburg is moving 1000 freight cars a day past No. Adams, but that 10,000 are waiting their turn at Rotterdam Junction. There is sad lack of motive power, and 50 engines are overdue from the equipment companies. He thinks however with J.J. Hill,[1] that there is a lack of trackage. The freight trains on the Fitchburg are short hauling only about 1200 tons, but they seemed to be constantly passing.

Passenger trains are now nearer schedule on the Fitchburg than on the B & A & travel generally is much pleasanter on the FRR.

1. James Jerome Hill (1838–1916) was the organizing genius behind the Great Northern Railroad system and, together with J. P. Morgan, contrived the Northern Securities Company to avoid a ruinous price war. Unlike some of the "robber barons," Hill is credited with being a good businessman, and his railroads were among the best in the country.

To:	Alfred Brandeis
Date:	June 18, 1907
Place:	Dedham, Massachusetts
Source:	Brandeis MSS

DEAR AL: The Senate voted yesterday 23 to 3 to order the Savings Insurance Bill to a third reading. That beats our record in the house. There was a slim attendance (the whole body is 40) as June 17 is a local holiday.

The bill should come up for engrossment today or tomorrow, and, in spite of rancorous opposition, ought not to meet any snags after yesterday's record.

The B & M–N Y & N H & H merger is in a less satisfactory shape.[1] It came up so suddenly that we have not had time to prepare for the fight. But our enemies are at least uncomfortable.

We settled the strike at Syracuse. I am experiencing a growing conviction that the labor men are the most congenial company. The intense materialism and luxuriousness of most of our other people makes their company quite irksome. Among the stokers at Syracuse I met a young fellow whose wife is a direct descendant (5th in descent) of Schiller[']s.[2]

Do you or Jenny remember anything of Schiller's family? This lad tells me that his wife['s] grandmother (?)—a Becker—came to America in 1840.

Hot weather has set in.

1. The attempted takeover of the Boston & Maine Railroad by the New York, New Haven & Hartford occupied a good part of LDB's time between 1907 and 1913 and propelled him into the national spotlight. When the New Haven began buying up Boston & Maine stock, a large public outcry arose—not so much because the people opposed monopoly, but rather because J. P. Morgan and New York financial interests controlled the New Haven, and Bay State pride objected to the Boston & Maine, a local institution, falling under "outside" or "foreign" interests. LDB, while sharing some of this sentiment, opposed the merger more on issues of ethics and monopoly. His research led him to uncover serious financial problems at the New Haven, which that line hoped to resolve through the injection of cash and earnings from the smaller but very profitable Boston & Maine.

As LDB became more involved, he found he could no longer attend to his practice; rather than have his partners suffer because of his reform activities, he arranged to pay the firm for the time he devoted to the antimerger fight (see LDB to E. Louise Malloch, 4 November 1907, BL).

There is no satisfactory account of the complete merger fight. The basic story is told in Henry Lee Staples and Alpheus T. Mason, *The Fall of a Railroad Empire: Brandeis and the New Haven Battle* (Syracuse, 1947), and in shorter form in Mason, *Brandeis,* ch. 12. Both accounts suffer from partisanship and a failure to place the events in the larger context and general economic trends in the country. Letters relating to the merger fight can be found primarily in volume 2 of BL.

2. Perhaps the great German writer Johann Friedrich von Schiller (1759–1805).

To: **Alfred Brandeis**
Date: **June 19, 1907**
Place: **Dedham, Massachusetts**
Source: **EBR**

DEAR AL: The enemy is still worrying us. At yesterday's Senate meeting a lot of amendments were introduced to the Savings Insurance Bill. Hope we shall brush them away without injury today.[1]

The merger is troublesome. Our business-men fail to grasp to [*sic*] the evils of monopoly and are cowards besides.[2] If we get time enough we may enlighten them, but it is too hot for much education.

I waded through a long dinner to the Chinese minister last evening.[3] (Effort of our cotton M[anu]f[acture]rs to win back the cotton trade) and was not delighted as I saw our business-nobility together. Though I would sacrifice myself just to get the feel of them on the Merger question.

It is much better fun coming out to Dedham for a ride with Susan. Country is in its best form with the early spring green still triumphant. Callahan came in for a moment today & promises to come in with you in Aug.

1. At 4 o'clock that afternoon LDB reported to his brother that the "Senate voted down all amendments and passed the Insurance bill to be engrossed by a vote of 28 to 4. It goes back to the house for enactment probably tomorrow" (BL).

2. The reasons for business support for the railroad merger have been explored by Richard Abrams in a significant article, "Brandeis and the New Haven–Boston & Maine Merger Battle Revisited," *Business History Review* 36 (Winter 1962): 408–30. Abrams suggests that many businessmen supported the merger because they believed a unified transportation system would aid Massachusetts in the competition with New York as a major port of shipment to Europe of goods and produce from the interior of the country. Economists have also argued that competition in transportation is wasteful, and many progressives—reformers and business leaders alike—believed strongly in consolidation.

3. Sir Chentang Liang Cheng was the Chinese minister to the United States.

To:	Alfred Brandeis
Date:	July 13, 1907
Place:	Dedham, Massachusetts
Source:	Brandeis MSS

DEAR AL: Had a charming letter from Uncle William [Taussig] this week acknowledging copy of Savings Insurance Bill. The Governor made the proper appointments for the Central Board which will doubtless be confirmed at the next council meeting on July 17.

Weather here is fine now, and I am working only moderately so as to taper off gently to the South Yarmouth days. I think you will be as well pleased with life there as you can be with anything outside Kentucky. The opportunities for loafing in various ways are good.

To:	Alfred Brandeis
Date:	August 23, 1907
Place:	South Yarmouth, Massachusetts
Source:	EBR

DEAR AL: We are very "homesick" for you—and are much depressed by the death of our good friend Dr. Folsom.

The wind blows hard from the South East; but the night is light with the full moon, which itself is not visible. We started a wood fire in the dining room to warm our shivering bodies and more to cheer us.

To-morrow the Wilde's [*sic*] are to have their flagraising with appropriate hospitalities which they regret you will not participate in. Prescott has gone to Falmouth in [**]. Lincoln Filene[1] came in his auto today from beyond Boston to talk over an important business matter and brought with him some friends who were here two hours. He reported Storrow[2] of Lee Higginson and Co. as talking blue of the financial situation, but that the Filene July–Aug. sales were largely in excess of 1906. Obviously the pinch is still only on the financial aristocracy.

Alice & I discovered an inland passage at high tide leading nearly up to the Bass River Light.

It was good to have you so long.

1. Abraham Lincoln Filene (1865–1957) and his brother Edward not only established the department store that bore their name but also shared a passion for social reform and experimentation. With LDB's suggestions and encouragement, Lincoln Filene directed his attention to the problems of employment and introduced a number of measures into his own business, such as minimum wages for women, employee organizations to bargain with management, profit-sharing, paid vacations, and other benefits. The two Filenes, especially Lincoln, would be associated with LDB in many reforms, and it was Lincoln who brought LDB in to mediate the great New York garment workers' strike of 1910.

2. James Jackson Storrow (1864–1926), although trained as a lawyer, achieved greater eminence as a banker with Lee, Higginson & Co. He joined that firm in 1906 and was among the first to capitalize on the expanding automobile industry. Involved in various civic measures, Storrow led the fight for the development and improvement of the Charles River basin, and the drive along the river is named after him.

To: **Alice Goldmark Brandeis**
Date: **August 30, 1907**
Place: **Dedham, Massachusetts**
Source: **Gilbert MSS**

DEAREST: Susan and I paddled this afternoon. It seemed hard to leave Elizabeth behind, but she submitted in silence, and sat with us cheerfully after her own supper when we returned.

Savings insurance has been active today and the prospect of carrying the Committee has improved much. Indeed many say it is only a question of the size of the majority. Our lobby is active. The Committee has set down the matter for discussion in Executive Session for Tuesday next and may decide its fate on that day.

Enclosed clipping of Fish's resignation[1] is interesting. He should accept the presidency of the Tech now. Theo. Vail was manager of the Bell Co. 20 years ago & was led off to another enterprise which ruined his health & fortune. He is rather old to assume these burdens.[2]

What say you to this of Symonds on that marvellous man Leo Battista Alberti of Rimini?[3]

"Alberti devoted his great faculties and all his wealth of genius to the study of the law, then as now the quicksand of the noblest natures."

I talked with Volenti today and am to hear more tomorrow.

1. Following the revelations of the insurance scandals, Stuyvesant Fish (1851–1923) was forced to resign as a trustee of the Mutual Life Insurance Company, on whose board

he had sat since 1883. For LDB's view of Fish, see LDB to Alfred Brandeis, 27 March 1908.

2. Theodore Newton Vail (1845–1920) was one of the pioneering organizers of the Bell Telephone Company and then of American Telephone & Telegraph. Ill health led him to retire in 1887, and the enforced rest soon cured his problems. In 1907, when AT&T faced major organizational difficulties, Vail returned to head the giant company and guided it safely through economic distress as well as World War I.

3. Leo Battista Alberti (1404–72) was originally educated in canon law but spent most of his life as a scholar and architect, executing commissions from many of the great families of Renaissance Italy. LDB is quoting from one of the books of the late-nineteenth-century Renaissance scholar John Addington Symonds (1840–93), one of his favorite writers.

To:	Alfred Brandeis
Date:	October 19, 1907
Place:	Dedham, Massachusetts
Source:	Brandeis MSS

DEAR AL: I had a chance for the Mayoralty the other day. The Republican City Com[mit]tee & the Good Government Association jointly requested me to make the run. Under our primary election law, the Republican nomination is, of course, not in the gift of the Committee, but they offered to put me up as the machine's candidate (Anything to beat Fitzgerald)[1] & to support me as thoroughly as possible.

I concluded that on the whole it was best to decline. I have the merger on hand, & shouldn't like to have that job interfered with. The New Haven & local public service corporations, or at least the Electric light Co. would have joined their forces against me. The main reason, however, that induced me to decline is the fact that we have a Finance Commission now at work, investigating city affairs, with obligation to report to the Legislature Jan 1/09, and I think it just as well to have a thorough job done & not attempt [to] palliate present ills. Furthermore the chances of a really good fight were not the best. My course in knocking heads right and left is not exactly such as to create an "available" candidate.

I am still struggling with the New Haven reports trying to find out its real financial condition & operation. I hope to get [a copy] of their report to the Interstate Commerce Comm. this week and if they have truthfully answered all questions, there ought to be some fun ahead bringing out the facts.

I think before we get through, the estimable gentlemen who scrambled for the chance of exchanging their B & M stock for New Haven will feel that they have been served to a gold brick.

At present stage of investigation it looks as if Mellen[2] had gone ahead like other Napoleons of finance joyously as long as borrowing was easy & that he will come up against a stone wall as soon as his borrowing capacity ends. There are some indications that it has ended, (with his stock at 139.), and that he is resorting to all kinds of devices to get money.

I have not been able to figure out yet from data available what he has done with all the money he raised & should not be at all surprised to find that some had already gone into dividends.

Sadie[3] returns Monday.

1. John Francis "Honey-Fitz" Fitzgerald (1863–1950) was a longtime Democratic leader in Boston and Massachusetts politics. He served as mayor several times, and Boston twice sent him to Congress. Fitzgerald epitomized for LDB and other good government advocates all that was wrong with machine politics. Fitzgerald was the grandfather of future president John Fitzgerald Kennedy.

2. Charles Sanger Mellen (1851–1927) started as a railroad clerk at age eighteen and rose to become one of the nation's most powerful railroad managers. In 1903 he left the presidency of the Northern Pacific to head the New Haven and immediately set about trying to absorb all of New England's transportation into the line, especially the Boston & Maine. LDB maintained his attack until his predictions came true—the railroad's shaky financial structure collapsed, leading to Mellen's forced resignation in 1913. For LDB's assessment of Mellen, see his letter to Norman Hapgood, 25 September 1911, BL.

3. Sadie Nicholson, born in Nova Scotia, was the Brandeis girls' nurse. She stayed on with the family, as a general assistant to AGB, even after the girls had outgrown their need for her.

To: Alice Goldmark Brandeis
Date: January 14, 1908
Place: Washington, D.C.
Source: Gilbert MSS

DEAREST: Had a half hour with Sen. Crane[1] yesterday afternoon, with shades carefully drawn. I was reminded of Anna Karenina's discovery of Oblonsky's long ears.

Peeped in at Justice Holmes for tea, & returned for a charming dinner with them à quarte [*sic*]—quite as of old. Between times I called at the Cordova where I saw the 4 Goldmarks & Mrs. Tompkins & Miss Sasis.

Had had half an hour with Henry at luncheon. He is not going to N.Y. this week as his boss is here from Panama. He seems well content with Panama prospects.[2]

[*] is expected from N.Y. today. Asa P. French[3] had an interview with Prest. [Roosevelt][4] yesterday. Have not seen him since.

Weather rainy yesterday, fine today. Case may not be reached until tomorrow.[5]

1. Winthrop Murray Crane (1853–1920) served as the Republican governor of Massachusetts from 1900 to 1902, when he met LDB and supported several of his causes. In 1904 he was elected to the United States Senate, where he remained until 1913.

2. Henry Goldmark was one of the designers of the Panama Canal locks system.

3. Asa Palmer French (1860–1935) was named U.S. attorney for Massachusetts in 1906; he would hold the office until 1914 and worked closely with LDB on the merger controversy.

4. Probably about the New Haven merger.

5. The next day LDB would argue one of the landmark cases in American constitutional development, *Muller v. Oregon,* 208 U.S. 412 (1908). The state of Oregon had enacted legislation limiting to ten the number of hours a day women could work in certain industries, and that law had been challenged in the courts by Curt Muller, a Portland laundry owner. Just a few years earlier the Supreme Court had struck down a New York law limiting the hours of bakery workers in *Lochner v. New York,* 198 U.S. 45 (1905). A five-to-four majority had overturned that statute on the grounds that it bore no relation to the health or safety of the workers and that it was unwarranted interference with the right to make contracts.

The National Consumers' League, which had helped pass the Oregon law, approached LDB to defend it before the Supreme Court. Working closely with his sister-in-law Josephine Goldmark and labor expert and social reformer Florence Kelley, LDB put together a unique brief. In just a few pages of traditional legal citation, he agreed that government should not interfere in the labor market unless conditions made it absolutely necessary to do so. He then provided over one hundred pages of references to labor studies done in the United States and Europe detailing the effect that long hours had on the health, family life, and morals of women, thus addressing the major issue the Court majority had raised in *Lochner.* The strategy worked: on 24 February the Court unanimously upheld the law, and Justice Brewer took the unusual step of praising LDB's brief.

According to Miss Goldmark "The distinguishing mark of Mr. Brandeis's argument was his complete mastery of the details of his subject and the marshaling of the evidence. Slowly, deliberately, without seeming to refer to a note, he built up his case from the particular to the general, describing conditions authoritatively reported, turning the pages of history, country by country, state by state, weaving in with artistic skill the human facts" (quoted in Mason, *Brandeis,* 250). The decision became the prime example of the so-called sociological jurisprudence called for by reformers like Holmes and Dean Roscoe Pound of the Harvard Law School, a jurisprudence that would recognize and take into account actual conditions in society and not rely on abstract theory.

To: **Alfred Brandeis**
Date: **February 2, 1908**
Place: **Boston, Massachusetts**
Source: **Brandeis MSS**

DEAR AL: Returned this morning from Washington where I spent yesterday. Went there to see the Asst. Secty. of Treas.[1] on a tariff matter for the Warrens, which left me time for other things, and had an interesting day. Henry Beach Needham[2] took me to see Roosevelt, to whom I wanted to talk merger, and who impressed me most favorably in every way—manners included. He is a great man and his special message expressed just my sentiments. You must have been pleased to have him use your quotation from Lincoln.[3]

Also spent an hour and a half with Prof. H.C. Adams[4] of the Interstate Commerce Comm., whom I am stirring up on New Haven accounting, and called on Asst. Atty. General Cooley[5] to have him get Purdy[6] into greater activity.

Needham says—he thinks that Taft[7] to be nominated, must win on the first ballot, and that if he doesn't, the most dangerous man is Cannon,[8] of whom he has a very poor opinion.

I suppose you read Hughes's[9] speech on Friday evening, which was, of course, good and fine as he is—but there is a counter current of dissatisfaction among his hitherto greatest admirers who think he is leaving unfinished his job. The New York World, hitherto his staunchest supporter and largely his inspiration in the Insurance fight, devoted Friday its whole editorial page to "Gov. Hughes' Unfulfilled Contract."[10]

Read the Lawson "Why I Gave Up the Fight" in the January Everybody. I think both his and Ridgeway's letters are genuine.[11] Ridgeway, I spent 8 hours with on the day before the Knickerbocker failure and was very favorably impressed with. He said to me much that comes out in one form or another in these letters.

Lawson's declarations tend to make clearer all the mystery of his fight hitherto. His dropping out, his grumbling at lack of gratitude, are as they should be in him. It would not have been Lawson if he had lived up to the exalted character some of his friends have pictured him to be.[12]

I don't believe in the reported "getting over the panic and business depression". Of course, business after a complete standstill must resume, but it can't resume at a higher enough percent of volume and continuousness to prevent serious bad business and much unemployment.

1. James Burton Reynolds was associated with LDB in the People's Lobby; he served as assistant secretary of the Treasury from 1905 to 1909.

2. Henry Beach Needham (1871–1915), after a brief law practice, joined the *New York Evening Post in* 1896 and the following year went over to the staff of *McClure's*. Eventually he left to become a freelance journalist and reformer until his death in an airplane accident in France during World War I.

3. President Roosevelt had delivered one of the most radical speeches of his presidency to Congress on 1 February. Condemning "predatory wealth," Roosevelt challenged the Congress to revise the Sherman Antitrust Act, to pass pro-labor legislation, and to impose restrictions upon the railroads. The *New York Times* reported that "Democrats and former Populists cheered and Republicans gasped as President Roosevelt's much-heralded 'buzz-saw message' today tore the air of Congress." Roosevelt closed with the "malice toward none and charity for all" passage of Lincoln's second inaugural. See *The Works of Theodore Roosevelt,* 20 vols. (New York, 1926), 7:1597ff.

4. Henry Carter Adams (1851–1921), professor of political economy at the University of Michigan, was the first person to receive a doctorate at the Johns Hopkins University. From 1887 to 1911 he served as chief statistician for the Interstate Commerce Commission.

5. Alfred Warriner Cooley (1873–1913), a New York lawyer then working in the Justice Department, would become an associate justice of the New Mexico Supreme Court in 1909.

6. Milton Dwight Purdy (1866–1937), then an assistant to the attorney general, would be appointed a federal district judge the following June.

7. The career of William Howard Taft (1857–1930) crossed paths with that of LDB at several points. A former federal judge and governor of the Philippines, he served as Roosevelt's secretary of war and was his hand-picked choice to succeed him as president. Taft had a conservative judge's temperament and despised politics, and his maladroitness in this area led him to stumble into the Pinchot-Ballinger imbroglio (see LDB to AGB, 12 January 1910, note 9) as well as several other political fiascos. Although often dismissed as a reactionary, Taft in fact had a solid progressive record as president, actively pursuing reform policies in the environment and enforcing the antitrust laws. In 1912 the hapless Taft finished third in the presidential election behind Roosevelt and Woodrow Wilson.

Taft always wanted to be on the Supreme Court, and he bitterly opposed LDB's nomination in 1916. Shortly after the war Taft accidentally met LDB in Washington. For LDB's charming account of that dramatic encounter, see his letter to AGB, 4 December 1918. In 1921 President Harding fulfilled Taft's lifelong ambition and named him Chief Justice and thus a colleague of LDB on the High Court. Just as in his presidential tenure, some of Taft's conservative opinions have obscured his very important contributions to reforming the administration of the federal court system. As members of the Supreme Court, Taft and LDB, despite their differences, maintained a polite and respectful relationship.

8. Joseph Gurney Cannon (1836–1927) was the crusty and controversial Speaker of the House of Representatives from 1903 to 1911. A virtual tyrant over House affairs, Cannon came to symbolize the GOP Old Guard. Taft did win the Republican nomination on the first ballot.

9. Charles Evans Hughes (1862–1948) ranks as one of America's great progressive statesmen. As a young New York lawyer he was swept up in the progressive movement and made a national reputation investigating gas and electric franchises and abuses in the insurance industry. LDB, in fact, relied heavily on Hughes's insurance work to buttress his own position. Hughes served as governor of New York from 1907 to 1910, when Taft named him to the Supreme Court, but he resigned to accept the Republican presidential nomination in 1916. After losing that race, Hughes returned to private practice until President Warren G. Harding named him secretary of state in 1921, a post he held for four years. In 1930 Hoover named Hughes to succeed Taft as Chief Justice, and he and LDB sat together during the turbulent decade of the New Deal. Hughes retired from the bench in 1941.

10. On 31 January Hughes appeared before an enthusiastic New York Republican Club, whose members touted him as Roosevelt's successor. In what many commentators described as an "acceptance" speech, Hughes talked about such national issues as the tariff, railroad regulation, employers' liability, and revision of the Sherman Act. The general enthusiasm for Hughes subsided in the face of Roosevelt's determination to place Taft in the White House, and he continued as governor for a second term until Taft named him to the Court.

11. The article is an exchange of letters between Thomas William Lawson (1857–1925), the colorful, sensation-seeking financier turned muckraker and the author of *Frenzied Finance* (1905), and Erman Jesse Ridgeway (1867–1943), the publisher of *Everybody's Magazine* and other periodicals. Lawson announced that he was dropping out of the fight to reform Amalgamated Copper, and Ridgeway, who had published many of Lawson's sensational exposure articles, begged him not to give up the fight.

12. Lawson had written to Ridgeway: "You talk of what I owe the people. What do I owe to the gelatin-spined shrimps? What have the saffron-blooded apes done for me or mine that I should halt any decisions to match their lightning-change ten-above-ten-below-zero chameleon-hued loyalty?"

To: Alfred Brandeis
Date: March 27, 1908
Place: Boston, Massachusetts
Source: Brandeis MSS

DEAR AL: I sat next to Stuyvesant Fish at the Economics Club Dinner this week where RRs & mergers were talked. I was not impressed by his mind & do not wonder that Harriman got the better of him.[1] He is a fine manly looking fellow, and something of a theorist, but his reasoning seems to me rather halting. He says for instance that there was an abundance of rolling stock in the country last year, but the difficulty lay in the hauling of empties. That is rather an overworking of a truth I think.

Our merger fight is growing red hot & no less interesting. The New Haven have [*sic*] at last come out into the speaking field. The [*sic*] have in Vice Pres[iden]t T.E. Byrnes an ex-lawyer & lobbyist who was with Mellen on the U[nion] P[acific,] quite a spellbinder, who combines the capacity of endless lying & unbounded promising with a charming personality and facility of speech.[2] So that we have a new element to deal with. We are getting the community well worked up now, and shall doubtless develop partisanship enough on each side to ensure everybody's keeping awake.

In which carriage were you on the drive to Miramar, i.e. with whom?

1. In 1906 Fish had been forced out of the presidency of the Illinois Central Railroad by Edward Henry Harriman (1848–1909), one of the most powerful and talented railroad barons in American history. Ironically, at LDB's confirmation hearings in 1916 unsubstantiated allegations arose that while battling against the New Haven merger he had been accepting fat fees from Harriman in the struggle against Fish. These charges merely echoed other allegations made against LDB at the time. See LDB to Joseph Walker, 19 May 1908, BL, and U.S. Senate, *Hearings before the Sub-Committee . . . on the Nomination of Louis D. Brandeis . . . ,* 64th Cong., 1st Sess. 2 vols. (Washington, D.C., 1916), 1:336–55.

2. Timothy Edward Byrnes (1853–1944), the New Haven's vice-president, was a practicing attorney and railroad lawyer before entering management in the 1890s. He and LDB embarked upon a series of debates before various business and civic organizations. See Staples and Mason, *Fall of a Railroad Empire,* 49–52.

To: Alice Goldmark Brandeis
Date: April 15, 1908
Place: New York, New York
Source: Gilbert MSS

DEAREST: Only a word of love for tomorrow, and all time. I should regret more being absent on this day,[1] were not all the year fete days.

1. AGB's birthday.

To: Alice Goldmark Brandeis
Date: April 19, 1908
Place: Washington, D.C.
Source: Gilbert MSS

DEAREST: We went out for a long walk with Henry [Goldmark] and Metcalf[1] this morning in the beautiful rolling country surrounding Washington. The beauty of this extraordinarily beautiful city I had not suspected. In road and park development and in architecture Washington has developed wonderfully since you were here, but it has dropped into luxury and to greater degree of insensibility to the sweetness of life. Though the sky has been mostly sunshine and the fresh green and blossoms are entrancing I have obviously been here too long or too often, and my heart yearns not only for you and the children but for our sterner life and climate.

We called on Mrs. [Nathaniel] Shaler yesterday and are to take supper with them this evening. There we met Prof. Schofield[2] (him of Berlin fame) and his wife.

I called on Lincoln [Filene] this morning whom Washington life has improved.

1. Probably Henry Clayton Metcalf (1867–1942), a professor at Tufts College who wrote widely on labor and industrial relations and who did some consulting for the Filenes.
2. William Henry Schofield (1870–1920) had taught English literature at Harvard since 1897, with a specialty in the medieval period.

To: **Alfred Brandeis**
Date: **June 20, 1908**
Place: **Boston, Massachusetts**
Source: **Brandeis MSS**

DEAR AL: Had a very charming letter from Uncle William.[1]

Yours about corn crop rec'd. I thought, remembering Father's attitude, that it was altogether too early to talk assured crops at this stage.

The Taft nomination assures one good candidate. I don't feel enthusiastic over Sherman.[2] Hughes, having made one mistake in saying he wouldn't be governor again, made a second in refusing the Vice Presidency.

I can't see sufficient justification for the views that business resumption is at hand. The Republican promise of extra sessions for tariff revision won't help matters.

I am dead against any tariff revision except a horizontal scaling down in annual installments, and maximum & minimum tariffs.[3]

1. William Taussig had written LDB about the New Haven fight; see LDB's response, 18 June 1908, BL.
2. James Schoolcraft Sherman (1855–1912) was nominated as Taft's running mate. A Republican congressman from New York, Sherman served out his vice-presidency, was renominated to run with Taft in 1912, but died at the close of the campaign.
3. See LDB to Woodrow Wilson, 1 August 1912, BL.

To: **Alfred Brandeis**
Date: **July 17, 1908**
Place: **Boston, Massachusetts**
Source: **Brandeis MSS**

MY DEAR AL: It seems to me clear that I ought not leave Alice this summer. She is gaining steadily but it would be more of a strain than is advisable to leave her alone with the children at So. Yarmouth, as [un]fortunately we have Miss Parker no longer with us.

As I must not go [to] Louisville, it seems to follow that you must come to South Yarmouth. You said last year that Jennie ought to be made to leave the [Ladless] Hill—and Madie[1] voiced the same sentiment when I last saw her.

Couldn't you induce her to come to So. Yarmouth with you. With Frank [Taussig] near and Walley[2] not very far off, the East ought to offer enough attractions to bring Jennie here—if "personally conducted."

We plan to go to So. Yarmouth July 31, & shall be ready for you and any members of the family on August 1st or soon thereafter as you can get there. Don't make it much later than Aug 1 & come then if you can. The first week of August is best. The waxing moon & the long days are then; & I want Jennie to see us at our best.

Tell Jennie we can give her and you the little house, with Ray's successor as Valet, and you can have as little of us as you like.

I want, inter alia, to talk over the merger fight with you before it grows stale.

The other day I was accosted in the train to Dedham by a Mr. Maynard (whom I didn't remember) formerly of Small Maynard & Co. who asked about Oscar[3] whom he lived with in Chicago 12 years ago. I see you advertised as fighting freight rate increase.[4]

1. "Madie" was Alfred's daughter Adele.
2. Walter Taussig was Jennie Brandeis's younger brother.
3. Oscar Wehle, a Chicago architect, designed Alfred Brandeis's farm at Ladless Hill.
4. The railroads wanted an across-the-board rate increase, and many commentators viewed this as the first test of the Hepburn Act, which had granted rate-setting powers to the Interstate Commerce Commission. Rumors abounded that both the ICC and President Roosevelt favored the increase in order to maintain labor wages; shippers like Alfred naturally opposed any rate increase. For LDB's role in the freight rate controversy, see LDB to Alfred Brandeis, 21 August 1910, BL.

To: **Alfred Brandeis**
Date: **September 20, 1908**
Place: **Dedham, Massachusetts**
Source: **Brandeis MSS**

DEAR AL: We are happily spending this Sunday at home. The children & I have just been nutting & returned heavily laden with hickory nuts & some butternuts to the girls' joy. Amy and Dorothy are expected next week. They may arrive in time for another expedition. Susan hopes the difficulties will surely be enhanced when the lower branches have been rifled.

Sen. Foraker has made a fine exhibit.[1] There is quite a little uneasiness in Republican ranks East about the campaign. New York, Conn., New Hampshire & Maine all show considerable dissention within Republican ranks, and much apathy toward the result, and I met a Springfield Ohio man who said much the same of Ohio, Ind., Ill., Iowa. At all events the interest is enhanced, and "dem Zuschauer is kein spiel zu hoch,"[2] as you rightly remark.

My office is pretty busy now, and even "Father" must work. This interrupts considerably my Savings Bank Insurance Campaign, which badly needs my prodding. I manage to get in a little lick most days, but it needs a lot of boosting to keep people in motion.

Pauline and Josephine [Goldmark] are expected toward the end of this week, Henry [Goldmark] will probably go to Panama about Oct 1.

We have endless forest fires in the East. Possibly this is to bring purification by fire.

1. Joseph Benson Foraker (1846–1917), after two terms as Ohio governor, served in the U.S. Senate from 1897 to 1909 and was a powerful figure in the Republican Party for many years. A few days earlier the Hearst newspapers had published facsimiles of letters between Foraker and officials of the Standard Oil Company that proved that Foraker had been on the Standard payroll during most of his tenure in the Senate. The disclosures greatly weakened Foraker's influence in the GOP and embarrassed party leaders in the midst of the presidential campaign.

2. "No game is too high for the casual observer."

To: Alfred Brandeis
Date: October 20, 1908
Place: Boston, Massachusetts
Source: Brandeis MSS

DEAR AL: Do you remember the thrill which we experienced when we came upon this?[1]

1. LDB enclosed a newspaper clipping about vandalism of a statue of George Washington in Lugano, Switzerland.

To: Alfred Brandeis
Date: November 4, 1908
Place: Boston, Massachusetts
Source: Brandeis MSS

DEAR AL: I voted for Taft, but am sorry he won by so large a majority.[1] I wish he had had a margin of not over 10.

As it is, I am glad the Republicans have the whole administration. There will be no divided responsibility. Taft is admirably qualified for the position & doubtless will—if he lives—prove a fine President, rather of the Cleveland type; but I fear the Republican Party will be less manageable than under Roosevelt & that we shall see much of the moneybags we abhor, & whom the V.P.[2] properly represents.

1. The Republicans easily won the 1908 elections, carrying both houses of Congress as well as the presidency. Taft defeated Bryan 7,679,006 to 6,409,106 in the popular vote and 321 to 162 in the Electoral College.
2. James S. Sherman.

To: Alfred Brandeis
Date: March 16, 1909
Place: Boston, Massachusetts
Source: Brandeis MSS

MY DEAR AL: I suppose your girls are starting East today, and your [sic] Italian journeyings will soon be beginning. I hope they may get as much lifelong enjoyment out of their trip as we did from ours.

I like to think of the possibility of going with Alice and the children in the next year or so. Get your farm organized, so that you & Jennie et al can join us when the time comes.

By the way, when you come to buying land, remember that I have a farm present to make you which is well overdue.[1]

I enclose letter from Charlie [Nagel].

1. See LDB to Alfred Brandeis, 21 March 1906.

To: Alfred Brandeis
Date: March 20, 1909
Place: Dedham, Massachusetts
Source: Brandeis MSS

MY DEAR AL: Thirty six years ago tonight we spent at Gratz;[1] and I should be quite ready to repeat the experiment—all except devouring those boxes of candies. Did any of us go to the theatre that night? I have an impression that Father et al. went & that I remained at the hotel with Mother. If any one went, what was the play?[2]

For lack of foreign travel, I am amusing myself with the New Haven a little again. Their lot is not an easy one, and as you would say: "Ich möchte wissen was er sich dabei denkt."[3] They are now just negotiating a $5,000,000 one year note issue. I had supposed they had enough money to last them until next Fall, but it costs something to pay unearned dividends.

However, this letter was designed as a bearer of our good wishes for the 23rd[4] and nothing more.

Hope you had a good trip on your RR expedition.

1. The capital of the Austrian province of Styria, Gratz (later Graz) is about ninety miles southwest of Vienna and is noted for the many medieval fortifications converted into promenades.
2. See LDB to Alfred, 27 March 1909, BL; Mrs. Brandeis did go to the theatre that evening.
3. "I would like to know what he thinks he is accomplishing by doing that."
4. Alfred's fifty-fifth birthday was on 23 March 1909.

To:	Alfred Brandeis
Date:	May 3, 1909
Place:	Boston, Massachusetts
Source:	Brandeis MSS

DEAR AL: Alice was not feeling well so we are spending Sunday in town. The children & I had planned a canoe trip upon our reorganized Charles River Basin to Watertown but the wind bloweth so hard all day, that we advanced no further than to the water's edge. So we proceeded by land to investigate the locks and canals which we had not before seen.

Now Susan & I are going to see some Spanish paintings (Sorolla's)[1] about which New York and Boston are very enthusiastic, and later Alice & I will perhaps drive a bit.

If you should ever be in Boston with us I want to show you a beech grove in Longwood—modern trees which will put Kentucky to its stirrups.

Pauline Goldmark expects to be in Washington Tuesday to see Charlie [Nagel] about Children's Bureau.[2]

1. Joaquín Sorolla y Bastida (1863–1923).
2. Thus LDB's sister-in-law was going to Washington to lobby LDB's brother-in-law! (Nagel was now Taft's secretary of commerce and labor.) Social workers had been trying since the turn of the century to establish a federal children's bureau. In January 1909 Theodore Roosevelt called a White House Conference on the Care of Dependent Children, but a bill to establish a children's bureau, drafted by Florence Kelley and Lillian Wald, did not pass Congress

until April 1912. Taft named Julia Lathrop as the first director. See Lillian Wald, "The Idea of the Federal Children's Bureau," *Proceedings of the National Conference of Social Work* (1932): 33–37.

To: **Alfred Brandeis**
Date: **June 6, 1909**
Place: **Dedham, Massachusetts**
Source: **Brandeis MSS**

DEAR AL: The merger fight will probably come to a head this week. Our situation is pretty desperate and only a miracle can land us safely. We could handle the New Haven & their money & monied friends well enough; but the Governor[1] & the Republican machine has [*sic*] joined forces with them unreservedly. That is piling Pelion upon Ossa.[2]

Norman White who has proved himself a good arithmatician [*sic*] in all previous battles, says we have got "the enemy licked." But I fear the effect of gold on our Democratic friends & of the Republican "third degree" on the insurgents. It is an interesting story which I hope to tell you before it gets stale.[3]

The general atmosphere is against us this year as it was with us last. There appears to me a resurgence of McKinleyistic materialism, & I think that worsens our chances much. But we are making a glorious fight, and are full of courage.

Herbert & Cleta [White] returned Friday.

1. Eben Sumner Draper (1858–1914), a textile manufacturer, was elected lieutenant governor in 1906 and two years later was elected governor.
2. In Greek legend when the giants made war upon the gods they piled Mount Ossa on Mount Olympus and Mount Pelion upon Ossa in an attempt to reach heaven.
3. See the next letter.

To: **Alfred Brandeis**
Date: **June 15, 1909**
Place: **Boston, Massachusetts**
Source: **Brandeis, MSS**

DEAR AL: I have yours about the Market St. house. Sorry you have had so much bother with it.

The expected happened today in the Merger fight. Amidst innumerable broken promises of support we got unmercifully licked but it took all the power of the Republican machine & of the Bankers' money to do it, and I am well content with the fight made. The aftermath of fighting continues.[1]

Was in Buffalo Saturday. Aunt Regina & Millie [Goldmark] are with us.

1. With the intercession of Governor Draper and intense lobbying by the New Haven, the battle had swung against LDB and his allies. The House approved a merger bill, the Senate followed suit, and the governor signed it into law on 18 June. Although Mellen and the New Haven backers were obviously pleased with this victory, as well as the dropping of a pending antitrust suit, LDB believed that in time he would be vindicated. Inevitably the juggling of figures, which so far only he had detected, would come out in the open; and when it did Mellen's house of cards would collapse for want of adequate financial underpinning. LDB had less than a year to wait before renewing his attack on the New Haven; see LDB to Alfred Brandeis, 13 April 1910, note 3, BL.

To: **Alice Goldmark Brandeis**
Date: **June 26, 1909**
Place: **Dayton, Ohio**
Source: **Gilbert MSS**

DEAREST: Susan is a good traveller and responds to all suggestions with a smile. The weather is tolerable—somewhat overcast—and rather better than yesterday in that. But oh, how dull this great Ohio paradise appears. I don't wonder its sons flock to Washington.

I am rereading the French Revolution. How different it was from the social revolution we are passing through. Did you notice that the President of Wisconsin University in his commencement address declared that the age of socialism and collectivism was at hand and bad[e] all prepare for it.[1]

If Christine is very enterprising possibly she may carry you automobilists to South Yarmouth, and you could inspect our maison.

We should reach Louisville 5:45. Let Elizabeth guess what will be my first pilgrimage.   Lovingly

1. Charles Richard Van Hise (1857–1918), the president of the University of Wisconsin, was a leading exponent of the idea of controlling trusts through federal regulation.

To: **Alice Goldmark Brandeis**
Date: **September 7, 1909**
Place: **Dedham, Massachusetts**
Source: **Gilbert MSS**

DEAREST: Elizabeth must be pleased to have Peary[1] reach the pole. Frolic took a long walk with me this afternoon (I took the 4:48 train out), and has behaved well ordinarily, but has occasional lapses from virtue which convince me that he should be muzzled. He does bite sometimes & we shall have claims made against us, if we don't act soon.

Susan will be delighted to find the garden so flourishing, but the apple crop is not promising.

Weather is fine.

The McClennens[2] moved up yesterday. Dunbar[3] returned to Maine this evening & is to bring his family home next Tuesday.

I can't say anything yet about the mountains.

1. Commander Robert Edwin Peary (1856–1920) had apparently won his race to be the first to reach the North Pole; he claimed to have achieved the goal on 6 April 1909, but news did not reach the United States until 7 September. For the expedition and the controversy surrounding it, see Dennis Rawlins, *Peary at the North Pole: Fact or Fiction?* (Washington, D.C., 1973).

2. Edward Francis McClennen (1874–1948) joined LDB's law firm in 1895 upon graduation from the Harvard Law School and stayed there until his death, becoming a full partner around 1900. Active in Boston law circles, he also undertook a number of government assignments between 1916 and 1940. LDB respected McClennen's ability and chose him to play a crucial role in the Supreme Court nomination hearings in 1916. McClennen had deep admiration for LDB, which one can see this in his reminiscence "Louis D. Brandeis as a Lawyer," 33 *Massachusetts Law Quarterly* 1 (1948).

3. William Harrison Dunbar (1862–1935) was one of the first lawyers Warren & Brandeis had taken into the firm as business prospered. After graduating from Harvard Law School, Dunbar clerked for Justice Gray for a year; he was active in numerous bar association committees and served as counsel to the Harvard Law School Association.

To:	Alice Goldmark Brandeis
Date:	October 21, 1909
Place:	On board the Overland Limited
Source:	Gilbert MSS

DEAREST: We are West of Omaha, really West.[1] The broad prairies, well harvested, are stretching out endlessly in their rich colors under beauteous, grateful sunshine and cloudless sky. Before night we should have passed the longitude of Salt Lake City, and then the Rocky Mountains. I feel almost as if it were a trip round the world.

Enclosed letters from Al will show why he disappointed us. The second letter did not reach us until late in the day, so we dawdled about the Auditorium Annex for an hour looking for Al or a telegram until 11:30, and a dreadful place it is. Everybody bustling, like a telephone exchange without evidence of any accomplishment except an essay in perpetual motion.

From there Herbert [White] went about his business, and I on interrupting others in their business which I did successfully until 5:30 P.M. Most of the time I spent with Walter Fisher[2] and William Kent.[3] Fisher told me the details of the Crane episode.[4] He was responsible with Crane for the publications and the provocation was great—Taft had indorsed Crane far more than appeared at first—and Knox's[5] course [was] more inexplicable and inexcusable than has appeared. Fisher and Kent are however even more stirred up on the conservation policy. They read me a lot of the correspondence between the Department of Agriculture and the Dept. of the Interior, and from Taft himself regarding one water power project, which is simply amazing.[6] It reminds strikingly of the Grant Administration episode, when the Pres[iden]t. was trying to shield his friends and considered every honest citizen who had courage to call his attention to conditions as a criminal libeller.[7]

Kent and others furnished me many letters to Californians which I shall doubtless be unable to use.

Kent says San Francisco affairs are far from hopeful. Calhoun[8] is the social leader. Heney[9] is making mistakes in his campaigning, hitting heads unnecessarily, and Spreckles[10] [*sic*] is wholly unable to do any team play. K. thinks Heney will be desperately beaten and Calhoun will never be convicted. Both F. & K. seem to find in Taft the same temptations too.

1. LDB loved to travel and when he married had hoped that AGB would be able to travel with him. Her health prevented their traveling together, but LDB would occasionally go off with his friend Herbert White, as on this trip across the country, and at other times sailing and hiking in Canada.

2. Walter Lowrie Fisher (1862–1935) was most famous as the man President Taft appointed to head the Interior Department following the Pinchot-Ballinger affair. A Chicago attorney, Fisher specialized in local transportation, railway law, and other municipal problems and served as special counsel to the city of Chicago from 1906 to 1911.

3. William Kent (1864–1928) worked in real estate and grain in Chicago until 1907, when he had returned to his native California. In 1911 he was elected to Congress and served there until President Wilson named him to the U.S. Tariff Commission in 1917.

4. Charles Richard Crane (1858–1939), a wealthy Chicago manufacturer, had numerous interests in the Far East and as a result was named minister designate to China. He then got into a public dispute with Secretary of State Knox (see the next note), following indiscreet remarks by Crane in which he indicated that the United States was examining the recent Sino-Japanese agreement on Manchuria and might object to some of its provisions. Knox considered this information a state secret and demanded Crane's resignation. Crane sent a letter of resignation not to Knox but to President Taft, hoping that Taft would decline to accept it. Instead Taft refused to communicate with Crane and directed Knox to accept the resignation. Partially as a result of this incident, Crane became more involved in Democratic Party affairs and would play a role in bringing LDB and Woodrow Wilson together in 1912. A warm friendship developed between Crane and LDB.

5. Philander Chase Knox (1853–1921) was the attorney general in the cabinets of McKinley and Roosevelt until appointed to fill an unexpired seat in the Senate from Pennsylvania in 1904. He was then reelected in his own right, but he resigned to become secretary of state in the Taft administration. He was reelected to the Senate in 1916 and died in office.

6. It is impossible to identify to which specific project LDB refers, but the previous day President Taft had given a speech in Corpus Christi, Texas, pronouncing himself in favor of an extensive system of deep waterways not only in the coastal areas but inland as well, where they would provide competition with the railroads.

7. The administration of Ulysses Simpson Grant (1822–85) was marked by several major scandals such as the Credit Mobilier (involving the Union Pacific Railroad) and the Whiskey

Ring. Grant showed poor judgment in placing his friends in high office and then continuing to defend them against charges of corruption long after the evidence had proven their guilt.

8. In a spectacular series of graft trials starting in late 1906, special prosecutor Francis Heney (see the next note) and district attorney William Langdon secured indictments against many of the city's public officials as well some prominent business and social leaders, including Patrick Calhoun (1856–1943), president of the United Railroads. The indictments of the so-called men in broadcloth split the support of the business community, which until then had been the firmest supporters of Langdon and Heney. In 1907, while on trial for bribery in connection with trolley franchises, Calhoun broke a strike against his streetcar operations. For details, see George Mowry, *The California Progressives* (Chicago, 1963), 32–36. Calhoun was acquitted of the charges.

9. Francis Joseph Heney (1859–1937), after serving as attorney general of Arizona in the early 1890s, moved to San Francisco, where he was soon caught up in the reform fight against the railroads' domination of the state. Despised by conservatives, he was also attacked by labor leaders for his refusal to support them in a bitter strike. Although he had the blessing of all the good-government groups, he was badly defeated in his race for district attorney. His loss, according to the *New York Times* (3 November 1909), was "the blackest eye that municipal reform has received in a good many years." See "The Election in San Francisco," *Outlook* 93 (20 November 1909): 610–11.

10. Rudolph Spreckels (1872–1958) made a fortune from the Hawaiian Sugar Company, which had been founded to oppose the sugar trust. He moved to San Francisco and was a leader in rebuilding the city after the earthquake, and he took a major role in financing the Heney investigations into municipal corruption.

To: **Alice Goldmark Brandeis**
Date: **October 22, 1909**
Place: **Wyoming**
Source: **Gilbert MSS**

DEAREST: We have been running through Wyoming the last twelve hours or more—at an altitude of from 6000 to 8000 feet. The sun shines out of an almost cloudless sky, and the temperature is about freezing. Glorious air & weather and an equally glorious expanse over endless miles of country. Herbert says it is almost exactly like the Sahara, possibly a little more rocky; although rock formations are exceptional feature here. Erosion is everywhere promint [*sic*] with the strangest results, often like huge fortresses formed on either hand. But unlike the Sahara there is at places much water—a veritable river—the Green River—flowing along calmly at an altitude of over 6000 feet with many forks. This part of the country is largely uninhabited. Occasionally one sees cattle or sheep ranging, and a distant coal mine (owned by the N[orthern]. P[acific].) but the main development is at division points of the Railroad which is all powerful here, and is pressing forward improvements (double tracking) all along the route.

It is a delight to think that there is still so much out of doors; and in the face of it N.Y. and the eastern cities with their congestion seem the more inexcusable.

William Kent say[s] the Japanese Exclusion Act[1] must come up soon & that the Japs are more feared & hated than the Chinese & with good reason.   Lovingly

1. By an 1894 treaty citizens of the United States and Japan were permitted mutual free entry, but by 1909 enormous anti-Japanese sentiment had spread throughout the Pacific states. Japan had inaugurated a policy of voluntary limitation of emigration, but it had not stopped the flow of emigrant workers to Hawaii, Canada, and Mexico, from whence they made their way into the United States. This led the western states to push for legislative exclusion of the Japanese, a move that would have been considered a major insult by Japan. To head off the crisis, Roosevelt negotiated a Gentlemen's Agreement with Japan in February 1907 halting further immigration. At the same time San Francisco dropped plans to segregate Japanese schoolchildren in separate schools. In 1909 the issue arose again, but Taft managed to thwart any formal legislative restrictions.

To: **Alice Goldmark Brandeis**
Date: **October 23, 1909**
Place: **Nevada**
Source: **Gilbert MSS**

DEAREST: As I peeped out of the Pullman this morning it was dawn, and in a few moments the sun rose over the veritable Nevada desert. An hour later we had passed into a region of fertile valleys amidst the high barren mountains, just before passing into California and the Sierras. The day is bright and clear again and the coloring would do honor to Monet.[1] Soon we are to descend to the Pacific.

I have been reading a bit in Queen's Necklace,[2] a wholly futile performance and nothing could be more incongruous.

It was far more interesting to talk with an American mining engineer who has been mainly in English employ in New Zealand, Australia, South & West Africa. He is not "gut zu reden auf der Deut[s]chen"[3] in So. W. Africa.

We have just entered into the region of pines.   Lovingly

1. The famous Impressionist Claude Monet (1840–1926) was well known for his use of light and color.
2. Alexandre Dumas, *The Queen's Necklace,* first published in 1850; there were several English editions that LDB might have perused, the latest being 1906.
3. "The one to speak to about the Germans."

To: **Alice Goldmark Brandeis**
Date: **October 1909**
Place: **California[1]**
Source: **Gilbert MSS**

DEAREST: We are again on sea-level, the elevation was only 34 feet at Sacramento which we passed a few moments ago, in a summer sun, and only a few hours before we were seeing the snow tipped Sierras. It is indeed a wonderful country, tempting one everywhere to stop—and do nothing. I can't imagine man really working here; and if trials are necessary for the elevation of the Soul, I should think these people would remain long below sea-level.

I chatted a long while today with a Berlin Assessor (Judge of 30) who is taking two months to see America. He is quite moderate-minded and obviously not a socialist; but he says the only way for Germany to avoid socialism is to persevere in adopting Socialist measures; and that now most activities are coming under Imperial, State or Municipal control.

We are due in San Francisco in 3 hours.

1. Although postmarked "Oakland," this letter was written closer to Sacramento and mailed when the train stopped in Oakland.

To:	Alice Goldmark Brandeis
Date:	October 27, 1909
Place:	Nearing Arizona
Source:	Gilbert MSS

DEAREST: We spent the night at Pasadena, amidst date palms and pepper and joyous flowers. Since, we have passed through orange plantations stretching out to the mountains bare and ragged, which rise on either hand. Now we are in the high desert lands. Even the cactus (huge trees they are) have ceased to dot the wide reaches of valley land, valleys where water has been in mass, and doubtless comes now at times, but which seem almost a desert waste. The sun beats down, as it should in a desert, according to Hoyle. I am learning a great deal of geography and much is made real of which we have vaguely heard.

Some day I want to introduce you and the children to this other world, so unlike our Eastern fringe.

We had a bit of South Africa yesterday in our visit to the Ostrich farm, where there are 150 birds, part of which come from Nubia.

To:	Alfred Brandeis
Date:	November 5, 1909
Place:	Entering Kansas
Source:	Brandeis MSS

MY DEAR AL: We have had a trip exceeding far in interest even my expectations. I feel that I have overcome much of my lamentable ignorance of the United States, and have now seen its most wonderful parts. West of Lincoln, my previous ultima Thule, the remarkable America really begins. There was hardly [a] day passed without expressing regret you were not with us.

Do arrange to take your family west soon and widen your American horizon.

I read with regret of the Republican defeat in Louisville[1] and generally throughout the State. Reformers have been roughly handled throughout the country. Tom Johnson's defeat in Cleveland[2] and Heney's in San Francisco[3] are lamentable. I have been [un]able to learn yet what our Boston Charter amendments[4] fate is but there is some satisfaction in the greatly reduced plurality of Draper & Frothingham.[5]

We have seen little of papers for a fortnight. The routine of life will doubtless have renewed interest on returning to Boston.

Tell Robert Brandeis[6]—I met at San Francisco his friend with whom he roomed a year in N.Y. I didn't get the name.

1. In a campaign decided mainly on racial issues, the Democrats won the mayoralty contest in Louisville and five out of eight legislative seats, five of seven magistrate seats, and five out of six seats on the school board. The Republican incumbent, James F. Grinstead, generally had a "reform" image, but the Republicans circulated letters in the black community mentioning "privileges for colored people." Although black wards gave Grinstead a wide margin, the Democratic candidate, William O. Head, won by 2,300 votes and immediately declared Louisville to be "a white city."

2. Tom Loftus Johnson (1854–1911), after amassing a fortune in franchise operations, went into politics as a reformer and single tax advocate. He served in Congress from 1891 to 1895 and then became Cleveland's mayor in 1901. Johnson may have lost his bid for reelection because the people, according to one contemporary commentator, got tired of his endless wars against the traction interests. See his book *My Story* (New York, 1911).

3. See LDB to AGB, 21 October 1909.

4. Despite the opposition of both parties, the Finance Commission's proposed reforms had been approved by the voters, 39,175 to 35,306; see LDB to Geoffrey B. Lehy, 14 February 1908, BL.

5. Governor Draper defeated James H. Vahey by only 8,000 votes, although a year earlier he had won by over 60,000. Louis Adams Frothingham (1871–1928), whose family roots traced back to the *Mayflower*, had been active in civic reform for several years. He served as a Republican member of the Massachusetts House from 1901 to 1905 and as Speaker the last two terms; he went on to become lieutenant governor and a member of Congress. Often allied with LDB, during his terms in the assembly he introduced a number of bills on behalf of reform groups. Frothingham defeated Eugene Foss for lieutenant governor by only 6,700 votes, despite a huge plurality of 96,000 in 1908. For LDB's opinion of Frothingham, see LDB to Henry S. Dewey, 13 November 1905, BL.

6. A cousin who lived in New York.

To:	Alfred Brandeis
Date:	December 4, 1909
Place:	Dedham, Massachusetts
Source:	Brandeis MSS

DEAR AL: Think I have never acknowledged the whiskey which came during my absence. It is a great comfort to know that so good a supply is near.

Also omitted to acknowledge the $3.50 draft re Fan. That is the whole debt. She was very economical & returned the balance of a $10 bill in cash.

By the way, let me know when the amount of my land payment is ascertained and due.[1]

I cleared my desk today for the first time since my return & feel "wie ein anderer Mensch."[2] I suppose when I go to argue the Illinois case there will be another relapse of arrears.[3] Haven't heard yet *when* that will be, & suppose it will be at Springfield, but I expect to take in Chicago in any event and hope to see you.

Your projected trip to Madison is interesting, should like to be with you. Short trips will go all right, but I assure you long ones are very demoralizing. It took me nearly a month to get over the effects of my western debauch & to be "gentle in harness again."

Had a business letter from George H. Kohn (who is at Cripple Creek). He spoke of his 1870 summer. The letter had rather the air of lack of prosperity. What do you know of him?

David Ives[4] was in Washington a few days ago to see Charlie [Nagel] & also saw Hildegarde [Nagel]. Had not seen Ives since the summer, & we hope to have them at dinner next Sunday. I like him much.

The Chicago Tribune seems to think the RR strike will spread. Labor has been extraordinarily quiet for 5 years, and I suppose a stormy season would not be surprising. The fact is, labor unionism has a pretty hard row to hoe with the larger aggregations of capital as employers, & may be making war as Napoleon III did, to maintain this dynasty.

Josephine [Goldmark] left us Wednesday, after the Illinois brief came from the printer.

1. See LDB to Alfred Brandeis, 21 March 1906.
2. "Like a different man."
3. After the Supreme Court upheld the constitutionality of the Oregon ten-hour law in *Muller v. Oregon* (see LDB to AGB, 14 January 1908, note 5), several states, including Illinois, passed similar statutes. In September 1909 W. C. Ritchie—the same man who had successfully opposed an earlier Illinois law (*Ritchie v. People,* 155 Ill. 98 [1895])—secured an injunction against the new ten-hour act. The Consumers' League again approached LDB, who agreed to represent them with the same conditions as in *Muller.* He argued the case before the Illinois Supreme Court in February 1910, and the Court upheld the statute the

following April in *Ritchie v. Wayman,* 244 Ill. 509 (1910). For LDB's evaluation of the case, see "The Living Law," 10 *Illinois Law Review* 461, 465 (1916).

4. David Otis Ives (1854–1914), after graduating from Harvard in 1879, went west and worked in railroad management. In 1909 he returned to Boston to manage the transportation division of the Chamber of Commerce. Ives later involved LDB in the freight rate cases; see LDB to Alfred Brandeis, 21 August 1910, BL.

To:	Alfred Brandeis
Date:	December 25, 1909
Place:	Dedham, Massachusetts
Source:	Brandeis MSS

MY DEAR AL: Alice[,] Elizabeth & I drove out yesterday afternoon and E. had her Xmas tree here.

Most of the day she has been absorbed in "The Two Royal Foes"[1] which Jennie sent her, and very happy with it. Susan writes joyous from New York. She will probably return Sunday with Bessie Evans.

We had a sunny day. I spent most of the morning walking and have loafed much of the balance of the day. This evening reading the "Master of Ballantrae"[2] with quite my original delight. It is fortunate to have "a grand memory for forgetting."[3]

Josephine is with Susie at N.Y.

1. Eva Annie Madden, *Two Royal Foes* (New York, 1907), dealt with Napoleon I and Louise, queen consort of Frederick William III, king of Prussia.
2. Robert Louis Stevenson, *The Master of Ballantrae* (New York, 1889).
3. Words spoken by Alan Breck in Robert Louis Stevenson's *Kidnapped* (1886), ch. 18.

To:	Alice Goldmark Brandeis
Date:	January 12, 1910
Place:	New York, New York
Source:	Gilbert MSS

DEAREST: Your diagnosis of the Storrow defeat is I think correct,[1] & the Evening Post seems of the same opinion.[2] The event should make the rich stop & think, if they were capable of the process.

Dined pleasantly at the Colliers'[3] yesterday. Mrs. C. is a delicate refined woman[4] & he an extraordinarily able & rare man. Mark Sullivan[5] was also there.

Today met Gifford Pinchot[6] & Ex. Sec. Garfield[7] & Geo. Wharton Pepper.[8] The job is interesting.[9]

I dined at Mother's. The New York contingent is fading out. Pauline [Goldmark] will probably not stay for Sunday & the Adlers will be represented only by Felix & he must be back for Sunday.

I wired Al to spend Sunday here & am awaiting reply.

Thanks for the tie

1. Storrow had narrowly lost the previous day's mayoral election to John F. Fitzgerald, 47,172 votes to 45,757. (See LDB to Charles Sumner Hamlin, 11 November 1909, BL, for his appraisal of Storrow.) The reform Citizens' Municipal League captured seven of the nine city council seats; however, it was unable to defeat James Michael Curley.

2. The *Post* carried a story that Republican voters had helped elect Fitzgerald, who had carried all of the regular Democratic wards and several of the normally Republican districts as well. In an editorial the paper praised Storrow for running an "able campaign" but noted that while he was "conspicuously qualified" the reformers would have done better had they chosen a candidate more representative of the people.

3. Robert Joseph Collier (1876–1918) took over the family publishing business upon the death of his father and as editor of *Collier's Weekly* made it one of the leading reform journals.

4. Collier married the former Sara Stewart Van Alen in 1902.

5. Mark Sullivan (1874–1952), after a short law career, entered a long and productive life in journalism. From 1906 until 1914 he was chief correspondent for *Collier's* and in 1914 took over the editor's chair. In 1919 he left the magazine to write a syndicated column and also to begin work on his important six-volume chronicle, *Our Times—The United States, 1900–1925* (New York, 1926–35).

6. Gifford Pinchot (1865–1946) was America's first professional forester and a lifelong advocate of conservation. He headed the Bureau of Forestry from 1898 to 1910 and had a major hand in withdrawing millions of acres of public land from the open market. He then served as president of the influential National Conservation Association and was governor of Pennsylvania from 1923 to 1927 and again from 1931 to 1935. While LDB and Pinchot worked together on a number of reforms and were in very close association during these years, they also had serious differences, most notably about bigness. LDB hated it, while Pinchot would be an ardent advocate of his friend Theodore Roosevelt's New Nationalism.

7. James Rudolph Garfield (1865–1950) was commissioner of corporations from 1903 to 1907 and then served as secretary of the interior during the last two years of the Roosevelt administration.

8. George Wharton Pepper (1867–1961), an extremely prestigious Philadelphia lawyer, would later serve as a senator from Pennsylvania; see his autobiography, *Philadelphia Lawyer* (Philadelphia and New York, 1944). Pepper was representing his friend Pinchot in the conflict with the Taft administration (see the next note), but Pinchot became increasingly unhappy with Pepper, who failed to understand that Pinchot was not interested primarily in legal advice but in how to make his case politically, a concept that LDB immediately grasped.

9. A few days earlier, at the request of *Collier's*, LDB became involved in one of the most controversial episodes of the progressive era, the so-called Pinchot-Ballinger affair. Although William Howard Taft promised to carry on Roosevelt's conservation policies, he aroused reformers' suspicions when he named Richard Achilles Ballinger as secretary of the interior. In August 1909 Louis R. Glavis, an Interior Department official, reported to Ballinger his doubts about the legality of the so-called Cunningham claims, which contained major coal fields that the Guggenheim mining interests wanted to develop. Ballinger, who at one time had acted as an attorney for the Guggenheims, dismissed Glavis's fears, and Glavis took his tale to Pinchot.

Pinchot then laid the charges before President Taft, who asked Ballinger for a response. Ballinger presented the president with a mass of materials; Taft issued a letter on 13 September 1909 exonerating Ballinger and authorizing him to dismiss Glavis from government employ. Although Taft hoped this would end the matter, he also recognized that it might endanger Republican unity, so he appealed to Pinchot to let the matter drop and not allow a minor dispute to mar their relationship. But both Pinchot and Glavis believed they were right; even while Taft was attempting to calm Pinchot, Glavis took his charges to *Collier's*, which printed them in its 13 November 1909 issue.

The public uproar over the article led to a congressional investigation of the charges, which the administration hoped to control. In order to protect his magazine's interests, Collier retained LDB at a fee of $25,000 plus expenses. Since Pinchot by now was also in open revolt against the Taft administration, he joined with Collier and several others to prepare a joint presentation.

LDB's involvement can be traced in volume two of BL, beginning with his letter to Norman Hapgood of 8 January 1910. For many years historians, following the view of pro-conservationist reformers, treated the Pinchot-Ballinger episode as a fairly straightforward tale of reformers attempting to protect the environment against big companies wanting to despoil it. We now see the issue as far more complex. Taft was not anti-conservation and in fact withdrew more forest and mineral lands for public use in his four years than Roosevelt had done in seven. Ballinger did want to exploit the Alaskan mineral preserves, but he also wanted to establish an orderly and sensible means of developing the huge territory. The only thing that is still agreed upon is Taft's clumsiness in handling the affair.

To:	Alice Goldmark Brandeis
Date:	January 15, 1910
Place:	New York, New York
Source:	Gilbert MSS

This, dearest, is to establish that I remember (as you desire) that I have a family. I don't know yet whether I shall have a brother here this P.M., but, on that account, am keeping open the evening.

There seems little probability of my returning to Boston for a few days at the least.

There is delay in getting together the material, & the witness Glavis[1] is expected here early next week & I want a whole day with him. The bag you are sending will hardly hold all the papers which are accumulating.

I walked up to Chris[tine Goldmark]'s house yesterday in spite of the storm & a large part of the way back, and am ready to enter the lists as a long distance walker at any rate.

Met the "Gloom" on 5th Ave yesterday & was invited to luncheon but postponed the pleasure. Indeed am going light on dissipations and strong on exercise, bearing in mind that I am off on a Sommer Kur[2] "as aforesaid".

Much love to the children, who are borne here in favorable remembrance.

Lovingly

1. Louis Russell Glavis (1884–19[?]) was chief of a field division for the General Land Office when he precipitated the controversy between conservationists and the Taft administration. Glavis's rather checkered later career is described in James L. Penick, Jr., "Louis Russell Glavis: A Postscript to the Ballinger-Pinchot Controversy," *Pacific Northwest Quarterly* 55 (April 1964): 67–75.

2. Summer cure.

To: **Alice Goldmark Brandeis**
Date: **January 30, 1910**
Place: **Washington, D.C.**
Source: **Gilbert MSS**

DEAREST: Another hearing tomorrow, possibly still another Wednesday.[1] Strenuous days but we have had a great time & there is certainly some "panicky" feeling in administration circles. Senator Crane called this A.M. to express his fervent admiration & gratitude for the help I had given him when Governor!

It looks now as if I should not get to Boston before next Sunday & will probably have to start for Illinois Tuesday night or Wednesday A.M. (Feb 8th or 9th).[2] It is a great comfort to know that Do is with you. Have not seen Hildegarde [Nagel] yet or even telephoned her. Saw Steffens[3] for a moment Friday night. Also Ray Stan. Baker,[4] Thomas Nelson Page[5] & other literary folk. But I was at the dinner only about 3/4 hour.   Lovingly

    1. On the Pinchot-Ballinger controversy.
    2. On 10 February LDB would argue the constitutionality of the Illinois women's ten-hour law; see LDB to William Bennett Munro, 24 November 1909, note 3, BL.
    3. Joseph Lincoln Steffens (1866–1936) was one of the nation's leading reformers and journalists. Born in California, he moved to New York in the 1890s and worked as a reporter and editor for several New York newspapers. He then joined *McClure's Magazine,* where his muckraking articles on municipal corruption, published as *The Shame of the Cities* (1904), earned him a national reputation. Steffens had enormous influence upon the younger generation of American reformers and social thinkers; see his monumental *Autobiography of Lincoln Steffens* (New York, 1931).
    4. Ray Stannard Baker (1870–1946) was another of journalism's luminaries. He had been lured from Chicago to New York to join *McClure's,* but in 1906 he had left to help found the *American Magazine,* which featured his exposés on factory conditions and also on race relations. He met Woodrow Wilson, served in his administration briefly, and then devoted the rest of his life to editing Wilson's papers and writing a multivolume biography of the president. He also wrote a sparkling memoir, *An American Chronicle* (New York, 1945).
    5. Thomas Nelson Page (1853–1922) wrote several novels about the Old South in general and Virginia in particular; Woodrow Wilson later named him ambassador to Italy.

To: **Alice Goldmark Brandeis**
Date: **January 31, 1910**
Place: **Washington, D.C.**
Source: **Gilbert MSS**

DEAREST: Your letter of Sunday has come & brings good home news.

The papers doubtless report our hearings, which you see keep me pretty busy; & last week I really worked hard; but am feeling much rested as compared with Jan 7th or 8th before this picnic began. It's more change of scene than the Great Divide & very entertaining.

We dined at the Pinchots last evening, talking [about the] case before & after dinner. Jim Garfield was there & Ass't Atty Woodruff.[1] Our next hearing comes Friday, but there is enough to occupy me in the meantime & I shall enjoy a few calm days à la New York.

What do you refer to in saying "Do is rather disgusted at the state of affairs"?   Lovingly

1. George Washington Woodruff (1864–1934) was the assistant attorney general assigned to the Interior Department while Garfield was secretary, and Roosevelt, who thought very highly of him, named him a federal district judge in 1909. But Woodruff resigned the following year to enter private practice. When Gifford Pinchot became active in Pennsylvania politics, Woodruff joined him, serving as attorney general of the state.

To: **Alice Goldmark Brandeis**
Date: **February 1, 1910**
Place: **Washington, D.C.**
Source: **Gilbert MSS**

DEAREST: Sorry to miss the Lee Dinner & some other things.

Have had a lull today after quite a stormy week. Am expecting to be busier tomorrow when a lot more papers are to be opened to us by the Interior Department.[1] The Administration is more troubled than the servile Eastern press will admit.

I hear quite generally that the sceptics are surprised at the strength of Glavis testimony, but we haven't yet many other transactions supporting the general propositions of improprieties. Glavis has certainly done more in maintaining the case than anyone expected, & I have confidence that in time we shall get hold of other transactions.

If Boston weren't so far off I should run home for a day.   Lovingly

1. LDB dunned the Interior Department (through the committee) for massive amounts of documentation; see, for example, his letter to Knute Nelson, 27 January 1910, BL.

To: **Alice Goldmark Brandeis**
Date: **February 5, 1910**
Place: **Washington D.C.**
Source: **Gilbert MSS**

DEAREST: Had a delightful evening at the La Follettes' yesterday.[1] They are quite our kind of people, and if I am here much shall be more apt to loaf with them than any one else. They received me like an old friend.

Tell Elizabeth that their son Bob[2] is a fine fellow about her age, also that I was glad to get her letter.

Papers report that Ballinger[3] et al have decided to be represented by Counsel & rumor has it that the Com[mit]tee (i.e. the Standpat Republicans— voiced by Root)[4] came down upon Ballinger like a load of bricks & compelled him to change his tactics & brought the matter up in Cabinet meeting. We have at least scared them. The Administration Scare on the increased cost of losing is also amusing. I may get La Follette to poke up Wickersham[5] on dismissing the merger suit.[6]   Lovingly

1. Robert Marion La Follette, Sr. (1855–1925), a towering figure of the progressive movement, became one of LDB's closest friends and allies. After establishing a reform movement in his native Wisconsin, La Follette came to Washington as a congressman from 1885 to 1891. In 1901 he finally overcame the entrenched Republican machine and was elected to the first of three highly successful terms as governor, during which time he pushed through a number of reform measures and earned for Wisconsin a reputation as the most progressive and enlightened state in the union. Among his most important accomplishments, he forged a coalition between the statehouse and the University of Wisconsin to provide his administration with the latest and best expertise in a number of areas.

In 1905 the voters sent La Follette to the U.S. Senate, where he quickly established himself as leader of the insurgent Republican forces. By 1910 he was making plans to run for the presidency, and many reformers, including LDB, rallied to his cause. But a physical collapse in 1911 put an end to these plans and cleared the way for Theodore Roosevelt to jump into the race.

La Follette originally supported Wilson's New Freedom but always believed Wilson could have done more and gone further and broke with him completely over the issues of American entry into the war and the League of Nations afterward. Following the Republican victory in the 1920 election, La Follette became the focal point for nearly all reformers trying to stem the conservative tide, and in 1924 he launched a third-party campaign for the presidency. Although he received 4.8 million votes, he had exhausted his strength in the battle and died the following year.

La Follette married Belle Case (1859–1931) in 1881. The first woman graduate of the University of Wisconsin Law School, she was an active partner in all her husband's ventures for more than four decades. A good part of the editing of *La Follette's Weekly* fell on her, and she assisted him in many political chores.

Following their first meeting, LDB and La Follette soon became good friends; and after AGB met Belle, the two families became close. LDB had a standing invitation for dinner at the senator's house whenever he was in Washington, and there they exchanged ideas on all the various issues troubling progressives. While the two men did not agree on everything (they disagreed, for example, on American entry into the war), nothing could mar the depths of a friendship based on so many shared interests and beliefs.

After the death of her husband, Belle did much of the research and wrote the first third of a two-volume biography of her husband, which her daughter Fola finished after Belle's death. In the acknowledgements to *Robert M. La Follette*, 2 vols. (New York, 1953), Fola wrote: "In addition to help on other aspects of the biography, Justice Louis D. Brandeis and Mrs. Brandeis made two financial contributions."

2. Mrs. La Follette once wrote to LDB, "The other day Robert [Jr.] said: 'Mother, I believe I like Mr. Brandeis the best of any one we know.' Then he qualified it—'Of course not better than Mr. Steffens but better than almost any one else' " (quoted in Mason, *Brandeis,* 368). LDB reciprocated the feeling toward Robert Marion La Follette, Jr. (1895–1953), who would serve as his father's secretary and then successor in the Senate. The voters of Wisconsin then returned the younger La Follette to the Senate in his own right three times, until he was defeated by Joseph McCarthy in 1946.

When LDB first met the La Follettes, he felt uncomfortable about the presence of the three children in the room while the adults discussed confidential political matters. According to Fola La Follette (*La Follette,* 295): "Years later, when Bob, Jr., became a candidate to fill his father's unexpired term, certain people protested to Brandeis that he was too young and had no political experience. To this Brandeis replied, 'Bob, Jr., and Phil have had more experience in politics than any boys since the days of the Roman Senators.'"

Elizabeth Brandeis would become a close friend of the La Follettes when she moved to Wisconsin to teach at the university.

3. Richard Achilles Ballinger (1858–1922) bore the brunt of the conservationist attack and for many years was considered anti-conservationist. In fact he had a long and distinguished career as a lawyer, as mayor of Seattle (1904–6) and as commissioner of the General Land Office before his appointment to head the Interior Department. Recent studies have argued that Ballinger's plans for land use fell within the parameters of what is now considered prudent management of public resources.

4. Elihu Root (1845–1937), an old-line patrician New York attorney, was secretary of war in McKinley's cabinet and secretary of state under Roosevelt. He was then elected senator from New York and became a leader of the conservative wing of the party.

5. George Woodward Wickersham (1858–1936), a successful New York lawyer, became attorney general in the Taft administration. Despite his business connections, Wickersham like Taft believed in the enforcement of the antitrust laws, and he prosecuted a number of big businesses, including Standard Oil, U.S. Steel, and the American Tobacco Company. After 1913 he returned to private practice, but Herbert Hoover named him to the National Commission on Law Observance and Law Enforcement (which became known as the Wickersham Commission), which declared the noble experiment of prohibition to be a disaster. As a result of their clash in the Pinchot-Ballinger controversy, LDB and Wickersham developed a strong and lasting dislike of one another.

6. The Justice Department dismissed its antitrust suit against the New Haven after Massachusetts enacted legislation that in effect legalized the merger of the New Haven and the Boston & Maine.

To: Alice Goldmark Brandeis
Date: February 11, 1910
Place: Washington, D.C.
Source: Gilbert MSS

DEAREST: It was a great comfort to find your letter (and the enclosures from Al) on arriving here this evening after an endlessly long journey from Chicago. The day was dark and snowy, but without any of the joy and brilliancy which attends our New England snow, and the endless vista of besmoked and bedevilled folk in the Ohio-Pennsylvania coal and iron districts was quite depressing. I occupied the day largely with Glavis papers, trying to [*] into my mind the facts which a few days of Illinois women's 10 hour law had tended to remove.[1]

There was a large mail awaiting me here, but I have not seen any of the Allies yet. Glavis I hear is in town & Cotton[2] returns Sunday morning.

The Ballinger lawyers are said to be concocting dynamite pills for us & Monday's hearing may be exciting.   Lovingly

1. LDB had just returned from Springfield, where he had argued *Ritchie v. Wayman;* see LDB to William Bennett Munro, 24 November 1909, note 3, BL.

2. Joseph Potter Cotton, Jr. (1875–1931), a New York attorney, was asked by *Collier's* to represent Glavis at the hearings. Cotton later became undersecretary of state during the Hoover administration.

To:	Alice Goldmark Brandeis
Date:	February 17, 1910
Place:	Washington, D.C.
Source:	Gilbert MSS

DEAREST: No hearing today, so I shall have a chance to rest out.

Taft's marvelous capacity for blundering has manifested itself in the selection of Vertrees[1] as Counsel. B[allinger]. had selected Carl Rash, who is there as assistant and would do far better; but, I fancy, he is not allowed any chance to do anything yet under Taft orders.

The complete surrender of the publicity feature of the Corporation bill under the guise of absence of appropriation[2] is another Taft-like condition, and the paralysis of his Postal Savings[3] & other bills "passt wie der Faust aufs Auge".[4]

I am becoming increasingly impressed by this capacity for doing the wrong thing.

I had a long talk with Ollie James.[5] He, Graham[6] and Madison[7] who are all with us are really very able and bother the administration faction considerably.

McCall[8] and Root are dead against us, though McCall hides his opposition. Root tries to, but his temper carries him off occasionally. The Administration men are having a very hard time in their effort to disbelieve Glavis. They would like to & are often ill-tempered at their judgment being convinced against their will. On the whole we have been gaining here steadily with the public & I think will take another step whenever we can get Hoyt[9] on the stand.

I am glad you had Miss Grady[10] in. Please repeat the dose soon. She needs your steadying hand. I am much pleased with Elizabeth's letter.

Lovingly

1. John J. Vertrees (1875–1944) represented Ballinger before the committee.

2. As part of progressive efforts to tame the powers of large corporations, a bill had been introduced during the Roosevelt administration providing for federal incorporation of interstate businesses. This would have resolved the problem of states like Delaware allowing corporations chartered there to do anything they pleased. The bill did not get out of committee, and it was reintroduced a number of times in both the Taft and Wilson years but never passed Congress. In its present iteration the Taft administration, while supporting the bill, did not ask for any funds to enforce its provisions.

3. Although both conservatives and reformers agreed on the need for a postal savings system, a fight had broken out, with the conservatives attempting to keep the interest rates low and to permit commercial banks to dump their low-interest government bonds on the system, while reformers fought for a higher rate as well as redeposit in commercial banks in interest-bearing accounts. Taft sided with the conservatives, and the bill passed later in the year. Taft's position earned him additional enmity from the insurgents, even though they had all started from the same position.

4. "Like getting socked in the eye."

5. Ollie Murray James (1871–1919), Democratic senator from Kentucky from 1913 until his death, in 1910 was serving the fourth of his five terms in the House of Representatives. James, who was on the investigating committee, proved to be a strong ally of LDB.

6. James McMahon Graham (1852–1945) represented Illinois in Congress from 1909 to 1915; LDB would later work closely with Graham's committee in investigating the Controller Bay leases. See LDB to Graham, 14 July 1911, BL.

7. Edmund Haggard Madison (1865–1911), an insurgent Republican, represented the Seventh District of Kansas.

8. Samuel Walker McCall (1851–1923) was for many years a Republican congressman from Massachusetts and would be elected to one term as governor of the state in 1916. A member of the investigating committee, he consistently backed the administration and voted to sustain Ballinger's conduct.

9. Henry Martyn Hoyt (1865–1910) was assistant attorney general and then solicitor general during the Roosevelt administration. In 1910 he was serving as counselor to the State Department. Hoyt had placed Glavis's charges regarding falsified land claims before Wickersham in 1909, and the attorney general at that time had stopped execution of those claims.

10. Alice Harriet Grady (1873–1934) entered the office of Warren & Brandeis as a young girl and soon became LDB's private secretary. As the firm expanded she assumed greater responsibilities and handled many of the details of LDB's reform work as an executive secretary. She was especially interested in savings bank insurance and became the financial secretary of the Massachusetts Savings Bank Insurance League. In 1920 she left the Brandeis firm to become deputy commissioner of the state program, which expanded considerably due to her efforts. At this time Grady was still unsure of herself and what she could or should do for the savings bank reform in LDB's absence, and there are constant references in LDB's letters to AGB urging her to have Grady in, reassure her, and essentially keep her working away on savings bank matters.

To:	Regina Wehle Goldmark
Date:	March 2, 1910
Place:	Washington, D.C.
Source:	Brandeis MSS

MY DEAR MOTHER: Much love and many good wishes.

I am delighted with the joyous reports of my delegation. From each member has come a separate letter telling of the beautiful days spent with you—and which, I am sure, brought you also much happiness.

Our investigation is moving along steadily, and very satisfactorily. The unfitness of Mr. Ballinger is being made more and more apparent, and the folly of the President more and more amazing.

We had left him the loop-hole by pointing out how he had been misled; but he insists that he knew and knows it all.

Meanwhile the people are led to think about conservation, are learning what it means; and the investigation must prove a very helpful education.

But I didn't intend to write an essay. With much love

To: **Alice Goldmark Brandeis**
Date: **March 4, 1910**
Place: **Washington, D.C.**
Source: **Gilbert MSS**

DEAREST: Louis Wehle brought good reports of the household. He certainly gets about and does the people knowing and seeing stunt most thoroughly, but one must wonder a bit whether he is over developing or merely utilizing to the full a great talent. It was a joy to see him.

I hope to have a quiet today [*sic*] today, which I purpose inaugurating with a haircut at 7 A.M. It is now 6.

This Convention habit is certainly as great a great [*sic*] revolution from the days when students studied and scientists were buried in laboratories. The apparent break up of the Railroad bill[1] and suppression of other Taft measures[2] is a great satisfaction. Like Indians, only dead Taft measures are safe.

Poor Paul Kellogg[3] is laboring for a substitute. Garfield and Prof. Freund[4] have declined & he and Dr. Favill[5] are in great distress, from which you may be assured I will not relieve them. With much love

1. Taft had little sympathy for the railroads and supported Roosevelt's efforts to strengthen the Interstate Commerce Commission's powers over the carriers. He proposed a special Commerce Court to hear appeals from the ICC's rate decisions and also wanted the ICC to have power over the issuance of railroad securities. The measures, which ultimately became the Mann-Elkins Act of 1910, really did give the ICC greater powers, but the Commerce Court was attacked by insurgents, who objected to the tribunal's broad jurisdiction as well as the suspension of certain aspects of the Sherman Act to allow mergers and other provisions they considered too favorable to the railroads. The House amended the bill and included telephone and telegraph companies as common carriers. The Commerce Court was barely saved by a tie vote. In the Senate Nelson Aldrich, the floor leader of the regular Republicans, made a deal with the Democrats to get around the insurgent opposition, and enough Democrats joined to support the administration bill. The Commerce Court was retained, but ICC power over physical evaluation as well as securities issues fell by the wayside. Nonetheless, the Mann-Elkins bill did prove a major advance in government regulation of railroads.

2. Other administration proposals in danger from insurgent opposition included the postal savings bank plan, the national incorporation bill, and revision of the tariff.

3. Paul Underwood Kellogg (1879–1958) edited the *Survey,* one of the leading social reform journals, from 1902 to 1942 and also served on the boards of numerous charitable and reform groups. In addition, he headed the famous Pittsburgh Survey, which provided invaluable data on industrial conditions in the steel industry. LDB's high regard for Kellogg and his colleagues led him to leave one-fourth of his residuary estate to the Survey Associates "for the maintenance of civil liberty and the promotion of workers' education in the United States" (quoted in Mason, *Brandeis,* 639).

4. Ernst Freund (1864–1932) exercised enormous influence over the generations of lawyers he helped to train at the University of Chicago, where he became an important advocate of "sociological jurisprudence." Freund was also active in the American Association for Labor Legislation.

5. Dr. Henry Baird Favill (1860–1916) was a well-known practitioner and advocate of preventive medicine and, like Freund, taught at the University of Chicago.

To: Alice Goldmark Brandeis
Date: March 5, 1910
Place: Washington, D.C.
Source: Gilbert MSS

DEAREST: Susan's box with dress-shirt shield arrived & contents worn to Justice's Holmes, where we dined aux trois as of old, with most cordial reception. (The bag has not appeared, but doubtless will early today.) So cordial that I was led to talk far more than is my wont, or, at least, intention. Indeed this Washington solitude is making me fearfully social. You will have to come on, when Do returns to B[oston]., & join in the whirl.

Thomas Nelson Page bad[e] me lunch with him Sunday which I shall do in honor of Marse [*].

The hearing went off really well yesterday, particularly in the afternoon. Garfield will, doubtless, be reached this morning & should prove a good witness, but there is none like Glavis in this modest world.

Mrs. Pepper[1] returned to Philadelphia yesterday & has her daughter and a friend come down [to] take care of Mr.

Tell Susan the daughter is to be 18 next week, & that the friend is Nancy Scott. Possibly Susan may meet them next year. Mrs. Pepper is a New Haven girl, who has quite a bit of New England in her still, hidden behind the thick-well-fed Philadelphia look. She said the other day that if a labor party came, she would be of it.

Weather yesterday was fine, had a walk with Pinchot after the hearing.

Lovingly

1. The former Charlotte R. Fisher.

To: Susan Brandeis
Date: March 24, 1910
Place: Washington, D.C.
Source: Gilbert MSS

DEAR SUSAN: Talking of things sartorial—please note that

1. I wore my gray spring suit in honor of the wedding-day.[1]
2. I had the black suit you love so pressed.

It should, doubtless, be considered also a special compliment to you that I called on your new cousin Sarah Dembitz. She appears to be a graduate of George Washington University, and, like yourself, is very fond of dancing, prefers it even to boating. Possibly you may find some occult bond of sympathy in the fact that she danced her first dance at age seventeen.

Massachusetts has assumed a new significance in the National Capitol through the extraordinary victory won by Foss over Lovering.[2] The standpat Republicans begin to doubt whether there is anywhere real solid ground under them. Perhaps they will have to import more Irish soil for their leaders to stand on.

Your vacations begin today, and I hope will be most joyous. My own plans for the days after Saturday are still entirely uncertain. We may have a hearing Tuesday.   With much love

1. The previous day had been the Brandeises' eighteenth wedding anniversary.
2. Eugene Noble Foss (1858–1939), a wealthy manufacturer and maverick Republican, had just won an upset victory running as a Democrat in a special election to fill the vacancy caused by the death of Republican William C. Lovering (1837–1910), who had been in the House since 1897. Foss served one term and then was thrice elected as governor of Massachusetts.

LDB like many others interpreted the Foss victory as a blow to the regular Republicans, but Foss only won because of a factional fight among Republicans in the district. Moreover, he had pledged during the campaign that he would be a nonpartisan congressman and would not run for election the following November. Foss thus gave the local Republicans a chance to punish their nominee, who had won the nomination after a bitter fight, without really losing too much—a seat in Congress for less than a year.

To: Alfred Brandeis
Date: March 27, 1910
Place: Washington, D.C.
Source: Brandeis MSS

DEAR AL: I thought the Ohio Gateway very effective. Hope to see Marble[1] this week. Lupton (whom you met) says he has been out of town. I delivered your regards to Pepper. Spooner[2] asked for you yesterday. The I.C.C. will decide the Pullman Case right & the report will be fine.[3]

My meeting with Charlie N. occurred Friday. He was walking on Penn. Ave. 9:30 A.M. from 10th toward the New Willard, as I went to the Capital (why he should be there at that hour moving in that direction I can't imagine)—But, we met & he couldn't escape—talked a few moments about Hildegarde & from a remark dropped I see he is "taking notice", widow-like, of the Ballinger inquiry. Charlie was pleasant enough; but he looks worn & troubled as compared with last summer—just as you found him recently. They are "up against it."[4] WHT[aft] can make more mistakes in a week than the rest of them can remedy in a year—if indeed they have any of the curative art.

I hope our last 2 days of Ballinger hearings were well reported. The enemy fell into every trap set. The refusal of B[allinger] to go on the stand now, either on direct or cross-examination, is better for us than if we had the immediate chance to flay him, which might have resulted in our getting some severe kicks.

But no report can give you an adequate idea of our fun on X-ex[amination] of Vertrees['s] first witness, Adolph Behrens.[5] A "Goat" is a "Hund dagegen"[6] and Keith's Continuous Vaudeville couldn't compete a minute.

There seems to be a mystery about my friend Cooper. Alice has pursued enquiry on the [*] end that doesn't check up either.

1. John Hobart Marble (1869–1913) had worked for the Interstate Commerce Commission since 1906, first as an investigator and then as secretary of the agency.

2. John Coit Spooner (1843–1919), a former senator from Wisconsin, now worked in the same New York law firm as Joseph P. Cotton.

3. The ICC was adjudicating a challenge to the rates charged by the Pullman Company for use of the beds in its sleeper cars. In the end the commission let the rates for the more desirable lower bunks stay, but reduced the rates for upper bunks. The opinion was written by Franklin K. Lane, who would be secretary of the interior in the Wilson administration and whom LDB greatly respected. See *George S. Loftus v. Pullman Co. et al.,* 18 ICC Rep. 135 (1910).

4. As secretary of commerce in the Taft administration, Nagel no doubt suffered from the general political troubles generated by the Pinchot-Ballinger hearings and from the fact that his own brother-in-law was taking such a prominent role in embarrassing the president.

5. Adolph Behrens (1860–19[?]) was a Seattle real estate speculator who was called by Vertrees in order to discredit a minor part of Glavis's testimony. Instead, in his cross-examination LDB discredited Behrens, showing his connection to fraudulent Alaskan land claims and catching him in several embarrassing lapses of memory. See I*nvestigation of the Department of the Interior and the Bureau of Forestry,* Senate Doc. 719, 61st Cong., 3d Sess., (Washington, D.C., 1911), 5:2393–2410.

6. A "dog by comparison."

To: **Alice Goldmark Brandeis**
Date: **March 27, 1910**
Place: **Washington, D.C.**
Source: **Gilbert MSS**

DEAREST: I hope sleep has come again, and also Do; so that you may be free to come on here if it seems best. There is so much work preparing for the X-examination that I deem it wise to stay here this week. We had a very good two days. The enemy fell into all traps set by the wayside, and Barnum's Show couldn't compare with the fun on my Cross-Examination of Vertrees' first witness, Behrens.[1] It kept me a laughing 6 hours long & I had to go out to the La Follettes to let off the accumulated merriment. It was a fitting sequel to Vertrees opening & denunciatory attack on Pinchot & Garfield which to my mind, seems as unwise as most of the Great Chief Taft's moves.

I was blessed with 3 dinner invitations for tonight; at the Pinchot's to meet Dolliver[2] which I shall accept; at the La Follettes to meet Judge B.B. Lindsey[3] & Ray Stannard Baker, for which I will substitute a late afternoon call as I want to get some information from Lindsey in our Ballinger enquiry; and at Mrs. Hoars' (our Mr. Rice's sister) which I have regretfully declined. I am going out now for a sunning & then shall return to burrow among paper & prepare traps for the unwary. As per fun; Behrens' plight, left the proverbial "goat" miles behind.

I suppose you read Garfield's Tippecanoe Club speech.[4] It looks to newer things. Met John Mitchell[5] & James Duncan[6] here yesterday. They looked a little weak to bear Labor[']s heavy burdens.

Lovingly

The enclosed financial news may interest you. I am glad to know Miss G[rady]'s work impresses you favorably. Please keep watch of her.

1. See the previous letter.
2. Jonathan Prentiss Dolliver (1858–1910), an Iowa lawyer, served in the House of Representatives from 1889 to 1901, when he went over to the Senate. There he allied himself with other insurgent midwesterners.
3. Benjamin Barr Lindsey (1869–1943) was judge of the Juvenile Court of Denver from 1900 to 1927 and a justice of the Superior Court of California from 1934 until his death. A leading reformer and muckraking writer, he is best remembered for his pioneering work in developing the juvenile courts system.
4. In a speech at the Tippecanoe Club in Cleveland, James Garfield attacked the Taft administration and said he would not run for governor of Ohio on a platform endorsing Taft's programs and principles.
5. John Mitchell (1870–1919), a self-educated coal miner, rose to be the president of the powerful United Mine Workers from 1898 to 1908 and a vice-president of the American Federation of Labor from 1898 to 1914. A widely recognized authority on labor problems, Mitchell lectured around the country and played a major role in the National Civic Federation.
6. James Duncan (1857–1928), another vice-president of the AFL, headed the granite workers' union.

To: Alice Goldmark Brandeis
Date: April 23, 1910
Place: Washington, D.C.
Source: Gilbert MSS

DEAREST: Yesterday was a terrible day. I felt almost like an executioner & was glad to have Norman Hapgood[1] here to share the responsibility. But it was an awful thing for Wickersham to have done & unfortunately the President (whom we have not mentioned) is as guilty as W.[2]

To date back that Attorney General's report so as to make it appear that it was prepared before the President's letter, when in fact it was written after Glavis' Collier Article Nov. 13, comes pretty near giving false testimony.

There was a fearful pall on the assembled company when the point was developed after two hours spent in riddling the report for its suppressions and misstatements. But no denial came of my suggestion & none has come since from W. or the White House or any other source.

On the other hand, I have had confirmation from one of the detective newspaper men, who appears to have known practically as much, from his contemporary observations in November.

Al turned up late yesterday at the hearing, after the crisis & will probably stay until tomorrow P.M. Louis B. W[ehle]. is coming next week & your cousin Willie Naumberg & Agnes are here now.

The Illinois victory is good.[3] I am particularly glad for Do's sake.

Norman H. will have a short notice in the May 7 issue of the Ill. decision.[4] It was a satisfaction to have him here. He left again at midnight, & was greatly disgusted with his Yale lecture Thursday evening.

Lovingly

1. Norman Hapgood (1868–1937) was an editor of *Collier's Magazine* when he first met LDB; the two would become allies and close friends. LDB often sent his articles to Hapgood first, for publication in *Collier's* and later in *Harper's Weekly*. Hapgood broke with Robert Collier in 1912 over Theodore Roosevelt's candidacy, and LDB helped Hapgood secure the editorship of *Harper's*, where LDB published his important series of articles on *Other People's Money*. When asked why he did not place his writings in other progressive journals with larger circulations, LDB replied: "I regard Mr. Hapgood as so important a factor in the American advance movement that if I have been of any service in helping *Harper's Weekly*, as his instrument, I shall feel well content with the decision made" (see LDB to J. R. Smith, 2 February 1914, BL). Hapgood remained an influential Democrat until his death and was an active advisor to Wilson, Alfred E. Smith, and Franklin D. Roosevelt, often serving as a confidential courier between LDB and the White House in the 1930s. For Hapgood's relations with LDB, see his memoirs, *The Changing Years* (New York, 1930), ch. 13.

2. In one of the most startling developments in the hearings, LDB showed that the attorney general had backdated his report clearing Ballinger. Wickersham's "Summary and Report," upon which Taft based his exoneration of Ballinger, was dated 11 September 1909, although the attorney general had received the original request to examine the evidence on 6 September. Supposedly Wickersham had read all of the evidence, amounting to more than a half-million words, and written a 74-page opinion in six days, the same time during which he also prepared a number of amendments to the Interstate Commerce Act.

LDB suspected that the summary had actually been written after Taft had decided to back Ballinger and that the statement had then been predated to 11 September, a date prior to Taft's personal interview with the interior secretary, thus giving the impression that the administration had made a thorough investigation of the charges before acting. In fact the Wickersham report was not made until November, as LDB suspected. Had the administration admitted this immediately, it would have been embarrassing but not critical; Taft and his advisors persisted in denying the charge until they were caught in a web of such conclusive evidence that they appeared guilty not only of lying but of more serious malpractices. See LDB to Abbott Lawrence Lowell, 16 June 1910, BL.

3. In defense of the ten-hour law for women in *Ritchie v. Wayman,* 244 Ill. 509 (1910); see LDB to Alfred Brandeis, 4 December 1909, note 3.

4. *Collier's* had a short article in its section "What the World Is Doing" that noted that the Illinois Supreme Court had upheld that state's ten-hour law for women and then sarcastically cited some comments from people opposed to the law. There was no mention of LDB in the article, "Protecting Women for the State," *Collier's* 545 (7 May 1910): 10.

To:	Alice Goldmark Brandeis
Date:	April 26, 1910
Place:	Washington, D.C.
Source:	Gilbert MSS

DEAREST: Show Susan the enclosed Census Report, which was handed to me, as becoming almost a Washingtonian.

I sent a long call for "papers" to Nelson (Chairman), which the Atty Genl is to furnish together with answers to some questions about the report.

Nelson has not transmitted it. Evidently it hurts, & we may have some rumpus about it Thursday. Everything points to our leaving them caught in a trap. This Nelson hesitation i.a. I think I shall see my compatriot [Ollie] James before the meeting & get him prepared to stand up for the liberties of Americans.

Hughes['s] appointment is fine & it is fine he has accepted.[1] He is quite conservative, but well equipped & progressive as compared with most of the mossbacks. His public service will be a great help to his understanding the questions he will be called upon to decide.

I am to dine at the Pinchots this evening.   Lovingly

1. Charles Evans Hughes had been named by Taft to succeed David Brewer as an Associate Justice on the United States Supreme Court.

To:	Alice Goldmark Brandeis
Date:	April 30, 1910
Place:	Washington, D.C.
Source:	Gilbert MSS

DEAREST: Ballinger did fairly well on his direct yesterday but makes the impression on me of one who will not grow stronger on the cross[-examination]. We may reach that this afternoon, possibly not at all today; & I shall not be sorry if I have a few days study on his testimony, in print, before beginning the cross.

The prime question now is the "papers." I shall at least emphasize the refusal, if refusal is persisted in. The Comm'tee will probably want to hear me on that in Executive Session. If they do, I shall insist upon a stenographer with liberty to disclose what takes place & that may end in not having a hearing at all. But, the majority will not find a willing tool in the game of suppression. The press may be controlled in large part, but I am quite sure the reporters are with me & some things will always leak out.

Louis Wehle is still here & doubtless will stay the day. His Supreme Court case[1] wasn't reached & really never had the ghost of a show of being.

Tell the children that under the spur of L.B.W. necessity I bought a new derby; & you may tell the great shopper Sadie [Nicholson] that I have achieved the impossible—a metal reinforced comb (price 25 cents).

Lovingly

I hope to see you in Dedham May 8.

1. Wehle was counsel for the plaintiffs in *Kentucky Union Co. v. Commonwealth of Kentucky,* 219 U.S. 140 (1911). The company claimed that the state's procedures on forfeiture of lands for failure to list and pay taxes violated the federal Constitution's Due Process Clause. The Court did not, in fact, hear the case until the end of October and on 3 January 1911 handed down a unanimous decision upholding the state.

To: Alfred Brandeis
Date: May 1, 1910
Place: Washington, D.C.
Source: Brandeis MSS

DEAR AL: Yours of 29 reached me after yesterday's hearing in which you see the Atty. Genl. episode played a leading part.

Your remarks are entirely pertinent—but I think not sound. There is nothing for us to do but to follow the trail of evil wherever it extends. Fiat Iustitia.[1] In the fight against special interest we shall receive no quarter and may as well make up our minds to give none. It is a hard fight. The man with the hatchet is the only one who has a chance of winning in the end. This chance is none too good. There is a chance—but a chance merely—that the people will now reverse all history and be able to control. The chance is worth taking, because there is nothing left for the self-respecting man to do. But every attempt to deal mercifully with the special interests *during the fight* simply results in their taking advantage of the merciful.

I think Wickersham and his acts are a fair sample & product of our special interest activities—what Wall St. and high finance make of a finely gifted and no doubt originally honorable man. If there ever was any doubt

150

as to his guilt in this particular—it should have been removed by yesterday's proceedings,—particularly by Vertree[s]'s talk.[2]

It *just occurs* to me that some work on the rate bill which Louis Wehle told me he did for La Follette may interfere with your Com[mit]tee plans. Better see him at once so that he can undo the work if you deem it advisable.

I concluded to stay here this week having much to do re Ballinger X ex[amination].

1. Let justice be done.
2. In a highly emotional statement, Ballinger's counsel, John Vertrees, had accused LDB not only of seeking to smear his client but also of wanting to discredit the entire administration, especially Attorney General Wickersham. See *Interior Dept. Hearings,* 7:3626–28.

To: **Alice Goldmark Brandeis**
Date: **May 1, 1910**
Place: **Washington, D.C.**
Source: **Gilbert MSS**

DEAREST: Papers report rain in Boston yesterday & I fear Elizabeth's picnic was interfered with. Weather was fine here, hot, & after the hearing I strolled alone over Potomac Park where the Marine Band was giv[ing] an out of door concert. It was quite European. Hundreds of vehicles with the gayly clad were passing slowly by or stopping within sound of the music.

For dinner I went to the Pinchots, to talk with Madame[1] & Amos P.[2] over the stirring events of the day.

Madame P. has abandoned her trip to Europe so as to remain in the midst of things, which she enjoys like an old stager.

Read yesterday's opening pages when the reports get to you. The majority have shown pretty clearly that "Protection not Investigation" is to be their motto hereafter, and I fancy from now on opposition to my enquiries will be more stubborn.

I have 4 days before the X examination of B[allinger]. begins; but abundant work to do; & I hope to break through his front of defiant respectability.

Norman Hapgood writes of his terrible grief at not being here. His unfortunate weekly Thursday lectures at Yale are interfering.

Lovingly

Louis B.W. escaped Friday night.

1. Mary Eno Pinchot (1837–1914) was the matriarch of the Pinchot family and after Gifford's rise to prominence spent much of her time in Washington.
2. Amos Richards Eno Pinchot (1873–1944), a New York attorney, was as uncompromisingly progressive as his brother. Although not in the front rank of reformers, he participated in nearly all of the major progressive undertakings of the era and was highly respected by fellow reformers. His pacifism during the war led him to closer contacts with some of the

more radical elements in American life. He and LDB worked together on several projects; and upon LDB's appointment to the Court Amos wrote a highly perceptive letter that summed up the mixed feelings of elation and regret that many progressives felt (see LDB to Amos Pinchot, 27 June 1916, BL). Pinchot's *History of the Progressive Party, 1912–1916* (New York, 1958) remains an important source for the period.

To: Alice Goldmark Brandeis
Date: May 5, 1910
Place: Washington, D.C.
Source: Gilbert MSS

DEAREST: Met Ollie James on Fifteenth St. last evening, and he tells me the House will pass the Harrison[1] resolution calling for the Atty Genl's papers.[2] Harrison butted in without conferring with the Com[mit]tee members, but James says he has talk[ed] with both Democratic & Insurgent House members since & he thinks it will be all right. At all events we shall get publicity out of it & people here & there are beginning to understand. Ben Flexner[3] saw without tutor or diagram where it leaves the President & even members of the N.Y. bar are beginning to take notice. I expect to get hold of Ballinger on X. today & hope there will be no slip. I have some good "dope".

Rublee[4] & Connolly [*sic*][5] & I dined with [*] hostess at the Tea Cup Inn yesterday & R. & I also the day before.   Lovingly

1. Francis Burton Harrison (1873–1957), a New York Democratic congressman, later served as governor-general of the Philippines.
2. The papers in question dealt with the attorney general (or one of his staff), who had prepared responses for Taft dealing with charges against Ballinger. On 2 May Harrison introduced a resolution calling upon the attorney general immediately to provide all such documents to the investigating committee. Harrison did not act unilaterally, however, but cleared his action with the ranking Democratic member, James Graham.
3. Bernard Flexner (1865–1945) was trained as a lawyer and practiced in Louisville and Chicago before moving to New York. He would be part of the coterie LDB brought in to work with him in the American Zionist movement beginning in 1914; Flexner would remain his lieutenant during the 1920s and 1930s, serving as a founder of the Palestine Economic Corporation (PEC). Flexner also never lost interest in Louisville affairs and particularly in the university. In 1938 he wrote a tribute to his friend, *Mr. Justice Brandeis and the University of Louisville* (Louisville, 1938). Alpheus Mason dedicated his biography of LDB to the memory of Bernard Flexner.
4. George Rublee (1868–1957), a member of the Cotton firm, would soon become LDB's right-hand man in Washington. A self-effacing person, Rublee worked well with LDB in drafting antitrust legislation and other laws. Wilson attempted to appoint Rublee to the Federal Trade Commission, but conservatives blocked the nomination in the Senate. He did serve Wilson and every succeeding president through Franklin D. Roosevelt on a number of special commissions and wartime agencies.
5. Christopher Powell Connoly (1863–1933) often contributed articles to *Collier's* on political and economic topics.

To: Alice Goldmark Brandeis
Date: May 13, 1910
Place: Washington, D.C.
Source: Gilbert MSS

DEAREST: Tell Elizabeth I will observe her "il faut"[1] if possible.

It looks now as if I could get off Saturday night even if we have to go on with another hearing Tuesday. That is, I could arrange to arrive Tuesday morning unless there were some terribly urgent matter on hand, which seems unlikely. Ballinger's examination is about ended and after the climax nothing will interest the Com[mit]tee or the public much, unless we should get Wickersham on the stand, which is unlikely.

The admission of W. as to antedating is coupled with lies; & Lawler's letter introduced yesterday indicates the extent to which men are driven when the path of deceit is entered upon.[2]

I think as ill of WHT[aft]'s morals now as of his intellect.

Saw La Follette last evening to talk over the situation. If only there were a Democratic party! But there isn't.   Lovingly

1. "One must" or "It is necessary."
2. Oscar Lawler was appointed by Ballinger as the Interior Department's chief lawyer; he prepared the memorandum upon which Taft based his exoneration of Ballinger.

To: Alice Goldmark Brandeis
Date: May 22, 1910
Place: New York, New York
Source: Gilbert MSS

DEAREST: It was good to get your letter. Next Saturday I expect to be with you in Dedham "for keeps"—and not to leave my hearth until we move to So. Yarmouth. It will be good to have a united family again.

I walked to Mother's & back yesterday, dining there with Felix [Adler], Nell & Henry [Goldmark], & talking (too much) Washington.

I want to walk up to Susie [Goldmark]'s this afternoon & then sup with the Burlinghams. I have been trying terribly hard to think on the argument[1] but without much avail. I know not whether it be weather or something else, but "Nichts Erfreuliches [*] heraus."[2] Indeed I don't like much this idea of opening. I think I could get along well enough if Vertrees starts in with his vituperation.

A wireless has just come from Norman, and another kind telegram from Paul Kellogg suggesting my going to St. Louis for tomorrow night. "Kleine andere Dinge."[3]

153

I hope to see Rublee tomorrow & get him to assume responsibility for the brief.[4] After Saturday it will be hard for me to keep my mind on Ballinger.   Lovingly

1. The closing argument before the Ballinger investigating committee.
2. "Nothing enjoyable will come out of it."
3. "Other small things."
4. The final written statement for the Pinchot side to be made part of the record and to be distributed to the public.

To:	Alfred Brandeis
Date:	June 5, 1910
Place:	Dedham, Massachusetts
Source:	Brandeis MSS

DEAR AL: This is a fine Sunday. The children and George Openhym[1] & I are going off for a day's paddle on the Charles. Shall probably be as lame as an old horse on my return. That Washington experience was pretty exerciseless.

That Indianapolis Sun editorial was probably written by Jas. A. Matthews [*sic*].[2]

If Watterson doesn't shoot soon, ask him why?[3]

My two speeches[4] made apparently a great impression on the hearers; but it must have been largely voice & manner. They read very poorly as you will see when the reports reach you. They are not printed yet.

It is pretty hard work returning to the office.

1. The son of AGB's widowed sister, Christine Goldmark Openhym.
2. James Abram Mathews (1881–1933), an Indianapolis newspaperman, eventually edited a number of midwestern papers.
3. LDB had been hoping for a strong anti-Ballinger editorial from Henry Watterson (1840–1921), the longtime editor and publisher of the *Louisville Courier-Journal,* perhaps the most influential southern newspaper in the country. Eventually Watterson published two editorials on the case (10 and 11 June). See LDB to Watterson, 25 May and 14 June 1910, BL, and to Alfred Brandeis, 14 June 1910, BL.
4. LDB's opening and closing arguments in the Pinchot-Ballinger investigation. The opening comments can be found in *Interior Dept. Hearings,* 9:4903–23, and the closing statement in ibid., 5005–21.

To:	Alfred Brandeis
Date:	July 31, 1910
Place:	New York, New York
Source:	Brandeis MSS

DEAR AL: Have been here since Thursday morning again trying to settle the Garment Workers Strike,[1] as Chairman of the Conference Com[mit]tee.

The outcome is doubtful with probabiles [*sic*] that there will be no settlement because of the union demand of an all-union shop.[2]

I go into conference with the lawyers tomorrow morning again.

The family was due to arrive at So. Yarmouth Saturday.

Lee Callahan called on me Tuesday. Met Louis Wehle here Thursday & Albert Brandeis Friday.

1. From 24 July 1910 until his appointment to the Supreme Court in 1916, LDB was heavily involved in labor-management relations in the women's garment industry in New York. The garment trade, consisting primarily of small establishments, was particularly anarchic, and laborers often worked under conditions that could only be described as horrible. By July 1910 walkouts had approached the level of a general strike in the trade, and A. Lincoln Filene moved to get LDB involved. First he sold the union and the manufacturer representatives on the idea of bringing in LDB as a neutral mediator. LDB responded positively, probably because he thought he could put into practice some of the ideas he had developed about labor-management relations over the preceding fifteen years: industrial self-government, mechanisms for settling disputes peacefully, and a spirit of equality and cooperation by both sides.

Throughout the controversy LDB faced two powerful obstacles: the unwillingness of the owners, who had formed the Cloak, Suit & Skirt Manufacturers' Protective Association on 7 July, to surrender any of the traditional rights of ownership and the unwillingness of the more radical elements in the union to settle for anything less than a "closed shop" agreement. Slowly, and with great tact and after much frustration, the negotiations came to fruition with the landmark "protocol of peace," which would provide for arbitration and self-government. See Mason, *Brandeis,* ch. 19.

2. LDB had moved the conference along smoothly, starting from the least controversial issues and working toward the more difficult points of contention. On 29 July there was optimism that the strike would soon be settled, but the next day the union members insisted upon bringing up the closed shop issue—despite their earlier assurances to LDB that the matter would not be raised. LDB was trying to get the unions to accept a "union shop" rather than a "closed shop." In the latter only union members could be hired; under LDB's plan, employers would give preference to union members but could hire nonunion workers if they were better qualified. At this stage in the negotiations the workers were unreceptive to the LDB proposal, and two days later LDB broke off the negotiations and resumed his vacation. For details of the settlement of the strike, see BL, beginning at 2:365.

To: Louis Brandeis Wehle
Date: October 1, 1910
Place: Boston, Massachusetts
Source: Brandeis MSS

MY DEAR LOUIS: Your gas article in the Louisville Herald of September 25th is excellent.[1]

Don't, however, let the Louisville people be misled in favor of a merger by the argument that monopoly in public service corporations is a good thing. A gas company with a monopoly may be a good thing; an electric company with a monopoly may be a good thing; but gas and electricity are different methods of supplying one's wants, and you cannot get the best results unless you maintain a competition between these two methods of lighting.

We are sure that our good results in the gas field are due, to a considerable extent, to the fact that gas and electric light companies are in keen competition.

In the smaller cities it is often desirable to consolidate the two methods of lighting partly because there are parts of the city to which the gas mains cannot be extended without undue expense, but in a large city the merger of gas and electric light companies is certainly an evil.

Don't let Louisville tie itself up either for a period of twenty years. I should infinitely rather have for Louisville municipal ownership, with all its dangers, than either a merger or a long term agreement. You will note that we thought it advisable not to make an agreement for a period of longer than ten years.

Great improvements in illumination, and great reduction in cost of distribution may be expected. Besides, it is quite on the cards that within a few years a dollar may be worth much more than it is today.

Your very truly

1. Wehle's article summarized the history and principal features of the Boston sliding-scale system and urged that a similar experiment be tried in Louisville, where, he claimed, the public had no safeguards against corporate wrongdoing

To: **Alice Goldmark Brandeis**
Date: **October 11, 1910**
Place: **Washington, D.C.**
Source: **Gilbert MSS**

DEAREST: It was good to get your Sunday letter.

Last evening's walk took me past the Pinchot house. To my surprise I found it illuminated & on going in found Gifford P. & some La Follettes. G.P. was in town only for the day. He is greatly exercised over T.R.'s N.Y. platform.[1] Hastened to Atlanta to see T.R. who says he didn't "realize what effect it would have"—"Had not thought much of the national" situation(!!) G.P. wasn't much taken in despite his friendship. Thinks it clear that insurgency will move on even if T.R. not the leader & doubts whether he will be, seems clear that he (G.P.) must steer his own course. Says Stimson[2] is very mildly progressive—G.P. is all right, but will, of course, support Stimson—but doesn't think Stimson will want him on the stump as G.P. would have to speak his mind.

156

G.P. says also T.R. would have been beaten in N.Y. but for his compromise with the Taft forces.

Saw Simon Flexner[3] here yesterday. He is here on cholera protection—doesn't expect much danger.

Tell the children there is fine chestnutting at the Lyons. Am deep in figures.

1. Theodore Roosevelt was eager to reenter politics and in 1910 was beginning to explore the possibility of running for president in 1912, a possibility that became a reality after the withdrawal of La Follette in early 1911. At the New York Republican convention in Saratoga on 28 September, Roosevelt had outmaneuvered the Old Guard and pushed through a program that called for a number of reforms, including a direct primary. Although the platform included an "unqualified endorsement of the Administrations of both President Taft and Governor Hughes," it was, in fact, a slap at the president—a fact that Taft and everybody else understood.

2. Henry Lewis Stimson (1867–1950) enjoyed a long and distinguished career in public service. As a no-nonsense U.S. attorney in New York (where Felix Frankfurter was one of his assistants), he agreed to Theodore Roosevelt's request that he run for governor in 1910, a race he lost. Taft did not hold the campaign against Stimson and named him secretary of war in 1911, and in 1929 Herbert Hoover called him back from private practice to be secretary of state. When World War II began, Franklin Roosevelt, at the suggestion of Frankfurter, called Stimson back to the war department, a post he held into the Truman administration. A man of unquestioned principle, Stimson was held in high esteem by both Democrats and Republicans.

3. Simon Flexner (1863–1946), the third of the Flexner brothers, had been head of the medical research laboratories at the Rockefeller Institute since 1903. For his work in pathology he would be honored with numerous degrees and citations from foreign governments.

To: **Josephine Clara Goldmark**
Date: **October 11, 1910**
Place: **Washington, D.C.**
Source: **EBR**

MY DEAR JOSEPHINE: My very best wishes; and I want you to know that we congratulate ourselves on your birthday.

I count it among the best fruits of our joint work, that we have had you with us so much, and that the children have had the rare privilege of your noble presence. It must prove an inspiration to them.

The year has brought much appreciation of your fine work; and it is sure to become fuller when that part in hand is finished.[1]

With much love

1. Josephine Goldmark was compiling the briefs and data in the several cases dealing with protective legislation, which would eventually be published as *Fatigue and Efficiency* (New York, 1912). See LDB to John M. Glenn, 30 November 1909, BL.

To: Alfred Brandeis
Date: December 5, 1910
Place: Boston, Massachusetts
Source: Brandeis MSS

MY DEAR AL: I have your letter of the 1st and have received a letter from Mr. Buckner and Mr. Taylor.[1] I should be delighted to speak before the Board of Trade under these circumstances, but I feel that I must not.

My long and frequent absences from Boston have already created a very great strain upon the patience of others who have prior rights to call upon me, and they might well feel that I was yielding too much to my own preference, should I extend my absences for a trip to Louisville.

I enclose you a copy of my letter to Mr. Taylor.[2]

I have your letter with clipping about Frank Schmitt. I had not known the nature of his death when I wrote you from Washington the other day.

I suppose you occasionally see the New York papers. I have been very pleasantly surprised at the support which we have had here in the East.[3] I rather expected support from the West, and worked hard with some of the New York papers myself, but we have had solid support from many which I did not approach, and from whom I only had expected to have sneers and abuses.

I expect to remain in Boston this week & probably longer.

   1. Marion R. Taylor was chairman of the Committee on Entertainment and Arrangements of the Louisville Board of Trade.

   2. See LDB to Marion Taylor, 5 December 1910, BL.

   3. Railroads had petitioned the Interstate Commerce Commission for a general increase in freight rates. LDB had been retained, along with other attorneys, to represent various coalitions of shippers opposed to the increase. At hearings earlier in the fall he had subjected railroad witnesses to an unmerciful examination of their finances, trying to show the ICC that the railroads were not as badly off as they claimed and, beyond that, that they were not being managed well. If the railroads adopted a more scientific mode of management, he claimed, they would not need a rate increase.

To: Alice Goldmark Brandeis
Date: January 4, 1911
Place: Washington, D.C.
Source: Gilbert MSS

DEAREST: I am just settling down to work, in a sunny comfortable room (741) on the 14th St. side[1] after a fine walk around the Potomac Basin which is partly frozen over. Day is clear, cold, wind North. On returning I went into the Bureau of American Republics,[2] the Carnegie[3] given building dedicated last spring which you may remember. It has a fine court, a la Gardiner Palace[4] in Spanish American architecture with tropical plants & fountain, a joyous bit of the South which you must see. As I stepped among the tropical plants, the first to catch my idea was my long beloved Yerba maté (Ilix Paraquaqeneis). Think of it. 128 million pounds exported from Brazil last year & I have never tasted a drop.

Now I must read Lyon's Brief.[5] Can't see him until I do.

Read the general brief of the RR attorneys (57 pp.) on my way to N.Y. It is uninteresting, & not over strong, & literally *says not a word* about scientific management or efficiency. Isn't that the scorn of silence?

Several of the Railroads have filed separate briefs which I have not yet examined.

You will note from enclosed that my brief was given first page notices.

Lovingly

I told George R[ublee]. to consult you as chief medical adviser. Mrs. was much delighted to have your letter.

Please mail me fur lined (Goldmark) gloves.

1. Of the New Willard Hotel.
2. Now known as the Pan American Union.
3. Andrew Carnegie (1835–1919) rose from a poor immigrant boy to become the world's greatest steelmaker as well as one of its richest men. LDB admired Carnegie as the embodiment of success through legitimate competition. After selling out his steel holdings to J. P. Morgan in 1901, Carnegie spent the rest of his life giving away his millions through a variety of charitable endeavors.
4. Isabella Stewart Gardiner (1840–1920) was an unorthodox and vivid leader of Boston society. Her home, now a museum, was a replica of a Renaissance Venetian palace, with art galleries opening on a flowered court.
5. Probably Frank Lyon, a Washington lawyer who had been intermittently associated with the Interstate Commerce Commission ever since its creation in 1887; the brief related to the rate hearings.

To:	Alice Goldmark Brandeis
Date:	January 5, 1911
Place:	Washington, D.C.
Source:	Gilbert MSS

DEAREST: Chas. Washburn's report is interesting but not surprising.[1]

Herbert White gave me such a catapultic bombardment Tuesday about overworking that I have loafed most of the time since.

Yesterday, walks achieved about 12 miles, lunched with Marble, supped at the La Follettes & talked with Lyon. Took several naps, & did little execution except reading Lyon's brief which is fine, immeasurably superior to the RR project.

Marble tells me he had a letter from Ives, which bore on the attack on him now. Also tha[t] Taft had intended putting a shippers' and a railroad traffic man on the Interstate C. Com'n, but refrained on account of the kicking in each case from the other side.

Mrs. La Follette is entirely well again, but the Senator is still rather under par & is pitching into work too hard. I signed the League,[2] deeming that the only chance for congenial political association. He was much pained to hear of Norman White's Lodgism.[3]

Fola[4] should now be at Mrs. Evans. I didn't get far with him on the RR problem[5] as he was called off by Bristow[6] & Beveridge[7] for a conference on the Lorimer situation.[8]

The La Follettes feel very sad about T.R.'s Saratoga performance.[9] So does Amos [Pinchot] but Gifford appears still to be loyal.

Tell Miss Wyatt to read her Koran.

"Ye who believe, hold fast to virtue"—i.e. the brief. And bear in mind Omar's disposition of all other repositories of knowledge.

Marble thinks that the Com'n will decide for the shippers.[10]

Lovingly

Having left my pajamas at home, I have purchased some flannelettes of dazzling beauty.

1. Charles Washburn (1857–1928) was a wealthy Massachusetts lawyer and business-man and a friend of Theodore Roosevelt. After serving in the state assembly, he was elected to Congress for three terms beginning in 1906. The report, delivered orally, probably dealt with the Ballinger hearings.

2. There had been discussion about creating a progressive Republican organization since 1909, and one finally took shape over the Christmas break in 1910. The National Progressive Republican League would be formally organized at La Follette's house on 21 January 1911 and announced to the press the next day. Oregon senator Jonathan Bourne, Jr., served as the president. In political circles it was widely assumed that the league would be the vehicle La Follette would use in his campaign for the 1912 Republican presidential nomination.

3. Norman Hill White (1871–19[?]) was the brother of LDB's close friend Herbert White. He was a member of the Massachusetts House of Representatives from 1907 to 1909 and was LDB's right-hand man in the struggles to establish savings bank insurance and against the New Haven–Boston & Maine merger. Independently wealthy, White may have found La Follette's progressivism too radical for his taste, preferring to stay with the more estab-lished leadership of the Republican Party, personified in Massachusetts by Senator Henry Cabot Lodge (see LDB to AGB, 21 March 1911).

4. Fola La Follette (1882–1970), the senator's daughter, took up an acting career after graduating with honors from the University of Wisconsin. She became an ardent suffra-gist and later collaborated with her mother in writing the two-volume biography of her father.

5. On 4 January the railroads had filed their briefs in support of their request for rate increases, ignoring LDB's suggestions regarding the economies that could be obtained through scientific management.

6. Joseph Little Bristow (1861–1944) was an insurgent Republican senator from Kansas.

7. Albert Jeremiah Beveridge (1862–1927), a well-known historian and insurgent sen-ator from Indiana, was a leading proponent of federal legislation to end child labor.

8. Illinois senator William Lorimer (1861–1934) had been charged with winning his seat through unethical and fraudulent methods. At the urging of La Follette and others, an eight-man committee—four friendly to Lorimer and four deemed unsympathetic—was named by the Senate to investigate. Rumors abounded that LDB had been asked by the committee to serve as counsel (see LDB to Alfred Brandeis, 10 June 1911, BL). In July 1912 the committee reported that the charges were indeed true; Lorimer resigned and returned to his business in Chicago.

9. See LDB to AGB, 11 October 1910, note 1.

10. On 23 February, in two unanimous decisions, the Interstate Commerce Commission turned down the railroads. The opinion noted that, while costs had risen, revenues had increased even more; in addition, the commission noted LDB's comments on scientific management, but said it was not the commission's function to pass on such matters.

To:	Alice Goldmark Brandeis
Date:	January 8, 1911
Place:	Washington, D.C.
Source:	Gilbert MSS

DEAREST: I have spoken for the room next to mine for Tuesday (No. 740) & think it will be OK at least no more than the best here. The hotel will be jammed with Tariff commission[1] crowds from the country over, under the aegis of John C. Cobb of Boston.[2]

I have been settling down to work after a haircut & walk in the Potomac Park, but have not done great stunts yet. Yesterday's results were better.

Miss Grady seems eager to come with you, but I have not encouraged her. There is plenty of Schildwach[3] duty on Savings Bank Insurance necessary. Miles Poindexter[4] seems a nice fellow, but not very strong. Indeed strength is not super abundant in this world of Pygmies. Amos Pinchot is on hand as you will see from the enclosed. I "Sheud" him off. Really what I need is a month or two more before argument.[5] Then it might be worth while.

Tell the children Buck Lathrop is in blooming health with appetite good. They live very pleasantly in the suburbs within a sign that vita Sunplesiina which one might have imagined.

I declined an invitation to the Pinchots tonight. Me for the simple life.

Au revoir   Lovingly

1. Representative Nicholas Longworth, with Taft's blessing, had proposed a salaried, five-member tariff commission (all of the members appointed by the president) to regulate tariffs. The House of Representatives passed the bill on 30 January, but it died in the Senate, where both insurgents and conservatives opposed it for different reasons. A tariff commission would eventually be created in 1916.

2. John Chandler Cobb (1858–1933) was a Boston shipping merchant who controlled Cobb & Company from 1892 until his death. He had organized and managed the South Bay Wharf & Terminal Company until it had been sold to the New Haven in 1907.

3. Sentry.

4. Miles Poindexter (1868–1946), a senator from Washington, was a particularly vocal critic of Ballinger during the hearings.

5. In the Advance Rate hearings.

To: **Alice Goldmark Brandeis**
Date: **March 21, 1911**
Place: **Nearing New York**
Source: **Gilbert MSS**

DEAREST: Elizabeth & Miss Grady have doubtless explained to you my sudden departure.[1]

Ives & Judge Bryan telephoned so plaintively that I felt obliged to put it up to Beatson[2] & to my surprise the latter yielded, not to me (because I didn't ask him) but to the situation.

I really think I shall not be of much use, but possibly I am mistaken.

The trip has been restful, in spite of some acquaintances. Among others my sometime Law School classmate George Plimpton[3] of Ginns whom I put to lecturing me on his collection of educational books etc. from the earliest times, the greatest in the world. Think of hav[ing] 3000 grammars, when one was too much for us. The children may be interested in the enclosed which Plimpton gave me showing the ascent of the pupil into the tower of knowledge.

Plimpton lives in N.Y., has an ancestral farm in Walpole adjoining the Birds.

The dining car conductor, an old friend, told me business is becoming pretty bad on the New Haven, only 112 on the train today instead of 145 the usual number until recently. And a broker whom I met told me that people are becoming afraid to hold New Haven stock, that he sold 1000 shares recently for a large trust that was afraid to continue to hold it. The truth is gradually permeating.

I lunched with Norman [White] to talk Pensions with him. He says he is making grand progress, realizes that he will get no support from Lodge[4] or Crane, says Lodge is controlled by Crane, but thinks well of Gussie Gardiner.[5]

Norman Hapgood writes i.a. that he had enjoyable dinner with us, & sends greetings.

Do writes the 8 hour law passed in California & is beginning to see visions of another brief.[6] Something for Lathrop.   Lovingly

1. To assist the ICC in the Advance Rate case.

2. J. W. Beatson was secretary of the Economic Club of Boston, a group that would have been vitally interested in the current railroad rate hearings.

3. George Arthur Plimpton (1855–1936), after studying at Amherst, spent only one year at the Harvard Law School and then left without taking a degree. He reputedly had the largest private collection of textbooks in the world, including works from the earliest days of printing as well as medieval manuscripts. He was an executive of Ginn & Company and wrote and lectured widely.

4. Henry Cabot Lodge (1850–1924), the scion of an old and distinguished Massachusetts family, represented the state in the U.S. Senate from 1893 until his death and dominated the state's Republican Party as well. Lodge led the opposition to the Treaty of Versailles in 1919.

5. Augustus Peabody Gardiner (1865–1918), a lawyer and former military man, represented Massachusetts in the House of Representatives from 1903 to 1917.

6. The California legislature enacted an eight-hour law for women workers, which Governor Hiram Johnson signed despite the bitter opposition of fruit growers, packers, and other industries that had large numbers of women employees. The California Supreme Court upheld the law in *In re Miller,* 162 Cal. 687 (1912), a case in which LDB played no part. He did, however, join the team defending the law when it was appealed to the U.S. Supreme Court, which sustained the measure in *Miller v. Wilson,* 236 U.S. 373 (1915).

To:	**Alice Goldmark Brandeis**
Date:	**May 19, 1911**
Place:	**Washington, D.C.**
Source:	**Gilbert MSS**

DEAREST: Spent last evening at the La Follettes' with Gifford P[inchot]. and [Francis] Heney. Of course we didn't get out the antitrust problem decently, but talked about LaF. candidacy. I am to lunch with G.P. & Heney today & meet them, Van Valkenburg[1] & Amos P. and Angus McSween[2] at 4 & the evening.

At 10:15 this A.M. I am to talk with Lenroot[3] & LaF. on antitrust, & at 12 A.M. to see Ashbrook,[4] Chairman of the Postal Com[mit]tee. See enclosed clippings which please preserve.

I don't intend to get bound up with this thing.[5] Some committeeman let this out, unauthorized & upon some misunderstanding. Unless this postal matter works out as result of joint enquiry with Insurgent Senators to the fore, it looks to me now that it is best to keep out of it. The rumor of my being in has spread some interest.

Gifford & I plan to call on His Honor the Secretary of the Interior[6] at 3 P.M.

Don't know yet when I shall leave. It is truly hot here.   Lovingly

1. Edward Augustus Van Valkenburg (1869–1932) was the editor of the *Philadelphia North American.*

2. Angus McSween was a reporter on the *Philadelphia North American.*

3. Irvine Luther Lenroot (1869–1949) was an ally of La Follette in Wisconsin, where he was speaker of the state assembly. He served in the House of Representatives from 1909 to 1918 and then in the Senate until 1927, when he was defeated for reelection. He was appointed to the Court of Customs and Patent Appeals in 1929 and retired in 1944.

4. William Albert Ashbrook (1867–1940) served as a congressman from Ohio from 1907 to 1921 and again from 1935 to 1939.

5. House Resolution 109 called for an investigation of the expenditures and services of the Post Office, and Ashbrook, as chairman of the House Post Office Committee, wanted LDB to serve as counsel to the committee during the investigation. LDB declined; see his letter to Ashbrook, 23 May 1911, BL.

6. Walter L. Fisher.

To: **Alice Goldmark Brandeis**
Date: May 20, 1911
Place: Washington, D.C.
Source: Gilbert MSS

DEAREST: Your letter came. Glad the wild west proved so attractive & that you talked with A.H.G[rady].

Albert[1] was here yesterday. Saw him for $1/2$ hour before his leaving for Louisville 11 P.M. He is enthusiastic over LBW's marriage romantique.[2] Says the wedding (50 present including Aunts Lottie & Julia) went off finely.

Am staying here to draft an amendment to the anti t[rust]. law which R.M. [La] F[ollette]. wants to introduce early next week.[3] The assembled party (including M.E. Clapp[4] & Bourne[5] & Congr. Lenroot & our civilian claque) being enthusiastic over the ideas suggested. Heney is helping me draft the bill. I rather expect to take the midnight train to N.Y. so as to meet you at supper Sunday in Boston or Dedham.

Enclosed from N.Y. Tribune bears the tone of Ballinger times.[6] I don't think I shall be drawn into that maelstorm.

1. LDB's cousin Albert Brandeis was the son of his uncle Samuel.

2. On 17 May Louis Brandeis Wehle married Mary Gray Patterson Liddell. See LDB to AGB, 2 June 1911.

3. On 16 May, following the Supreme Court's decision in the *Standard Oil* case that only "unreasonable" restraints of commerce were illegal under the Sherman Act, La Follette had telegraphed to LDB: "We need you to consider next important step. . . . Come immediately if possible." The decision, La Follette believed, opened the door to endless special pleadings by big corporations that their actions were not "unreasonable." Following several meetings, LDB, Heney, and Lenroot agreed to draft a bill to supplement the Sherman Act; after weeks of hurried preparation, La Follette introduced the bill in the Senate and Lenroot sponsored it in the House. The measure died, but see LDB to E. A. Grozier, 19 September 1911, BL, for its main provisions.

4. Moses Edwin Clapp (1851–1929) was an insurgent senator from Minnesota, part of the growing nucleus of anti-Taft Republicans. His committee would provide LDB a sympathetic forum in which to present his antitrust views. See LDB to Moses Edwin Clapp, 22 June 1911, BL.

5. Jonathan Bourne, Jr. (1855–1940), the progressive senator from Oregon, would head up the National Progressive Republican League, the organization La Follette hoped to use to win the GOP nomination for the presidency in 1912.

6. An editorial in the *New York Tribune* of the previous day, entitled "Brandeis after Lime-light," claimed that LDB, "who achieved a certain kind of fame as the attorney for L. R. Glavis in the Ballinger-Pinchot investigation, and who acquired a large amount of free advertising by offering to save the railroads $1,000,000 a day . . . now offers his time and efforts free to the Democratic committee of the House which is to investigate the Post Office Department."

To: **Susan Brandeis**
Date: **June 2, 1911**
Place: **New York, New York**
Source: **Gilbert MSS**

MY VERY DEAREST SUSAN: Good courage to you, and keep your good wits about you. You will then have what is called "good luck". I am sure you know enough.[1]   With ever so much love

1. Susan was apparently taking college placement examinations; see LDB to AGB, 4 June 1911.

To: **Alice Goldmark Brandeis**
Date: **June 2, 1911**
Place: **New York, New York**
Source: **Gilbert MSS**

DEAREST: I quite sympathized with what you say of L[ouis] & M[ary Wehle]. Mary's youth impressed me as the most conspicuous fact. I didn't get a chance to talk really with her at all. Am quite anxious to hear what the children say. Louis seemed to leave an impression of not being over wise at the moment, with perhaps the primordial view of a honeymoon as a spree.

McClennen turned up this morning and we having [*sic*] been discussing the Case most of the day. It isn't nearly as interesting, as Antitrust, or Shoe Machinery, Wage-Earners Insurance or the like. One feels the trammel of the law. I suppose Denman[1] would say that only legislation is constructive, law is but the interpretation of what others have said & done. Some other rot could also be said on the subject as to which you shall be spared.

I supposed you noticed Root—the Root of all evil—in Gary's Steel testimony.[2]

McClennen & I are going to walk now & to dine at Mothers.

Lovingly

I wrote Susan to Bessie [Evans]'s today.

1. William Denman (1872–1959), a California progressive, would later be named by Franklin Roosevelt to the Court of Appeals for the Ninth Circuit.
2. In hearings before the Stanley Committee, Elbert Henry Gary (1846–1927), the head of the U.S. Steel Corporation, was questioned about the many subdivisions owned by the

gigantic firm and admitted that these companies were wholly controlled by U.S. Steel, that their markets were no longer competitive, and that their profits went entirely to the parent company. He denied, however, that the American Steel Institute, which he also headed, attempted to fix prices or control the market. When questioned about U.S. Steel's purchase of Tennessee Iron & Coal in 1907, he told the committee that he had consulted not only with President Roosevelt but with Secretary Elihu Root as well.

To: Alice Goldmark Brandeis
Date: June 4, 1911
Place: New York, New York
Source: Gilbert MSS

DEAREST: I am delighted to hear that Friday's examination seemed to Susie [Goldmark] to go off well. Her trial is constantly in my mind. I trust she is not mistaken.

Grandma was on the sofa in her room yesterday, troubled somewhat with throat & not feeling so vigorous. She has decided not to go to [*] or to us, but instead to [*] Long Island.

Thelma & Sam were at Mother's also & T. played quite a little, not as enjoyably as I should have expected. She isn't really musical. Josephine can play much better, even if the fingers won't always move as desired.

We have been working literally on law all day, & the old man has been able to show the Junior that there are points not thought of in his philosophy.[1] We are going to print a little supplement to the brief tomorrow.

It is some satisfaction for the arduous labor on private business to find out that there is some use in grubbing up the case.   Lovingly

1. "There are more things in heaven and earth, Horatio, Than are dreamt of in your philosophy." Shakespeare, *Hamlet,* I, 5:166.

To: Alice Goldmark Brandeis
Date::   July 28, 1911
Place: Washington, D.C.
Source: Gilbert MSS

DEAREST: Am not certain yet when I shall get away, certainly not before Saturday P.M. & may not reach home before Monday morning.

There is much to look into. I have [had] a look in & am sure there is only one solution for Alaska.[1] A most comprehensive plan of Govt. ownership, Railroads, Utilities—with leasing only of most lands, & then a complete separation of the industrial property state from the political state. Control the property of the people of the U.S. from Washington, & give the inhabitants of Alaska otherwise home rule.

The great event of yesterday was the La Follette wool victory.[2] We visited him in the evening & talked a little about that & mainly of my Alaska ideas. The antitrust bill is promised introduction next week.[3]

Matz[4] it seems will not get out of the Directors before the suits against USMCo begin.[5]

Lovingly

Am glad you called on the Hurleys.

1. In mid-July a sensational story broke charging that the Taft administration had secretly handed over to the Morgan-Guggenheim interests the valuable Controller Bay area in Alaska. The bay was a strategic outlet for coal and therefore invaluable to mining interests wishing to exploit the Alaska fields. LDB was first approached by Representative James Graham, whose Committee on the Interior Department was looking into these charges (see LDB to Graham, 14 July 1911, BL). LDB spent a fair amount of time on the Alaska issue. For his thoughts on overall development of the territory, see his letters to Robert M. La Follette and Gifford Pinchot, both 29 July 1911, BL. For his conclusions on the charges against the administration, see LDB to James Graham, 27 November 1911, BL.

2. The previous day a Senate coalition of insurgent Republicans and Democrats had passed a wool tariff making substantial reductions in the existing rate schedules. Taft, however, vetoed the final version of the bill the following month, and the House sustained his veto.

3. See LDB to AGB, 20 May 1911.

4. Rudolph Matz (1860–1917) was a Chicago lawyer married to Florence Henderson, whose family-owned business had been one of the companies merged to form the United Shoe Machinery Company.

5. Although LDB had at one time done work for United Shoe, he eventually came to see its practices as monopolistic. He became a bitter critic of the company and pushed for an antitrust suit against the firm. See Mason, *Brandeis,* ch. 14, for details of LDB's complicated relations with and subsequent fights against the company.

To:	Louis Brandeis Wehle
Date:	July 31, 1911
Place:	Boston, Massachusetts
Source:	Brandeis MSS

MY DEAR LOUIS: You may be interested to know that your friend Congressman Buckley [sic] introduced himself to me while I was in Washington last week, and I had an interesting talk with him.[1] He appears to be a good Progressive, and to make clear the fact that there is no difference, except in name, between a Progressive Republican and a Progressive Democrat.

1. Undoubtedly Robert John Bulkley (1880–1965), the Democratic representative from Ohio who later served in the Senate as well; Bulkley had attended Harvard with Wehle.

To: Alice Goldmark Brandeis
Date: August 29, 1911
Place: Boston, Massachusetts
Source: Gilbert MSS

DEAREST: Nothing from you yet. Hope the day went well.

I slipped away from the Union Club in search of more Insurgent companions & dined at the City Club with Julian Mack.[1]

He is quite an up to date Federal Judge, who think[s] inferior court judges should not be permitted to declare laws unconstitutional & that a decision by a large majority (at least) of the Supreme Court ought to be required to nullify an act of the [state] legislature or of Congress.

Have cleared my desk of extraneous matter, dictated my letters & am ready now to take up Controller Bay literature. There appears to be little of moment collected by my so called assistants. Amos [Pinchot] has too much nurse-duty.

Wigmore[2] was in today. Had thoughts of transferring his Criminal Law Institute to Boston, but I advised Madison, Wisconsin as a more fertile soil. Think of radical changes in the law via the Boston Bar!

I am going to dine with E.A.F[ilene]. to be brought up to date[3] & then go early to the Polo Club for the night.

Dedham is looking green. Our flower beds seem from a distance quite resplendent considering the time of year.

The Sunday paper article sent by Aunt Julia was from the syndicated Sunday magazine. It brought me a [*] of letters from unfortunates, i.a. inmates of insane hospitals and prisons.

Miss Grady is enthusiastic about Canada, & the Sav. Bank Ins. situation seems quite favorable.

Lovingly

As to "tips"—Susan would say:

"signs of nobleness like stars should shine on all deservers."[4]

Did you note the Transcript's blast on N.H.?[5]

1. Julian William Mack (1866–1943) became one of LDB's most trusted friends. He had just been appointed to the Court of Appeals for the Seventh Circuit in Chicago and held that position until 1941, during which time he gained a reputation as a fine jurist. Mack and LDB first met through agencies such as Survey Associates and the American Association for Labor Legislation, but their most important ties were through the Zionist movement, where Mack served as LDB's lieutenant; Mack would ultimately be head of both the American Jewish Congress and the Zionist Organization of America (ZOA) but would resign from those posts along with other Brandeisians in the 1921 clash with Chaim Weizmann.

2. John Henry Wigmore (1863–1943) was dean of the Northwestern University Law School for more than three decades and one of the acknowledged authorities in the field of evidence.

3. On the situation in the New York garment industry's protocol.

4. Shakespeare, *Macbeth*, I, 4.

5. On 29 August the *Transcript* had called for an independent tribunal to investigate the cause of an accident on the New Haven line in Middletown, Connecticut, where there had been a clash between railroad officials, who claimed that vandals had caused the mishap by tampering with the switches, and the local police chief, who said there was no evidence of any such tampering. The chief believed the rails had buckled due to their inability to support the heavy weight of the locomotive. The paper wanted an investigation to determine if the line was maintaining its rails and beds properly. LDB, of course, had been saying for years that the New Haven had been skimping on maintenance.

To:	Susan Brandeis
Date:	October 3, 1911
Place:	Boston, Massachusetts
Source:	Gilbert MSS

MY DEAREST SUSAN: I trust the first day at College has been beautiful, and full of that promise of happiness and usefulness which we wish for you.[1]

Take very good care of yourself and be full of courage. You will find it quite possible to accomplish all that the College demands—even in English.

I enclose New York draft two hundred dollars so that you may open your bank account at once.

With much love

Please acknowledge receipt.

1. Susan, like her Goldmark aunts, attended Bryn Mawr College.

To:	Alice Goldmark Brandeis
Date:	October 17, 1911
Place:	New York, New York
Source:	Gilbert MSS

DEAREST: Don't worry about me. Think I have fairly cleared the decks now & gotten rid of clients, associates, Com[mit]tees, delegates, & newspaper men et al. who have prevented "thought having a clearness."[1]

A.H.G[rady]. foolishly called me up this A.M. to tell me of a telegram from Gov. of Wisc.[2] asking me to aid their Atty Genl[3] on constitutionality of Waterpower law (conservation), but as briefs are to be filed in Nov. & case argued in early Dec. I told her to answer I could not. Incidentally I told her not to bother me with telephones unnecessarily—as this clearly was. She probably was somewhat hurt. If you can, invite her in for some time tomorrow and try to steady her etc. while I am away. She needs about weekly doses.

Sam Untermeyer [*sic*] is, of course, much chagrined; & he will try to do "his darndest", but I guess he is sidetracked for the moment & perhaps his enmity may be not less helpful than his alleged cooperation.

I have set my allies to some definite tasks which should, at least, occupy them & I hope may give me more aid than came from A[mos].P[inchot]. et al. re Alaska.

Walked to Mother's & back yesterday & am alarmed a la Sugar Broker. My waist measurement is 37 as per allow.[4] Think Paul[ine] will join us at Bryn Mawr. I have a good sunny suite here.

Lovingly

Please preserve for A.H.G. any clippings sent you.

1. Shakespeare, *Macbeth*, III, 1.
2. Francis Edward McGovern (1866–1946) served as Wisconsin governor from 1911 to 1915 and during his first two terms oversaw the enactment of a wide range of progressive legislation.
3. Levi Horace Bancroft (1861–1948), a Richland Center attorney who had been speaker of the Wisconsin House, served as the state's attorney general from 1910 to 1912 and later as a judge of the state's Fifth Circuit Court. There is no record of such a case in either the Wisconsin reports or those of the U.S. Supreme Court.
4. See LDB to AGB, 23 October 1911.

To:	Alice Goldmark Brandeis
Date:	October 19, 1911
Place:	Washington, D.C.
Source:	Gilbert MSS

DEAREST: My plan of 48 hours solitude has been rudely & completely shattered. But (strictly confidential) the Coal Case hearings[1] are going over to November, so I shall be able to restore my mind to tobacco.[2] At the moment, I have little mind to restore, as I found myself pretty tired & have been letting the reservoir fill up, which it is doing.

Have just had a soothing luncheon with Gilson Gardner[3] who returned today from the West. He talks like [a] suckling dove in gentleness, but is very determined in statements about Taft. Says his Western trip was an unquestioned frost & that he cannot be nominated. Asserts that the West is almost solidly for La Follette, that the Middle West is divided & that even the mercenary Southern delegates are about to waver as to whether there is not more chance of fat for them in the La Follette ranks than to go down in Taft defeat. He thinks La Follette, if nominated, would win over everyone except Woodrow Wilson.[4] Gardner is going to see TR tomorrow.

I have thought it wise to shore up my press friends on Tobacco, & am trying to influence the Department of Justice via Layman [*sic*], the Solicitor General.[5] It may be possible to make G.W.[6] afraid not to vigorously oppose the plan.

Albert Brandeis reports his mother et al. already in the new house, also rumors of the Louis Wehles having moved to apartments.

Copious enquiries are made for you here, on all sides, and I am being introduced to innumerable wives on account of the pleasure other gents had in meeting you here.

Saw the Wendell Holmes, in the dining room—semper idem.[7] Have not seen the La Follettes & doubtless shall not today as I don't want to be lured into any late hours.

These Washington trolleys can almost hold their own in noise with the N.Y. Elevated.

Me for a lodge in some vast wilderness. Thermometers 80°—plenty of water—all sunshine and no mosquitos. Let's try it in Hawaii.

Summon A.H.G[rady].   Lovingly

1. Regarding the Controller Bay leases, see LDB to AGB, 28 July 1911, note 1.

2. In May the Supreme Court had handed down its decision in *United States v. American Tobacco Co.*, 221 U.S. 106 (1911), supporting the government's contention that the company had acted illegally in restraint of trade. The justices remanded the case to a lower court to oversee a reorganization of the giant firm; throughout October there was considerable attention in the popular and business press to the form the reorganization should take. LDB represented the National Cigar Leaf Company and the New York Leaf Tobacco Association in the reorganization hearings.

3. Gilson Gardner (1869–1935) was the Washington correspondent for the Newspaper Enterprise Association and would be closely associated with LDB in progressive politics over the next few years.

4. Thomas Woodrow Wilson (1856–1924) would play a crucial role in LDB's life for the next decade. After a successful career as a scholar, Wilson won the governorship of New Jersey in 1910 in a strong progressive campaign. After winning, he surprised everyone by carrying out his promises: he easily divorced himself from the Democratic machine and clamped down on corporate abuses. Wilson then set his sights on what had always been his dream, the presidency. Wilson was a magnificent speaker, whose talks clearly reflected his deep moral passion.

Originally a Grover Cleveland Democrat, by 1911 Wilson had moved much closer to the Bryanite reform wing of the party, but he found himself unable to articulate a clear message about what he considered the major economic problem of the times, the danger of monopoly to the American economic and political system. In August 1912 he would meet with LDB, who provided him with the rationale for an antitrust program, the regulation of competition as opposed to Theodore Roosevelt's call to regulate monopolies. (See LDB to Alfred Brandeis, 29 August 1912, and to Wilson, 30 September 1912, BL.) There is evidence that Wilson never completely understood the Brandeisian philosophy, but he trusted the man and soon came to rely on him for advice. LDB thus had a major hand in shaping Wilson's program, and Wilson's leading biographer, Arthur S. Link, called LDB the "intellectual architect of the New Freedom" (*Wilson: The Road to the White House* [Princeton, 1947], 489). After deciding not to name LDB to a cabinet position in 1913, Wilson nominated him to the Supreme Court three years later.

5. Frederick William Lehmann (1853–1931) had a successful law practice and civic career in St. Louis before becoming solicitor general in 1910. During his tenure he enjoyed a reputation as an honest and independent agent, highly thought of by reformers otherwise disenchanted with the Taft administration.

6. George Wickersham, the attorney general.

7. Always the same.

To: Alice Goldmark Brandeis
Date: October 21, 1911
Place: New York, New York
Source: Gilbert MSS

DEAREST: Be sure to get hold of A.H.G[rady]. soon & straighten her out, & remember the treatment requires periodical doses.

Had a pleasant talk at the La Follettes last evening. He looks finely, never better & has settled (as per Associated Press Despatch [*sic*] of today) the Western tour with a No. He is just finishing Article No. 5, has just begun Article No. 6. So you see he will need all of December to complete the 10.[1]

Sere Matthews say LaF. can't be nominated, but Taft can be defeated for nomination, but W. Wilson cannot.

Arthur W. Drum says Taft will be nominated & elected. Gilson Gardner's views you know. So now take your choice.

LaF's have Gilbert Rowe's [*sic*][2] 5 year old boy with them for a month—to accommodate the Rowes & are very happy with him. A cousin's son (Rep. La F. of Washington State[3] being the cousin) was also there, with a fine Western spirit that make[s] one tired of the "effete East."

I heard a little Southern Oratory today from the Atty's General of the Great South,[4] & then fled for a two hour tramp in the most miserable weather. Wet. Muggy dark, but the aftermath of a long tramp is always good, & I treated myself to complete seclusion for dinner—dining chez moi.

The suitcase had not reached Washington when I left & I am approaching famine, but I suppose it will be here Monday.

I lunched [with] Frankfurter[5] yesterday, who called me up & brought with him Asst. Atty. Denison,[5] who has had a terrible case of typhoid. After 6 months he is little good & the Doctor says it will take him 2 years to get back his strength.[7] I got in a little work I think toward the Atty Genl re Tobacco through them.   Lovingly

172

1. La Follette's autobiography ran in the *American Magazine* between October 1911 and July 1912 and was written by La Follette with the help of Ray Stannard Baker. It had been planned as a campaign document for La Follette's run for the Republican presidential nomination, a project aborted by La Follette's health in early 1912. The articles appeared in book form in 1913.

2. Gilbert Ernstein Roe (1865–1929), then a New York attorney, had once been La Follette's law partner in Wisconsin and continued to work closely with him on political and reform matters.

3. William L. La Follette (1860–1934) grew up in Indiana but moved west at age seventeen to be a farmer and stock grower. He served in the Washington House of Representatives from 1899 to 1901 and in the U.S. House of Representatives from 1911 to 1919.

4. The southern officials had come to New York in regard to the tobacco reorganization; see LDB to AGB, 19 October 1911, note 2.

5. The relationship with Felix Frankfurter (1882–1965) would be one of the closest and most important of LDB's life. Born in Vienna, Frankfurter came to the United States as a child of twelve. He attended City College and then went on to a brilliant career at Harvard Law School. After a brief and unhappy stint in a private firm, he joined Henry Stimson's staff as an assistant U.S. attorney for the Southern District of New York and then followed Stimson to Washington, where he was currently working in the Bureau of Insular Affairs.

Frankfurter and LDB soon became close friends, and it was LDB who helped persuade Frankfurter to accept a position at the Harvard Law School, where he taught until appointed to the Supreme Court in 1939. While there Frankfurter became LDB's surrogate, both in Zionist affairs (where he played a minor role) and most importantly in carrying on reform work during the 1920s and 1930s. The relationship has been explored in Bruce Allen Murphy's *The Brandeis/Frankfurter Connection* (New York, 1982), but a somewhat different interpretation can be inferred from the documents, which are collected in Urofsky and Levy, eds., *"Half Brother, Half Son": The Letters of Louis D. Brandeis to Felix Frankfurter* (Norman, 1991).

6. Winfred Thaxter Denison (1873–1919), a New York attorney, served in a number of government positions. He was then in the Justice Department and shared quarters with Frankfurter, Robert Valentine, and other young progressives at 1727 Nineteenth Street, dubbed "The House of Truth," a place that LDB would often visit on his increasingly frequent trips to Washington.

7. Denison's health never fully recovered, and he died during the great influenza epidemic in 1919.

To:	Alice Goldmark Brandeis
Date:	October 23, 1911
Place:	New York, New York
Source:	Gilbert MSS

DEAREST: As yet nothing from you since Friday's letter. Possibly I may find something this evening.

My suitcase has come & my lightweight shoes have been resoled & heeled. The sun shone properly today & I walked to Wall St. & back & considerable besides so I feel quite virtuous & can assure you that the avoir du pois has not increased in the last week.[1]

Had a long talk with Ass[istan]t Atty Genl McReynolds[2] who ought to be running the Tobacco Case & is not allowed to. He tried to say little, but

I am sure has no more confidence in G[eorge]. W[ickersham].'s doing what "the people" want than a rampant insurgent. The proof of my objections has come back & I am looking it over in solitude. Indeed I shall probably have some time for study now. The Southern Attys General have departed. Another Southern delegation leaves tonight & with diminishing forces, "thought may have its required clearness."[3]

Hope to hear good reports of the Dedham Sunday.　　　　　Lovingly

1. See LDB to AGB, 17 October 1911.

2. James Clark McReynolds (1862–1946) first gained public attention when he resigned as an assistant attorney general during the Roosevelt administration in protest against what he considered ineffective enforcement of the antitrust law. He was currently dividing his time between private practice in New York and service as a special prosecutor in the American Tobacco antitrust case. His reputation as a foe of monopoly would lead Wilson to name him as attorney general, but this proved a major error. McReynolds, aside from his hatred of trusts, was no progressive; quite the contrary, he was conservative to the point of reaction. To get him out of the cabinet Wilson named him to the Supreme Court in 1914, and for the next twenty-seven years he anchored the conservative bloc on the Court. Relations between McReynolds and LDB were never warm and took a downturn when the anti-Semitic McReynolds found LDB as a colleague after 1916.

3. Shakespeare, *Macbeth*, III, 1.

To:	Alice Goldmark Brandeis
Date:	November 14, 1911
Place:	Washington, D.C.
Source:	Gilbert MSS

DEAREST: Wade Ellis[1] fortunately had an unfinished case in the Supreme Court,[2] and our conference was adjourned until two today. This gave me a chance for a long longed for walk, doubly welcome after a strenuous yesterday; and I had a stiff 8 mile tramp along the Potomac—mainly where the extended Park is to be. It will be an extraordinarily fine park when once completed. The retaining wall is finished.

This Antitrust fight will be a hard one, and our own friends much divided—more or less imbued with the idea of monopoly inevitableness. I think it probable that we shall get some valuable thinking on the subject at any rate. That the country will repeal the Sherman Law seems to me almost impossible; but it is highly probable that some changes will be made, mainly in respect to the Court's powers & discretion. The recent Commerce Court decision enjoining the order of the Commission in the Spokane Case[3] is exciting much adverse comment & may lead to the abolition of the Court, to the creation of which there was much opposition—a Taft measure.

Nothing yet from you today.

　　　　　Lovingly

Has Do or the office heard from the Atty Genl of Ohio?[4]
Tomorrow is Mother's Birthday.

1. Wade H. Ellis (1866–1948), originally a Cincinnati lawyer, was attorney general of Ohio from 1904 to 1908 and assistant to the U.S. attorney general from 1908 to 1910. He then stayed on to practice law in Washington.

2. *United States v. Eckstein,* 222 U.S. 130 (1911), dealt with whether the Board of Customs had properly classified artificial horsehair for tariff duties; Ellis's client had appealed the decision and lost in the High Court.

3. On 4 January 1910 the Interstate Commerce Commission ordered the railroad companies to cease charging lower rates for coal intended for railway consumption than were charged against other users. The railroads appealed to the Commerce Court, which, among other powers, had the power to review and reverse orders of the ICC. The court reversed this order, saying that the ICC had exceeded its authority and that the railroads had justification to charge themselves a lower rate for coal they used. The ICC appealed the ruling, and the Supreme Court reversed, finding in favor of the commission. *Interstate Commerce Commission v. Baltimore & Ohio Railroad Co. et al.,* 225 U.S. 326 (1912).

4. LDB had been invited to defend the Ohio nine-hour law, and he did so successfully in the Ohio Supreme Court in *Ex parte Anna Hawley,* 85 Ohio 495 (1911). The constitutionality of the act was then appealed to the U.S. Supreme Court, where LDB again prepared the brief and took part in oral argument. The High Court upheld the law in *Hawley v. Walker,* 232 U.S. 718 (1914).

To:	Alice Goldmark Brandeis
Date:	November 15, 1911
Place:	Washington, D.C.
Source:	Gilbert MSS

DEAREST: My letters seemed to bunch. The late arrival of the Nov 10 reflects discredit on the Twentieth Century Limited. It should have been mailed according to schedule—at Elkhart, Indiana.

The Trust discussion won't let me in peace. Ray Stannard Baker called me up yesterday to talk bonus which we did at dinner at the Tea Cup with Felix Frankfurter as accidental companion. Later La Follette called me up to say he was arranging to have Van Hise & Commons[1] here Sunday for discussion & a call came also from Senator Clapp who was in this morning for an hour to discuss the subject. I think there will be a battle royal. I am dead against the Middle of the Road. No regulated private monopoly of the capitalists. Either competition or State Socialism. Regulate competition, not monopoly is my slogan.[2] We have trouble enough with vested right, let us not begin with vested wrongs.

Lovingly

1. John Rogers Commons (1862–1944), a professor of economics at the University of Wisconsin, was one of the leading authorities on labor law and economics. He worked closely with La Follette and other progressives in drafting numerous bills and oversaw a number of studies on working conditions that provided factual material for reform efforts.

175

Perhaps his most famous work was the *History of Labor in the United States*, 4 vols. (New York, 1935), of which LDB's daughter Elizabeth wrote a part.

2. See LDB to Woodrow Wilson, 30 September 1912, BL.

To: Alice Goldmark Brandeis
Date: November 16, 1911
Place: Washington, D.C.
Source: Gilbert MSS

DEAREST: Well T.R. has burst into the Trust problem now[1] and that will help keeping it in the lime-light. But I don't think it greatly needs artificial publicity. It won't down, and if I had nothing else today, I could devote day & night to those who want to talk about it. My idea is to say nothing before the Senate Com[mit]tee[2] until *we* progressives have agreed fully on a program & then set it out in its entirety. We must have competition, even if we have to combine to get it.

At 2 today Pinchot, Gardner, Lathrop & I are to meet at Graham's to discuss Controller Bay, to the finish I trust.

In Tobacco Wickersham & Taft have behave[d] à la their mode.[3] As Ollie James says, "Left-handed with both hands."

Last evening I had to spend (a deferred dinner) at the Wade Ellis'. It was restful thanks to Mrs. E's engagement with the shampooer which with her [*]. She claimed to have met us—with the Mr. & Mrs. Davenports here last year & I think she is right. Although a Kentuckian, she is the least interested & interesting wife I have seen here.

Hope you will have a good Sunday.   Lovingly

1. On 26 October the Justice Department filed an antitrust suit against the U.S. Steel Corporation and in the bill of particulars implied that company officials had hoodwinked Roosevelt in 1907, when he had agreed to their request to buy the Tennessee Iron & Coal Company, supposedly to avert a panic on Wall Street. Roosevelt responded in an article in the *Outlook* in which he justified his actions in approving the purchase. He then went on to lambast Taft's "archaic" efforts to restore the competitive process by filing lawsuits against the great corporations, an effort he denounced as no more logical than a return "to the flintlocks of Washington's Continentals " The only way to cure the industrial problems of the country was to accept the inevitability, in fact the necessity, of industrial combination in modern life. This theme, of course, would be the core of the debate between Roosevelt and Wilson in the 1912 campaign. Theodore Roosevelt, "The Trusts, the People and the Square Deal," *Outlook* 99 (18 November 1911): 649–56.

2. The Senate Committee on Interstate Commerce was then holding hearings on the trust issue; in fact, LDB did testify before it for three days the following month, 14–16 December. Excerpts of the testimony can be found in Alfred Lief, ed., *The Social and Economic Views of Mr. Justice Brandeis* (New York, 1930), 372–75.

3. Despite pleas from independent tobacco producers as well as several of the southern state attorneys general, neither Taft nor Wickersham objected to the proposed settlement of the antitrust suit against the American Tobacco Company, which left much of the trust's

power intact. Taft had defended the Supreme Court decision as well as the settlement in a speech in South Dakota in late October; Wickersham had explicitly approved the settlement at the beginning of November and a few days earlier had announced that the government would not appeal the settlement.

To: **Alice Goldmark Brandeis**
Date: **November 18, 1911**
Place: **Washington, D.C.**
Source: **Gilbert MSS**

DEAREST: I am glad to hear E. Boston is moving along, and hope you are making Miss F. dance. Remember if the years work is compressed into 6 months it should be intense.

Do get A.H.G. in again soon. She needs the guide & the necessity of confronting an account of achievement. All she & her two aid[es] are doing for me (when away) other than S[avings].B[ank].I[nsurance] ought not to occupy one person's time more than 2 hrs. a day. S.B.I. reports seem encouraging in a number of respects & it seems a better time for push than any in the past.

Do's staying in Boston to complete the work is fortunate, & must be a special joy to Elizabeth.

I talked over with La Follette, Matt Hale[1] & E. Smith.[2] He had already heard from Houser[3] & was much pleased.

Dined with Gifford last evening & then went with him to LaF, as I heard H.K. Smith[4] was to be there to talk Trust Laws. We found Commons there also. On the whole it was I who did the talking. It was intentional as I have some apprehension of heresy on LaF's part & I want to forestall. This necessity of converting doubters has greatly aided me in clarifying my own views & improving my presentation. Am almost ready to talk in public & would be delighted at the chance of joint debate, e.g. with Garfield who has been misleading T.R. By the way, G's deluge was because he would not sign as favoring Initiative & Referendum. Just met Sen. Spooner here. It is 22 years this month since we first met him before I went to Louisville to see you. Also met Will Van Dyke[5] yesterday who has been seeing Howard Morris.[6]

Lovingly

Ainsworth Parker just enquired about you & the daughters.

1. Matthew Hale (1882–1925) worked for a year at LDB's law firm and then opened his own office; at this time he was one of the leading younger progressives in Massachusetts. Officially committed to La Follette's candidacy, he privately hoped that Theodore Roosevelt (whose children he had tutored) would enter the race. When Roosevelt did so in February 1912, Hale was one of the first to announce his support. LDB had probably discussed with La Follette bringing in Hale and Smith to work full-time on the campaign.

2. Ellison DuRant Smith (1864–1944) helped organize one of the largest cotton growers' associations in the South; he represented South Carolina in the U.S. Senate from 1909 until his death.

3. Walter L. Houser (1855–1928) was elected Wisconsin secretary of state and served in that office from 1903 to 1907 before returning to newspaper work. He had managed La Follette's recent senatorial campaign and would be in charge of his presidential bid.

4. Herbert Knox Smith (1869–1931), the federal commissioner of corporations, opposed antitrust laws. Under Theodore Roosevelt he had helped arrange the entente between big business and the administration that precluded antitrust attacks on the large Morgan interests.

5. William Duncan Van Dyke (1856–1932) was a Wisconsin lawyer and president of the Northwestern Mutual Life Insurance Co. Although a conservative in business matters and in his personal life, Van Dyke supported some progressive measures.

6. Howard Morris (1856–1922) was general counsel and vice-president of the Wisconsin Central Railroad.

To: **Alice Goldmark Brandeis**
Date: **November 18, 1911**
Place: **Washington, D.C.**
Source: **Gilbert MSS**

DEAREST: The C[ontroller]. B[ay]. conference came off satisfactorily yesterday. All present including Henry George Jr.[1] are reconciled. The Democratic majority are to be called together in about ten days & when they are converted, full Com[mit]tee is to meet & result be sprung. So there seems a high probability that that mine of work may be closed soon.

Forgot to tell you that I have entered upon the Walter Child[2] chest exercises and you may be prepared for a real chest development, which will overcome even your incredulity. The first two or three days I felt as much exercised as if I had been off on an all day paddle. You shall have an exhibit on my return.

My associate Felix H. Livy[3] is progressing finely in his self-advertising campaign. I doubt whether he is accomplishing much more, but the mere mention of protest against the Tobacco decree is valuable.

Cong. Stanley[4] (he of the Steel enquiry) of Ky. sent word he wanted to talk with me re Tobacco & I saw him while at the Capitol on C.B. matters. He would be quite ready to have me "aid" in concocting some legislation which he wants to introduce. Altogether I might well become a sort of Mother's Assistant to congressional legislators.

My meeting with Com'r. of Corp. Smith at LaF's was worthwhile. He telephoned me today, saying he wanted to call & talk over some questions, & later did so. It proves that he is in substantial accord with my views & left with the understanding that he would endeavor to draft a bill embodying them. His coincidence of view should be a potent leverage in keeping G.P[inchot]., La Follette & other progressives in line.

Wade Ellis interfered with my solitary walk by suggesting that he go with me, but he was really interested in a rather confidential talk, in which he expressed his views very freely about Taft and Wickersham, and altho a marked administration man has really reached the same opinions of them that we have. He seems also to have a realizing sense of the underlying movement in America which seemed to me rather to be a possession of the insurgent. He was Taft's manager in Ohio in 1910.

Jud Welliver[5] dined with me to pump me for an article on the Trust decision result which he is writing for Munseys, and in which my view will doubtless appear in a somewhat lurid form.[6] He is certain[ly] a pretty lively insurgent, and longing for greater freedom of expression. The surprising thing is that Munsey[7] with his 30 millions should let him write at all for his publications.

This evening Senator Clapp is coming in to talk Antitrust & particularly [the] Tobacco decision.[8] That noble issue of the Court's brain is certainly receiving quite comprehensive damning from all sides save Wall St. It will make fine kindling for Congressional oratory.

Senator Clapp came in & was [so] full of indignation that it took $2\frac{1}{2}$ hours to empty the cask. It is difficult to see just what ought to be done, but there will be plenty, apparently, eager to take a hand.

Felix H. [Livy] is to be here today Sunday in preparation of his instructing the Com[mit]tee tomorrow.[9] Samuel Untermeyer [sic] did so yesterday as the Ev. Transcript doubtless advised you.[10]

Despite varied interest the week has greatly rested me & I am in fine shape. The multitude of counsel may not conduce to safety, but in the Coal Case it relieves from responsibility.

Lovingly

The denial of oral argument by the Ct. in Ohio is quite a labor saver for me though rather unfortunate for the Const[itution].[11]

---

1. Henry George, Jr. (1862–1916), the son of the famous single tax advocate, was a newspaperman and a member of the House of Representatives from New York from 1911 to 1915.

2. Horace Walter Child was a prosperous shoe manufacturer and expert on orchids who lived in Worcester, Massachusetts. LDB met him shortly after coming to Cambridge, and the two men remained life-long friends. He was the father of the noted writer and diplomat Richard Washburn Child. For LDB's affectionate view of him, see LDB to Alfred Brandeis, 19 June 1927.

3. Felix H. Livy was a New York attorney and co-counsel with LDB for the independent tobacco growers and manufacturers who objected to the proposed tobacco settlement that would still have left enormous power in the hands of the giant companies like American Tobacco.

4. Augustus Owsley Stanley (1867–1958) served in the House of Representatives from 1903 to 1915. After one term as governor of Kentucky, he returned to the Congress as a senator from 1919 to 1925. Stanley had presided over the House hearings into the steel trust and in 1914 would work closely with LDB in the preparation of the Clayton Antitrust Act.

5. Judson Churchill Welliver (1870–1943), originally an Iowa journalist, now wrote out of Washington and had important ties within the Republican Party. During the 1920 presidential campaign he directed publicity for Warren G. Harding and in the following decade advised Harding, Coolidge, and Hoover.

6. Welliver did not write such an article for *Munsey's*. He did, however, write a flattering portrait of LDB in "Louis D. Brandeis: Troublemaker." *World Today* 21 (January 1912): 1603–7.

7. Frank Andrew Munsey (1854–1925) published not only the magazine that bore his name but several newspapers as well. He was a strong supporter of Theodore Roosevelt in 1912.

8. See LDB to AGB, 19 October 1911, note 2.

9. The Senate Committee on Interstate Commerce, which was holding antitrust hearings. Livy's testimony dealt primarily with the impact the proposed tobacco settlement would have on small growers and manufacturers.

10. On 18 November Samuel Untermyer spent several hours before the Senate Committee on Interstate and Foreign Commerce attacking both the steel and tobacco trusts. "The Steel Trust," he said, "is the most flagrant violation of law ever known" (*New York Times,* 19 November 1911). As for the tobacco settlement, which allegedly broke up the monopoly, it had proven completely ineffective.

11. See LDB to AGB, 14 November 1911, note 4.

To: **Alice Goldmark Brandeis**
Date: **November 20, 1911**
Place: **Washington, D.C.**
Source: **Gilbert MSS**

DEAREST: Some of the Cabinet are not as fearful of contagion as C[harles]. N[agel]. Met Stimson yesterday on the street. He stopped to express his thanks for the aid my article "Organized Labor & Efficiency"[1] had been to him & asked me to lunch today. I had to decline because of the coal case, but told him I should take the liberty of letting him know as soon as I was free.

The conference at LaF's proceeded yesterday—Van Hise, Commons, George L. Record,[2] R[ay]. S[tannard]. Baker & I. The agony is over & LaF's statement whenever made will be for competition.[3] Commons has been here 10 days & helped him prepare it. V.H.'s view was quite narrow, although of course intelligent. He claimed for it much professorial & some financier support, but he got little from us & I pitched it to him hard.

Of course this is not the end of the Wisc. Movement, but I think the Senator is safe.

Now for coal.   Lovingly

1. *Survey,* 26 (22 April 1911): 148–51.
2. George Lawrence Record (1859–1933) was perhaps the most important figure in New Jersey progressivism before Woodrow Wilson came on the scene. He took part in shaping nearly every major reform in the state after 1890.

3. La Follette had been unsure of whether to follow LDB's advice regarding the regulation of competition or that put forward by Van Hise and the Wisconsin school, which favored regulation of monopolies. See LDB to AGB, 15 and 18 November 1911.

To: **Alice Goldmark Brandeis**
Date: **November 25, 1911**
Place: **Washington, D.C.**
Source: **Gilbert MSS**

DEAREST: The Symphony program is fine. I wish I might join you.

The morning papers bring out a rather faint denial by T.R. which is quite aggravating.[1] One feels almost a sympathy for the Mephistophelean attack of William Randolph Hearst.[2] It would be so easy to give a positive denial, & set his "friends" at rest.

It is quite possible that the coal hearings may end today. It will be a relief—daily hearings of anything are a nuisance, even if one take[s] a languid part. I am to examine your friend Mr. Muller today on 136 pp. exhibit.

Wade Ellis is a pretty good fellow, able and thorough with some nice traits that go down deep. His friendship for the fat man[3] don't blind him to his shortcomings nor to those of Atty Genl.

Auf baldiges wiedersehen,[4]   Lovingly

1. Roosevelt continued to deny that he intended running for the Republican nomination for president in 1912. Although some scholars believe Roosevelt was sincere in this view, at least until early 1912, LDB and other La Follette supporters suspected that despite his denials he intended to make the run.
2. William Randolph Hearst (1863–1951), the flamboyant newspaper editor and publisher, built up a chain of papers by exploiting the public's insatiable desire for sensationalism. He served a term in Congress, but thereafter his various attempts to win elected office were unsuccessful.
3. President Taft.
4. See you shortly.

To: **Alice Goldmark Brandeis**
Date: **December 14, 1911**
Place: **Washington, D.C.**
Source: **Gilbert MSS**

DEAREST: Yes Susan's letter is amusing. She is fine [in] her tribulations & her joys.

Listened most of yesterday to George W. Perkins[1] before the Senate Interstate Commerce Com[mit]tee—the weakest rot man ever uttered. It was hard to keep quiet under it, & I should rejoice to go through the country on joint debate with him.[2] I think I could stand a continuous performance with him & [Elbert H.] Gary—for a season.

I am to talk, i.e. testify today myself, and must be off. I should rather make a speech, but perhaps it will fall into something like that.[3]

Lovingly

1. George Walbridge Perkins (1862–1920) rose from insurance clerk to a partnership in the House of Morgan before he was thirty, and he aided Morgan in organizing some of the great trusts, including U.S. Steel and International Harvester. In 1912 Perkins would be a principal architect and financial backer of Theodore Roosevelt's Progressive Party.

2. The Perkins testimony may be found in U.S. Senate, Committee on Interstate Commerce, *Hearings* . . . , 62d Cong., 2d Sess. (Washington, D.C., 1912), 15:1089–1145. Perkins believed in rationalizing business and argued that cooperation should take the place of competition in the market, a position diametrically opposed to that of LDB.

3. In fact, LDB would be on the stand for three days. His testimony can be found in *Hearings,* 16:1146–1291.

To: **Alice Goldmark Brandeis**
Date: **December 16, 1911**
Place: **Washington, D.C.**
Source: **Gilbert MSS**

DEAREST: You may have seen from the papers that I spent the whole of yesterday also "on the stand", and the Senators were not quite ready to let me go when the Com[mit]tee adjourned last evening so I shall be on for a little while at least this morning.

About all, or a fair share of all my social economic views are being embalmed in the Com[mit]tee records & you will have quite a task catching up when the printed volume reaches you. Think of ten hours fairly rapid talk so embalmed. There is good evidence that a deep impression has been made upon them. Even upon the Standpatters. My dear friend, the Junior Senator of Mass.,[1] feels it his duty to be constantly present & he has been most of the time & listens with pretended satisfaction.

It was fortun[at]e that my talk came after Gary & Perkins, and the many sky travelling palavers who preceded me. The Tobacco Trust & Shoe Machinery have been well explained, & I think most of the Com[mit]tee's faith in Bigness been jarred.

Lovingly

1. Winthrop Murray Crane.

To: **Alice Goldmark Brandeis**
Date: **January 4, 1912**
Place: **Minneapolis, Minnesota**
Source: **Gilbert MSS**

DEAREST: My luncheon talk at Chicago before 500 was declared a "howling success"—indeed an "unequalled [*]" & the luncheon talk here before

200 likewise.[1] It was of a wholly different character than the Chicago one. My talk at Madison last night (after 6 hours travelling from C.) before some 1500 or 2000 students et al was much less successful but not very bad. Tonight I talk again here & then start for Chicago.

I think I am better known in this country than in most of New England. Minneapolis is an insurgent nest.

Weather 30° below, now 20° is exhilarating to such a degree that one feels neither the cold nor man though I have been multifariously personally conducted every moment of the day.

Goodnight   Lovingly

1. At the urging of La Follette and his campaign managers, LDB agreed to go on a speaking tour in favor of the senator's candidacy. Despite protests that he had never engaged in political campaigning, LDB drew large crowds and generally favorable reviews. See Mason, *Brandeis,* 371–72.

To: Alice Goldmark Brandeis
Date: January 7, 1912
Place: Washington, D.C.
Source: Gilbert MSS

DEAREST: Met Glavis today. He is here on behalf of the State of California looking up titles in the land office, & Bill Kent tells me that when [Walter] Fisher heard of it, he gave a "Bureau" with six clerks at his disposal & also sent for Dennett[1] to direct him to aid Glavis in every way. Such is the whirligig of time.

I have concluded to give the Stanley Com[mit]tee[2] a talk of Steel Trust Labor Policy in a few weeks. That will give me the chance to talk of "Pension Peonage".[3]

Glavis is very nice, but one can't help feeling on meeting him now somewhat as if one were seeing the stage heroes the next day, with paint washed off in ordinary clothes, and a little washed out look.

Have been out for a walk with beautiful sunshine, upon the snow, wearing the rain coat. By this afternoon the Sham[4] may be in order.

I am to lunch with Gifford [Pinchot] at 1 o'clock, & am anxious to hear his latest about Ohio & T.R.[5] At 4 I am to meet Lenroot & shall probably drop in at Bob [La Follette]'s who should return by that time; & between luncheon & 4 I am to see Stanley's accountant to learn some Steel Corp. matters.

Lovingly

Let A.H.G[rady]. give you a copy of my talk before the Senate Committee.[6]

1. Fred Dennett (1863–1928) was appointed by Roosevelt and retained by Taft as commissioner of the General Land Office.

2. The growing antitrust movement led a House Committee headed by Augustus Stanley of Kentucky to begin extensive investigations into the activities of the U.S. Steel Corporation in late 1911. The hearings focused on the dealings of Andrew Carnegie, J. P. Morgan, and other financiers, and especially the negotiations involving then-president Roosevelt that led to U.S. Steel's takeover of Tennessee Coal & Iron Co. in 1907. See House Special Committee, *United States Steel Corporation: Hearings . . . ,* 62d Cong., 1st Sess. (Washington, D.C., 1912).

3. LDB testified before the committee on 29 and 30 January 1912; his testimony is in *Hearings,* 2835–72. In his testimony LDB analyzed the much-discussed pension and profit-sharing plan that U.S. Steel had inaugurated. The pensions were given at the discretion of the company, however, and workers had no accrued rights. Thus a worker who joined a union or protested working conditions could be denied a pension, even after serving the company faithfully for many years. LDB charged that by tying the pension to conduct, U.S. Steel reduced employees to a status little better than slavery. He proposed instead a system in which a pension depended solely on an investment in an annuity and in which the worker had vested rights. He condensed the testimony and published it as "Our New Peonage: Discretionary Pensions," *Independent* 73 (25 July 1912): 187–91.

4. A light-weight coat.

5. With Roosevelt acting more and more like a candidate, progressive forces, especially in the Midwest, began calling on him formally to enter the race for the Republican nomination. Ohio insurgents were supportive of the colonel's nascent candidacy, especially since Ohio was President Taft's home state.

6. LDB's testimony before the Senate Committee on Interstate Commerce, delivered 14–16 December; see LDB to AGB, 14 and 16 December 1911.

To: **Alice Goldmark Brandeis**
Date: **January 10, 1912**
Place: **Washington D.C.**
Source: **Gilbert MSS**

DEAREST: I went up to La Follettes after dinner yesterday & found the Senator quite rehabilitated.[1] He had sent for me to talk more antitrust legislation with the Wisconsin contingent, but I found him reading to the assembled company one of his favorite Irish stories, & his reading continued for a good part of an hour—marvellous recuperative powers.

The Coal Case[2] promises to finish tomorrow & I must try to be in N.Y. Friday on Steam Block[er] matters,[3] having been visited here last evening by one of them.

I made a long intimate visit on Mrs. Shaler yesterday.

Have just seen Frank Lyon who sends his greetings & met Walter Fisher whom I shall call on if time [*].

Expect to leave here tomorrow night.

Lovingly

Albert [Brandeis] is here.

1. La Follette was suffering from exhaustion, which would eventually lead to his ill-tempered speech before the Magazine Publishers' Association in Philadelphia on 2 February. See the next letter.

2. For the background of the case, see LDB to AGB, 14 November 1911, note 3. It would be argued on 12 and 15 January, and a decision handed down on 7 June. In an opinion for a unanimous Court, Justice McKenna had ruled that the ICC had the appropriate authority and reversed the Commerce Court.

3. LDB was still involved in trying to make the New York garment industry protocol work.

To:	**Alice Goldmark Brandeis**
Date:	**February 3, 1912**
Place:	**Kearney, Nebraska**
Source:	**Gilbert MSS**

DEAREST: Two speeches at York yesterday & 2 at Hastings today & another here this evening—with the thermometer today below zero and breeze blowing that would do honor to Otis Place.[1] The pull politically is a pretty hard one. The York meetings were as meetings great successes, the only ones that can be termed such, and I should not feel that the trip was worthwhile except as giving La Follette some moral support when he was most in need of it.[2]

Pretty much all the world is progressive here. La Follette would have an easy time with T.R. out of the way to see Nebraska at the primaries & would be surer of election with a large Democratic support. Many of those at the meeting are Democrats & not a few Socialists & many are declaring that the separation of Republican Progressives from the Democratic Progressives ought to cease. But the love for T.R. lies deep.

I feel off in the wilderness—No New York paper since last Tuesday & only occasional Chicago dailies. I see Bob has raised (doubtless unwisely) the ire of Don Seitz.[3] The [New York] World will have had [a] time deciding between its enmities—T.R. & La Follette—and at times Taft.

Lovingly

1. LDB was on another campaign swing for La Follette, starting in Chicago on 31 January and ending with his return to Dedham on 11 February. Otis Place was the Brandeises' residence.

2. The evening before La Follette had succumbed to nervousness and exhaustion. Heavy speaking and writing obligations had worn down his physical reserves, and then his younger daughter Mary was taken ill and scheduled for a dangerous operation on 3 February. Although he wanted to cancel the engagement, La Follette reluctantly agreed to speak at the Periodical Publishers' banquet in Philadelphia. He arrived late and was suffering from nausea when he arose to speak. Rather than giving the relatively short political speech that had been expected, La Follette launched into a rambling indictment of the press in general and of the way he had been treated. Rumors immediately spread that he had suffered a nervous breakdown, and they gained credence when he remained in seclusion for the next few

weeks. Although he never formally withdrew from the race, the episode marked the end of any viable candidacy. On 7 February LDB wrote to his brother: "The news from La Follette is of course distressing, but if the smash is not a bad one, it may be all for the best to have him completely out of the Presidential race. I was sorry when he concluded to enter it. Personally I shall be glad to have no political obligations."

3. Don Carlos Seitz (1862–1935) was the business manager of the *New York World* and the author of a number of books. Seitz was the toastmaster at the catastrophic Philadelphia meeting where La Follette broke down. After the rambling speech was over, Seitz rose and apologized for what he called La Follette's unfounded, irresponsible, and "wicked" attack on the members of the press (many of whom were invited guests). In their biography of the senator, Belle and Fola La Follette closed their account of the episode with this paragraph: "While in the West Brandeis had read the newspapers, and on the train from St. Louis to New York he wrote a little note to Belle. 'My thoughts have been much with you and Bob and the children,' he said, 'and I long to be East where I may hear something authentic. Only make Bob take the rest he needs and make a pleasure trip out of this necessity. When he comes back we will take up the good fight again together. With much love.' In the midst of misrepresentation and desertion, it was a comfort to Bob and Belle to have this assurance of love and loyalty." La Follette and La Follette, *La Follette*, 406.

To:	Alice Goldmark Brandeis
Date:	February 4, 1912
Place:	Kearney, Nebraska
Source:	Gilbert MSS

DEAREST: At 11:45 A.M. I am to start East—for Omaha—& this evening am to leave there for Kansas City. Next Sunday I hope to be with you at Dedham, and after my next excursions to Washington re Coal[1] and Old Dominion cases[2] hope to cling near to threshold of 6 Otis Place.

I feel at the moment remote from all the world. Such glimpses of Eastern life which the local papers afford make the distance seem even greater than if I were left in utter darkness.

The fat man [Taft] has made a fatuous suggestion of the Government building an Alaskan railroad to be operated by private capitalists, which will make attacks upon him easy and the carrying out of the project very difficult.[3] His endorsement of the Industrial Commission project,[4] which in some form was drafted by Dr. Devine,[5] seems at this distance rather swollen inter alias. If something is to come of it Borah[6] had better be the champion.

There was quite a good attendance last night in spite of below zero weather & good attention. But Nebraskan freemen are certainly not demonstrative. Lovingly

1. See LDB to AGB, 14 November 1911, note 3, and 10 January 1912, note 2.
2. Albert S. Bigelow and an associate named Lewisohn, while officers of the Old Dominion Mining & Smelting Company, sold some of the company's assets, secretly acquiring great profit for themselves. Later new officers of the company sued to recover those

profits, which they alleged properly belonged to the company. They filed a suit against Lewisohn in New York court and an identical bill in a Massachusetts court against Bigelow. The New York suit was decided first, with both the trial court and the court of appeals deciding that Lewisohn had done nothing illegal. Bigelow, represented by LDB, then claimed that the New York decision served as a bar against further proceedings in Massachusetts, since the Massachusetts court under Article IV's Full Faith and Credit Clause had to treat the New York decision as a final decision in the entire matter. The Massachusetts court disagreed, and Bigelow appealed, finally reaching the Supreme Court. There, by an 8–0 decision, the Court held that since Bigelow had been neither a party to nor privy to the New York suit the Massachusetts court had acted correctly in not considering the New York decision as a bar. *Albert S. Bigelow v. Old Dominion Mining & Smelting Co.,* 225 U.S. 111 (1912).

3. The Taft plan, ultimately announced on 20 March, called for the army, not private companies, to bisect Alaska by a new railroad, using the equipment left over from construction of the Panama Canal. See *New York Times,* 21 March 1912.

4. On 30 December 1911 LDB and thirty-eight other prominent progressives sent a letter to Taft urging him to establish a federal commission to look into the causes of industrial unrest. Taft had already been considering some form of industrial investigation and may also have been drawn to the idea by the hope of gaining political credits with social workers in the 1912 election. In his State of the Union message on 2 February, Taft formally requested Congress to establish a Commission on Industrial Relations. After intense lobbying efforts by labor and social justice groups, Congress approved the proposal, and Taft signed it into law on 23 August 1912. His nominees for the commission, however, aroused such resentment in the Senate that it fell to Woodrow Wilson to name the members.

5. Edward Thomas Devine (1867–1948) was editor of the *Survey* and was involved with many of the social justice groups around the country.

6. William Edgar Borah (1865–1940) was then serving the first of his six terms as United States senator from Idaho. A leading progressive Republican, Borah is mainly remembered for his isolationist fights against American entry into the League of Nations and his determination to keep America out of any involvement with European affairs in the 1920s and 1930s.

To: **Alice Goldmark Brandeis**
Date: **February 7, 1912**
Place: **En route to New York**
Source: **Gilbert MSS**

DEAREST: The day at St. Louis was a success. I was delighted to have the time with Uncle William [Taussig], and a nice visit in the afternoon with Aunt Adele, whom the nurses brought down, clad in gorgeous black silk as of old. Her memory seems perfect and but for her regrets about herself (which were ever present in her mind but not expressed) she would have seemed quite her old self—only older.

I also had moment's visit at James Taussig's. He lost his wife recently. His son Ben was my companion & escort from the lunch hour until I left at 5.

Walt Fishel & Walter McClubb and many others I saw for a moment at the luncheon, which seemed to go off very well. They say they never had a larger crowd (even when Taft spoke) although the Club members didn't receive their notices of the meeting until that morning. The greatest compliment paid me was from my new friend Judge Amidon[1] of South [*sic*] Dakota, the Federal District Judge (appointed by Cleveland & intimate of T.R.) who subjected himself to the full treatment again yesterday in St. Louis after having sat through the session in Kansas City. Amidon has been in much communication with T.R. on the Presidency & thinks *he* thinks that he is necessary to prevent a reactionary President—Taft or Harmon[2] being elected.

Shall hope for a letter from you this evening.

1. Charles Fremont Amidon (1856–1937) served as United States district court judge in North Dakota from 1896 to 1928.
2. Judson Harmon (1846–1927) was attorney general in Cleveland's second term. In 1909 he was elected to the first of two terms as governor of Ohio and was one of the early contenders for the 1912 Democratic presidential nomination.

To: Alice Goldmark Brandeis
Date: February 8, 1912
Place: New York, New York
Source: Gilbert MSS

DEAREST: As I wrote you, arrived at 7:30. Then I walked up & saw Mother & Millie for a little, & later disposed (I hope) of Charles Henry[1] from whom 3 letters were awaiting me.

I have been busy all morning with engagements, strangely most of them business matters. Think I may return to some private business if La Follette drops out of the race.[2] No others [*sic*] politics for me.

Expect to go to Mothers to talk legislation with Do this evening.

Moskowitz[3] is waiting below to lunch with me   Lovingly

1. Perhaps Charles Lewis Henry (1849–1927), a former Indiana congressman and electric traction magnate and president of the American Electric Railway Association. He frequently testified before the ICC and congressional committees on matters of interest to the association.
2. La Follette never formally withdrew, but his candidacy was no longer viable.
3. Henry Moskowitz (1879–1936) was closely associated with LDB as secretary of the Board of Arbitration established under the garment industry protocol. An important social worker, Moskowitz was active not only in labor relations but in the settlement house movement, civic reform, and Jewish communal work.

To: Alice Goldmark Brandeis
Date: February 9, 1912
Place: New York, New York
Source: Gilbert MSS

DEAREST: I am longing for Sunday morning with you, & wishing I might "jump["] tonight & tomorrow. Perhaps this evening's performance may make N.Y. overcome its desire to hear me.

Max Eastman[1] has been after me for the Suffrage Meeting, Howe[2] for a Carnegie Hall Trust talk, Hilquit [*sic*][3] for an Intercollegiate Social[ist] Trust talk, Percy Grant[4] for his Church talk, but I am obdurate. I have no talk engagement between now & June 19.

I do hope Bob will go abroad & I wish Bess [Evans] would go with him & of course he should start at once & finish the autobiography there.[5]

Impress Bess with this & let her hammer Belle.

Up to the moment I have escaped my progressive friends except the newspaper men. George Rublee came down to breakfast with me. The private practice is becoming wearisome—particularly Bigelow.[6] He is veering to Woodrow Wilson.   Lovingly

1. Max Forrester Eastman (1883–1969) was one of the nation's leading Socialists and the next year would begin his editorship of the influential journal *The Masses*. Over his long lifetime Eastman was a prolific writer on political and cultural issues.

2. Frederic Clemson Howe (1867–1940), a pioneer muckraker and urban reformer, was best known for his book *The City, the Hope of Democracy* (New York, 1905). He was also secretary of the National Progressive Republican League.

3. Morris Hillquit (1869–1933), a leading Socialist, was involved in the garment workers' protocol and in 1915 became counsel to the International Ladies' Garment Workers' Union (ILGWU).

4. Percy Stickney Grant (1860–1927) was born and educated in New England; in 1893 he was called to New York to become rector of the Church of the Ascension. He was the author of several books on the moral and religious aspects of contemporary social issues.

5. *La Follette's Autobiography: A Personal Narrative of Political Experiences* would be published early in 1913.

6. Albert Bigelow, LDB's client in the Old Dominion case; see LDB to AGB, 4 February 1912.

To: **Alice Goldmark Brandeis**
Date: **March 2, 1912**
Place: **Washington, D.C.**
Source: **Gilbert MSS**

DEAREST: Just finished short argument in Coal Case.[1] I don't feel particularly satisfied with it & don't feel as if I had contributed to the case, but I think we ought to get fairly favorable decision.

The John Graham Brooks[es][2] leave this afternoon for Boston. Possibly you may see them before I return. Our Old Dominion Case is on the list Monday but is not likely to be reached before the latter part of the week.[3] I wish it might go over a little longer, so as to get Pitney[4] on the bench. He probably will take his seat on the Monday following March 11.[5] It would be too bad to get in just before he takes [the] seat.

Called on Pinchot last evening. Was glad to find he had left for the west the day before.

Lovingly

1. See LDB to AGB, 14 November 1911, note 3, and 10 January 1912, note 2.

2. John Graham Brooks (1846–1938) was one of the nation's leading labor sociologists and reformers and an old friend of LDB's. A former Unitarian minister, he had given up the pulpit and moved to Cambridge in 1891 where, for the next four decades, he devoted himself to studying labor conditions and writing widely about his findings.

3. In fact the Court heard oral argument on the following Tuesday and Wednesday, 5 and 6 March; for the case, see LDB to AGB, 4 February 1912.

4. Mahlon Pitney (1858–1924) served in the New Jersey legislature, the House of Representatives, and the New Jersey Supreme Court and as chancellor of the state before Taft named him to the United States Supreme Court. There he earned a reputation as a reactionary for his antilabor opinions.

5. LDB was correct. Pitney was sworn in on 18 March 1912.

To: Alfred Brandeis
Date: April 30, 1912
Place: Boston, Massachusetts
Source: Brandeis MSS

DEAR AL: Today will probably settle matters between Taft & T.R.—with chances in the latter's favor. Certainly if Taft is defeated in Mass[achusetts], his goose seems cooked.[1] There is a fine fight here, and I am sad that I can't be in it. It is a real "Wenn's Gold regnet."[2]

If we could only have had such an impasse between conservatism & progress—instead of the issue of T.R.!

The Missouri outcome must be a special grief to Charlie [Nagel].[3] Altogether it is "a fine day for the lizard." Gifford P[inchot] dined with us today. Sen. Clapp was in yesterday. It is possible he may want me in Washington soon on the La Follette Bill. But there is little legislation in this Congress & I doubt it.

It looks as if Mass. Democracy would go for Clark.[4]

1. Despite strenuous campaigning by Theodore Roosevelt, Taft outpolled his rival in the Massachusetts presidential preference vote 86,722 to 83,099; La Follette received less than 2,000 votes. Confusion in the selection of delegates, however, gave Roosevelt all eight at-large seats, thus splitting the delegation at eighteen apiece.

2. "When it rains gold," i.e., an ideal time that will never be.

3. At the Missouri Republican state convention, Nagel tried to forge a compromise between the Taft and Roosevelt supporters to avoid a bitter fight. But TR's backers decided to fight and easily captured a majority of the state's delegates to the national convention. Some of the party regulars blamed Nagel for Taft's loss, claiming he had prevented them from using the full strength of the party apparatus.

4. In the preferential vote, Speaker of the House James Beauchamp "Champ" Clark (1850–1921) of Missouri easily outpolled Woodrow Wilson, 34,575 to 15,002, and carried all of the state's delegates to the Democratic national convention.

To: Alice Goldmark Brandeis
Date: June 8, 1912
Place: Washington, D.C.
Source: Gilbert MSS

DEAREST: Miss Grady doubtless telephoned you that I leave tonight for Hot Springs & am to be here again Monday morning, as I want to attend the Supreme Court sitting—the last of the season. Tyler[1] will probably file some motion to tie up the Old Dominion judgement until October.[2] I don't imagine I can prevent it; but it seems best to be on hand. That will give me two days with Al instead of one.

Spent last evening with George R[ublee]. Norman [Hapgood] was at Bryn Mawr. Also saw Hamilton Holt.[3] He says the Pension Article will appear this month.[4] He wanted to see about another matter.

Saw Gifford today, Gilson Gardner, H.B. Needham, Clapp, Bristow, Oldfield,[5] Stanley & Frank Lyon & Sere Matthews, & am to dine at the La Follette's. T.R. is not sure, & there is good probability that if he doesn't get the nomination he will bolt.[6]

I guess I made a good enough escape from being embroiled in the Boston El. labor war.[7] They tried to reach me this A.M. to defend the strikers.

Gifford had the T.R. platform with him, which I fancy is largely his & [*] & M's[8] with a N[orman]. H[apgood]. composite.

Talked with Bob over telephone this morning. He seemed in good shape & John Hannan[9] says he is.   Lovingly

1. Charles Hitchcock Tyler (1863–1931), after graduation from Harvard College and Boston University Law School, practiced in the city for many years, originally with Owen D. Young before Young went off to head General Electric. Hitchcock was also a well-known dog breeder.

2. The decision would be handed down on 27 May 1912; see LDB to AGB, 4 February 1912.

3. Hamilton Holt (1872–1951) had been the managing editor of the *Independent* since he was twenty-five and would be with the magazine until 1921. He interested himself in a large number of civic and political activities. In 1925 he became president of Rollins College.

4. See LDB to AGB, 7 January 1912, note 3.

5. William Allan Oldfield (1847–1928) represented the Second Arkansas District in the House of Representatives from 1909 until his death.

6. At the Republican National Convention which met in Chicago on 18 June, Taft's control of the party machinery secured him a majority of the delegates, although Roosevelt had defeated the president in almost every state where there had been a popular primary. Claiming that he had been cheated out of the nomination, TR ordered his followers to walk out of the convention, and in early August Roosevelt supporters returned to Chicago and organized the Progressive Party, naming Roosevelt as their presidential candidate.

7. The Boston Elevated Railroad Conductors, Motormen, Shop and Barn Employees Union demanded union recognition and a pay increase, both of which the company rejected. On 3 June a pitched battled erupted between police and union demonstrators, with seven people injured. The company declared it would protect its "loyal employees," those

not affiliated with the union. On 6 June the union formally went on strike, and the company stopped service the next day while it imported strike-breakers from New York and elsewhere. Considerable violence followed, with trolley cars derailed and wrecked. But despite the violence, the company managed to restore service and break the strike.

8. Probably the publisher Frank Munsey, who would later be one of the chief financial backers of Roosevelt's Progressive Party.

9. John Joseph Hannan (1866–1946) was a reporter in Wisconsin before becoming La Follette's private secretary in 1903, a position he held until 1920. Later he was secretary of the state's board of control and helped to reform the prison system.

To:	Alfred Brandeis
Date:	July 10, 1912
Place:	Boston, Massachusetts
Source:	Brandeis MSS

MY DEAR AL: Nothing from Louisville of a later date than July 2.—I trust this means an individual so happy as to have no history. You remember your blast at Fannie—on the "rarified air" of the McAdams House,[1] as affecting her correspondence.

I am coming out for Wilson.[2] Unfortunately most of my progressive friends will stand by T.R. Charles R. Crane called me up from New York Saturday & says he is for Wilson, so much so that he will stay here abandoning his trip to Russia which had been planned for the summer; says he has not been so much interested since Cleveland days.

Heney and Merriam[3] of Chicago, whom I also talked with over the telephone are in serious doubt. Local political needs will probably turn them to the TR party.

I declared my views to Charles S. Bird[4] & other local progressives who wanted me for Governor or Senator & ended that agony.

I tried to reach Hattie or the Robbins after Mr. Speed's death,[5]—i.e. sent them word to call on me if I could help them, but have heard nothing.

I suppose Jean [Brandeis] told you of the Brenner[6] the Speeds selected for me & possibly Louis Wehle has told you that arrived some weeks ago—a very large piece which we like better as time teaches us its beauties. It seemed at first less beautiful than some of the smaller pieces.

It is hot enough here to make man pause in exertion.

Enclosed is my article on Business—A Profession in the form in which it is to appear in System.[7]

1. The McAdams House in New Hampshire had been a favorite vacation place for Fannie and Charles Nagel.

2. On this day LDB issued a statement announcing his support for Wilson and calling on all progressives to support the New Jersey governor. "Without loyal support from the progressives of the country Wilson's war upon unjust privilege must be futile. The progres-

sive cause can succeed only if it has loyal support from the progressives. It can fail only if the progressives fail in their duty of giving to Wilson that full support" (quoted in Mason, *Brandeis,* 376).

3. Charles Edward Merriam (1874–1953) was a professor of political science at the University of Chicago who wrote widely on various aspects of democratic government. Involved with the Republican insurgents, he ran unsuccessfully for mayor of Chicago in 1911.

4. Charles Sumner Bird (1855–1927), a paper manufacturer, was one of Roosevelt's leading supporters in Massachusetts and later in the year would run unsuccessfully for governor on the Bull Moose ticket.

5. James Breckinridge Speed (1844–1912), the husband of LDB's childhood friend Hattie Bishop, had recently died. See LDB to Alfred Brandeis, 4 October 1912.

6. An oil painting of the Kentucky woods, *Beeches in Autumn,* painted by Carl Christ Brenner (1838–88). Later LDB and AGB donated the picture to the J. B. Speed Memorial Museum in Louisville.

7. One of LDB's most important and widely cited articles, "Business—a Profession," grew out of the commencement speech he had given the previous month at Brown University. In it LDB tried to sum up his views on the proper goals and conduct of business, which, he claimed, ought to be considered a profession, akin to law or medicine. He dismissed those who only sought to make money as not being real businessmen, since true success is to be found in utilizing one's skills to make the market and the world a better place. He cited as his example his longtime friend and client, the late William H. McElwain, who not only made money but, more importantly, pioneered in labor relations and in trying to eliminate the curse of irregular employment. See "Business—a Profession," *System* 22 (October 1912): 365–69, reprinted in *Business—a Profession,* 1–12.

To:	Alfred Brandeis
Date:	August 14, 1912
Place:	South Yarmouth, Massachusetts
Source:	Brandeis MSS

DEAR AL: Do keep away from the office until you reach 130—or better 140 lbs.[1] Office presents no molocha[2] for a man in your fix. Ladless Farm, So. Yarmouth or the Mountains is much fitter. We could show you some more interesting folk than Dick Dedi here. I had, by chance, one of the original Zionists[3] at luncheon yesterday, who told a better story (Susan & Elizabeth will so testify) even than Capt. Baker.

Bessie Evans is here for a few days, & we are off now for a paddle.

1. Alfred, recuperating from an illness, had reported his weight at 124 pounds. See the next letter and LDB to AGB, 13 January 1913.

2. Yiddish for "work."

3. Jacob Judah Aaron deHaas (1872–1937) changed LDB's life significantly by introducing him to Zionism, helping him assume command of the American movement, and serving as his loyal lieutenant for more than two decades. DeHaas had been a secretary to the founder of the Zionist movement, Theodor Herzl, who had sent him to America to help establish the movement there. A journalist, deHaas earned his living as editor of the *Boston Jewish Advocate,* and it was as a reporter that he came to South Yarmouth for that fateful meeting with LDB.

To: Alfred Brandeis
Date: August 29, 1912
Place: South Yarmouth, Massachusetts
Source: Brandeis MSS

DEAR [AL]: The 130 lbs. is fine, but you ought to make it 140 before you try work.

I can beat your 1872 reminiscences "all hollow." [Charles R.] Crane telegraphed me Monday Gov. Wilson wanted to see me. So I went to N.Y. & Sea Girt (leaving here Tuesday P.M.)—breakfasted at the Albermarle Hotel (just opposite Democratic Headquarters) (Old Fifth Ave. Hotel)—passed Long Branch on the way to Sea Girt. I had gone to N.Y. via the Fall River line so passed by Newport.

Was very favorably impressed with Wilson. He is strong, simple, serious, openminded, eager to learn and deliberate. I suppose your papers carried some account of my visit.[1] I was very cordially received at the N.Y. headquarters. There are a lot of fine fellows in charge there. I dined with Congressman Redfield[2] and returned to Boston on the night train and came here on the 9:38 A.M.

    1. During luncheon and a three-hour meeting afterward, LDB and Wilson hammered out the basic tenets of the candidate's platform, the New Freedom. Although Wilson had moved steadily toward the progressive cause, he had never really thought out the problem of the trusts. Like LDB he believed them basically bad and inimical to American democracy, but he did not know what to do about them. He opposed big government and so could not accept Roosevelt's so-called New Nationalism, which posited a powerful national government serving to keep the trusts under control. LDB convinced Wilson that the answer lay in reestablishing competition and then enacting strong antitrust laws to make sure that big companies could not use their power unfairly. Wilson immediately seized on this notion, but he never fully understood LDB's thought. Years later, in an interview with Ray Stannard Baker, LDB said that Wilson had attacked monopoly rather than bigness, because Americans hated monopolies and loved bigness.
    2. William Cox Redfield (1885–1932), a Brooklyn iron manufacturer, was elected to Congress in 1910. Wilson would name him secretary of commerce, and he is given credit for suggesting to Wilson the idea that tariffs be reduced at the rate of five percent a year.

To: Alfred Brandeis
Date: September 15, 1912
Place: Dedham, Massachusetts
Source: Brandeis MSS

DEAR AL: I am glad you and the family like the Collier articles.[1] I think they are creating some trouble for the enemy. *Entre nous* I have Norman supplied with editorials—through the October 19th number & shall probably add two more to make the full measure. Have been at work this week on a labor-trust speech to be delivered before the State Branch A.F. of L. at Fitchburg Wednesday.[2]

That, probably, will be my only speech until October. I expect to make the tour of the N.E. quarter of the country then, speaking, practically only before Economic Clubs & Chambers of Commerce & the like & only on trusts.[3] I think it will be rather a unique political campaign. Shall probably devote the whole month to this.

Buckner is wrong on the Atty Genl matter.[4] It would bother me as much as it would the Governor [Wilson]. But I am glad to know Buckner thinks so.

Take good care of yourself.

1. LDB had agreed to supply Norman Hapgood with a series of articles attacking the new party, and the first one had just appeared: "Trusts, Efficiency and the New Party," *Collier's Weekly* 49 (14 September 1912): 14–15. The following week the journal published "Trusts, the Export Trade and the New Party," *Collier's* (21 September 1912): 10–11, 33. No further articles were printed, however, because the owner of the publication, Robert Collier, a Roosevelt backer, fired Norman Hapgood from the editorship. See LDB to AGB, 20 October 1912.

2. LDB's speech was a thorough-going attack on Roosevelt and the Progressive Party trust program, which LDB argued would be inimical to the best interests of labor. See LDB's explication of that talk in his letter to the editor of the *Boston Journal,* 24 September 1912, BL, published in the paper the following day.

3. For LDB's speaking schedule for Wilson, see LDB to William Gibbs McAdoo, 2 October 1912, BL.

4. Ever since LDB had come out for Wilson, rumors had circulated that should Wilson win LDB would be a member of the cabinet, probably as attorney general. In fact, Wilson did try to get LDB into that post, but pressure from Democratic politicians blocked the appointment. See LDB to Alfred Brandeis, 2 March 1913. Probably Alfred Brandeis's friend Mr. Buckner, from the Louisville Chamber of Commerce (see LDB to Alfred Brandeis, 5 December 1910), had made a remark on the possibility, which Alfred repeated to his brother.

To:	Alfred Brandeis
Date:	October 4, 1912
Place:	Portland, Maine
Source:	Brandeis MSS

DEAR AL: Here speaking before Economic Club—of course on trusts.

I must tell you of the rare pleasure which a little visit from Hattie B. S[peed]. the other day gave me. She is a fine woman and the sacrifices incident to her married life have enobled [*sic*] her, as she undoubtedly enobled Mr. Speed. Her visit was one of the best things that have come my way for a long time. I could see her only twenty minutes, as our R.R. hearings before Prouty[1] were on. We had 3 successful days & it looks as if we should make some real progress in getting from the I.C.C., a real show up of the situation, & an honest report on the results of monopoly.

Prouty set our next hearings for October 28th which will—if it stands— put a "strich[2] through my California trip". I know [* * *]. I wanted to go only because W[illiam]. J[ennings]. Bryan was very insistent I should. Those California folk are almost irresistible when they want anything & pull all available strings.

Enclosed clipping about Charlie. He evidently doesn't take his cue from your friend of the confessional who didn't come to boast.

Expect to be in Cin[cinna]ti Sunday Oct 13. Couldn't you come up that afternoon and spend the night? I should like to have a quiet talk and sit with you alone after a strenuous week.

1. Charles Azro Prouty (1853–1921) was appointed to the Interstate Commerce Commission in 1896 and served on the ICC until 1914, the last two years as chair. After an unsuccessful political bid, Prouty would rejoin the ICC as director of valuation.
2. Stroke.

To: **Alice Goldmark Brandeis**
Date: **October 17, 1912**
Place: **Cleveland, Ohio**
Source: **Gilbert MSS**

DEAREST: You seem to be busier than I now. I am having a real rest & am being complimented quite as much upon my youth & fitness as upon my speaking, which is not bad now. Indeed 12 miles a day, at a good clip, in the sunshine, & the good sweat & baths, is bringing out my complexion so that a debutante might be proud.

I am making quite an impression in Cleveland, in one way or another I think this stay worthwhile. The A[ssociated].P[ress]. will probably put out my letter on what to do with the trusts.[1] I have added a paragraph. They may cut it a little, but will leave it long enough to give a clearer idea than this week's Collier's editorial.

The weather has been most kind, sunshine unbroken; tho most people talk of having had much rain of late.

I am just up from an hour's nap after a hearty luncheon following my morning's walk and am not quite awake yet, but awake enough to know that my limbs are really exercised. So you see I am not moving at the speaking gait of a presidential candidate.

Lovingly

The news of Bessie is very reassuring.

1. In order to clarify his own thinking on the trust issue, Wilson asked LDB to write him a memo stating his views on what to do about monopolies and how they differed from the

positions advocated by Roosevelt. LDB did so, and the letter was used by the Wilson forces to illustrate their stance on the trusts. See LDB to Woodrow Wilson, 30 September 1912, BL.

To: Alice Goldmark Brandeis
Date: October 18, 1912
Place: Cleveland, Ohio
Source: Gilbert MSS

DEAREST: I am to leave for Buffalo at 11:30. Have been strolling about Euclid Ave. these two hours. It is almost too warm to walk hard—wind graciously southwest and I am thinking how some folks are toiling.

The audience last evening was not large, but listened most attentively. Among them was Myrta Jones & her sister Miss Jones, whom I talked with a moment after the talk. Cleveland is really full of progressivism, but the forces are as little united as one might expect in Boston. Indeed I was the occasion of introducing some to one another who reminded of Tourgenieff's Benevolence & Gratitude.[1]

Note my trip is half over in time, though there is considerable distance. I have been thinking this morning about what I shall say to the students of University of Minnesota whom I am to address next Thursday. I have concluded that such seed so sown is, on the whole, most fruitful. I am meeting here & there men who heard my lecture to the Law Students at Fogg Museum or at Brooks House years ago & say it wholly changed their point of view.[2]   Lovingly

1. Ivan Sergeyevich Turgenev (1818–83) was a well-known Russian novelist, poet, essayist, and short story writer.
2. LDB's talk at Brooks House (Harvard) was one of his most famous, "The Opportunity in the Law," published in 39 *American Law Review* 555 (1905) and republished in *Business—a Profession,* 88–98. In it LDB called upon lawyers and those studying to become lawyers to represent the public, to cease being the hired hands of business and reclaim their rightful place in society as impartial servants of the public good.

To: Alice Goldmark Brandeis
Date: October 20, 1912
Place: Pittsburgh, Pennsylvania
Source: Gilbert MSS

DEAREST: Your two letters to P[ittsburgh] have come. I am sad about the Collier break.[1] Have just written NH. Collier probably thinks: "My poverty, that my will consents."[2] I almost think frugality instead of cleanliness stands next to godliness.

The talk here is said to have been a great success. Found quite a lot of old law school acquaintances here. They seem much older than I. Had a good walk over the hills this morning. Off tonight for Toledo, no [*] afternoon trips for me. Shall dine with A. Leo Weil.[3] Due Chicago Tuesday morning.

Lovingly

Isn't T.R. trust statement great!![4]

1. On 14 October Collier fired Hapgood and in that day's issue of *Collier's* came out personally in favor of Roosevelt. Moreover, he apologized for the biased treatment that the magazine had given to Roosevelt and opened its pages so that the colonel could reply. Since LDB felt partially responsible for the incident and believed Hapgood was an important asset for reform forces, he spent the next several months first trying to cool the feud between Collier and Hapgood and then helping Hapgood take over *Harper's Weekly*. See LDB to AGB, 6 January 1913.

2. The correct wording, from Shakespeare's Romeo and Juliet, V, 1, is:

Apothecary: My poverty, but not my will, consents.
Romeo: I pay thy poverty, and not thy will.

3. A. Leo Weil (1858–1938) was a Pittsburgh lawyer active in civic reform of the "good government" type.

4. After being wounded in an assassination attempt on 14 October, Roosevelt, while recuperating, issued no statements and made no speeches until his appearance in Madison Square Garden in New York on 30 October. It is possible that LDB may have had an advance look at the letter Roosevelt wrote to *Collier's*, in which he lauded the magazine's change of policy toward him, without, however, mentioning the recent firing of Norman Hapgood. In the statement, which appeared on 28 October, Roosevelt declared that he stood by the same position he had always espoused: "I am not for monopoly. We intend to restore competition. We intend to do away with the conditions that make for monopoly. My plan was pretty well laid out before I left the White House."

To:	Alice Goldmark Brandeis
Date:	October 22, 1912
Place:	Chicago, Illinois
Source:	Gilbert MSS

DEAREST: I am [in] C.R.C[rane].'s room at the Chicago Club, & he has gone down to get my mail. I have just come from my luncheon talk to the Ill[inois]. Mfrs. which they say went well. They looked impressed & some of them heard what they needed—some perhaps what they liked. There are some things I wanted to say but forgot at the moment.

Charles C. says he tried in vain to reach you on tel. before coming West. He says Norman had 6 good offers before [the] Saturday which made public his severance ended. C.R.C. wants to go to the Balkans as soon as the election is over & take Norman (& me) with him.

Richard[1] is getting on so finely that Charles sees the possibility now of taking an office if it is offered him.

People here think Ill. will go for Teddy; but California is very doubtful.[2] Still they have wholesome respect for T.R.'s power. Lovingly

1. Charles Crane's son, Richard Teller Crane (1882–1938), entered public service after working in the family business. For a while he served as private secretary to Robert Lansing in the State Department and was later named minister to Czechoslovakia.

2. In the election Wilson carried Illinois and received all but eight of California's electoral votes.

To:	Alfred Brandeis
Date:	November 2, 1912
Place:	New York, New York
Source:	Brandeis MSS

DEAR AL: I closed my speaking campaign at the Economic Club here last evening, & am told it went off satisfactorily. Am glad to have the talkfest over & to get down to some other affairs for a while. I am staying over to consider with Hapgood his future.

Alice and Elizabeth went with Pauline to Bryn Mawr for lantern night & are due here Sunday. Elizabeth & I plan to return Sunday night & I hope Alice will stay with Aunt Regina a few days.

It looks pretty certain Wilsonway now but I shall feel relieved when the vote is in. The redoubtable Colonel is too formidable an opponent. That shooting[1] stopped his waning tide, if it didn't help him positively.

Hope your Chicago trip turned out well.

1. On 14 October, while speaking in Milwaukee, Roosevelt was shot by an anti-third term fanatic. He insisted on delivering his speech and was furious when Wilson announced that he would stop campaigning until Roosevelt recovered.

To:	Alice Goldmark Brandeis
Date:	November 2, 1912
Place:	New York, New York
Source:	Gilbert MSS

DEAREST: The speech apparently went off well. My most tolerant critic, Norman, said it was "great" & that T.R.'s eternal Lincoln could not have made "a deeper impression". In fact, it was not as good as several of my western ones, but it was better than Van Hise's & Williams; and at all events it brought V.H. & me nearer together instead of widening the breach. He abjured monopoly & asserted he was not defending the New Party. After the affair he came up to me & said he thought we were much nearer together than when we met at LaF's & that he thought we could agree on a bill.

I saw many acquaintances, but did not see Pauline [Goldmark] in the box. I hope that means she joined you yesterday.

Day fine. Shall walk much unless an abrasion due to walking in the wet yesterday prevents.

Give my love to Susan & E[lizabeth]. It cleared here by 6:30, so I assume you had a good evening after all.

Lovingly

Let me know when you are to arrive in N.Y.

To:　　　　**Alfred Brandeis**
Date:　　　November 7, 1912
Place:　　　Boston, Massachusetts
Source:　　**Brandeis MSS**

MY DEAR AL: Well—Wilson certainly got a broad sweep.[1] And what pleases me most is T.R.'s defeat in the really progressive strongholds—Oregon, California, Iowa, Nebraska, Kansas, Wisconsin, the Dakotas & our eastern Progressive New Hampshire. Most of the Progressives who went over to T.R.—little Governors & the like—are left without support, & my friend Ben Lindsey among them.

I wired La Follette my congratulations & rather hope McGovern is beaten altho' LaF. came out for him.[2]

1. Wilson polled 6,286,214 votes to 4,126,020 for Roosevelt, 3,483,922 for Taft, and 897,011 for the Socialist candidate, Eugene Debs. But although he had less than a majority of the popular vote, Wilson had a stunning electoral victory, 435 to 88 for Roosevelt and 8 for Taft, the largest electoral landslide in American history up to that point.
2. Francis Edward McGovern had just been elected to his second term as governor of Wisconsin. He had a clear majority of 179,360 against the combined total of 153,977 for his two Democratic opponents.

To:　　　　**Alfred Brandeis**
Date:　　　November 13, 1912
Place:　　　Boston, Massachusetts
Source:　　**Brandeis, MSS**

DEAR AL: Grusse to Mother's Birthday.

Your greeting came this morning. You are wise in your statement as to my future activity. [David O.] Ives saw Charlie N[agel]. last week in Washington. Says he looks well & didn't seem particularly unhappy. Is disgruntled because Wilson would [not] answer the questions put by Charlie in his speeches—of which presumably WW never heard: "Would you have signed the Tariff bills Taft vetoed?" Still, Republicans and Progressives have all grounds for congratulation—the Republicans that T.R. was beaten & the Progressives that Taft was. So we may enter upon one of those perilous eras of good feeling.

They are both talking about Wilson being a "minority" president. Your historical study will confirm Sue in saying, so was the blessed Lincoln they talk so much about.

To:	Alice Goldmark Brandeis
Date:	November 21, 1912
Place:	New York, New York
Source:	Gilbert MSS

DEAREST: I am going now for my walk until dinnertime at Mothers & then want to see Felix [Adler] if he is in.

Till now the day has been peopleful, or until 3, when I sauntered down to the Penn. Fifth Ave. Ticket Office to get my accommodations. The day has not been New Havenless. The I.C.C. examiner was with me $1^1/_2$ hour & I think he is steered straight & then at luncheon I talked of New Haven with Dan Martin, at his instance, to the effect that he says he will write on the subject. Even the Village Blacksmith might be satisfied.

House of Texas[1] who was the occasion of the luncheon is a good friend of Wilson's apparently & D.M. says he is a very good fellow (which he appears to be) & influential.

Norman lunched with us & also breakfasted with me. Leslie's seems to be waning.[2] I learn of a new Cabinet possibility for me—Secy of the Interior which is supposed to be a Gore[3] suggestion. It is almost time for the Army & Navy post.   Lovingly

1. Edward Mandel House (1859–1938) was for several years Woodrow Wilson's closest advisor. A self-effacing man who delighted in his shadowy role behind the scenes, he was consulted by the president on nearly every major issue. He broke with Wilson in 1919 over the conduct of the Paris peace conference. His involvement with almost all aspects of New Freedom policies and politics can be seen in Charles Seymour, ed., *The Intimate Papers of Colonel House*, 4 vols. (Boston, 1926–28).

2. Following the break with Collier, Hapgood and LDB had been searching for a magazine that might be available for purchase so that Hapgood could continue his journalistic work. Among the possibilities was *Leslie's Weekly*. Eventually arrangements were made for the purchase of *Harper's*. See LDB to AGB, 6 January 1913, note 4.

3. Thomas Pryor Gore (1870–1949) was a blind senator from Oklahoma from 1907 to 1921 and again from 1931 to 1937.

To:	Alice Goldmark Brandeis
Date:	December 18, 1912
Place:	New York, New York
Source:	Gilbert MSS

DEAREST: Wilson's declaration last evening[1] was great—not a speech—not a sermon, but a solemn, frank noble statement of his purpose to carry out—without fear or favor—his promises to the American people. It breathed determination; there was neither nook nor corner in which compromise could find lodgement, and a making clear that the business was too serious to brook delay or to justify the diversions of etiquette.

No one who heard him could doubt that he would do or die; that he neither expected nor feared death; but was content to do battle and, if need be, go down smiling assured of the victory that must follow. There was not a word of temporizing with thing[s] material.

I am to lunch with Norman et al and start at 2:45 for Chicago (Sherman House). Don't know yet how long I shall stay there, but shall probably return in any event to N.Y.

Lovingly

The report on Bessie is fine.

1. Wilson had spoken to the Southern Society of New York and in a widely quoted phrase promised "a gibbet as high as Haman's" for any financial oligarchs who tried to oppose reform. "Men have got to stand up now and be counted," he said, "and I want to appeal to you, gentlemen, to conceive of yourselves as trustees of those interests of the nation with which your personal interests have nothing to do." For the entire speech, see Arthur S. Link, ed., *The Papers of Woodrow Wilson* (Princeton, 1978), 25:593–603.

To:	Alfred Brandeis
Date:	December 27, 1912
Place:	Boston, Massachusetts
Source:	Brandeis MSS

MY DEAR AL: Upon my return to the city I have a letter from Rudolph Brandeis dated December 14th, asking for a loan of $50 to be returned January 15th. I have sent him that amount.

In view of his positive promise to return this, I think it best to hold him to it, and if he does not return the amount in January, I plan to deduct it from the March 1st payment.

I have your letter in which you speak of Solicitor-General Bullock's [sic][1] note on shoe machinery. I did not see that in the paper, but suppose it had to do with the submission of the brief to the Supreme Court.[2] I have not yet seen any copy of the much discussed attack of Mellen on me.[3] I came back yesterday and have not been able to catch up with matters yet.

With best wishes for the New Year,   Yours

1. William Marshall Bullitt (1873–1957), a Louisville native, served as solicitor general during the last year of the Taft administration; he would later become one of the nation's leading constitutional lawyers.

2. The government had lost its antitrust suit against United Shoe Machinery and was appealing to the Supreme Court; see *United States v. Winslow,* 227 U.S. 202 (1913).

3. On 30 December Mellen issued a scathing indictment of LDB and blamed him for the many ills that had befallen the New Haven Railroad. He specifically denounced LDB's use of train wrecks as evidence of poor management and claimed that the line had been sabotaged (although he did not directly accuse LDB of that).

To: **Alice Goldmark Brandeis**
Date: **January 4, 1913**
Place: **En route to Chicago**
Source: **Gilbert MSS**

DEAREST: Nearing Chicago. At Albany I was joined by Richard Crane, Rogers and Stephens (their Chicago lawyer) & soon Charles D. Norton[1] turned up so we spent the evening in long—too long—converse. I was interested in observing Charles Norton, & pained by the necessity of refraining from asking him questions which he might have answered to our great enlightenment. Of course the New Haven situation was discussed and I took occasion to drop some pearls of wisdom which I thought might ultimately find their way to his Lord and Master J.P. Morgan—Patron of Arts.[2]

This week's Collier[']s has the first of Carl Snyder's two articles.[3] It is pretty well done. I will bring you my copy, but you needn't read it, as you have so much Zionist literature awaiting.[4]

Lovingly

Mellen will be maddened again as LDB is referred to as the guide to all Snyder's knowledge.[5]

1. Charles Dyer Norton (1871–1922) was assistant secretary of the treasury in the Taft administration and then private secretary to the president.

2. John Pierpont Morgan, Sr. (1837–1913) was from the 1890s until his death later in 1913 the most powerful financier in the country. Building upon the banking base created by his father, Morgan became a master at creating mergers and then controlling those creations through his appointees to the boards of trustees. He had engineered the New Haven–Boston & Maine merger that LDB had opposed for many years.

3. Carl Snyder (1869–1946), a statistician and economist who wrote widely on business matters, wrote two articles essentially restating LDB's argument against Mellen, Morgan, and their management of the New Haven. See "Charles S. Mellen to the Bar," *Collier's* 50 (4 January 1913): 8–9, 30; and "Mellen's Wonderful Top," ibid. (11 January 1913): 8–9.

4. This casual mention of Zionist literature confirms suspicions that the visit of Jacob deHaas in the summer of 1912 began LDB's long interest in the Zionist movement.

5. Actually, Snyder made only one or two references to LDB. In one of them he wrote: "Almost at the beginning, Mr. Brandeis had exposed the methods of bookkeeping to which Mr. Mellen was compelled to resort to conceal the true financial condition of the New Haven. But New England had listened to the voice of its 'conservative business men.' . . . Now it angrily refuses to pay the price of its folly" (4 January article, p. 30).

To: **Alice Goldmark Brandeis**
Date: **January 5, 1913**
Place: **Chicago, Illinois**
Source: **Gilbert MSS**

DEAREST: Have had some good much needed walking today. The cold is coming on & there is a slight snow which gives piquancy to the air.

Henry [Goldmark] is here & Mlle Leon[1] & others were in to dine and for luncheon I was carried off by Crane to an affair given by Julius Rosenwald[2] to a most extraordinary Rumanian Palestinean Jew—Aaron Aaronsohn[3] who spoke on his discovery in Palestine of "wild wheat", and the possibilities it opens of increasing the world's Food Supply.[4] I think it was the most thrilling talk I have ever heard & I shall try to tell you the tale when I return.

I was unfortunately lured into saying I would say a little at the Lincoln Centre Emancipation meeting with [sic] Jenkin Lloyd Jones[5] has on for this evening. Shall talk about the liberation of man, but I wish I had not said yes.[6]

I shall not be able to leave here before Tuesday evening & think it probable that I can't before Wednesday evening.

Mr. & Mrs. Lillie[7] dined here yesterday also a Mrs. Flint who succeeded to her husband['s] Professorship in English at the Un. of Chicago after his death.

1. Perhaps Eva Leon, a pioneer in bringing nursing to Palestine, an associate of Aaron Aaronsohn (see note 3 below) and a sister of the pioneering American Zionist Richard Gottheil.

2. Julius Rosenwald (1862–1932) became president of Sears, Roebuck & Co. in 1910. An extremely wealthy man, Rosenwald supported a variety of philanthropic activities, including Jewish colonization in Palestine, the YMCA and YWCA, and African-American education.

3. Aaron Aaronsohn (1876–1919), an important pioneer in Palestinian agriculture, developed a strain of wild wheat well suited to the arid conditions of the Middle East. LDB and he would get to know each other much better over the next several years as LDB became more involved in Zionist affairs. LDB often referred to this talk by Aaronsohn as one of the events that led to his interest in Palestine and Zionism. Aaronsohn was killed in an airplane crash shortly after the end of the war.

4. See *Agricultural and Botanical Explorations in Palestine,* U.S. Dept. of Agriculture, Bureau of Plant Industry, Bulletin No. 180 (Washington, D.C., 1910).

5. Jenkin Lloyd Jones (1843–1918) wrote numerous books on religion and the life of Jesus. He was pastor of the All Souls Church in Chicago as well as head of the Abraham Lincoln Centre there.

6. See the next letter.

7. Frances Crane Lillie (1870–1958), a social worker and philanthropist, was the sister of Charles R. Crane and the wife of the well-known University of Chicago zoologist Frank Rattray Lillie (1870–1947).

To: Alice Goldmark Brandeis
Date: January 6, 1913
Place: Chicago, Illinois
Source: Gilbert MSS

DEAREST: The talk last night didn't seem to me worthwhile; but others say it was. At all events no one suffered severely, as I talked less than 10 minutes in view of the terrifyingly long program.[1]

The Palestinian friend Mille Leon is still here, & as she was to appeal to her race yesterday afternoon for funds, the Cranes and I had to attend. Indeed I am becoming quite an assistant Zionist—unawares.

The more I think of Aaronsohn's wild wheat address the more inspiring it seems. I wish you might have heard it. Even your archeological Prof. Clark(?) could not have stirred you more. It is interesting to think of two Jews, Dr. Lubin[2] & Aaronsohn, as the great aid to agriculture—with the Jewish reputation of being incapable of farm life. Perhaps with farming becoming a science this may change.

The Crane will matters are still absorbing most attention;[3] but Norman's affairs[4] are receiving some and I hope may move a bit—within the next day or two.

I don't know that I am helping the Cranes much, but they feel that I am & the situation is certainly serious.

                                                        Lovingly

Elizabeth's postal received.

1. After the opening prayers, LDB was the first of several speakers to address the audience in a program marking the fiftieth anniversary of the Emancipation Proclamation. He spoke about new conditions caused by industrialization that deprived people of opportunity. "Each social and industrial wrong must be subjected to diagnosis. We must find the cause of all the misery. Little has been done to remove social and industrial wrongs." The meeting and LDB's brief remarks were reported in the *Chicago Tribune* (6 January 1913).

2. David Lubin (1849–1919) was a Sacramento merchant deeply involved in agricultural reform and agricultural science. Among other achievements, Lubin introduced the idea of rural credits in the United States.

3. Charles R. Crane and his brother Richard Teller Crane, Jr. (1873–1931) were embroiled in a legal tangle over the $10 million estate left by their father, elevator manufacturer Richard Teller Crane (1832–1912). The elder Crane had arranged for the two sons to have equal control of the business and over time had distributed his stock to them accord-

ingly. But Charles's brother had sold off some of the stock prior to the father's death, thus impeding the idea of "equal control." LDB attempted to mediate the dispute to avoid having to go into litigation and in late February managed to resolve the issue.

4. See LDB to AGB, 20 October 1912, note 1. At the end of December 1912 Hapgood met with Thomas Lamont, who, according to Hapgood (Hapgood to LDB, 31 December 1912, BL), practically asked him to make an offer for *Harper's Weekly*. Although Hapgood initially said no, within a short time he changed his mind; negotiations began, involving Hapgood, Lamont, LDB, and Charles Crane (who helped finance the deal). Not until May 1913 were the arrangements concluded, in which Hapgood purchased *Harper's* for $100,000, provided by Crane. For further details, see the many letters between LDB and Hapgood from January through May 1913, BL.

To: **Alice Goldmark Brandeis**
Date: **January 9, 1913**
Place: **Chicago, Illinois**
Source: **Gilbert MSS**

DEAREST: Charles Crane bids me say something very nice for him to you & Elizabeth "before the postscript." Consider the nicest possible things said. The Cranes are certainly lovely folk. Mrs. Crane quite as much so as he. And there is a beautiful family spirit.

Unfortunately their will tangle is very knotty and it looks now as if I should [not] escape from here until after Sunday. And meanwhile Norman's matter also is hanging fire, as it is impossible to divert the mind of Crane, or indeed my own, from the will problems to another.

If I have to remain over Sunday, I shall probably run down to Louisville for Sunday both because I want to see Al and because I don't want to go to the Wilson dinner Saturday evening.[1] There is so much Brandeis Cabinet talk that I think it just as well to be absent.

I didn't like the sound of Al's letter. It seems as if he were not as well as he seemed to be some months ago.[2]

Lovingly

Am I to lunch with [*] & his financial-currency friend Halbut.

1. At a dinner attended by many of the business leaders in the Midwest, Wilson held out both a carrot and a stick. "The business future of the country," he declared, "does not depend on the Government of the country but on the businessmen of the country." However, unless business behaved more ethically and followed rules of honest competition, the government would have no choice but to step in to preserve the public interest.

2. See LDB to AGB, 13 January 1913.

To: **Alice Goldmark Brandeis**
Date: **January 10, 1913**
Place: **Chicago, Illinois**
Source: **Gilbert MSS**

206

DEAREST: Perseus (if that was the gentleman) overcoming the Python[1] is a "Hund dagegen"[2] compared with your grapple with colds. I have had something of a one myself for nearly a week which manifested itself earward, but seems to have vanished only today, so I can't count myself in your class.

The Crane imbroglio is not straightened out yet. At the moment it looks as if progress had been made, the clouds have lifted a bit, but there is an element in the situation which reminds of the Warren tragedy—indeed a number of factors.[3] Meanwhile Norman's affair is stalled.

Then you know my charming Prince Florijelt was ultimately dispossessed of his throne, for which we liked him the better, but it "wasn't business".

You probably noticed that the Washington dispatches are persistently naming me as Secretary of Commerce. I have no doubt the enemy is doing what it can to make public opinion to the effect that I am not to be Attorney General.

Suppose you noticed Supreme Court in the Union Pacific–Southern Pac. case has taken the position I insisted on in the Tobacco case that the shares in the would be competing company should go to others than the stockholders in the main company.[4]   Lovingly

1. Neither Perseus nor Heracles wrestled with a python, although both did grapple with a snakelike creature. Perseus had to overcome a "sea monster" in order to marry Andromeda, and one of the twelve labors of Heracles was to slay the Lernaean hydra, a snake with nine heads. Every time Heracles cut one off, two grew in its place.

2. "A dog by comparison" (i.e., nothing).

3. After the suicide of LDB's friend and former law partner Samuel D. Warren, a controversy arose among his siblings over the disposition and control of the family-owned paper mills. LDB, one of the trustees of Sam's estate, attempted to serve as a neutral mediator, only to have one member of the family accuse him of unethical behavior—a charge that took a great deal of time during the hearings over his appointment to the Supreme Court in 1916.

4. In *United States v. Union Pacific Railroad Co.,* 226 U.S. 61 (1912), decided the previous December, the Supreme Court upheld the government's contention that the Union Pacific's purchase of 46 percent of the stock of the Southern Pacific line violated the Sherman Antitrust Act and remanded the case to a lower court to work out how the Union Pacific should divest itself of that stock. The railroad proposed that since it was not feasible to get the original sellers of the stock, heirs of E. H. Harriman, to repurchase it, the stock should be issued as a form of stock dividend to stockholders of the Union Pacific in proportion to the number of shares they held of Union Pacific stock. On 6 January a unanimous Court (with Justice Willis Van Devanter abstaining) denied the request; see *United States v. Union Pacific Railroad Co.,* 226 U.S. 470 (1913). Justice William R. Day explained that, since the largest shareholders of the Union Pacific would get the largest number of shares of the Southern Pacific, they would be in a position to elect identical boards and thus in effect still control both lines in violation of the Sherman Act.

In *United States v. American Tobacco Co.,* 221 U.S. 106 (1911), the Court found the company a monopoly acting in restraint of trade but, instead of ordering its complete dissolution, ordered a reorganization. As a result, the same large shareholders now controlled several companies instead of one and were still able, in effect, to act in a monopolistic manner. For LDB's views, see his letter to Edwin A. Grozier, 19 September 1911, BL.

To: Alice Goldmark Brandeis
Date: January 13, 1913
Place: Chicago, Illinois
Source: Gilbert MSS

DEAREST: Just back from Louisville & have not yet gotten my mail. The trip was a complete success & I feel rested by the outing. Al is doing finely. He looks well and says he is all right if he takes care of himself, and that he has found out how to do it & intends to. I think he is taking the health problem with becoming seriousness, and it looks now as if he would really look out for himself.[1] He is going to St. Louis tonight for his old railroad matters, but says this does not mean he is going to be lured into excesses.

Louis Wehle has at last "gotten his gait" professionally, and seems quite elated. The money has not come in in large quantity; but he is really gaining recognition & sufficient publicity so that he may become the fashion. Mary had an operation some two months or so ago, I think, & is slowly getting back to strength.

Louis's visit to Madison was to try to secure his papa-in-law an appointment, with Senator La Follette's aid, & he had a long talk with the Senator, going with him from Chicago to Madison, & had an interview with Van Hise.

The Ladless Hill House[2] is pretty near completion. It may take some months to clear up odds & ends; but it is wholly livable and is really a beautiful place, only rather grand for "unser eins."[3] Al feels pretty guilty about it; but Jennie & the others [are] very happy. Jennie says "their friends are quite as faithful to them as heretofore."

Amy's young man, a Mr. McCreary[4] and a Mr. Lewis (young lawyer) attending on Madie were there spending night & day. Only Fan seemed manless. Amy looked very well & McCreary clung to her as if matters were serious, but "mir hat man nichts gesagt."[5] And I heard nothing about Walter Fischel except that he had not been in Louisville since Thanksgiving.

The high water made access to Ladless very difficult and circuitous, and only by motor. So I breakfasted at the Wehles' (Louis met me at station) & went for a walk with Otto & the car did not arrive until 10:30. Then Al, Fan, Louis & I called for a moment at Mary's. Had lunch & a nap at Ladless, returned at 4 with Al & Louis Wehle to the Wehles, where we supped & spent the evening, after making duty call on the Dembitz's & Belle, and a most charming call on Hattie [Speed] and the Robbins who seemed very happy together.

Wilson seems to have charmed, but "fazed" the Chicago business men, & from what I have learned seems to have reiterated the good doctrine of the earlier post election speeches.[6] From the papers I should think he hadn't been as strong on conservation as he should be. If that is a weak spot in his armor, he is in great danger. For the Pinchot sharpshooter[s] will be out for him & they are experienced war men.[7]

I hope today will decide something as to my plans—or rather how long I must remain here. Lovingly

1. See LDB to Alfred Brandeis, 14 August 1912.
2. Ladless Hill, the house Alfred built on what was then the outskirts of Louisville, was a working farm as well as a residence. A streetcar line ran past the hill, so the family could get into town in less than twenty minutes. Ladless was three stories high with a full basement that contained, among other things, an "ice room" and was rather a grand house for the time. It was surrounded by about 100 acres, on which horses and cows grazed, and Alfred also raised and butchered hogs, providing the family, including LDB, with a constant supply of country hams. The residential area took up about ten acres and included a tennis court as well as extensive flower gardens that his daughter Madie supervised. The farm labor was provided during Alfred's lifetime by the Nichols family, who had their own house on the property. This, and further information, was provided by Eric Tachau in a letter to the editors, 19 February 1998.
3. "People like us."
4. William Harold McCreary (1885–1946) taught English at the Louisville Male High School and published several volumes of poetry. He would wed Amy Brandeis; see the next letter.
5. "No one said anything to me."
6. See LDB to AGB, 9 January 1913, note 1.
7. LDB is referring to Taft's experience: his allegedly weak conservation policies led Amos and Gifford Pinchot to attack him, culminating in the Pinchot-Ballinger affair, which severely damaged the president's reputation.

To: **Alfred Brandeis**
Date: **March 2, 1913**
Place: **Boston, Massachusetts**
Source: **Brandeis MSS**

MY DEAR AL: We are very happy over Amy's engagement.[1] It seems to me the two are unusually well mated, and it is fine to have the family supplemented by a son.

Madie's mind is thus turned to the contemplation of matrimony; and I cannot but think she will eventually yield.[2]

Today's papers will have removed the mystery as to the Cabinet. As you know I had great doubts as for it's [sic] being desirable for me; so I concluded to literally let nature take its course and to do nothing either to get called or to stop the talk, although some of my friends were quite active. State Street, Wall Street and the local Democratic bosses did six months' unremitting work; but seem not to have prevailed until the last moment. The local Democratic bosses were swayed partly by their connections in the financial district, partly by the fear of being opposed in job-seeking. It is almost, indeed quite, amusing how much they fear me, attributing to me power and influence which I in no respect possess.[3]

I shall know more when I go to New York and probably Washington the end of this week.

Do let me know, at once, about enclosed letter from Otto Fleishner. I can almost remember something about a Lederer somewhere: How else should Fleishner hit on the early seventies.

Madie will travel to N.Y. in Herbert White's company tomorrow.

1. To William McCreary; see the previous letter.
2. Adele Brandeis never married.
3. Rumors that LDB would be appointed to the cabinet circulated even before the election (see LDB to Alfred Brandeis, 15 September 1912), and Wilson seriously contemplated naming LDB as attorney general. Progressives of all kinds inundated Wilson with letters urging the appointment, and La Follette sent word through Charles R. Crane that LDB could "pull together the progressives—whether La Follette, Democratic or Bull Mooser—and harmonize progressive legislation" (quoted in Mason, *Brandeis,* 390). At the same time, business and financial interests also let Wilson know that they objected to LDB in any high federal position, and the conservative press predicted that LDB's appointment to the Justice Department would trigger a depression (*Boston Journal,* 21 November 1912). In the end Wilson yielded to the advice of Col. Edward M. House; although he toyed for a while with the idea of naming LDB to the Commerce Department, he finally abandoned that notion as well.

To: **Alice Goldmark Brandeis**
Date: **March 8, 1913**
Place: **Washington, D.C.**
Source: **Gilbert MSS**

DEAREST: Have had a busy day. Charlie Crane-ing with many folks. Saw Jud Welliver, Gilson Gardner, Henry Beach Needham, Senators Clapp, Bourne, James, etc. etc. Am to see Lane[1] at 4:30. Had long talk with Prouty and Marble this morning which will I think advance New Haven matters materially and am to have this evening with La Follette, & starting my interlocking directorate campaign.[2] There is work ahead without end, & when I see the crowds of office seekers & the like besieging the Secretaries my contentment with existing things as to myself is confirmed.

Met Hildegard[e] by chance this morning. She was as stiff as her Grandmother wasn't.[3]

Louis Wehle breakfasted with me & has been trudging about all day with me.

Lovingly

Have appointment 9:30 Monday with Prouty & examiners on New Haven matters.[4] I am at the [Hotel] Gordon.

210

1. Franklin Knight Lane (1864–1921), a California lawyer and politician, was named to the Interstate Commerce Commission in 1905 and served there until Wilson made him secretary of the interior. LDB considered Lane one of the best men on the commission and just a few weeks earlier had written to praise him on a report he had done on express rates and revenues, calling it "the finest piece of work of its kind that I know." LDB to Lane, 1 February 1913, BL.

2. One of LDB's pet crusades was against interlocking directorates, where the same individuals representing particular interests sat on the boards of competing corporations or of firms doing business with one another that should have an arm's-length relationship. He constantly used the case of the New Haven, where Morgan's appointees also sat on the boards of competing lines as well as on those of companies that supplied the New Haven with items such as steel rails, engines, and cars. The most explicit statement of LDB's views can be found in "The Endless Chain: Interlocking Directorates," *Harper's Weekly* 58 (6 December 1913): 13–17, the third part of the series he wrote on "the Money Trust," which is also chapter 3 of *Other People's Money, and How the Bankers Use It* (New York, 1914).

3. Hildegarde Nagel's grandmother was Frederika, LDB's own mother.

4. LDB's long campaign against the New Haven merger was nearing an end as ICC examiners, following his lead, began to confirm his accusations against the road.

To: **Alice Goldmark Brandeis**
Date: **March 9, 1913**
Place: **Washington, D.C.**
Source: **Gilbert MSS**

DEAREST: I am expecting Bessie [Evans] & Lynn Haynes at 10. At 10:30 I am to see MacFarland[1] who apparently won't be able to head of[f] the Olney appointment.[2] At 1:30 I lunch with the Pinchots & at 7 dine with the Frankfurter contingent. The day is lovely & warm & I plan a long walk in intervals. Had a quiet talk a deux with La Follette last evening. He is pretty grim. W[oodrow].W[ilson]. will not be taken on faith by him. He is open to conviction; but every move will be scanned, strongly endorsed if proved satisfactory, & fought if not. LaF. thinks W. took the "easier way". Says LaF was constantly overhearing talk on this issue for months in the cloak rooms.[3]

We laid out a good plan in the rough for undermining the interest[s] & shall shape up some legislation which we hope will prove as useful as the La Follette Antitrust Bill.

Talk with Lane was very satisfactory. The way is open to me to help run the Interior [Department] and (via Marble) the Interstate Commerce Com[mission, but no office for me. "Me for the simple life".   Lovingly

1. Grenville Stanley MacFarland (1878–1924) was an editorial writer for the Hearst newspaper chain.

2. Wilson, in order to maintain ties with the conservative wing of the Democratic Party, would on the next day offer the ambassadorship to Great Britain to Richard Olney, who had been Cleveland's secretary of state. Olney, now seventy-seven years old,

declined the offer on 16 March, and Wilson immediately named Walter Hines Page to the post.

3. About the possibility of LDB receiving a cabinet appointment.

To: Alfred Brandeis
Date: March 10, 1913
Place: Washington, D.C.
Source: Brandeis MSS

DEAR AL: Louis Wehle has told you doubtless of our day together.

Since he left, I have been engaged largely in promoting the entent [sic] cordiale with the Administration. Had a good private talk with the President this evening for an hour—and with Lane, Redfield, Bryan, and McReynolds today—inter alia pushing along New Haven and Shoe Machinery matters[1]— & spent this morning at the I.C.C. on New Haven matters. There is no lack of occupation. Heard quite a little gossip about Charlie Nagel last evening.

He was as near the Supreme Court as this: Taft told the Chief Justice[2] Charlie would be appointed the next day. The C.J. called on Charlie 10 P.M. to welcome him for coming event. The next day another name was sent in. Taft also treated Charlie atrociously on dit.[3] in respect to O'Keefe's discharge.

Same inside source says Charlie had substantially no influence on Taft or the Administration. He is a great admirer of Charlie personally and intimate with him. Says Charlie was fearfully harried by his Chief's qualities.

1. Although LDB had started out as counsel to the United Shoe Machinery Company, he and the large firm parted ways in 1907; and afterward he became an increasingly vocal critic of the company's monopolistic practices. In 1911 the government began dissolution proceedings against United Shoe, and LDB testified before various congressional committees on the firm's pricing practices. This opened him to repeated charges of "inconsistency" from both the company and his own critics, who used LDB's prior defense of the firm as proof that he was now wrong; his change of mind would also be flung back at him in the confirmation hearings in 1916. For the progress of the shoe company conflict, see Mason, Brandeis, ch. 14.

2. Edward Douglass White (1845–1921), after a brief stint as a senator from Louisiana, was named to the Supreme Court by Grover Cleveland in 1894; Taft elevated him to Chief Justice in 1910.

3. It is said.

To: Alice Goldmark Brandeis
Date: April 4, 1913
Place: Washington, D.C.
Source: Gilbert MSS

DEAREST: Have just come from an hour with the President on efficiency.[1] He looks better than when I saw him last; but said he was tired out by the

212

Free Sugar wrangle[2] & I guess he is right. But then I was rather tired myself. The cold & throat are better but not hergestellt[3] yet, & I have had treatment continued by the throat man here, so as to settle this matter as prompt[ly] as possible.

Weather hot here, & I long for summer suit. Do is here. We were invited to Frankfurters for dinner, but I concluded (despite Aaron Aaronsohn) to stay quietly at home after a busy day with I.C.C.   Lovingly

1. LDB had long argued that big companies ran inefficiently and could charge less for their goods and services if they simply adopted the practices of scientific management. See LDB, "The Inefficiency of the Oligarchs," *Harper's Weekly* 59 (17 January 1914): 18–21, which is also ch. 9 of *Other People's Money.*

2. To fulfill his campaign pledge to lower the tariff, Wilson called a special session of Congress, and on 8 April he would personally address this session—the first president to speak directly to Congress since John Adams. In the negotiations already going on over what would become the Underwood Tariff, Wilson had to battle representatives from his own party who sought to retain a protective tariff for sugar. Wilson would agree to no more than a penny a pound tariff for three years, after which sugar had to go on the free list.

3. Not fully recovered.

To:	Alfred Brandeis
Date:	April 9, 1913
Place:	Boston, Massachusetts
Source:	Brandeis MSS

DEAR AL: Returned to Boston yesterday, having spent Monday in N.Y. on way from Washington. Nothing specially thrilling in W. Was there mainly on New Haven matters. The Co. & its backers are fighting hard—the inevitable & me—with increasing bitterness. But arithmetic must ultimately prevail, even over false accounting.

Everybody seems well satisfied with Wilson. Heard almost no criticism of him in W., but the talk about some members of the Cabinet has already begun & I guess no administration can escape without its trouble—particularly if we have a bit of hard times.

To:	Susan Brandeis
Date:	April 24, 1913
Place:	Boston, Massachusetts
Source:	Gilbert MSS

MY DEAREST SUSAN: I am delighted that the English examination is fortunately disposed of. The proviso that you shall continue the tutoring seems to me entirely satisfactory. You will undoubtedly gain much from it, if you can arrange so that your subjects are those you are really interested in—sociological, political or practical—subjects on which you naturally would have something to write about.

After all, the purpose of the course is to enable you to express your thoughts, and to compel you to think clearly and effectively.

The mere task of composition may continue difficult for you, as it has always been for me. But that is no terrible misfortunate [*sic*]. The important thing is to have something to say and to learn how to say it. And I have no doubt you will, in due time, have plenty to say, and that what you say will be worthwhile, because what you do is high-minded and noble.

We are very happy over your development.

With much love

You have not asked for funds lately. Remember, we want you to be in a position to contribute your liberal share to all college activities you are interested in.

To:	Alice Goldmark Brandeis
Date:	June 10, 1913
Place:	Washington, D.C.
Source:	Gilbert MSS

DEAREST: Made good progress yesterday on One price Article campaign,[1] first with Redfield who is thoroughly with me. He made appointment for us to see the Pres[iden]t. together which we did from 4:30 to 5:15. Prest was converted from dense ignorance to the light, wants me to make the educational campaign, & to have the Administration come out with a bill in Dec. Redfield & I are to see the Atty Genl at 10:45 today to try to get him to be quiescent on prosecution, a harder task.

Had long talk with Corporation Com[missione]r Davies[2] who will probably take up the investigation into facts I proposed.

On New Haven matters—saw Prouty, Marble & Meyer,[3] & some others at I.C.C. Don't feel so sure they will do the wise thing. Their "partial" report will probably appear between June 20th & 30th.[4] Had satisfactory talk with Gregory[5] who I am to spend hours with today.

Was at La Follettes after dinner. Bob was busy on the Magazine at first & Mrs. Bishop was there so we had only meaningless chat. Am to dine there & spend the evening in more serious talk today.

I expect to leave here 12:30 (noon) tomorrow—to talk at Baltimore[6] & hope to be home Thursday A.M. Lovingly

1. As part of his campaign against cutthroat pricing as a form of unfair competition, LDB suggested that manufacturers be allowed to set a price on their goods that would be

uniform throughout a marketing area. See "On Maintaining Makers' Prices," *Harper's Weekly* 57 (14 June 1913): 6.

2. Joseph Edward Davies (1876–1958) practiced law in Wisconsin before becoming commissioner of corporations in Wilson's administration. In 1915 the president named him to the Federal Trade Commission. Davies later held a number of special posts, including ambassador to Moscow and Franklin Roosevelt's personal envoy to Joseph Stalin.

3. Balthasar Henry Meyer (1866–1954), an economist at the University of Wisconsin and an expert on railway regulation, was appointed a commissioner of the Interstate Commerce Commission in 1911 and served until 1939. He then opened a private consulting business in Washington.

4. The ICC report did not come out until 9 July, and it fully endorsed LDB's charges about the poor financial practices followed by Mellen. Perhaps as a sop to the business community and in an effort not to deflate the already dropping price of New Haven stock, the report concluded that "[t]he financial condition of the company calls for careful consideration and prudent action, but gives no occasion for hysteria." For a full summary of the report, with copious quotations, see the *New York Times,* 10 July 1913.

5. Thomas Watt Gregory (1861–1933), a Texas attorney and protégé of Col. House, was brought into the Justice Department as a special assistant attorney general in charge of prosecuting the New Haven for antitrust violations. In 1914 he succeeded McReynolds as attorney general.

6. LDB spoke before what was billed as an "Inspirational Meeting" of more than 3,000 advertising professionals in Baltimore. In his speech LDB wove together two of his constant themes: the need for business leaders to act ethically and the merits of fair pricing (see note 1 above).

To: **Alfred Brandeis**
Date: **July 9, 1913**
Place: **Boston, Massachusetts**
Source: **Brandeis MSS**

DEAR AL: Was just on the point of writing you about Uncle William's marvellous improvements when yours of Monday came.[1] Hope your St. Louis trip won't tire you too much.

Mellen's resignation from the B. & M. is interesting.[2] I enclose Journal clipping & Herald editorial.[3] The latter is particularly interesting, as accepting my principle of merit of efficiency, as it has been & is my bitterest foe here, being controlled by Shoe Machinery & New Haven interests.

Yr $225 draft received.

1. The next day William Taussig, Alfred's father-in-law, died in St. Louis.

2. The previous day Mellen had resigned as head of the Boston & Maine, explaining that being president of that line as well as of the New Haven had been too heavy a load and that he would devote his time to the New Haven alone. Antimerger critics claimed, however, that Mellen was trying to avert further investigation and antitrust prosecution. In a statement to the press LDB said: "The action today is a step in the right direction, but it does not go far enough. The traveling public will not be entirely satisfied until there is a complete severance of the control of the Boston & Maine and Maine Central by the New Haven Road" (quoted in Mason, *Brandeis,* 208–9).

3. The *Herald*, in an editorial on 9 July, ignored nearly all of the arguments put forth by opponents of the merger and suggested that the problems of the two lines were different—therefore a capable man was needed at the helm of each road. Without mentioning LDB at all, the paper in essence echoed his argument that one individual could not efficiently perform too many tasks without a loss in the quality of work.

To:	Alfred Brandeis
Date:	September 2, 1913
Place:	Dedham, Massachusetts
Source:	Brandeis MSS

DEAR AL: Nothing from you for a long time, and I didn't get a chance to ask Madie about you on Wednesday.

Have had a rather quiet time since South Yarmouth, trying to write some articles on the money trust for Harper's.[1] There will be some crys [*sic*] of "Holy Murder" if the legislation I propose ever gets past [*sic*]; but less than that will do little good.

New Haven matters are active as ever. The government lawyers are steadily at work and we should get some action before the middle of October.[2]

1. These articles, printed in *Harper's Weekly* in the last months of 1913 and through January 1914 as "Breaking the Money Trust," were compiled and published as *Other People's Money, and How the Bankers Use It* by Frederick A. Stokes in 1914 and reprinted several times since. The articles summarized and popularized the findings of the Pujo Committee (see LDB to Samuel Untermyer, 18 March 1913, note 2, BL) and revealed the extent to which American business was dominated by what LDB called, in his first chapter, "our financial oligarchy." The articles included many of the themes LDB had emphasized for the past several years—the evils of monopoly, the inefficiency of big corporations, the autocratic power of the bankers, and the threat that industrialization on a large scale posed to traditional American values. They appeared in *Harper's* because LDB had played a major hand in securing that magazine for Norman Hapgood.

2. New Haven matters had never been far from LDB's mind ever since he had opposed the merger of the Boston & Maine with the New Haven. Under Roosevelt and Taft the Justice Department had not been sympathetic to LDB's call for an antitrust investigation, but Attorney General McReynolds, long a foe of monopoly, quickly picked up on LDB's suggestion while the Interstate Commerce Commission also investigated the road's finances; LDB was closely involved with both investigations. In December 1913 the road passed its dividend for the first time in its history; the following spring the Senate Committee on Interstate Commerce began hearings on the road and on the role of J. P. Morgan in its management. The Justice Department filed a bill for dissolution of the merger, and on 11 August 1914 the company capitulated, never recovering from the financial mismanagement that LDB had warned about so clearly.

To:	Alice Goldmark Brandeis
Date:	November 11, 1913
Place:	Washington, D.C.
Source:	Gilbert MSS

DEAREST: Your Sunday letter has come. Sorry you too had so poor a day, but that oncoming cold doubtless pleases you more than it does me, tho' there is fine sunshine here.

Lunched very pleasantly with McAdoo[1] alone at his home on Mass. Ave. (1¼ hours), gained no special information, but think he is full of fight.

I kept my promise & dined with E.G. Lowry[2] at the Cosmos, got some interesting sidelights, but there is not much of value in him. He is really wrong headed, in rather a nice way. He says the Even[ing]. Post let up on the New Haven really for lack of funds. He didn't have any appropriation to follow up his lead (Lowry is a tremendous admirer of Murray Crane[']s—that about measures him). He says everyone here is practically against Wilson's Mexican policy.[3] Says it is without warrant in international law or practical policies. Thinks John Basset [sic] Moore[4] is of that opinion too, but Lowry rather thinks Wilson will carry it through by sheer force of will—that is Huerta will resign. Lowry talked much of Wilson's isolatedness, says he wants no advice & will take none, that Cabinet members have nothing to say in any matters Wilson takes up (even McAdoo re Currency bill)[5] & that Wilson, on the other hand, lets them shift for themselves as in Lane & Houston's[6] departments; & that W. don't want to see anyone.

Lowry say[s] W. is thoroughly imbued with Walter Bagehot[7] & that one ought to have B. always at hand in order to understand W's actions. Also say[s] W. is urging Prouty not to resign as W. has no one satisfactory to fill his place.[8] Also that he probably will not reappoint Clements.[9] L. thinks W. fills most of his callers with fear by his intelligence, but that he is not great—lacks simpleness, that he is always courteous, but does not have or want friends, that the currency bill will pass by Xmas,[10] but that W. will meet his rebuffs on the trust legislation.

I must be off.

Lovingly

The Putnams are here again.

---

1. William Gibbs McAdoo (1863–1941) was the most able member of the Wilson cabinet. A lawyer, he was attracted to transportation problems and organized the company that built the first tunnel under the Hudson River. The president named McAdoo, an early Wilson supporter, as secretary of the treasury; Wilson's confidence in him grew after he married the president's daughter Eleanor in 1914. McAdoo and LDB hit it off well, and each respected the other's considerable abilities. During the war LDB urged Wilson to appoint McAdoo to head the Railroad Administration, which took over control of the country's lines and ran them as a unified system. After the war McAdoo moved to California to practice law and in 1932 won one term as U.S. senator. He was frequently mentioned as a possible Democratic candidate for the presidency but never received the party's nomination. See his memoirs, *Crowded Years* (Boston, 1931).

2. Edward George Lowry (1876–1943) was the managing editor of the *New York Evening Post*.

3. The old and corrupt regime of Porfirio Díaz in Mexico had been overthrown in 1911 by a reformer, Francisco Madero. Madero tried to effect real reforms, which triggered counterrevolutions by the established groups, especially the large landowners and business interests. In early February 1913 Madero was overthrown by one of his chief lieutenants, Victoriano Huerta. Wilson, of course, inherited this situation; although he had said he would not intervene in Mexican affairs, his burning desire to establish a constitutional democracy there eventually led him to send troops. Wilson refused to recognize the Huerta regime—"I will not recognize a government of butchers'—and his personal animosity was matched and supported by American business interests who wanted to see a more friendly government installed. A few days earlier Wilson had issued a circular note informing the governments of the world that had recognized Huerta that it was "his immediate duty to require Huerta's retirement from the Mexican government" and that the United States would "now proceed to employ such means as may be necessary to secure this result" (Arthur S. Link, *Wilson: The New Freedom* [Princeton, 1956], ch. 11). Huerta refused to be cowed and gave the United States its opportunity to use force when armed bandits along Mexico's northern borders began forays into Texas. The following spring United States forces occupied Vera Cruz, and war was averted when both countries agreed to arbitration by Argentina, Brazil, and Chile. Wilson was widely condemned for his Mexican policy and antagonized many of his supporters.

4. John Bassett Moore (1860–1947) was counselor of the State Department and a widely recognized authority on international law. Moore had been consulted by Wilson before issuing the 7 November note on Mexico.

5. One of the most important pieces of legislation in Wilson's New Freedom was the Federal Reserve Act, which reformed the American banking system and made currency issue solely a government function. LDB must have smiled when listening to Lowry, because he himself had been consulted by Wilson on the currency question (see LDB to Wilson, 14 June 1913, BL), and McAdoo had also played a key role in convincing Wilson that a strong Federal Reserve Board had to be created and that currency issue had to taken away from the banks.

6. David Franklin Houston (1866–1940) was Wilson's secretary of agriculture; the former president of the University of Texas was named to the position because of his friendship with Colonel House. He was one of the more conservative members of the cabinet, and Arthur Link called him "something of a misfit in a progressive administration" (*The New Freedom,* 137). Nonetheless, he served through both of Wilson's terms. See his *Eight Years with Wilson's Cabinet, 1913–1920* (Garden City, 1926).

7. Walter Bagehot (1826–77), the English economist and journalist, had been a major intellectual influence in Wilson's life since his graduate school days. Bagehot's *The English Constitution,* published in the United States in 1873, was the model for Wilson's doctoral dissertation, *Congressional Government* (New York, 1885). Like Bagehot, Wilson considered the British cabinet model of government far superior to the American system since the ministers' responsibility for particular areas of government, and their accountability to the prime minister, made for both effective party leadership and effective government.

8. Prouty remained on the ICC until 1914, serving in both 1913 and 1914 as chair.

9. On 23 December Wilson did, in fact, reappoint Judson C. Clements (1846–1917) to the Interstate Commerce Commission. Clements represented the Seventh Georgia District in the House of Representatives from 1881 to 1891; in 1892 he was appointed to the ICC and served on that board until his death.

10. On this Lowry was correct. Congress passed the final version of the measure on 23 December, and Wilson signed it into law immediately.

To: Alice Goldmark Brandeis
Date: November 12, 1913
Place: Washington, D.C.
Source: Gilbert MSS

218

DEAREST: Greetings to the birthday which you have made worthwhile.[1]

It looks now as if I had better stay here until Saturday night, spend Sunday in N.Y., Monday & Tuesday in Boston, Wednesday in New York and back here again for Thursday of next week. I am getting considerable work started through I.C.C. men[2] and it looks now as if I were quite as well off without [Joseph B.] Eastman. He might have raised jealousies.

I have not heard from Norman since my letter, but after yours, suggested he confer with George Rublee who should be in N.Y. & also wrote George. The cuts Norman was proposing[3] are not as serious in character as you probably suppose, though quite copious in quantity. They were mainly quotations, (which I though[t] gave life to the article, rather than the reverse). However, I am always rather afraid of having *too much* influence with Norman.

Lunched with Welliver yesterday. He thinks he may be put at the head of the Washington Times which would result in "fur-flying".

Welliver is quite impatient with the President. Says, Wilson is so much a party man that he is deliberately throwing away all progressive and newspaper support, and is making considerable future trouble for himself. It is evident that Wilson's political philosophy is that none but Democrats need apply, that the Democrats have the responsibility, that they must legislate, that all minority Democrats must yield, & I my Lords embody the Democratic party. That seems to be the impression so far gained here on this visit.[4]   Lovingly

1. The next day would be LDB's fifty-seventh birthday.

2. Although they lost in their first attempt to secure higher freight rates in 1910–11, the railroads made a second attempt in May 1913. They now claimed that they needed an average five percent increase. On 15 August the ICC asked LDB to enter the case. This time, however, he would represent neither the carriers nor the shippers but "the public." His task was to see that all sides of the question were fairly presented. In view of his previous record as a critic of the railroads, and the ambiguity of his assignment in the second rate hearings, LDB's conclusion that eastern railroads did, in fact, need a rate increase was met with anger and charges of bad faith by some shippers and some other opponents of the railroads. These charges of betrayal surfaced in the hearings over LDB's nomination to the Supreme Court in 1916. For the details of the Second Advanced Rate hearings before the ICC, see Mason, *Brandeis,* ch. 21.

3. LDB's forthcoming article, "Our Financial Oligarchy," the first installment of "Breaking the Money Trust," appeared in *Harper's Weekly* 58 (22 November 1913): 10–13.

4. Political affiliation certainly dominated the Wilson administration's appointments, since there were many hungry Democrats clamoring for jobs after sixteen years in the political wilderness. Nowhere was party loyalty more valued over ability than in the State Department, where William Jennings Bryan sacked dozens of career officials and replaced them with incompetent party hacks. Wilson's autocratic tendencies had shown up as early as his tenure as president of Princeton and would lead to his downfall in the battle over the League of Nations in 1919.

To: Alice Goldmark Brandeis
Date: November 14, 1913
Place: Washington, D.C.
Source: Gilbert MSS

DEAREST: I spent the birthday largely loafing. It was warm & lured to labor-lessness & as my assistant Carmalt[1] was absent there was no compulsion to work. To begin with I followed Susan's advice & visited Dr. Meade Moore, a competent throat man, whom [Winfred] Denison recommended & shall give him a chance to restore my mellifluous voice. Then I talked merger & advance rate data with Adkins[2] and advance rate material & price maintenance with Com[missione]r Davies with whom I later lunched at the Cosmos. (He is a fine progressive). Had also a talk with Redfield, who may cooperate in some cloakmakers investigation, called on Norman [Hapgood]'s parents & found père at home & after a chat with Pullman[3] while I was eating at the Tea Cup Inn, went to the La Follettes, but Belle & Phil were at the theatre. The Senator is still atalking in the South & I should think would have to talk an extra night or two to cover the increased rent of their new house which is very attractive outside and finely situated. It is about a mile further out (3320 Ave of the Presidents).

Prof. Bemis[4] is greatly disturbed over the prospect that the President will appoint as I.C. Commission[er] Daniels[5] former Princeton professor whom Wilson appointed N.J. Public Service Com[missione]r.

I think I see some material available for the advance rate case in several of the Dept[s]. & am planning new requisitions.

Poor old New Haven seems to have dropped another peg yesterday.

Lovingly

Susan's long letter shows increasing self reliance.

1. James Walton Carmalt (1872–1937) was an attorney with the ICC. The following year he would become the commission's chief examiner. He worked closely with LDB in preparing for the advanced rate hearings.

2. Jesse Corcoran Adkins (1879–1955) was serving his second term as assistant attorney general; in 1930 he was appointed to the supreme court for the District of Columbia.

3. Raymond Wellington Pullman (1883–1920) was a publicity agent in the Forestry Service in the days of the Pinchot-Ballinger fight and an ally of LDB in the hearings.

4. Edward Webster Bemis (1860–1930) taught statistics at Vanderbilt and the University of Chicago and then became superintendent of the water department in Cleveland. He also wrote several books on municipal franchises.

5. Winthrop More Daniels (1867–1944) went to Princeton as an assistant professor of political economy in 1892 and was a full professor by 1897. In 1911 then governor Wilson named him to the Board of Public Utility Commissioners of New Jersey, and in 1914 President Wilson appointed him to the Interstate Commerce Commission, where he served until 1923. He then taught at Yale until his retirement in 1936. Daniels was the author of numerous books and articles.

To: Alice Goldmark Brandeis
Date: November 22, 1913
Place: Washington, D.C.
Source: Gilbert MSS

DEAREST: All the newspaper men here are terribly down on Senator Owen.[1] Say he is utterly unreliably [*sic*], that he lies & even charge him with corruption & say that the President's difficulties with the currency bill are largely due to Owen's being chairman.[2] Also that all the brains & study & most of the virtue on the Com[mit]tee is on the side of the opposition, including Hitchcock.[3] (Hollis[4] they say is still an unknown quantity.) I am told this is [the] view (regardless of party) of the newspaper men. Angus McSween, Kirby of the N.Y. World[5] & Dunlap of the Sun & Jud Welliver seem to agree on this. Have seen these & Stoddard[6] & gotten them interested in money trust & advance rate matters & you may see some results in the Transcript. "This sort of thing takes a deal of training."

[David] Ives called me up early yesterday & I saw him before he went to Lane's. He was weak & thinner, but better than I expected.

Called on Stanley, in view of his talk with the President on trust. S. says he told the Prest. he (S) couldn't follow me on new administrative board.[7] The Prest. broke in & said stop, "I have the highest opinion of Mr. Brandeis' judgement on these matters etc." & W. had apparently been reading my Nov 8 article.[8] Then I saw Oldfield to get him in line on Price Maintenance. I think he will be amenable.[9] He said he had been to the President & had urged my appointment as Commissioner of Patents; and the President replied, Nothing would suit him better, but the trouble with me was I would not accept any office.

Ives had a 3 hour talk with the Atty Genl yesterday & I am to hear this morning what occurred.

Think it would be well for you to have Miss Grady come in for an evening's talk if you can arrange it.

The currency bill, Kirby says will not pass before March 1 & then substantially the Glass bill will be put thro' by Democratic caucus.[10]

Lovingly

Please send me some of my white ties.

Ives and I are very sad about John Marble's death.

    1. Robert Latham Owen (1856–1947) was a liberal Democrat who served as senator from Oklahoma from 1907 to 1925.
    2. Owen sided with McAdoo and Secretary of State Bryan in insisting that the Federal Reserve System be controlled by the federal government and not by the banks. In June Owen succeeded in scuttling the more conservative Glass bill, which Wilson had

originally approved. In the end Owen and his allies, including LDB, got nearly everything they considered important in the bill.

3. Gilbert Monell Hitchcock (1859–1934), an Omaha lawyer and newspaper publisher, represented Nebraska in the House of Representatives from 1907 to 1911 and then in the Senate from 1911 to 1923. In early September Hitchcock, along with James A. Reed of Missouri and James O'Gorman of New York, bolted from the Democratic caucus in support of the banking bill and insisted on a series of lengthy hearings that took up most of two months.

4. Henry French Hollis (1869–1949) had been elected the previous November to his only term as senator from New Hampshire.

5. Probably Rollin Kirby (1875–1952), the cartoonist at the *World* who thrice won the Pulitzer Prize. It was Kirby who drew the famous cartoon entitled "The Blow That Almost Killed Father," showing a Wall Street financier in shock at a newspaper headline that LDB had been named to the Supreme Court (see BL, vol. 4, opposite p. 294).

6. Possibly William Leavitt Stoddard (1884–1954), a young writer whose primary career would be in public relations. A close associate of E. A. Filene, Stoddard would later serve as executive secretary of the Savings Bank Insurance League.

7. Although he had initially opposed the idea of a federal agency to interpret a new antitrust act, LDB slowly came around to see the need for one. The Wilson antitrust program initially consisted of three measures. The Clayton bill provided for a strengthening of the Sherman Act; the Covington bill provided for an expansion of the then existing Bureau of Corporations but would not have significant enforcement powers; the Rayburn bill would have given the ICC power over the issuance of railroad stocks and securities.

8. LDB, "The Solution of the Trust Problem: A Program," *Harper's Weekly* 58 (8 November 1913): 18–19. In the article LDB endorsed the administration's efforts to strengthen the Sherman Act. He said that the critical things needed were to remove the uncertainties of the Sherman Act, to facilitate its enforcement by the courts, to create a board to aid in administering the Sherman Act, and to secure the approval of trade agreements that enhanced competition.

9. A bill drawn by Rublee and LDB was eventually introduced by Congressman Raymond B. Stevens, and Congress even held hearings on it in January 1915. But, like much other legislation aimed at regulating the economy, it was forgotten as the United States prepared for and then entered World War I. The idea of price maintenance was reintroduced in 1924 and again in 1931, but to no avail. LDB did, however, live to see Congress enact the measure as the Miller-Tydings Act of 1937.

10. See LDB to AGB, 11 November 1913, note 5.

To: Alice Goldmark Brandeis
Date: November 23, 1913
Place: Washington, D.C.
Source: Gilbert MSS

DEAREST: Dined last evening at the Pinchots to get Gifford to write the Water Trust article.[1] Of course I took G[eorge].R[ublee]. & we met the Cranes there.

Evening before dined with the Cranes at the Shoreham (took George & had D[avid].O.I[ves]. invited, but he was too tired to go.) Gov. Folk[2] and the Poindexter[s] were there. Folk told things about Mexican situation which rather confirmed my views on Wilson's policy. Says Middle & Southern Mexico is practically unanimous for Huerta & that H. is keeping order there; that Northern Mexico is practically unanimous against Huerta, but that no one keeps order there, every village having practically a separate rebel chief; & that between these two sections is largely a desert land.

Charles [Crane] said last night that [Senator] Owen expects to pass Currency bill by Xmas.

Lady Johnson [sic][3] was with us a part of last evening. "Mir wenigstens gefällt sie nicht."[4] Very modern & English & her gown would be appropriate for the Kismet performance.

I shall lunch with Frankfurter & Denison & dine with D.O.I. this evening.

Lovingly

Please send Mrs. C.R. Crane, 31 W. 12th St., a copy of the volume of William James containing his essay on the Substitute for War,[5] & send to Miss Morgan c/o Mrs. Pinchot, 1605 R.I. Ave the volume of E.E. Hale containing "My Double & How he undid me."[6]

The Harper's articles are much talked about.

Think I did a good job yesterday with Stratton, Director of Bureau of Standards.[7]

1. LDB was probably aware of a series of eight unsigned newspaper articles that Pinchot had written for the *Philadelphia North American* in February and March 1911 on the water power monopoly in Pennsylvania. Pinchot did not write on this subject again, however, until many years later. He published a pamphlet, "The Power Monopoly: Its Makeup and Its Menace," in 1929 and also wrote several articles on the subject between 1929 and 1932.

2. Joseph Wingate Folk (1869–1923) was the St. Louis lawyer whose crusade against municipal corruption attracted national attention. He had served a term as governor of Missouri and in 1913 was counselor to the State Department. The following year he became chief counsel to the ICC.

3. Antoniette Eno Pinchot (1868–19[?]), the younger sister of Gifford Pinchot, married the Hon. Sir Alan Johnstone, the British minister to Copenhagen.

4. "She doesn't please *me* at all." For LDB's reevaluation of Lady Johnstone, see LDB to AGB, 8 January 1914.

5. Shortly before his death, William James (1842–1910), the noted Harvard psychologist and philosopher, wrote "The Moral Equivalent of War" for the American Association for International Conciliation. In it he proposed a national conscription of young men for a "war against nature." All men, he argued, are pugnacious by nature and will fight unless there is an adequate outlet to divert their aggressiveness. The trick is to channel those instincts to worthier purposes than warfare.

6. Edward Everett Hale (1822–1909) was the longtime minister of South Congregational Church in Boston as well as a noted writer of essays and short stories, of which the two most famous are "The Man without a Country" and "My Double and How He Undid Me," which first appeared in *Atlantic Monthly* in 1859. The story is about a minister who, bored with all the meaningless meetings he has to attend, finds a man who looks just like him. The double, who is somewhat dim-witted, is taught a few basic responses, which seem to serve all purposes for a whole year until he fumbles one of the cliches and is discovered.

7. Samuel Wesley Stratton (1861–1931), a physicist, headed the National Bureau of Standards until 1923, when he became president of the Massachusetts Institute of Technology.

To: Alice Goldmark Brandeis
Date: November 24, 1913
Place: Washington, D.C.
Source: Gilbert MSS

DEAREST: The interview with the Atty. Genl. lasted 3 hours & only a part of the ground he wanted to cover was exhausted. Much of our time was taken in discussing conditions which you & I talked over after the Fowler-Gregg dinner. I am to have a further conference with McReynolds later in the week.

I lunch with the Frankfurter/Denison household,[1] which was augmented by Christie,[2] the Stanley Kings,[3] the artist Bergland [sic][4] and one Bissell,[5] who is in the Dept. of Justice. Stanley K. has been here having his eye operated on—by Dr. Wilmer—thus does Boston greatness pass. Mrs. King seemed to me much more attractive & interesting than when newly married & he the less so. You are right about Frankfurter's excessive sociability. McReynolds criticised [Winfred] Denison also on that score.

The Marble service was simple, but not beautiful. Secretary Lane seemed almost crushed. Marble was apparently not particularly overworked. He died of Bright's Disease, of long standing.

I dined most quietly with Ives at the Willard. His prospects are not brilliant, but there is still hope. The President will probably have to act soon.

I hope soon to get through with my preliminary work & to settle down to some quiet study of material which is beginning to lumber up my room. There are a lot of leads to be followed up.

Grenville McFarlane [sic] writes of my first article[6] that it is "too condensed". Thus is one hounded by conflicting criticism.

The Chamber of Commerce victory[7] ought to encourage the progressives & should lead to many resignations. That would improve matters considerably. I suppose E.A.F.[8] feels much set up.

It was good to have Elizabeth's letter.   Lovingly

1. Frankfurter lived at 1727 Nineteenth Street, a house owned by the brilliant Robert G. Valentine, commissioner of Indian affairs during the Taft administration. Other residents included Winfred Denison, Loring C. Christie (see the next note), and Lord Eustace Percy, posted to the British embassy. Known as "the House of Truth," the house became one of the best-known salons in Washington, where at almost any time of the night or day good conversation with interesting people could be found.

2. Loring Cheney Christie (1885–1941), although a Canadian citizen, served as an assistant to the United States solicitor general; he would later be a legal advisor to the Canadian government and minister to the United States.

3. Stanley King (1883–1951) had been a special assistant in the War Department and would later be president of Amherst College from 1932 to 1946. He was married to the former Gertrude Louisa Besse (d. 1923).

4. Gutzon Borglum (1871–1941), already a celebrated sculptor, would be remembered primarily for his monumental carvings on Mount Rushmore. He was a frequent guest at the House of Truth.

5. Louis G. Bissell was an attorney in the Office of the Assistant Attorney General for the Court of Claims Division.

6. In LDB's "Breaking the Money Trust" series for *Harper's Weekly;* see LDB to AGB, 12 November 1913.

7. On 20 November a new executive director of the chamber, Frank J. Ludwy, was elected. There apparently had been a sharp fight over the selection, and LDB may have been anticipating that the losers might resign.

8. Edward Albert Filene (1860–1937) was a client of LDB as well as a close friend and associate in various Massachusetts reform efforts. He and his brother had taken over their father's small store and built it into one of Boston's leading department stores. He was also a pioneer in employee relations and with LDB's encouragement and advice set up health care programs, profit sharing, and other programs. For LDB's view of Filene, see *Business— a Profession,* 9–12; for Filene's view of LDB, see "Louis D. Brandeis As We Know Him," *Boston Post,* 4 March 1916.

To:	Alice Goldmark Brandeis
Date:	November 25, 1913
Place:	Washington, D.C.
Source:	Gilbert MSS

DEAREST: Another request to publish the articles in book form has come, this from the Century.[1]

The RR hearings began yesterday.[2] The RRs are well prepared this time and make a good *prima facie* case, and are doubtless telling largely the truth, but not the whole truth. The amount of work to be done is growing apace & I don't see how this job, including the necessary legislation, will be out of the way before another Summer. It is a pity we could not have postponed it until 1914–15, when Elizabeth's Radcliffe plans would have suggested a month in Washington. George Rublee and probably D.O.I[ves]. will spend Thanksgiving here also; not wholly the result of Evil Example. Charles R. [Crane] et uxor[3] leave for Asheville tonight. I declined an urgent invitation to dine with Hamlin last night & began my nap at 8:30.

Lovingly

Yours of Sunday just recd. You should have had a special delivery letter.

1. LDB eventually agreed to allow Frederick A. Stokes of Boston to publish his *Harper's* articles in book form.

2. The Second Advanced Rate hearings before the Interstate Commerce Commission would occupy much of LDB's time for the next several months. See LDB to AGB, 12 November 1913, note 2.

3. And wife.

To:　　　Alice Goldmark Brandeis
Date:　　November 26, 1913
Place:　　Washington, D.C.
Source:　Gilbert MSS

DEAREST: Wired you yesterday about Ives as we through [sic] newspapers might have some reference to his illness which would alarm Mrs. Ives. He was quite comfortable when I left him last evening protected by a nurse who I (à la Goldmarks) advised the doctor to instal. It did not seem necessary, but illness now is mostly nerves anyhow & I was sure he would sleep better if he knew he could have aid in case he needed it. The pull of the last $3^1/_2$ years has been too hard on him, & if it weren't for this cussed office he wants,[1] the Chamber of Com. victory would have set him up.[2] But the present uncertainty & that old rebate sentence worry him.

I enclose letter from Louis Wehle who is having his troubles too.

Lunched with Charles [Crane] & William Hard[3] yesterday for a few moments, between visits on Dave Ives & saw [Carl] Snyder and Garrett [sic][4] for a little last evening. The Times Annalist has a page on my Price Maintenance article. Met Lynn Haynes at the New Willard lunching with McDonald & will send you McD. letter on the Mich Strike. Haynes telephoned me this morning after reading the financial oligarchy[5] that he thought it the most remarkable feat of clear statement ever done, etc.

Lovingly

A joyous Thanksgiving to you three.

1. LDB was working to get Ives appointed to the Interstate Commerce Commission to replace Charles Prouty, who had announced his intention to resign. See LDB to Woodrow Wilson, 10 October 1913, BL. Despite intense pressure from New England, Wilson passed Ives over, and then Ives unexpectedly died in March 1914.

2. See LDB to AGB, 24 November 1913.

3. William Hard (1878–1962), a prolific freelance writer, was a friend to many progressive politicians and reformers. See Hard's "Brandeis," *Outlook* 113 (31 May 1916): 271–77.

4. Garet Garret (1878–1954) was, at various times, the financial editor of several of the leading New York newspapers; presently he was the editor of the *New York Times Annalist*.

5. The first article in LDB's money trust series.

To:　　　Alice Goldmark Brandeis
Date:　　November 27, 1913
Place:　　Washington, D.C.
Source:　Gilbert MSS

DEAREST: Ives seemed much better this morning. Said he had slept finely, felt as if he could eat a pound of beefsteak and that if he weren't under the doctor's orders would get up. He is game too about his heart and work and hasn't let himself be depressed by the doctors' prognostications. If things continue to improve so, there ought to be no difficulty in our getting off to New York Monday noon.

Had a nice walk in the Potomac Park and a good nap thereafter. Expect to dine quietly with G[eorge].R[ublee]. I am sometimes reminded of [*].

Lovingly

To:	Alice Goldmark Brandeis
Date:	December 5, 1913
Place:	Washington, D.C.
Source:	Gilbert MSS

DEAREST: About Crowly [sic],[1] I forgot to say that the success of a weekly edited by him seems to me improbable. To appearances, he lacks most of the necessary qualifications & I should think he doesn't have but a slight idea of the work involved. He is preeminently of the recluse type of worker & it is difficult to see how he could manage men & affairs. Besides, his wife is forbidding. She is very nice, except that she smokes.[2]

I went for a couple of hours dine—8 to 10:15—at the Borden Harriman's,[3] as I wanted to land Moscowitz [sic] etc. She is a well meaning worker, but the President showed his failure to grasp the significance of social work.[4]

Senator Newlands[5] wanted me to take supper with him & Com[missione]r Davies tomorrow to talk trusts etc., but I have commuted the sentence to a luncheon with him & House members some time next week.

Untermyer was at the Henry Clayton,[6] Davies luncheon yesterday. Clayton wants me to submit bills galore & they all want my cooperation most intensively. Henry is a fine fellow in desire. I can't quite make up my mind about U.

You might have added to your gallery of horrors of women's dress from the Harriman's last evening. She is [of] a handsome womanly nature, but her get up & that of her guests was [beneath] contempt.[7]

A Mr. Fletcher[8] Minister to Chile, & previously in the diplomatic service in China etc. was interestingly informing, & the dinner was not tiring, but give me "papers" for steady diet.

Had a long talk on trust, money trust & price maintenance with McAdoo today & am to dine with him Tuesday 7:30 alone to map out an administration policy.

Redfield wants to see me Monday. Livy Richard[9] arrived today. I have seen him but a moment

Lovingly

1. Herbert Croly (1869–1930), like LDB, had given a great deal of thought to the problems created by industrialization. But unlike LDB, Croly came to the conclusion that bigness had to be accepted and a new political philosophy developed, blending the democratic idealism of Jefferson with the Hamiltonian notion of a strong central government. His important book *The Promise of American Life* (New York, 1909) caught the eye of Theodore Roosevelt and became the basis for his New Nationalism. In 1914, with the help of Dorothy and Willard Straight, Croly founded and became the editor of the *New Republic,* which for many years was the leading journal of liberal thought in the United States.

2. Louise Emory Croly (1866–1945), the daughter of a well-established Baltimore family, met Croly while she was studying at what was then known as the Harvard Annex, now Radcliffe. She was a perfect counterpart to Croly, gregarious where he was shy, intelligent, well read, and admired by all of his friends.

3. J. Borden Harriman (1864–1914) was a banker and stockbroker before ill health (possibly stomach cancer) forced him to retire from business in February 1913.

4. LDB's phrasing does not make it clear whether he is discussing Florence Jaffray Hurst Harriman (1870–1967) or Belle Lindner Israels Moskowitz (1877–1933). Harriman, despite LDB's poor impression of her, became one of the more important women reformers of the day. Wilson had recently named her as the only woman member of the Industrial Commission; Franklin Roosevelt later appointed her as ambassador to Denmark prior to World War II (where, at the age of sixty-nine, she escaped the invading Nazis by hiding out in the woods for several weeks with Danish partisans); and in 1963 John F. Kennedy chose her as the first person to receive the newly created Citation of Merit for Distinguished Service. Moskowitz was a well-known social worker and New York activist, the wife of LDB's Garment Workers ally Henry Moskowitz. Belle became a warm adherent of Governor Alfred E. Smith and remained loyal to him until her death.

5. Francis Griffith Newlands (1848–1917) went to Nevada as a young man and became involved in politics there. He served five terms in the House of Representatives and in 1902 was elected to the first of his three terms in the Senate.

6. Henry DeLamar Clayton (1857–1929) represented the Third Alabama District in Congress from 1897 to 1915, when Wilson named him a U.S. district judge. Clayton was considered the antitrust expert in the House of Representatives, and LDB would work closely with him in developing the Wilson administration's antitrust bill.

7. Here LDB wrote the word "contempt" at the bottom of the page with an arrow coming underneath that word—obviously indicating "beneath contempt."

8. Henry Prather Fletcher (1873–1959), a Pennsylvania lawyer, joined the Rough Riders in the Spanish-American War and then went on to a distinguished diplomatic career that began in Theodore Roosevelt's administration and ended during Harry S. Truman's, when Fletcher was one of the American representatives to the Dumbarton Oaks conference that established the details for founding the United Nations. In 1916 Fletcher served as ambassador to Mexico, helping to restore better relations between the two countries.

9. Livy Strong Richard (1872–1935) was editor of the *Boston Common;* from 1915 to 1928 he edited the *Boston Advertiser.*

To: **Alice Goldmark Brandeis**
Date: **December 8, 1913**
Place: **Washington, D.C.**
Source: **Gilbert MSS**

DEAREST: Your good postal has come & trust you found yourself in good shape on reaching home. Have had a fine time this A.M. in my sunny room [at the Hotel Gordon] over "papers" quite uninterrupted & have planned to work here with Carmalt & Burnside tomorrow when the draft of questions is supposed to be ready for my first formal revision.

Yesterday morning was devoted to Livy R[ichard]. & to Moscowitz [*sic*] & correcting proof for Harpers.

I declined 3 luncheon invites, spent the lunch hour over N.Y. Times at Cosmos Club & after a nap walked out for ex[ercise]. Landed at La Follettes for supper & left there at 8:30 for a walk home & was in bed at 10. (Tell Bessie [Evans] I was wrong about their house having no window etc. in rear. It has considerable access to sun there.)

I am a bit alarmed about the President's alleged Central American policy,[1] which as described is quite near a protectorate & in harmony with his Mexican attitude,[2] & I am also afraid he is being frightened by increasing signs of business arrest, although this is worldwide—all South America e.g.

Lovingly

Fine cold weather today.

Wayne MacVeagh[3] was very critical of the Administration & says he is glad I am not in the Cabinet.

1. Since the Spanish-American War, the U.S. government had been taking an increasingly active role in Latin America, extending over it what amounted to a sphere of influence. In order to promote political stability and protect U.S. investments, the government on a number of occasions sent the military to impose order. Since Democrats had been critical of the policies of Roosevelt and Taft, Latin American countries expected that the Wilson administration would be more respectful of their national autonomy, and the early pronouncements of Wilson and Bryan championed the cause of nonintervention. But as Arthur Link notes, "the administration, with the best intentions, found itself so entangled by previous commitments and especially by its own inconsistencies that it violated all its generous professions in its relations with Mexico, Central America and the island countries. The years 1913 to 1921 witnessed intervention by the State Department and the navy on a scale that had never before been contemplated" (*Woodrow Wilson and the Progressive Era* [New York, 1954], 93). At this time, the United States and Nicaragua were negotiating a treaty that would give the United States an option to build a second isthmian canal but would also have made Nicaragua into little more than a protectorate of the United States.

2. See LDB to AGB, 11 November 1913, note 3.

3. Isaac Wayne MacVeagh (1833–1917), an old and experienced Washington insider, held a number of important positions in various administrations, including attorney general, ambassador to Italy, and chief counsel before the Hague tribunal.

To: **Alice Goldmark Brandeis**
Date: **December 9, 1913**
Place: **Washington, D.C.**
Source: **Gilbert MSS**

DEAREST: I am greatly disturbed about Felix [Adler] & shall write Do for news.

Norman's remarks about the Water Power Cos. is a manifestation of one of his weaknesses.

1. I had written him *Nov 18* striking out the whole thing (after agreeing with him that G[ifford]. P[inchot]. should write on that subject.)[1]
2. I had talked with him before Nov 18 & twice since about doing it.

The money matter is more serious. I concluded to wire Walter Rogers[2] urgently today to raise $25,000 quick and am awaiting reply.

I went in to dine with the Rublees (leaving at 9) & to talk a little Price Maintenance with G[eorge]. They are nicely housed & Mrs. R. very eager to see you. Offered me a residence as have some others here, but "me for the simple life." Think I shall have to abandon the Cosmos Club soon, too much "talkie" at breakfast. It is pretty hard finding a place where reading light is good and man is absent.

The "interests" are having a little fling at Wilson. Note enclosed Creelman article.[3] McAdoo is being greatly attacked by the N.Y. Tribune on the US Trust Co–Munsey deal.[4] I hope these episodes will convince them that fight—fight—fight is the thing.

Suppose you will have seen in today's Transcript that Gen. Crozier[5] comes out strong (in his annual report) on Scientific Management. Hope to get some good from that in railroad case. My deputies are due here in a few moments. For Friday evening I have promised to talk to the I.C.C. employees on my ideas of the Commission's work in the future.

Mrs. Rublee was greatly delighted with the President at yesterday's session of the suffrage visitors. It is pretty clear "that he put it over" on the fair sex, saying "nothing in particular" "very well". But some people are beginning to comment on that.[6] Did you see the Providence Journal Editorial?[7]

Love to Elizabeth

1. See LDB to AGB, 23 November 1913, note 1.
2. Walter Stowell Rogers (1877–1965) was Charles Crane's assistant and was heavily involved in the financial arrangements for the purchase of *Harper's*. He also helped Hapgood on questions involving financial management of the magazine.
3. It is difficult to determine to what article LDB refers. James Creelman (1859–1915) wrote widely for the periodical press, but because of illness no magazine articles signed by him appeared between the end of 1911 and his death.
4. In an editorial that day entitled "A Transaction with an Ugly Look That Needs Investigation," the *New York Tribune* attacked an effort by the government to save depositors' interests in the financially troubled United States Trust Company of Washington by depositing one million dollars of government funds in the Munsey Trust Company, which was buying the Washington bank. There were too many unanswered questions, the editorial claimed, as well as the troubling fact that a director of the Munsey Trust had a brother who was assistant secretary of the treasury. The whole arrangement needed a full and open investigation.
5. Brig. Gen. William Crozier (1855–1942) rose through the Indian campaigns to teaching at West Point then to the presidency of the Army War College. At this time he was chief of ordnance. In his annual report he recommended, on grounds of efficiency, that the government should not attempt to produce smokeless gunpowder but should enter into contracts with private manufacturers.

6. Woodrow Wilson was not an advocate of women's suffrage, calling his own judgment "an uncertain balance" and preferring to leave the issue to the states rather than to a constitutional amendment. Not until 1918, when the country was engaged in a war to make the world safe for democracy, did Wilson reluctantly come to support votes for women.

7. On 3 December the *Providence Journal* attacked Wilson's message on antitrust as being too pro-labor, pro-farmer, pro-railroad employee and very indifferent or hostile to the legitimate interests of railroads and the great industries that were the backbone of the nation's strength and prosperity.

To:	Alice Goldmark Brandeis
Date:	December 14, 1913
Place:	Washington, D.C.
Source:	Gilbert MSS

DEAREST: Weather has been indescribably beautiful here both day and night. The moon ravishing. Had some fine walks yesterday, i.a. back from La Follettes after dinner (Belle and David Thompson[1] were there. Bob at his Currency Bill at the Senate.)[2]

Matters are sizzling here in Merger, I.C.C. & Trust Matters & I think it fortunate I am here. Nothing could be done without being in daily contact as the emergencies are arising every moment most unexpectedly. Howard Eliot [*sic*][3] is due at Dep. of Justice at 10:30. Have just talked with Gregory.

And I.C.C. needed very especial steering yesterday which I hope has kept the vessel on its true course.

Harper's is troublesome, but then there is little peace in mundane sphere.

A.H.G. is pretty "perky", but she is doing good work & is the saving factor.[4]

Much love to Elizabeth. I may arrange to leave here Friday midnight & drive you to Dedham 2:30 P.M. Saturday. Let me hear about N.Y.

Lovingly

As soon as you know about N.Y. better have E.D.P.[5] get 3 seats on 1 P.M. for both 23rd & 24th.

1. J. David Thompson (1873–1932) was currently the law librarian at the Library of Congress. He and his wife, Lulu Daniels, had been very close friends of the La Follettes since the days when Belle and Lulu were undergraduates together at the University of Wisconsin.

2. La Follette believed the Federal Reserve bill, now almost in its final form, still left too much power in the hands of the private bankers and worked in vain to substitute his own bill creating much stronger regulation of the banking industry.

3. Howard Elliott (1860–1928), the president of the Northern Pacific line, was chosen by the New Haven directors to replace Mellen. Although Elliott eschewed Mellen's efforts to monopolize New England transportation, he proved to be just as fiscally irresponsible. During his tenure (although he had inherited the situation), the New Haven stopped paying dividends altogether.

4. Alice Grady became more and more involved in the affairs of Savings Bank Life Insurance and would eventually head the system.

5. Elizabeth Peabody was one of LDB's longtime secretaries.

To:	Alice Goldmark Brandeis
Date:	December 26, 1913
Place:	Washington, D.C.
Source:	Gilbert MSS

DEAREST: Only a word to tell you how good were the days together. There are lots of interesting things to tell you which must await tomorrow, as I must go up now to the La Follettes (to dinner) to make our peace with Belle, who was greatly disappointed at my telephone about Susan.

Lovingly

To:	Alice Goldmark Brandeis
Date:	December 28, 1913
Place:	Washington, D.C.
Source:	EBR

DEAREST: Nothing from you today, but Friday's letter tells of your plan of returning Monday to Boston. Bon Voyage.

Have had a quiet day & after a good walk some hours on my papers—then $1^{1}/_{4}$ hours with McReynolds, lunch with [Jesse C.] Adkins, a nap (yesterday it was $1^{1}/_{2}$ hours at that—quite equalling you & Do) & now some more papers.

Belle [La Follette] has just telephoned me to be sure to come to supper this evening as John R. Commons is there. I shall be glad to hear what he will say on the Moyer episode.[1] It looks as if we might have a new trouble there. Cong. McDonald [sic][2] has started for Mich. to look into the situation further. He wants a Congressional enquiry that would offer an opportunity for the Industrial Commission as an alternative; but the Court declared some time ago against further investigations.

Spent last evening in my room alone, after a dinner at the Tea Cup Inn which looks forlorn.

Resisted an invite to lunch at the Hamlins.

Lovingly

Please ask Josephine to send Senator La Follette (3320 Ave. of Presidents) copy of the opinion of the Oregon judge on minimum wages.[3]

1. The Moyer incident grew out of the long, bitter strike in the copper mines of Calumet, Michigan. After a Christmas eve tragedy that involved a panic in a workers' meeting that left

a number of people dead, the Western Federation of Miners president, Charles H. Moyer, was accosted and "deported" from the area by a group of "citizens."

2. Congressman William Josiah MacDonald (1873–1946), a one-term Progressive representative from Michigan, went home to look into the situation for himself.

3. The state of Oregon passed a minimum wage law, and the first challenge was heard in Portland in the Circuit Court for Multnomah County. Judge T. J. Cleeton upheld the law, ruling that the Supreme Court's decision in *Lochner v. New York* (1905) did not apply. The case went on appeal to the Supreme Court of Oregon, which affirmed the lower court; *Stettler v. O'Hara,* 69 Ore. 519 (1914). Frank C. Stettler appealed to the U.S. Supreme Court, and the National Consumers' League and the state asked LDB to defend the law, as he had the hours law in *Muller v. Oregon* (1908). LDB agreed; but before the case was heard, Wilson named LDB to the Supreme Court. When that tribunal heard the appeal, LDB recused himself; the Court by a 4–4 vote upheld the Oregon decision. *Stettler v. O'Hara,* 243 U.S. 629 (1916).

To:	Alice Goldmark Brandeis
Date:	December 30, 1913
Place:	Washington, D.C.
Source:	EBR

DEAREST: My yesterday was quiet enough to suit even your taste—three meals and a walk alone, & most of the hours day & evening in my room except for a brief visit at the I.C.C. & on Gregory in the morning & drop in on the Social Insurance Meeting in the afternoon, leaving shortly after the business session began.

Miss Kelley[1] was there—after morning with the Industrial Relations Com[mit]tee, which she was hopeless about—and Ann [*sic*] Morgan[2] strode in with her air of dashing royalty; and sonerous [*sic*] Gompers[3] appeared after 2 days in New York wrestling with Hourwich[4] and then all the small fry—Lee K. Frankel[5] and Fredk. Hoffman[6] of Old Savings Bank Insurance days—with finally James Lowell,[7] Henry Dennison[8] and Prof. Doten[9] of Boston to give real respectability. Business began some 3/4 hours after called time—& I, after encountering Easley[10] and Arthur Williams,[11] flew to Potomac Park.   Lovingly

1. Florence Kelley (1859–1932) was one of the most influential women reformers of the time. A former resident of Hull House, she first met LDB when she helped gather the materials for his brief in *Muller v. Oregon;* by that time Kelley had become the executive director of the National Consumers' League. LDB's sister-in-law Josephine Goldmark wrote a biography of her, *Impatient Crusader* (Urbana, 1953); but see the definitive study by Kathryn Kish Sklar, *Florence Kelley and the Nation's Work* (New Haven, 1995).

2. Anne Morgan (1874–1952), the daughter of J. P. Morgan, was active in a large number of social reform and philanthropic movements.

3. Samuel Gompers (1850–1924) was a founder and the longtime president of the American Federation of Labor. LDB had known him for many years and had debated against him in 1902 on the question of the incorporation of labor unions. See LDB to John Graham

Brooks, 8 April 1903, BL, and LDB, "The Incorporation of Trades Unions," *Green Bag* 15 (January 1903): 11–14.

4. Isaac A. Hourwich (1860–1924), a revisionist Marxist labor leader, was a founder of the Yiddish daily *Forward* and chief clerk of the International Ladies' Garment Workers Union. LDB had worked with and fought against Hourwich in the protocol negotiations.

5. Lee Kaufer Frankel (1867–1931) was involved in a number of social agencies before joining Metropolitan Life, where he eventually became a vice-president.

6. Frederick Ludwig Hoffman (1865–1946) was a consulting statistician at the Prudential Insurance Company and wrote widely on the statistical aspects of various social and health problems.

7. James Arnold Lowell (1869–1933) was a longtime member of the Massachusetts House of Representatives and had been chair of its Judiciary Committee during its antitrust hearings on the United Shoe Machinery Company. In 1922 he would be appointed a federal district judge.

8. Henry Sturgis Dennison (1877–1952), a Massachusetts manufacturer, wrote several books on industrial problems and served on a number of federal commissions.

9. Carroll Warren Doten (1871–1942) was a professor of economics at the Massachusetts Institute of Technology and was involved in workers' compensation issues.

10. Ralph Montgomery Easley (1856–1939) organized and headed the Civic Federation of Chicago and in 1900 founded and became executive chair of the influential National Civic Federation.

11. Arthur Williams (1868–1937), an engineer and former vice-president of the Edison Company, was also a director of the Metropolitan Insurance Company.

To:	Alice Goldmark Brandeis
Date:	January 3, 1914
Place:	Washington, D.C.
Source:	EBR

DEAREST: That was a lovely New Years letter.

And I am glad you called on Mrs. Angell. There are not many of the old generation left. Brand Whitlock[1] quoted Mr. Howells[2] yesterday as saying: "All the people I know ar[e] dea[d]." I met Whitlock, (or rather he met me), as I was leaving the Commission yesterday afternoon and we had a nice walk together in Potomac Park. He is a charming fellow, a real democratic [*sic*] in feeling, and in manner and bearing the distinguished gentleman. We must see him in new post as Minister to Belgium. He says he has had to listen daily to my praises from his townsman Ashley,[3] who you will recall has furnished funds for subscriptions of Harpers to the Ohio libraries.

Is J.P.M. Co. directorate withdrawal interesting?[4] Kuhn, Loeb & Co. should follow and will be kicking themselves they didn't lead.

I dined with Watson & after dinner discussed RR with Congressman Sims[5] of the Comm[it]tee on Interstate & Foreign Commerce. Mat Hale has written for an appointment to discuss "an important matter" for which he will come to W[ashington] next week. If it's money for the Journal he will have his trouble for his pains.

234

The Govt. Printing Office is still unable to cope with the demands of our questions. I think University Press could have done as well.

1. Brand Whitlock (1869–1934) served as reform mayor of Toledo, Ohio, and was one of the country's best-known reformers. Wilson appointed him ambassador to Belgium, and Whitlock spent most of the rest of his life in diplomatic service in Europe.

2. William Dean Howells (1837–1920) was one of the most prolific and influential American critics and novelists of the late nineteenth century.

3. H. W. Ashley of Toledo.

4. On the previous day, the first business day of the new year, J. P. Morgan had announced that he and his vice-presidents would voluntarily resign from thirty directorships in banking, transportation, and industrial firms. The move was widely attributed to the growing antitrust sentiment in the public and in Congress, which was then considering strong legislation against interlocking directorates.

5. Thetus Willrette Sims (1852–1939) was a Democratic representative from Tennessee.

To: **Alfred Brandeis**
Date: **January 3, 1914**
Place: **Washington, D.C.**
Source: **Brandeis MSS**

DEAR AL: G.G. Hull's letter duly rec'd. Please tell him so. Dr. L. exaggerates. I met him twice, but, of course, love him as a brother. I don't know his project, but whatever it is, I want to divert your funds to another cause for the moment.

I conceived the idea that the best way to help Harper's influence & give it some financial support is to make sure that for a year it is in all the public libraries & to this end to arrange that it be sent to all that were not already subscribers. I provided for all New England & got other to provide for the middle Atlantic states, Ohio, Illinois & the North Western states. I have hopes of covering N.C., Ga. and Fla. I thought you might care to take Ky. I will let you have soon the list of libraries not already subscribers. The cost is $3 per subscription.[1]

When we meet I will tell you of my recent talks with Lamont[2] (of J.P. Morgan & Co.) about withdrawal from directors.[3]

1. Kentucky had a mere twelve unsubscribed libraries and Tennessee only eleven, so LDB sent his brother a list of libraries in other southern states. See LDB to Alfred Brandeis, 11 January 1914, BL.

2. Thomas William Lamont (1870–1948) was both a journalist and a member of the House of Morgan. He eventually headed the great banking house after the death of J. P. Morgan, Jr. It was Lamont who sold *Harper's Magazine* (which he had utilized as an organ to defend big business) to Norman Hapgood for $100,000 in a deal negotiated by LDB and bankrolled by Charles R. Crane. See his memoirs, *My Boyhood in a Parsonage* (New York, 1946).

3. See the previous letter.

To: Alice Goldmark Brandeis
Date: January 5, 1914
Place: Washington, D.C.
Source: Gilbert MSS

DEAREST: I am wearing the beautiful tie in honor of returning sunshine. The afternoon paper tells of Miss Grady's fire escape. I trust there will be no ill effects.[1]

Walter Rogers is in. He had done nothing about money in spite of my telegrams and letters, but left for C[hicago] today & promised to act promptly. Meanwhile I have written Charles [Crane] as per enclosed. The proposition seems to me essentially sound financially. It is merely a question of adequate preliminary capital & management. It looks to me as if now we were having neither.[2]

Pres[iden]t. Willard[3] is to see the and Harlan [*sic*][4] this afternoon. I suppose there will be some bitter complaint of some kind. But the questions are out, and I don't see how the Com[missio]n can go back on them now. Nor do I see at the moment any disposition to do so. Meanwhile I have about 60 men of the Comn at work.[5]

Lovingly

I suppose the financial world wishes I was in the Cabinet.[6]

1. A fire in the fourth-floor office of the Common Sense Gum Company, one of the tenants in the Compton Building (where LDB's law firm had offices on the eleventh floor), sent smoke billowing throughout the building and trapped Alice Grady on the eleventh floor. The firemen's regular ladders only reached to the seventh floor, and they had to use scaling ladders to reach Miss Grady, described in one newspaper as "the highest salaried woman in Boston." The story and accompanying pictures made the front pages of all the Boston afternoon papers.

2. In regard to the Crane financing of Hapgood's purchase of *Harper's*, see LDB to AGB, 6 January 1913.

3. Daniel Willard (1861–1942) was president of the Baltimore & Ohio Railroad from 1910 until 1941; he would at times appear to be the most receptive of all the railroad officials to LDB's ideas on scientific management.

4. James S. Harlan (1861–1927) was named to the Interstate Commerce Commission in 1906.

5. LDB remained at work in the Advanced Rate case; see LDB to AGB, 12 November 1913, note 2.

6. Had LDB gone into the cabinet, he would not have been able to speak out as forcefully on various economic matters (as he had in the money trust articles) or sit in judgment over railroad requests for increased rates as he was now doing.

To: **Alice Goldmark Brandeis**
Date: **January 8, 1914**
Place: **Washington, D.C.**
Source: **Gilbert MSS**

DEAREST: George [Rublee] and I went to Great Falls yesterday morning, and I shall be quite competent to act as Cicerone when you choose to make the trip. It is something over an hour's trolley ride, and when you arrive about ³/₄ mile further to the canoe ground. (There is another canoe possibility much nearer—at Georgetown.) There is a delightful opportunity for the Government to establish a Forest Park in connection with the falls, & this is being talked of, as well as developing the falls for the purpose of supplying Washington with light and power.[1]

George and I had promised to dine at the Pinchots' to meet Gifford. Later we learned G. was to leave at 3, & as George wanted to talk with P. about the Lane position it resulted in our both lunching & dining there. Mrs. P. was extremely feeble, but plucky beyond compare.[2]

Amos was there also & will be here I think throughout the week. He is held in leash now by Gifford's candidacy[3] but will be ready to break loose after November elections.

I have come to think very much better of Lady Johnston [*sic*].[4] Her devotion to her Mother is very beautiful & if she wouldn't smoke I could forgive much. She has probably the best of the Pinchot minds.

The work is I think telling on George. He seems to be affected as in the Ballinger Lane days.   Lovingly

1. The Great Falls of the Potomac River is located about ten miles northwest of Washington. Many years later it became part of the C & O Canal National Park.
2. Mrs. Pinchot would die at the end of August 1914.
3. Pinchot had entered the Pennsylvania senatorial race as a Progressive Party candidate in an effort to defeat Republican boss Boies Penrose. In the November election, Penrose won easily, receiving 489,346 votes to 252,853 for Pinchot and 251,433 for the Democratic candidate, A. Mitchell Palmer.
4. See LDB to AGB, 23 November 1913.

To: **Alice Goldmark Brandeis**
Date: **January 14, 1914**
Place: **Chicago, Illinois**
Source: **Gilbert MSS**

DEAREST: Don't you intend to have Susan come home for the New Year holidays? I suppose you could arrange a young folk's dinner, if not a dinner dance.

I went with the Cranes and Walter Rogers to the Irish Players this evening to see "The Patriots,"[1] & left at 10. for a good night['] s rest, without awaiting "The Rising of the Moon."[2] It was noble, natural, effective acting, a fine contrast to much of the modern stuff.

Can't tell yet about my start home but hope to know more tomorrow.

I guess you did right to go on to the Suffrage Com[mit]tee.[3]

The Progressives' New Haven program is interesting. You will remember Charlie Bird's attitude in 1908–09.   Lovingly

1. Possibly the play by John Hartley Manners and William Collier, first produced in 1908.
2. A popular Irish folk ballad; apparently the cast sang this and other songs at the end of the performance.
3. AGB had long been an advocate of women's right to vote but had not taken a public stance on the matter. Over the next three decades she would be more forthcoming in her advocacy of particular causes. She made no secret of her support for Sacco and Vanzetti and openly worked for the election of Robert M. La Follette in 1924 and Alfred E. Smith in 1928.

To: **Alfred Brandeis**
Date: **January 23, 1914**
Place: **Washington, D.C.**
Source: **Brandeis MSS**

DEAR AL: You are right about the Pres[iden]t's message.[1] He has paved the way for about all I have asked for & some of the provisions specifically are what I got into his mind at my first interview.[2]

Confidentially I think he rather overdid the era of good feeling.[3] I am convinced that the Wall St. gents are playing a game—want to unload their securities on the men with hoarded money & they have to appear pleased. Doubtless the Prest is playing his game a little as well as they & he is a fine player.

I have yours about Transit; hope we can do something with that some day.

Saw Thruston Ballard[4] last week at the Industrial Relations Com[mit]tee.

1. On 20 January Woodrow Wilson appeared before a joint session of Congress to announce the third prong of the New Freedom, antitrust legislation. Some of the proposals he made could be traced directly to LDB, and there was little in the speech that LDB could not endorse. Wilson called for a ban on interlocking directorates, attacked the bankers' use of other people's money, and demanded tighter regulation by the ICC of railroad securities, a better definition of what constituted monopolistic practices, as well as a commission to help businesses comply with the law. The text of Wilson's speech is in the *New York Times,* 21 January 1914.
2. See LDB to Alfred Brandeis, 29 August 1912.
3. In a letter to Alice two days earlier, LDB wrote that Wilson "really overdoes a bit his *suaviter in modo* [sweetness of manner]; but that balance has its uses & makes it possible for the big interests to swallow his pills more easily." Professor Link also comments on Wilson's use of "honeyed words," as Wilson talked about "[t]he atmosphere of accommodation and mutual understanding which we now breathe with so much refreshment. . . . The antagonism between business and government is over."
4. LDB probably knew Samuel Thruston Ballard (1855–1926) from Louisville, where Ballard headed one of the large flour mills. Wilson appointed him as a member of the National Industrial Commission, and Ballard would later serve as lieutenant governor of Kentucky.

238

To: Alice Goldmark Brandeis
Date: February 5, 1914
Place: Washington, D.C.
Source: Brandeis MSS

DEAREST: Elizabeth's free days and your theatre dissipations make me quite envious. I should be delighted to be off for a few days & collect my thoughts. This business of general guide, counsellor and friend grows a bit wearisome—particularly when friends stop at the Gordon [Hotel]. Anderson[1] was here & has left. Mrs. B.H. Meyer[2] longs to call on you, as does Mrs. Adolph Miller[3] who bad[e] me to dine (in vain) for this evening as did Mrs. Thruston Ballard last.

ICC affairs are proving intensely interesting.[4]

I must be off to the General Croziers.   Lovingly

1. George Weston Anderson (1861–1938) was a longtime friend and reform ally of LDB during his Boston years. He was named to the Interstate Commerce Commission and was later a judge of the United States Court of Appeals for the Second Circuit. Anderson and LDB did not agree on all issues, but LDB commented that of all the men who had ever crossed swords with him on public issues, only Anderson supported him in the nomination fight.

2. The wife of Balthasar Henry Meyer, a former professor at the University of Wisconsin who then joined the ICC as an economist.

3. The wife of Adolph Caspar Miller, another former college professor then serving as assistant to the secretary of the interior, who would soon begin a 22-year stint in the Federal Reserve Bank.

4. Many people mistakenly assumed that LDB had been retained to represent the shippers against the railroads, when in fact he had been hired by the ICC to advise it and to represent the public's interest. As a result, many shippers were surprised when LDB started asking them discomfiting questions about issues such as the better rates enjoyed by the large shippers. Moreover, while the railroads and the shippers focused on—and disagreed about—the question of whether existing rates yielded adequate revenue, LDB and the commission also wanted to know what course the carriers should follow to remedy the situation if revenues were inadequate. LDB, of course, pushed for greater scientific management just as he had in the first Advanced Rate hearings three years earlier. See Mason, *Brandeis,* chs. 20 and 21.

To: Alfred Brandeis
Date: February 7, 1914
Place: Washington, D.C.
Source: Brandeis MSS

DEAR AL: Don't believe all you hear about the B & M Chairmanship.[1] There was a suggestion somewhat about of that character. I refused to admit or deny or to be communicated with simply to "tease" those Boston folks.

Interstate Commerce Commission matters seem to be progressing well, except that we lost out on Ives.[2] I think the rebate indictment did it.

1. Rumors had begun to fly that LDB would be appointed a trustee of the Boston & Maine, perhaps even chairman of the board. See for example, the *New York Times,* 7 February 1914. There was more to the rumors than LDB let on to Alfred, however. Two days later George W. Anderson, who had been handling negotiations on the reconstitution of the Boston & Maine board, telegraphed LDB: "Apparent agreement on you. Wire suggestions for names and number of desired associates." See LDB to Anderson, 9 February 1914, BL.

2. LDB had lost his four-month struggle to get David O. Ives appointed to the ICC to succeed Charles Prouty. Six weeks later Ives died.

To: **Alice Goldmark Brandeis**
Date: **February 26, 1914**
Place: **Washington, D.C.**
Source: **Gilbert MSS**

DEAREST: I am about to write Susan.[1] Her development was slow for a time, but now her future seems full of promise to become a noble, generous hearted, helpful woman. It was a good day 21 years ago, and I am happy at the thought of the days you had here with her recently.

As you left the hotel, a summons to the Department [of Justice] came. I was there until quarter past one, and must go to meet the Atty. Genl., Anderson et al this evening at 8. But being dentist-free I revenged myself by a joyous afternoon. First a luncheon with N.Y. Times and Annalist at our old table at the Knickerbocker. (Harvey Chase[2] came in as I was finishing my lemon custard pie and wanted to talk National budget, but I fled.) Then after a short visit at the Com[missio]n, largely devoted to Gov. Folk, I had a perfect walk over the Potomac Park flats, & then a good nap from which I have just risen at 6:10. Triple dinner invitations—George R[ublee]., Anderson and Folk are declined & I shall steal away & read Annalist or the like.

It was fine to have you. I don't blame Elizabeth for being lonesome.

Lovingly

1. The following day was Susan Brandeis's twenty-first birthday. See the next letter.

2. Perhaps Harvey S. Chase, an accountant who served for a time as an unofficial auditor of city accounts and whose work LDB admired.

To: **Susan Brandeis**
Date: **February 26, 1914**
Place: **Washington, D.C.**
Source: **Gilbert MSS**

MY DEAREST SUSAN: Every good wish for tomorrow and for all the days to come. May the day always bring you as much happiness as it has us.

At no time have we looked forward to your future with as much confidence as now; for we see in your development the promise of a noble, generous hearted useful woman. That development gives us assurance that you will use your new freedom well; and as aid to your development we want you to have the responsibilities of financial independence. We have, therefore, concluded (as I suggested some weeks ago) to give you an allowance large enough to defray your college as well as your personal expenses, and also furnish means for reasonable gifts and contributions to such public causes as you may be interested in. We think $1800 a year will do that. Which sum will be sent you in monthly instalments of $150, except that next October you will receive $450 to cover October, November, & December so that you need have no embarrassment in meeting the college bills.

I enclose now check for $150.

You know how important accounting is, in my opinion. With the allowance fixed you should carefully prepare your budget in advance. We want you to spend the money as seems to you best, but I must ask you to prepare and send me not later than 8th of each month an account of the disbursements of the preceding month classified as:

1. College expense
2. Dress
3. Travelling
4. Amusements
5. Gifts (to relations or friends)
6. Contributions to public causes
7. Sundries

(& any other subdivisions you may desire) & showing balance-on-hand & expenditures for the year (beginning March 1) to the end of the month reported on, as I showed you in the account last Summer. I want you to keep a copy of the account for your own file.

This all sounds very business-like, my dearest Susan, but you know how important a proper system & good habits of life seem to me.

Mother had a wearisome cold; but the days with her were fine, and she said she have [*sic*] never enjoyed any days with you so much as your recent visit here. With no end of love

To:	Alice Goldmark Brandeis
Date:	March 2, 1914
Place:	Washington, D.C.
Source:	Gilbert MSS

DEAREST: McReynolds was very intelligent in his criticisms of the bill & much more helpful than my coadjutor,[1] but he is very conservative. We didn't get very far, despite 3 hrs. conference, partly because he is a great time waster, by the way & largely because he is so tired out that he ought to be off in some vast wilderness. He is really pretty sick of his job & realizes that the volume of work imposes upon him the impossible.

His real tiredoutness developed as I lunched with him at the Shoreham. I, virtuous man, had had a good walk before our conference, another after luncheon, then 1½ hour sleep & a still another airing before dinner (with Julius Henry[2] & the Conference) & a breather before going to bed.

Julius Henry talk enabled me to lay before him his grievous mistake in charging huge fees & he was I think sincerely surprised, but it will do good.

The situation in both associations is very troublesome, but it looks as if it would work out.[3]

Louis Israels impressed me as very able.

I couldn't go to Mrs. Pinchot as her brother John died Friday. I wrote her, & Howard Morris, & of course Mother.[4]

Lovingly

The Springfield postal, mailed at Boston 9:20 is the last yet from you. The morning mail is not yet in.

1. George Rublee, who was working with LDB on the antitrust and trade commission bills. For an example of how closely LDB was working with McReynolds in shaping the antitrust bill, see LDB to McReynolds, 22 February 1914, BL.
2. Julius Henry Cohen (1873–1950) was a prominent New York City attorney. He was the lawyer for the manufacturers in the 1910 garment workers' strike, which LDB had been called in to arbitrate.
3. The protocol that LDB had worked out in the garment trade was never free from criticism from its two major components, the manufacturers' associations and the trade unions. For the eventual demise of the protocol, see Mason, *Brandeis,* 310–14.
4. This was the birthday of Regina Goldmark, AGB's mother.

To:	Alice Goldmark Brandeis
Date:	March 12, 1914
Place:	Washington, D.C.
Source:	Gilbert MSS

DEAREST: Hope this is my last before seeing you. Hearings are on daily, but the labor has not been very strenuous as Clifford Thorne[1] has lectured for the past three days. He has done an extraordinary amount of work & knows a great deal, not always drawing safe deductions, but very intelligent and he has visibly disturbed the poor railroad men.[2]

Garret [sic] says Morgan et al have really learned nothing and are quite incapable of learning.[3] That, if true, is our only safety. It looks, on the other hand, as if this period of apparent docility were about over, & I judge the President will find that Christian Science won't settle our economic contests.

We of the I.C.C. are having to brave a great rebellion of the big shippers.[4] It reminds of attempts to reform the tariff.[5]

Lovingly

Weather has been unpardonable.

1. Clifford Thorne (1878–1923) would develop into one of LDB's bitterest enemies because he thought that LDB had betrayed his principles in the Advanced Rate hearings. Thorne spent his whole career defending the interests of shippers against the railroads, and he believed that LDB would be fighting alongside him in this cause. But LDB represented neither shippers nor lines and was working with the ICC to secure a rate fair to both sides. For Thorne's views, see his testimony during LDB's confirmation fight, U.S. Senate, *Hearings before the Subcommittee of the Committee of the Judiciary . . . on the Nomination of Louis D. Brandeis to Be an Associate Justice of the Supreme Court of the United States*, 64th Cong., 1st Sess., 2 vols. (Washington, D.C., 1916), 1:5–62.

2. Thorne's "lectures" began on 9 March; see *Five Percent Case (1913–1914)*, Senate Document 466, 63d Cong., 2d Sess. (Washington, D.C., 1914), pt. 3, 2995ff.

3. See the anecdote about the elder Morgan and his refusal to pay any attention to LDB's pamphlet in the New Haven matter in Mason, *Brandeis,* 212.

4. Because of the commission's—and LDB's—view that certain railroad rates were too low and also because of questions being raised about the big shippers receiving lower rates.

5. See Arthur Link, *Woodrow Wilson and the Progressive Era,* 35–43, for a brief analysis of the tariff fight.

To: Alice Goldmark Brandeis
Date: March 18, 1914
Place: Washington, D.C.
Source: Gilbert MSS

DEAREST: It was lovely weather yesterday & as Al would say, "A fine day for the Lizard."

Matters are a bit troubled at the I.C.C. In Harlan's absence last week things went quite a bit askew, and my absence didn't help, though it might not have aided. Among other things there are apparently some jealousies of him & of me.[1] I trust not serious but that they can be ironed out.

I had an hour & a half with McReynolds on the trust bill & then another hour & a half walking & talking nothings on the Potomac flats. His trust discussion was intelligent but not courageous, & we shall not agree on what should be done re interlocking directors. He stands practically by the Pujo Com[mit]tee. His greatest desire is to have things over & let Congress adjourn. Says everybody, particularly the President, is tired out.

I am to see Clayton et al at 2:30 & George R[ublee]. is to be present. I guess I can dump that job on to him.[2] I have no time to follow it up & it would need about all my time to do it effectively.   Lovingly

1. See the next letter.
2. Although LDB would continue to play an important role in drafting the antitrust and trade commission bills, Rublee did take on a larger share of the work.

To: **Alice Goldmark Brandeis**
Date: **March 24, 1914**
Place: **Washington, D.C.**
Source: **Gilbert MSS**

DEAREST: Your wedding day letter has not come yet; doubtless [it] will be in on the early mail.

We had a "Strich durch die Rechnung"[1] at headquarters, but there are said to be several ways of shuffling off the mortal coil of a cat and the obstacles interposed may prove mere pleasing hurdles. I am not sure whether jealousy or fear or lack of clear thinking or some other of the elemental defects of man are the explanation.[2]

Went up to Bob [La Follette]'s for dinner. He is in pretty poor shape, and Belle looks even more troubled than usual. Bob got on to the magazine.[3] He now sees that the only thing possible is to treat it as an endowed institution & that it takes $12,000 a year to meet the deficit. Hannan has been for some time west trying to raise a 5 year contribution list, among friends of the cause in Wisc., Minn. & Illinois & Gilbert Roe is to work in N.Y. Bob expects Spreckles [*sic*] to help.

I told Bob this was a really business like plan, but that it must be so arranged that no deficit should fall upon him to bear & that on this plan I should be delighted to subscribe one thousand a year for five years, if Hannan succeeds in his canvas. Bob was much pleased & I was greatly relieved myself, as I had felt, as you know, anxious to do something for them. Indeed I should be glad to subscribe more, if necessary. I think it clear now that as Belle said, it would be a fearful thing for him to give up the magazine. He should feel really "down and out."

The President has no easy sailing on the Panama Tolls bill. There is a bare chance he may lose, if the opponents succeed in their efforts at delay.[4]

The party is terribly afraid of the fall election. Carlin[5] said to me that he did not think they could hold more than 30 majority in the house.[6]

Lovingly

I have Watson at work on several chores.

1. "Something that upset our calculations."
2. See the previous letter.
3. La Follette's personal organ, *La Follette's Weekly Magazine,* had always skated along on thin financial ice, and the senator was currently exploring various ways to keep the progressive journal afloat.
4. In August 1912 Congress had exempted American ships engaged in coastal trade (that is, going between the two American coasts) from payment of tolls through the Panama Canal, and the Democratic platform that year strongly endorsed the exemption. But the British lodged a protest, claiming that the exemption violated the 1901 Hay-Paunceforte Treaty, which promised equal rates for all nations. Wilson came to believe that the British were correct and that national honor required repeal of the exemption. He did not move on the matter, however, until after passage of the Federal Reserve Act. On 26 January 1914 he met with the Senate Foreign Relations Committee, urging repeal. He then waited for Congress to act. When warned that unless he took personal leadership the measure would fail, he addressed Congress on 5 March. The subsequent battle almost split the Democratic Party, with its strong Irish-American constituency opposing the British position. The bill finally passed the House at the end of March and the Senate on 11 June.
5. Charles Creighton Carlin (1866–1938), a Democrat, represented the Eighth District of Virginia in the House of Representatives from 1907 to 1921.
6. In fact the Democrats did even worse, with their majority in the House of Representatives reduced from seventy-three to twenty-five. In the Senate, however, despite some changes in seats, the numbers remained the same, a Democratic majority of six.

To: **Alice Goldmark Brandeis**
Date: **March 27, 1914**
Place: **Washington, D.C.**
Source: **Gilbert MSS**

DEAREST: I enclose draft of will. Please look it over soon & let me have your suggestions. The ultimate residency clause is the one about which I should have most doubts. Perhaps some better suggestions may occur to you, & there is no reason why any good individuals or causes should not be added.

Dined quietly with [Angus] McSween and Hansen[1] last evening. (The La Follettes had autoed by to get me for dinner—in vain.) They tell lurid tales of the trading of offices which is going on now in aid of the Canal toll repeal.[2] Hansen, who was during the campaign a most strenuous Wilson man, is particularly sad. I guess W.W. has made a serious blunder in this as in each other of the preceding steps in the Mexican policy. He will probably carry the bill, but there will be much heartburn after & the rift between Progressives & Republicans is the saving of the Democratic majority, as it now looks.[3]

Lovingly

245

1. Elisha Hansen (1888–1962) was then a Washington correspondent for the *Chicago Tribune* and later served as secretary to Senator Medill McCormack. In 1924 he opened a law practice in the District of Columbia.

2. The stories were quite true. Postmaster General Albert S. Burleson, the administration's chief dispenser of patronage, worked the House of Representatives steadily during the debate.

3. LDB was correct in that regular Republicans joined with enough Democrats to pass the repeal bill, while many of the progressive Republicans opposed it.

To: **Alice Goldmark Brandeis**
Date: **March 28, 1914**
Place: **Washington, D.C.**
Source: **Gilbert MSS**

DEAREST: Your coming with Do on the 5th is an admirable idea. Elizabeth will feel proud at her emancipation.

Copy of "Other People's Money"[1] has come to me & doubtless to you. Zimmern[2] is more entertaining. The Greek word for "unemployment" is "leisure"—what a happy land that. You remember the man from Home says "the Negro is our leisure class.["] That is perhaps why they are so much more agreeable than most folks.

There is no leisure class life while rate advance case lasts; but I am pretty philosophical about it.

I don't much like the "gag rule" adopted on the Panama tolls;[3] but vidremino.[4]

Hope you will have a good Sunday & be well over that cold.

Lovingly

When you come please bring (1) belt
    (2) shortsleeve underwear
    (3) cotton socks
       blue serge suit if good enough

1. See LDB to Alfred Brandeis, 2 September 1913, note 1.

2. Sir Alfred Zimmern (1879–1957) was an English student of foreign relations as well as the author of the highly influential *The Greek Commonwealth,* published in England in 1911. According to one scholar, it was Zimmern's description of ancient Greek life that helped to shape LDB's view of Zionism, in which the new Jewish commonwealth in Palestine would have the virtues of both ancient Athens and republican America. See Philippa Strum, *Brandeis: Beyond Progressivism* (Lawrence, Kans., 1993), 102–6.

3. See LDB to AGB, 24 March 1914, note 4. On the previous day the House had adopted a rule limiting debate on the Panama Canal tolls exemption repeal to twenty hours, with no amendments allowed. At the end of that time the House would have to vote the measure up or down.

4. We shall see.

To: Alice Goldmark Brandeis
Date: April 1, 1914
Place: Washington, D.C.
Source: Gilbert MSS

DEAREST: The John Graham Brookses are eager for your arrival. I arranged with Mr. to review "Business a Profession" instead of "Other People's Money".[1]

Mrs. Harriman says there is great complaint of Democratic appointments going to machine reactionaries instead of to the progressive wing & that Mitchel[2] is disgusted with the N.Y. situation. He wired Pres[iden]t. protesting again over Kelly[3] as Brooklyn postmaster, offering to come to Washington for the purpose; & no attention was paid to his telegram. Mrs. H. says Garrison[4] is quite free in giving his advice to the Prest. also and [Franklin K.] Lane; that no one else does & that even G. and L. don't press theirs. She thinks Col. House may be responsible for the refusal to recognize Huerta, & that the Prest. had favored H's recognition up to about April 1913.[5] [And] That Col. House drops pearls of wisdom, but don't press his views.   Lovingly

1. There is no evidence that Brooks reviewed either book, at least not in a signed review.

2. John Purroy Mitchel (1879–1918) had joined Wilson's war against Tammany Hall and, with the president's backing, had been elected mayor of New York the preceding November. Mitchel worked with LDB in 1915 trying to save the garment industry protocol. During the war he enlisted in the Aviation Corps and was killed in an airplane accident in Louisiana.

3. Following Mitchel's election, Washington had waited to see how the administration would support the mayor in his battle against Tammany. Although Wilson and his advisors engaged in discussions about forming a new Democratic Party in New York, the president could not afford to alienate the party regulars in New York or elsewhere. Fearing that continued anti-Tammany agitation would lead to an overwhelming Democratic defeat in the 1914 congressional elections, Wilson agreed to a compromise plan that appeared to be anti-Tammany on the surface but in effect left the organization alone. Moreover, through Postmaster General Burleson, who had no sympathy for anti-Tammany activities, the administration began feeding important patronage appointments through Senator James O'Gorman and other party regulars. The important Brooklyn postmaster's job went to William H. Kelly, an old-line Democrat clearly aligned with Tammany. Mitchel, who had until recently seen himself as Wilson's point man in the battle against Tammany, found himself practically frozen out by the administration.

4. Lindley Miller Garrison (1864–1932) was a lawyer in New Jersey and a member of the Chancery Court before Wilson named him as his secretary of war. Garrison was a competent administrator but proved unable to make necessary political adjustments; he resigned in 1916 when Wilson refused to accept the preparedness plan that he and the army staff had devised.

5. According to Arthur Link, Wilson from the very beginning detested Huerta and had no intention of extending *de jure* recognition to him. See Link, *Wilson: The New Freedom,* 349.

To: Alice Goldmark Brandeis
Date: May 21, 1914
Place: Washington, D.C.
Source: Gilbert MSS

DEAREST: Staying over in Boston another week sounds very leisurely—and wise.

As a favor to George R[ublee]. I joined him, Stevens,[1] [Frank] Walsh, McCarty [sic][2] in the visit to the President yesterday & was glad I went. He seemed just as open-minded and quick-intelligenced as when I saw him at Sea Girt in 1912 & his manner was excellent. He looked well, vigorous almost, as he sat in his tent without a book or paper near except a few sheets on which he was writing. He seemed more serious. He was frank and as easy in his talk and manner, including some slight digressions, as in any private talk among friends. I felt as if his errors had been those of judgement merely, or of intellectual habit. In other words that his failure to confer is a fault of judgement and likewise that his apparent lack of courage in some industrial lines is a fault of the mind & not of the heart.[3]

Of course Bob [La Follette] (with whom I dined last evening) & Belle to some extent, are much less tolerant & Bob declares he cares not for sincerity which leads into wrong paths. I should like someday to find out how W.W. squares his views with putting forth Richard Olney.[4]

I suppose you saw Mellen's testimony that (as I surmised) R.O. had given his opinion that the B & M purchase was legal.[5]   Lovingly

1. Raymond Bartlett Stevens (1874–1942) was then serving his only term as a member of the House of Representatives from New Hampshire. He worked closely with LDB in drafting and struggling to pass the Clayton Antitrust Act. Wilson later tried to name Stevens to the Federal Trade Commission, but political biases in the Senate led to his rejection. Franklin Roosevelt, however, did appoint Stevens to the FTC and then to the United States Tariff Commission, of which he was the chair after 1937. From 1926 to 1935 Stevens served as special advisor to the government of Siam (now Thailand).

2. Probably Charles McCarthy (1873–1921), who organized the first bill-drafting service in Wisconsin under La Follette and who was often called upon in Washington and elsewhere for help in drafting legislation.

3. The meeting was probably to discuss the antitrust and trade commission legislation then under consideration in Congress; see LDB to AGB, 10 June 1914.

4. Wilson had offered the former secretary of state, who was almost eighty, a governorship on the Federal Reserve Board as a gesture to show that the administration was not hostile to Wall Street. Olney, however, declined the appointment.

5. In continuing testimony before the ICC on the Boston & Maine-New Haven merger, Charles Mellen blamed J. P. Morgan and the officials of the Morgan firm, including Olney, as the people responsible for pushing ahead with the merger.

To:	Alice Goldmark Brandeis
Date:	May 23, 1914
Place:	Washington, D.C.
Source:	Gilbert MSS

DEAREST: I made my dinner engagement at the Frank Lyons['] in [the] most beautiful country yesterday, motoring out at 5:30 with F.L., & taking in his countryside. It is really a wonderful location, only 4 miles from the Capitol & about 450 feet above the Washington level. Mrs. Lyon is a fine woman, worthwhile you seeing her when you are next here.

I feel now as if the "next" would be postponed until Fall. Even if the decision is disposed of right there will be a general desire on the part of all concerned to clear out & take up the new troubles after a vacation. There is so much to be done, that a little touch now would accomplish nothing worthwhile.

The attacks on McR. are fierce, & not justified. Except, of course, that he is a standpatter without a particle of sympathy with insurgent methods. Bob [La Follette] has little patience with my sympathetic judgment of him & thinks it does little credit to my intelligence.[1]   Lovingly

1. In later years, when LDB and McReynolds served together on the Supreme Court, it is questionable whether LDB would feel so sympathetic. McReynolds was a nasty and crude bigot who made numerous anti-Semitic comments and would often leave the conference room when LDB spoke. When LDB retired from the Court in 1939, McReynolds alone refused to sign the customary letter of praise and farewell from the other brethren.

To:	Alice Goldmark Brandeis
Date:	May 26, 1914
Place:	Washington, D.C.
Source:	Gilbert MSS

MY DEAREST: I shall have quite a breakfast party. Norman [Hapgood] reserved a seat when I last saw him, & now come Do and [Joseph] Eastman. D. arrived last evening. Eastman came on a wire from Folk. [George] Anderson had suggested he might be valuable as a witness(!)[1] I told F. he should retain him, if possible, and I guess F. realizes well enough now the shallows of his own knowledge on this subject to want all the help he can get. I had several talks with him during the past few days.

Enclosed from the Saturday Even. Post[2] led me to Bob to talk matters over last evening. The idea of going in to Mexico to change their land system is really a "touch beyond." No doubt the change is essential to Mexican well being & perhaps well being may bring internal peace. But here the American people are going into Mexico to secure [the] most fundamental changes in their government—the most altruistic enterprise nation ever entered upon—without the people ever having had a word to say about it or a word of public discussion. If there ever was an *ultra vires*[3] act in government we seem to have it here. It is really an astounding exercise of absolute power.

While at Bob's, Billy Kent happily strolled in, I fancy the first time he did that since the 1912 break. Surely the first time in the new house. Kent is an intense admirer of Lenroot & I hope there will be further rapprochement to Bob.   Lovingly

1. In the Advanced Rate hearings. Eastman was extremely knowledgeable on railroad finance.

2. Samuel G. Blythe, "Mexico: The Record of a Conversation with President Wilson," *Saturday Evening Post* 186 (23 May 1914): 3–4, 71. In the interview Wilson argued that democracy can never come from the top down but must always develop from the people. For democracy to survive and grow in Mexico, Wilson argued, there had to be true grassroots reform, including land redistribution.

3. Beyond permitted or normal powers.

To:	Alfred Brandeis
Date:	May 30, 1914
Place:	Boston, Massachusetts
Source:	Brandeis MSS

MY DEAR AL: We seem to have returned to very primitive conditions when all communications are per messenger by word of mouth. Louis Wehle brought some word of you, and yesterday Com[missione]r Hall[1] introduced me to his Louisville brother who had some vague data. If you don't speed up and let me know something about yourself I may be forced to run down to Kentuck myself and begin an investigation.

I am afraid Dan Willard didn't like my enquiry of yesterday into the CH & D.[2] The financial end puts a terrible strain on their operating men.

Gruesse aus die Familie.[3]

1. Henry Clay Hall (1860–1936) was a Colorado lawyer who served on the Interstate Commerce Commission from 1914 to 1928.

2. The ICC, after being alerted by an Illinois congressman who suspected fraud, was looking into the complicated financial dealings between Willard's Baltimore & Ohio line and the Cincinnati, Hamilton & Dayton Railroad. For details, see LDB to Norman Hapgood, 1 June 1914, BL.

3. Greetings from the family.

To:	Alice Goldmark Brandeis
Date:	June 6, 1914
Place:	Washington, D.C.
Source:	Gilbert MSS

DEAREST: Too bad about Bessie [Evans]'s voice, but she has a wonderful recuperative power & will doubtless disappoint her specialist as she has so often done.

I am glad Elizabeth has achieved a horse & shall hope for some good rides with her soon, although there is little Harlan movement yet and Carmalt seems quite impatient. Meanwhile I am continuing my studies in railroading.

George [Rublee] had a busy day at the Capitol yesterday and is exhibiting energy and persistence in spite of himself. I had to submit last evening to a long session with George, Stevens and Covington.[1] Newlands is the despair of mankind. I think his shortcomings may now be ascribed to senility, & I am reminded of Mahaffy's reference of the Spartan Ephors.[2] Bob is busy with his Wisconsin folk & that tolls speech lags. He is the greatest of procrastinators.[3]

Had Examiner Brown[4] lunch with me yesterday. He is not "gut auf Folk zu reden."[5]   Lovingly

1. James Harry Covington (1870–1942), a Maryland lawyer, was then serving his second term in Congress and was the sponsor of the original trade commission bill. At the end of the year he resigned from the House when Wilson named him chief judge of the D.C. Supreme Court. In 1918 he returned to private practice.
2. Sir John Pentland Edwards Mahaffy (1839–1919) wrote numerous popular books about ancient Greece and Rome. The Ephors were men chosen by the Spartans to be a council of state in an effort to prevent the aristocracy from imposing a dictatorship on the city-state.
3. La Follette did not give a speech in the Senate on the Panama tolls proposal.
4. David E. Brown was a longtime employee of the ICC.
5. "An easy person to talk with."

To: Alice Goldmark Brandeis
Date: June 9, 1914
Place: Washington, D.C.
Source: Gilbert MSS

DEAREST: If I must stay here it would be fine to have you come, provided the heat would not try you unduly. Yesterday was pretty hot. Today it is comfortable and overcast after a thunder storm.

New York is not tempting as a resort. If it seems wise to leave here at all, Boston would be a better meeting ground.

I will have a talk with Harlan before the week is over & see what the prospects are. Carmalt thought yesterday matters might drag on so until July 1.

The Atty. General asked me yesterday to act as Special Counsel to take charge of his Southern Pacific–Central Pacific dissolution case.[1] I told him

[I] felt myself bound to I.C.C. to finish the investigation there & suggested McClennen. I have no special appetite for that job anyhow. It isn't "constructive."

It's amusing now to have Sherman Whipple come out as a great man on New Haven.[2]

Gilson Gardner joined George [Rublee] & me after dinner at the Tea Cup last evening, & then took us in his motor to the Potomac & otherwise for a drive. Ending (let Susan & Eliz. note) with an ice cream chocolate soda at Huglers.

George is well content with the tolls bill—Norris amended—that is prefers to have Wilson win—the sting being taken out.[3] I can't be so content.

Lovingly

1. McReynolds, while unsympathetic to much progressive reform, was unyielding in his opposition to trusts and saw antitrust prosecution as the central task of his department. In response to the Supreme Court decision of 2 December 1912 (see LDB to AGB, 10 January 1913, note 4), McReynolds decided to seek the dissolution of the combine. After LDB turned him down, McReynolds brought in Thomas W. Gregory to handle the case, and the government won a dissolution decree on 30 June 1913.

2. Sherman Leland Whipple (1862–1930) was a leading Boston trial attorney who had been involved with LDB in the Lenox will case. Although Whipple disagreed with LDB, at the confirmation hearings in 1916 he nonetheless praised LDB's character and integrity. For details, see LDB to Edward Francis McClennen, 9 March 1916, note 1, BL. On 6 June Whipple, acting for the directors of the Boston & Maine, brought suit for $25 million against the New Haven to recover losses that the B & M had suffered while under New Haven control. This move came about the same time as stories that the alleged New Haven surplus was not real but was the result of accounting stratagems.

3. Despite some opposition in the Senate, the Panama Canal tolls repeal moved easily through the upper house. To avoid a bitter debate, Wilson gave opponents a sop by accepting an amendment supported by a number of senators that really meant nothing, namely that the United States reserved all rights it had enjoyed under the old Hay-Paunceforte Treaty. The Senate approved the bill on 11 June, the House accepted the Senate amendment the following day, and Wilson signed the measure into law on 15 June 1914.

To: **Alice Goldmark Brandeis**
Date: **June 10, 1914**
Place: **Washington, D.C.**
Source: **Gilbert MSS**

DEAREST: I have $2/3$ of a notion that I shall leave here tomorrow or Friday for about 5 days at home. It looks now as if I shall be needed here most between the 20th & the 4th of July and that I had better take a chance for days at home now than later. Will have a talk with Harlan probably tomorrow morning & decide then.

George [Rublee], Stevens, Hollis & I dined together at the Tea Cup last evening to talk over Trust Legislation, preparatory to another descent upon the President this morning.[1] I felt that I had to take some hand at trusts for George's sake, & indeed, also to prevent some very bad legislation. George was in distress with dear old Mr. Clapp, so I went up to the Senate to see him yesterday. He is terribly disgusted with the "Morgan in the White House," believe[s] in his motives, etc. but thinks he is endangering democracy etc. However, I have cajoled a promise that he will cooperate on the trust bill.

Vrooman[2] turned up & lunched with me yesterday. He came on to try to get Bryan & the Pres[iden]t to help him against Roger Sullivan,[3] all other candidates being eliminated. The Prest. says [he is] leaving it to B.& B. is disposed to compromise on an "available" third man. V. says also Norman [Hapgood] has let up on his attacks on Roger Sullivan & V. thinks that is at the Prest. request via C[harles]. R. C[rane]. I warned V. against hasty inference.

Lovingly

V. says [if] he is turned down for [*sic*] the Senate he will then devote himself again to Railroads.[4]

1. As part of the New Freedom attack on trusts, Wilson had proposed three bills—a strengthening of the Sherman Act, a commission to advise businesses on the legality of their practices, and stricter regulation of railroad securities by the ICC. The first proposal, on which LDB worked closely with the administration and congressional leaders, became the Clayton Antitrust Act of 1914. The last proposal, the Rayburn bill, died after war broke out and the administration feared the bill would upset the already fragile securities market. LDB was originally unhappy with the trade commission bill, fearing it smacked too much of Theodore Roosevelt's proposal to give the government power to regulate business, and on 5 June a weakened Covington bill passed the House of Representatives. According to Rublee, this group then went to see Wilson to get him to strengthen the measure, so that the trade commission would be able to enforce the antitrust provisions. They asked LDB to go along, expecting that—given his antipathy to strong government—he would not necessarily support their views, but that his presence would get Wilson to take their suggestions seriously. To everyone's surprise, LDB did speak up for a stronger commission and convinced Wilson of the need to have a mechanism to implement the Clayton measures without always having to go to court. Wilson agreed; the Senate adopted and the House agreed to the strengthened commission.

2. Carl Schurz Vrooman (1872–1966) was a publicist and writer specializing in agricultural issues.

3. Roger C. Sullivan (1861–1920) was the "boss" of the Cook County Democratic organization in Chicago as well as a member of the Democratic National Committee. He did not receive a federal appointment.

4. Wilson had just nominated Vrooman as assistant secretary of agriculture, an appointment easily confirmed in the Senate.

To: Alice Goldmark Brandeis
Date: June 27, 1914
Place: Washington, D.C.
Source: Gilbert MSS

DEAREST: Morris L. Cooke[1] dined with the three musketeers at the Tea Cup. He is a most active & apparently effective insurgent & think of it coming from Philadelphia where [he] is apparently getting abundant support financial & otherwise. There seems to be the same regenerative & recuperative power in man as in the exhausted soils. I suppose that after the rotting of enough scattered leaves over our own Massachusetts folk even they will rise to action.

Cooke's present project is a counter combination of the cities to fight the Electric Light etc. combination which is wondrous effective as compared with the combination of railroads. After the dinner we called on Scripps[2] when Victor Murdock,[3] Rep. Bryan of Washington[4] & Gilson Gardner were sitting around. Scripps is interesting, no[t] particularly powerful intellectually & getting lots of new ideas here. He told Gilson he had lain awake till 3 A.M. after our talk Thursday night thinking it over.

Hope Susan's face is mending.

Lovingly

Terrible tragedy. The box arrived shattered—without the knife.
George [Rublee] is troubled about the debates on the Trade Com[missio]n bill & we are terribly in need of Bob [La Follette] there & impatient at his weekly which has kept him hors de combat.[5]

1. Morris Llewellyn Cooke (1872–1960) was a consulting engineer and efficiency expert closely associated with Frederick W. Taylor. He was Philadelphia's director of Public Works. Cooke served in a variety of positions, but his most important was as administrator of the New Deal's Rural Electrification Agency.

2. Edward Wyllis Scripps (1854–1926) was a founder of the Scripps-Howard newspaper chain; he also headed the United Press Association and the Newspaper Enterprise Association.

3. Victor Murdock (1871–1945) was a progressive congressman from Kansas between 1905 and 1915. Wilson appointed him to the Federal Trade Commission in 1917, and he resigned from the FTC in 1925.

4. James Wesley Bryan (1874–1956) was a Bremerton, Washington, attorney. He had been elected in 1912 to his only term in Congress on the Progressive Party ticket.

5. Out of action. For the senator's difficulties with *La Follette's Weekly,* see LDB to AGB, 24 March 1914.

To:	Alice Goldmark Brandeis
Date:	July 5, 1914
Place:	Washington, D.C.
Source:	Gilbert MSS

DEAREST: Matters moved quite rapidly within the past week, & it looks now as I should get through here well before your time limit of Aug 1—perhaps by July 20.

Enclosed from Delano[1] will interest you. No blow ever struck them so hard as the New Haven, & the RR men, like bankers, are suffering now for their cowardly compliance or silence. The only trouble is that they may be waking up too late to save the day. The Govt. ownership movement has received a tremendous impetus.

Washington has seemed quite deserted these two days. People are away and their absence emphasized the greyness. We cannot cope with your coldness, but it has been cool enough for me to take long walks.

The RR men say that my substitute RR securities bill will be accepted by the Senate Com[mit]tee even though W.W. is reported as wanting the other thing. I doubt the latter, but the chances of the Com[mit]tee adopting my plan seem good.[2]

You never told me how Susan did on her exams. "Mir sagt man nichts."[3]

Lovingly

1. Frederic Adrian Delano (1863–1953) was for many years president of the Wabash Railroad and then of the Chicago, Indianapolis & Louisville. Wilson appointed him as one of the employer representatives on the U.S. Industrial Commission. For LDB's positive view of him, see LDB to Katherine Buell, 6 July 1914, BL. Perhaps Delano had sent LDB a copy of a pamphlet he had just written, "Some Suggestions for the Owners of Railway Securities and Railway Officials," which contained ideas for self-management that LDB approved of.

2. In addition to a revision of the Sherman Act and the establishment of a trade commission, the third part of the administration's antitrust program consisted of a bill sponsored by Representatives William C. Adamson and Sam Rayburn and drafted primarily by LDB. Known as the Rayburn bill, it gave the ICC authority over issuance of new securities by the railroads. The bill was introduced in the House on 7 May 1914 and, in part because of the New Haven scandal, easily passed on 5 June. It then ran into opposition from a variety of groups, including railroad officials, states' rights southerners, and radical progressives like La Follette, who charged it would lead to government sponsorship of railroad financing. The only other measure introduced was a bill prepared by Samuel Untermyer and Senator Robert Owen, which would have established federal control over stock exchanges. This proposal, as LDB suggested, did not have Wilson's support. The Rayburn bill, which looked as if it would pass the Senate, fell victim to the panic that overtook American securities markets when war broke out in Europe later in the summer.

3. "No one tells me anything."

To: **Alice Goldmark Brandeis**
Date: **July 6, 1914**
Place: **Washington, D.C.**
Source: **Gilbert MSS**

DEAREST: That is fine about Susan. In her developed stage she ought to realize your quiet wisdom; and I am hoping for much gain from her long talks with you.

My walk was interrupted yesterday by Kent, who picked me up in his auto, having just shipped off the family. I am to dine with him this evening.

He says Heney's chances are nil for Senatorship.[1] Kent is glad T.R. is blowing himself out,[2] & that the enormity of our Panama behaviour is coming out.[3] Common talk here is that the Navy could a tale unfold, which would bring the blush of shame to the most shameless.

Kent is greatly excited re water power bills which he says Secy Garrison and [*] are endeavoring to foist on the country. He says Lane & Garrison had it out hot, & W.W. had to come to the rescue.[4]

Having missed my walk because of Kent, I trotted C.H. Winslow[5] out & took his lecture peripatetically.

Lovingly

Met Phil [La Follette] & Nellie D. today. They say Bob is better, but he can't see anyone yet.

1. Francis Heney, running on the Progressive Party ticket, lost his bid to become a United States senator from California.

2. On 18 July LDB wrote to his wife that Charles Crane had "told me confidential[ly] yesterday he had a long talk with Mark Sullivan the day before & that Sullivan had spent the day before that with T.R. and was haunted with the thought T.R.'s mind was affected. S[ullivan] said that he had had some of that feeling when he saw T.R. a month before (probably earlier), but the feeling was much stronger now."

3. After leaving the White House Theodore Roosevelt gave a speech in which he said that, while Congress dithered, "I took the Canal Zone." The Senate began holding hearings on Panama in 1912, and the hearings confirmed not only Roosevelt's high-handedness but also the machinations of lawyers like William Nelson Cromwell who made vast sums of money off the subsequent licensing arrangements. In 1914 the Wilson administration offered to atone for Roosevelt's sins in a treaty with Colombia (from which Panama had been taken), expressing "sincere regret" and paying an indemnity of $25 million. The offer enraged Roosevelt and increased his already considerable hatred of Wilson. In the end, the Thomson-Urrotia Treaty was not ratified by the Senate until 20 April 1921 and, while it paid the money, did not include any expression of regret. For the details of the Senate hearings, see Senate Document 471, *The Panama Canal and Our Relations with Colombia,* 63d Cong., 2d Sess. (Washington, D.C., 1914).

4. Congressman Adamson in January introduced a bill prepared by Garrison that would have given the secretary of war authority to license dams on navigable rivers, provided the states in which the dams were located had established adequate machinery to regulate electric power rates. The bill drew fire from conservationists, who considered the language too vague. They backed a measure drafted by Secretary of the Interior Lane to control construction of hydroelectric projects in the public domain, national parks, and forests, which had a fifty-year limit on the lease and a government buy-back provision. The rivalry between the two factions threatened to undercut any power bill. Finally Wilson called all the parties to the White House on 2 July. There he helped prepare amendments to the Adamson bill that would meet conservationist demands. The revised Adamson bill passed the House in early August, but determined opposition from power lobbies and their allies blocked the measure in the Senate. Then war intervened, and the administration did not press for a comprehensive water power bill again until 1920, when it secured most of the provisions of the revised Adamson measure.

5. Charles H. Winslow (1866–19[?]) was a special agent in the Bureau of Labor Statistics with expertise in the garment industry. He was the chief author of a statistical study of the garment industry protocol, a study LDB helped arrange. See LDB to Walter Weyl, 3 November 1913, BL, and Winslow, *Conciliation, Arbitration and Sanitation in the Dress*

and Waist Industry of New York (Washington, D.C., 1914). On this walk Winslow may well have been giving LDB the early results of the study.

To: **Alice Goldmark Brandeis**
Date: **July 8, 1914**
Place: **Washington, D.C.**
Source: **Gilbert MSS**

DEAREST: Gregory was in for 1½ [hours] yesterday (his telephone call waking me from a nap) to talk over New Haven affair with his usual charm. He read me Anderson's letter to Storey[1] (which has doubtless been published) urging the N[ew]. H[aven]. to accept the string bill.[2] By the same mail came a letter to G. from Storey saying they wouldn't. So G. expects to begin suit on the 16th.[3]

McR[eynolds]. & G. are very much aggrieved over the Folk incident.[4] G. wants to put Anderson on the Federal Trade Commission.[5]

I had Hansen (the Chicago Tribune correspondent) & a Cornell Senior (his friend & classmate) who wanted to talk to me about a thesis he is writing, for dinner at the Tea Cup. The[n] we walked down to the Potomac Basin to look at the full moon on the water. It was a beautiful summer night.

I am the possessor of several additional teeth purchased at the cost of considerable time & an as yet unknown number of dollars. We shall see whether it was a good bargain. Dr. G. is highly pleased.

Lovingly

You should re[ad] the enclosed on Panama.

1. Moorfield Storey (1845–1929) was a leading Boston attorney, a former president of the American Bar Association, and a pioneer in civil rights; he was at this time counsel to the New Haven Railroad.

2. In January 1914 the Justice Department had insisted that the New Haven sell the Boston & Maine in order to avert a threatened antitrust suit. The arrangement agreed upon required the Massachusetts legislature to pass enabling legislation to allow the Boston Railroad Holding Company (which held the B & M shares for the New Haven) to sell the B & M stock. The legislature passed the required law but tacked on a requirement that every stock certificate of the B & M should be stamped, informing the purchaser that the shares would always be subject to purchase by the state. The New Haven immediately protested this so-called string, and both LDB and Commissioner Anderson thought the provision unwise. It conferred no real legal advantage since the state could always take the stock by eminent domain. With a settlement apparently within grasp, Anderson urged the railroad to ignore the string. He wrote a strongly worded letter to Storey in which he warned that failure to accept the provisions would be unwise not only from the public's viewpoint but from that of the railroad as well. Anderson then wrote to LDB urging him to try to convince the board, and LDB wrote to James L. Richards, a member of the board with whom he had good relations (see LDB to Richards, 9 July 1914, BL). In the end the board refused to accept the string, and on Attorney General McReynolds's recommendation President Wilson approved the filing of an antitrust suit on 21 July 1914.

3. McReynolds, no doubt with urging from LDB, had decided to destroy Morgan's New England railroad empire and over a year earlier had appointed Thomas Gregory as special attorney. The government had such a strong case that the New Haven directors decided to surrender rather than risk a fight in the courts and promised McReynolds that they would dispose of the company's holdings in the Boston & Maine and various trolley and steamship lines. Then they balked, hoping that fears of forcing the company into bankruptcy would lead the government to abandon its suit. Instead the attorney general charged the directors with bad faith and, acting on Wilson's direct orders, filed a dissolution suit in federal court on 23 July 1914. The case never came to trial because the directors agreed to the government's terms on 11 August, and the Justice Department withdrew its suit on 17 October 1914.

4. Although the government abandoned its dissolution suit, it had also intended to bring criminal prosecutions against New Haven officials under the Sherman Act. But this plan was foiled because the chief target of the prosecution, Charles S. Mellen, had obtained immunity for his testimony before the ICC that spring, under a relentless examination by former Missouri governor Joseph Folk.

5. Wilson did appoint Anderson to the new trade commission later in the summer.

To: Alice Goldmark Brandeis
Date: July 14, 1914
Place: Washington, D.C.
Source: Gilbert MSS

DEAREST: Mother would have criticized the Kraft Ausdrücke[1] in the New Haven report. It isn't a particularly dignified document, but its net result will help in the country as a whole. I doubt whether anything can help our beloved New England except the passing of a generation & glorious hope bringing spring after a winter of discontent.

Richards, Gregory & Anderson wanted me to meet them in N.Y. Wednesday. The Atty Genl wrote the N[ew]. H[aven]. a pretty strong letter & there is a chance of their reconsidering their refusal to accept the Mass. Act. at a Directors meeting to be held Thursday,[2] & they wanted to talk matters over with me before. But the situation here is such that it seems, at this moment, unwise to leave even for a day.

"But the world's wise are not wise."

McCarthy poured out his hopes and fears in good measure last evening. There is [a] chance, I think, that Bob [La Follette]'s feelings may be obscuring his vision as to Wisconsin affairs.

"Und ich hüll mich in den Mantel um zu schlafen mit den Göttern"[3] was perhaps a wise decision.

1. Strong language.
2. See the previous letter.
3. Literally, "And I cover myself with a coat in order to sleep with the gods." A more colloquial translation would be "I will close my eyes to get along with the powers that be."

258

To: Alice Goldmark Brandeis
Date: July 15, 1914
Place: Washington, D.C.
Source: Gilbert MSS

DEAREST: John Bright[1] was a man of wisdom. But as I see the performance of Senators et al. I begin to have more sympathy with the disinclination of W.W. to advise with anybody. Heine has made clear the danger of "Gedankenaustausch"[2] under certain circumstances.

George [Rublee], Stevens, Caffey (Solicitor of the Agricultural Dept)[3] & I motored with Hitz[4] to Great Falls & dined at a little club called Lock Tavern, formerly a real Tavern on the Chesapeake & Potomac Canal. It was the nearest thing to the old inns in the Tyrol or Switzerland which I have ever found in this country.

These evening parties are a sort of Boccaccio tale.[5] Excursions amidst the plagues of an unregenerate working world.

Hitz is troubled that Felix [Frankfurter] does not work more.

Lovingly

1. John Bright (1811–89) was an English orator and politician.
2. "Exchange of ideas."
3. Francis Gordon Caffey (1868–1951), an Alabama lawyer and graduate of the Harvard Law School, moved to New York to practice. In 1913 Wilson named him solicitor of the Department of Agriculture, and in 1917 he became U.S. attorney for the southern district of New York. He returned to private practice in 1921 and in 1929 became a federal district judge in New York, a position he held until 1947.
4. William Hitz (1872–1935) was then working as a lawyer in the Justice Department; two years later he began a fifteen-year tenure on the Supreme Court for the District of Columbia. In 1931 he would be named to the Court of Appeals for the District of Columbia Circuit. Hitz was one federal judge who was greatly respected by both LDB and Felix Frankfurter.
5. A reference to the *Decameron,* one hundred tales published by the Italian writer Giovanni Boccaccio in 1353. Supposedly a band of travelers, trying to avoid the Black Death, tell each other ten tales a day to pass the time.

To: Alice Goldmark Brandeis
Date: July 19, 1914
Place: Washington, D.C.
Source: Gilbert MSS

DEAREST: Your Wednesday letter arrived Saturday morning. In whose pocket did it tarry?

You can't draw any tears from me on your reduced train service. It's the punishment which fits the crime & there are no folk who need punishment more than these smug "Wenn Gott uns auch gesund erhelt"[1] suburbanites.

I called at Bob [La Follette]'s last night, but did not see him. He is still in poor shape, but has passed on to cereals. He walked the other day (owing to auto tire giving out) about 2 blocks & was entirely exhausted. Also thinks his liver isn't working right. Hannan has gone to San Francisco to see Spreckles [*sic*].[2] This magazine is worse than drink or women—almost—for dragging a man down. Met Lenroot on way back. He thinks Hannan will not succeed with Spreckles & that it is best so.

Lenroot is very well satisfied with the Water power "compromise".[3]

Lovingly

Weather cool. Have ret[urne]d to grey suit. Dined at Cosmos with scientists last evening. Heard about Tennant Lee from his friend Townsend.

1. "If God will only keep us in good health."
2. For support of *La Follette's Weekly*, see LDB to AGB, 24 March 1914.
3. See LDB to AGB, 6 July 1914, note 4.

To: **Alice Goldmark Brandeis**
Date: **July 24, 1914**
Place: **Washington, D.C.**
Source: **Gilbert MSS**

DEAREST: Talked with young Bob [La Follette] yesterday. He assures me that his father is progressing satisfactorily, but that he is not able to see anyone yet. Bob Jr. seems to be in sole charge now. Fola is Chatauquaing until early in August.

We had ¾ hour with W[oodrow].W[ilson]. yesterday—mainly on the RR bill. He was as fine as ever, but impressed us all as if his sense of power over Congress was gone, and later in the P.M. I heard from LaRue Brown[1] that he had withdrawn the Jones nomination.[2] The RR & Clayton bills are both in very bad shape, but we may be able to get them somewhat improved.

George [Rublee], Stevens & I dined in the Raleigh Roof Garden & I returned at 9 to see LaRue, who wanted to talk about New Haven & other matters.

Date of leaving here still uncertain, but it looks now as if I could leave Monday midnight.[3] As Wednesday is Canal Day,[4] we couldn't go to So. Yarmouth before Thursday in any event.

Washington would resent very much your calling it "material."

Lovingly

1. Herman LaRue Brown (1883–1969) graduated from Harvard Law School and then entered a career of public service. He chaired, among other things, the Massachusetts Minimum Wage Board, was counsel to the state's Public Service Commission, and in 1918 and

1919 was assistant attorney general of the United States. For LDB's opinion of Brown, see LDB to James C. McReynolds, 13 September 1913, BL.

2. On 15 June Wilson sent the Senate his nominations for the Board of Governors of the new Federal Reserve Board. Two names shocked the insurgents—Paul M. Warburg, a partner in the great Wall Street banking house of Kuhn, Loeb & Co., and Thomas Davies Jones (1851–1930), the owner of the so-called Zinc Trust, a director of International Harvester, and former trustee of Princeton and a close friend of President Wilson. Although Wilson did what he could to secure the nominations, in the end he had to ask Jones to withdraw. The Senate confirmed Warburg only after he agreed to appear before the Banking Committee. See LDB to AGB, 27 July 1914.

3. This was a theme in LDB's letters to his wife for most of the latter part of July: each day he expressed his hope of an early departure from Washington, to be followed by news that it was not yet to be. He finally managed to get away at the very end of the month, intending to spend all of August on Cape Cod.

4. Although there had been many proposals for a canal connecting Cape Cod and Buzzard's Bay since the seventeenth century (thus making it unnecessary for ships from Boston to sail around the cape), nothing came of this talk until August Belmont interested himself in the project in 1906. Work began in 1909, and the eight-mile canal would be formally opened on 29 July 1914.

To: **Alice Goldmark Brandeis**
Date: **July 26, 1914**
Place: **Washington, D.C.**
Source: **Gilbert MSS**

DEAREST: The pictures of the girls are very good, and as you say characteristic. Hope Susan will have a really fine time at Silver Lake & in the mountains, but am glad you will have another chance at her in September.

Had an all too long telephone call from Garrett Garrett [*sic*] who wanted me to write on the future of the New Haven for Everybody's [Magazine]. I politely declined, as I do most things these days. The President's correspondence on N[ew]. H[aven]. matters[1] has elicited much adverse comment from the standfasters. I think his & McR[eynolds]'s charge of bad faith in declining to accept the act was unfounded & that the Directors' refusal was simple wretched judgement. Still the editorial comment shows that New England generally is as impervious to understanding on this subject as Henry L. Higginson.[2]

Saw David Lubin last evening. An extraordinary Jew, in a way world compelling and filled with a somewhat original conception of the Jewish Mission. Really an extraordinary man, doing his work as a work of pain, rather than of joy. Lying on his table were well thumbed copies of Plato and Spinoza and writings of the Jewish medieval teachers—this a former California storekeeper.

Father & Mother's engagement day.
Very sorry to hear about poor Susie's added pain.

1. In his correspondence with McReynolds on the New Haven (see LDB to AGB, 14 July 1914), Wilson used strong language in denouncing the New Haven directors. The letter is printed in the *New York Times*, 22 July 1914.

2. Henry Lee Higginson (1834–1919) directed the influential Boston banking firm of Lee Higginson & Co., considered a rival to the Morgan bank in financing new industries. LDB and Higginson had been on opposite sides of the New Haven merger from the very beginning. See Irving Katz, "Henry Lee Higginson vs. Louis Dembitz Brandeis," *New England Quarterly*, 41 (1968): 67–81.

To: **Alice Goldmark Brandeis**
Date: **July 27, 1914**
Place: **Washington, D.C.**
Source: **Gilbert MSS**

DEAREST: Yesterday's letter has come. You are right about W.W. letter on Jones.[1] He isn't a good loser, & that defect will make him less courageous I fear, & perhaps not more careful. The general effect will probably be to make him fear progressives more, treating all opposition as cantankerousness. There are some views on one of his appointees that I defer telling you about until we meet.

European war news is terrible.[2] It must be a fearful strain on nerves, revenues, & business. Even if they don't fight.

George [Rublee] returned after 2 days tennising on Long Island refreshed but tired.

Your Salem thought seems quite enterprising.

Shall not know anything re I.C.C. before tomorrow P.M.   Lovingly

1. In reply to attacks on Thomas Jones, Wilson sent a public letter to the Senate Banking Committee defending Jones and declaring that his friend had gone onto the board of International Harvester to help bring that company into compliance with the law. Jones, however, then went before the committee, said he had not gone onto the board to reform it, and moreover approved everything the Harvester Trust had done since he had become a director. As a result the committee refused to approve the nomination, and Wilson had no choice but to ask Jones to withdraw.

2. On 28 June Archduke Franz Ferdinand, heir to the throne of the Austrian-Hungarian Empire, and his wife were assassinated by a Serbian nationalist while on a state visit in Sarajevo. What might have been a localized incident soon escalated across Europe. Germany pressured Austria-Hungary to launch a punitive assault on Serbia, which in turn called upon Russia for aid. The Russians began mobilizing their forces on 30 July, and by 3 August Germany had declared war on both Russia and France and had invaded Belgium. The following day Great Britain entered the war against Germany. Italy, the Ottoman Empire, and a number of smaller nations joined the conflict in the next few months. By the time LDB wrote this letter, it seemed certain to most observers that war could not be avoided.

To: Alice Goldmark Brandeis
Date: July 31, 1914
Place: Washington, D.C.
Source: Gilbert MSS

DEAREST: The war news is terrible.[1] Slowly the proper social conditions have risen for a half century & now comes worse than arrest.

As I feared when I wired the office last evening, I must stay here another day, which means Monday instead of Saturday at the office. We seem to be really progressing & one long chapter about closing. The rest I leave for talk.

Hope you travelled yesterday & are well settled in So. Yarmouth by this time.

George [Rublee] expects to spend Sat. & Sunday on Long Island again.

Lovingly

1. See the preceding letter.

To: Alice Goldmark Brandeis
Date: September 12, 1914
Place: New York, New York[1]
Source: Gilbert MSS

DEAREST: No letter from you today, I trust the head is not troublesome. It has been sunny and cold, & I spent much of the day out of doors, walking and alone, & in part trying to think.

New York seems subdued. It may be partly imagination, but I am sure that there is less of the pleasure seeking air, and the world-struggle seems to have made these materialists thoughtful. One feels here much nearer the war than elsewhere. Nearly every one has some direct tie with the war-zone, even the Old American stock through its foreign business connections.

The business end of the war came forcibly home to me yesterday when Levin[2] showed me a line in a letter from Berlin from his wife (the first recd. which was mailed by an American from Holland) in which she spoke of all being quiet and calm "aber niemand hat Geld".[3] That was Aug 20— after 3 weeks of war. Think what the situation will be there later, if the war lasts long. As the Socialist organ pointed out, what can German industries do with the supply of cotton, silk, rubber & copper cut off?

Last evening I dined at Prof. Gottheil's,[4] & spent the time in cross examining Mr. Leon[5] on Mexico where he had spent much of the last 5 years. (He was a free talker & needed leading rather than pumping). Leon thinks the prospects of peace are good & that the wealth in natural resources is such that a few years of peace would make Mexico prosperous. But he considers the Administration's policy absolutely fatuous, and this because it is ignoring all facts & endeavors to apply American standards to conditions as unlike ours as the Orient.

The prospects of peace [in Mexico] he declares good because practically all possible trouble makers have been killed off. He says we have no conception of the extent of the proscription which has been resorted to by the Revolutionists (with which he was in sympathy). Leon declares that the Wilson policy was Huerta's greatest asset, that he could not have maintained himself for three months if the administration had recognized him at the start. But that the attitude of the administration in taking part in Mexican internal affairs turned to Huerta a large number of persons who had been his bitter enemies, & that the final act of occupying Vera Cruz[6] has resulted in Mexicans hating the United States unreservedly & he thinks—deservedly.

Leon asserts that the Revolution was due to about 5000 persons, that the desire for land distribution is widespread, but that otherwise there is little interest in poli[ti]cs, and that an election in Mexico is the most ridiculous of farces. Madero[7] he says was really public spirited, practically the only public-spirited man in recent years, but absolutely incompetent, and ridiculous as a president.

He says Huerta was one of a junta of 11 which disposed of Madero, but that there was nothing unusual in the act, that it was & is the custom of the country which any set of leaders would resort to.

Com[mit]tee meeting this evening.

Hope Susan is at her German & that the Sunday guests will not interfere too much.   Lovingly

1. LDB was in New York because of a dramatic and permanent new concern in his life. While vacationing in South Yarmouth, he received an urgent message to attend an emergency meeting in New York to deal with the devastating impact of the war on the Jewish agricultural colonies in Palestine. LDB had maintained an interest in Zionism ever since meeting Jacob deHaas in 1912 (see LDB to Alfred Brandeis, 14 August 1912); but aside from some monetary gifts and an occasional talk, he had little contact with the movement and no part of its leadership. For reasons still not clear, LDB accepted the invitation to attend the meeting on 30 August, at which the Provisional Executive Committee for General Zionist Affairs was founded. With the disruption of the European branches of Zionism, this committee became the central office of the world movement during the war. The delegates elected LDB as chair, expecting that he would make a short speech, give some money, and then leave the work to the old-line cadre. Instead, he literally took over the committee, kept it in session, reorganized it, and over the next four years turned it into a powerful political instrument that played a key role in securing the British Mandate for a Jewish homeland. The Zionist cause would absorb much of LDB's thought and effort for the rest of his life.

2. Schmarya (or Schmaryahu) Levin (1867–1935), a Russian-born Jew, had been active in the Zionist movement even before Herzl. Forced out of Russia, he settled in Germany,

then the headquarters of the World Zionist Organization. He was in the United States raising money when the war stranded him, and he became the link between the new American leaders and the world organization. See his three-volume memoir, *Forward from Exile* (New York, 1967).

3. "But no one has money."

4. Richard James Horatio Gottheil (1862–1936) was professor of Semitic studies at Columbia and a pillar of the early American Zionist movement. A reluctant leader, he gladly welcomed LDB's direction. His book *Zionism* (New York, 1914) was for many years the standard volume on the subject.

5. Maurice Leon (1880–1952), Gottheil's stepson, was a New York lawyer who traveled extensively overseas.

6. To prevent the entry of a shipment of German munitions into Mexico in late April, Wilson, without seeking congressional approval, ordered the navy to occupy Vera Cruz on 21 April 1914. The Mexicans put up a spirited resistance, leading to the deaths of 126 Mexican naval cadets and civilians and 195 wounded; the North Americans suffered 19 fatalities and 72 wounded.

7. Francisco Ignacio Madero (1873–1913) led the reform movement that overthrew the old regime of Porfirio Díaz in 1911; he was in turn betrayed, deposed, and executed by his chief general, Victoriano Huerta.

To: **Alice Goldmark Brandeis**
Date: **October 14, 1914**
Place: **Cincinnati, Ohio**
Source: **Gilbert MSS**

DEAREST: From enclosed you will see that but for Al, Cincinnati trip was worse than a Fool's Errand, but it is all a part of the day's work,[1] and Al & I have had a real Zusammensein.[2]

He is fine in every way & I think we are nearer to one another than ever before.

The women suffragists are pretty alert. They have been on my trail again & in the Cin[cinna]ti Enquirer (which is not at hand) I have a little of an interview.[3]

Business is rather worse here than in New England, this part of the country being affected particularly by the South. The war news grows worse and worse, and the end ever more distant. It seems ignoble to think of our own troubles.

Al says they are having through Walter Taussig most interesting reports from Germany & terrible ones.

Lovingly

Hope the head is behaving passably.

1. Cincinnati, the home of the Hebrew Union College and the heart of Reform Judaism in America, was dominated by the Reform German Jews, who were strongly anti-Zionist. LDB was received politely, but little more, and he later described the trip to Jacob deHaas as "quite embarrassing" (LDB to deHaas, 23 October 1914, BL). It would take many years before Zionism would make any headway in Cincinnati.

2. Meeting.

3. In an interview with reporters, LDB spoke mainly about Zionism, but when asked about votes for women replied: "We cannot have real democracy without woman's suffrage, which is to be voted on in your state next month. Not only do I advocate it as a fundamental right of woman to have an equal voice with men in the government of which they are a part, but for the good which would result in the community. Our problems are half feminine ones, and the woman's vote is needed to help us solve them. In my social work among industrial workers I have found woman's aid to be invaluable" (*Cincinnati Enquirer,* 14 October 1914).

To:	Alice Goldmark Brandeis
Date:	October 14, 1914
Place:	Cincinnati, Ohio
Source:	Gilbert MSS

DEAREST: I wrote to N.Y. today and am only sending this greeting to Boston to bid you bon voyage in case the trip has been delayed.

Al and I are catching up again, but a year's separation at our age is too long.

Al is quite emphatic about Oscar, & I guess with all possible avenues for charity uses now, it will be best not to begin with that load.[1]

People say here women's suffrage will be beaten, and also *probably* the Wets.[2]   Lovingly

1. A Brandeis relative apparently in need; see, however, LDB to Alfred Brandeis, 27 November 1914.

2. Ohio voters turned down women's suffrage, narrowly defeated prohibition (thanks to a large negative vote in the cities), and also defeated a local option plan that would have allowed individual counties to go dry.

To:	Alfred Brandeis
Date:	October 16, 1914
Place:	Detroit, Michigan
Source:	Brandeis MSS

DEAR AL: Ran into Carmalt and some other I.C.C. men here of which I was glad, as it enabled me to talk over the Washington situation in advance of my going there. Es ist nicht sehr erfreulich.[1] "Man delights me not,"[2]—and my appreciation of Bob son of Battle grows.[3]

At this hotel I was introduced to the modernist stunt of having not only an orchestra at dinner & singers, but also dancers. Pompeii & Alexandria are being emulated. I guess a heavy batch of adversity wouldn't hurt American morals.

By the way, Anti-Semitism seems to have reached its American pinnacle here. New Athletic Club with 5000 members & no Jew need apply. Ich könnte es Ihnen kaum übel nehmen[4]—if the other 4600 were excluded also. But as Percy Lowell said of our Athletic Club: "It is the most inclusive club in Boston."

Off for Washt. 11:55 P.M.

1. It isn't very satisfactory. Claiming that they were confronted by unprecedented financial conditions aggravated by the war, the railroads had petitioned for a rehearing on their application for a five percent rate increase. For further details, see LDB to Alfred Brandeis, 21 October 1914, note 2, BL.

2. *Hamlet*, II, 2:321.

3. Alfred Ollivant, *Bob, Son of Battle* (New York, 1898), was a popular children's book about horses. It was also the name of LDB's horse.

4. I couldn't take offense.

To: **Alice Goldmark Brandeis**
Date: **October 18, 1914**
Place: **Washington, D.C.**
Source: **Gilbert MSS**

DEAREST: Nothing from you today. I hope the head is mending.

I had some telephone talk with Harlan. He is at Atlantic City and will not come to the hearings & I shall have to see him there soon. There is no knowing what to expect in I.C.C. matters until after Monday['] & Tuesday['] hearings.

Bob [La Follette] seems well, but not in good frame of mind. I suppose the Weekly is bothering him as well as Wisconsin policies. He and Phil are pro-German. So Al remains, but not virulent. Al talks Russian alliances and the inevitableness of race competition.

There was joyous time in my room, & if one must inhabit cities instead of South Sea islands, let it be Washington instead of Detroit & Cincinnati.

The dress clothes are pretty smelly. I am airing them out for tomorrow dinners.   Lovingly

To: **Alfred Brandeis**
Date: **October 24, 1914**
Place: **Philadelphia, Pennsylvania**
Source: **Brandeis MSS**

DEAR AL: I came over on the midnight [train], on my way to Atlantic City to have a little talk with Harlan & then to N.Y., where Alice & Susan are.

Tomorrow, unfortunately, must be devoted to Zionism. Then I return (with Alice I hope) to Washington for about a week. The arguments begin Thursday; & we shall go back to Boston to vote. The later moves are not yet settled, but shall probably return to Washington after election for a[t] least a short time.

The RRs & Bankers did not do themselves much credit. If they have their way they will utterly break down the [Interstate Commerce] Commission & even if they are beaten they will have succeeded in greatly impairing its standing and their own defense against lawlessness and public ownership.

To: Alfred Brandeis
Date: November 1, 1914
Place: Washington, D.C.
Source: Brandeis MSS

DEAR AL: 42 years ago today we were on the Huzzarrenberg.[1] (I am not quite sure which to double, the z's or the r's.) Those were better days for poor Europe—and for Austria in particular.

I omitted to tell you that [Schmarya] Levin described his Cincinnati meeting as a "Reinfall,"[2] & was quite as disgusted with the local material as we were.

Alice & I plan to leave on the Federal today,—should have left yesterday, but for her annoying headache, which Alice thought would be humored into decency by a day's waiting. May be back here again before many days. The railroads made a pretty poor showing in many respects,—in wisdom as well as in earning.

    1. One of the Austrian Alps. The impression made on the Brandeis boys back in 1872, when they encountered this mountain, was a lasting one; LDB regularly reminded his brother of the occasion in letters.
    2. "Disappointment" or "letdown."

To: Susan Brandeis
Date: November 10, 1914
Place: Boston, Massachusetts
Source: Gilbert MSS

MY DEAR SUSAN: Your letter arrived during my absence in New York:

First: I will write you about law schools after I talk with Prof. Frankfurter. It may be that University of Michigan should be considered.

Second: As to Miss Brown's studying law. The study of law is an admirable preparation for many occupations; but I should doubt whether Miss

B. (even if she got her training at Harvard or Columbia) would find the way open to a profitable law practice. The profitable work in law is apt to be connected with important business transactions, and there is little likelihood that in the near future men of business will take women for their lawyers, much as they may like them as assistants. Even woman doctors have advanced but slowly, although the path would seem a much easier one in the medical profession. Of course there will be important and profitable work about law offices such as Miss Malloch and Miss Grady have done, but a legal education is not an essential for that.

I am glad Miss Thomas was so well satisfied with your German, and I have no doubt that your present study of German will make your next appearance at orals a joy. Aunt Do reports to me on the "Cats" situation Sunday.

The elections show an unmistakable reactionary trend,[1] but there are some bright spots—William Kent in California, and you must rejoice in Meyer London the Socialist congressman elected from New York.[2] He is the attorney for the garment workers with whom I have had many dealings & much admiration for 4 years.

Miss Amidon's[3] father is one of the most progressive judges in America, a very fine man. O. Butterfield[4] is counsel of the New York Central of whom I have seen much in the advance rate cases.   With much love

1. In the midterm elections the Democrats lost nearly fifty House seats, and Republicans either swept back into power or retained control of important states like New York, Illinois, Pennsylvania, Ohio, Kansas, New Jersey, and even Wisconsin. The vote was misleading, however, because in many states the return of the Bull Moose Progressives to the Republican Party gave the GOP the majority it had enjoyed prior to 1912.
2. Meyer London (1871–1926) served as attorney for the unions in the protocol. He was elected to Congress as a Socialist in 1914 and reelected in 1916 and 1920.
3. Beulah Amidon (1895–1958) became a talented and prolific writer, specializing in labor, social work, and educational topics. She was an associate editor of the *Survey* from 1926 until it ceased publication in 1952.
4. Ora Elmer Butterfield (1870–1916), a Michigan railway attorney, became assistant solicitor for the New York Central in 1909.

To: Alfred Brandeis
Date: November 27, 1914
Place: Boston, Massachusetts
Source: Brandeis MSS

MY DEAR AL: Your letter of the 25th is so searching in some of its inquiries that I am resorting to a stenographer.

First: The Chicago experience was as successful as the Cincinnati was unsuccessful. In fact Chicago was successful far beyond expectation.

Dr. Hirsch,[1] who is ordinarily a pretty difficult factor to deal with, and has declared himself repeatedly, non-Zionist, was helpful in every way, and the meeting at his Temple was really a perfect meeting. There were 2200 present, and my talk which I limited to thirty-five minutes was unquestionably effective. [Julius] Rosenwald, who had been quite anti-Zionist in his inclinations recently, was not content with a mere call for immediate relief, but insisted that the donors should bind themselves to continue contributions, and he rose and stated that he would give $1000 a month during the war and for twelve months thereafter. A number of others gave contributions of similar character in small amounts, and Dr. Hirsch himself said he would make small monthly contributions for life. The other meetings,—the mass meeting Sunday evening, and the luncheon with the reformed rabbis on Monday, were also successful. In addition there was a banquet on Saturday evening, and a Menorah talk at the University on Monday afternoon. The general feeling was that we had captured the town, and I don't think the editorial in the Chicago Tribune,[2] which you doubtless saw, will do any harm. There must be people who won't agree with us, and it is well enough to have the subject definitely discussed.

The Milwaukee meeting also was successful. We had a dinner before the meeting with the Germans, who really had no sympathy with the Zionist movement, and who came in to it merely out of personal regard for me,—one of them being interested in the Independent Shoe Machinery fight,—another in the Fair Trade.[3] The leader of the German community there stated to me at the dinner that he was opposed to Zionism, and no argument could move him; but when I got through my talk, he said that I had converted him, and I think that was true of some of the others.

The B'nai Brith men are very friendly. [Schmarya] Levin is to talk at the Annual Convention in Chicago, December 26th, and I had a very urgent letter from Samuel Sale[4] of St. Louis asking me to speak there in his Temple at a joint meeting of the Temple and the St. Louis B'nai Brith,—their annual meeting. In the Southwestern States Dannenbaum[5] of Texas is working in cooperation with the B'nai Brith in joint meetings, on the basis of their taking one-quarter of the proceeds, and similar arrangement has been made with the B'nai Brith in Norfolk. It occurs to me that something of that sort might be worked up in Louisville. What do you think?

Second: I believe that when the war is over there will be great increase in immigration, and particularly of the Jews. The indications are that if the Polish monarchy is re-established, the condition there will be worse than it now is. Of course the possession of means will probably be the only serious limit upon the volume of immigration. Hirsch, in his talk which followed mine, bore heavily upon the subject of immigration, and the importance of keeping Palestine open for this purpose. Of course immigration to Palestine would involve far less initial cost than to America.

Third: Mrs. R.C. Nicholson, 5471 Kimbark Avenue, who you remember was Oscar [Brandeis]'s landlady, sent me a letter while I was in Chicago, telling me that he was in the hospital, and suggesting that I see her and her husband, which I did on Monday morning. I was very favorably impressed with them. He seemed a very nice fellow, and she a fine woman, and they speak in the highest possible terms of Oscar. I told her that I had not communicated with her before because I did not care to say how the family had felt about him. I did tell her substantially the family feeling, and why they had not given relief. On the whole I was firm that I would not take over his support, but I told her I would send her $100 to be used in her discretion for Oscar; but I did not want Oscar to know that I had sent it. I have sent her that sum. She says that Oscar was operated on, and the doctors thinking that there was one chance in four that he would recover; but that the operation was successful, and he seems now on the road to recovery. She said that she was convinced that it was nothing but ill health that stood in Oscar's way; that whenever he was well, he had good positions, and was most highly thought of. She wanted to know whether she should keep me advised in regard to Oscar, and I told her I might write her again on the subject. I have relieved my feeling a little by sending the $100 but I don't feel very comfortable in not doing more,— particularly as I am inclined to think Oscar is now being helped by the Nicholsons and other friends who are probably less able to help him. The immediate situation is doubtless taken care of.

Let me know what you think.

Met young Fisher brother on the Twentieth Century of which he is conductor. He told me he recognized me by my resemblance to you & treated me quite royally.

Had intended each day while west to write to you but was excessively occupied. The Cincinnatians are pretty unhappy over Phillipson's [*sic*][6] performance & have been trying to get me down there for the Intercollegiate Menorah meeting, but they won't.

1. Emil Gustav Hirsch (1851–1923) had been rabbi of the prestigious Sinai Congregation in Chicago since 1880 as well as professor of rabbinical philosophy at the University of Chicago. He stood among the more liberal Reform rabbis and, despite LDB's characterization, was consistently friendly toward Zionism.

2. The editorial of 25 November, entitled "Patriotism Begins at Home," attacked LDB's contention that the lack of a homeland was responsible for the rise of crime among Jews.

The paper said that the Jews had maintained high ethical principles for two thousand years without a homeland and that immigrants must adopt the United States as their homeland.

3. For United Shoe, see LDB to Moses E. Clapp, 24 February 1912, and LDB to George Carroll Todd, 24 September 1915, both in BL; for price maintenance (fair trade), see LDB, "On Maintaining Makers' Prices," *Harper's Weekly* 57 (14 June 1913): 6.

4. Samuel Sale (1854–1937) had been rabbi of Congregation Shaare Emeth in St. Louis since 1887.

5. Harry Dannenbaum was an official of the Texas B'nai Brith. He suggested that his organization assume the fund-raising responsibilities for the Zionist movement in the South because of the absence of Zionist organizations there.

6. David Philipson (1862–1949) was one of the leading Reform rabbis in the country and served the B'ne Israel Congregation in Cincinnati from 1888 to 1938. He was also the most outspoken opponent of Zionism; long after most of the Reform movement had embraced the Zionist cause, he continued to resist it.

To: **Alfred Brandeis**
Date: **December 12, 1914**
Place: **Washington, D.C.**
Source: **Brandeis MSS**

DEAR AL: I have yours of 8th with copy of letter from Cornelius. I don't think grain rates are high enough, but they may be absolutely unfair otherwise & I have no faith in the RRs or Chicago & see no reason why you shouldn't fight if you have a mind to. I told Harlan of your letter. Anytime you are here he will no doubt be glad to talk with you on grain matters. Am confirmed in views expressed to you in October about I.C.C.

The Cranes, Rublees & we (including Josephine) dined at the LaFollettes last evening. Wisconsin situation is pretty bad,[1] and reactionaries are pretty well buttressed the country over.

Terrible stories of suffering in Palestine & generally. The Jews are having a sad time—Frank included.[2]

1. The Wisconsin reform candidates backed by La Follette had done poorly in the November elections. The candidate for lieutenant governor, John J. Blaine, finished a weak third, while Paul Hastings defeated Governor McGovern, an ally of La Follette, in the race for the Senate.

2. Leo Max Frank (1884–1915) was a superintendent in his uncle's pencil factory in Atlanta, Georgia. On 26 April 1913 the body of Mary Phagan was found in the plant; based on testimony of one of the workers, it appeared that Frank had been the last person to see her alive. (Years later that testimony was proven false.) Frank was accused and tried amidst a wave of anti-Semitism; during the trial his defense was almost incompetent, and the judge did nothing to prevent mobs outside the courthouse from chanting, "Hang the Jew." After his conviction, he was sentenced to death, and at that point northern civil rights lawyers began working on appeals. Governor John Slaton, recognizing the gross improprieties of the trial, commuted Frank's sentence to life imprisonment. In prison Frank was almost killed by another inmate, and then on 16 August 1915 a mob plucked him from the hospital where he was recuperating and lynched him.

To: Alfred Brandeis
Date: December 23, 1914
Place: Boston, Massachusetts
Source: Brandeis MSS

DEAR AL: My Xmas greetings.

I have yours about A.J.R.C. collection. It is pretty hard raising money now for any purpose.[1] We have our first try here at a Com[mit]tee meeting this evening. The cry of home needs is loud, but men must realize that even taxes do not yield to customary standards. The situation abroad among the Jews is worse than man can tell.

Alice & Susan arrived today. Haven't seen either yet.

Confidential: The I.C.C. decision will prove a misfortune to both the RR's and the Comm[issio]n & will do much to hasten government ownership.[2]

Shall be in St. Louis January 3 & 4.

1. The American Jewish Relief Committee did a rather remarkable job of fund-raising, but the bulk of the money came from the wealthy German-American Jews affiliated with the American Jewish Committee.
2. Under the pressure of the railroads' claims of unusually high expenses caused by the war, the ICC reversed itself on 16 December and agreed to a general five percent rate increase in all classifications.

To: Alfred Brandeis
Date: February 3, 1915
Place: Washington, D.C.
Source: Brandeis MSS

DEAR AL: Nothing from you here. We start this afternoon for N.Y. Shall be there until Thursday. Elizabeth is to be at [*].

Democrats becoming rather doubtful of passing Ship bill, & generally as to political outlook.[1]

We dined with Justices last evening at the Atty General's invitation. Have known of as interesting dinners with less distinguished guests.

Wheat is behaving disreputably.[2]

1. In an effort to meet the economic crisis caused by the war, Wilson asked Congress for $30 million to purchase and operate a government shipping line. Since the only vessels available were interned German boats, the measure sparked a fierce debate. Conservatives led by Henry Cabot Lodge and Elihu Root opposed it on grounds that the government should not get into an area traditionally run by private enterprise. They and others also feared the move would embroil the United States in the European war. Despite intense lobbying by the administration, the bill was defeated in early March.
2. The price of wheat climbed steeply in January because of greatly increased European demand. On 17 January Wilson ordered an investigation following widespread protests by housewives, and the next day wheat prices dropped considerably.

To: Alfred Brandeis
Date: February 24, 1915
Place: Boston, Massachusetts
Source: Brandeis MSS

MY DEAR AL: I had not suspected when I was prodding you so persistently for a letter that you had not been well. It is too bad that you should have had such pain again . Obviously you and I ought to adopt Father's policy of frequent resort to the Medicine-Man. I am sure he was very wise in this. Man ought at least to treat himself as well as a Machine.

It was good to have Fannie's assurance that you are taking the needed rest, and to know that for you exile from business, which means confinement to the farm, is not irksome.

I am off for N.Y. tonight, after more than a fortnight here. My longest stay since—well it must be more than a year. Expect to spend Thursday in N.Y., Friday in Washington, Saturday again in N.Y. Sunday I speak in Providence & Monday am due here again. Activities now are quite largely Jewish relief. We are getting our community well organized & they are contributing quite liberally. Had an invitation from Fechheimer[1] and Max Senior[2] to talk Zionism in Cincinnati, but wrote them I *deemed* public controversy so unwise for the Jews that I could not go unless Phillipson [sic] joins in invitation—which I suppose will prove an effective obstacle.

Thank Jennie for her letter.

Tell Otto [Wehle] Harry was in Monday. He seems in excellent condition physically & mentally. You may tell Louis (Wehle) I met Rem Ogilby's[3] brother on train from W[ashington].

1. Samuel Marcus Fechheimer (1864–1932) was a Cincinnati clothing manufacturer with strong Zionist sympathies.
2. Max Senior (1862–1939), a Cincinnati businessman and philanthropist, was president of the city's United Jewish Charities as well as president of the National Conference of Jewish Charities.
3. Charles Fitz Randolph Ogilby (1879–1962) had recently opened a law practice in Washington.

To: Alfred Brandeis
Date: March 6, 1915
Place: Boston, Massachusetts
Source: Brandeis MSS

DEAR AL: Enclosed must have been intended for you. The only farming I am engaged in is in Palestine & these books throw no light on that problem.

After you have mastered farming in Kentucky should like to secure your services as expert to study Palestinian conditions.

Things Jewish have been occupying my time largely. Boston is doing well on relief funds & we are getting the Jewish Community stirred [*] to attempts at Zionistic organization. Have raised between $60–$70,000 here for one fund or another & expect to bring it up pretty near $100,000 before we stop.

Cincinnatians (Max Senior, Fecheimer [*sic*] et al) have been very pressing with invitation, but I have resisted saying I don't want a public controversy with Philipson.

My greetings to the family.

To:	Alfred Brandeis
Date:	March 21, 1915
Place:	New York, New York
Source:	Brandeis MSS

MY DEAR AL: Delighted to have your report of condition. But Go Slow. As father used to say: Qui va piano etc.[1]

42 years ago today we arrived at Trieste. It was a happier time despite the impending crises.

Has the Jitney[2] invade[d] Louisville? It is striking our trolley lines with consternation. Stephen Edwards[3] tells me 200 swooped down on Providence like an army of locusts the other day & struck terror into the security laden trolley system which the New Haven bought the worthless equity of for 24 millions.

Yesterday saw Rudolph Spreckels (who is trying to engineer purchase by State of California of the Western Pacific). He says the San Francisco trolleys are losing $2,000 a day by the 500 jitneys which have sprung out of the earth, mostly light Fords. If this continues the trolley companies will be squealing as hard and shrilly as the railroads.

I speak in Hartford this evening—then back to Boston.

1. He who goes quietly, etc.
2. Motorized taxis.
3. Stephen Ostrom Edwards (1855–1916) was a prominent Providence, R.I., attorney and president of the Providence & Worcester Railroad Company.

To:	Susan Brandeis
Date:	March 23, 1915
Place:	New York, New York
Source:	Gilbert MSS

MY DEAR SUSAN: The Wedding Day

I am delighted to know that your Dardonelles are safely passed, and I look forward to safe navigation on the Sea of Marmora.[1]

Your class standing brings me no disappointment. You have made good use of your years at college, and have grown most during the past year. I have no doubt but that you will give good account of yourself after graduation, in the law school[2] and in life. With good health, tact and the avoidance of unnecessary enmities you will accomplish much.

We are planning a joyous day. Elizabeth is coming in to dine.

I saw Harry G[oldmark]. with his parents at Grandmother[']s Sunday & promised Harry to report to you.   With much love

1. Susan was finishing up her college work at Bryn Mawr.
2. After taking a year off, Susan would enter the University of Chicago Law School.

To: **Alice Goldmark Brandeis**
Date: **July 12, 1915**
Place: **New York, New York**
Source: **Gilbert MSS**

DEAREST: Breakfasted with Norman [Hapgood] & George Porter,[1] lunched with Eugene Meyer, Jr.[2] at Yale Club & dined with F[elix]. F[rankfurter]. & Francis Hackett[3] here.[4] The rest of the day was Zionistic, except that Moskowitz saw me a moment & is coming in later—& that I visited my N.Y. specialist to ward off an inchoate boil which I discovered on my wrist & took an injection. Thus does the Evil one surround mortals.

Dr. Fordyce told me that my dear Carmichael has just emerged from the hospital himself after an appendix operation and similar pleasantries.

It was very interesting hearing Francis Hackett pour forth his pent up Irish hate for English injustice long continued.

It has been cool here & most pleasant.

Poor Norman seems much troubled, domestically as well as professionally. Only F.F. is joyously concerned with the world's affairs. My greeting to Elizabeth.   Lovingly

1. George French Porter (1881–1927) was a midwestern financier who was active in the Progressive Party.
2. Eugene Meyer, Jr. (1875–1959) devoted his long life to public service. He was appointed to various federal positions by every president from Wilson through Dwight Eisenhower. In 1933 he purchased the *Washington Post* and began the process of turning that paper into one of the nation's finest daily publications.

276

3. Francis Hackett (1883–1962) was born in Ireland. After coming to America he practiced law for a while before finding his life's calling as a journalist and literary critic. At the time he was an associate editor of the new liberal periodical the *New Republic.*

4. The City Club in New York.

To:	Alice Goldmark Brandeis
Date:	July 18, 1915
Place:	New York, New York
Source:	Gilbert MSS

DEAREST: Nothing from you today. Breakfasted with Ray Stannard Baker who enquired about Susan's contemplated law studies, and [I] lunched with Emory Buckner[1] et al., instead of going to the Millionaires' Club to lunch with George Porter before his leaving for the West. He returns soon to go to Plattsburg training camp.[2] Thus is the militaristic spirit abroad.

The heat moderated a bit last night, so that it has been reasonable summer weather today with a good breeze blowing & New Yorkers enjoying the Fifth Ave. stage ride with the abandon which used to characterize the European pleasure seekers.

Felix and I have gotten on finely so far, I doing a little steering occasionally and pushing him into all prominence & work.[3] The outlook is encouraging & we still hope to finish Tuesday.   Lovingly

1. Emory Roy Buckner (1877–1941) was an important and influential New York attorney in the firm headed by Elihu Root. From time to time Buckner was enlisted to serve on various investigative committees.

2. In 1913 two summer camps were begun to extend the Reserve Officer Training Program. In 1915, with war raging in Europe, Secretary of War Garrison proposed a federal volunteer force of 250,000 men, but Congress would not approve. General Leonard Wood, with Garrison's approval, then expanded the summer training camps to allow patriotic business and professional men to get officer training as well. Wood's own encampment was at Plattsburgh, New York, which gave its name to the movement. In 1915 some 4,000 volunteers received training at four camps; by the following year the number had grown to 10,000. The program was highly controversial, with Democrats charging that the camps were hotbeds of Republican militarists eager to get the United States embroiled in the war. After the country entered the war in April 1917, a high percentage of the Plattsburgh program graduates received commissions as junior officers.

3. LDB was in New York City trying to prevent the Garment Workers' Protocol from unraveling under the pressures of the war economy. In a last-ditch effort to maintain the fragile peace in the garment industry, Mayor Mitchel—at the request of both the unions and the manufacturers—appointed a conciliation council chaired by LDB's brother-in-law Felix Adler. Other members included Professor George W. Kirchwey of the Columbia Law School, Charles L. Bernheimer of the Chamber of Commerce, Judge Walter Noyes, and LDB. The council met from 13–23 July; as Alpheus T. Mason notes, "though present at all twenty sessions, Brandeis was conspicuously silent." The group postponed the inevitable, but the protocol eventually floundered the following April when the manufacturers locked out about 25,000 workers and the union retaliated by calling out another 60,000 on strike. For the details, see Mason, *Brandeis,* 313–14.

To: Alice Goldmark Brandeis
Date: July 19, 1915
Place: New York, New York
Source: Gilbert MSS

DEAREST: It now looks as if we should not finish tomorrow & that my return to Boston will be Thursday morning.

You may tell Susan that Prof. Kirchwey[1] says, that in his opinion the Columbia Law Faculty will, at its September meeting, reverse its vote of 6 to 3 against admitting women & will vote in favor of admitting them.

He says the Faculty has the power to do so independently of the Trustees; but that the Trustees have the power to order it done; that there is reason to believe that the Trustees will so vote, if the Faculty does not, & that the Dean[2] is inclined to vote for admission of women, rather than be ordered to admit women by the Trustees. Dean Gildersleve [sic][3] of Barnard wants women admitted & is supposed to have been active lobbying.[4]

Lovingly

Glad the Salem trip was accomplished.

1. George Washington Kirchwey (1885–1941) taught law at Columbia. Particularly interested in criminology, Kirchwey wrote widely on the subject and served on many investigating commissions. He and LDB were thrown together in the effort to save the Garment Workers' Protocol (see the preceding letter, note 3).
2. The dean of the Columbia Law School from 1910 to 1923 was Harlan Fiske Stone.
3. The formidable Virginia Crocheron Gildersleeve (1877–1965) was the dean of Barnard College from 1911 to 1947 and a champion of higher education for women.
4. Although agitation to admit women to Columbia went on for a number of years, the first two women were admitted under a special dispensation in the fall of 1927. The faculty finally voted to admit women fully in October 1928.

To: Alice Goldmark Brandeis
Date: July 21, 1915
Place: New York, New York
Source: Gilbert MSS

DEAREST: It looks now like Saturday arrival in Boston. We are making progress, but it [is] as slow as cold molasses.

Last evening I went down to Henry St. somewhat reluctantly to see Miss Adams [sic][1] after a long day, but decency seemed to demand it. Kirchwey and Paul Kellogg also were there & had been for dinner. Miss Addams said rather little & of course I couldn't add much by way of encouragement. One felt in her, of course, the terrible horror of war and the sympathy with suffering, but even she and Kellogg seemed to agree that nothing could be done now.

Charles [Crane] turned up for breakfast this hour. His thought now is of Richard III for Asst Secy of State or Asst to the Secy of State.[2] Jos. E. Davies is responsible for the suggestion. Asst Secy Osborne[3] (Bryan's special friend) wants to retire.

Frank Scott[4] interposed a doubt whether it might not embarrass somewhat Charles' free relations with the Administration. Charles has talked with William Phillips[5] & House & may go to Washington to see how the thing looks.

Norman & I didn't say much. Felix Frankfurter is coming in later.

Lovingly

1. Jane Addams (1860–1935) was one of the foremost figures of the progressive movement and a leading reformer, humanitarian, and social worker for more than forty years. Best known as the founder and leader of Chicago's Hull House settlement, she was also one of the country's leading pacifists: she was horrified by the events of the summer and feared that the United States would enter the war.

2. The young Richard Crane became secretary of state Robert Lansing's private secretary and was later named minister to Czechoslovakia.

3. John Eugene Osborne (1858–1943) was governor of Wyoming from 1893 to 1895 and then served one term as a member of the House of Representatives; a strong supporter of Bryan, he received a patronage appointment as assistant secretary of state and served from 1913 to 1916.

4. Frank Hamline Scott (1857–1931) was a Chicago attorney and a friend of Crane.

5. William Phillips (1878–1968) was one of the first career officers in the foreign service. He held a number of positions in the State Department as well as ambassadorial posts during a distinguished career.

To: **Alice Goldmark Brandeis**
Date: **September 4, 1915**
Place: **Boston, Massachusetts**
Source: **Gilbert MSS**

DEAREST: I hope the sleep came at last. It surely would, had you such a bed as awaits me here.[1] It seems royal; and indeed, all Boston as strange, as if I had been absent an age.

Susan has doubtless talked with you of her invitation to go suffraging in Western Mass. I suggested she could join the party Wednesday, but she felt she must not leave you while Elizabeth is away. I told her to talk the matter over with you. I am confirmed in the belief that you are right that she had better spend the next year at home with regular work, & I should think suffrage campaigning an excellent beginning.

Susan refused to take the Aug & Sept. checks saying she had money enough. (She found $20 more in her bank a/c than she could account for.)

A Hyannis oculist (a Prussian Jew with a German education) who came to America 9 years ago (& is naturalized) says that after war began he was

politely invited to register at the [German] Consulate for military service.
The all seeing eye.   Lovingly

1. The Union Club in Boston.

To: **Alice Goldmark Brandeis**
Date: **September 25, 1915**
Place: **New York, New York**
Source: **Gilbert MSS**

DEAREST: N[orman]. H[apgood]. turned up & with him Chas R. [Crane.]
(Norman's father is about the same.) C.R. wanted to talk over Armenians,[1]
but particularly a larger project in domestic affairs. [Col.] House, &
W[oodrow].W[ilson]., have suggested that he become Chairman of the
Democratic Nat[iona]l Com[mit]tee, a pretty big job. He (and Norman) are
disposed to his acceptance provided he can get good assistants. House
thinks Sen. Owen, McAdoo & others stand ready. House & W.W. think the
progressive-minded Progressives & others may be won over thus. Norman
has hopes even of Heney & Gifford [Pinchot]. C.R. says for him the reelection of W.W. is the most important thing in the world at present.[2] (He has
just been in Washington for a few days & says Richard is very happy in his
job.)[3]

Spent most of the day at Zionist headquarters but lunched with Charles
at his apartments. Am leaving for Philadelphia at 7 P.M.   Lovingly

1. The Christian Armenian subjects of the Ottoman Empire had been oppressed before
the war; but when the Ottomans joined the Central Powers and non-Ottoman Armenians
backed Russia, oppression turned into genocide. Starting in April 1915 the Ottoman government set about the wholesale slaughter of its Armenian subjects. Depending on sources,
somewhere between 600,000 and 1,500,000 Armenians out of a population of 2,500,000
were killed.

2. Crane did not become head of the Democratic National Committee, but he did serve
as chairman of the Wilson Business Men's National League during the 1916 campaign.

3. See LDB to AGB, 21 July 1915.

To: **Alice Goldmark Brandeis**
Date: **September 26, 1915**
Place: **Philadelphia, Pennsylvania**
Source: **Gilbert MSS**

DEAREST: Note how English we are.

There is a lowering sky, not quite the weather for an excursion into the
realm of a Farm School, but the sun has peeped out & perhaps it will have
more courage later.

I have just come back from a little walk on Broad St. which seems as peaceful as Dedham on this Sunday morning.

Charles R. [Crane] is becoming so Russian that he now has only Russian servants at the apartments & he addresses them in the vernacular which they pretend to understand.[1] I have my suspicion that this is merely evidence of Russian peasant servility. His maid was of a fine type of land folk.

Expect to leave for Washington 3:30.   Lovingly

1. Crane had long been involved in business in Russia and was well acquainted with Russian affairs. Like many of his colleagues, he believed that the overthrow of the tsar would open up great business opportunities for Americans.

To: **Alice Goldmark Brandeis**
Date: **October 3, 1915**
Place: **New York, New York**
Source: **Gilbert MSS**

DEAREST: George Rublee turned up just as I was going to bed. He has left now for his train to Washington. He is full of gloom about the [Federal Trade] Com[missio]n—thinks his Burling[1] will not be appointed and disclosed much reason for gloom there.

Breakfasted with Norman, & he is to breakfast with me again tomorrow.

Spent the day in conference about the Congress[2] and the evening in Zionist Com[mit]tee. The greatest achievement of the day was a haircut at the Harvard Club, which relieved mind and body.

Good night.

Lovingly

The RR conference last night was long & inconclusive. Man is a trying and futile creature.

1. Edward Burnham Burling (1870–1966), a Chicago lawyer, was being pushed by many for appointment as the FTC's general counsel; see LDB to Charles R. Crane, 9 October 1913, BL. In the end, after the position had been filled for nearly two years on an interim basis, Wilson named John Walsh, a Wisconsin attorney. Burling graduated from the Harvard Law School in 1891. After wartime service in Washington, D.C., he remained in the city and was a partner of the prestigious law firm of Covington & Burling from 1919 until his death.

2. Within a short time LDB found his Zionist work seriously hampered by the anti-Zionist attitude of the American Jewish Committee. Composed of wealthy and primarily German-Jewish Americans such as Jacob Schiff and Louis Marshall, the committee had access to the money needed for overseas relief. But it also strongly opposed Zionism, believing it to be un-American and a threat to the full acceptance of Jews in American society. As a result, most of the money raised by the American Jewish Relief Committee was earmarked for Europe and little went to the Palestinian colonies. Marshall and others raised the specter of "dual loyalty," claiming that one could not be loyal both to the cause of a Jewish homeland in Palestine and to the United States. To counter the committee, LDB

needed an organization that was not controlled by the Zionists but would be supportive of their goals, and he hit upon the idea of calling for a democratically elected Jewish Congress. This, he believed, would show up the American Jewish Committee for what it was, an elite, self-appointed group that lacked broad support among the masses of American Jews, especially those of eastern European origin. The committee vigorously opposed the congress idea but could not come up with a convincing rebuttal to the call for democracy in Jewish life. A preliminary planning organization met in 1916, and a full congress was scheduled to meet in 1917. American entry into the war, however, led the Wilson administration to suggest that the congress be put off until after the cessation of the conflict. The congress did meet in December 1918; although it was only supposed to be a one-time affair, it was revivified in the early 1920s under the leadership of LDB's lieutenant, Stephen S. Wise.

To: **Alfred Brandeis**
Date: **October 22, 1915**
Place: **New York, New York**
Source: **Brandeis MSS**

DEAR AL: Was glad to have a glimpse of Jean last week & am promised more soon.

Met Walter Child Wednesday. He bids me to express to you his distinguished consideration & included in his greeting the several members of your family including the grandson.[1]

Have been supplementing Jewish activities by woman suffrage, gubernatorial, garment workers arbitration and public franchise excursions. Am today going to Philadelphia for Frederic Winsor [sic] Taylor Memorial Meeting.[2] Thus is the honest practice of a profession interfered with. Still as the world is topsy-turvey there is no good reason for expecting peace on earth since there is no good will among men.

1. Alfred's daughter Amy Brandeis McCreary had given birth to her first son, Alfred, on 24 August 1914.
2. The meeting was being held to honor Frederick Winslow Taylor (1856–1915), who had died on 21 March. Taylor was the best-known and most active evangelist for scientific management and efficiency in the United States. LDB's speech for the occasion, "Efficiency by Consent," was published in *Harper's Weekly* 61 (11 December 1915): 568, and can also be found in the 1925 edition of *Business—a Profession*, 51–56.

To: **Alfred Brandeis**
Date: **January 28, 1916**
Place: **Washington, D.C.**
Source: **Brandeis MSS**

DEAR AL: Thanks for the telegram.[1] I am not entirely sure that I am to be congratulated, but I am glad the President wanted to make the appointment & I am convinced, all things considered, that I ought to accept.[2]

282

N.B. My coming here was for the McAdoo's dinner before any thought of this.[3]

1. "Our congratulations to you and Alice. What about this appointment?" See the next note.

2. Shortly after noon on this day President Wilson sent to the Senate the nomination of LDB to the Supreme Court to succeed the late Justice Joseph Rucker Lamar, thus triggering one of the longest and most bitter confirmation fights in the nation's history. The full story of the fight and its successful conclusion can be found in Mason, *Brandeis,* chs. 30 and 31, and A. L. Todd, *Justice on Trial: The Case of Louis D. Brandeis* (Chicago, 1964). For LDB's views and participation in the confirmation battle, see volume 4 of BL, letters from 28 January through early June 1916.

3. Prior to leaving on a ten-day speaking tour to garner popular support for his preparedness program, President Wilson was given a dinner by his son-in-law and treasury secretary, William Gibbs McAdoo. In attendance were some of the current members of the Court, including Wilson's first appointee, James McReynolds. Noting the former attorney general's hostility, Wilson allegedly took him by the arm and said, "Let me introduce you to Mr. Brandeis, your next colleague on the Bench" (Mason, *Brandeis,* 466).

To: Alice Goldmark Brandeis
Date: February 2, 1916
Place: Washington, D.C.
Source: Gilbert MSS

DEAREST: Arrived on time.[1] Weather miserable. Norman [Hapgood] met us on arrival then I saw Chantland,[2] George [Rublee], [Raymond] Stevens, Atty Genl[3] & some Senators later— with telephone interlude from [William] Hitz.

Gregory seems confident & thinks it is merely a question of method.

Telegram & letter from Louis Wehle who is eager to come on & do something as are many others.

Hope you got home comfortably. [George] Anderson is due tomorrow A.M.   Lovingly

1. LDB came down to Washington to meet with key senators, members of the administration, and supporters who would be responsible for coordinating the confirmation process and rebutting any charges against him. Although LDB kept in constant touch with this team, ultimately headed by his law partner, Edward McClennen, he stayed in Boston through most of the four-month ordeal. At that time nominees did not appear before Senate committees deliberating their appointments.

2. William T. Chantland was a special assistant attorney connected with the Department of Justice.

3. Thomas W. Gregory.

To: Alice Goldmark Brandeis
Date: February 5, 1916
Place: New York, New York
Source: Gilbert MSS

DEAREST: Your yesterday's letter rec'd. Entirely uncertain still what next. Unless there is a hearing I shall return to Boston. If there is a hearing shall probably go to W. or remain here until called; if likely to be called soon.

It is delightfully quiet here, & Mother is doing finely.

I am off now for a walk & then comes work with Do.[1]   Lovingly

1. LDB and his sister-in-law Josephine Goldmark were working on still another case for the National Consumers' League. In 1912 Oregon had established an Industrial Welfare Commission to fix minimum wages and maximum hours for women and children. The law had been challenged and upheld in the state's high court and then went on appeal to the U.S. Supreme Court, at which time the Consumers' League asked LDB to handle the law's defense. It is unclear whether LDB withdrew from the defense during the confirmation hearings or soon after, but the league secured the services of Felix Frankfurter to argue the case, LDB of course recused, and the Court split, 4 to 4, upholding the lower court decision but not enunciating any clear constitutional rule. *Stettler v. O'Hara*, 243 U.S. 629 (1917).

To:	Alfred Brandeis
Date:	February 10, 1916
Place:	Boston, Massachusetts
Source:	Brandeis MSS

MY DEAR AL: I am sending herewith:

1. A letter from S. Grayson of Rockford, Illinois about Madison together with a copy of my reply.[1]
2. A letter from Sarah Silverman Joseph.[2]
3. A letter from Drury of St. Louis, in which you will be interested.[3]

Return these to me at your convenience.

It is rather amusing that one who is not of judicial tenor should be bombarded on the one hand by the financiers for opposing the railroads, and on the other, by Thorne for favoring the railroads.[4]

The hearings seems to be a fit method of clearing the atmosphere. However, it is not my fight.

I was in Washington for a day for conference recently, but shall not go down again unless requested by the Committee.

1. The letter came from a man who identified himself as an old newspaper reporter, who recalled seeing a sign in the 1850s in Madison, Indiana, marked "L.D. Brandeis" and wanted to know if LDB was the same man. LDB's reply is LDB to S. Grayson, 10 February 1916, BL.

2. Sarah Silverman Joseph was a friend of LDB and Alfred from their youth in Louisville; see LDB to AGB, 15 June 1918.

3. There is no copy of the Joseph letter in the Brandeis MSS. The letter from J. B. Drury, dated 25 January 1916, recalled: "I hadn't seen you since I worked in grain business in Louisville with your Dad when you were 8 yrs. old. I was a grain buyer."

Adolph Brandeis, ca. 1865

Frederika Dembitz Brandeis, ca. 1865

Louis and Alfred Brandeis, 1881

Susan and Elizabeth Brandeis, 1898

LDB and Alfred Brandeis, mid-1920s

LDB, Chatham, 1931

Susan Brandeis
Gilbert, LDB, and
Elizabeth Brandeis
Raushenbush,
Chatham, 1931

LDB and grand-
children, early 1930s

LDB and niece Fannie
Brandeis, ca. 1930

LDB's son-in-law Paul
Raushenbush, 1933

LDB's son-in-law Jacob Gilbert, 1947

Alice and LDB and their four grandchildren, Chatham, mid-1930s

Walter Brandeis
Raushenbush,
Elizabeth Brandeis
Raushenbush, and
LDB, ca. 1935

Walter and Elizabeth Raushenbush with Louis, Alice, and Frank
Gilbert, Chatham, 1939

Alice and Louis
Brandeis, late 1930s

4. Clifford Thorne was the first witness when the confirmation hearings opened the previous day. Thorne never forgave LDB for not taking the shippers' side in the advanced rate case and believed he had committed fraud by claiming to be acting for the ICC and the public. Thorne argued that LDB had fooled the public and sold out to the railroads. See his testimony in U.S. Senate, *Hearings before the Sub-Committee of the Committee of the Judiciary . . . on the Nomination of Louis D. Brandeis to be an Associate Justice of the Supreme Court of the United States,* 64th Cong., 1st Sess., 2 vols. (Washington, D.C., 1916), 1:5–62.

To: **Alfred Brandeis (fragment)**
Date: **February 12, 1916**
Place: **Boston, Massachusetts**
Source: **Mason,** *Brandeis,* **469**

The Justiceship ist ein bischen langweilig,[1] but I am leaving the fight to others and we are getting a pretty nice issue built up. As you correctly divined, I should have preferred to be let alone until sixty-five. . . . But the fight that has come up shows clearly that my instinct that I could not afford to decline was correct.[2] It would have been, in effect, deserting the progressive forces. Now my feeling is rather—'Go it husband, go it Bear' with my self as 'interested spectator.'

Nothing could demonstrate more clearly the concentrated power of the interests than some of the incidents, which I will tell you about when we meet.

1. Is a little boring.
2. On 31 January AGB had written to Alfred: "Louis wrote you on Friday but you & Jennie, I know, will be wanting to hear more of last week's happenings. The whole thing went most rapidly—it is barely a week since Louis was asked whether he would consider the appointment. I had some misgivings for Louis has been such a 'free man' all these years but as you suggested, his days of 'knight erranting' must have, in the nature of things, been over before long. It is of course a great opportunity for service & all our friends here feel that he is the one man to bring to the Court what it greatly needs in the way of strengthening . . ." (quoted in Mason, *Brandeis,* 466).

To: **Louis Brandeis Wehle**
Date: **May 28, 1916**
Place: **Dedham, Massachusetts**
Source: **Wehle MSS**

MY DEAR LOUIS: It was good to get your letter & hope it will not be long before I see you somewhere or other.

Miss Grady has given you more report of us than mere letter can carry & something of you and Mary has filtered through her talk.[1]

Your father made a complete conquest. She says she would "like to sit and listen to Mr. Wehle a whole month."[2]

I am off for N.Y. again tonight for a couple of days at Zionism and the Jewish Congress affairs which are ever with us & present problems galore. A few problems like these would have supplied worlds of occupation for the Great Alexander and saved his fighting.

1. Alice Grady had gone to Louisville to gather information about LDB's youth there for publicity purposes.
2. Otto Wehle, LDB's brother-in-law.

To:	Alice Goldmark Brandeis
Date:	July 16, 1916[1]
Place:	New York, New York
Source:	Gilbert MSS

DEAREST: 6:15 P.M.—

Up to date there is nichts erfreuliches[2] except a southerly wind unduly humid & the prospect of dining with Felix [Frankfurter] and Walter Lippmann.[3]

The dove of peace is not likely to light on the Jewish factions and the association with the "respectability" for 3 hours this afternoon is not to [be] counted among the summer's joys. Louis Marshall was the best behaved & did his utmost to keep the eminent speakers within the bounds of wisdom & decency! We have come to that.[4]

The boat ride had its points of interest but I remain a landlubber by preference, though the moon was beautiful & the Canal trip one one wishes to have made & the digging of the Canal a most reasonable proposition. It is a marvel that it should have been so long delayed.[5]

I still plan to return tomorrow night & hope this trip will end my public appearances in the Jewish world—for the present.

Poor Mack.[6] The peacemaker looked unhappy.

Hope the revolution you thought you discovered a brewing subsided.

Lovingly

1. There is no gap in letters to AGB. For the first time in several years LDB stayed home in Boston and broke this routine only with a few short trips, many of them just overnight, to New York for Zionist business.
2. Nothing pleasant.
3. Walter Lippmann (1889–1974) was one of the young luminaries of the progressive era. In 1914 he was one of the founding editors of the *New Republic*. That same year he published *Drift and Mastery* (New York, 1914), which firmly established his reputation as a social critic and thinker. Later on Lippmann would become one of the most influential syndicated columnists in the United States. For many years, LDB tried to interest Lippmann in the Zionist movement, but always in vain.
4. On this day LDB walked into a trap set for him by the anti-Zionist leaders of the American Jewish Committee. After having been defeated in its effort to avert an American

Jewish Congress, the committee met with LDB and other leaders of the congress movement at the Hotel Astor in New York to see how they would be able to play a role. At the meeting representatives of the committee, especially Judah Magnes, were deliberately rude to LDB; attacks on him and on the congress mounted until Louis Marshall, chairing the meeting, suggested that personalities be left out. The indignities to which LDB had been subjected immediately aroused the ire of the Yiddish press (strong defenders of the congress movement), but the *New York Times*, whose owners were closely associated with the committee, noted that it was LDB who was out of place. In an editorial on 18 July, the paper took LDB to task for violating the custom "faithfully honored by observance, for the Justices of the Supreme Court of the United States, upon taking office, to withdraw from many activities of a political or social nature, in which as private citizens they were free to engage." Although the Zionists had worried that LDB might withdraw from leadership upon going on the Court, until this point he had given no indication that he felt such a move was necessary. Now he moved swiftly; on 21 July, without consulting any of his associates, he resigned all his offices in the American Jewish Congress, the Joint Distribution Committee, the American Jewish Relief Committee, and the Provisional Executive Committee for General Zionist Affairs (see LDB to Hugo Pam, 21 July 1916, BL). He acknowledged that the Hotel Astor incident, even though deliberately provoked, had shown him that he could no longer act as if he were a private citizen. Although now formally out of office, LDB would nonetheless be the guiding spirit and de facto leader of American Zionism until 1921.

5. LDB had taken the night boat from Boston, which, before the digging of the Cape Cod canal in 1914 between Sagamore and Point Grey, went around Provincetown and Chatham before heading toward New York.

6. Judge Mack, who became LDB's right arm in the Zionist movement, was also a member of the American Jewish Committee, one of its few pro-Zionist members. He had tried in vain to keep peace between the committee and the congress advocates, to the satisfaction of neither side.

To: **Alice Goldmark Brandeis**
Date: **August 13, 1916**
Place: **New York, New York**
Source: **Gilbert MSS**

MY DEAREST: This is a painful decision. I am bringing Gregory back from his Blue Ridge a day earlier to meet me at 9:30 for he is largely responsible for the original cause of all the trouble.[1]

Felix [Frankfurter] is spending the day with me, first discussing the Mexican matter at breakfast & after until 11 (the last $1^1/_2$ hours of which I was trying to get you on the telephone) then at Zionist Congress Conference. This evening he & Laski[2] are to dine with me, & I plan to take my sleep near 10, as the past nights have not been over sleepful. The Adirondack night trips are not soporific at best.

The Whiteface [*] population & generally that of Lake Placid were depressing in the extreme.[3] The only redeeming feature (beside the Chief J[ustice]. & much sullied nature) was a Zionist whom I met at the station & who recognized me. He was the real thing. I never felt more, the chasm between me & the prosperous gentility, than that day at Lake Placid & it was a wonderous [*sic*] relief to find "one of my own people" who, by the way, told some interesting South African things.

I shall try to return tomorrow on the Congressional & take the midnight for Boston & 7:35 for So. Yarmouth Tuesday.   Lovingly

    1. LDB was vacationing at South Yarmouth when he learned that President Wilson had named him to serve with secretary of the interior Franklin Lane and another still unnamed individual as a commission to meet with Mexican officials over border disputes. See note 3 below.

    2. Harold Joseph Laski (1893–1950), an English intellectual, was one of the most important political theorists of the first half of the twentieth century. Unable to serve in the war because of a heart ailment, he wound up in 1916 at Harvard, where he stayed until 1920. LDB's daughter Elizabeth was a student of Laski's when she attended Radcliffe. While at Harvard, Laski developed strong friendships with Frankfurter, Oliver Wendell Holmes, and LDB. He then began a lengthy tenure at the London School of Economics and served as the chief intellectual architect of the Labour Party.

    3. LDB, especially after the Hotel Astor incident, worried whether it would be proper for him to accept the appointment, and he hurriedly made arrangements to go to Lake Placid to confer with Chief Justice Edward Douglass White (1845–1921). White convinced LDB that it would be detrimental to the business of the Court for him to take an assignment that might keep him away from Washington for an indefinite period. On 14 August LDB wrote to Wilson declining the appointment, using the argument that White had made about the pressing business of the Court.

To: **Louis Brandeis Wehle**
Date: **September 10, 1916**
Place: **Dedham, Massachusetts**
Source: **Wehle MSS**

MY DEAR LOUIS: Our good wishes go to you most appropriately this evening; for we have been living in memories of the beginnings of the Otto Wehle family—reading letters from your mother and father written in the seventies and early eighties.[1] Some are enclosed.

Susan and Elizabeth are so interested in them that all other literature is being neglected. Even the daily papers with thrilling news is [*sic*] suffering from the competition.

We missed you and Mary greatly this summer. There was much to talk over. And your stay at Madison—of which I heard incidents from Mr. Crane and Felix Frankfurter—must have given you much to think and talk about. Possibly some I.C.C. case may bring you to Washington again soon. We are due there about Oct 5th.

There is a long list of important cases assigned for the beginning of the term. The Solicitor General[2] tells me the government cases may occupy three weeks nearly and there should be much of deep interest awaiting us.

Give my love to Mary, and let me hear what you are doing and planning.

1. LDB's side of this correspondence may be found in volume 1 of BL; for LDB's reaction to the birth of his nephew and the fact that the baby was to be named after him, see LDB to Amy and Otto A. Wehle, 16 September 1880.

2. John William Davis (1873–1955) was a lawyer and former congressman from West Virginia. He served as solicitor general from 1913 until 1918, when he became ambassador to Great Britain. He then entered a very lucrative private practice in New York and was the unsuccessful 1924 Democratic candidate for president against Calvin Coolidge.

To: Susan Brandeis
Date: September 29, 1916
Place: Boston, Massachusetts
Source: Gilbert MSS

MY DEAREST SUSAN: My welcome to the realm of Legal Study.[1] May the next year be filled with happiness and usefulness.

Your last year, rich in experiences, showed the fine stuff in you.[2] You have only to be true to yourself, and in time there will be fine accomplishment.

With much love

1. Susan had just begun studying law at the University of Chicago Law School.

2. Susan spent the year before entering law school working for the women's suffrage movement.

To: Susan Brandeis
Date: October 9, 1916
Place: Washington, D.C.
Source: Gilbert MSS

MY DEAREST SUSAN: Have just come from the opening day of court when Justice Clark [sic][1] was sworn in and many motions presented. We hear our first case, an important one, tomorrow,[2] and then steady grind for the next eight months and more. The amount of work piled up is stupendous. Shall try to keep Master Magruder[3] fully occupied.

Hope all goes well with you.

Lovingly

1. John Hessian Clarke (1857–1945) was a liberal Ohio lawyer whom Wilson had appointed to the Court only a few weeks after LDB's confirmation. Clarke resigned in 1922 to work in the peace movement and to seek American involvement in the League of Nations.

2. Apparently the court calendar changed at the last minute, because the Justices heard no cases argued on 10 October. The only business reported was the resignation of the Court reporter, Charles Henry Butler, the Court's acceptance of the resignation, and the appointment of a new reporter, Ernest Knaebel.

3. Calvert Magruder (1893–1968) was LDB's first law clerk, serving during the October 1916 term. After leaving LDB, Magruder worked for the wartime administration and then joined the army. He later returned to the Harvard Law School and taught there until Franklin Roosevelt named him to the Court of Appeals for the First Circuit. President Kennedy called him out of retirement to head a panel investigating ethics in government.

To: Susan Brandeis
Date: November 15, 1916
Place: Washington, D.C.
Source: Gilbert MSS

MY DEAREST SUSAN: Grandma Brandeis' Birthday.

It was very good to have your letter for my birthday.[1]

41 years ago I was studying the same subjects with which you are wrestling now; & I too found them thrillingly interesting.[2] It is fine that you have the opportunity of discussing the questions with congenial classmates.

As to the points on which you ask advice:

First: As to Hadassah. Be liberal with your money; but very economical of your time and vitality. Good law training now will enable you to do better Zionist work later.

Second: There is only one place to study law for the law student; and that is at the law school. To spend time next summer "studying law" in Judd's office or any other—or at home—would be time absolutely wasted. I have given similar advice to law students galore, for a score of years or more.

Mr. Rublee and Mr. Dennison dined with us yesterday. The day before Mr. Crane was in for tea, and Mrs. [Florence] Kelly [*sic*] and Co.

Mr. Gregory enquired most solicitously for you last week.

Lovingly

1. Two days earlier LDB had celebrated his sixtieth birthday.
2. See, for example, LDB to Otto A. Wehle, 12 March 1876.

To: Alice Goldmark Brandeis
Date: November 27, 1916
Place: Washington, D.C.
Source: EBR

DEAREST: The day is perfect without; but the apartment is less beautiful. Norman lunched with me today, & left this afternoon for Indianapolis on his father's business.—He is due here again Dec. 10–11 & is to sail 14th. Ruth[1] is to sail Dec 30. Can you find a chaperone. She is to be in W[ashington]. with grandparents before sailing.

[John R.] Commons—who occurred to me in the street—is to dine with me alone, upon the understanding that I have an engagement at 9 with Morpheus.

Had 1¼ hours with the C[hief]. J[ustice]., half on his, half on my cases. He has a cold & was quite doleful. I have 4 opinions in printers hands[2] &

300

feel over the peak of the load. Two more in process & then a raft of others to peruse.

Lovingly

I will reserve section in my name to Boston for Sunday night so that Eliz. may be sure of a berth. There will be great travel then.

1. Ruth Hapgood was the young daughter of Norman Hapgood.

2. On 4 December 1916 LDB handed down five opinions in which he spoke for a unanimous Court: *Hutchinson Ice Cream Co. et al. v. Iowa,* 242 U.S. 153 (upholding a state law requiring minimum amount of butter fat in any product labeled as "ice cream"); *Kane v. New Jersey,* 242 U.S. 160 (upholding a state law requiring out-of-state motor vehicle drivers to appoint a state official as an agent upon whom process could be served); *Baltimore & Ohio Railroad Co. v. Whitacre,* 242 U.S. 169 (letting stand a lower court ruling allowing a negligence case to go to trial); *Kryger v. Wilson et al.,* 242 U.S. 171 (holding that in a breach of contract suit the quieting of title to disputed land should be settled under state law); and *United States et al. v. Merchants & Manufacturers Traffic Association of Sacramento,* 242 U.S. 178 (upholding rate findings and rules of the Interstate Commerce Commission).

To: Alice Goldmark Brandeis
Date: March 9, 1917
Place: Washington, D.C.
Source: EBR

DEAREST: It was good to get your postal & I hope the change of air will have worked its usual tonic.

The Steel case[1] came on at 1, so I walked home for luncheon (alone). On the way I met Bob Wooley [sic],[2] who said that Daniels[3] had said (yesterday or today) that he could [not?] see how war could be averted. I guess he would be as likely to see peace ahead as any living man, if it were visible.[4]

The press is full of German plots which I fancy the British publicity Bureau is feeding. At all events it is a comfort to have the British within 12 miles of Bagdad & if they can take it, much prestige will be gained. Besides they are evidently moving forward also toward or in Palestine.[5]

Bob's filibuster[6] has brought its first beneficent fruit. Perhaps an early extra session will follow.

Your suggestion re Rob Barretts[7] had been anticipated. I called at 6:30 yesterday & they were out.

I deposited $150. for you in the Nat. S.&D. a/c today, my balance in Cosmopolitan a/c. Let me know if you want more before the checks naturally come on for signature.

The Chief [Justice] was up most of last night with a sick dog, which left for the Vet. Hospital at 5 A.M. Thus are great affairs of man dependent upon beasts. Love to E[lizabeth] B.

1. In 1911 the Taft administration had begun an antitrust suit against the United States Steel Corporation: in 1917, after several appeals, the case reached the High Court. LDB and McReynolds both recused, the latter because as attorney general he had taken part in the prosecution of the case and LDB because he had been such a vocal critic of the company. A few weeks later the United States entered the war, and the country's need for steel became a paramount war priority. As a result the Justice Department asked Chief Justice White to hold the case over until the war had ended. In 1920, by a 4–3 vote, the Court held U.S. Steel not in violation of the antitrust laws. *United States v. United States Steel Corporation et al.,* 251 U.S. 417 (1920).

2. Robert Wickliffe Woolley (1871–1958), a former newspaper reporter, was chief investigator for the Stanley Committee in 1911. Wilson gave him a position in the Treasury Department and in 1917 named him to the Interstate Commerce Commission.

3. Josephus Daniels (1862–1948) was the embodiment of southern progressivism. He made his newspaper, the *Raleigh News & Observer,* a crusading organ that attacked tobacco and other entrenched interests. Originally a supporter of Bryan, he helped bring Bryan and Wilson together, and Wilson rewarded him with the Navy Department.

4. Daniels had long been a pacifist. As war approached there was a great deal of criticism directed at Wilson for keeping Daniels as navy head. But Daniels proved to be an excellent administrator, and during the war the navy functioned as well as any of the other branches.

5. British forces under Gen. Edmund H. H. Allenby had entered Palestine, but they did not capture Jerusalem until the end of the year. See LDB to Regina Wehle Goldmark, 20 December 1917.

6. On 26 February Wilson asked Congress for authority to arm merchant ships with defensive weapons. Robert La Follette and other antiwar senators opposed the bill both for the extensive grant of power it made to the president and also because they were sure this would involve the United States in a war against Germany. They launched a successful filibuster, tying up the measure until Congress adjourned on 4 March. La Follette became the target of intense criticism, especially from those eager to have the country join the Allies. Wilson branded him and his followers "a little group of willful men." Wilson was expected to call a special session of Congress to deal with arming merchant ships, but the rapid pace of events led him to call Congress back for the purpose of receiving his war message in early April.

7. Robert Edward Barrett (1881–1954) was a consulting engineer from Boston who later headed one of New England's largest public utilities.

To: **Alfred Brandeis**
Date: **March 23, 1917**
Place: **Washington, D.C.**
Source: **Brandeis MSS**

MY DEAR AL: I trust that you and Jennie are sharing, on the birthday,[1] some of the elation we feel over the Russian Revolution. Charles Crane was in last evening to say goodbye before sailing (on Tuesday) for Russia. It has been his stamping ground for 18 years[2] & he was one of the earliest discoverers of Milyukoff [*sic*][3]—brought him to America to lecture at Chicago University years ago. Crane thinks the Russian Cabinet is the ablest body of men in the world & that Russia will teach the world democracy. Says their local self government, and cooperative system, with which 15,000,000 people are connected, is greatest essay in practical democracy the world knows today—& Crane is generally as happy as a clam over the outlook.

It also looks as if the Jews would get relief; but my confidence that Zionism is the only way out, remains.

Gruesse

1. Alfred Brandeis turned sixty-three on this date.

2. Crane helped organize the Westinghouse Electric Corporation interests in Russia as early as 1898 and witnessed the abortive revolt in 1905. Wilson offered him the ambassadorship in 1913, but Crane declined. Now he was going to Russia as a member of commission headed by Elihu Root to investigate conditions and report back to the president. Wilson, however, chose to ignore all of their recommendations. LDB asked Crane to pay particular attention to Jewish affairs, and Jacob deHaas gave him a list of contacts.

3. Pavel Nikolaevich Milyukov (1859–1943), a leading Russian historian, intellectual, and political activist, was the great hope of the constitutional liberals in Russia. But Milyukov was outmaneuvered by Alexander Kerensky. He served for a while as foreign minister but was forced to resign in May 1917 and shortly thereafter emigrated to Paris.

To:	Susan Brandeis
Date:	April 15, 1917
Place:	Washington, D.C.
Source:	Gilbert MSS

MY DEAREST SUSAN: I have your Thursday letter and am delighted to know that the [*] devolution has been satisfactorily effected.

You are entirely right in your remark that you must face the world, as if you were my son, and that experience is, *in the main,* our best teacher.

Elizabeth arrived this morning in bad shape, and we may go to the country later, as the sun is shining joyously—although it is still cold.

I am sorry the war still proves depressing.[1] To me the world seems more full of hope and promise than at any time since the joyous days of '48,[2] when liberalism came with its manifold proposals. Aunt Bessie [Evans] is here, vigorously pacifying and seems encouraged by her efforts before the Congressional Com[mit]tee & elsewhere.

I trust you gave all my greetings to Miss McDowell.[3]

Had a letter from Prof. Ernst Freund & am rather expecting to see him here.

Lovingly

1. The United States entered the war against Germany on 6 April.

2. LDB is referring to the uprisings that rocked Europe in 1848, in which liberal forces imposed at least temporary reforms on the reactionary governments of central Europe. Although in most instances the efforts failed, and many of the liberals fled to the United States, they did mark the arrival of a more liberal consciousness in Europe.

3. Mary E. McDowell (1854–1936) had headed the University of Chicago Settlement in the stockyards area since 1893. She was active in a number of reform movements, including the National Association for the Advancement of Colored People (NAACP), the Urban League, and the Immigrants' Protective League.

To: Alfred Brandeis
Date: April 25, 1917
Place: Washington, D.C.
Source: Brandeis MSS

DEAR AL: Met [Carl] Vrooman at the Balfour reception last evening.[1] He spoke enthusiastically of his visit to your home. I hope you and your neighbors are showing this year that it is worthwhile being a farmer. The country looks to you for the prime service. I mean to go on an inspection tour to Ky after June 11 to see what Ladless can do.

    1. Actually, the reception had been on 23 April. Arthur James Balfour (1848–1930) was England's prime minister from 1902 to 1905 and now served as foreign secretary in the coalition government, a position that thrust him into the center of Zionist affairs. It was a note from him to Lord Lionel Walter Rothschild on 2 November 1917, known as the Balfour Declaration, that promised the Jews a homeland in Palestine after the war. Balfour came to Washington immediately after the United States declared war against Germany to begin extensive consultations with the Wilson administration. For LDB's personal meeting with Balfour, see LDB to Jacob deHaas, 8 May 1917, BL.

To: Susan Brandeis
Date: May 14, 1917
Place: Washington, D.C.
Source: Gilbert MSS

MY DEAREST SUSAN:

1. Account received. I enclose check for $35 as requested on dentist a/c. Mother paid the $14 bill.
2. I am glad to hear of the new opinion & brief. I enclose the briefs sent last week.
3. Act on your own judgement as to Congress. The withdrawal (ignominious) of the workmen is being severely criticized.
4. Mr. L.E. Kirstein[1] wants you to let him know (care Filenes') if you decide to go to the Baltimore Zionist convention. If you do, he will bring his daughter.
5. I should think Judge Mack the best man for your Zionist study circle if you can get him. I don't think Shulman[2] would be what you want. Zolotkoff[3] would be better. If he, make him tell the history of the movement. He was an early adherent.
6. I doubt whether I can make any valuable suggestion on Criminal Law. I found Stephen's (James Fitzjames S.) stimulating—both the Digest & the larger work.[4]

7. I am glad you find something of value in my old law notes. They may be good to review by.

It is fine to know that your law studies are growing ever more fascinating. It is a great field, and there is no question but that it will be wide open to women by the time you are fully equipped through study & experience.

With much love

1. Louis Edward Kirstein (1867–1942) worked his way up through the ranks at Filene's and was also a director of the nationwide Federated Department Stores. He was active in both civic and Jewish activities in Boston and would later head the American Jewish Committee.
2. Max Shulman (1853–1937) was a lawyer and also president of the Community State Bank of Chicago. He was a vice-president of the Chicago Zionist Association and would later be a vice-president of the Zionist Organization of America.
3. Leon Zolotkoff (1885–1938), a Russian-born Zionist leader, settled in Chicago, where he founded and published the *Chicago Jewish Courier*. Zolotkoff was also grand master of the Order of the Sons of Zion but would be best known for his writing in the *Jewish Daily News* when he later moved to New York.
4. Sir James Fitzjames Stephen (1829–94) was the leading figure in English legal theory in the nineteenth century, and his works on criminal law and evidence went through many editions, remaining the definitive works well into the twentieth century. LDB is referring to Stephen's *A Digest of the Criminal Law (Crimes and Punishment),* first published in London in 1877, and *A General View of the Criminal Law of England,* first published in 1863.

To: Alice Goldmark Brandeis
Date: July 6, 1917
Place: Washington, D.C.
Source: Gilbert MSS

DEAREST: Your postal of Tuesday & letter of Wednesday have come, & I am glad you are having some Adirondack joy & hope you will feel invigorated in eyes and otherwise.

Walter Lippmann has just been in; LaRue Brown also, & Herbert [White], & I had an hour with McAdoo. Herbert has also been about. Lunched Magruder at the Cosmos & am planning to interview Bobby[1] in Potomac Park.

More & more of the world is settling here, i.e. Prof. Marks[2] and a fragment of the Mass. Minimum Wage board. There are a lot of things I should like to tell you about, that can't be put on paper. It is too bad you are not a salamander.

Note—The new grey suit was inaugurated today & the world looks on in amazement.

Herbert has just come in.   Lovingly

1. Bobby was LDB's horse, Bob, Son of Battle, and the "interview" was LDB's regular afternoon exercise.

2. Perhaps Lionel Simeon Marks (1871–1955), professor of engineering at Harvard. Born and initially educated in England, Marks came to the United States in 1893 on a traveling fellowship to visit the Chicago World's Fair. He stayed to take an engineering degree at Cornell and in 1894 began teaching at Harvard. A pioneer in the development of the internal combustion engine, Marks advised the armed forces on aeronautical issues during World War I.

To:	Alice Goldmark Brandeis
Date:	July 10, 1917
Place:	Washington, D.C.
Source:	Gilbert MSS

DEAREST: Nothing from you since Friday's letter & this is Tuesday. The Adirondacks are very far away; and we are having such cool weather here that even you would enjoy it. Herbert [White] reports Boston too cold.

George Rublee turned up yesterday afternoon, and in the evening we dined together with Covington at the Cosmos.

First Citizens are still gathering here i.a. Endicott[1] & Preston Clark[2] summoned by Hoover.[3]

The A[ttorney].G[eneral]. who called me for some consultation today tells me his family leave tomorrow. Many of the Cabinet are still here. As I rode yesterday in Potomac Park I saw the Burlesons and the Lanes horse-drawn. The McAdoo's [sic] also "occurred to me" in auto.

Eugene Meyer was in today with a long protest against the administration's delay in deciding where to rest authority to make purchases & contracts. It certainly is taking W.W. a long time to decide, & there seems to be no lessening of the questions which go to him for decision.[4] The only person who seems to go forward is Hoover who has no authority in law for anything practically.   Lovingly

1. Henry Bradford Endicott (1853–1920) was a shoe manufacturer and the founder of the Endicott Johnson Company, with plants in new England and New York. Endicott had a reputation as a good employer and was often called upon to act as a mediator in labor disputes.

2. This is either Benjamin Preston Clark (1860–1939), a Boston businessman, or his son.

3. Herbert Clark Hoover (1874–1964), after a successful career as a mining engineer, jumped into international prominence when he organized relief programs in Belgium at the outbreak of the war. Wilson named him as food administrator, and Hoover emerged during the war as perhaps the most capable man in the government. He served as secretary of commerce in the Harding and Coolidge administrations and then was elected president in 1928. His ideological rigidity, however, left him helpless before the needs of the Great Depression, and he was defeated in his bid for reelection in 1932 by Franklin Roosevelt. After 1945 Harry Truman turned to Hoover to head several commissions looking into reorganization of the federal government.

Hoover first came to LDB's attention through Norman Hapgood, and the two men met shortly after Hoover returned to the United States from Belgium. "In one hour," LDB later told Professor Mason, "I learned more from Hoover than from all the persons I had seen in connection with war matters heretofore." During the 1920s LDB was often critical of Hoover's policies, but the two men enjoyed cordial relations; LDB found Hoover's responses to the Depression inadequate and wrong-headed.

4. Wilson, philosophically committed to the idea of small government, had difficulty adjusting to the fact that war demands extensive governmental control of the economy. In the fall of 1917 LDB helped convince Wilson to name his son-in-law, William Gibbs McAdoo, as director of the nation's railroad system. The blockages in production complained of by Eugene Meyer grew worse, and finally Wilson again turned to LDB for advice, this time through the agency of Colonel House. LDB's assurances that central direction and control were necessary led Wilson to reorganize the War Industries Board and make Bernard Baruch its director (see LDB to E. M. House, 9 January 1918, BL).

To: **Alice Goldmark Brandeis**
Date: **July 14, 1917**
Place: **Washington, D.C.**
Source: **Gilbert MSS**

DEAREST: It will seem much nearer to have you in Dedham.

The photo of Susan has been found & sent her. But it was not in the left hand bureau drawer. The only ones there were of your parents & Bessie [Evans]. I found the one of Susan in the drawer of the pamphlet case. What a time you would have had laying your hand on it in the dark blindfolded!!

I had my ride yesterday & the day before, but it looks now as if there should be none today. It is storming mit Wolkenbruch.[1]

Lunched with Louis W[ehle]. (Percy,[2] Lowry, & Anderson also) & promise[d] L. to dine with him and Mary at their new house tomorrow. Louis II has gained 5 ounces this week.

Saw Baker[3] today. He looks calm but W.W. who passed in his auto seemed to me a bit worn. I should think he might be. Zionist trouble aplenty.

German rumors are interesting.

1. With a cloudburst.
2. Eustace Sutherland Campbell Percy (1887–1958; later Baron Percy of Newcastle) was part of the British delegation to the United States, and LDB probably met him through Felix Frankfurter. Percy would go on to have a long and distinguished career not only in government but in education as well.
3. Newton Diehl Baker (1871–1937), a leading Ohio progressive, was mayor of Cleveland from 1912 until Wilson named him secretary of war in 1916. Although reputed to be a pacifist, Baker proved an able and effective administrator. After the war Baker returned to a profitable law practice in Cleveland, and in 1928 Coolidge named him to the Permanent Court of Arbitration in the Hague. He was often mentioned as a possible presidential candidate for the Democratic Party but never received the nomination.

To: **Alice Goldmark Brandeis**
Date: July 25, 1917
Place: Washington, D.C.
Source: Gilbert MSS

DEAREST: Sunday and Monday letters have come. I am glad for Susan.

My talks with Stimson seem to have landed Herbert safely in his lap. S. is I think really the head of the War Intelligence Service, though not such ostensibly. H. remarked yesterday that he had advanced more in his work in a day than heretofore in four months. He is to have a commission, but with unusual freedom befitting his task.

The President has solved happily & in the only way possible satisfactorily, the Denman-Goethals controversy. "A curse on both your houses."[1] Herbert will probably work now also with the Shipping Board.

The Russian retreat[2] adds to our task. I see no basis for Felix Adler's prediction of a relatively early peace. Every German victory makes it more difficult to end the war.

I note the Palestine war activity. The Turkish report of defeat makes me think the British have made a dent.

Stimson thinks there is hope in the revived Roumanian army of 350,000 men under French officers. It seems incredible.

Lovingly

The Russian freedom makes one think of Gregory's definition of an independent—as one who cannot be depended upon.

1. A struggle had been brewing for several months between Gen. George Washington Goethals (1858–1928), who had been the chief engineer in the building of the Panama Canal and then the first civil governor of the Canal Zone and who in April 1917 became general manager of the Emergency Fleet Corporation, and William Denman, chairman of the Shipping Board. Denman, in an effort to speed up ship production, called for the building of wooden ships, since steel was in short supply; Goethals, however, derided the wooden ship idea and maintained that there was adequate steel to build a modern fleet. In the meantime few if any ships were being built. Wilson suggested on several occasions that the two men resolve their differences and, when that did not occur, finally stepped in and asked both men to resign their positions.

2. In what appeared to be a coup for Germany, working with its agents inside the new Russian government, Russian troops were falling away from the front line and beating a hasty retreat toward Petrograd. News reports from the front pictured a fractured Russian military command unsure of who was in charge of the government and what its battle plan was supposed to be.

To: **Alice Goldmark Brandeis**
Date: August 24, 1917
Place: Washington, D.C.
Source: Gilbert MSS

DEAREST: Yesterday's visitors were—Walter Meyer,[1] Mack, Lewin-Epstein,[2] Price, Eugene Meyer, Boynton[3] and the A[ttorney].G[eneral]. Boynton has recently returned from Russia (where he saw C[harles].R.C[rane]. often). He is hopeful. Says our Com[missio]n mission did not create even a ripple there. It was deemed best not to let them operate publicly, for fear of being considered as "butting in."

The dinner[4] had only this merit: It was strictly limited to 8 to 10 & we were not a[t] table more than an hour. Menu—cantaloupe, soup, chicken with 2 vegetables, Ham & celery salad, ice cream, fruit. Wine was served, but little taken. I sat between [*] & another Japanese even more taciturn. Talked after dinner & before with many Senators et al. including Senator Lodge. [Joseph G.] Cannon said, I looked "ten years younger than he supposed I was." I asked him how young I looked & his answer was 38. "You will say at 82 one's eyesight weakens."

The President looks fit, but Baker, McAdoo & the A.G. & Hoover besides "der Kleinste der Kleinen"[5] like Redfield look all fagged out. Baker & Hoover most of all.

The War Industries Commissioners—[Frank] Scott, Brookings,[6] Lovett,[7] & Baruch[8] I also talked with. They looked hale & hearty.

Add Pears "40 Years at Constantinople"[9] to the books to be brought here. Have ridden every day.

1. Walter E. Meyer (1882–1957), Eugene's brother, was a New York attorney who later became a director of the St. Louis & Southwestern Railroad. For LDB's view of Walter Meyer, see LDB to Jacob H. Gilbert, 24 October 1930.

2. Elias Wolf Lewin-Epstein (1863–1932) was one of the early settlers in Palestine. He came to the United States in 1900 as a representative of the Carmel Wine Company and immediately became active in Zionist affairs. During the war he went to Europe on a diplomatic mission for American Zionists and in 1918 headed the American Zionist medical mission to Palestine.

3. Charles Hudson Boynton (1868–1935), a former newspaperman turned stockbroker and financier, was also the president of the American-Russian Chamber of Commerce. He had just returned from Petrograd and told newspaper reporters that the Provisional Government under Kerensky was strong and would endure.

4. At the White House.

5. "The smallest of the small."

6. Robert Somers Brookings (1850–1932) was a businessman who made his fortune early and then devoted the rest of his life to philanthropy. Wilson named him to the War Industries Board (WIB), where he headed the Price Fixing Committee. After the war he founded the famous Brookings Institution in Washington.

7. Robert Scott Lovett (1860–1932) was a lawyer who became president of the Union Pacific railroad. He was a member of the WIB and headed the section dealing with setting priorities.

8. Bernard Mannes Baruch (1870–1965) was best known as an unusually astute stock speculator. Because of his intimate knowledge of the American economy, especially raw materials, Wilson named him to the War Industries Board and after 1918 put him in charge of war production. Few civilians in the United States exercised as much power as Baruch

during World War I. He gained a reputation as an astute administrator and was regularly consulted by succeeding presidents. From time to time LDB would try to interest him in Zionism but never successfully.

9. *Forty Years in Constantinople: The Recollections of Sir Edwin Pears, 1873–1915* (New York, 1916). Pears was a British lawyer who lived and worked in Constantinople; his book was not a history but a collection of reminiscences relating to people he had known and events he had witnessed.

To:	Alice Goldmark Brandeis
Date:	August 30, 1917
Place:	Washington, D.C.
Source:	Gilbert MSS

DEAREST: Was with President half hour on I.C.C. nominations. He is thinking much on future of RRs & would be for Govt ownership but for the political power of organized RR employees. Had a word with him also on international affairs.

Mark Sullivan called, very interesting. Five years after the [*] comes, he is being driven out of Colliers. by being unwilling to be a sufficiently compliant tool of the interests. He was ready to suppress, but not affirmatively to attack the right. I was more than sound in my advice to Mc. on Allen. He is far more dangerous than I supposed. The 5 years have dealt hardly with M.S.—the compliance has degenerated him. There is a flabbiness in appearance, corresponding with the moral degeneration. I feel as if his call on me had in it something of the drunkard's determination to free himself. More of this when we meet.

Stevens says Magruder has left for the officers training camp.

Mark S. says that he has come to my views on Money Power & the suppression of individual liberty & looks for social upheaval here after the war.

Lovingly

Louis [Wehle] has not rec'd his Commission yet, but has an ever growing circle of admirers, including Hurley[1] and Stevens.

1. Edward Nash Hurley (1864–1933), a tool manufacturer, had been named chairman of the United States Shipping Board.

To:	Alice Goldmark Brandeis
Date:	September 1, 1917
Place:	Washington, D.C.
Source:	Gilbert MSS

DEAREST: E.W. Scripps has been drawn from his mountain fastness by the war & has taken a house for some months at least in Washington, in order to be in the midst of affairs. He came in yesterday for a long talk, to talk out his doubts and fears and asked leave on parting to come in more. He is an interesting character, with ideas extending like his top-boots, into the prewar (Civil War) period & forward into the 21st Century.

I ran across the Gilson Gardners yesterday also. She looks battered and defiant—insists her gardening is not to help the war. He, too, looks less rosy.

I dined at the Cosmos yesterday without pre-arrangement, & became inextricably attached, for a while, to Oswald Garrison Villard[1] (whom I should like to consign to burning oil) and on escaping from him fell in with Bainbridge Colby[2] (who has not improved since Anno X.) whom Gregory and Hitz had in tow. The A[ttorney].G[eneral]. plans a Maine Woods vacation beginning Tuesday.

Lunched with Louis [Wehle], who is now labor counsel for the Emergency Fleet Corporation & has a promise of salary from Hurley.

My love to Susan.

1. Oswald Garrison Villard (1872–1949), the grandson of the famous abolitionist William Lloyd Garrison, was editor and publisher of the *New York Evening Post* from 1897 to 1918 and then editor of the influential progressive journal the *Nation*. Villard, who vehemently opposed the war, wrote on numerous liberal causes; see his autobiography, *Fighting Years* (New York, 1939).

2. Bainbridge Colby (1869–1950) had been a Roosevelt Republican from New Jersey. Wilson named him to the Shipping Board in 1917. He soon impressed the president, and upon Robert Lansing's resignation as secretary of state in March 1920 Wilson appointed the compliant Colby to take his place. After Wilson left office in 1921, he and Colby opened a law practice in Washington.

To:	Alfred Brandeis
Date:	September 16, 1917
Place:	Washington, D.C.
Source:	Brandeis MSS

DEAR AL: Your letters to Barnes[1] puts [*sic*] the question with great clearness & I shall be glad to see his answer. This price fixing job is about the hardest economic problem ever tackled. The world has been at it from time to time for thousands of years—never with great success. My own opinion is that in America—inducing lessened consumption through education & exhortation—difficult as the task is—is the factor which will tend most toward a satisfactory solution. But it is comforting to know that Hoover and Barnes are on the job. No men can do better than they—with such help as they are sure to get from loyal supporters.[2]

Coal men are yelling loud. The probability is that soft coal prices are largely too low and anthracite too high. Coal saving has not been started.

The easiest way of all is to pass a Day Light Saving bill providing for steps from 1 to 2 hours—seven months in the year.[3]

Send to the Library for Abbott's "The Common People of Ancient Rome" (Scribners 1911) & read the chapter "Diocletian's Edict & the High Cost of Living."[4]

1. Julius Howland Barnes (1873–1959) was in charge of wheat production for Hoover's Food Administration.

2. Shortly after this letter Alfred Brandeis went to Washington personally to present his ideas on wheat production to Hoover, who was impressed with them and immediately offered to put them into effect if Alfred would stay on and work with him as a special assistant. Alfred agreed and served during the war as a "dollar-a-year" man, accepting no salary for his war service.

3. A one-hour Daylight Savings Time act was passed as a war measure to conserve coal supplies.

4. Frank Frost Abbott, *The Common People of Ancient Rome* (New York, 1911), 145–79. Abbott concluded that Emperor Diocletian's radical attempt to control wages and prices had been a disastrous failure.

To: Alice Goldmark Brandeis
Date: September 17, 1917
Place: Washington, D.C.
Source: Gilbert MSS

DEAREST: Had a busy day yesterday. Read law all morning; & of course I rode in the afternoon. Lunched with Lords Northcliffe[1] & Reading[2]—we three alone. After luncheon N. went off for Golf & the L[ord]. C[hief]. J[ustice]. & I had a confidential talk. He is a charming combination of Englishman & Jew, with no more of the latter than is essential to great charm. He is most refined in speech & manner, with an inoffensively keen intellect and exquisite gentlemanliness. These qualities are heightened by youth and agileness physically & a most agreeable voice.

The dinner with Holman[3] & Louis [Wehle] was agreeable & informing. H. had also been Minister of Railways in Australia. Had much to tell, in answer to enquiries, about his own country & much about England. Ll. George,[4] Smuts,[5] Winston Churchill[6] and Rhodes[7] he considers big men. The underlings he thinks are most inefficient—unter dem Hund.[8]

Later in the evening Asst Secy Crosby[9] came in to talk Treasury matters. The task is—all around—of a seriousness to tax all our resources, in brains, money and manliness.   Lovingly

1. Alfred Charles William Harmsworth, 1st Viscount Northcliffe (1865–1922), was a leading publisher and chairman of the British War Mission to the United States in 1917 and 1918.

2. Rufus Daniel Isaacs, 1st Marquess of Reading (1860–1935), was a renowned lawyer, first elected to Parliament in 1904 and named Lord Chief Justice in 1913, the first Jew to hold

that office. He made several trips to the United States during the war and was then in Washington to urge the immediate transport of American troops to France. In 1920 he became viceroy of India, a position he held for six years. Isaacs was a committed Zionist.

3. Probably William Arthur Holman (1871–1934), the Labour premier of New South Wales, Australia, who was then in the United States on a war mission.

4. David Lloyd George (1863–1945) became prime minister of Great Britain in 1916. He was favorably disposed toward Zionism and played a key role in producing the Balfour Declaration.

5. Jan Christian Smuts (1870–1950) rose to prominence in South Africa because of his leadership during the Boer Rebellion. He would be one of the leaders of South Africa's government for nearly the rest of his life. At Paris he worked for a humane peace settlement and later blasted the Versailles Treaty as a folly.

6. Winston Leonard Spencer Churchill (1874–1965) was then first lord of the Admiralty; he would gain his greatest fame, of course, as prime minister, leading England through World War II.

7. Although he was now dead, Cecil John Rhodes (1853–1902), more than any other man, developed British interests in southern Africa and was the chief imperial officer there from 1890 to 1896, when he served as premier of the Cape Colony (later South Africa).

8. Less than a dog.

9. Oscar Terry Crosby (1861–1947), after a career as an army engineer, became interested in the practical applications of electricity. He worked for Hoover in Belgium in 1915, and Wilson named him assistant secretary of the treasury in 1917.

To: **Alfred Brandeis**
Date: **October 14, 1917**
Place: **Washington, D.C.**
Source: **Brandeis MSS**

MY DEAR AL: Alice has gone to New York for Ruth Goldmark's funeral.[1] She died of pneumonia following the exhaustion 6 days after the son was born. It is a tragedy. The marriage was an exceedingly happy one which had brought to both much development.

I have been reading today some Czecho-Slovak literature—historical political. The Hapsburg monarchy has done them grave wrongs, and our Viennese contracted contempt most unfounded.

You would find Steed's Hapsburg Monarchy[2] and Prof. Masaryk's[3] writings interesting. Father's horror of the Austrian regime was most justified. The marvel is that the Empire should have lasted so long.

The Jews have played there an ignoble part.

1. Ruth Goldmark was the wife of LDB's brother-in-law Charles J. Goldmark, a well-known electrical and consulting engineer specializing in transportation problems.

2. Henry Wickham Steed, *The Hapsburg Monarchy* (New York, 1913).

3. Thomas Garrigue Masaryk (1850–1937) was a Czech intellectual and patriot who became the principal founder and first president of the new republic of Czechoslovakia in 1918. He was married to an American. The next year Masaryk visited the United States and met LDB; see Masaryk, *The Making of a State, Memories and Observations, 1914–1918* (New York, 1927), 236.

To: Alice Goldmark Brandeis
Date: October 14, 1917
Place: Washington, D.C.
Source: EBR

DEAREST: It was hard to have you go. I walked to the Stoneleigh.[1]

Did not succeed in getting Miss McKinley—worked a bit on law (the C[hief] J[ustice] has not assigned any case to me yet)—and read Czech history at & after luncheon. It is a grievous story of Hapsburg-German wrong-doing and a fine tale of national idealism. Me for the small nations.

The sun was so inviting and the Stoneleigh so dreary, that I overcame my trepidation & summoned Robert Son of Battle for 1½ hours in Potomac Park. Now I am to clear my desk again and take another nibble at law.

My love to Charles.

It is indeed a tragedy.[2]

Lovingly

1. The apartment building where the Brandeises lived.
2. See the preceding letter.

To: Alfred Brandeis
Date: November 26, 1917
Place: Washington, D.C.
Source: Brandeis MSS

MY DEAR AL: Thanks for 2 letters—I am returning to Otto [Wehle] the ancient one from myself.

Herbert [White] came back from France & England with reports of very optimistic feeling in both countries, and another observer, who came back last week, says the same. Very great changes in feeling there as compared with last January says Herbert & due largely to their confidence in what America will do & what she has done in relieving their financial strain (which was great) & in assuring their supplies of food & otherwise.

They feel that the U. Boat, tho still a very serious matter, is no longer a menace to success. Destroyers, convoys, & improvement in handling the situation—including Depth Bombs—have greatly changed the situation. Of course, shipping is a very great need & would be for the next year, if not a single merchantman were destroyed; the demands for shipping are so greatly increased.

U.S. plans to send 50,000 men a month. The Vaterland (Leviathan) took 12,000-16,000 on her first trip over.[1]

The transportation problem (domestic) is giving much concern—as is the coal problem.

314

1. The gigantic German merchant ship *Vaterland* was one of ninety-seven German vessels interned by the United States. Renamed the *Leviathan,* it was used to carry American troops to Europe beginning in late 1917.

To: **Regina Wehle Goldmark**
Date: **December 20, 1917**
Place: **Washington, D.C.**
Source: **EBR**

MY DEAR MOTHER: It was sweet of you to send me congratulations on the Liberation of Jerusalem.[1] The work for Zionism has seemed to me, on the whole, the most worthwhile of all I have attempted; and it is a great satisfaction to see the world gradually acquiescing in its realization.[2]

Alfred enjoyed much seeing you and the girls. Susan and Elizabeth are with us today and all send much love.

1. After weeks of anticipation, the British army under General Allenby captured Jerusalem with little bloodshed and almost no destruction of the city's holy sites.
2. To his associates in the movement, LDB was less sentimental. He wrote Jacob deHaas: "I note your telegram, fall of Jerusalem creating 'Big Sensation.' Is it creating big 'Money & Members'?" (LDB to deHaas, 20 December 1917, Jacob deHaas MSS Zionist Archives and Library, New York City).

To: **Elizabeth Brandeis**
Date: **April 25, 1918**
Place: **Washington, D.C.**
Source: **Gilbert MSS**

MY DEAREST ELIZABETH: You made the last year beautiful for yourself and for us by development in character and in mind and by the happiness which you have given others.

I cannot wish better for you or for ourselves than that his development and loving helpfulness may continue.[1]   With many kisses

1. Two days earlier LDB had written to his daughter: "For your birthday I can wish you and us nothing better than that you shall continue to develop as nobly as you have heretofore and enjoy as much happiness as you are giving us." This date marked her twenty-second birthday.

To: **Alice Goldmark Brandeis**
Date: **June 15, 1918**
Place: **Washington, D.C.**
Source: **Gilbert MSS**

DEAREST: This is to exhibit my new paper.[1] George R[ublee]. dined with me & spent the evening. Al & Louis W[ehle]. dined & left shortly after. L has returned to P. & expects to be back here Tuesday.

Al saw Sarah Silverman Joseph in N.Y. & much enjoyed talking with her of their last meeting 50 years ago, when she married.

Hoover has a more important job for Al. Not yet developed.[2]

George R. tells me he expects to return to England with Hoover & Stetinnius[3] early in July.

Eugene Meyer was in this A.M., later Edgar Davis.[4] Otherwise the morning has been occupied with reading the Weizman [sic] Report (& 20 Appendices) which is very interesting.[5] Felix finishes it today & then [it] goes to DeHaas.

I made my adieux to Judge Holmes yesterday. It was sad to see him. With the work of the term over he relaxed & grew old over night. A disillusionment like seeing the prima donna the next day in bright daylight with curlpins en dishabille. His anxiety about travelling arrangements reminded of Father. He properly designated his state as train fear.

FF tells me Josephine is due today.

1. LDB had a new letterhead printed that read "Stoneleigh Court, Washington, D.C."

2. Alfred continued to serve as a special advisor to Hoover in the Food Commission.

3. Edward Reilly Stettinius (1865–1925), a banker and manufacturer affiliated with the Morgan firm, was assistant secretary of war and served as the American representative on the Interallied Munitions Council. His son of the same name became Franklin Roosevelt's last secretary of state.

4. Possibly Henry Edgar Davis (b. 1855), a Washington, D.C., attorney, former assistant U.S. attorney for the District of Columbia, and a professor of law at George Washington University.

5. Chaim Weizmann (1874–1952) devoted his life to creating a Jewish homeland in Palestine. Born in Russia, he trained as a chemist and then worked through World War II at the university in Manchester. In England he not only became the unofficial leader of the British Zionists but also cultivated important contacts with government figures. With the outbreak of World War I and the isolation of German and other continental leaders, Weizmann assumed de facto leadership of the World Zionist Organization. In early 1918 Great Britain asked him to lead a commission to Palestine to study conditions there and to prepare the groundwork for an eventual British mandate over the country. (It was the report of this commission, laden with facts about economic and social conditions in Palestine, that LDB was now reading.) While in Palestine, in an important symbolic act, Weizmann laid the cornerstone of what would become the Hebrew University in Jerusalem.

LDB corresponded with Weizmann from the time he took over as head of the Provisional Executive Committee, but the two men would not meet until LDB's trip to Europe and Palestine in the summer of 1919. The inevitable and bitter clash between them grew out of differing views on where the movement should go following the war as well as differing views of what Zionism meant. By 1921 they were open opponents, and their followers were engaged in a struggle to control the American Zionist movement.

To: Alice Goldmark Brandeis
Date: June 19, 1918
Place: Washington, D.C.
Source: Gilbert MSS

DEAREST: Your Monday & Tuesday's letters have come. I trust this day won't be too tiring. You must have had an avalanche of letters from me on Tuesday or today.

Last evening McCarthy brought in [*], who is connected with the Japanese Embassy. It was an illuminating evening "aber nicht erfreulich."[1] The Japanese situation has in it nothing of promise for the future. They are the Germans of the East without a doubt & I never felt so clearly how serious would be the results if we approved of their entry into Siberia. On the other hand the denial to them of Manchurian expansion is serious also. It is the Anglo-German situation of 1878–84 over again.[2]

Today Do & Felix [Frankfurter] are coming in for dinner. Tomorrow Al & Louis [Wehle] are coming in to dine and Friday, if Frank [Taussig]'s plans persevere, Al will move over, so he would be in charge while I am at Pittsburg.

Charles R. [Crane] is enthusiastic over his Cape Cod crops—thinks the land as good for rye, barley & oats as any anywhere. So we may look forward to Mass. as an agricultural state again, if Bessie [Evans] will continue her labors.

Susan was in for a moment. She looks less fresh than Sunday.

I am walking around the basin or its equivalent.   Lovingly

1. "But not very pleasant."
2. After its defeat of Russia in the Russo-Japanese War of 1904, Japan rebuilt and modernized its industry and began a policy of expansion in Asia, primarily into China. In 1914 Japan took Shantung and looked to expand into Manchuria. In 1917, in a secret treaty, the Allies transferred Germany's rights in China to Japan. Following the Russian Revolution, Japan also sought to win control over part of Siberia. At the Paris Peace conference the Japanese had to give up many of these gains, which only fueled their bitterness toward the West.

To: Alice Goldmark Brandeis
Date: June 26, 1918
Place: Pittsburgh, Pennsylvania
Source: Gilbert MSS

DEAREST: It is good you have Elizabeth, and that the Italians are doing so well. DeHaas and Levin think the Zionists are also. The "Stimmung"[1] is excellent & there is some performance. And after much storming at the Consolidation & District plan & threats of all evils present & future, it has gone through [and] made unanimous.[2]

Syrkin,[3] who is here as reporter for the Poale Zion paper thinks we have stolen their thunder, & the Mizrachi are quite bewildered.[4]

We raised $175,000 for the bank last night & it seems probable we shall get as much more which is what is needed now. One almost unknown Brooklyner, Schweitzer,[5] subscribed for $90,000 of stock. I took (anonymously) $12,500 which I told DeH & Wise[6] (privately) I shall give for the [Hebrew] University when paid for.

This morning I have been listening to William Rosenblatt[7] on Russia who has just returned (sailing from Christiana June 4). He is intensely anti-bolshevistic (& anti Thompson) as in his letter which you will remember.

Susan told me that Alexander Sachs[8] was coming to Washington to spend the week end. He & Magnus[9] appear to be pursuing diligently. As Susan talks (judging by standards of others) one would think she didn't care greatly for either but more for M.

Felix wires, I should not delay return after Friday, & it is my expectation to rejoice again at Stoneleigh then.

1. "Spirit" or "enthusiasm"—a term LDB often used with bemusement or even contempt.
2. LDB had long disliked the organizational structure of American Zionism. The Provisional Executive Committee was an umbrella body that allowed for some coordination but left each constituent agency completely autonomous. He wanted a single Zionist Organization of America, to which all Zionists belonged; they could also then join other groups such as Hadassah or B'nai Zion. The smaller groups did not want to give up their autonomy, but LDB forced the plan through at the Pittsburgh meeting. He also secured the so-called Pittsburgh Programme, which set out the Zionists' aims for the future.
3. Nachman Syrkin (1867–1924) was a leader of the Poale Zion (see the next note) and an early adherent of the Zionist movement. He moved to America in 1907 and supported himself as a journalist. During the war he worked to found the American Jewish Congress and was a member of the Jewish delegation to the Paris Peace Conference.
4. Poale Zion was the socialist labor organization in Zionism; the orthodox Mizrachi wing of the movement wanted the Jewish homeland governed by orthodox religious law and tradition.
5. Peter J. Schweitzer (1874–1922) was born in Russia. He came to the United States, made a fortune manufacturing cigarette paper, and became a generous supporter of Zionist causes.
6. Rabbi Stephen Samuel Wise (1874–1949), leader of the Free Synagogue in New York City, was one of the first Americans to become a Zionist. He was not only an outstanding Jewish leader but also an important reformer both locally and nationally. He was a founder and the longtime president of both the American Jewish Congress and the World Jewish Congress, the founder of the Jewish Institute of Religion, and one of the last great orators in Jewish life. Wise was devoted to LDB and served, for a quarter-century, as his loyal lieutenant in the Zionist movement.
7. William Rosenblatt (1893–1981), a young Philadelphian, had gone to Russia as a representative of a syndicate of American banks. He had witnessed the 1917 Revolution and had just returned to the United States. Rosenblatt later founded and directed the Postal Telegraph and Cable Company.
8. Alexander Sachs (1893–1973) worked as an economist for Lee, Higginson and later for the Lehman Brothers. He was also an economist for the National Recovery Administration. He served on the political economy committee of the ZOA. Sachs became close to

Franklin Roosevelt and is credited with carrying to FDR Albert Einstein's message advocating the development of the atomic bomb. At this time, apparently, Sachs was courting Susan Brandeis.

9. Magnus Block Rosenberg was one year ahead of Susan Brandeis at the University of Chicago Law School and seemed also to be a suitor.

To:	Alice Goldmark Brandeis
Date:	July 4, 1918
Place:	Washington, D.C.
Source:	Gilbert MSS

A Glorious Fourth '18

DEAREST: Sir Henry Fowler[1] (at F[elix]F[rankfurter]'s) proved the least attractive of Englishmen. He is an aircraft man—thinks sailing [*sic*] to Europe to save the ship space is easy.

Charles Day[2] is enthusiastic on ship prospects. He goes to England next week also.

Baruch came in at FF's after dinner, & was pleased at cutting down the beer possibilities. All the Big Business men now completely in Gov. service are becoming fierce on their former fellows. B. said, "I used to say you were 90% right, now I feel you are 100%."

Gov. [Eugene] Foss was most emphatic in his denunciation & surprised that he should have lived so long among the business-man & known so little of his wickedness.

Al is coming in for luncheon, & Chief Justice McCoy[3] for dinner.

Lovingly

1. Sir Henry Fowler (1870–1938) was one of Britain's leading engineers; he held a number of important positions in the Ministry of Munitions during the war.

2. Charles Day was a mechanical engineer from Philadelphia, who would undertake various missions to the Allies from the secretary of war in regard to war production. The secretary of the navy hired him to inspect naval yards for efficiency.

3. Walter Irving McCoy (1859–1933), a New York lawyer, served in Congress as a representative from New Jersey from 1911 to 1915. Wilson then named him chief judge of the Supreme Court of the District of Columbia, a position he held until retirement in 1929.

To:	Alice Goldmark Brandeis
Date:	July 18, 1918
Place:	Washington, D.C.
Source:	Gilbert MSS

DEAREST: Your yesterday letter has come & I have wired you:

"Act on your own good judgment after further consultation with surgeon."

I think your judgment, enriched by his, is very much better than mine. If it is clear that there is trouble, it would seem wise to remove the cause while place and conditions are favorable.[1]

If you want me, of course I will come immediately, but I don't think I can add anything to your judgment in my ignorance of such things.

I really haven't an intelligent opinion.   Lovingly

1. It appears that the Brandeises' younger daughter, Elizabeth, was ill, and the doctors were considering surgery. Other letters at this time indicate that in the end surgery was either not elected or not needed; see LDB to AGB, 23 July 1918.

To: Alice Goldmark Brandeis
Date: July 21, 1918
Place: Washington, D.C.
Source: Gilbert MSS

DEAREST: Nothing from you yesterday or today. Shall hope tomorrow to hear what you and Elizabeth have decided.[1]

This day has been employed on the law. So far without interruption, as Susan telephone[d] me this morning that she would come in at 4:30 instead of for luncheon, and no one else even trespassed so far as to telephone (Susan stayed out at Glen Echo to play tennis altho the day is warmer than Aug[ust] for a long time.)

I have had a jolly good time writing a dissenting opinion (in advance— as V.D.,[2] who writes for the majority, has not yet sent in his) and I have practically sketched it out.[3] Shall probably send the draft to the printer tomorrow, as a basis for further work; but don't expect to spend [a] very long time on this job in any event. I have another legal problem which may occupy me for the next few days.

DeHaas [*] away restfully last evening, & I had a good night. It is evident [that] 80 in the shade is my heaven.   Lovingly

1. See the preceding letter and next letter.
2. Willis Van Devanter (1859–1941) was a Wyoming railroad lawyer when he was appointed to the Court of Appeals for the Eighth Circuit in 1903 by Theodore Roosevelt. In 1910, after heavy-handed lobbying by Wyoming senator Francis E. Warren, President Taft named Van Devanter to the Supreme Court. Although he suffered from a writer's block, Van Devanter became one of the more influential members of the conservative faction on the High Court because of his skills in framing the issues in conference, and LDB once compared him (favorably) to a Jesuit cardinal in his abilities. Van Devanter was, of course, one of the Four Horsemen opponents of the New Deal, and he left little in the way of a jurisprudential legacy. Despite their obvious differences in philosophy, LDB and Van Devanter maintained friendly relations based on mutual respect.
3. There is no opinion by Van Devanter during this term to which LDB dissented. It is possible that the case was reassigned (Van Devanter wrote far fewer opinions than his

brethren because of his difficulty in writing). LDB may be referring to his dissent in *International News Service v. Associated Press,* 248 U.S. 215 (1918), which had been argued the previous spring. The Associated Press had filed a copyright complaint against its rival, INS, claiming that AP stories had been pirated (by using AP bulletin boards or early editions of AP papers) and then sent out over INS wires. Mahlon Pitney, for a 5–3 majority, affirmed the lower court injunction against the practices of the INS largely on the ground that the organization was appropriating "property" that had been paid for and for which labor had been expended. LDB in a lengthy dissent (at 248) argued that there was no property right in "news." "The general rule of law is, that the noblest of human productions—knowledge, truths ascertained, conceptions, and ideas—become, after voluntary communication to others, free as the air to common use" (250). LDB also acknowledged that this was an entirely new and fresh problem for the Court and that "courts are ill-equipped to make the investigations which should precede a determination of the limitations which should be set upon any property right in news. . . ." Under those circumstances the High Court should "decline to establish a new rule of law in the effort to redress a newly disclosed wrong, although the propriety of some remedy appears to be clear" (267).

To: **Alice Goldmark Brandeis**
Date: July 23, 1918
Place: Washington, D.C.
Source: Gilbert MSS

DEAREST: I have yours of Sat. & Sunday & am myself rather relieved at Elizabeth's decision. It certainly was for her to decide.[1]

Susan was really charming this A.M. She referred to my dressing down of Sunday in a most delightful way in connection with some really tactful thinking & acting concerning the matter which had led to it.

I am steadily pursuing the discharge of my obligations to the great. Sec[retar]y Daniels lunched with me yesterday. Secy Baker comes today for luncheon. DeBilly[2] comes tomorrow for luncheon. The Solicitor General[3] (who being a lawyer was not interesting) dined with me last evening. Acting Secretary Polk[4] escaped a luncheon, because he is still under invalid orders. (He calls it hen-pecked) & goes home for lunch & a rest.

What say you to that list?

Susan reports that the La Follettes have gone to Hot Springs. Isn't that fine? I begin to think Dedham & the Aberdeen[5] are near.

Al & Jennie left yesterday.   Lovingly

1. See LDB to AGB, 18 July 1918.
2. Possibly Edouard DeBilly, deputy French high commissioner to the United States.
3. John W. Davis.
4. Frank Lyon Polk (1871–1943), a New York lawyer and reformer, became counselor to the State Department in 1915, taking Lansing's place when the latter became secretary of state. He became undersecretary in 1919 and was a member of the delegation that negotiated the peace treaty at Paris. After the war he returned to private practice and public service in New York.
5. The Aberdeen Hall hotel at Point Gammon in Hyannis, on Cape Cod.

To: Alice Goldmark Brandeis
Date: July 24, 1918
Place: Washington, D.C.
Source: Gilbert MSS

DEAREST: The Susan dinner went off happily, she & others behaving very well. I had to retire at 9 to 809[1] to see Major Wolfe & then was constrained to take a walk.

Had a very nice luncheon with Baker who was much impressed with my plan for a military campaign which he will submit to his strategist.

Bob Bass[2] was in again, beautifully attired. Later Palfrey[3] called me up. He has come down to aid Bass. It seems a good deal like giving cold molasses a treacle accompaniment.

Morris L. Cooke was in the day before. His Frau seems to be with him.

Tell Elizabeth I had a call from an 1872 classmate whom I had [not] seen since 1876 & thereby hangs an amusing tale.   Lovingly

    1. The Brandeis apartment at the Stoneleigh.
    2. Robert Perkins Bass (1873–1960) served one term as governor of New Hampshire and was later active in various conservation groups.
    3. John Gorham Palfrey (1875–1945), the son of the well-known historian, worked in LDB's law firm from 1901 to 1904, when he left to establish his own practice.

To: Alice Goldmark Brandeis
Date: August 19, 1918
Place: Washington, D.C.
Source: Gilbert MSS

DEAREST: Called up Dr. Collins. He has sent buggy to shop. Thinks Bob [Son of Battle] getting on all right, has seen him for 2 or 3 weeks. Will let me know after next visit.

Tell Eliz. I have now given up sugar for breakfast—salt on oatmeal, nothing in coffee.

Susan was quite charming yesterday. Al & I walked with her to 26th & P after luncheon & he was with me to 4:30. Then I returned to law work.

Crowder[1] was in to dine. He is not happy & I think has reason, which is unfortunate. The same is true of Goethals.

Cables galore from Weizmann with ever new needs or demands; and N.Y. reports but slight performance.

Susan is still without definite word about the Law School in October & seems to think she will get no definite word before October.[2] The Uni-

322

versity will certainly be greatly shrunken. This is a great time for revolutionizing our college & high school habits, banishing loafing & saving two or three years of boys['] time. And perish the long vacation.

I opened up this to McLaurin [*sic*]³ et al.   Lovingly

1. Gen. Enoch Herbert Crowder (1859–1932) was a professional soldier who battled Indians, fought in the Philippines, and rose to provost marshal general during World War I. In 1923 President Harding appointed him ambassador to Cuba.

2. The University of Chicago was considering shortening the school year because of the war, but according to the current archivist there is no record that this happened.

3. Richard Cockburn MacLaurin (1870–1920), a Scottish-born mathematician, became president of the Massachusetts Institute of Technology in 1909.

To:	**Alice Goldmark Brandeis**
Date:	**September 4, 1918**
Place:	**Washington, D.C.**
Source:	**Gilbert MSS**

DEAREST: September 4, 1890–1918¹

Your Monday letter has come. I trust Susan arrived safely and has opened her stay with you as fairly as she closed hers here.

Walked with Al. yesterday p.m. & this morning. He told me of the Frank-Laura affair & I shall write them today.

F[elix]F[rankfurter]. was in last evening to report on recent interview with the Col. [House].

Be on the lookout Friday A.M. for the President's letter to Wise on Zionism which was arranged for when W. was here last week. That is we drafted the letter to be submitted, but didn't know until yesterday that W.W. had consented. It should cheer N.Y. and abroad & help us in raising money which is sorely needed. The letter is coming out Friday as that is the Jewish New Year.²

H.B. Endicott was just in.   Lovingly

1. Apparently 4 September 1890 marked a significant milestone in the courtship of LDB and AGB (perhaps the day they became engaged or reached an informal "understanding" about their futures together), and LDB wished to remind her of the anniversary.

2. Following the Balfour Declaration in November 1917, American Zionists pleaded with President Wilson formally to endorse the pledge that there would be a Jewish homeland in Palestine after the war. The State Department, however, adamantly opposed this request, pointing out to Wilson that the United States was not at war with the Ottoman Empire. Wilson finally decided to yield to Jewish requests and, without consulting the State Department, addressed a Jewish New Year's greeting to the Jewish people through Stephen Wise, dated 31 August 1918. In the letter Wilson approved the Zionist program, the Balfour Declaration, and the work of the Weizmann Commission in Palestine.

To: Alice Goldmark
Date: September 21, 1918
Place: Washington, D.C.
Source: Gilbert MSS

DEAREST: Isn't the news from Palestine glorious this morning.[1] I am expecting [Aaron] Aaronsohn in later to interpret it. This swing should result in Allenby[2] cleaning the Turks out of Northern Palestine. Then we shall have some new demands for money which we don't raise. Another appeal from W[eizmann]. yesterday.

Al was in yesterday (9 P.M.), summoned by us after my consultation with FF ended. Regular Adirondack weather. Miss Grady is doubtless reporting today to you on yesterday's performance. The incursion was taxing, but my cold vanished as suddenly as it came.

1. Newspapers that morning headlined the fact that General Allenby (see the next note) had resumed his drive to rid Palestine of Turkish forces and on the first day of battle had broken through Turkish lines and advanced more than twelve miles.
2. Edmund Henry Hynman Allenby, 1st Viscount Allenby (1861–1936), led the British Expeditionary Force in Egypt during the war and in a series of brilliant maneuvers drove the Turks out of Palestine and Syria. He dramatically entered Jerusalem on foot in December 1917, an action interpreted by the Zionists as putting the final seal on the Balfour Declaration.

To: Susan Brandeis
Date: November 5, 1918
Place: Washington, D.C.
Source: Gilbert MSS

MY DEAREST SUSAN: Elizabeth is still abed and seems no better.[1] The temperature hovers about 106°, and Dr. Parker has no adequate explanation yet. Dr. Meade Moore has been at work on the sinus trouble with some success, although only a little. Mother is of course devoting about all her time to Elizabeth's care and entertainment; the latter mainly by reading her the day[']s news.

The prevailing opinion here is that the war will be over (that is the fighting) in a few days. But, of course, this is prophecy only.[2] What Germany will do, you have as good a guess on as anyone else.

Our court resumed its regular sessions yesterday, and LaRue Brown was before us in an important case and argued well.[3]

Some other lawyers make me feel the truth of what I wrote you recently—the paramount importance of clear statement. Take *and make* every opportunity possible to practice that.   With much love

1. The great epidemic of Spanish influenza struck the United States in mid-September 1918, and over the next two months more than 300,000 Americans died; worldwide the epidemic left 20 million dead, a number equal to the Black Death of the Middle Ages. In early 1919 the flu disappeared as mysteriously as it had arrived.

2. Negotiations over an armistice finally led to the cessation of hostilities less than a week later, at 11 A.M. on 11 November 1918.

3. *Dillon v. Strathearn S.S. Co.,* 248 U.S. 182 (1918). John Dillon had filed a libel against the steamship company claiming $125 in wages due to him as a ship's carpenter. Brown, as assistant attorney general, represented the United States because the constitutionality of a federal statute, the La Follette Seamen's Act of 1916, had been challenged. The case was dismissed on technical grounds and returned to the lower court. It returned to the Court (252 U.S. 348 [1920]). On that occasion LDB wrote an important memorandum touching directly on the interpretation of statutes by studying their legislative histories. Instead of publishing his dissent, however, he merely joined in the dissent of Justice Joseph McKenna on different grounds. The whole matter is illuminatingly discussed by Alexander Bickel in his *The Unpublished Opinions of Mr. Justice Brandeis* (Chicago, 1957), ch. 3.

To:	Susan Brandeis
Date:	November 14, 1918
Place:	Washington, D.C.
Source:	Gilbert MSS

MY DEAREST SUSAN: The faithful mail brought your letter [*] for the greeting yesterday.[1] [****] this read it to Elizabeth.[2]

E. is about the same. The temperature continues, mostly under 100° but Mother is less anxious as we had Dr. Barker of Baltimore for consultation & he is certain of the recovery after a little delay & that Dr. Parker has handled the situation finely. E. is not suffering any to speak of except ennui, which Mother, Aunt Pauline [Goldmark], daily papers and the mail are relieving.

Peace has brought a new world in the making—with problems galore, and more difficult than the making of war. At least [***] But you should have a pretty interesting time the next twenty five years taking part in the reshaping. And I am glad that you concluded to study law which will be a great aid in fitting you for the task. You may be interested in reading again my "Living Law" in the February 1916 Illinois Law Review.[3]

Work at the Court is in full swing & the days seem short.   Lovingly

1. For LDB's sixty-second birthday.

2. The manuscript is torn here, rendering parts of this paragraph and of the third paragraph impossible to read.

3. LDB, "The Living Law," 10 *Illinois Law Review* 461 (1916). Not since his 1905 address on "The Opportunity in the Law" had LDB spoken so comprehensively about the law and the legal profession. In particular he called upon judges to understand and take into account the rapid social and economic changes taking place around them in the larger society, a philosophy he himself would put into practice on the Supreme Court.

To: Regina Wehle Goldmark
Date: November 17, 1918
Place: Washington, D.C.
Source: EBR

DEAREST MOTHER: It was fine to get your birthday greeting, with those of the girls and Charles, and to hear of your valliant [*sic*] entry into political life.[1] Your voting is a great satisfaction to all of us. Your granddaughter Susan was also much excited by her voting; and took the responsibility of decision with appropriate seriousness.

Alice and I are joyous today over a marked improvement in Elizabeth's condition. Her temperature was normal for the first time in nearly four weeks, and her cough is distinctly better. She will doubtless have a week more of bed to put up with; but that will be easy to bear.

Washington shows already signs of the transformation from war to peace. The tension is relaxed; and the evidences of return to the easy-going are developing on all sides. The warm weather has contributed a bit to the restoration of the pre-war mental attitude. Soon doubtless we shall take tottering thrones and overturned governments as matters of course, like Latin American revolutions. But the new world is ushered in with endless problems which are knocking at our door for solution.

I am glad Pauline is here to help.   With much love

1. New York had recently granted women the suffrage, and Mrs. Goldmark had cast her first ballot in the November elections.

To: Alice Goldmark Brandeis
Date: December 2, 1918
Place: Washington, D.C.
Source: EBR

DEAREST: Nothing yet from you. [Herbert] Croly and Felix [Frankfurter] were in at 3 yesterday for an hour & a half, & C. seemed to think he had gained in wisdom & encouragement. At 6:30 Samuel McCune Lindsay[1] was in [*] about the meeting to consider Reconstruction problems. The President thinks, apparently, there are none of great moment.[2]

After dinner Stotz was in for an hour. The rest of the day I was alone. Had some brisk walking & made some progress on opinions. And having had a haircut before breakfast today, feel as if I were "stripped for action."

The event of the day was, of course, the President's message, which Holmes, Pitney, McReynolds, Clarke & I attended. The President was obviously nervous at start & much of the audience obviously hostile. But both parties behaved well. There was enough applause for decency & not enough to belie the existing dissatisfaction.

The message was, as you will see, beautifully phrased, and in some ways a clever presentation of needs for Congressional activity, as if to make them feel that they have plenty to work at while he is being abroad. But I incline to think the actual silence in regard to his plans will anger the Senate the most.[3]

Letter from George Rublee today; also a long one from G[eorge]. W. A[nderson]. who is much troubled over many things. The main trouble impending here is that I have a letter from a Florida planter saying he is sending me a box of oranges & grapefruits. It won't do for you to stay away too long.   Lovingly

1. Samuel McCune Lindsay (1869–1959) was professor of social legislation at Columbia University; from 1910 to 1930 he served as president of the American Academy of Political Science.

2. Wilson, his mind totally focused on Paris and the forthcoming peace conference, resolutely refused to consider postwar domestic issues, such as converting the country back from a war to a peacetime economy. This task he asked the Congress to handle (see the next note), and the Congress did nothing. As a result government agencies were disbanded almost overnight, contracts canceled in mid-production, and personnel stranded with no idea of what they were to do. The postwar recession was created and then aggravated by this policy.

3. One day before sailing for Europe, Wilson addressed a joint session of Congress. Many senators openly grumbled about their exclusion from the American delegation, pointedly reminding Wilson that any treaty he negotiated would have to be ratified in the Senate. A number of senators, in fact, threatened to interrupt the president's speech with heckling questions; but when the time came, cooler heads prevailed. Wilson limited his talk to praising American soldiers, advocating women's suffrage, and urging Congress to study the economic problems of the postwar conversion.

To: Alice Goldmark Brandeis
Date: December 4, 1918
Place: Washington, D.C.
Source: EBR

DEAREST: Had an experience yesterday which I did not expect to encounter in this life. As I was walking toward the Stoneleigh about 1 P.M., [William Howard] Taft & I met. There was a moment's hesitation, & when he'd almost passed, he stopped & said in a charming manner: "Isn't this Justice Brandeis? I don't think we have ever met." I answered: "Yes, we met at Harvard after your return from the Philippines." He at once began to talk about my views on regularity of employment. After a moment I asked him to come in with me. He spent a half hour in 809 [Stoneleigh], talking labor & War Labor board experiences. Was most confidential—at one point put his hand on my knee. I told him of the great service he had rendered the country by his action on the Labor Board. & we parted with his saying in effect—He hoped we would meet often.

John Davis in for 3/4 hour to have me talk Zionism (at my request) & [*]. FF was in, well crushed by the President's expressions on Reconstruction.[1] There is nothing for F.F. to do, but demobilize his reconstruction group & devote his energies to the U.S. Employment Service. Miss Mortonson will become sec[retar]y for the [*] Board.

Had an hour at Gearhart's & 1/2 hour at Justice Holmes on a dissenting opinion I want him to write.[2]

Eugene & Mrs. Meyer were in for a half hour to talk his future.

So you see my poor opinions have suffered neglect.　　　　Lovingly

1. See the previous letter.
2. There was no case during this term in which Holmes and LDB joined in dissent.

To:　　　　**Susan Brandeis**
Date:　　　　**February 24, 1919**
Place:　　　　**Washington, D.C.**
Source:　　　　**Gilbert MSS**

MY DEAREST SUSAN: The year now ending brought you much in development and in happiness; and I cannot send a better birthday wish than that there be continuance of both.[1] Trials and difficulties are sure to come; but with your noble ideals they should serve only to strengthen the fibre of character through which is wrought the life worthwhile.

You have been happily born into an age ripe for change; and your own horror of injustice properly beckons you to take an active part in effecting it. In laying your plans, bear in mind that time, the indispensable, is a potent factor, and that your own effectiveness is to be measured in terms of a life-time; and that you should have before you half a century of persistent, well directed effort with ever growing power and influence. Be not impatient of time spent in educating yourself for the task, nor at the slowness of that education of others which must precede real progress. Patience is as necessary as persistence and the undeviating aim.

This sounds fearfully solemn and must not be permitted to mar the day which should be full of joy and sunshine; but I can never think of your future without this vision of a noble, useful and significant life.

I hope the law exams are getting on well. Have you heard yet about Trusts?

I was not amazed by Phil's[2] referring the possible employer to me; but I should have advised against his doing so if he had written before doing it. All I could say in answer to the enquiry was my "high opinion" of him. As to his special business qualifications I have, of course, no knowledge.

Mother will have written you—or Elizabeth—about our Old Point experiences. Both of them enjoyed the outing & I got a much-longed-for riddance of the thoughts that inhere in Washington life.

Just think of this: "I didn't read a newspaper or periodical for a whole week" & I did read St. Ives "Greek Traditions"[3] & "Romeo & Juliet". Now, I am toying with the thought of a trip to Palestine starting immediately upon the adjournment of court (June 9) with Mr. DeHaas.[4] He is still abroad, but I hope will be back by April 1st at latest. We need him much, but he is much needed abroad also.

Felix [Frankfurter] should be arriving in London today.

With much love

1. Susan Brandeis was to become twenty-six on 27 February.

2. It is impossible to determine the identification of this person, who may have been one of Susan Brandeis's fellow students at Chicago and perhaps a suitor. Her son, Frank Gilbert, reported that he never heard his mother mention a "Phil" as a college friend.

3. The only book listed in the Library of Congress catalogue by this title that LDB might have read was by A. K. Thomson, published in London and New York in 1915.

4. Aside from his own desire to see Palestine, LDB was under pressure from European and American Zionists, as well as Palestinian settlers, to make the trip. In addition, it was felt that his presence at the Paris peace conference that summer would enhance the Jewish position, not only in terms of effectuating the Balfour Declaration, but also to bring relief to Jews in eastern Europe. Moreover, growing tensions between the European Zionists, who now wanted to assert their prewar domination of the movement, and the Americans, the main source of funding for Zionism, demanded that LDB meet with the Europeans in an effort to restore peace. Although LDB mentions the possibility of the trip rather blithely here, in fact the logistics and the final decision itself were far from simple; he almost canceled the trip on more than one occasion. See details in letters to Felix Frankfurter, 16 and 19 May and 5 and 9 June 1919, in Urofsky and Levy, *"Half Brother, Half Son."*

To:	**Alfred Brandeis**
Date:	**March 25, 1919**
Place:	**Washington, D.C.**
Source:	**Brandeis MSS**

DEAR AL: Nothing yet from you, but Elizabeth's letter from the train describes your charming travelling companions. Saturday evening the Ray Stevens were in for dinner. He talked considerably about your Chief,[1] on the lines of recent home-comers, only more emphatic. Sunday evening two Russians of importance, connected with the cooperative movement, were in & confirmed my views on the situation there.[2]

"Nichts Erfreuliches."[3] I fear that the Allies since the Germans surren-
dered are making as great errors as the Germans did in starting the war.
The Russians fear a Napoleon will develop there. To understand affairs
read the story of the French Revolution & thereafter, instead of the Daily
Press.

DeHaas wants $500,000 quick. Kleinischkeit.[4]

1. Herbert Hoover.
2. One of them was Alexander Birkenheim, the vice-president of the All Russian Central Union of Consumer Societies.
3. "Nothing pleasant."
4. A small matter.

To: Alice Goldmark Brandeis
Date: June 13, 1919
Place: New York, New York
Source: EBR

DEAREST: The session with [Jacob] Schiff was about as fruitless as that of a
year and half ago in W[ashington].[1] It was followed by one at Nathan
Straus' (our) office with N.S., who will supply me with milk and butter for
the voyage.[2] There was a brief interview with Prof. Gottheil, sad & diplo-
matically courteous,[3] & a quiet luncheon with DeHaas and Mack (and a
glass of Budweiser) here. And now I have had an hour's nap. Flexner is
en-route to America. Mack will put up to him the taking of the responsibility for the financial supervision of the American Organization with the
title of Treasurer.

Mack says that Croly told him he had resigned from the New School
and that C. thinks will not last long.[4] Mack has shown me recent letters
from Pound,[5] in the same vein as his to me, and repeating that they are
gunning hard for Felix. Apparently Felix's attitude on the Mooney case is
being much discussed.[6] Shall doubtless hear all details from Pound.[7]

I got my nap before dinner yesterday & slept so long that I had to take
a taxi to Mother's. Do seemed much less weary, her decision having been
made. She & Madie Hopkins declare that the *ms* must be in Washington
by Wednesday & wholly out of their hands by June 30.[8] I called up Fannie DeHaas this A.M. & shall try to telephone Jim & Thelda [Goldmark]. In
my talk with Felix [Adler], Palestine was not mentioned, & Wilson referred
to only once, in a gentle [*] by F. which was allowed to pass with a smile
on my part.

The morning news on Kolshack [*sic*] is about the worst yet on W.W.'s
doings.[9] Altogether there is little joy in men's performances.

I understand that the trip on the P[acific] & O[rient] from Marseilles to Port Said is without a stop & takes 5 days. From there to Jerusalem is a night's journey by rail. So that we expect to spend Fourth of July in Jerusalem.[10]

I got a pair of Keds at Rogers Peet, not as good at the [*].

Nothing yet from you.

Lovingly

After leaving Mother's last evening I walked to the Ansonia where Mack was giving a Zionist goodbye. Mrs. Fels[11] & Susan are to have a stateroom together.

1. Throughout the war the Zionists had attempted to win over the leaders of the American Jewish Committee to the cause of rebuilding Palestine. Despite LDB's pessimism here, within a relatively short time the effort bore fruit. Although Louis Marshall, Schiff, and other committee members never became Zionists, they did agree that all Jews bore a responsibility in the rebuilding of the Jewish homeland in Palestine. In January 1920, for example, Schiff made a large donation to help purchase the Technion campus in Haifa.

2. Nathan Straus (1848–1931) had been the head of the R. H. Macy department store since 1896. He was a devoted Zionist, and his philanthropy helped many Zionist projects, especially in public health and education. One of Straus's best-known gifts helped provide fresh milk and butter to both Jewish and Arab children in Palestine.

3. The reorganization of the ZOA at Pittsburgh had led some of the older Zionists to withdraw from the movement or, as in Gottheil's case, to be gently shoved aside.

4. For the origins of the New School for Social Research, an institution modeled after the London School of Economics, and for Croly's role in its beginnings, see Alvin S. Johnson, *Pioneer's Progress: An Autobiography* (New York, 1953), ch. 27. Despite Croly's prediction, the New School prospered and is still extant.

5. Roscoe Pound (1870–1964) was dean of the Harvard Law School from 1916 to 1936. He greatly influenced American jurisprudence by his insistence that the law take sociological factors into account, a direction followed by LDB in his Muller brief as well as during his tenure on the Court.

6. On Preparedness Day 1916 (22 July) a bomb exploded in San Francisco, killing nine persons and wounding forty. Several radical labor leaders, including Thomas J. Mooney, were arrested and charged with murder. Mooney and Warren K. Billings were convicted, but a number of liberals claimed that there had been perjury on the part of some of the prosecution witnesses. Frankfurter was among those fighting for a new trial, and this was the "proof" offered by conservative Boston brahmins that Frankfurter was unfit to hold a chair at Harvard.

7. See the next letter.

8. Josephine Goldmark and Mary Della Hopkins had been working for several months on a study of fatigue and efficiency under the auspices of the United States Public Health Service. See *Comparison of an Eight-Hour Plant and a Ten-Hour Plant* (Washington, D.C., 1920).

9. Admiral Alexander Kolchak (1873–1920), whom many considered a reactionary, was leading the White Russian forces in their fight against the Bolshevik government of V. I. Lenin. Kolchak secured large amounts of aid from the Allies, and the previous day the Big Four had agreed to extend even more help, an act that some saw as a de facto recognition of the White government at Omsk. Kolchak's efforts proved vain, and in 1920 he was captured and executed by the Lenin government. For LDB's criticism of Wilson's behavior toward Russia, see LDB to Edwin A. Alderman, 11 May 1924, BL.

10. LDB was to be held up for several days in Egypt awaiting General Allenby's return and did not reach Palestine until 10 July.

11. Mary Fels (1863–1953), the widow of soapmaker Joseph Fels, carried on his philanthropic work, much of which was centered on Palestine.

To: Alice Goldmark Brandeis
Date: June 14, 1919
Place: New York, New York
Source: EBR

DEAREST: Pound was with me from 6:30 to 10:30 P.M. & I think I really did some good. I am sure the sympathy helped him & I think I hit upon advice which fits the occasion & which he will follow.[1] This is clear: Old Boston is unregenerate and I am not sorry to have escaped a struggle there that would have been as nasty as it is unending. F[elix].F[rankfurter]. is evidently considered by the elect as "dangerous" as I was; and it looks as if some whom F. considered his friends are as unrelenting as were some who were called mine.

Your letter via Susan has not reached me yet as I have communicated with her only over the telephone. She seems to have had a joyous day with Phil, was at [*] at 5:30 & then at the Arlors, & Alexander S[achs]. has been doing her chores.

James G[oldmark]. was in yesterday afternoon. Otherwise my only afternoon occupation was a walk, buying a beautiful light dress shirt, and reading the Book of Esther which tells of this wise provision in the reign of Ahasuerus:[2]

"And the drinking was according to the law: none could compel; for so the king had appointed to all the officers of the house; that they should do according to every man's pleasure."

At ten I am leaving for the Mauretania which sails at 12. Au revoir.

With no end of love to you and Elizabeth.

I have sent laundry by parcel post.

We sail for Southampton.

DeHaas had given directions to have copies of all cables and letters from us mailed to you at Dedham, unless you supply other address, & the office will always have our best address. Either Charles Cowen,[3] Alexander Sachs or Miss Blanche Jacobson[4] or all of them will be there to answer any enquiries.

1. LDB had earlier requested Pound not to do anything hasty until he had an opportunity to see him (LDB to Pound, 28 May 1919, BL). At the meeting LDB reassured Pound that the best way to fight intolerance at Harvard was to stay there and not resign.

2. Esther 1:8.

3. Charles Cowen (1881–1953) graduated from the New York University Law School and practiced for a few years before devoting himself entirely to Jewish communal work. He was currently a staff member at the ZOA New York office but moved on to many positions of responsibility in Jewish and Zionist affairs. Two years before his death, he moved to Israel.

4. Blanche Jacobson was deHaas's secretary at the ZOA's New York office.

To:	Alice Goldmark Brandeis
Date:	June 18, 1919
Place:	On board RMS *Mauretania*
Source:	EBR

DEAREST: This is Wednesday. The sea, weather and temperature have been ideal, Susan comme il faut,[1] stateroom and food excellent, the steamer as well appointed and run as the latest New York hotel, my immediate travelling companions most agreeable, and the rest of the ship's company, so far as explored, entirely unobjectionable. But life has been without a thrill much as if I had taken the day trip to Norfolk—without you. The non-stop fly across the Atlantic[2] reported by wireless leaves one untouched and there is only a mild sense of shame at so much genteel comfort (repulsive luxury there is none) with crying need in Europe. It is like existence in the Packard limousine of our most respectable bourgeois pillars of society. When I think of that day with Louis [Wehle] on the Canal and the hour on [*] Creek, the [*] at the gate and the longing for Paradise is appreciated; and I understand Carlyle's "respectability with its thousand eyes."

I have read again Paul Goodman's little history of the Jews,[3] which accompanied us to Quebec in 1913 and yesterday the Book of Daniel in which I found some acquaintances. The Rabbis showed what Allen would call their "penetrations," in accepting it hesitatingly.

With DeHaas' scope in education I am more and more impressed, and also with his broadly thoughtful view of life. Mrs. also has educated herself and is a woman of significance. They must have led, among the crude materialistic Boston Jews, a most lonesome life. You would be much pleased with the [*] of her motherhood.

Great love to Elizabeth.

On dit[4] that I am looking very well, & very different (!) from a few days ago.

1. As necessary; proper. There is some evidence that Susan had been reluctant to make this trip.

2. The *London Daily Mail* offered a prize of $50,000 for the first nonstop flight across the Atlantic. On 15–16 June 1919 Captain John Alcock, an Englishman, and his American navigator, Lieutenant Arthur Brown, piloted an Vimy-Vickers monoplane across the ocean, landing in an Irish bog to win the prize.

3. Paul Goodman, *A History of the Jews* (London, 1911).

4. It is said.

To: **Alfred Brandeis**
Date: June 20, 1919
Place: On board RMS *Mauretania*
Source: Brandeis MSS

MY DEAR AL: We should arrive at Southampton at 4:30 and dine in London today.

The trip has been, in weather, much as in 1872; but 47 years has made a change in other things than the size and appointment of ships. All, including traveling companions, has been unexceptionable; but there has been an entire lack of thrills, which the uninitiated youths experienced on the "Adriatic."[1] I dare say, if you had been with me, it would have been different; at least you would have revived thrilling memories now dormant. And I am sure you would have found much paydirt in the "Lounge" and some acquaintances. One Kentuckian, John ?, who is to help crown King George with Masonic honors, is of the delegation which America send[s], apparently from every State. The other Americans seem largely composed of buyers and sellers. The Britishers aboard are from all parts of the Empire. A young girl—"so mir nichts, dir nichts"[2]—from South Africa, and another from Australia or New Zealand, as if it were a Katzensprung.[3] But the Wandering Jew is hardly less in evidence. One returning to his family at Archangel via Bergen, and many others no less detached.

You may assure Julius Barnes that Mauretania passengers don't need his wheat.

My love to the family, including *two* grandsons.

1. A reference to the memorable 1872–74 extended tour of Europe by the Adolph Brandeis family. With the exception of a trip he had made to England in 1887 on business for the Warren firm, this was LDB's first trip abroad since that trip a half-century earlier.

2. "As bold as brass."

3. A cat's leap, i.e., a stone's throw.

To: **Alice Goldmark Brandeis**
Date: June 22, 1919
Place: London, England
Source: Brandeis MSS

DEAREST: I wish I had the six idle days of the voyage in which to tell you of the last forty-eight hours. There is an infinitude of the interesting.

First. London is civilization, & it would be worth millions of men's lives to preserve it. Our American cities are business machines; London is living. All the horrors of bigness are absent. From Southampton to this hotel, everything is for man and is man's size, & beautiful in its adaptation to his needs. In addition the weather has been ideal, sunshine & reasonably cool, or warm shall I say. And here it would still be possible for us to jog about with Bob in the heart of the city. It is simply joyous.

Secondly. My coming was very much needed, more than I could have conceived possible, & I feel that I may be of real value all along the line, with the British quite as much as with our own people.

Third. The P[acific]. & O[rient]. sailing date is now Wednesday, so we leave here tomorrow 8:50 A.M. [to] spend the day (Tuesday) in Paris & sail Wednesday (25) from Marseilles.

Fourth. Our stay in P[alestine]. will probably not exceed a month. We shall need weeks here and are arranging our sailing from here for August 31.

Fifth. Susan was talking latterly still of returning before I do; but I fancy she will change her attitude. It is not yet joyous, but the interest seems to be taking hold. Last evening we dined here (Weizmann, Felix [Frankfurter], Flexner, Major Ormsby Gore & Lady Gore)[1] and Susan (quite reluctantly) but she seemed happy over it this A.M. when we breakfasted together & went out for a short walk. This evening she & I are going with Felix to the Graham Wallas'[2] for a diversion from Zionism.

Sixth. Weizmann is neither as great nor as objectionable as he was painted; but he is very much of [a] man & *much* bigger than most of his fellows.

Seventh. Felix, Flexner and Ben Rosenblatt[3] were at Southampton to meet us & we spent the night there, partly for an uninterrupted talk before meeting the forces here. F[rankfurter]. & F[lexner]. are as blue as men can be over the Peace Treaty, and the League to Enforce Peace.

Lovingly

I could fill a scrap book with clippings of interest in the two days' papers, which I have had time only to glance at.

1. William George Arthur Ormsby-Gore, 4th Baron of Harlech (1885–1964), first came into contact with Zionism during the war when he served with the Arab Bureau in Egypt. In 1917 he took a hand in drafting the Balfour Declaration and the following year served as liaison between British officials and the Weizmann Commission. He would later be colonial secretary. His wife was the former Lady Beatrice Cecil, daughter of Lord Salisbury.

2. Graham Wallas (1858–1932), a writer and social critic, was one of the early Fabians and a founder of and teacher at the London School of Economics.

3. Bernard A. Rosenblatt (1886–1969) was a New York lawyer and then magistrate, but his life's passion was Zionism. He worked closely with LDB for more than three decades, spent time in Palestine, and was the first American elected to the World Zionist Executive in 1921. He had helped LDB draft the Pittsburgh Program the year before.

To: Alice Goldmark Brandeis
Date: June 24, 1919
Place: Paris, France
Source: Brandeis MSS

DEAREST: Here we arrived last evening & we plan to leave this [evening]. After a latter dinner & seeing a few folks briefly, Felix and I walked off to the Champs Elysees—the Boulevard—& the Seine. A new world for me of beauty. There was a faint effort of rejoicing over the peace, but it was microscopic in size. Every one is dissatisfied & each pretty nearly with everybody. But there are here most interesting people and problems, & with the early summer upon us & sunshine it is hard to be gloomy. Our own problems are sufficiently serious, but one bears them with becoming lightness in the world of gloom.

Lewis Strauss[1] says everything east of Switzerland is in much worse condition than when the Armistice was made, and the prospect of Austria, with its burdens amidst amputation almost is worst of all.

Percy was in on our arrival and I expect to see a raft of Englishmen today, including Mr. Balfour & all at their suggestion. My purpose had been to await with interviews until my return.[2]

Marshall was happy over his achievements. He has experienced human religion & all speak admiringly of his conduct throughout these months.[3]

Hoover and Lewis Strauss are Felix's heroes. H. is to breakfast with me.

Lovingly

1. Lewis Lichtenstein Strauss (1896–1974) was Herbert Hoover's personal secretary until the end of the war, when he became an investment banker with Kuhn, Loeb & Co. He later served on the Atomic Energy Commission under President Truman and was its chair under Eisenhower.
2. See the next letter, however.
3. Louis Marshall labored valiantly as head of the combined Jewish delegation to the peace conference to bring order out of chaos. He was only partially successful, but without his presence the big powers would have paid little attention to Jewish demands for equal rights in eastern Europe.

To: Alice Goldmark Brandeis
Date: June 25, 1919
Place: Marseilles, France
Source: Brandeis MSS

DEAREST: Only a few words before sailing. We are surely at the Mediterranean Sea with its heterogeneous population, half Asiatic. The crew are of lascars[1] and Indians and there is throughout the P[acific]. & O[rient]. an air of fiction and autobiography.

The day in Paris was uncomfortably full but profitable.[2] My interview with Balfour very delightful & satisfactory[3] & a pleasant one with Col. House and M. Tardieu,[4] who enquired most solicitously of you. [Lincoln] Steffens I saw at the Orion, also Frank Taussig, who looked worn as do most of those engaged in treatyfying, like [Herbert] Hoover who talked interestingly. The Baron de Rothschild,[5] deHaas thinks is a cross between [Jacob] Schiff & Nathan Straus. Not a bad characterization. Shepardson[6] and Mrs. House[7] also send their greetings. Many others now looking longingly homeward. Left cards on DeBilly and Monod a la mode.

France interesting. But Hail Brittania [*sic*]. We are delighted to be on this ship after French dirt. Lovingly

1. East Indian sailors.
2. Many of the World Zionist Organization (WZO) leaders were in Paris for the conference and insisted on tendering LDB a reception. Although he had met Nahum Sokolow and Levin in the United States, LDB knew many of these men solely through reputation or correspondence.
3. LDB, Balfour, Frankfurter, and Lord Eustace Percy had spent nearly two hours discussing Zionism the previous day. The Americans were pushing Balfour for larger boundaries for Palestine, demands quite consistent with British plans in the region.
4. André Tardieu (1876–1935), after a brilliant career as a newspaperman, entered government during the war and was an aide to Georges Clemenceau at the peace conference. He would later serve as premier three times and as a minister in several cabinets.
5. Baron Edmund de Rothschild (1845–1934), although nominally opposed to political Zionism, was a major figure in developing the Palestinian colonies. He donated millions, bought 125,000 acres, established wineries, and sent numerous experts to assist the colonists. Toward the end of his life he accepted the honorary presidency of the Jewish Agency.
6. Whitney Hart Shepardson (1890–1966) was in Paris as a special assistant to Colonel House. A lawyer, he would often interrupt his career to answer calls for public service.
7. Loulie Hunter House (1859–1940), a native of New Orleans, married House in 1881.

To: Alice Goldmark Brandeis
Date: June 27, 1919
Place: On board the *Malwa*
Source: Brandeis MSS

DEAREST: Vive the Mediterranean. Next June we must make this voyage together. The Gulf of Lyons at Marseilles is more beautiful and interesting than the Bay of Naples as I recollect it, and the water of this Sea grows more luminously & marvellously blue as we proceed eastward. Yesterday we skirted along Sardinia, overly mountainous, and as I awoke this morning we were passing along the Island of Pantellaria. There was the air and temperature of Miramar and smooth sea & clear sky and the sense of the infinite, all pervading past. And all this undisturbed by any excrescences of the present in the ship which is bearing us. Excellence in the essentials; an absence of frills; of nothing too much; the sense of modesty which attends uncontested mastery. Yes, we must go by the P[acific]. & O[rient]., unless some transatlantic service bears us directly here avoiding trip to Marseilles.

The night yesterday was bright starlight, even more glorious than the day. Wednesday night had been cold, with the wind westerly as we left Marseilles and colder than at any time on the Atlantic. Today it blows as yesterday, from the South.

Today it is warmer, but entirely comfortable, for the life we are leading under the covered deck, walking, reading, talking; reading and talking Palestine and much else with [Alfred] Zimmern who is not only interesting but a congenial, gemütlich travelling companion.

I am rather ashamed that we were so glad to leave France. There is much of beauty, although a long drought had done much to obscure it; but I appreciate better the feeling of the English, and I am growing dangerously pro-British myself.

Now we are passing south of Malta, which is not itself in sight for now.

To: Alfred Brandeis
Date: June 30, 1919
Place: Port Said, Egypt
Source: Brandeis MSS

DEAR AL: On the Mediterranean there are no lack of thrills, and here one is completely immersed into the New Old World, or rather a melange of all the worlds, so far as diverse continents can supply the elements.

The Mediterranean trip has been perfect. Water, sky, temperature and the boat. We should all have been content to have the days extended indefinitely. Most of the voyage we were out of sight of land and there was a surprising lack of shipping visible. Days passed without our seeing a single one. But the water with its luminous blue was an endless delight, and there was not a moment when it was too warm even for my warmer-blooded companions. Most of the time (including this morning) there has been a light breeze which has fanned one in Oriental luxury.

We are still awaiting our directions. Doubtless we shall go to Cairo and see the British officials, as I have letter from Balfour to Allenby, & we may not start for Palestine before tomorrow.

To Americans accustomed to the Negro, the color scheme is less surprising than to others, but these yellow men are far more picturesque than anything we can offer. The Indians in particular [have] a wonderously [sic] fine look. Au revoir and gruesse,

Saw Frank [Taussig] for a moment in Paris. He looked tired, like the rest.

338

To: Alice Goldmark Brandeis
Date: July 1, 1919
Place: Cairo, Egypt
Source: Brandeis MSS

DEAREST: So here we are at Cairo. We arrived at 11:30 last evening having spent the day until 6 P.M. at Port Said, as passport and permit requirements and luggage moving prevented our getting the 12:30 train, although we anchored midstream at 8:30 A.M. But in the East delays are natural and no doubt heaven sent. It gave us the opportunity of becoming acquainted with Port Said, and it will not in fact delay our arrival in Palestine, as General Allenby will not return to Egypt from Syria until July 4 (in the morning) and we must in any event see him before leaving for Palestine. Meanwhile there is much to see and to do, and quite a willingness to do nothing where it is so ordained.

The reception on our arrival here was stirring and politically encouraging. At the moment the train stopped the first note of the Hatikva[1] was sounded by a band of 23 pieces, a Zionist military (?) band which led the Maccabees and the boy scouts and the Civilian Com[mit]tee, which had gotten together the arrangements although they did not know of our coming until a few hours before. They bore their heads high and the backs were straight and they bore the blue and white like a free and independent people. We and the civilian leaders motored to Shepheard's[2] and a little later, the procession which had marched from the station, brought up before the hotel. The Hatikva was repeated and at midnight we retired to our luxurious apartments.

This morning (at 9 A.M.), Major Whaley, who had been Ormsby-Gore's second-in-command in Palestine and now succeeds him, called; and after a brief talk took us to Col. French, who is acting political officer in General Clayton's[3] absence in Europe. We are to leave on the 3rd for Alexandria, to have conferences there with Lord Dalmany, Roseberry's son[4] who is nearest in charge of Palestinian affairs under General Allenby; & the Commander in Chief, to whom we have a good letter from Mr. Balfour, is to see us soon after his arrival on July 4. We hope to leave Alexandria that evening; & Major Whaley will probably join us in Palestine a week later, & spend 10 days with us there. Before we leave here we shall go over his data with him so as to know the learnable before reaching Palestine, & further data as to most recent events will be brought from our Commission. Whaley speaks highly of Dr. Friedenwald's[5] and Szold's[6] services. They have had laborious and troubled days and nights, but have undoubtedly learned much in the process. The problems are severe, of course, but no more so than we anticipated; and, of course, they will be solved, if only the British and we bear constantly in mind, that it is a question not of whether, but of how and when Palestine shall become in fact the Jewish Homeland; and that the irreducible minimum is a Palestine large enough with the water, land and ports requisite to a self-supporting & reasonably self-sufficient community.

The most pervading impression of the East is the dreariness, in comparison, of our American civilization in all save the virtues. In those, America and Great Britain excels [*sic*]; and one feels constantly their superiority in moral, mental and physical cleanliness. But why our lack of beauty and joyousness which life here is full of? And why should western *women* have made such a lamentable failure in utilizing the colors and the flowing gowns with which *man* here makes every moment interesting and every scene a picture? Even the blackened coal loaders are entrancing in their agile grace. Even they remember the law of folds as they place the basket on their shoulders and hurry up the gangplank. And every human, rich or poor, shows that color schemes are ever in his mind. The long flowing gowns are borne so nobly that I am almost reconciled to the habit of priests and acolytes, which used to fill me with unspeakable horror, and which a peep into the Roman Catholic Church (with Zimmern) has served to revive. If only dress makers and milliners and their fashions could be completely exterminated there would be hope.

The hopeful in the Zionist problem is as present in quite as great a degree as the problems. It met us almost on landing at Port Said, in the form of a young medical student, graduate of Tomsk University, who had just arrived from Vladivostok via Japan and the Red Sea (42 days en route) who was so attractive that we were tempted to annex him at once. He is awaiting a permit to enter the Promised Land, & he says he comes merely as advance agent of many more well equipped with money. At Port Said we met also a Palestinian girl, daughter of a Rishon-le-Zion family returning from England where she had been marooned during the war, a fine specimen too.

But I must close to catch the mail. Lovingly

1. Hatikvah (The Hope) was the Zionist anthem; it later became the national anthem of Israel.

2. Shepheard's, where LDB stayed, was the most luxurious hotel in Cairo.

3. Sir Gilbert Falkingham Clayton (1875–1929) served under Kitchener in the Nile campaign and after retirement in 1910 stayed on to enter the Sudan service. Recalled to active service in 1914, he headed British intelligence in Cairo. An Arabist, Clayton was not friendly toward the Zionists and would be a thorn in their side during his tenure as chief secretary in Palestine from 1922 to 1925.

4. Albert Edward Harry Meyer Archibald Primrose, Lord Dalmany and later 6th Earl of Roseberry (1882–1974), was a member of the Grenadier Guards during the war. He became a notable breeder of horses and served briefly as secretary of state for Scotland. His father,

Archibald Philip Primrose, 5th Earl of Roseberry (1847–1929), was more interested in public service, held several cabinet positions, and was prime minister in 1894 and 1895.

5. Harry Friedenwald (1864–1950) was a pioneering American Zionist, active in the movement from the 1890s onward. From 1904 to 1910 he was the president of the Federation of American Zionists, the predecessor organization to the American Zionist Organization (AZO). Friedenwald was a Baltimore ophthalmologist and teacher of medicine; he was also an authority on the history of Jews in medicine.

6. Robert Szold (1889–1977), a New York lawyer, became an extremely important figure in American Zionism after being recruited to the cause by LDB. During the 1920s and 1930s he would be the chief lieutenant of the Brandeis-Mack forces, eventually regaining control of American Zionism in the 1930s. He had been in Palestine as an agent of the ZOA to confirm some of the findings of the Weizmann Commission and to oversee some of the ZOA projects.

To: **Susan Brandeis**
Date: **July 1, 1919**[1]
Place: **Cairo, Egypt**
Source: **Gilbert MSS**

MY DEAREST SUSAN: Voila. Nous sommes ici.[2]

French and Italian are nothing to us, but English serves fairly well, if supported by the requisite supply of coin which Mr. DeHaas must have ever in hand.

Of our movements he has doubtless kept Mrs. DeHaas fully advised and thus you.[3] We are moving on as planned, with no greater annoyance than the passport and permit regulations which survived the war intact. They are enough to make a pacifist or internationalist out of the most belligerent of mortals, but the East and the heat make a man patient and a fatalist.

I hope you are growing as enthusiastically pro-British as I am. Certainly you would if all these fine clean looking young officers and Tommies whom one sees all along the route were as prominent at home as they are here. One feels as if they had been born to lead. There is an entire absence of swagger or of frills. On the other hand the samples of real Palestinian Jews whom we have met are also refreshing. At Port Said a young woman whom I had seen on our P[acific] & O[rient]. steamer, and here a young lieutenant, graduate in law at Constantinople and student later in Paris. The girl was from Rishon [le Zion], the colony of which Mr. Lewin-Epstein was a leader. She had gone to Europe in 1914 to study music, was first in Belgium and happened to have reached London two days before the war broke out. There she was marooned until last week. She had two brothers in the French army. Our young Palestinian lieutenant was also in the French army; entered as volunteer with 10,000 others of whom all but 500 were either killed or wounded. He was for 18

341

months at the French front, for a like time on the Serbian front, and then with the Palestine legion. He came here at the insistence of the Zionist mission to serve us.

Hope all goes well with you.

1. LDB dated this letter 4 July, but the party appears to have left for Alexandria on the third.

2. We are here!

3. Both Mrs. deHaas and Susan Brandeis had remained in England while the rest of the party proceeded to France, Egypt, and Palestine.

To: Elizabeth Brandeis
Date: July 1, 1919
Place: Cairo, Egypt
Source: EBR

MY DEAREST ELIZABETH: I have written from here both Mother and Susan, letters which will doubtless reach you, but I must send a word direct to tell you how often days and places suggest joyous things we might do together. In Northern France it was many Inland Voyages.[1] Like most Americans, we came away without enthusiasm for the inhabitants or their customs; but their little rivers are alluring and seem, like so much in Europe, quite man's size. "Quite" among the English is altogether the most important word, by the way. It serves fully as many purposes as bien in French and appears to be the first of the British insignia which an American assumes.

And as I am talking of doing, let me record some facts about the temperature. At Port Said it was 82 to 85 with a pretty steady north west breeze. Here it is warmer and the breeze less, but for an enured Washingtonian, it has no terrors. The great advantage here is that men adapt themselves to nature. The siesta is comme il faut.[2] At Port Said, the Permit Office, manned mainly by Englishmen closed at 12 and re-opened at 4 P.M. More usual is it to re-open at 3 P.M. The evenings are delicious and are more fully utilized. The ride here from Port Said, partly over a desert country and partly over the Delta, occupied 5 1/2 hours, from 6 to 11:30 P.M., and was most comfortable throughout. Railway travel, here as in England, is much easier than with us in summer. There is neither dirt nor noise so we could keep the two windows in our compartment wide open throughout the journey and converse without an effort. I suppose it must be the light cars which makes this possible. Here we probably had an oil-burning engine, but the result was the same on the journey from Southampton to London and from there to Folkstone. The comfort was due, in part, to our travelling First Class. We had the compartment to ourselves, a privilege which a pourboire[3] readily secures.

Felix [Frankfurter] was much pleased with the candy.   Lovingly

1. Robert Louis Stevenson, *An Inland Voyage* (Boston, 1883), an account of a canoe trip from Antwerp, Belgium, to Pontoise, France.
2. Necessary.
3. Tip.

To: **Alice Goldmark Brandeis**
Date: **July 4, 1919**
Place: **Alexandria, Egypt**
Source: **Brandeis MSS**

DEAREST: The General [Allenby]'s delay in returning from Syria is giving us idle days in Egypt, here as well as in Cairo, and a chance to know something of the country's present and past. We had a wonderful hour at the Pyramids, the Sphinx, and the Temple and have assumed an air of acquaintance with the country. The strangest thing of all is that it does not seem at all strange to be here. That is in part, I suppose, because one has read and seen so much in description & pictures and partly because there is so much of the omnipresent new world interlaced with the old.

The present is not very cheering. The population has increased from 6 millions to 13 millions in the 37 years of British control and wealth has probably much more than quadrupled, but happiness has not come; and the fact that it has not is perhaps the most hopeful indication. The Egyptians feel that they are in tutelage and they don't like it. Graduates of Oxford and Cambridge among them think they should have a share in the effective government, and have succeed[ed] in convincing the fellahin[1] that present conditions do not serve even them. So all classes share in the discontent and the British administrators with their customary honesty admit that the Government's policy hitherto that [*sic*] been extremely unwise. It is really a great compliment to human nature that the Egyptians did rise recently.[2] It shows that nature has not wholly subdued man; but one feels that man here is engaged in an unequal contest in which his victories can, at best, be short lived. The forces that made Cleopatra and overcame Anthony and Caesar are still operative. The climate, the unearned wealth, the plethoric population would certainly demoralize if they didn't disgust. The natives of low degree—fellahin and Negro—attractive; the higher class natives—yellow or white—are nichts erfreuliches.[3] Quite unexpectedly we find the Jews an exception to this rule, so far as we have come in contact with them. Their adaptability seems to have served them well here, and they have shown a real interest in Jewish affairs. We think we may get considerable help from them in much needed personnel for Palestine as well as in connection with the forwarding of immigrants.

This hotel[4] is on the sea, and you would be compensated by the surf bathing for much you would dislike. In some respect, the hotel & surroundings are like the great Florida and Southern California resorts, but the ever picturesque Arabs and Egyptians relieve the agony. The prevalence of the ass and the camel amidst Victorias and Motor Cars has ceased to seem strange, but remains most cheering. One has literally always at hand pictures of 2000 years ago, and a sense of the eternal in Eastern civilization, like that Meredith Townsend[5] and others give when they describe the ever recurrent wanderings of the Bedouin from oasis to oasis.

This peep at the East is immensely informing and would make much more intelligible much of history past and present.

My two companions are most agreeable. My opinion of deHaas' breadth of knowledge and of views grows further, and Zimmern is like one of the family, more Jewish in looks than a half-gentile is entitled to be, but not more so than Lord Dalmany, Roseberry's son-in-law [*sic*] whom you could see reproduced a thousand times in the Rosenbaums, Greenbergs and Wurzburgers of New York City.

Today it is three weeks since we sailed. There have been but few work days in that period; and I fancy Palestine will be less leisurely. However, I had not found that there was any tiredness to overcome. Your persistent care seems to have restored me to the normal before vacation time.

We are far more removed from Paris and Peace affairs than was possible in America, or even thinkable there. Little comes through to Egypt in the way of news, and that which comes (except for Smuts' statement)[6] gives little reason for joy. Lloyd George's report to Parliament, as given, seems shocking.[7]

July 5—Gen'l Allenby is to return this morning. We hope to leave for Palestine not later than tomorrow at 4 P.M. by rail. Enclosed may amuse you as coming from an Egyptian paper.

I shall hope for something from you when we reach Palestine.

1. Arab peasants.
2. The arrest of a number of leaders of the Wafd, an Egyptian nationalist movement, had triggered several student-led riots.
3. Not pleasing.
4. The Hotel Casino San Stefano.
5. Meredith White Townsend (1831–1911) wrote numerous books about the Middle East.
6. On 29 June Smuts announced that he had signed the peace treaty involuntarily and only as a formal means of ending the war. He charged the document with being too harsh on the losers and declared that a real and lasting peace had not been achieved.

7. On 3 July Lloyd George defended the treaty before a cheering Parliament. He condemned the entire German people as guilty of the war and announced that the government was giving serious consideration to bringing ex-kaiser Wilhelm II to London to stand trial as a treaty breaker.

To:	Alfred Brandeis
Date:	July 6, 1919
Place:	Alexandria, Egypt
Source:	Brandeis MSS

MY DEAR AL: This may interest you: The best cotton land is selling at $1000 to $1500 an acre and rents for $100 or more an acre. The highest taxes on any cotton land is about $15 an acre, which includes water rights. About half the land is owned in tracts of less than five acres and tilled by the owners. The balance owned by large land owners who are to a considerable extent charging rack rents. There has been a terrific rise in land values during the last five years, and both the fellahin and the wealthier Egyptians have grown rich, relatively, and are largely without uses for their money. Among the poorer much of the money is buried in the soil.

Unlike the Negro, there is no marked tendency at imitation among the masses and the primitiveness of their living arrangements are almost inconceivable. Within five minutes walk of this hotel, in the most fashionable spot, you can reach hundreds of natives living in reed or *mud* shacks, such as the poorest American Negro would not be content with even for a night's lodging, and living apparently with dignity and satisfaction. This country makes one pretty doubtful of the blessings of civilization, and superimposed good government, and the condition of the educated is most pitiable. They could not compete with Europeans in the things Europeans do best, partly because they are not interested in them, and our standards of success are not theirs. And all need of manual work being removed, they are really without an occupation. Perhaps there was a time when religion was an adequate occupation. But it is obviously not such now and *nationalism,* a European substitute, is not a comfortable substitute. It seems sufficient to create discontent without being intense enough to fill their lives.

This year there will be a very serious crop failure, due largely to the diversion of water incident to suppressing the incipient rebellion, and partly to lack of the usual heat required to mature the crops.

Much of the irrigation is primitive and the blind-folded horse at the water wheel functions still.   Gruesse

To: Alice Goldmark Brandeis
Date: July 6, 1919
Place: Alexandria, Egypt
Source: Brandeis MSS

DEAREST: Please send enclosed to Al after perusal.

Our Egyptian bondage is to end today. Allenby returned yesterday. I dined with him, Lady Allenby and half a dozen British officers and officials at 8:45 P.M. and had talk with him on Palestine from about 10:15 to midnight. The problems grow no simpler, and there are a number of stone walls which must be burrowed through or under or be scaled. Both Allenby and my lady are unusually attractive folk. He a man of charm and refinement as well as of strength and intelligence and still with the glow of youth. Lady A. told me that she had seen Mr. Crane before leaving Beyruit [sic], that he had come down from the mountains to see them off. Also that she and General Allenby had had a most interesting trip to Palmyra, spending two nights in [*] on the way there and back, having motored from Homs. The ruins are said to be very fine, in a fair state of preservation and to cover a mile of territory.

Sheldon Amos[1] turned up yesterday, having heard somewhere of my being here, & his first enquiry was for you. He is acting judicial adviser and spoke informingly of Egyptian affairs, much to the same effect as we had heard from Col. Lawrence[2] and others. I forgot whether I told you that Lawrence had come out here on a seven weeks flying trip from England, stopping at other Arabian countries between. Sheldon asked me to tea, and the local Jewish magnates had asked me to a school commencement. I compromised by staying at the hotel & taking an $1\frac{1}{2}$ [hour] siesta while Zimmern went to the Amoses and deHaas to the commencement. We are to leave here at 3:15 P.M. and are due in Jerusalem at noon tomorrow, travelling by train to the [Suez] Canal, by motor over it, and then by train to Lud which is about 40 miles from Jerusalem and from there (where Friedenwald is to meet us) by motor. The train connections there would consume more time. I tell deHaas re Palestine: "Was Du geerbt von deinem Vatern hast, Erwirb es, um es zu besitzen."[3] It will be well earned when gotten.

Lovingly

1. Sir Percy Maurice MacLardie Sheldon Amos (1872–1940) spent most of his life as a judge in the Egyptian courts established by the British, until he was recalled for giving a decision in favor of a native child over a white child. During the war he had been sent by Balfour on several missions to the United States. In 1919 he was serving as a judicial advisor to the Egyptian government.

2. Thomas Edward Lawrence (1888–1935), the legendary Lawrence of Arabia, was assigned to the Arab Bureau in Cairo in 1916 but then managed to be sent as an advisor to

King Faisal. He helped lead the Arab revolt against the Turks and became Allenby's chief advisor on Arab affairs.

3. The quotation, slightly modified, is from Johann Wolfgang von Goethe's *Faust*. Bayard Taylor's translation is "What from your father's heritage is lent, / Earn it anew, to really possess it."

To:	Alice Goldmark Brandeis
Date:	July 10, 1919
Place:	Jerusalem, Palestine
Source:	Brandeis MSS

DEAREST: We have been in Palestine 48 hours. The first day was spent on the way to Jerusalem; the second here. It is a wonderful country, a wonderful city. Aaronsohn was right. It is a miniature California, but a California endowed with all the interest which the history of man can contribute and the deepest emotions which can stir a people. The ages-long longing, the love is all explicable now. It has also the great advantage over California of being small. The marvelous contrasts of nature are in close juxtaposition. Not only the mind but the eye may grasp them within a single picture, and the marvelous quality of the air brings considerable distances into it. What I saw of California and the Grand Canyon seemed less beautiful than the view from the Mount of Olives upon the Dead Sea and the country beyond. And yet all say that northern Palestine is far more beautiful, and that in this extra-dry season we are seeing the country at its worst.

It was a joy from the moment we reached it at Rafia. Many enter south of Gaza, and even in the hot plains the quality of the air was bracing. To my surprise, I have experienced no inconvenience from altitude (about 2500 feet) here, and I have seen nothing in the country yet which should deter even such lovers as you of the cool to avoid summering here. The nights are always cool. In Jerusalem it is comfortable at mid-day in the shade, and there is almost constant breeze.

We are living here most pleasantly with Friedenwald, Szold, and Sonneborn[1] and I am taken care of much in the manner of a Swiss landlady. Living conditions couldn't be better.

The problems are serious and numerous. The way is long, the path difficult and uncertain; but the struggle is worthwhile. It is indeed a Holy Land.

Lovingly

1. Rudolph Goldschmidt Sonneborn (1898–1986), after serving as a flier in the war, came to Paris as a member of the Zionist Commission despite the fact that he was only twenty-one years old. The scion of a prominent Baltimore family, he would later make a fortune as a manufacturer. He was well connected among American Jewry (being the

son-in-law of Jacob Schiff). His greatest contribution to Zionism came through the fictitious "Sonneborn Institute," which arranged the purchase of illegal arms for the fledgling state of Israel in 1947 and 1948.

To: Alice Goldmark Brandeis
Date: August 1, 1919
Place: Nearing Marseilles
Source: Brandeis MSS

DEAREST: Transportation conditions are such that it is much easier to go to Palestine than to get away. On July 21 a wire from the Government folks at Cairo informed us that unless we took this steamer, sailing July 26 from Port Said, we could not sail before the 6th of August. So our stay was cut short, and interesting tours in process abandoned, so as to reach Egypt in time. The *Teutonic,* an old White Star Liner converted into a cruiser, was further converted into a transport; and we are on her, by special favor, with some thousands of officers and men. We means deHaas, Rosof [sic],[1] Friedenwald, Szold, Sonneborn, Zimmern & I. We are en route to Paris & London & perhaps the Hague if the Actions Com[mit]tee meeting is to be held there.[2] Palestine is as remote from Europe as from America still, and censorship & wartime lack of mail & cable communication prevails, so that we know practically nothing of what has happened in Europe, America or the rest of the world, since we sailed from Marseilles June 25. Fortunately, some letters of yours came through; those of the end of June inclusive; & I am glad Susie [Goldmark] has been with you and the Powder Point & Keene Valley plans were proceeding. Susan's last was mailed July 9 & still threatened return to A[merica]. before me.

Our Palestine stay—only 16½ days—was crowded with impressions and most informing. I feel that we really know the main problems and the difficulties and possibilities.[3] What we saw and heard there has been supplement[ed] by the constant conferences since with our associates; also all my previous reading has become vitalized; so that the 16 days represent in some respects years of acquisitiveness. We saw practically all the country; all the cities and 23 of the 43 Jewish colonies. I have been converted to the food & found long auto travel agreeable and not fatiguing.

My opinion as to the future was summed up in a letter to General Allenby substantially as follows: "What I have seen and heard strengthen greatly my conviction that Palestine can and must become the Jewish Homeland as promised in the Balfour Declaration. The problems and the difficulties are serious and numerous, even more so than I had anticipated;

but there is none which will not be solved & overcome by the indomitable spirit of the Jews here and elsewhere."

What Friedenwald and Szold wrote in the letter received by you June 14 we found substantially confirmed, but I cannot believe that the Home Govt. is in any sense a party, & I look forward to satisfactory talks with Mr. Balfour and others whom I promised to see on my return.[4] The Palestinian officials extended to me every courtesy personally. Felix [Frankfurter] was very wise in insisting upon our coming. There was, in fact, no basis whatsoever for a different view.[5]

With much love to you & E. B.[6]

1. Israel Binyamin Rosov (1869–1948), a Russian oil engineer, was a member of the early Zionist movement and emigrated to Palestine in 1919.
2. The Actions Committee meeting was held in London.
3. Weizmann, on the other hand, believed LDB did not understand Palestinian conditions at all, since his short stay did not give him any opportunity to make a thorough survey of conditions. Scholars of the Zionist movement, however, have noted that LDB's analysis of the situation, and of the need for large-scale sanitation to eradicate malaria, proved essentially correct.
4. LDB had discovered that the anti-Zionism, and indeed anti-Semitism, of many British officers led to an attitude that nullified the implied promises of the Balfour Declaration. The army officers especially showed a marked preference for the Arabs. LDB's report to Balfour led to a more vigorous enunciation of British policy and the reassignment of many officers.
5. See LDB to Susan Brandeis, 24 February 1919, note 4.
6. Elizabeth Brandeis was universally known, by family and friends alike, as E. B.

To:	Alice Goldmark Brandeis
Date:	August 8, 1919
Place:	London, England
Source:	Brandeis MSS

DEAREST: I had three busy and profitable days in Paris where I lunched effectively with Mr. Balfour & breakfasted with the American Peace Commissioners & have supplement[ed] work there with two busy & effective days in London. The authorities here are unreservedly with us & Palestine problems are being rapidly mended. There is much to tell. On the whole I think Zionist affairs about the most hopeful of all the world's problems. The labor however is only begun & there is apt to be an adjournment of the international problems (so far as mandate etc. is concerned) to the United States. As to our internal Zionist international and other problems we have no end [of things] to discuss and decide.

Please note. I didn't make speeches in Palestine. The most I said on any one occasion did not exceed a few short sentences. There were few such occasions & when I spoke I said mainly sweet nothings. At Paris & here, at the Actions Com[mit]tee meetings, I have however labored hard *in German* and at length. It is a very wearing performance to me[1] & doubtless to the others although I have recovered a bit of my fluency.

Susan was to have sailed today on the Carmania, but embarkation has been indefinitely postponed on account of the strike.[2] The world is certainly out of joint. I suppose American problems will tend to further delay action on the Treaty & thus prolong and intensify the agony here.[3] Hoover is in the depth of gloom. Col. House is less gloomy generally, but like all other Americans severe on most that has been done.

Shall probably be here most of the time until Aug. 30, when we expect to sail on the Adriatic, with the aid of the British authorities who are most courteous and helpful.

I hope you are happily with Mother now. Your July 25 letter has come.

Lovingly

1. Not just language problems made the Actions Committee meeting difficult for LDB. Accustomed to the rapid and efficient meetings he had led in reform movements, he was stunned by the verbosity and concentration on minutiae in which the Europeans gloried. The meeting was a "talkfest" as far as he was concerned, and he felt that European Zionists spoke around everything and never got to the point. The Europeans, however, saw his efforts to move things along as "dictatorial," and they resented his indifference to questions of philosophy and ideology. In addition, there was a growing rift between the Europeans and Americans over what practical policies to pursue in Palestine.

2. American workers in coastal shipping had gone on strike, demanding higher wages and union recognition. The work stoppage tied up east coast docks most of the summer; the strikers won higher wages but not union recognition.

3. The Zionists hoped that the victorious Allies would get on to the business of assigning the mandates, but the fight in the United States over ratification of the treaty would delay the award of mandates for many months.

To: **Alice Goldmark Brandeis**
Date: **August 15, 1919**
Place: **London, England**
Source: **EBR**

DEAREST: Susan plans to leave tonight for Liverpool. She will tell you all of my doings in London during the past ten days, and I hope to supplement the story soon.

The trouble of which Friedenwald and Szold wrote in May has been overcome and some other progress made.[1] Internal problems are less easy of solution, and there is much labor ahead, but the will to do is present among these Zionists. The spirit is willing, and the flesh strong enough, but the East Europeans have much to learn in practical affairs.[2]

Susan has been sweet and helpful. I think she found much of interest here and that she will consider the trip worthwhile. I am sure that, later at least, she will realize that this experience has enriched her life.

Your latest letter was of Aug. 1.

Much love to you & Elizabeth

1. See LDB to AGB, 1 August 1919, note 4.
2. See the preceding letter, note 1.

To: Alice Goldmark Brandeis
Date: August 20, 1919
Place: London, England
Source: Brandeis MSS

DEAREST: Susan will, I trust, have brought you full reports of me before this reaches you, but sailings are so delayed & her route via Halifax may prevent. I feel quite lonesome without her. She was very thoughtful and in much better mood than on her arrival in England. It was doubtless the longing for P[hil]. which took her home.

We still hope to sail not later than the 30th, but the American dock strikes have sadly disarranged schedules; & if we get off it will be on some other steamer than contemplated; & by grace of the British officials.

I made my first emergence from strictly Zionist circles by teaing at the Hobsons[1] Sunday & lunching with Nation-Elders Monday; (where the omnipresent Ratcliffe[2] appeared & sends you greetings). That evening F[elix]. F[rankfurter]., Capt. Armstrong & I went off to talk with F.W. Hirst[3] (Burlingham's friend of the "Economist"); & yesterday Mrs. Fels brought in George Lansbury.[4] So I have gotten a bit of the Radical and Labor flavor; but it is not much relief. Their problems are quite as serious as our[s]. All the world curses Lloyd George and the Peace Performances. Still there is much joy in London and England and the English, who are really a delightful people; and despite all croaking and doubts, it is difficult to believe that they will not work out of their troubles satisfactorily. We are, of course, watching American affairs, so far as the English papers permit. The President has his hands pretty full, and even my revered associates on the Bench (of whom I rarely think) must begin to realize that we are not living in the Nineteenth Century.

The task of steering the Zionist ship safely for the moment is not an easy one. Fortunately on financial matters I find in the Dutch safe leadership,[5] so I think we shall be able to keep Ben Flexner in America for the present at least, and impose upon him the responsibility for the financial

351

management of the American Organization. That will be a great comfort for me; & I rather think we can install Howard Gans[6] as his aid.

I am hoping Ruppin[7] will be able to come here; and perhaps the Germans may be safely entrusted with carrying out of industrial and agricultural policies. Weizmann, who stands admirably with the British at home can handle the political here. My doubts are as to the effects [of] his presence in Palestine, where he may go in a few weeks. The Russians are fine in spirit, but not housebroken. And all the Europeans take a bit unkindly to our social-economic ideas & even to those of administration.

Enough for today.

Lovingly

1. John Atkinson Hobson (1858–1940) was a British Liberal intellectual and an economist whose work anticipated some of John Maynard Keynes's general theory. He was well known for many of his works on social topics, but especially for his pioneering work *Imperialism: A Study* (London, 1902).

2. Samuel Kerkham Ratcliffe (1868–1958) edited the influential *Sociological Review*; he then became a journalist and lecturer, often traveling in the United States, and a frequent contributor to popular journals.

3. Francis Wrigley Hirst (1873–1953), an economist and writer, edited the *Economist* from 1907 to 1916, when he was forced to resign because of his pacifism.

4. George Lansbury (1859–1940) was formerly editor of the *London Daily Herald*. Unlike Hobson and Hirst (who were Liberals), Lansbury was a Socialist and for many years was a Labour leader in Parliament.

5. LDB is probably referring to Jacobus Kahn, the Dutch banker who handled many of the Zionists' financial affairs.

6. Howard Schiffer Gans (1871–1945) was a New York lawyer who served on the War Labor Policies Board, where he met and impressed Frankfurter. Although he later withdrew from the Zionist movement, during 1919 and part of 1920 he devoted himself to the cause on a full-time basis.

7. Arthur Ruppin (1876–1943) was a sociologist who pioneered in the collection of data regarding the Jews and in doing so helped elevate the study of the Jewish people above the level of stereotype, myth, or mere cultural patriotism. He went to Palestine on a study in 1907 and became an active Zionist, head of the Jaffa office from 1908 until his death. He was responsible for land purchase and day-to-day development of Jewish settlements. Ruppin was one of the few European Zionists LDB trusted, because Ruppin dealt primarily in facts and numbers, not theories. See Alex Bein, ed., *Arthur Ruppin: Memoirs, Diaries, Letters* (New York, 1972).

To:	Susan Goldmark
Date:	December 7, 1919
Place:	Washington, D.C.
Source:	EBR

MY DEAR SUSIE: A fortnight ago I hoped to deliver you in person my thanks for the birthday greetings and to show you the tie in situ; but you were off with joyous Jonathan.[1]

What charming photographs the latest are which have just come to Alice.

I am glad the young man is, despite all precocity, still unable to appreciate how unworthily his countrymen are behaving these days. I have been daily renewing my apologies to Signor Torquemada[2] for all the evil impressions I had harbored. He was doubtless a thorough patriot. The intensity of the frenzy is the most hopeful feature of this disgraceful exhibition;—of hysterical, unintelligent fear—which is quite foreign to the generous American nature.[3] It will pass like the Knownothing[4] days, but the sense of shame and of sin should endure. But don't tell Jonathan.

With much love

1. Jonathan Goldmark, the son of Charles and his late wife Ruth, would grow up to become an attorney. He settled in the state of Washington, where he also engaged in ranching.

2. Tomás de Torquemada (1420–98), a Dominican friar, was the inquisitor-general of the Spanish Inquisition, responsible for the expulsion of hundreds of thousands of Jews and Moors from Spain.

3. LDB is here comparing the Spanish Inquisition to the American Red Scare, an outburst of anti-radical, anti-immigrant sentiment led by attorney general A. Mitchell Palmer, who probably hoped to use the publicity to capture the 1920 Democratic presidential nomination.

4. In the 1850s America experienced its first great wave of nativist hysteria, led by the anti-immigrant, anti-Catholic Order of the Star Spangled Banner, a secret organization. It got its nickname because whenever members were asked questions they claimed to "know nothing." The movement enjoyed a brief moment in the sun but was soon eclipsed by the coming of the Civil War.

To:	Alice Goldmark Brandeis
Date:	April 20, 1920
Place:	Washington, D.C.
Source:	EBR

DEAREST: Nothing from you yet. Hope the stay continues joyous. Bessie [Evans] was to see [*] this morning, Elizabeth tells me, & then starts for N.Y. She thinks very poorly of America & of Courts.

Harold Laski turned up this A.M., for which I am very glad on Holmes' account & I impressed upon him that he must see as much of H. as he can, & that means that he should dine there. If he is not permitted to do so he will dine with us. Alfred is here, & of course will.

Harold says Felix F[rankfurter] is doing better work at the Law School than ever before, & is showing more concentration & lecturing with more brilliancy. He says, however, that Felix is not at the Law School as much since marriage[1] & has not as much hold on the individual students as formerly. Harold says Pound stands first in their affection—easily—then comes Chaffee [sic],[2] & that Felix is hardly an easy third. Thus does matrimony mar!!

Harold thinks radicalism will not disturb Felix's position, that Pound & he will be firmly seated, but that the difficulty will come in getting others seated, that is new men.[3]

He also says Gere[4] might not be impossible now, but that [*] advises him against settling now definitely at teaching; also that Learned Hand[5] might be a possibility, but he thinks Mrs. H.[6] could not be induced to leave N.Y. But Magruder has been appointed, as a professor, I think.

Harold looks very well, & is cheerful.

Lovingly

Ralph tells Eliz[abeth]. that Lenroot is entirely squelched & that Bob has all but 2 delegates.[7]

1. The previous December Frankfurter had married Marion A. Denman (1891–1975), the daughter of a Congregational minister from Longmeadow, Massachusetts. Although suffering from nervous illnesses during much of their marriage, Mrs. Frankfurter edited many of her husband's nonjudicial writings and also was co-editor of the letters of Sacco and Vanzetti.

2. Zechariah Chafee, Jr. (1885–1957), the son of a well-to-do Rhode Island family, began a 40-year teaching career at the Harvard Law School in 1916. The author of numerous books and articles, he is best known for his pioneering work *Freedom of Speech* (New York, 1920). For LDB's approval of Chafee's work, as well as his courage in defending unpopular causes, see LDB to Chafee, 5 June 1921, BL.

3. Conservatives on the Harvard Law School's Board of Visitors had managed to block the appointment of Frankfurter as Byrne Professor of Administrative Law because of his allegedly radical views. They claimed they were particularly worried about how he would teach constitutional law. Thanks to the pressure exerted by Roscoe Pound, who threatened to resign unless the faculty's nomination of Frankfurter was confirmed, the Harvard Corporation named Frankfurter to the chair on 1 June 1920.

4. Gerard C. Henderson (1891–1927), a great favorite of both LDB and Frankfurter, graduated from Harvard in 1912 and then went to law school. He wrote two books on administrative law and served as counsel to the War Finance Corporation from 1921 to 1925.

5. Billings Learned Hand (1872–1962) was the most respected lower court judge in America for more than a half-century. Appointed to the U.S. District Court in 1909, he was elevated to the Court of Appeals for the Second Circuit in 1924 and sat on that bench until his retirement. He was mentioned as a possibility almost every time a vacancy appeared on the United States Supreme Court.

6. Frances Fincke (1876–1963), a Bryn Mawr graduate, artist, and early feminist, married Hand in 1902.

7. La Follette supporters in Wisconsin triumphed in the 6 April primary election. La Follette campaigned strenuously in this first test of his political strength since he had opposed the war, and the Lenroot-Philipp wing of the party was defeated soundly, even in Superior, Lenroot's home city.

To: **Alfred Brandeis**
Date: **June 20, 1920**
Place: **On board SS *Lapland***
Source: **Brandeis MSS**

MY DEAR AL: We[1] have had eight beautiful days at sea. The Adriatic & August 1872 could not do better, and we should have been quite content to pardon the intrusion of the 48 insolvent years if you had joined us with your eternal youth.

We have had a bit of old Kentucky with us, however, whom we have enjoyed much. Dr. Simon Flexner, who sends you his greeting. It is a great joy to run across a mind so finely attuned, clothed in a personality so adequate.

I have also had some interesting talk with Col. House, with whom I find myself in close agreement on things political, national, and international. America would have had a different place in the world and the world would have been quite differently set, at the moment, if his views had prevailed.[2]

The elevation of Harding and Coolidge,[3] and the rejection of Hoover, is a sad story of American political irresponsibility. My hope is in the very extremeness of our present unworthiness. It is essentially un-American and when we awake, we shall cast aside in shame our present mistakes.

Elizabeth has enjoyed the voyage, and I think Alice has also, in part, although she has not been quite so perky, as on the Potomac.

Unsere gruesse to Jennie et al.

1. On this trip to England to attend the *Jahreskonferenz* of the World Zionist Organization (a meeting of important Zionist officials, greater than the Actions Committee but less than a full-fledged Congress), LDB was accompanied by his wife and younger daughter. The meeting was notable for the increased friction between the American and European delegations, a warm-up for the all-out fight that would take place the following year in Cleveland.

2. When Wilson returned to the United States after his first trip to the Peace Conference, House stayed behind as Wilson's alter ego. Apparently House indicated to the European leaders that Wilson would be willing to separate the League of Nations from the overall peace treaty. Upon Wilson's return to Paris in March he learned of this from House and immediately repudiated the idea. After that relations between the two men were never close again.

3. The Republicans nominated Warren Gamaliel Harding (1865–1923), an undistinguished senator from Ohio, and Calvin Coolidge (1872–1933), the governor of Massachusetts, as their presidential ticket for 1920. The two men were clearly not in the league of Theodore Roosevelt or William Howard Taft, but conservative business leaders made sure that stronger figures such as Hoover were effectively blocked out. The platform was the most conservative in the GOP's history to that point.

To:	Susan Brandeis
Date:	June 21, 1920
Place:	Southampton, England
Source:	Gilbert MSS

MY DEAREST SUSAN: We are in Southampton harbor, and should reach London for a late luncheon. Our thoughts have been much of you, and in our idle days there was some relief to know that, at least, one of the family has been at work.

Elizabeth has, I think, had days of abundant interest. Mother has not been over-well, but has enjoyed at times the glorious days, and some interesting people, particularly Dr. Simon Flexner, who has been with us much.

We have had considerable Zionist talk aboard, particularly with Julius Simon[1] & I am sure have gained much by his coming to America. He will understand much better than any one else aboard did our condition and possibilities and the difficulties with which we labor. No doubt he will become not only our interpreter to his associates but also, in large part, our advocate.

Felix [Frankfurter] has been interesting & interested as always. Eager for men and things. With Colonel House I have had some good talks. Of reading there has been little among us. Mother had the appearance of grappling with modern French literature & Elizabeth devoured some poor novel. I read to a finish only a campaign life of Debs[2] which ought have been much better done. But I dipped also into Miss Follett's "New State"[3] &, to a less degree, into some other books, but very cautiously. Mother insists I have exceeded all past exhibition of indolence.

The only real excitement of the voyage has been the loss of Mr. DeHaas' suit case, which still persists in hiding. It is a tale of distress & humiliation for one who brought 30 pieces successfully from Jerusalem to the worlds end. With much love

1. Julius Simon (1875–1969), an early follower of Herzl, held important Zionist positions throughout his life. Born in Germany, he lived in the Netherlands, England, and the United States before moving to Palestine in 1934. LDB trusted him implicitly, and Simon was a founder and longtime president of the LDB-backed Palestine Economic Corporation.

2. Eugene Victor Debs (1855–1926) was the leader of American socialism and a perennial candidate for president on the Socialist ticket. The campaign biography is probably David Karsner, *Debs: His Authorized Life and Letters from Woodstock Prison to Atlanta* (New York, 1919).

3. Mary Parker Follett, *The New State, Group Organization the Solution of Popular Government* (New York, 1918), argued that professional public administration, with government in the hands of professional bureaucrats, would solve many of the problems of democratic government.

To: Susan Brandeis
Date: September 18, 1920
Place: Washington, D.C.
Source: Gilbert MSS

DEAREST SUSAN: You were right in not telegraphing but we were relieved to have your letter this morning.

You were wise in deciding to spend your holidays in study for the exams, although it would have been fine to have had you here to play with us.

The prospects are that we shall not take up any of your time in N.Y. until after the exams. There will be much of importance coming up at the Zionist meeting Sept 29, but, as you know, I deem it wiser to have matters fought out without my being present. It seems clear, in any event, that the Z.O.A. will be subjected to needed reorganization, and that an attempt will be made to secure a compact efficient administration.[1] Mr. [Bernard] Flexner & Felix [Frankfurter] due today will doubtless bring much new light on London and Palestine darkness.

Elizabeth went to the theatre last evening & was at Glenn Echo the evening before.

I am glad Jerry is back for your great study.   Lovingly

1. Following the London conference, LDB found himself in a constant battle raging within the ZOA between his followers, who accepted the Americanized version of Zionism that he had preached since 1914 and that was embodied in the 1918 Pittsburgh Program, and the followers of Chaim Weizmann and the ideologies of European Zionism. Part of the debate raged around who would lead the movement. Had LDB been willing to step down from the Court, he would have remained the acknowledged and unchallenged leader of American Zionism; moreover, Weizmann and the Europeans had offered to step aside if he would take on the leadership of the world movement. But LDB believed that if he did resign it would do little more than confirm the old charges of the German-Jewish elite that one could not be a good American and a Zionist at the same time. Nevertheless, at the Buffalo convention that November, when faced with a possibility that LDB would resign, the delegates voted overwhelmingly to support his program and his plans for reorganization.

To: Alfred Brandeis
Date: September 26, 1920
Place: Washington, D.C.
Source: Brandeis MSS

DEAR AL: I had seen the Ford notice, but not the full statement. It is a significant act & shows the business genius.[1]

Am watching grain market carefully. Is the whole corn crop safe from frost? & why will not wheat go below $2.? I guess sanity will come back now; but its long delay is not a [testimony] to our intelligence & I fear will result in much suffering by individuals.

You may tell Alfred[2] that he will have to be very steadfast in accompanying you, if he wishes to reach Aunt Alice's record. We have now had 15 consecutive days driving & 15 consecutive days canoeing & like Washington as a summer resort.

Norman Hapgood was here 2 days & Miss Grady one.

1. On 11 September 1920 Henry Ford (1863–1947) announced that the prices of all Ford motor cars would be rolled back to prewar levels. The move was cheered throughout the country as a positive step in combating the rampant postwar inflation then afflicting the United States.

2. Alfred Brandeis McCreary (b. 1914) was Alfred's first grandchild.

To: Alfred Brandeis
Date: October 7, 1920
Place: Washington, D.C.
Source: Brandeis MSS

DEAR AL: We were much interested in your grain report & quite envy the routine of your musical forces. We sought consolation in our wee Victrola, and a new record Alice had just secured.

It just occurs to me that there is some joint account disbursement *re* the N.Y. Brandeises which I have not settled. Let me know the amount.

Louis W[ehle]. was here this week & dined with us Monday & Tuesday. His professional future is still unsettled. That would not be serious—for he could always earn a decent living with his many connections—but he is really hopelessly extravagant considering that he is only beginning his career & has saved nothing. If he could reduce his expenses to $5000 a year there would be no problem.

To: Alfred Brandeis
Date: December 27, 1920
Place: Washington, D.C.
Source: Brandeis MSS

MY DEAR AL: Walter Child was in to dine yesterday and of course his talk was much of you and the family in its several generations. He asked particularly about Alfred II & was delighted to hear of Bruce.[1] He revelled in the old days, beginning with your reading of [**] on his bed at the hotel while he was dressing. He was much interested in the photos of the house, & of Fan & Jean musicking—which are uncommonly good.

Walter looks quite like a young old man—white hair & moustache; but he is full of youthful enthusiasm & says he is enjoying life copiously. He is pursuing his orchids with unabated fervor.

He was visiting his son Richard[2] who, Walter says, was not secretary to the President—thinks Harding's entourage would not permit an ardent Roosevelt man to fill that position & also thinks Richard should not give up his moneymaking career until he amasses a fortune. (W. says Richard can earn now $35,000 to $50,000 a year. It reminds of H.G. Wells'[3] remark when looking at the residence of one of our writers: "Nowadays writers live—formerly their works did.")

Dr. Rowe[4] who was also dining with us, when looking over the photo of your house, said—"That's the place the ham comes from which I enjoyed here last year." You see Ladless is getting a reputation like some Rhenish Weinberg,—or as the lady said at the Centennial Exhibition when the prize porker was being admired: "I am somewhat acquainted in the town that pig comes from."

Love to Jennie et al.

1. Alfred's second grandson was William Bruce McCreary.
2. Richard Washburn Child (1881–1935) served in secretarial positions with Harding during the campaign. After the election, Harding rewarded him with an ambassadorship to Italy. Child also wrote widely, especially on foreign affairs, and was later a founder of the Council on Foreign Relations.
3. Herbert George Wells (1866–1946) was the immensely prolific British novelist, social reformer, socialist, and historian.
4. Possibly Leo S. Rowe (1871–1946), a well-known economist, lawyer, and public official, then in Washington serving as assistant secretary of the treasury.

To	**Alfred Brandeis**
Date:	**March 1, 1921**
Place:	**Washington, D.C.**
Source:	**Brandeis MSS**

DEAR AL: I trust that Amy's convalescence is proceeding satisfactorily. You must have had quite a scare—despite modern advances in medical science.

Thanks for the data on grain freights. What part of present Chicago prices would you say are due to freight rate increases?

The talk here on RR finances is very dark. On dit[1] that they will have to seek Govt. ownership or bust. Certainly these last six months have been pretty lean.

Teal leaves the Shipping Board this week.[2] His figures show a terrific out of pocket loss for 1921—about 50 percent of the steel ships & all the wooden ones are laid up now.

Hoover is landed in the Cabinet. Speculation is whether he will be able to stay.[3] He can contribute much in many ways if allowed to. But his temper is feared, & he has many enemies in the Senate. Sen. Walsh of Montana[4]—who dined with us a few days ago— said "He hasn't a friend in the Senate." He has plans on labor, as well as on foreign affairs which he would like to put over; but the obstacles will be many.

1. It is said.

2. Joseph Nathan Teal (1858–1929), a prominent Portland, Oregon, attorney who specialized in transportation issues, had just completed a brief term as a commissioner of the United States Shipping Board.

3. Herbert Hoover remained in the cabinet as secretary of commerce until 1928, when he successfully ran for the presidency.

4. Thomas James Walsh (1859–1933) was a leading liberal in the U.S. Senate from 1912 until his death. He was a warm supporter of LDB during the confirmation hearings of 1916, and the two men became friendly. Walsh was soon to start on his most important national service as the crusading investigator of the Teapot Dome scandals in the Harding administration.

To: Regina Wehle Goldmark
Date: March 1, 1921
Place: Washington, D.C.
Source: Brandeis MSS

MY DEAR MOTHER: Sun and sky are gladsome today. The trees are jutting forth buds; the grass its tenderest leaves. And the birds are singing their sweetest love songs—all preparation for your birthday.[1] Even the impending gloom of a Republican Administration cannot dampen their ardor or suppress their joyousness.

The Party of Peace and Prosperity will have to lead us through long stretches of Purgatory before they land us in Paradise. And there will not be idle, carefree days for Mr. Harding and his Cabinet. Even the doleful, outgoing Administration (Democratic) impressed with the ingratitude of republics—may feel some relief in laying down the burdens of Government at this time.

You have doubtless heard that the Great Einstein[2] is coming to America soon with Dr. Weizmann, our Zionist Chief. Palestine may need something more now than a new conception of the Universe or of several additional dimensions; but it is well to remind the Gentile world, when the wave of anti-Semitism is rising, that in the world of thought the conspicuous contributions are being made by Jews.

Mr. Teale [sic] (Portland, Ore.) bids us notify Pauline that when he lays down his shipping Board honors the end of this week he plans for a play day in New York.   With much love

1. LDB's mother-in-law was about to become eighty-six.
2. Albert Einstein (1879–1955) was already the best-known scientific genius of the twentieth century. His four pathbreaking articles of 1905 revolutionized modern physics. This year he would receive the Nobel Prize. His eminence did not save him from the animosity of Adolf Hitler, however; with the help of LDB's friend Bernard Flexner, Einstein came to the United States and eventually took up residence at the Princeton Institute for Advanced Study. Einstein was instrumental during World War II in suggesting the development of atomic energy to President Franklin D. Roosevelt. The great physicist was on his way to

America with Chaim Weizmann, to work for the development of Hebrew University in Jerusalem. He had little knowledge of the quarrels that were about to split American Zionism, with one faction backing LDB and the other Weizmann. On the ship he accepted Weizmann's interpretation and in his one public statement on Zionism said that Weizmann was the Zionist leader and that all should follow him. At the urging of Jacques Loeb of the Rockefeller Institute, however, Einstein agreed to meet with LDB in May and, after hearing the jurist's views, remained neutral in the struggle. See LDB to AGB, 27 April 1921; see also LDB to Mack et al., 27 April 1921, BL.

To: **Alfred Brandeis**
Date: **March 8, 1921**
Place: **Washington, D.C.**
Source: **Brandeis MSS**

DEAR AL: As Alice wrote Amy we had a very friendly & informal dinner with the Hoovers yesterday, only Gregory of San Francisco,[1] an old Food Adm[inistration] man, being there also. H. was in fine form—full of ideas, plans and facts—most of the plans spoken of did not relate to official matters. He has evidently gotten into his own Department deep enough to know many of its failings. He says it is arranged so that he is to have a free hand there.

He told me our monthly figures of exports & important [sic] are far distant from the facts—that the Jan '21 reports contain items of exports actually made in Sept. Oct. & Nov.

He also says known Mexican oil pools are reported within 18 months of exhaustion—this by the best engineering authority.

H. has collected or has assured the whole $33,000,000 [sic] he set out to get for child relief.[2] He is a wonder. He talks quite as freely as ever; & evidently means to make himself felt.

Norman H[apgood]. had an hour with Harding Sunday & was favorably impressed. I too think he will do his best, but he has a tough job.

Enclosed about Levitt may interest you.

1. Thomas Tingey Craven Gregory (1878–1933) was a San Francisco attorney before joining Hoover's Food Administration. He maintained a deep interest in international relief work after the war.
2. See LDB to Alfred Brandeis, 27 November 1920, BL.

To: **Alfred Brandeis**
Date: **March 23, 1921**
Place: **Washington, D.C.**
Source: **Brandeis MSS**

DEAR AL: Very sorry Billy is still so far from well.

Redlich[1] was most interesting. Amidst much that is depressing, he told this: Manufacturing [in Austria] has taken a great turn upward, & owing to the exchange situation they are able to export where other favored countries cannot. I asked what. He said they are manufacturing all sorts of things, e.g., are sending cars & locomotives & automobiles to neighboring countries.

This morning I came across the enclosed clipping. The world looked better 48 years ago in Venice. I feel the thrill of the Doge's Palace & San Marco as we came on deck.

Have just learned of indications that there is something like a storm in the Cabinet over Hoover's statement on Russian trade, & that something may soon appear which will be a slap in his face & that both Hughes & the President will be heard from.[2]

The newspapermen have the impression that the powers at both ends of Pennsylvania Ave. have been counting on his hanging himself by some such indiscretion.

Perhaps something on this may appear before this reaches you.

1. Josef Redlich (1869–1936), a former Austrian minister of finance, was an authority on law and administration. During the 1920s he was professor of comparative law at Harvard but was recalled to serve again as Austria's finance minister. Redlich wrote the preface to Josephine Goldmark's *Pilgrims of '48*. He was visiting the United States in 1921 to acquaint American officials with the Austrian economic situation. See his article "Austria: A World Problem," *New Republic* 25 (9 February 1921): 310–12.

2. Two days earlier Hoover had issued a statement rejecting the Russian suggestion for trade with the Soviet Union. He denounced the economic measures of the Bolsheviks and saw no chance for an improvement until they were gone. The cabinet uproar that LDB predicts here did not occur, despite Hoover's encroachment into the territory normally reserved for the secretary of state, Charles Evans Hughes. Hughes also issued a statement rejecting the Russian suggestion. Thus the hard-line policy against the Bolsheviks that the Wilson administration had adopted continued unaffected.

To: Alfred Brandeis
Date: March 26, 1921
Place: Washington, D.C.
Source: Brandeis, MSS

DEAR AL: We are greatly relieved to know that Billy's operation is over & so successfully.

Your suggestion about McCauley's New Zealander is "nicht ohne."[1] I guess we shall do little for Europe & it looks as if we were determined that no other country should do much for us. The tariff game, as it is to be played,[2] will I think run up against reactions hitherto unknown to us. And our whole policy seems directed toward enabling England & Germany to get control of trade elsewhere. I can't imagine that Canada, Australia & the Argentine will sit quietly by & see us place embargoes on their raw material, without kicking back against our manufactured products. On the whole, U.S.A. has little to be proud of in its conduct. We have slipped back badly in 25 years, in order—security to life & property; in liberty of speech, action, & assembly; in culture; &, in many respects, morality. Father would have said "Pfui."

I hope I was not justified in the impression of Lewis Straus[s].[3]

1. "Not without [merit]."
2. At the end of the Wilson administration, the farm bloc in Congress had pushed through an emergency tariff, but it fell to the president's veto. The Republicans now in power were more sympathetic to high tariffs; with Harding's approval, Congress passed prohibitive tariffs on twenty-eight agricultural products. The measure was due to become effective in May. The law had little effect on farm income, but it did commit farm state legislators to vote for high tariffs. The next year Congress passed the Fordney-McCumber tariff, revising all tariff rates upward.
3. On 19 March LDB had written to his brother: "Lewis Straus[s] just called. He has lost much of his fine look. The spirituality is largely out of his face & there has crept in a good deal of the gemeiner Jude [the common Jew]. I don't know whether aging or occupation & environment are responsible. He is still an attractive fellow, but it was sad to see him so changed."

To:	**Alfred Brandeis**
Date:	**April 23, 1921**
Place:	**Washington, D.C.**
Source:	**Brandeis, MSS**

MY DEAR AL: Several interesting letters have come from you this week.

The figures on corn prices & freights are illuminating. Eugene Meyer spoke to me on the subject the day after your letter came. And I fancy the same [*] prevented Hoover dining with us as promised, Tuesday evening at the Adolph Millers.[1] When the RR's can't raise rates there [*sic*] are really up against it.

The Zionist [*] was inevitable. It was one resulting from differences in standards. The Easterners—like many Russian Jews in this country—don't know what honesty is & we simply won't entrust our money to them. Weizmann does know what honesty is—but weakly yields to his numerous Russian associates. Hence the split.[2] But the work goes on & I enclose a number of [the New] Palestine so that you may read p. 24.[3] Please return it.

Thanks for the enclosures on the milling trade. Please let me know about Little and his one man mills. How have the high freight rates affected them—and what is their present condition?

I don't see where the Europeans are going to get the cash to buy much from us & it doesn't look as if our people would let them send us any of their products.

1. Adolph Caspar Miller (1866–1953) went from teaching economics at the University of California to government service. After 1914 he was a member of the Federal Reserve Board, where he would serve for twenty-two years.

2. On 17 April negotiations suddenly broke down between the two factions within the American Zionist movement. The ostensible issue was the proposal to establish a new endowment fund, the Keren Hayesod, to help in the upbuilding of Palestine. LDB and his lieutenants objected to the lax accounting and fiscal methods that the Europeans, led by Chaim Weizmann, proposed. The east European Zionists soon made the issue into a test of loyalty to the world movement. Upon breaking off the April negotiations, Weizmann, without consulting Julian Mack and the American leadership, boldly announced the creation of the Keren Hayesod in America. LDB always believed that Weizmann was under enormous pressure from his own followers in America, who were opposed to any compromise and bent on taking over leadership of the American organization from the Brandeis-Mack group. In reality, the issue was simply the focal point of a larger and deeper set of emotional and temperamental differences between the eastern European Zionists and the Americanized followers of LDB. From this point, events marched inevitably to the gigantic struggle at the June convention in Cleveland, where LDB and his followers were deposed.

3. No doubt LDB meant to refer his brother to pp. 2–4 of the *New Palestine* for 22 April 1921, which gave Julian Mack's version of the breakdown of negotiations with Weizmann and his followers.

To: Alice Goldmark Brandeis
Date: April 27, 1921
Place: Washington, D.C.
Source: EBR

DEAREST: Your train postal came yesterday P.M. Prof. & Mrs. Einstein are simple lovely folk.[1] I will tell you about our talk when we can talk. It proved impossible to avoid some discussion of the "break," though they are not in [it]. They specialize on the University.

As enclosed will show you, the Zionist ferment continues.[2] W[eizmann]. is indeed a lost soul, but Palestine lives, of course. The appeals to me to assume the World leadership are not wanting—Schöene World[3] beset by assassins of reason & of character.

But the U[nited]. S[tates]. S[upreme]. C[ourt]. goes merrily on. The main discussion at luncheon was of shirts, where, when & how satisfactory ones may be secured & you fail to appreciate the judicial shirt. Why not a chapter, like Carlyle in Fred[er]ick the Great, "The King of France changes his Shirt."[4]   Lovingly

1. See LDB to Regina Wehle Goldmark, 1 March 1921. The meeting between the Einsteins and LDB was probably arranged by Abraham Flexner and took place on the morning of 26 April. Bernard Flexner later wrote to Felix Frankfurter about the meeting: "Einstein

went off with [Jacques] Loeb and asked him his opinion of L.D.B. He was utterly astounded at what Loeb had to say of L.D.B. and told Loeb that Weizman [*sic*] had given him an utterly different opinion and had urged him not to go to see L.D.B. when they were in Washington. After having heard Loeb's opinion, he made up his mind as did also his wife, to call on L.D.B. When he came back from the meeting with L.D.B. amazed and delighted, he said unequivocably to Loeb that he would stand to the uttermost with L.D.B. and the Americans against Weizmann; that he was utterly sick of what Weizman [*sic*] had done and was trying to do. He asked L.D.B. how he, Einstein, could be of help and reported that L.D.b. said that he could help in the university matter upon insisting on the right sort of committee." Flexner to Frankfurter, 2 May 1921, Brandeis MSS.

2. See the preceding letter, note 2.

3. The world of fashion.

4. In the fourth volume of his ten-volume work *The History of Frederick II of Prussia* (1858–65), Thomas Carlyle entitled his seventh chapter "At Versailles, the Most Christian Majesty Changes His Shirt . . ."

To:	**Alfred Brandeis**
Date:	**May 6, 1921**
Place:	**Washington, D.C.**
Source:	**Brandeis MSS**

DEAR AL:

1. I enclose chk $50 for Rudolph [Brandeis]. I think—all things considered—he has handled himself well.

2. Our crossing letters testify to agreement of opinion on Hoover's Germany talk.[1] My greatest grievance against him is that 18 months have elapsed since he said he would grapple with the irregularity of production in the coal industry & nihil fit.[2] That is the bottom trouble. Sen. Elkins[3] says wages per ton are $1.70 higher than in 1914 & freight rates $1.50 per ton higher. But employment is so irregular that miners can't average more than a living now & the rail coal equipment etc. is not utilized & the RR's have high costs etc. It is the worst of all evidences of man's inability to organize society.

3. I guess we & the Entente Allies are behaving so stupidly that Germany will run away with the industrial field ultimately. Whatever her handicaps, Europe & South America & China will be open to her I guess—as well as other odds and ends.

4. We beat you on sugar. The A&P[4] are selling granulated here at 7 cents.

1. Perhaps LDB is referring to a 28 April address before the national convention of Chambers of Commerce in which Hoover warned against increasing militancy on the part of Germany and other nations in trade policy—a militancy, he said, that might call for some remedy on our own part.

2. Nothing has been done.

3. Davis Elkins (1876–1959) was the son of West Virginia's former senator, Stephen B. Elkins (1841–1911). He returned from the Spanish-American War to enter the family's coal business. At his father's death, he was appointed to fill out his senatorial term. In 1918, while he was fighting in France, he was elected to a full term in his own right.

4. The Atlantic & Pacific grocery store chain.

To: **Alfred Brandeis**
Date: **May 14, 1921**
Place: **Washington, D.C.**
Source: **Brandeis MSS**

DEAR AL: Hoover has shown his efficiency in bringing out the Foreign Trade figures on the eleventh instead of 27th or 28 or later as his predecessors did.

You doubtless noted that our m[erchan]d[i]s[e] export balance during past two months is just about equal to gold imports. It looks as if our foreign credits were not being expanded further.

Today's report that Hoover will publish mfrs, jobbers & retailers prices hereafter will give some aches to the retailers who are holding back on price reductions.

At all events, I am safe. I bought a fine pair of Navy officers shoes (high) for $6.50 yesterday.

                                           Gruesse

To: **Alfred Brandeis**
Date: **June 17, 1921**
Place: **Woods Hole, Massachusetts**
Source: **Brandeis, MSS**

DEAR AL: Reached here duly Wednesday F.M. after comfortable trip to B[oston]. & pleasurable day there.

Weather lovely here & we shall probably stay in or near the Breakwater. Had some lovely canoeing yesterday & today & are seriously contemplating bathing although the water is said to be 64.°

The N.Y. Times gives interesting grain reports etc. Altogether the captains of industry & finance the world over "haben sich arg planiert."[1] When the Governors of mankind make such huge errors, it is clear we are not fit for organized society & should dissolve into the primordial atoms.

Elizabeth should be with Catherine today,   Gruesse

1. "Have plotted the mischief themselves."

To: Susan Brandeis
Date: June 21, 1921
Place: Woods Hole, Massachusetts
Source: Gilbert MSS

DEAREST SUSAN: I am glad to know from your yesterday's letter that you have had some further court experience & that you are enjoying it so much. It is fine to have experience to test and stimulate one's law study. And you are getting it now also in business affairs through the receiverships. Whenever you have time, put in some on the law of evidence. That is a branch which one must have at the finger tips.

Weather here has been fine & until today not too windy for canoeing & even today we have had bathing.

I plan to go to Pittsburg. Mr. DeHaas will know the train & day. If your practice permits your starting as early [as] I may have to, or my affairs permit me to defer starting until the evening of July 2, we should have the trip together both ways.   Lovingly

To: Alice Goldmark Brandeis
Date: July 16, 1921
Place: New York City, New York
Source: Raushenbush MSS

DEAREST: Your & Elizabeth's warnings were not wholly groundless.

Buzzard's Bay sailing was entirely comfortable, but an hour & a half out from New Bedford we encountered considerable swell & even Mrs. Houston's[1] prophylactic did not give joy, although I escaped external manifestations of discomfort.

Weather fine here today after terrific rainstorm yesterday.

Talked with Susan on the telephone. She is coming up for luncheon & I have set her to work studying Tegamini folder & travelling possibilities.

I find a most businesslike note from Norman [Hapgood] awaiting me, about appointments for our meeting. Elizabeth[2] is with him.

Now I am off for the Bar Assn. I failed to catch your eye (I on the second deck) before you turned your back on the boat.

I didn't dream of Mrs. Houston. But her revered husband figured most prominently in an absurd dream.

                                      Lovingly

Hope Eliz. found the idea promising.

1. Wilson's secretary of agriculture, David F. Houston, married Helen Beall in December 1895.
2. Elizabeth Hapgood was the daughter of Norman Hapgood and his second wife.

To: Alice Goldmark Brandeis
Date: July 24, 1921
Place: Toronto, Canada
Source: Raushenbush MSS

DEAREST: Susan has been quite charming & interesting—eager to see & most reasonable.

It is warm, but there is a cooling northwest wind. We spent the morning strolling about town, sitting in the parks or university grounds, sight seeing most leisurely with a sense of dolce far niente.[1]

The town is mainly American in character, but there is here & there a touch of England in a cluster of buildings and more frequently in names and faces. But one feel[s] the new world and even more than now in America that it [is] the young men's country.

Some progress [has] been made in the New York [Zionist] gathering; but the pace is slow & art is long, & there is much backsliding even among the faithful.

Lovingly

Please rescue my bathing shoes from No. 60.

    1. Sweet nothing; idleness.

To: Alice Goldmark Brandeis
Date: July 27, 1921
Place: Bear Island, Canada
Source: Raushenbush MSS

DEAREST: Susan wrote you doubtless of our yesterday's doings & the simple life al fresco. Some might have thought it too warm to paddle, for there was, much of the time, not even a light breeze. But it was worth braving the sun for the joyous shade along the rocks and under the red pines.

Susan exhibited capacity for silence as well as speech & lay contentedly on the rocks looking heavenward while I read Wells.[1]

This morning there is more wind than we should have ordered; but the day is still young & as the direction appears to be Southwest & there are specks of blue sky, nature may be exhibiting merely a passing frown.

There is a shack or more on nearly every island we have viewed; & I am told that Americans own most of them—i.e. the shacks only, as the govt wisely leases the islands.

368

The storekeeper says this is the quietest season he has known & suggests that people haven't the money to come. Perhaps.

We are expecting a letter from you today.

I wrote Miss Grady to Falmouth Arms.   Lovingly

1. Perhaps LDB was reading H. G. Wells's famous *Outline of History,* which had appeared in two volumes the year before.

To: Alice Goldmark Brandeis
Date: August 2, 1921
Place: Bear Island, Canada
Source: Raushenbush MSS

DEAREST: Your Friday letter has come. Hope your household gathered as per schedule & that you are enjoying the house. Too bad Fan can't join you. But I am glad you asked her.

Our day at Gull Lake was interesting, but guides are as great a nuisance as waiters at meals & we shall doubtless confine our further trips to those in which there are no portages so that we can dispense with guides' services.

Susan is always good company—an interesting talker [and] an interested listener and most considerate & contented.

She has passed far beyond the period of grievances for treatment of the family, and is rather inclined to overestimate what she has gained from us or been permitted to enjoy.   Lovingly

To: Alfred Brandeis
Date: August 9, 1921
Place: New York, New York
Source: Brandeis MSS

DEAR AL: Glad to get your letter here. We had most satisfactory outing in Canada, & I enjoyed much having a solid fortnight uninterruptedly with Susan. Hadn't seen so much of her for ten years.

Sunday afternoon we spent at Niagra [*sic*]. The old International is still in ruins after the fire, & the Cataract House is just as it was in 1865 apparently except for the natural wear, which is great. It seemed strange to find any where in America such a survival of the early ages. The only fine hotel at Niagra appears to be the Clayton on the Canadian side.

But the falls are still fun, despite obstructions for power which are discernible.

We went under the falls from the Canadian side, through a tunnel built in 1904. Susan & I had been in Niagra in 1909, & I not since. You will recall I was there with Alice in 1903.

I am off by the New Bedford boat this P.M. for Woods Hole.

Gruesse

To: Susan Brandeis
Date: August 10, 1921
Place: Woods Hole, Massachusetts
Source: Gilbert MSS

DEAREST SUSAN:

Felicium avunculum memento[1]
(Latin not Guaranteed)

A good passage here closed a beautiful outing with you, fittingly. We finally had ample opportunity for "Gedankenaustausch."[2] (I don't know the Greek term—hence am driven to German—Pardon, Mademoiselle.)

And know that the scissors have been sharpened—an itinerant artist pushing his wheel from door to door appeared at the opportune moment & the deed was done.

Otherwise haircut & a bath are my only achievements today. But this evening we go to Naushon for supper at your friend's Mrs. Forbes. And tomorrow we are to lunch at Quissett—at the Clements, with Mrs. Willard Straight.[3]

Read a thrilling essay by Toynbee, "The tragedy of Greece"[4]—on the boat—(Alex. Sachs whom I met at City Club, left it for me at the office.)

Aunt Bessie [Evans] & Mrs. [David O.] Ives send greetings.   Lovingly

1. The Latin phrase means "remember your happy [or blessed] uncle." LDB's meaning is unclear, but perhaps Susan, upon leaving LDB after their trip together, was to visit one of her uncles in Louisville or New York City.

2. "An exchange of thoughts."

3. Dorothy Whitney Straight (1887–1968) used her great inherited wealth for philanthropic and politically progressive purposes. She and her husband Willard had established the *New Republic* under Herbert Croly; after Willard's death in the influenza epidemic of 1918, she was continuing to sustain it. In 1925 she would marry an English economist and reformer, Leonard Elmhirst, and move to England, where the couple pursued experiments in agricultural and educational reform.

4. Arnold Toynbee, *The Tragedy of Greece, a Lecture Delivered for the Professor of Greek to Candidates for Honours in Literae Humaniores at Oxford in May, 1920* (Oxford, 1921), 1–42.

To: **Alfred Brandeis**
Date: **September 6, 1921**
Place: **Washington, D.C.**
Source: **Brandeis MSS**

DEAR AL:

1. I entirely agree with you as to our Foreign Trade. Because some or most European countries need it, we foolishly pursue it, like the lady who wanted a mortgage on her house, as all the neighbors had one. Hoover had much that view once—talked with me in 1919 at length on the folly of increasing our manufactures etc.
2. I am sorry to say, your impression as to Hoover is shared by many here who have been watching affairs this summer. They speak of "his insatiable and absurd graspingness" and "insane longing for publicity"; & it is said this is common talk among newspaper men.
3. I had not noticed Nat Myers' death, but judging from what I saw of him during the war, I think he should have been glad to go.[1]
4. The La Follettes were in good form—the Senator looks finely, & is in great fighting trim. He & his friends are giving the administration severe headaches. He says, in substance, that the President is an automaton worked by the Old Guard, & that these constant statements of what the President wants are all prepared feed, put out to effectuate their purpose.
5. Susan returned to N.Y. last night & is to start out in her own office (140 Nassau St.) today. She has good courage.

Gruesse

1. Nathaniel Myers (1848–1921), an important New York City corporation lawyer extremely active in Jewish philanthropic work, died on 31 August.

To: **Alfred Brandeis**
Date: **September 16, 1921**
Place: **Washington, D.C.**
Source: **Brandeis MSS**

MY DEAR AL: Re. yours of 14th.

1. Yes, that is an uncommonly satisfactory report on Hildegarde [Nagel] & a nice letter altogether from Charlie [Nagel]. I am very

glad he got so much out of his visit to you. The remark about "thinking aloud" is pathetic.[1]

2. As to the check for Annette: I enclose Otto [Wehle]'s letter and mine to him, which letter please return after perusal. In it I have answered for the present about Lincoln [Dembitz]'s family.[2] I suggest that you might find out through the commercial agencies if available to you, something about the West family circumstances.[3] I will make enquiries if opportunity offers from some Washington folk.

3. I am sorry to learn that you and Otto sent the $350 to Annette last spring without letting me know. I think you had better let me take care (through you) of any amounts which may be required for the relatives hereafter—be they Brandeis, Dembitz or Wehle. And if you will let me know any regular amounts you are now sending to any of the relatives & the dates, I will have the quarterly (?) checks which are now being sent you by the Boston office on like account, increased by the amount of your own present contributions. You must remember that you have four daughters and I only two.

4. The President made another "strich durch die Rechnung"[4] as to my dining with Hoover. I guess H. must be suffering like a [*] on this play voyage with the President.[5] I am quite sure Bridge, Whist, and escorting Mrs. Harding while the President plays golf isn't Hoover's favorite sport. I spent the evening with Adolf Caspar Miller pleasantly enough chatting on things political & economic, but can't recall any additions to my knowledge which you would be enriched by.

5. We leave for N.Y. this afternoon. Hope to see Frank T[aussig] before we go.

Gruesse

If DeHaas has not sent you a copy of the statement of the outgoing Zionist administration (127pp), write him to 31 Union Square, R1103, to send you a copy.[6]

1. Charles Nagel had written to LDB's brother Alfred: "I remember with so much pleasure our visit with you. It means something to be once more where you can feel and think aloud."
2. LDB's cousin Abraham Lincoln Dembitz had died, inaugurating an extensive correspondence between LDB, Alfred Brandeis, and Otto Wehle over the financial needs of the family and who should supply them. Annette was Lincoln's sister.
3. Sara West Dembitz was Lincoln's widow.
4. "Disruption of plans."

5. President Harding had invited Hoover on his Chesapeake Bay cruise aboard the presidential yacht, USS *Mayflower*.

6. This was probably the statement justifying the Brandeis-Mack group's position that was delivered at the Zionist Conference in Carlsbad by Julius Simon. Some of the delegates requested that Weizmann try to patch things up with the alienated Americans, but he ignored the request.

To: Susan Brandeis
Date: October 9, 1921
Place: Washington, D.C.
Source: Gilbert MSS

DEAREST SUSAN: The interesting letters you enclosed are returned herewith. It is very sad about Mrs. Simon.[1] She was a fine woman; thoroughly in sympathy with his Zionist work and a great help to him in every way. You may recall that they first met at a Zionist Congress. She was there as [a] newspaper reporter.

I am glad to hear how interesting you find the Accounting Course. It is no end important. Accounting is the language of business & largely of Government, and much more accurate as a means of expression than words.

It is fine that Mrs. L.[2] is working so effectively. There is great need of her putting on all possible steam, so that we may hasten—by getting together the $250,000—Mr. Rosenbloom's departure for Palestine.[3]

It is good to know that Learned Hand is returning to the bench. I hope, through him, others of his associates may learn how good a receiver is available.[4] Everybody seems to admire your courage in starting alone. That will help.

My greetings to Mr. Zimmern. I shall write him.

Lovingly

You & I each have Room 809.

1. Julius Simon's first wife, the former Johanna Friedberg, had just died.

2. Probably Mrs. Irma Levy Lindheim (1886–1978), an important leader in Hadassah, the women's Zionist organization. Hadassah was devotedly loyal to the Brandeis-Mack wing of the American Zionist movement throughout these years.

3. Upon being removed from power, the Brandeis-Mack faction hoped to continue Zionist work through a new organization to be called the Palestine Development Council. The council was determined to raise $500,000 for Palestine projects, and it was agreed that as soon as half of that sum was raised Solomon Rosenbloom (1866–1925), a Pittsburgh banker and Jewish activist, would be sent to Palestine to explore possible projects for the effective use of the funds. Rosenbloom finally left on his mission in January 1922.

4. A goodly portion of Susan Brandeis's early law practice consisted of receiverships assigned to her by various judges.

To: Alfred Brandeis
Date: October 11, 1921
Place: Washington, D.C.
Source: Brandeis MSS

DEAR AL: We have sold the Dedham house to Maynard who buys for his son Haskell & will alter it, making the front door on the side facing the Maynard house.

Price, $11,875, which is $2125 less than I was offered 2¹/₂ years ago & about $1000 less than the cost 22¹/₂ years ago, plus alterations then & cost of additional strip of land about 9 years ago. Still considering other shrinkages from 1919 & the customary ones on residences, it is not very bad. We have not even painted it since some years before 1916.

Dedham by reason of cutting of RR train service, the increased trolley fares & the opening of wider suburban country through the auto, is less valuable real estate than it was.

Alice is planning a cottage on Cape Cod.[1] Sadie [Nicholson] and Bessie Evans are to take care of the house contents for us, some of which we shall sell, some store & the books have brought here. Alice was entirely ready to sell; Elizabeth sighed but would never go near it. Susan not yet heard from. But when she was in B[oston] last May, did not, I think, go out to Dedham.

As to your enquiry about Chinese loan—"Kann dienen."[2] The Pacific development took its bonds at 81. They haven't sold any & are likely to go into receiver's hands (confidential). The Continental I guess took the bonds at about the same figure. It seems that there is much Chinese & international politics in this & that the Chinese bankers are financing the Southern Republic & are ready to have the Pekin government go broke.[3]

I thought I would politely called [sic] Eugene Meyer's bluff[4] & asked him (1) for a list of loans to farmers by states and (2) how much cash he had advanced to Cooperatives. The press bureau data I am sending under another cover. His letter enclosed bears out your views.

Elizabeth's party had to change their objective. And they started at 3:30 A.M. today on the train to Linden Va, in the day coach. Das zeigt dass es ja noch Kinder gebt.[5]

Enclosed from Louis B. W[ehle] will show that he is not yet out of the woods.[6]

1. After spending several summers on Cape Cod, LDB was to purchase a large house near Oyster Pond in Chatham. His daughter Susan and her future husband, Jacob Gilbert, were to build their own summer home a short distance away. The Brandeis family spent summers there for many years after LDB's death in 1941; and while LDB was alive, the Chatham cottage was visited by numerous public officials, Zionists, intellectuals, and others

who wished to consult with LDB about one matter or another. In August 1974 the National Park Service declared the Chatham house a national historic landmark.

2. "Can serve."

3. By late 1921 rumors circulated that the Chinese government, threatened by the civil war there, would default on its debts. On November 1 it did, in fact, default on a $5.5 million loan from the Continental and Commercial Trust of Chicago. The Chinese government paid the interest but not the principal on another loan from the Pacific Development Corporation. See LDB to Alfred Brandeis, 5 November 1921.

4. The "bluff" LDB refers to is Meyer's boast about how loans from his agency, the War Finance Corporation, were helping farmers and cattle raisers. See the *New York Times,* 2 and 8 October 1921.

5. This shows that they are still children.

6. LDB's nephew Louis was experiencing financial difficulties. On 3 December LDB wrote his brother: "I am disturbed by his being 'beset by bills'. He has had from me $2000 in 30 days—and a month earlier $500—in all $6250. Of course, it doesn't do me any harm; but I am much troubled about him and his future." Five days later, however, LDB received assurances from Wehle that the financial picture was not so bleak as LDB had feared. See LDB to Alfred Brandeis, 8 December 1921, BL.

To: **Susan Brandeis**
Date: **October 14, 1921**
Place: **Washington, D.C.**
Source: **Gilbert MSS**

MY DEAREST SUSAN: I have yours of 13th.

I know nothing about the building combination prosecutions in New York except the fact that there are such;[1] but I also know of no reason why you should not act as special assistant to the District Atty. if you are offered the job.[2] L.S.P.[3] will know much better than I whether there is any objection. On the face of it I should say you would find it a valuable experience, and useful in the building of a practice.

I am delighted to hear of so much business coming in. It is a fine reward for your courage, & it is good to see that Judge Mack and Judge Hand have not forgotten their receiver.   Lovingly

1. At the end of 1921 dozens of individuals in the building materials industry found themselves indicted for violations of the Sherman Antitrust Act. Before the year was over heavy fines were levied against many of them by Judge Learned Hand.

2. On 1 November Susan Brandeis was appointed special assistant to David Podell (1884–1947). She had once worked for Podell, a well-known New York trial lawyer, who had just become a special assistant to the attorney general in the southern district of New York. He was in charge of antitrust cases and would later write on antitrust law. See LDB to Alfred Brandeis, 5 November 1921.

3. Louis Samuel Posner (1878–19[?]) was an English-born New York City lawyer who specialized in housing matters. Posner was also active in several city agencies and was a committed Zionist. He was a delegate to the World Zionist Conference in London in 1920.

To: Alfred Brandeis
Date: October 15, 1921
Place: Washington, D.C.
Source: Brandeis MSS

DEAR AL:

1. John Dudley seems to be as expert in making commercial reports as in providing eggs. We are getting another customer for him (Senator Bristow) if he has products available. I guess Otto won't miss this particular chance for worry, when the factory is working day & night shifts.
2. The ham has come. Sorry it didn't arrive a few days earlier, so as to have been shared with Hoover who dined with us the other evening. He was in good form, talkative and interesting. The net result was that "Every prospect pleases only man is vile"[1]—or rather inexpressibly stupid.

Among his specifications were:

The worst outlook is attributable to the coal situation. He had been trying to get some agreement between operators & men—in vain. Says that a strike April 1 is probable[2] & that in a month business will get its preliminary jolt, because no one will be able to know that he can get coal to carry through building projects etc etc. He says union coal operators (bituminous) haven't earned 4% on cash invested during the last 10 years, on the average, & that they are about desperate. Very many are losing money now, with the mines operating on small tonnage, & that the men are not getting more than 2 days a week work &, in the year, 140 days.

On the other hand the 20% who are not union are running 6 days a week & the miners at $4 a day are earning $24 a week as against $14 ($7 a day) in union mines.

There are now 80% of the miners unionized as against 70% a short time ago. A majority of these want nationalization of mines & their leaders do not represent the men's wishes & hence are afraid to stand up for reduction in wages, although they really believe in it. The operators would be content with a strike because they think this is a good time to fight to a finish. The men because they want to show what a rumpus they can make. Hoover hopes that fear of a strike April 1 will induce consumers to stock up meanwhile.

1. Reginald Heber, "Missionary Hymn," stanza 2.

2. Within three months Hoover would be offering this forecast to the public, and it turned out to be accurate. United Mine Workers chief John L. Lewis ordered a strike in late March 1922.

To:	Alfred Brandeis
Date:	November 5, 1921
Place:	Washington, D.C.
Source:	Brandeis MSS

DEAR AL: The [Edward] Burlings & Carl Weston had to be substituted for the Delanos and Rublee as your dinner guests with the Bob Woolleys, but did well. R. Walton Moore,[1] who might a [sic] learnt a thing or two about Louis [B. Wehle], was prevented by a political engagement from joining us.

When I suggested the corn growers utilizing more of the crop at home, I had in mind, not only hog raising, but also packing. The only escape from the packing monopoly has seemed to me to lie in many packing plants distributed through cooperatives like the Danish, over the farming region.

I notice Minneapolis patent at $6.90 yesterday.[2] I remember a Boston case when they were selling by the carload at $4.50.

How much of the wheat is still in farmers' hands & where? i.e. in what states.

Herbert White was in yesterday. He was here again on Pacific Development Co. matters. They have also a $5,000,000 Chinese loan which is likely to have on Dec 1 the same fate that the Continental & C[ommercial] B[ank] of Chicago's had. Herbert is having ample insight into the ways of the great international bankers. Pawn brokers are a "Hund dagegen."[3]

Yes, Susan was very happy over her appointment.[4] I don't know where it originated. But I think not from among her friends. "The office sought the woman." Podell, the Asst. U.S. Att[orne]y, came to Posner (her former employer) supposing she was still there.

Susan is free to continue with her private practice. The U.S. is only one of her clients. She is "special Asst." in certain cases only. Thanks to her many little receiverships and her modest living & office expenses she is paying her way now & had been before this new opportunity came.

Bob Woolley told interesting tales of the Democratic Nat[ional]. Com[mit]tee meet at St Louis & how their McAdoo party captured the chairmanship.

1. Robert Walton Moore (1859–1941) was a Democratic congressman from Virginia. Franklin Roosevelt named him to the State Department in 1933.

2. As a result of the general drop in the price paid for wheat, high-grade patent flour dropped below $7.00 a barrel for the first time in more than five years.

3. A "dog by comparison." See LDB to Alfred Brandeis, 11 October 1921, note 3.

4. See LDB to Susan Brandeis, 14 October 1921.

To: Susan Brandeis
Date: November 13, 1921
Place: Washington, D.C.
Source: Gilbert MSS

MY DEAREST SUSAN: Your two letters bring fitting birthday cheer.[1] Your own development during the past year is our greatest gift, and the happiness you have found in professional work a constant source of satisfaction.

Elizabeth is off on her long hike. Greetings came from Boyce, Va. But we shall have a choice gathering of friends, for the dinner. The Hapgoods, George Rublee, Judge Anderson, Ray Stannard Baker and Dean Acheson.[2] There will be rejoicing over Secretary Hughes' admirable start.[3] It was nobly and effectively done. Mother & I attend[ed] the opening session, and last evening the reception at the White House.   Lovingly

1. This was LDB's sixty-fifth birthday.

2. Dean Gooderham Acheson (1893–1971) served as LDB's legal secretary from 1919 to 1921 after his graduation from Harvard Law School. He then joined the Washington, D.C., law firm of Covington & Burling. Roosevelt named him undersecretary of the treasury in 1933, but a dispute over policy caused him to resign. In 1941 Roosevelt appointed him assistant secretary of state. President Harry Truman named him secretary of state in 1949. In that position he was instrumental in implementing the Marshall Plan, the North Atlantic Treaty Organization (NATO) agreement, and the containment policy against the Soviet Union. He and LDB had a warm personal friendship until the latter's death. For Acheson's side of the relationship, see chapter 5 ("Working with Brandeis") in his memoir, *Morning and Noon* (Boston, 1965).

3. Secretary of State Charles Evans Hughes had, the day before, opened the Washington Conference to consider the need for naval disarmament. Alarmed at the growing arms race, America took the lead in bringing the great naval powers of the world together to explore the possibilities of reducing their fleets. Hughes began the conference by proposing a ten-year "holiday" in the construction of battleships and that some ships even be destroyed. Over the next few months he successfully negotiated a number of arms-reduction treaties, the most important of which set a ratio of capital ships between the naval powers. See the next letter.

To: Susan Goldmark
Date: November 13, 1921
Place: Washington, D.C.
Source: EBR

MY DEAR SUSIE: The tie bringing your good wishes gleams with beauty as if to celebrate the long step forward made yesterday through Secretary

Hughes['] admirable practical proposal.[1] It was a master stroke, presented with simple directness and simplicity, impressive and persuasive almost to the point of demonstration. One felt that it left to "the Allied & Associated Powers" hardly an option. In form a proposal, it was in substance a command.

Of course curtailment of armament is what each nation wants; because it is for all an imperative domestic need. And men readily find a way of doing that which they desire. The more difficult task will come when the Far Eastern problem is approached, and the nations are urged to do what they really deem a sacrifice—though erroneously. For it would be best for all the Westerners to commence now the orderly retreat from their Asiatic excursions. The East has been awakened from its sleep. The doubt of our wisdom and of our superior virtue is widespread, as is the conviction that we are not invincible. And I fancy it is not Japan but China and India which will be standard-bearers of Asiatic civilizations. Japan's strength is that borrowed from the West, in large part, and to be rejected.

You see how the calm even of anticipated disarmament stimulates speculation.
                                                                With much love

1. See the previous letter, note 3.

To: Susan Brandeis
Date: May 18, 1922
Place: Washington, D.C.
Source: Gilbert MSS

DEAREST SUSAN: Re yours of 16.

1. I think you show good judgement in not "rushing" for the new US Att[orne]y Asst job. When your present special Asst job will have run its course, you will doubtless have gotten all the benefit you can from such a job—experience, reputation, acquaintance. Your search will be for good regular private clients & new experiences. There is danger of demoralization in easy jobs & easy money; & it is much better to feel that you have been underpaid than that you were overpaid.

2. The opinions are to go to you today. To see the full import— study the Child Labor[1] and Future Trading Act[2] opinions, in connection with the Stockyard case.[3] Our good friends, like Mrs. Kelly [sic] & Julia Lathrop[4] will be very unhappy.[5] But I am convinced that the immediate loss will result in great gain later. If we

may hope to carry out our ideals in America, it will be by development through the State and local Governments. Centralization will kill—only decentralization of social functions can help. In the 19th Century nationalization was the keynote & the 20th should bring local development in States & cities.

3. You will be interested also in the Gas cases—in Referees' fees.[6]

4. Dave Podell telephoned to give you greetings. I asked him to come up, but he said he was with friends & hadn't time.

5. Aunt Belle [La Follette] says she didn't get your card.

1. After the Supreme Court struck down the first federal child labor law in 1918 (*Hammer v. Dagenhart,* 248 U.S. 251), on the grounds that it exceeded the power of Congress to regulate interstate commerce, Congress tried again. This time it rested the case on the taxing power. But the Court once again declared the act unconstitutional in *Bailey v. Drexel Furniture Company,* 259 U.S. 20 (1922). LDB joined with Chief Justice Taft's majority opinion, which argued that Congress had not created a legitimate tax but a "penalty" in order to regulate labor practices in plants that were local and not engaged in interstate commerce. Not until 1941 (*U.S. v. Darby,* 312 U.S. 100) would the Court uphold a child labor law.

2. In August 1921 Congress passed the Future Trading Act to prevent gambling in grain futures at the Chicago Board of Trade. Once more Congress's method was to impose a heavy tax on that kind of trading. In *Hill v. Wallace,* 259 U.S. 44 (1922), the Court declared that this was not a proper use of the tax power and that futures trading in Chicago was not interstate commerce and therefore was not subject to regulation by the Congress. Taft again gave the majority decision, but this time LDB issued a concurring opinion.

3. Three weeks earlier, on 1 May, however, the Court—again speaking through Taft and with LDB in agreement with the majority—upheld the constitutionality of the Packers and Stockyard Regulation Act of 1921. In this case, *Stafford, et al. v. Wallace,* 258 U.S. 495 (1922), the stockyard business was ruled to be within the definition of interstate commerce.

4. Like LDB's old comrade-in-arms Florence Kelley, Julia Clifford Lathrop (1858–1932) was a social worker deeply interested in welfare legislation, particularly as it applied to children. Long associated with Jane Addams at Hull House, Lathrop was appointed by President Taft as the first director of the Department of Labor's Children's Bureau.

5. LDB's point here is that, although it was social welfare legislation that was nullified in the *Bailey* decision, the key issue was not social welfare but the proper allocation of powers to the federal government. In a letter to Frankfurter on 16 May, LDB wrote: "The N[ew].R[epublic]., The Survey & like periodicals should not be permitted to misunderstand yesterday's decision on The Child Labor and Board of Trade cases, & should be made to see that holding these Acts void is wholly unlike holding invalid the ordinary welfare legislation. That is—that we here deal (1) With distribution of functions between State & Federal Governments [and] (2) With the attempt at dishonest use of the taxing powers" (Urofsky and Levy, *"Half Brother, Half Son,"* 100).

6. Justice McReynolds, speaking for a unanimous Court, declared that receivers' fees are subject to judicial review and that in a series of eight cases decided together the payment to the receivers was excessive. See *Newton v. Consolidated Gas Co.,* 259 U.S. 101 (1922).

To: Susan Goldmark
Date: November 14, 1922
Place: Washington, D.C.
Source: Brandeis MSS

MY DEAR SUSIE: The tie is charming—and even aged[1] I may give myself the pleasure of wearing it—evenings—when off duty.

We had a cheering gathering of friends for Alice's first Monday afternoon yesterday, but it was hard to do without Pauline [Goldmark] and the Norman Hapgoods to whom we had acquired almost a vested right for such occasions.

There was, of course, much talk of the elections.[2] Gov. Allen of Kansas[3] (who happily has less chances now for presidential nomination) said cleverly: "Discontent seeks another sacrifice."

The last two years prove that it is easier to put an administration out, than to keep [one] in. The problems of government have become so difficult, and the progress in solving them is so slow—if any is made—that even wished for overthrows do not satisfy. But there is satisfaction in quite a number of defeats (Kellogg, Beveridge, Calder et al.)[4]—and in the election of Al. Smith as essentially a Goldmark possession.[5]

Much love

1. On the day before, LDB had turned sixty-six.

2. The 1922 congressional elections were a major setback for the Republicans. The enormous majority that Harding had won in 1920 was largely negated as the Democrats came roaring back, gaining six seats in the Senate and seventy-five in the House. Many commentators believed the results threw into jeopardy Harding's chances for reelection in 1924.

3. Henry Justin Allen (1868–1950) was a liberal Republican who had followed Theodore Roosevelt out of the 1912 convention. While serving in France in 1918, he was overwhelmingly elected governor of Kansas. In 1920 he passed up the chance to run as Harding's vice-president.

4. Frank Billings Kellogg (1856–1937) had just been unseated in the Minnesota senatorial race, losing to Henrik Shipstead, the Farmer-Labor candidate, by 80,000 votes. Calvin Coolidge named him secretary of state in 1925, and he would be the architect of the famous Kellogg-Briand Peace Pact. He served as a judge at the Permanent Court of International Justice in the 1930s. Albert Beveridge, who was trying to return to the Senate, was defeated in Indiana by a former governor of the state, Samuel M. Ralston. And in New York William Musgrave Calder (1869–1945), a veteran Republican who had been in Congress since 1905, was unseated by Democrat Royal S. Copeland.

5. Alfred Emanuel Smith (1873–1944) was one of the most colorful and influential politicians of his generation. He had risen from the streets of the Lower East Side to a prominence in New York State politics that catapulted him into the governorship in 1918. For more than a decade he had been closely associated with a group of prominent New York social activists and social workers whose membership included the Goldmark sisters, LDB's sisters-in-law. On the basis of a sterling record as a progressive, Governor Smith ran unsuccessfully for the presidential nomination in 1924 (when Franklin Roosevelt, in nominating him, coined the epithet "the Happy Warrior"); and in 1928 Smith became the first Roman Catholic to run as a major party candidate for the presidency of the United States. His Catholicism probably played a part in his defeat by Herbert Hoover, but the prosperity of the 1920s made it unlikely that anyone could have defeated the Republican candidate in 1928. After that defeat, Smith grew increasingly conservative and ultimately broke with his old friend Roosevelt; he became a bitter and harsh critic of the New Deal.

To: Alfred Brandeis
Date: January 3, 1923
Place: Washington, D.C.
Source: Brandeis MSS

DEAR AL: Re yours 29.

The Hadassah is all right—but the Keren H[ayesod]. is all wrong and I think, as they combine the two, you may properly decline.[1]

Alice is delighted to hear that Fanny has also discovered the Goldmark Concerto. We did, two months ago through the Victor catalogue.[2]

I can't understand where all this (and other) money comes from.[3] We are certainly not earning it as a nation. I think we must be exploiting about 80 percent of Americans, for the benefit of the other 20 percent. And that all the new bonds—national, state, and municipal—are simply a mortgage held by the few on the many.

1. The Louisville Jewish community had organized a joint Keren Hayesod and Hadassah fund drive, and Alfred had asked his brother's opinion about contributing to it.
2. Perhaps a recording of the *Violin Concerto in A Minor,* by Karl Goldmark (1830–1915).
3. LDB sent his brother a clipping about the rapid increase in automobile production in 1922. In only eleven months auto manufacturers had produced 2.3 million units, compared to 2.2 million for all of 1920, which had been the best year in the history of the industry. The November 1922 total doubled the November 1920 total of automobiles produced.

To: Alfred Brandeis
Date: June 2, 1923
Place: Washington, D.C.
Source: Brandeis MSS

DEAR AL:

1. The 2 days with the Zionists were, unexpectedly, very gratifying.
2. I have sent to Judge Seymour & to Otto [Wehle] the photos.
3. I entirely agree with you about an essay in foreign shipping. We should limit ourselves to coastwise & inland waters.[1]
4. You can't escape auto statistic[s]. Here are some more.[2]

I too can't figure where the money we are spending comes from. But I fancy it is:

(a) Partly exhaustion of natural resources (timber, natural gas & oil, which should be largely charged against the nation's capital account)
(b) "Kiting checks"[3]

382

We have practically mobilized all our wealth, converting it into bonds & notes. The farms are now being blown in, following in inverse order:

Mercantile, manufacturing, mining, public utilities, national, state & municipal loans.

And through the banks all m[erchan]d[i]se. That is, deposits means largely debts *due* the banks. When we established the Federal Reserve System, we came pretty near doubling the possible loans.

Thus we have endless securities. But I can't see great additions to wealth. That would have to be evidenced either

(1) By large investments (solvent) abroad
(2) Additions to property here, or
(3) Facilities of some kind for increased production.

I don't see them in large volume.

Eliz[abeth] plans to go to Boston on Tuesday's Federal & to take Alice to Chatham Wednesday.

1. See LDB to Alfred Brandeis, 6 September 1921, and to Felix Frankfurter, 20 September 1921, BL.

2. See the previous letter, note 3.

3. "Kiting" checks is the practice of drawing against insufficient funds and redepositing in order to create a false balance. It is made possible by the delay needed for collection.

To:	Elizabeth Brandeis
Date:	August 7, 1923
Place:	Chatham, Massachusetts
Source:	Raushenbush MSS

DEAREST ELIZABETH: I have yours of 4th.

1. What you say about the Potomac & Canal trip is most encouraging & as Susan (judging from her letter from St. Paul) is content to leave time etc. to me, I think we may as well fix defin[ite]ly that we will start about Sept 1. Please have [*] get all available data. It will be entirely agreeable to me to sleep in any house (or barn) and in any bed (if we have blankets with us). I guess I had better not try camping, unless an emergency arises. So prepare detailed, comprehensive instructions for me. I guess some food (as insurance) should be taken.

I suppose [*], if he is to be in W[ashington]. could most effectively arrange to have an appropriate canoe shipped up. If not, I guess my friends Foley

& Dempsey could (with Poindexter's[1] supervision) be relied upon to supply the canoe & ship it.

    2. As to three of your problems, I have definite advice.

(a) It clearly is not necessary on Mother's account that you should remain in Washington this winter. I told Mother, some time ago, of the talk you & I had on this subject; and she agreed entirely with the advice I had given you. Moreover, Mother's progress, although slow, is pretty steady. I have confidence that by October, or middle of September, she will have advanced far beyond the present stage (if all goes well) and that she will be able to run the household as of old; and be the better for having the responsibility of doing so.

(b) I think the combination of law and economics is a good one. If you pursue economics as a teaching career, or otherwise, I shall look forward to your doing important work some day, for which your abilities fit you. And, whether it be in teaching, in writing or in administration, knowledge of the law, and of its processes, is almost an indispensable for first class work. Perhaps, some day you may conceive to do for the Massachusetts textile industry, with its Lowell and Lawrence and Fall River, what the Hammonds have done in "The Town Labourer"; an admirable book,[2]—or the Webbs in the Cooperative Movement.[3] If you go into research, it should be on your own account, not as part of a machine, but to enable you to present the results of your own thinking in the best possible form.

(c) I have no doubt that the Wisconsin Law School is good enough for your purposes, and should think it probable that you would find economics instruction, and, doubtless, other conditions more sympathetic there than at Yale. The next few years are apt to be tinged with a radical hue; and it will be particularly satisfying to live in an atmosphere which breathes La Follette air.

As to Dave I am, as you assume, unable to advise.

Mother is, doubtless, keeping you posted of our quiet days and being. The bird-migrations have begun and bring a new, and thrilling and beautiful interest. Mother is getting real pleasure in stimulating Miss Jardine's interest in birds and flowers. It is rewarding and vivifying her own.

I happily escaped going to Washington for the funeral.[4] The Chief didn't request it; simply enquired whether I was coming & I thought it permissible to treat attendance as impossible.

It is good to think of Susan being with you today.   With much love

384

1. William Poindexter was LDB's "messenger," provided by the Supreme Court; Elizabeth Brandeis, however, described him as "a very helpful member of the household."

2. John L. Hammond and Barbara Hammond, *The Town Labourer* (London, 1917).

3. Beatrice (Potter) Webb, *The Co-operative Movement in Great Britain* (London, 1891). Although she often published with her husband Sidney, this book appeared under her name alone.

4. President Warren G. Harding died in San Francisco on 2 August while touring the West. His body arrived in Washington, D.C., for an elaborate memorial service on 8 August; two days later he was buried in Marion, Ohio.

To:	Elizabeth Brandeis
Date:	February 8, 1924
Place:	Washington, D.C.
Source:	EBR

DEAREST ELIZABETH: Yours of the 6th has come.

My advice is to accept the job at Smith.[1] Pres[iden]t Neilson[2] evidently wants you. He is one of the finest of college presidents. And if you do as well as I expect you to do in the Labor course you would give, there is pretty sure to be a call by him to more & higher service.

Moreover, if it should happen that a distinctly more desirable opportunity offers elsewhere, before the summer, I have no doubt that Prest Neilson—being what he is—will be glad to release you.

Smith seems to me not at all an undesirable place—in spite of being a girls college. It is in a beautiful country—a small place which you like—near enough Amherst to be in touch with men folk. And it has a reputation which would make it a good stepping-stone to another job.

What I am eager for you is to have next year the opportunity of showing somewhere what you can do;—which, I think, is unusually good work.

Mother is quite prepared to have you take an immediate job anywhere in the United States. She approved my talking with Mr. [Joseph N.] Teal about the University of Oregon, and I think wrote you to write Clara [Goldmark] about the University of California. She has asked Dr. [*] to write Prest Comstock[3] about Radcliffe; & I think has written Bessie [Evans] & Pauline [Goldmark] about Bryn Mawr. So you see [she] is bent on having you make the trial this fall.[4]   Lovingly

1. While completing her M.A. in economics at Wisconsin, Elizabeth Brandeis was hunting for a job for the coming fall. There had been some suggestion of her teaching at Smith.

2. William Allan Neilson (1869–1946), an English professor, assumed the presidency at Smith College in 1917 and retained it until 1939. He was active in many liberal and civil rights causes.

3. Ada Louise Comstock (1876–1973) had been a dean at Smith College but accepted the presidency of Radcliffe in 1923. She stayed in that position until 1943, when she left it to marry the historian Wallace Notestein.

4. In the end Elizabeth Brandeis decided to remain in Wisconsin as a graduate student and a teaching assistant.

To: Susan Brandeis
Date: March 9, 1924
Place: Washington, D.C.
Source: Gilbert MSS

MY DEAR SUSAN: Re yours of 7th.

1. I think it clearly wise that you and Ben[1] should continue to occupy the Woolworth Bldg offices—even if you should have to pay the expense, unaided by another occupant.
2. I also think it clearly wise that you two should not accept another partner in Sam's[2] place until you two are sure he is the right man. It would be a good way to find out whether a prospect is desirable as a partner, by having him as an occupant of the vacated office, if opportunity for that should occur.
3. I assume that you and Ben will continue as partners in any event. I think a partnership is (other things being about equal) distinctly preferable to going it alone.

In any event stay together in the Woolworth Bldg offices.

Under Grandpa Goldmark's will your mother had an interest which she never accepted, leaving Grandmother Goldmark to have the income and always intending that Aunt Susie should have the principal later. Those funds under Grandpa Goldmark's will, will, I assume, be distributed among the beneficiaries soon. I am writing Uncle Charles (who has had the management of the property) to confer with you about drafting an appropriate instrument for assigning to Aunt Susie mother's interest in the estate.

Lovingly

1. Benjamin Sollow Kirsh (1898–19[?]) was Susan Brandeis's law partner. He had been chair of the Trucking Commission of the Labor Board during World War I and, like Susan Brandeis, a special assistant to the U.S. attorney in New York for the prosecution of antitrust cases. He wrote on law and economics, including *Automation and Collective Bargaining* (Brooklyn, 1964).
2. The third partner in Kirsh, Rosenman & Brandeis until recently had been Samuel Irving Rosenman (1896–1973), a Columbia graduate and a member of the New York state legislature. Rosenman was a close friend and advisor of Franklin Roosevelt, who appointed him to the New York Supreme Court in 1932. He resigned that position to become a special counsel to Roosevelt and then to President Truman. Rosenman was the editor of a multi-volume edition of the public papers and addresses of Franklin Roosevelt.

To: Susan Brandeis
Date: March 12, 1924
Place: Washington, D.C.
Source: Gilbert MSS

DEAREST SUSAN: I am very glad to know that you & Ben [Kirsh] are extending your lease 2 years, & that there is a prospect of Sam [Rosenman]'s remaining with you at least locally. It will be a considerable gain to have him do that, leaving the firm name unchanged, even if earnings are not pooled by him.

A three legged firm name is better than a two nowadays & it is undesirable to make a change in name so early in the firm's career.

Elizabeth expects to teach at the Bryn Mawr summer school, June 13 to Aug 9. That would give her good experience & ought to make it easier to get the regular position elsewhere in the fall.[1]

I note the Pres[iden]t has denied the Rumely pardon, & assume that includes N. in the denial.[2]   Lovingly

    1. See LDB to Elizabeth Brandeis, 8 February 1924.
    2. Edward A. Rumely (1882–1964) was the publisher of the *New York Evening Mail*. He had been convicted of failing to report that the paper was German-owned, thereby violating the terms of the Trading with the Enemy Act. With Coolidge's refusal to pardon him, Rumely began to serve his sentence of one year and one day. The "N" that LDB mentions is undoubtedly Norvin Rudolf Lindheim (1880–1930), Rumley's lawyer, who was convicted for his own failure to report the matter. Norvin Lindheim, and especially his wife, Irma, were allies of LDB in the Zionist movement.

To: Susan Brandeis
Date: March 18, 1924
Place: Washington, D.C.
Source: Gilbert MSS

DEAREST SUSAN: Enclosed opinion may interest you.

Rose Rothenberg[1] of your bar was admitted to our Court today. Her next friend ought to have supplied her own lack of the sense of propriety in coming into Court, with ²/₃ short sleeves, & decollete & a long necklace!!!

    1. Rose Rothenberg came to America from Romania at an early age. She graduated from the New York University Law School in 1914, practiced law in New York City, and was active in Jewish charities and in Democratic politics. She married Dr. M. W. Goldstein.

To: Susan Brandeis
Date: July 13, 1924
Place: Chatham, Massachusetts
Source: Gilbert MSS

DEAREST SUSAN: Glad you have planned an enjoyable weekend. Our weather was perfect yesterday and Friday. Today it is grey again. We are deep in endless political discussions. If Senator La Follette keeps his health during the next four months, election day may bring great surprises.[1] The farmer discontent is apt to be matched by that of labor with increasing unemployment; & even the small tradesmen are apt to think that a new deal had better be tried. The existence of labor governments abroad is calculated to encourage imitation here.[2]

If you have time & inclination for work on a legal article, it would be most valuable to limit your study to a very narrow topic, so that you could feel, when it is done, that you know all that is to be known in the jurisdiction (say, N.Y. or federal) on that subject. Lovingly

1. On 4 July Senator Robert M. La Follette, responding to the urgings of many progressives, announced that he would be an independent candidate for the presidency. The new Progressive Party immediately nominated him and Burton K. Wheeler of Montana as his running-mate, and the two mounted a campaign vaguely reminiscent in its platform of the campaign of 1912. Despite LDB's optimism here and in the following letter, and despite the senator's valiant effort and the wide support from disaffected progressives, socialists, and reformers from all over the country, La Follette's finish was disappointing. He received 4.8 million votes (13 electoral) compared to 15.7 million for Calvin Coolidge and 8.3 million for the Democrat candidate, John W. Davis.
2. Ramsay MacDonald became prime minister in Great Britain's first Labour government in January 1924. LDB could not know it, of course, but Labour would be removed from power even before the November elections in the United States.

To: **Alfred Brandeis**
Date: **July 19, 1924**
Place: **Chatham, Massachusetts**
Source: **Brandeis MSS**

DEAR AL: Here are some of the N. R. editorials. There will be more.[1] The Senator will have (if he keeps his health) a grand fight. If I had several watertight compartment lives, I should have liked to be in it.[2] The enemies are vulnerable & the times ripe.

The Chicago consolidation doesn't look to me very promising for the farmers.[3]

Will return the Cal[ifornia] wires from Reece later. I think I remember Miss R.

1. The *New Republic*, disappointed by the Democrats' nomination of John W. Davis, was unrestrained in its support of Senator La Follette. For example, see "The Meaning of La Follette's Candidacy," *New Republic* 39 (16 July 1924): 196–98, and Robert Littell, "La Follette for President," ibid.: 201–2.
2. There had been strong rumors that La Follette had asked LDB to run with him as vice-president (see *New York Times,* 18 March and 3, 14, and 19 July 1924). La Follette never

discussed the matter directly with LDB, but sent Gilson Gardner to Chatham to explore the possibility. LDB, preferring his life as a Supreme Court Justice, declined the offer. See La Follette and La Follette, *La Follette*, 2:1115–16.

3. On 16 July the Grain Marketing Company was formed by consolidating several leading Chicago grain operations. Farm organizations denounced the merger even though it was touted as a "cooperative." Even the Farmers' Cooperative Marketing Association called the merger a trick on the nation's farmers. See the next letter.

To: **Alfred Brandeis**
Date: **July 26, 1924**
Place: **Chatham, Massachusetts**
Source: **EBR**

DEAR AL: The parents['] engagement day.

The hog meat has come. Thanks.

Your letters & enclosures about the grain deal are all interesting.[1] It simmers down to: "I don't know what to think." Frank [Taussig] is coming over next week to talk it over. The further Minneapolis offer adds to the [*] of nations.

Fate is making us the owner of this estate. The owner concluded to sell, had an offer, and we had to buy to "protect the home". The papers have been signed (subject to Miss Malloch's scrutiny to be made) & we think fate dealt kindly with us. At all events, as Father said to Aunt Julia: "Ich füge mich in mein Schicksal."[2]

The price is only $15,000—the acreage 12^1/$_{10}$ (twelve). Now we enjoy nearer twelve hundred, stretching out over the unoccupied land North, South, East & West of us on either side of Oyster Road. As the village is a mile and half away, we shall hope other folk will be slow in buying.

Emma Erving was here yesterday.[3] She is always a great comfort in need & a joy when there is none. Fortunately Alice seems to be gaining pretty steadily.

The talk of the household is largely of politics, with Mrs. Evans high in national duties, Felix Frankfurter very active in writing & thinking & the rest of us hardly less keen in our interest. Wheeler[4] has helped much in taking the second place. Bob ought to make a fine fight & a great beginning for the future tussle.

If [John W.] Davis gets the licking which the Democrats deserve for hitching their horse in Wall St., we may get the country divided on these new lines of Conservative & Progressive & get some honest thinking into our political & social problems.

Susan is due here today to stay until Monday P.M.

I hope things go well with Jennie.

1. See the preceding letter. Thirty-six additional grain companies in the Northwest offered to sell their holdings to the American Farm Bureau Federation on 22 July.
2. "I succumb to my fate." Aunt Julia was Julia Wehle Oettinger, Regina Goldmark's sister.
3. Emma Lootz Erving, the daughter of a Norwegian diplomat, was a Washington, D.C., orthopedist and a close personal friend of the Brandeises.
4. Burton Kendall Wheeler (1882–1975), La Follette's running mate, served as a Democratic senator from Montana from 1922 to 1947. He is best remembered for his strict isolationism and his opposition to Franklin D. Roosevelt's foreign policy in the late 1930s.

To: Susan Brandeis
Date: July 29, 1924
Place: Chatham, Massachusetts
Source: Gilbert MSS

DEAREST SUSAN: That was a lovely visit, and a great satisfaction to note your steady development. Mother, too, is very happy over what your are doing with yourself.

We had a thrilling chapter read by Felix last evening from the Hammonds' "Life of Lord Shaftesbury",[1] which acted as a sedative on Auntie B's political excitation.[2] It is an extraordinary thing to get from authors such a combination of research, judgment and style—a performance, in this respect, much like Alfred Zimmern's "Greek Commonwealth."[3]

Auntie B. has been busy all morning cultivating her garden patch. She leaves for Boston on the afternoon train to be gone some days.

Hope you are finding N.Y. weather bearable.   Lovingly

1. J. L. Hammond and Barbara Hammond, *Lord Shaftesbury* (New York, 1924).
2. Elizabeth Glendower Evans was deeply involved in La Follette's presidential campaign.
3. Alfred Zimmern, *The Greek Commonwealth, Politics and Economics in Fifth Century Athens* (Oxford, 1911).

To: Susan Brandeis
Date: August 25, 1924
Place: Chatham, Massachusetts
Source: Gilbert MSS

DEAREST SUSAN: Our greetings for the homecoming; and hope that the stay in England has been in every way delightful.

Life goes on here much as you knew it. Elizabeth, after two abortive essays, reached Monomoy Point in the Water Witch and spent about 24 hours in camp there with Eva and Connie, looking out upon the loud resounding Atlantic, in which they had two (cold) dips. It was a good test of E's seamanship and she is evidently pleased with the achievement.[1]

Mother and I have been busy in husbandry—planting on bare spots on our bluff. I guess it is nearly as hard a job as making the hair grow on a Bismarkian head. Today we plan to photograph the bluff so as to be in a position to make comparisons next season.

Norman Hapgood will have an article on La Follette in the Oct Hearst's.[2]

Lovingly

Wrote you c/o Margery that your first week end with us will probably be in W[ashington].

1. Monomoy Point is the southernmost point of land off of Chatham, a narrow stretch that separates Nantucket Sound from the Atlantic Ocean.

2. No article by Hapgood appeared in the October *Hearst's*. Hapgood instead published his views in "Why I Shall Vote for La Follette," *New Republic* 40 (15 October 1924): 168–69.

To:	Susan Brandeis
Date:	October 4, 1924
Place:	Washington, D.C.
Source:	Gilbert MSS

DEAREST SUSAN: Your two letters report fine progress in practice. These retainers for trials are the best thing that could come; and the small cases the proper road to important ones later.

Your client's effervescent letter (returned herewith) is really significant. Of course, it is bombastic and amuses. But it is such enthusiasms "among the lowly" which eventually will bring the most desirable support.

At the dinner of the Circuit Judges, given by the C[hief].J[ustice]. Thursday, Judge Rogers[1] spoke of you & showed that he (and doubtless others) are keeping tabs. He said you had not yet argued in his court, but that you seem to be much in the District Court, that Learned Hand cares a lot for you, and "Judge Mack also".

The latter I am to see here tomorrow A.M.

Lovingly

You certainly carried forward the family [*] promotion.

1. Henry Wade Rogers (1853–1926) taught at the University of Michigan law school and was president of Northwestern University. He was named judge of the Second Circuit Court of Appeals in 1913.

To: Susan Brandeis
Date: October 14, 1924
Place: Washington, D.C.
Source: Gilbert MSS

DEAREST SUSAN: I planned long ago to send you at some time two law books which I thought you would value.

(a) An edition of Daniels' [*sic*] Chancery Practice (3 vols) containing interleaved notes made by me in 1887 (of which I told you in connection with the Wisconsin experience).[1]

(b) The first edition of Morawetz on Corporations (1881)[2] given me then by M. with an inscription to remind of our discussions at the law school & his stay with me on Pinckney St. while he was correcting the proof.

The other day I wrote Miss Malloch to send them to you. She does not find them in their place & suggests the possibility that I may have sent them to you so long ago that I have forgotten about it.

Will you kindly write her on receipt of this whether you have received from me either or both these books. If not already received, further search will be made.   Lovingly

1. Edmund Robert Daniell, *Pleading and Practice of the High Court of Chancery*. Perhaps LDB had purchased the fifth American edition (Boston, 1879). LDB's "Wisconsin experience" was his connection with the Wisconsin Central Railroad, beginning in November 1889 and leading to his first appearance as a young attorney before the United States Supreme Court. See Mason, *Brandeis*, 70–71.

2. Victor Morawetz, *A Treatise in the Law of Private Corporations Other Than Charitable*, was actually published in 1882. Morawetz (1859–1938) was two years behind LDB at Harvard. He wrote several textbooks on commercial law and became what LDB called "the controlling intellect of the great Atchison Railroad system." LDB pointed to Morawetz as a prime example of how legal training prepared young men for important work in society in his 1905 address before the Harvard Ethical Society, "Opportunity in the Law."

To: Fannie Brandeis
Date: October 20, 1924
Place: Washington, D.C.
Source: Brandeis MSS

MY DEAR FANNIE: Until the University of Louisville shall be equipped to promote the study of the fine arts and music, one of its important functions must remain unperformed. Doubtless many years will elapse before adequate provision for this can be made. But it is not too early to begin, now, to dream what might be; and to plan what shall be. Moreover, any concrete steps toward realization taken now, however modest they be, will, as overt acts, manifest the purpose of the University, and may be the means of securing from others needed cooperation. I hope you will care to do some of this planning and will undertake the small beginnings which I want to suggest.[1]

First. The beginning of a departmental library. The University gives now some instruction in Greek and Latin and in Ancient history. Obviously, the earlier civilizations cannot be understood without full appreciation of their contributions to the fine arts. Access to the rich and ever growing fruits of archeological exploration is essential to an intimate knowledge of the life of the older peoples. Thus, books on ancient arts and archaeology are primal needs of instructors who seek to awaken in students an interest in the achievements of a great past and to feed the hope for a greater future.

If the University authorities approve, Aunt Alice and I will be glad to place at your disposal, from time to time, funds to be applied in the purchase, for this purpose, of such books as you and the appropriate members of the faculty deem necessary; and for the attendant expense of shelving, binding, and cataloguing. We should expect also to help, through you, in like manner, in the acquisition of the books on art required for an adequate study of the Renaissance and the later period; and eventually to lay a wee corner-stone for a library of music. To learn modern history implies understanding of the culture of the several peoples and knowledge of such contributions as each has made to civilization.

Second. The beginning of an art collection. Living among things of beauty is a help toward culture and the life worthwhile. But the function of the University in respect to the fine arts is not limited to promoting understanding and appreciation. It should strive to awaken the slumbering creative instinct, to encourage its exercise and development, to stimulate production. There is reason to think that Kentuckians have, among their many gifts, imagination and creative power. There seems to me no reason why this should not express itself in the fine arts. The Brenner which your Aunt Hattie and Mr. Speed generously gave me is an example of Kentucky art, finely achieved.[2] With her approval, I should be glad to give it to the University, through you, as an encourager of effort in others.

These are functions of the University which would have made the strongest appeal to your two grandmothers and your Aunt Fannie. They must interest deeply also your mother, Maidie and Jean. And I am sure your cousin Harry would be ever ready to give his expert advice.[3]

Your uncle

1. In the fall of 1924 LDB began to interest himself in the task of improving the University of Louisville—a project that he entered with his customary energy and attention to detail and that occupied him throughout the 1920s. Because of his judicial duties and his distance from the scene, he operated through various intermediaries—both officials of the university and, principally, members of the Louisville branch of the Brandeis family—his brother Alfred and members of Alfred's family. (For another example of this effort, see LDB to Frederick Wehle, 28 October 1924.) After Alfred's death, LDB's niece Fannie Brandeis served as his chief representative in implementing his plans for the university. LDB's efforts soon became focused on two projects within the university: improving the law school and building up the university libraries. (In 1997 the University officially renamed its law school "The Louis D. Brandeis School of Law.") For the most complete statement of his underlying thinking in this undertaking, see his letter to Alfred Brandeis, 18 February 1925. Also see the numerous letters to Alfred, Fannie, and Adele Brandeis and to Frederick Wehle and Charles and William Tachau in BL. The details of LDB's involvement are thoroughly recounted by his friend and associate Bernard Flexner, *Mr. Justice Brandeis and the University of Louisville* (Louisville, 1938). It should be noted that this work on behalf of the University of Louisville was closely tied to LDB's fear of the overcentralization of American life and his increasingly passionate and urgent belief that if America was to be saved it would need to develop diversity in its various locales. For LDB this meant encouraging local experiments in social and political life and local centers of cultural and educational vitality. For that reason, he insisted that the responsibility for building a great university in Louisville would always remain with the faculty, the administration, and the citizenry of the city.

2. In 1912 James and Hattie Bishop Speed had presented LDB and his wife with an oil painting of the Kentucky woods, *Beeches in Autumn,* by Carl Christ Brenner (1838–88). The painting was eventually donated to the J. B. Speed Memorial Museum in Louisville. See LDB to Fannie Brandeis, 14 February 1925.

3. LDB's nephew Harry Brandeis Wehle (1887–1969) worked at the Metropolitan Museum of Art in New York City.

To: Susan Brandeis
Date: October 27, 1924
Place: Washington, D.C.
Source: Gilbert MSS

DEAREST SUSAN:

1. Your letter reached me Saturday after mine to you had been mailed. Glad to know that you are expecting to prepare the Sanitary etc. brief. Hope your week end was as enjoyable as Valhalla usually is.

2. Please let me know, by return mail, whether Aunt Susie can vote by mail Tuesday; & if so send the necessary blanks & instructions.

If not, ask Uncle Henry whether he is going to vote for Coolidge; & if so, whether he would be willing to pair with Aunt Susie. If yes, ask him to write Aunt Susie offering to do so.

Please do not let him (or others) say anything about my having suggested this. Aunt Susie is having an uncommonly happy time with us; but thinks she ought to go home Friday in order to vote Tuesday. We don't propose to dissuade her from doing so, but want to see that the alternatives, if any, are presented to her.

3. Enclosed opinion may interest you because of its brevity.

Lovingly

To: Frederick Wehle
Date: October 28, 1924
Place: Washington, D.C.
Source: Brandeis MSS

MY DEAR FRED:[1] The World War has wrought epochal changes. Every phase and incident of the stupendous struggle and of the efforts at readjustment will become the subject of special research and of interpretation. To understand the causes of the war, its conduct and its consequences will hereafter be essential to statesmanlike conduct of our public affairs. To study them will be a necessary part of a liberal education. Opportunity for this study must be afforded Kentuckians if they are to be fitted for tasks which await them. The ambition of the University of Louisville should rest even higher. It should seek to become truly a seat of learning; a place where historical research may be pursued and histories be written. It is only by affording facilities for such study and research that it may hope to attract to its faculty, and retain, men and women who will bring to students not instruction merely, but inspiration; teachers through whom, indirectly, history is made.

To this end the University must possess an adequate library of the war and the post-war period. This library must include not merely the tools necessary for undergraduates, but so far as possible, also the mass of publications which constitute the new material for historical research. Most of the unpublished papers bearing upon the period will necessarily remain in the official archives of belligerents or neutrals, or will be made available only through the world's greatest libraries. But materials which most concerns [sic] Americans is not of that unique character. We shall learn most by unprejudiced, painstaking study of our own strengths and weaknesses; by enquiries into our own achievements and shortcomings. It is thus that we may best learn how great are the possibilities of high accomplishment in the future; and what are the real dangers with which we shall be confronted. The rich material for these enquiries may be obtained by the University, if the members of its department of history and political science care enough to build up such a library to be willing to make the necessary effort. For the publications required for this purpose—partly official, partly private in origins—were widely circulated in the United States. Copies of most of these are still procurable. And probably copies could be obtained from some sources without resort to purchase.

My own collection of such books and papers might serve as the nucleus for such a library of the war and post-war period. It is quite large; and is comprehensive. It includes a fair number of books on the causes of the war, its conduct and its results; on the birth of the new nations; on the proposals for ending war. It includes publications of the numerous war—agencies established or utilized by our Government in the prosecution of the war and in the adjustments made after the Armistice; publications emanating from foreign Governments or their nationals which were circulated in this country; and publications of societies or individuals seeking to advance our interests in the war, a satisfactory solution of foreign problems, or the World peace. But my collection would serve as a skeleton merely. It is, in no respect, complete. For there has been no conscious effort on my part to build a library. What I possess of this character is an aggregation of books and papers which I procured, from time to time, because I was interested in the general subject or was called upon to advise in respect to some specific matter. Some of these publications came to me unsolicited—indeed many of them.

In order to develop my aggregation of books and papers into a worthy library on the war and the post-war period, much work would have to be done. The files of publications which I have must be completed. Of other publications, not represented in my collection, the full files would have to be sought. Publications soon to appear must be obtained when issued. To this end, members of the faculty would have to familiarize themselves with the existing and available material, and to enquire into and consider carefully the sources from which such material could be obtained without purchase. If the task of obtaining such material is entered upon promptly and efforts are pursued unremittingly, Kentuckians within and without the State can be counted on for furnishing such aid as may prove to be needed.

If the University authorities approve of making such a collection, if the appropriate members of the faculty are willing to assume the task suggested, and if you are to aid them in it, Aunt Alice and I will be glad to give the University now my collection of books and published papers on the war and post-war period, together with sums required to defray the expense of cataloguing, binding, and shelving and the purely clerical disbursements incident to the immediate efforts to complete and supplement the files of publications as indicated. At a later time we should expect to give to the University some unpublished documents relating to the war which seem to have historic interest, but should, for the present, be treated as confidential.

Your father's life-long study of history and government leads us to hope that he will join you in lending aid to the faculty in this task. We hope, also, that some day Fred Jr.[2] and his cousins will, as students at the University, find valuable the material which you will bring to it.

Your Uncle

1. Frederick Wehle (1896–1973) was the third child of LDB's sister Amy and her husband, Otto Wehle. He was the only one of the Wehle children to remain in Louisville.
2. Frederick Wehle, Jr. (b. 1919) is the eldest son of Frederick Wehle. He has worked for various companies around Louisville.

To: Frederick Wehle
Date: November 19, 1924
Place: Washington, D.C.
Source: Brandeis MSS

MY DEAR FRED: I have yours of 16th.

I assumed that the University is poor in possessions—including the instructors. What I aim to do is to make them rich in ideals and eager in the desire to attain them. I want the authorities to dream of the University as it should be; and I hope to encourage this dreaming by making possible the first steps toward realization. The only assurance I care to exact is that a desire for high standards is felt, and that an effort will be made to carry out the project as suggested. Teachers are largely a meek, downtrodden, unappreciated body of men. To know that others believe in them, consider them capable of high thinking and doing, and are willing to help them rise—may enable them to accomplish more than even they think possible.

Your Uncle

To: Susan Brandeis
Date: December 6, 1924
Place: Washington, D.C.
Source: Gilbert MSS

DEAREST SUSAN: It's fine to have the reports of your court experiences. I feel like a superannuated war-horse at the sound of martial music.

I vaguely remember Paul Abelson.[1]

I suppose you noticed Mabel's[2] triumph over U.S. Atty Harris of Mass. It looks as if she wouldn't return to Los Angeles March 4.[3]

Your admission to U.S.S.C. seems to have awakened transcontinental memories & I have no doubt will result in business.[4]

Your clientage is evidently becoming international—perhaps more accurately, interracial.

Lovingly

We are to have Progressives in to dine. The Edward Keatings (Labor),[5] the John M. Nelsons[6] & Grace Abbott[7]—the defeated.[8]

The distinguished atty. for Jeanne should have been [*].

Lovingly

1. Paul Abelson (1878–1953) was a veteran of the settlement house movement in New York City. He and LDB were drawn together between 1911 and 1914, when Abelson was a member of the conciliation staff for the garment industry's Protocol of Peace. Afterward Abelson helped to set up arbitration machinery in other industries.

2. One of Susan Brandeis's good friends was Mabel Walker Willebrandt (1889–1963), a California lawyer and Republican progressive. She was appointed assistant attorney general in 1921 and placed in charge of prohibition enforcement. She retained the position until 1929. During the 1920s Willebrandt was a frequent dinner guest of LDB and his wife.

3. Robert Orr Harris (1854–1926) was a Boston attorney and justice of the Massachusetts Supreme Court from 1902 to 1911, when he resigned to serve one term in Congress. He then became the U.S. attorney for Boston. He and Mabel Willebrandt crossed swords over his lax enforcement of the prohibition law. Harris criticized Willebrandt publicly (perhaps thinking that the change in administrations would undercut her position); but Willebrandt won the battle, and on 3 December President Coolidge sent a letter to Harris removing him from office.

4. Susan Brandeis was admitted to practice before the United States Supreme Court on 20 November 1924.

5. Edward Keating (1875–1965) was a Democrat from Colorado. After serving in Congress from 1913 to 1919, he stayed in Washington to edit *Labor*, the magazine of the railroad brotherhoods.

6. John Mandt Nelson (1870–1955) was a La Follette Republican from Madison, Wisconsin. A member of the House of Representatives from 1906 to 1919 and again from 1921 to 1933, Nelson probably would have had considerable influence in the Congress in the unlikely event of a Progressive Party victory in 1924.

7. Grace Abbott (1878–1939) spent nine years with Jane Addams at Hull House and developed into a leading figure in numerous civic and industrial reform efforts. She is best known for her work in the United States Children's Bureau and succeeded Julia C. Lathrop as chief of the bureau in 1921.

8. For the conversation at this dinner of defeated La Follette supporters, see LDB to Felix Frankfurter, 1 January 1925, in Urofsky and Levy, *"Half Brother, Half Son,"* 187.

To: Susan Brandeis
Date: January 17, 1925
Place: Washington, D.C.
Source: Gilbert MSS

DEAREST SUSAN: It's fine that Elsie Williams is so enthusiastic a client. Who is, or was, her father?

As to enthusiastic clients, you recall Heine's: "Solch einen liebenswürdigen Jüngling kann ich nicht genug verehren etc."[1]

When you see the Throckmorton, remember that there is (or was) a prominent Kentucky family of that name.

I am glad you are to see Cousin Clara [Goldmark].

I always found so much of romance and of adventure in securing a new client and in their confidences that the ordinarily [*sic*] essays of the imagination presented by all but the best novels or stories seemed pretty poor by comparison.   Lovingly

1. "Such an amiable youth I cannot honor enough, etc."

To: Susan Brandeis
Date: February 6, 1925
Place: Washington, D.C.
Source: Gilbert MSS

MY DEAREST SUSAN: Your letter, which has just come, brings a great surprise.

There is nothing which we could wish more for you than a husband worthy of you whom you deeply love. And we have confidence in your mature judgement.[1]

It is fine that you will be here in a few days. And then we can hear all about it—and him.

Let me know, as soon as you know, whether it will be Wednesday evening or Thursday morning that you arrive. I assume you will be here Wednesday night. A room will be ready then & the key at the desk, if you come late.

With much love

Your train letter has also come. I am glad you cared so much to go.

1. Susan Brandeis had informed her parents of a tentative engagement to Jacob H. Gilbert (1883–1966), also an attorney. The two first met in New York, when they opposed one another in a minor litigation. See LDB to Susan Brandeis, 23 October 1925.

To: Fannie Brandeis
Date: February 14, 1925
Place: Washington, D.C.
Source: Brandeis MSS

MY DEAR FAN: We are delighted to hear of Aunt Hattie's gift.[1] In honor of it, Aunt Alice is sending you today by Amer. Ry Express (receipt enclosed) a piece of old Japanese lacquer, which we are told is of large value artistically and financially.

Its ancient history we cannot, at the moment give you. Doubtless you will divine it, after you have mastered those "uncut leaves."

The recent history is this: It was given us by Percival Lowell (brother of A. L. L.)[2] who, as your father will remember, was, nearly half a century ago, the secretary of the mission of Japan to the United States. (P.L. wrote three books on Japan.)[3]

Aunt Alice and I, in our ignorance, gave this piece what we thought was a place of honor in our Boston home. Denman Ross saw it there & was shocked at the sacrilege—told us of its value and that it should be exhibited only under glass.

So it has been carefully preserved awaiting the day when Aunt Alice should send it to you for the University.[4]

Affectionately

I hope to answer your letter tomorrow.

1. To honor the memory of her husband, Hattie Bishop Speed donated the J. B. Speed Memorial Museum to the University of Louisville.

2. Abbott Lawrence Lowell (1856–1943) graduated from the Harvard Law School in 1880 and eventually became a professor of government at Harvard University. Upon the retirement of Charles W. Eliot in 1909, Lowell ascended to the presidency of Harvard, a position he held until 1933. Lowell, a classic Boston brahmin conservative, was frequently at odds with LDB, and in 1916 few men opposed LDB's appointment to the Supreme Court with greater vehemence.

3. Percival Lowell's works on Japan were *The Soul of the Far East* (1888), *Noto: An Unexplored Corner of Japan* (1891), and *Occult Japan; or the Way of the Gods . . .* (1895).

4. LDB and his wife eventually gave the Speed Museum a number of items that they had collected over the years, ranging from two volumes of Plutarch to a fourteenth-century Japanese sword.

To: Fannie Brandeis
Date: February 17, 1925
Place: Washington, D.C.
Source: Brandeis MSS

MY DEAR FAN: Your letter gave Aunt Alice and me much pleasure.

1. "The Fine Arts Library of the University of Louisville" seems to us admirable for the book plate. Do not let the Louis D. Brandeis name creep in there or in the Museum, as Aunt Hattie has so generously suggested. We have been willing that it should be used in the publicity solely because, in view of my official position, it appeared to be effective as a lever to move others to aid. But any

use of the name in a more permanent way would tend to defeat the purposes we have in mind. We want to stimulate action, and to this end it is important that others have the memorials. This is of particular significance because of other plans we have in mind about which I am writing your father.[1]

2. Aunt Alice & I think it would be better for you to write Mr. Currall for the Journal & the Bulletin. A letter written by you on University paper would doubtless be effective

We hope that the express package arrived safely.   Your Uncle

1. See LDB to Alfred Brandeis, 18 February 1925.

To:	Susan Brandeis
Date:	February 17, 1925
Place:	Washington, D.C.
Source:	Gilbert MSS

MY DEAREST SUSAN: It is a great satisfaction to have your yesterday's letter about Jack.[1]

No doubt my standards seem to some exacting. But my insistence results largely from my faith in man's possibilities and in his perfectibility.

That was very good advice you gave Miss Martin.   Lovingly

1. Susan's fiancé, Jacob Gilbert, was often called "Jack."

To:	Alfred Brandeis
Date:	February 18, 1925
Place:	Washington, D.C.
Source:	Brandeis MSS

MY DEAR AL: What has been started through Maidie and Fanny, and what was attempted through Fred [Wehle], are but parts of a larger plan to lay broad and deep the foundation of the University. It is a task befitting the Adolf Brandeis family, which for nearly three-quarters of a century has stood in Louisville for culture and, at least in Uncle Lewis [Dembitz], for learning. For this undertaking conditions seem favorable now. It would be fine if all the grandchildren could take an active part. But six of them are disqualified, for the present, by non-residence; and Fred has declared himself ineligible for another reason. So the task devolves upon your family—yourself, Jennie, the girls and the sons-in-law—and upon Alice and me. If we elders can have ten years to work in, the preliminary work will have been done. The rest can be left wholly to your descendants and the centuries.

Money alone cannot build a worthy university. Too much money, or too quick money, may mar one; particularly if it is foreign money. To become great, a university must express the people whom it serves, and must express the people and the community at their best. The aim must be high and the vision broad; the goal seemingly attainable but beyond the immediate reach. It was with these requisites in mind that I made the three essays referred to. To indicate, through the Department of Sociology, the purpose to influence the life of the State socially and economically. To indicate, through a Department of Fine Arts and of Music, the purpose to provide that development which is comprised in the term culture. To indicate, through the proposal concerning the World War history, the purpose, not only to encourage research and learning, but to influence the political life of the State and the nation by a deep and far-reaching study of history, an enquiry into the causes and consequences of present ills, and a consideration of the proper aspirations of the United States and of the functions of the State. History teaches, I believe, that the present tendency toward centralization must be arrested, if we are to attain the American ideals, and that for it must be substituted intense development of life through activities in the several states and localities. The problem is a very difficult one; but the local university is the most hopeful instrument for any attempt at solution.

Our university can become great, and serve this end, only if it is essentially Kentuckian—an institution for Kentuckians, developed by Kentuckians. For this reason, everything in the life of the State is worthy of special enquiry. Every noble memory must be cherished. Thus, the detail of Kentucky history, political, economic and social, become factors of ultimate importance. The biographies of its distinguished sons and daughters, including as such, Kentuckians who have lived and achieved elsewhere, are matters of significance. The University library should grow rich in Kentuckiana. It should become a depositary [*sic*] of unpublished manuscripts and like possessions associated with the life of the State and the achievements of Kentuckians.

Growth cannot be imposed upon the University. It must proceed mainly from within. The desire for worthy growth must be deeply felt by the executive officers and members of the faculty. It must be they who raise the University to standards and extend its usefulness. But the desire may be stimulated by suggestion; and achievement may be furthered by friendly aid. Thus, there is a large field for the efforts of those outside the University whose capacity, experience and position gives them a wider view and bolder vision; whose position enables them to secure for the University's projects the approval and support of the community; and whose means enable them to furnish financial aid. From them may come also the encouragement without which few achieve and that informed, friendly supervision, without which few persevere in the most painstaking labors.

If the development is to be both sound and fine, it is essential that the growth be gradual, continuous and manifold. Every department must be improved; some expanded, some divided. From time to time, new departments must be added and the functions of the University must be enlarged. This can be accomplished, in part, by single acts—specific gifts of buildings or the establishment of endowments, general or special. The recent Speed gifts are sure to be followed by similar ones from other persons. Alice and I think that the Adolf Brandeis family is equipped to promote the development of the University by a continuous service which, while less conspicuous, will be no less useful and should prove of enduring value. It is to take the part of the ever helpful sympathetic friend who, with thought, tact and patience, will awaken aspiration and encourage effort on the part of officers and members of the faculty; and also those without the University who may join in advancing the high purposes of the University. The family service which we have in mind is, in its general character, similar to that which is already being performed by Fanny and Maidie. If you and your Angehörigen[1] are willing to extend your operations, Alice and I will be glad to aid with our suggestions and with such part of our surplus income as may be wisely applied in the undertaking. The money required will doubtless increase with the expanding functions and intensive character of the work. But in this connection the service of money will resemble that of water in agriculture, always indispensable, always beneficent to the point where it becomes excessive, but of little avail unless the soil be rich, naturally or through fertilizers, unless there be appropriate cultivation, and unless the operations be conducted with good judgment.

This letter has grown so long that I must leave for another letter some suggestions which we wish make for immediate activities.

1. Relations.

To: Susan Brandeis
Date: March 20, 1925
Place: Washington, D.C.
Source: Gilbert MSS

DEAREST SUSAN: I supposed you noticed that I yielded the Second Circuit to Justice Stone;[1] so that you won't be embarrassed by my presence when you have to apply for a writ of error to that Circuit. I am in the 3rd now, so for your N.J. cases you will have to go to Stone J.[2]

Your not-beloved Rush Holland has resigned; Seymour is to go soon; and Beck, it is said, will resign in April.[3]

Yes, I recall your East Boston Finkelsteins.

Your N.Y. building situation seems rather to worsen than improve.[4]

That's a nice letter of Elsie Hills.   Lovingly

1. Harlan Fiske Stone (1872–1946) was dean of the Columbia University Law School until April 1924, when President Coolidge named him to be attorney general. In January 1925 Joseph McKenna resigned from the Supreme Court; after a few weeks Coolidge nominated Stone to the vacancy. The Senate confirmed him on 5 February. Despite some earlier connections to Wall Street (including J. P. Morgan & Co.), Stone became an ally of LDB while on the bench and during the 1930s was counted among the liberals on the Court. In June 1941 President Roosevelt elevated him to Chief Justice.

2. Although they had been freed from "riding circuit" since 1891, each Supreme Court justice was assigned to one of the Circuit Courts of Appeals (there were nine in 1925). The Second Circuit, which LDB had just left to Justice Stone, encompassed Vermont, Connecticut, and New York; the Third Circuit, to which he now moved, encompassed New Jersey (hence LDB's warning to his daughter that any of her cases arising there and requiring Circuit Court services would have to be brought to Stone), Pennsylvania, and Delaware. The justices' duties in the circuits were now limited to matters such has issuing injunctions, granting bail, and first hearing requests to stay executions.

3. In the wake of Stone's appointment to the High Court, the Justice Department experienced a major shake-up. Rush LaMotte Holland (1867–1944), a Colorado attorney, resigned as assistant attorney general on 19 March. Augustus Theodore Seymour (1873–1926), an Ohio lawyer, resigned his position as assistant to the attorney general later this month. And James Montgomery Beck (1861–1936), a noted conservative lawyer from New York and a constitutional authority, resigned the solicitor generalship on 29 April. Beck went on to serve as a congressman from Pennsylvania from 1929 to 1934.

4. LDB is probably referring to the spread of already serious strike activity among the building trades unions of New York City. The strike activity began in January, spread to the ironworkers in February, and was moving to plasterers and others in March. On this date the U.S. labor department sent a mediator to the city to help negotiate a settlement.

To: Susan Brandeis
Date: April 12, 1925
Place: Washington, D.C.
Source: Gilbert MSS

DEAREST:

1. That is an informing paper on Women Jurors. It will doubtless be used before the next session of the General Court.

2. Mother suggests that your "Mrs. Bayard" was probably Florence Bayard Hillis of Del.—wife (still I think) of quite a prominent lawyer.[1] She was the next younger sister of Mrs. Sam Warren (Mrs. W. died last year.) Mrs. Hillis [*sic*] has been very a very [*sic*] active member of the Woman's Party. I knew her well 40 years ago.

3. Elizabeth has talked over the place, time, and manner of the marriage. (She objects to the word, wedding).[2] It is to be at Chicago—near the end of June, probably, Dr. Hayden officiating. We (Mother & I) are not to be present. Eliz. & P. plan to come to Chatham on or before Aug 1, & before then to spend the time mainly in the Canadian Woods & probably some in Rochester.[3]

4. The above facts are presumably to be held in confidence. But the fact of the engagement is discussed freely.

5. Eliz. R.[4] says she called up your office & understood you were not to return until "Tuesday". She hopes to see you when next in N.Y.

6. Yes, as you assume, silence as to P. means that we like him very much.

7. We have heard nothing from Marion Calkins. Possibly Eliz. has & hasn't mentioned it. She & the others are hiking today.

Lovingly

1. The sister-in-law of LDB's former law partner and the daughter of former secretary of state Thomas F. Bayard, Florence Bayard married William Samuel Hilles (1865–1928), a Wilmington lawyer, in 1898.

2. Elizabeth Brandeis was about to announce her engagement to Paul Arthur Raushenbush (1898–1980), the son of the well-known Social Gospel minister and theologian Walter Rauschenbush. The two met at the University of Wisconsin and were to teach together there in the Economics Department for a short time. Paul Raushenbush then taught in the university's Experimental College but soon went into public service. He was a leader in the fight to win unemployment compensation benefits for Wisconsin workers and, during the 1930s, for American workers in general.

3. The Rauschenbusch family lived in Rochester, New York.

4. Perhaps Elisabeth Rauschenbusch, Paul's sister.

To: Susan Brandeis
Date: May 4, 1925
Place: Washington, D.C.
Source: Gilbert MSS

DEAREST SUSAN: That was a nice visit. Hope you found much joyous work awaiting you.

When we were talking yesterday afternoon, there came into my mind this passage from Pliny's letters no. X (which I have been reading recently in a 1747 edition Mother found for me).[1] Speaking of Euphrates: "Distinguished as he is by the sanctity of his manners, he is no less so by his polite and affable address. He points his eloquence against the vices, not the persons of mankind, and without chastising reclaims the wanderer."

Perhaps Jack has Pliny among his old books.

Godfrey Goldmark made a good short argument today.[2] He was fully prepared, & was evidently granted the opportunity by the lawyer in another case because of his superior qualifications. We had refused to grant him leave to argue his (advanced) case orally.   Lovingly

1. *The Letters of Pliny the Consul* (Cambridge, 1747). Pliny the Younger (61–113 A.D.) was a Roman administrator and man of letters.
2. Godfrey Goldmark (1880–1968) was the son of Ida Wehle and Adolf Goldmark. He was a New York City corporation lawyer. The case he argued was *Price v. U.S.*, 268 U.S. 685.

To: Susan Brandeis
Date: May 7, 1925
Place: Washington, D.C.
Source: Gilbert MSS

DEAREST SUSAN: You certainly seem to be a wonder on getting jobs.

And you select very good company for your Press Club associates.

Hope the Baltimore lady will appear with the funds.

I find that I haven't a blessed individual picture of myself. But I have one of the whole Court, duly signed, taken before Stone J. ascended to it. That I am sending to you under another cover.

Perhaps it is fortunate that none of my individual pictures remain, as Mother thought they were atrocious (and I did also).

I suppose the Court will subject itself soon to the photographer, as it is customary to do so after every ascension to the bench. And I plan to make a try then for an individual photograph.   Lovingly

To: Susan Brandeis
Date: May 14, 1925
Place: Washington, D.C.
Source: Gilbert MSS

MY DEAREST SUSAN: Re yours of yesterday:

406

1) If Jack is as familiar with his Schiller as with his Pliny, he will recall this from the Capucines [*sic*] in Wallenstein's Lager, Scene 8:

"Muss man den Mund doch, ich sollte meinen,
Nicht weiter aufmachen zu einem, Helf Gott,
Als zu einem Kreuz Sacherlot!"[1]

Everyone of any prominence, and most others, are subjected to interruptions and to unjustified and often impertinent requests, but such acts do not justify one subjecting the applicant to insult. Courteous refusal is a part of the law of noblesse oblige. Failure to exhibit courtesy is more degrading to him who fails to practice it, than it is to the victim.

2) Please get from Clara [Goldmark] the names & addresses of the other members of the Brandeis family to whom Eliz. announcement should be sent. We want to be careful not to offend anyone.
3) I don't think Eliz. would be happy in accepting much cash now. But later there may be occasion to enable her to get something that she will want.
4) We are delighted to know that Hapgoods are moving to Washington.

Lovingly

1. The lines LDB quotes are from "Wallenstein's Camp," the first section of the three-part historical drama *Wallenstein* by the great German dramatist and poet Friedrich Schiller (1759–1805). This passage is part of a denunciation, delivered by a Capuchin monk, of blasphemy. In Jeanne Willson's translation it reads: "It's just as easy, in my opinion, to ask God's help as to be crude and damn another by God's blood."

To:	Susan Brandeis
Date:	June 27, 1925
Place:	Chatham, Massachusetts
Source:	Gilbert MSS

DEAREST SUSAN: It's fine that you are to have so much time with Elizabeth on Wednesday and Thursday.

Dick Boekel [*sic*][1] and Auntie B. left this morning. The latter for a few days absence; (to see Mrs. Hodder[2] and Sacco and Vanzetti[3] incidentally) and mainly to move Miss Eugenia Gardiner[4] to Rockport. We expect Auntie B. back at latest on Thursday. Until then we expect to be alone, unless possibly Herman [*sic*] Blumgart[5] should turn up.

The McClennen (parents) are coming over for supper this evening; Persis,[6] who has developed finely, may come also.

Most of your tools (including 2 saws) have been sharpened; & I am about to engage in removing the rust. The old canoe has been painted by me & 2 coats of varnish given the outside. The inside remains to be sandpapered & varnished. You see how active and self-reliant we are. Auntie B. sets so fine an example.   Lovingly

1. Richard Martin Boeckel (1892–1975), an experienced Washington correspondent, founded *Editorial Research Reports* in 1923 and served as its editorial director. The organization supplied materials to numerous newspapers across the United States.

2. Mrs. Hodder was a friend of Elizabeth Glendower Evans ("Auntie B.").

3. Nicola Sacco and Bartolomeo Vanzetti were the principals in one of the most celebrated and controversial trials in American history. They were arrested and accused of murder in connection with the 1920 robbery of a payroll truck in South Braintree, Massachusetts. The two men were Italian immigrants, draft dodgers, and radicals. They were quickly convicted of the charges of robbery and murder. But the case was taken up by sympathetic liberals, radicals, writers, artists, civil libertarians, and many others. Their defenders claimed that the two were convicted because they were radicals and that the trial was characterized by great unfairness and obvious bias. After every legal maneuver was attempted and after every appeal for clemency denied, the two men were executed in August 1927. One of the earliest and most active participants in the attempt to gain a new trial for Sacco and Vanzetti was the Brandeises' friend Elizabeth Glendower Evans. LDB was sympathetic to the cause of Sacco and Vanzetti, but disqualified himself from entering the case hours before the execution, because two of his closest friends, Felix Frankfurter and Mrs. Evans, were deeply involved on behalf of Sacco and Vanzetti as were his wife, Alice, and daughter Elizabeth.

4. Eugenia Gardiner was Elizabeth Glendower Evans's sister.

5. Hermann Ludwig Blumgart (1895–1977) was a Boston physician and professor of medicine at Harvard. He became attached to LDB through his friendship with Felix Frankfurter.

6. Persis McClennen was the daughter of LDB's former law partner, Edward F. McClennen, and his wife. In 1927 she married Chester T. Lane, an English-born attorney practicing in New York City.

To: **Susan Brandeis**
Date: **June 29, 1925**
Place: **Chatham, Massachusetts**
Source: **Gilbert MSS**

DEAREST SUSAN: Hope you left New York as planned, had a good trip out, and will have joyous days at Chicago.[1]

We are having our first days alone. There has been much wind and weather, but not so much but that paddling was possible each day for a while; and there is much work about the place which requires attention. Our bald bluff has not yet acquired its green covering, & we are striving mightily despite a cloud of mosquitos.

Note enclosed letter from Uncle Al. After the ceremony, please write him a few lines about it. We have not told him either of the day or place or of the manner; and I should not like him to know of it first from the papers without details arriving more promptly than my letter would.

Lovingly

1. Susan had gone to Chicago to attend the marriage ceremony of her sister and Paul Raushenbush.

To: Susan Brandeis
Date: July 6, 1925
Place: Chatham, Massachusetts
Source: Gilbert MSS

DEAREST SUSAN: Your letter of the 3rd telling of Alice Greenacre's great case has come. I am writing before any mail from New York could have come, as I am going to the station to meet Mr. R. C. Ballard Thruston of Louisville, a great collector of Kentuckiana, with whom I want to discuss building up the University of Louisville & who is coming here at my suggestion. I hope I may induce him to help, as he can mightily.

From Elizabeth came a letter from Temagami Station where they arrived on time with nine (9) pieces of baggage. I guess the canoe will be heavily laden. Fortunately the occupants are light weights. They planned to lunch at the Hotel (which they must have regretted, unless a revolution set in there)[1] and to set out immediately thereafter.

Possibly you have heard all this & more.   Lovingly

1. In July 1921 LDB and Susan had camped and canoed in the same area of Canada where the Raushenbushes were now honeymooning.

To: Susan Brandeis
Date: July 12, 1925
Place: Chatham, Massachusetts
Source: Gilbert MSS

DEAREST SUSAN: I think there is a bus running from Wood's Hole to Chatham every 2 hours, through Hyannis, which would bring you here about 10 A.M.; or there may be some other bus connection made with the Cape Cod train which would serve you better. I will enquire & let you know.

Auntie B. washed the floor of your house carefully & the first coat of paint went on it yesterday, put there by her. I am oiling the walls which begin to look like rich mahogany. The job is not near done as it involves sand papering.

Jack must feel greatly encouraged with being able to stand on his foot, and the good progress made.

I am enjoying reading Goethe's "Italienische Reise"[1]—enjoying particularly the quality of the man which it exhibits, &, of course, also the memories of our stay in Italy   52 years ago.

Lovingly

President Eliot[2] at 91 just acknowledged the wedding card with a nice note.

1. Johann Wolfgang von Goethe, *Italienische Reise* (1816–17), was the reminiscence and travel account of his sojourn in Italy (1786–88) by the great German dramatist, poet, and philosopher (1749–1832).

2. Charles William Eliot (1834–1926) was the president of Harvard from 1869 until 1909. His success in transforming the school from a provincial college to the nation's leading university made him one of the most significant figures in the history of American higher education. LDB greatly admired Eliot from his days as a Harvard Law School student and his work on behalf of the Law School Association from 1886 until his appointment to the Supreme Court. Likewise, Eliot always maintained a cordial relationship to LDB; because of Eliot's national stature, his warm letter of praise on behalf of LDB's nomination in 1916 was an important moment in the long and acrimonious hearings. For Eliot's letter, see LDB to Stephen S. Wise, 18 May 1916, note 1, BL.

To:	Susan Brandeis
Date:	September 29, 1925
Place:	Washington, D.C.
Source:	Gilbert MSS

DEAREST SUSAN: Hope you arrived in good form & enjoyed the trial. You will recall the advice given me in 1878 by a wise litigant:

"Don't expect to win all your good cases or to lose all your bad ones."

Lovingly

To:	Susan Brandeis
Date:	October 6, 1925
Place:	Washington, D.C.
Source:	Gilbert MSS

DEAREST SUSAN:

1. Enclosed telegram from Mr. Charles R. Crane, and the cards from him & Mrs. Crane, accompanying a box of most beautiful flowers, came this afternoon.[1] You will have to write them your prettiest.

The roses Mother & I are keeping on commission.

2. Justice Van Devanter says you represented your case clearly, defined well the issue, and generally handled yourself well & tactfully.

3. Justice Sanford[2] said you presented your case well, clear and logically & that he had nothing to suggest except that you let your voice fall at times, so that he sitting at the end of the bench, could not hear. Have heard nothing from the others except Judge Holmes, as to which Mother reported.

4. I hope the welcome on return to your office will give promise of much interesting work during the coming year.

Lovingly

1. On 5 October 1925 Susan Brandeis argued a case before the United States Supreme Court. She and her partner Benjamin S. Kirsh represented Joseph P. Margolin, a New York attorney. Margolin was convicted in the Federal Court for the Southern District of New York and fined $250 for charging a fee more than the legally stipulated $3 for his services in filing an insurance claim to the U.S. Veterans' Bureau (Margolin had received $1,500 for his services). The Court of Appeals for the Second Circuit affirmed his conviction, even though the court acknowledged that Margolin had rendered services "worth many times the sum of $3," including conferences, a trip to Washington, D.C., railroad fare and hotel expenses, and a considerable investigation. Margolin's client, Mrs. Yetta Cohen, eventually recovered more than $12,000, with interest. Ms. Brandeis, who joined the case only at the final stage, the appeal to the Supreme Court, argued that the statute was erroneously construed by the Circuit Court of Appeals and that Congress intended to stipulate the $3 fee only for filing the necessary papers but never intended the law to prevent a lawyer from charging more for such extensive services. On 16 November 1925 the Court, speaking through Justice McReynolds, rejected the argument, stated that there was no reason to doubt "the plain language" of the statute regarding the $3 fee, and affirmed the decision of the lower court. See *Margolin v. U.S.*, 269 U.S. 93. Although no law required it, LDB recused himself from hearing the case and took no part in the deliberation. Susan Brandeis's appearance received national notice, including front page stories in the Boston newspapers and the *New York Times* (6 October 1925).

2. Edward Terry Sanford (1865–1930) graduated from Harvard Law School in 1889 and was a district court judge from Tennessee when President Harding nominated him to the Supreme Court. Closely allied with his longtime friend Chief Justice Taft (the two men were to die on the same day in 1930), Sanford served from 1923 until his death.

To: Susan Brandeis
Date: October 23, 1925
Place: Washington, D.C.
Source: Gilbert MSS

MY DEAREST SUSAN: This day brings us your letters of 21st and of 22d. We are happy to know that your heart and mind are at rest, and that the decision has come after full opportunity for consideration.[1]

A very wise man said to me many years ago: "Take all the time necessary for deliberation; but when you have decided, act thereon for life without doubting." Much change has come in the world since those words were spoken. But I fancy they embodied an eternal truth.

We shall be glad to see Jack any day. Court recess begins on Monday and continues three weeks.

It will be all right for you to come for Sunday Nov 1st as you suggest.

Do you know Alexander B. Siegel? He made a very good presentation in a somewhat complicated case.[2] Knew well his record and the law, and stated his position clearly, forceably [*sic*] and tactfully.   Lovingly[3]

1. See LDB to Susan Brandeis, 6 February 1925. After a period of reflection, Susan Brandeis and Jacob ("Jack") Gilbert decided to marry. The couple announced their engagement on 9 December, and the ceremony took place on 29 December. Felix Adler, leader of the Ethical Culture Society and the bride's uncle, performed the ceremony at his "meeting house" on Central Park West and 64th Street. Adler, of course, was the one who had joined Susan's parents in marriage back in 1891.

2. Alexander Bernard Siegel (1885–1954) was a New York attorney and senior partner in Siegel & Brownstein. He was also an expert in the game of bridge and wrote on that subject (under the name W. W. Wentworth). On 22 and 23 October Siegel had argued a multifaceted case involving a suit against the Alien Property Custodian. See *Hicks v. Guiness,* 269 U.S. 71 (1925).

3. At the end of this letter AGB appended the following note: "I was very glad to get yr two letters & I think we understand. It will be good to see you. My love always, Mother."

To: **Susan Brandeis**
Date: **December 20, 1925**
Place: **Washington, D.C.**
Source: **Gilbert MSS**

DEAREST SUSAN: We shall expect you for dinner Tuesday.

Hope Mother will be well along toward recovery—from a stomach upset which came last night & was sufficiently painful to have had us call Dr. Ecker[1] at 6 this morning. It was of the same character as the upset in Chatham in August, but seems to have been much lighter; and Mother has had good hold of herself. Dr. Erving[2] was in later & will come again today.

Mr. Ray Stevens was in Friday (with Mr. Rublee) to pay his obeisance to Mother—as his "Kingmaker". He has been appointed counselor to the King of Siam—as the result of her suggestion I submitted to Felix F[rankfurter]. at Mother's request; Felix to Prof. Sayre;[3] & Prof Sayre to the King. (S. had been his counselor for 2 years & succeeded in abrogating all the treaties with the Europeans for extra-territorial rights & tariff subjection).[4]

Lovingly

Please make sure that the marriage notice to Prof. Calvert Magruder, Cambridge, includes Mrs. Magruder and to Mr. Robert N. Miller,[5] Southern Bldg. Washington, Mrs. Miller. Both of these married in October.

1. Dr. Ecker was the Brandeises' family physician.

2. Emma Erving, a Washington orthopedist, was a close friend of LDB and his wife.

3. Francis Bowes Sayre (1885–1972) was a professor at the Harvard Law School. He married Woodrow Wilson's daughter Jessie in 1913 and was an insider in Democratic politics. In the 1930s President Roosevelt named him assistant secretary of state. Sayre's work with the Siamese government occurred from 1923 to 1925.

4. Ray Stevens served as counselor to the king of Siam from 1926 to 1935.

5. Robert Netherland Miller (1879–1968) was a tax lawyer. Originally from Louisville, Miller maintained offices both there and in Washington, D.C. Along with Felix Frankfurter, he was soon to become a chief consultant and ally in LDB's attempt to build up the University of Louisville School of Law.

To: **Susan Brandeis Gilbert**
Date: **January 1, 1926**
Place: **Washington, D.C.**
Source: **Gilbert MSS**

DEAREST SUSAN:

1. I am very glad that you are addressing your letters jointly to Mother & myself.

2. Mother sends enclosed cards.

3. It's good to hear of Jack's getting "an immense kick out of" (which I interpret as "approval of") my "Mrs. Susan Brandeis Gilbert[.]" I am sure that trade name would avert many a prejudice on the part of court, jury or client, as well as many a misunderstanding which Miss S.B. would encounter or lead to.

4. I didn't see the Thursday's Times. But I guess what you complain of was largely due to the failure of Jack's memo to reach the Times on Tuesday.[1] Elizabeth reports via the Adlers that two Times reporters made repeated essays on the Adlers Tuesday P.M. (& I think Wednesday) & were much put out at their not being advised etc.

5. Mother & I had an hour on the tow-path this morning—after I greeted the President etc.[2]

Lovingly

1. The *New York Times* did not report the Brandeis-Gilbert wedding, which occurred on 29 December, until its issue of 31 December.

2. Earlier in the day the Coolidges had hosted a gigantic New Year's Day reception at the White House for more than 3,000 dignitaries.

To: **Alfred Brandeis**
Date: February 6, 1926
Place: Washington, D.C.
Source: **Brandeis MSS**

DEAR AL: Glad to hear such good report of Jennie and Frank [Taussig].

I guess you are right about Iowa banks. Eugene Meyer told me some years ago that blue-sky investments[1] had so crippled them (holding hundreds of millions) that they would have failed in 1920–21, bringing down some large Chicago banks, but for War Corporation help.

Elwood Mead[2] was strong on Iowa over-valuation as a cause of farm troubles there; and Alvin Johnson[3] says its [*sic*] true of his native state, Nebraska. He says his father's farm, valued in his youth at $25 an acre, is really worth $75 now (based on earning power)—but was sold a few years ago at $250 an acre. He says, however, that nobody wants to foreclosure [*sic*], although mortgages are badly in default & that if the farms were deflated, the whole of the North & Middle West territory would go broke. [Carl S.] Vrooman admitted as much.

I wish to record my utter inability to understand why a lot of other folk don['t] go broke. These consolidations, & security flotations—plus the building boom, beat my comprehension—unless there is a break coming within the year.

    1. Investments that are unwise or fraudulent.
    2. Elwood Mead (1858–1936) was a well-known agricultural engineer. Because of his expertise in irrigation, he was employed by American Zionists to aid in several Palestine projects and became an authority on that country.
    3. Alvin Saunders Johnson (1874–1971), an important progressive economist, left teaching to work for the *New Republic* from 1917 to 1923, when he became head of the New School for Social Science Research in New York City. He retained that position until 1945. Johnson was also co-editor of the important *Encyclopedia of the Social Sciences.*

To: **Charles Gabriel Tachau**
Date: February 20, 1926
Place: Washington, D.C.
Source: **Brandeis MSS**

MY DEAR CHARLES: Re yours of 16th.

I wired you yesterday: "I approve. Glad to see Miss Flexner at nine thirty any day before March first."[1]

On that day our Court reconvenes & its work will be engrossing.

I approve of all save your expression "your libraries." Alice and I will aid. But if the libraries attain the worth we dream of, the achievement will be the work of the Louisville family—work which we hope will go forward long after we shall have passed away.

1. Mary Flexner (1873–1947), sister of LDB's friend Bernard, was considering assuming the duties of special librarian at the University of Louisville (but see the next letter). She graduated from Bryn Mawr in 1893 and earned a master's degree at Columbia in 1906. She spent most of her life as a teacher, but she and Bernard, both unmarried, were constant companions at the end of their lives.

To: Charles Gabriel Tachau
Date: February 24, 1926
Place: Washington, D.C.
Source: Brandeis MSS

MY DEAR CHARLES: Re yours of Feb 22.

You are entirely right in assuming that I approved generally of the plan for a special librarian,[1] and that my approval was not conditioned upon acceptance by Miss Flexner.

I am sorry she did not accept; because aside from her purely personal qualities, she possesses two qualifications of which, at least the first, seems almost essential to the achievement of what we have in mind. *First* she has the local knowledge. Some knowledge of Kentucky and Kentuckians will be required at almost every turn. *Second* she is a woman; and my experience in this kind of works [*sic*] leads me to think that we are more likely to get the results for an enduring task from a devoted woman than from the men who would ordinarily be available for work of this character. However, I am content to leave wholly to you and Dean Anderson[2] the selection of the special librarian. So you will consider what I have said merely as suggestions—not as conditions.

1. For the University of Louisville; see the previous letter.
2. Warwick Miller Anderson (1872–1943), a Louisville native, returned to his hometown—after doing graduate work at Johns Hopkins and the University of Chicago—to teach physics at the University of Louisville. He was appointed dean of the College of Liberal Arts in 1924.

To: Susan Brandeis Gilbert
Date: February 25, 1926
Place: Washington, D.C.
Source: Gilbert MSS

DEAREST SUSAN: Answering your enquiry:

1) I don't know anybody better suited to talk with B. G. Richards[1] than yourself.

I do not habitually contribute anything to the American Jewish Congress. I did give them $200 last year via Mr. deHaas to meet their deficit incurred by the Washington meeting, but I do not know whether my name was used by deHaas in making the gift.

> 2) I guess (because of Judicial office) I had better not see your anti-injunction bill.[2]

Don't fail to return the issue of the U.S. Daily for my files.

It was good to see Jack with his clients in tow. I was reminded of Father Brown with Flandreau.[3]   Lovingly

1. Bernard Gerson Richards (1877–1971) was a Lithuanian immigrant active in the Zionist movement. He was the editor of the Jewish periodical the *Maccabaean* and a leading force in the American Jewish Congress movement.

2. Perhaps Susan Gilbert was involved in drafting a bill to limit injunctions in labor disputes for the New Jersey legislature. Such a bill was introduced and passed in March.

3. Flandreau was the arch-criminal who plagued Father Brown, G. K. Chesterton's famous fictional detective.

To: **Susan Brandeis Gilbert**
Date: **February 26, 1926**
Place: **Washington, D.C.**
Source: **Gilbert MSS**

DEAREST SUSAN: Our loving greeting.[1]

It seems fitting that your first birthday after marriage should be spent at your birthplace among friends of the family, tried and true.

Father

I have written Auntie B. via Felix.[2]

1. On 27 February Susan would be thirty-three years old.

2. Susan Gilbert was in Boston for the seventieth birthday celebration of Elizabeth Glendower Evans, commemorated by a gala dinner in her honor, organized by Felix Frankfurter. LDB sent Frankfurter a letter to be read at the dinner.

To: **Susan Brandeis Gilbert**
Date: **March 8, 1926**
Place: **Washington, D.C.**
Source: **Gilbert MSS**

DEAREST SUSAN: Nothing from you since Friday except the Manchester Guardian. Has it taken you all this time to recover from the dinner that evening?

416

Judge Holmes on the 85th birthday was in fine form.[1] He seems good for 10 years more as Mr. Hapgood suggested in his article today.[2] By the way, I saw your copy of his "Common Law"[3] in Elizabeth's room. Do you want it sent on?

Hope you had a good week end.

Mother and I are reading F.W. Hirst's "Jefferson,"[4] an informing book.

Lovingly

1. On 14 March LDB wrote to Frankfurter: "OWH bore his birthday week in the pink of condition physically & mentally and in the most joyous spirits—despite heavy court work and nearly 100 letters answered. Your beautiful piece in the N[ew]R[epublic] will add to his happiness" (Urofsky and Levy, *"Half Brother, Half Son,"* 235).

2. Which one of the many anonymous articles commemorating Justice Oliver Wendell Holmes's eighty-fifth birthday on this date was written by Norman Hapgood is not known.

3. Oliver Wendell Holmes, Jr., *The Common Law* (Boston, 1881), was everywhere regarded as one of the great classics of American legal scholarship and an important contribution to the modernization of legal philosophy.

4. Francis W. Hirst, *The Life and Letters of Thomas Jefferson* (New York, 1926).

To: **Susan Brandeis Gilbert**
Date: **March 9, 1926**
Place: **Washington, D.C.**
Source: **Gilbert MSS**

DEAREST SUSAN: Mother and I are delighted to know that an office has been found satisfactory to you and Jack, and I am much relieved to hear that it is one with a good light.[1]

I sent to Jack today, as you suggested, Vol. I. of the Warren U.S.S.C. in History.[2]

It was nice to hear that the evening at Uncle Felix [Adler] went off so well. I thought he would seclude Jack, as he always did me after a dinner.

Elizabeth writes with great joy of the success of their first Open Forum meeting.   Lovingly

1. Ever since law school and his own traumatic experience with failing vision, LDB had been profoundly concerned with measures to conserve eyesight. See for example, LDB to Amy B. Wehle, 20 January 1877, and to Walter B. Douglas, 31 January 1878, BL.

2. Charles Warren, *The Supreme Court in United States History,* 3 vols. (Boston, 1922).

To: **Susan Brandeis Gilbert**
Date: **March 10, 1926**
Place: **Washington, D.C.**
Source: **Gilbert MSS**

DEAREST SUSAN: Is your new office in the Woolworth Bldg. If so, in what story? And are you actually in the tower? And when do you expect to move in? What becomes of Ben [Kirsh]?

Mabel made another good argument before us today. This time it was a corporation capital tax case.[1] The argument was closely knit, well reasoned and forcefully put. She has grown distinctly. The Solicitor General[2] was present—in the background, presumably to hear and see how she performed.   Lovingly

1. Assistant attorney general Mabel Willebrandt argued on this date *Edwards, Collector, v. Chile Copper Co.,* 270 U.S. 452. The case turned on whether the corporation was actually "engaged in business" in the years 1917–20 and therefore liable to the tax laws. The Court, through Justice Holmes, ruled that it was in fact in business and, as Willebrandt contended in her argument, was required to pay tax, thereby reversing two lower court judgments.

2. The solicitor general was William DeWitt Mitchell (1874–1955). Mitchell, whose work LDB greatly admired, was a Minnesota lawyer who was appointed solicitor general in 1925 and eventually served as Herbert Hoover's attorney general. Mitchell was to be the chief counsel to the congressional committee that investigated the attack on Pearl Harbor.

To: **Alfred Brandeis**
Date: **March 20, 1926**
Place: **Washington, D.C.**
Source: **Brandeis MSS**

MY DEAR AL: Today our birthday wishes go to you. I hope the day may bring joyous Zusammensein.[1]

My recollection is that we left Vienna between 9 & 10 A.M. on March 20 [1872], arrived in Gratz [*sic*] that evening, spent the night there, started, between 8 & 10 A.M. Mch 21 and arrived in Trieste about 5 P.M. Spent March 22 mainly in visit to Miramar. Took the steamer before supper, having supper on board, and arrived off Venice after 6 A.M. March 23 & land[ed] there before 8 A.M.

I am glad Hattie [Speed] is getting so much recognition for her U of L[ouisville] gifts.[2] Also that the Jews are becoming active givers.

1. Gathering. LDB's brother Alfred was seventy-two.
2. See LDB to Fannie Brandeis, 14 February 1925.

To: **Alfred Brandeis**
Date: **March 23, 1926**
Place: **Washington, D.C.**
Source: **Brandeis MSS**

DEAR AL: Your greetings[1] came by the morning's mail.

You seem to remember the Italian days [of 1872] so well, perhaps you can say definitely:

   (a) How long we had Mueller as guide & where
   (b) How long & where Buchler was with us.

Frank [Taussig] called today. We were sorry to miss him & to find that he had "checked out" of the Cosmos [Club] before we could telephone there.

I called at Dudley's office & was very glad to find him there at 4 P.M. &, as he says, in better shape than at any time in 2 years—due to "transfusion" treatment, ultimately tried by the Johns Hopkins folk. I saw his wife also (and a child) who had come for him in the car.

Alice bids me tell you that Washington Flour, which she uses religiously under your instructions, is not obtainable anywhere in the city.

The terrific fluctuations in grains lead me to enquire whether the world has really gotten much benefit from the International Institute of Agriculture & other statistic-collecting agencies. It was said that knowledge so derived would prevent speculation & bring stability of prices.

   1. This was the thirty-fifth wedding anniversary of Alice and Louis Brandeis.

To:	Alfred Brandeis
Date:	March 28, 1926
Place:	Washington, D.C.
Source:	Brandeis, MSS

MY DEAR AL: I was interested in Gov. Bramlette's message[1]—and am glad to hear of Judge Kerr.[2] Will try to get into touch with him, but will leave the matter of Librarian[3] out of our talk, as this is for Charles [Tachau] & Dean Anderson.

Herbert White blew in the other evening. He is looking finely—much younger than recently, not so fat.

He told us much of Storrow[4] (who he thinks amassed a fortune of $40,000,000). From his estate, Herbert is to have Storrow's half of the boat & an endowed fund to cover the expense of running it.

Herbert was South with Storrow this winter—a part of the time at a small rich-man's club in No. Carolina (60,000 acres) and then visiting a friend in South Carolina (30,000). Lucullus was ein Hund dagegen.[5] Father would have said: "Nichts erfreuliches".[6] It is evident, you & I are relics of a past world—which I prefer.

Herbert is quite his old good self, not visibly affected by his rich associations (& no riches himself)—But he is also quite the same unregenerate boy whom I met 30 years ago.

The Frank Lyons are coming in to dine. He has won a great I[nterstate]. C[ommerce].C[ommission]. victory before the I.C.C. re Canal traffic and transcontinental rates.

[Edward F.] McClennen & wife turned up 10 days ago, having motored down from Boston. He argued a case in N.Y. En route & was to argue one here but our Court recessed before it was reached. We sent them back via Gettysburg & they were delighted with the trip.

1. Alfred had evidently sent his brother a message uncovered in one of his explorations of Kentucky history. Thomas E. Bramlette (1817–75) was the Civil War governor of Kentucky, 1863–67. Upon the completion of his term he moved to Louisville to practice law.

2. Charles Kerr (1863–1950), a Kentucky lawyer, served as judge of a Kentucky circuit court. Harding named him judge of the district court of the Canal Zone. Kerr was also interested in Kentucky history and edited a multivolume history of the state.

3. For the University of Louisville; see LDB to Charles Gabriel Tachau, 24 February 1926.

4. James J. Storrow died on 13 March 1926.

5. A dog by comparison. Lucius Licinius Lucullus (ca. 110–56 b.c.) was an immensely wealthy Roman military and political figure at the time of Pompey and Sulla.

6. "Not very pleasant."

To: Elizabeth Brandeis Raushenbush
Date: April 8, 1926
Place: Washington, D.C.
Source: EBR

DEAREST ELIZABETH: It is three weeks since your letter came.

1. Harold Laski has been in Monday, Tuesday, & Wednesday. We have had considerable talk & [I] find him one of the few surviving who hold Felix's & my views on current American problems. He further ingratiated himself with me by bringing a copy of the Hammonds' "Rise of Modern Industry,"[1] & by speaking most enthusiastically of your Eileen Power.[2] He says she is as beautiful and charming as she [is] talented & learned; & dresses uncommonly well. Her great book, he says, is the volume on the nunneries.[3]

You & Paul and Phil & Isen[4] will be interested to learn (what I suppose, is quasi-confidential) that the Faculty of London University declined—almost unanimously—an offer from the Rockefellers of 8 new professorships & provision for research work. Harold is almost as skeptical about the value of research endowments as I am. You & Paul, who are confronted with American niggardliness in university salaries, may be able to tell those in authority that poor England pays Harold 1000 pounds a year. Harold says that the University is determined to restrict numbers to 2500. There is more of his talk that must await Chatham.

2. While Harold was with me Tuesday Sidney Hil[l]man[5] came in & we three had an hour together. Of the S.H. attitude, I shall have much to tell when we meet. He is not as democratic as I had supposed.
3. I had a further talk with Mr. Hamilton.[6] I then told him of your urgent call for teachers as against researchers. He expressed himself definitely of that opinion, favoring research largely as a means of training & educating teachers.
4. I should think an employment insurance plank would be a more appealing campaign for the workers than cheap life insurance. But I suppose Mr. Eckern [*sic*] might fear the interests' opposition.[7] Of course, cheap life insurance is about the easiest way of saving money conceivable. But the "interests" fight strenuously against it. Miss [Alice H.] Grady has had a running feud on her job these six months,[8] but it looks as if the enemy would have a large casualty list. She is a wonderful fighter. Quite equal to Allan Breck.[9]

The enclosed statement shows the rapid rate of growth in recent years.[10] The current year's growth is even better. In March the premium income gained 42 percent over last year.

It is my hope, however, that *no* other state will try anything very like Saving Bank Insurance for some years to come.[11] It will be better for all that Mass[achusetts]. should have become thoroughly permeated with S.B.I. before it is tried anywhere else.   Lovingly

1. John L. Hammond and Barbara Hammond, *The Rise of Modern Industry* (London, 1925).
2. Eileen Edna Power (1889–1940), Laski's colleague at the London School of Economics since 1921, specialized in the social and economic history of medieval England.
3. *Medieval English Nunneries, c. 1275–1535* (Cambridge, 1922).
4. Philip Fox La Follette (1897–1965), the second son of LDB's old friend Robert La Follette, was already a rising figure in Wisconsin politics. Currently the district attorney for Dane County (Madison) and a lecturer at the University of Wisconsin Law School, he would serve as governor of the state (1931–33 and 1935–39). He was a close friend of Elizabeth and Paul Raushenbush, whose son Walter Brandeis Raushenbush was to write *Wisconsin under Governor Philip La Follette: A Study in Creative Government* (Cambridge, Mass., 1950). After a long engagement, he married "Isen," Isabel Bacon of Utah, on 14 April 1923.
5. Sidney Hillman (1887–1946) had known LDB since his service as chief clerk of the Garment Workers' Protocol in 1914. In 1915 Hillman became president of the Amalgamated Clothing Workers union, a position he held until his death. In the 1930s he was one of the

leaders of the breakaway Congress of Industrial Organizations and served as the CIO's vice-president. He was an important link between President Franklin Roosevelt and organized labor and became an unofficial advisor to the president.

6. Walton Hale Hamilton (1881–1958) was a close friend and frequent dinner guest of the Brandeises during these years. An economist and lawyer, he was presently at the Brookings Institution, but in 1928 he began a lengthy career at the Yale Law School. He wrote on both law and economics.

7. Herman Lewis Ekern (1872–1954) was a Wisconsin lawyer and political figure. He had been Speaker of the State House of Representatives in 1907. Ekern was involved in unemployment and insurance issues and was to be an important ally of the Raushenbushes in attempts to reform Wisconsin social welfare legislation.

8. LDB's former private secretary Alice Grady was named deputy commissioner of the Massachusetts Savings Bank Insurance system in 1920.

9. The bold outlaw in Robert Lewis Stevenson's 1886 novel *Kidnapped.*

10. In 1920 four banks were writing Savings Bank Insurance policies, and there were 30,834 policies in effect; in 1926 ten banks were participating, and there were 55,822 policies.

11. Not until 1938 did a second state, New York, adopt savings bank insurance.

To: **Stella and Emily Dembitz**
Date: **April 22, 1926**
Place: **Washington, D.C.**
Source: **Brandeis MSS**

MY DEAR STELLA AND EMILY:[1] In discussing, last year, with President Ford[2] the project of developing at the University [of Louisville] a worthy World War Library, I made the following suggestion which seemed to impress him deeply.

The liberation of lesser nationalities is prominent among the hopeful results of the War, and yet, their independence was won less by arms than by the slow process of education. It was largely the work of far seeing, patient, persistent, devoted men and women, who awakened in the rising generation an interest in the language, the literature, the traditions of their people, and through the acquisition of knowledge, developed the striving for liberty and opportunity and the fuller life. This is true of the liberation of Czechs, Slovaks, and Yugoslavs; of the Finns, Letts, Esthonians and Lithuanians; of the Irish and the Poles; and of other peoples. In these victories of ideas, America had an important part. Our War of Independence was an inspiration and an encouragement. And, throughout long years, there came from men and women of these nationalities living in happier America, money and other supplies for these campaigns of education. Finally when the war came, committees of these nationals, formed in America, lent, in many ways, important aid.

These struggles, rich in heroic incident and noble achievement, present material for some of the most promising chapters in the [history] of mankind. The University should have in its library, not only the books in which

422

the events are summarized, but, so far as possible, the contemporary publications which were themselves acts in the process of liberation, or which record in detail events of importance. Louisville has among its citizens men and women of many of the liberated nationalities; and among these, doubtless, some who aided materially in their struggles for independence. That the University purposed making such collections and desired their cooperation to that end, of these of its citizens, when announced, [would] be an event of civic significance. It would indicate the breadth of Louisville's hospitality; its appreciation of all contributions to civilization, regardless of the nationality of those who made them, and that what was noble and fine in the tradition of all the peoples of which its population is composed, is to be cherished as a subject for generous study. Thus would be made clear that the University is the University of all, regardless of race, or creed, and however recent their migration to America; and that all should endeavor to work through it for the city's finest development.

Among the peoples to whom the war brought the opportunity of liberty and development are the Jews of Eastern Europe and of other lands of oppression. Through the Balfour Declaration, the ages long dream of the Jewish Homeland became possible of realization. Through my connection with the Zionist movement during the last fourteen years, I chance to have made a collection of the publications in which, to a considerable extent, the ideas and events are recorded which have led to the Rebirth of Palestine. These, with some unpublished documents of historic value I purpose offering to the University; and also funds to provide for the necessary cataloguing[,] binding, shelving and purchases to supplement the collection. All would be an appropriate addition to the books on Jewish life and thought which the generous gift of Adath Israel Congregation is bringing to the University. The collection would surely be enriched, in course of time, by many valuable contributions of other volumes and documents. And it is reasonable to expect that these gifts will lead Louisvillians of other nationalities to aid similarly in the efforts of the University to develop a worthy World War Library.

I should like that this offer to the University be made through you, with the suggestion that if it is accepted, you will share the burden of supervision by associating with yourselves some member of the faculty, or other member of the community, having special interest in this subject.[3] That the offer should be made through you seems peculiarly fitting for the following reason. To your father the recent growth of the University would have given great joy. To those of my generation he was a living university. With him, life was unending intellectual ferment. He grappled eagerly with the most difficult problems in mathematics and the sciences, in economics, government and politics. In the diversity of his intellectual interests, in his longing to discover truths, in his pleasure in argumentation and in the process of thinking, he reminded of the Athenians. He loved books as a vehicle of knowledge and an inciter to thought; and he made his love contagious. It is appropriate that his influence should be remembered in the library where he would have worked. A collection of books is the memorial for which he would have cared most. And the collection which tells of Palestine's rebirth seems the most appropriate.

For the deepest of his studies were those allied to the Jewish religion. He was orthodox. He observed the law. But he was not satisfied with merely observing it. He sought to understand the law. And to find its reason, he studied deeply in the history of the Jewish people. His was not the drive of intellectual curiosity with the realm of dead knowledge. He recognized in the past the mirror of the future—a noble and glorious one for his people. It was natural that he should have been among the first in America to support Herzl in his effort to build a New Palestine.

If it will be agreeable to you to aid in this undertaking, I shall send you later the details as to the collection, and some suggestions for supplementing it. Your cousin

1. Stella and Emily Dembitz were daughters of LDB's favorite uncle, Lewis Naphtali Dembitz (1833–1907), a man who had been a formative influence on the young LDB. A brilliant scholar and accomplished lawyer, Dembitz practiced in Louisville and wrote several legal treatises. He was also a devout Jew and scholar of Jewish life. To honor his uncle and to recognize what his example had meant to him, LDB changed his middle name from "David" to "Dembitz."

2. Arthur Younger Ford (1861–1926), a journalist and businessman, became the president of the University of Louisville in 1922.

3. Rabbi Joseph Rauch (1881–1957), longtime leader of Louisville's Adath Israel Congregation, agreed to serve in this capacity.

To: Alfred Brandeis
Date: May 2, 1926
Place: Washington, D.C.
Source: Brandeis MSS

MY DEAR AL: Alice shipped her nurse yesterday 8 P.M. & we celebrated today with two hours on the Potomac in heavenly weather.

Ben Flexner's report on Palestine was encouraging. Relations with Arabs so friendly that there is at present no Arab problem. The English army has been withdrawn & there is only a very moderate police in the country. The budget of the Mandate territory is, I, understand, balanced.

Malaria situation eminently satisfactory. Immigration about 2500 a month. That is quite as large as it should be, making a percentage addition to the Jewish population of about 20 to 25 percent a year.

I have written Jessie C[ochran] as James Speed desired.

I saw your friend Judge Kerr today, & Walker Hines[1] the day before. H. looks blooming.

Gruesse

1. Walker Downer Hines (1870–1934) was a Kentucky-born lawyer who specialized in railroad affairs. Long associated with the Louisville & Nashville and the Atchison, Topeka, & Santa Fe, Hines worked in railroad regulation during World War I.

To:　　　**Susan Brandeis Gilbert**
Date:　　**May 11, 1926**
Place:　　**Washington, D.C.**
Source:　**Gilbert MSS**

DEAREST SUSAN: It is fine to have your reports on Madison, and of the homecoming.

There goes to you by express today a box containing some Victor Records which Mother unearthed & in which you and Jack may be interested; also some papers of yours re War Activities which you may care to have or to destroy.[1]

Mother has unearthed also a group photograph of the Court, as it was constituted in the 1916 Term—my first on the Court. I should be glad to send it to you, if you & Jack care to have it.

We were on the Potomac today for an hour in beautiful sunshine.

Has Elizabeth reported to you fully on our "New Fall Styles"?

Lovingly

1. The Brandeises were about to move to new apartments, and in the process of packing up their possessions AGB earmarked numerous items, in this and other letters in the spring of 1926, for possible shipment to her newly married daughters. See LDB to Alfred Brandeis, 11 September 1926.

To:　　　**Susan Brandeis Gilbert**
Date:　　**June 2, 1926**
Place:　　**Washington, D.C.**
Source:　**Gilbert MSS**

DEAREST SUSAN: Mother bids me say:

   A. She is sending you
      (a) Your silver napkin-ring.

(b) The amber hair-pin which she got from Grandma Brandeis (& which Eliz. used to wear occasionally). She thinks Jack will like to see it in your hair.

B. She wants to send you, if you & Jack would like them, all or any of the following:

(a) The Vienna brass coffee-machine (for use at table) which Grandma Brandeis gave us.

(b) The Barrie [*sic*] lion[1] (plaster) which Margaret Deland gave us.

(c) Two small silver-plated single candle sticks & two double candle sticks for use at dining table.

C. She suggests that she send you the heavy double hair mattress to be made over (with a little additional hair) into two mattresses for the new beds. She says she did the like for Elizabeth & that it yielded a saving of $30 or $40 as against two new mattresses. If you approve please let us know promptly to what address in N.Y. the mattresses shall be sent.

Also let Mother know about B. *supra* so that the packing can be attended to before we leave [for Chatham]. Lovingly

1. Antoine Louis Barye (1795–1875) was a French sculptor and painter who specialized in sculpting animals in the romantic style. He was thought to be one of the most accomplished animal sculptors in history.

To: **Susan Brandeis Gilbert**
Date: **June 7, 1926**
Place: **Washington, D.C.**
Source: **Gilbert MSS**

DEAREST SUSAN: Jack may care to see the above clipping and Oliver Garrett (whose article in this week's N.R. you have doubtless seen)[1] may care to have it.

Mother has unearthed the wrought-iron stand for the hanging kettle (given us by Mr. Wigglesworth) which used to stand at 6 Otis Place[2] in our dining room & thinks you & Jack may like it. Poindexter has instructions so that he can pack & ship it on request.

I am venturing to send you (with the plaster cast whence it goes) my certificate of entry into the Zionist Golden book; also my first certificate of admission to the bar—Louisville Oct 24, 1878; also my Harvard Diplomas, as you have become the custodian of the family mementos. To Jack I am sending the copy of O.W. Holmes addresses (1891)[3] given me then by O.W.H.

You & Jack may be interested in enclosed copies of letters to Stella [Dembitz] & Dean Anderson & memo of Collections on Liberation of Lesser Nationalities (which please return).[4]

The sun shines again today after much gray cold weather.

We still plan to leave on the Federal today.[5] Boston address—Hotel Bellevue.

Lovingly

1. Oliver Hart Palmer Garrett (1897–1952) was a reporter for the *New York World*. In 1927, however, he would begin his long career as a Hollywood screenwriter. His article "Politics and Crime in Chicago," *New Republic* 47 (9 June 1926): 78–80, was an examination of the connections between gangsters and politicians. The piece was occasioned by a new grand jury investigation of the murder of assistant state's attorney William H. McSwiggin, gunned down in a dive while in the company of a known gangster and ward politician.

2. The Brandeises' address in Boston, before 1916. The gift was from George Wigglesworth, LDB's old friend and ally in the Savings Bank Insurance fight. By a coincidence, LDB and Wigglesworth lunched together in Boston on the day after this letter was written.

3. *Speeches by Oliver Wendell Holmes, Jr.* (Boston, 1891). See also LDB to Holmes, 25 October 1891, BL.

4. See LDB to Stella and Emily Dembitz, 22 April 1926.

5. For Chatham, with an overnight stay in Boston.

To:	Susan Brandeis Gilbert
Date:	June 12, 1926
Place:	Chatham, Massachusetts
Source:	Gilbert MSS

DEAREST SUSAN: Mother & I opened your house in solemn state yesterday & found it and contents in perfect condition. Due doubtless in part to Paul [Raushenbush]'s skil[l]ful carpentry, the house seems to have been rain and wind tight, although the gales & storms have been fierce in this region. Much of the brush we put on the bluff has been blown far away.

We had some asparagus yesterday from our patch; and Auntie B. reports that a large supply of radishes may be expected.

Quite a large boat (in wrecked condition) has been swept ashore near our bath house—as appropriate an addition to the landscape as a cow on the hill-side.

Mother appreciates your and Jack's thoughtfulness in suggesting a Victrola, but it will be better not to bring one. We considered, some time ago, the proper distribution of the world's goods & enjoyments & concluded that the Victrola should be limited to the Washington season.

Lovingly

To:	Susan Brandeis Gilbert
Date:	August 21, 1926
Place:	Chatham, Massachusetts
Source:	Gilbert MSS

DEAREST SUSAN: Mother bids me say that it will be fine to have you and Jack here again—arriving Friday morning before Labor Day and leaving Tuesday P.M. after Labor Day. Mrs. Hodder will probably be here then.

Yes[ter]day was exceptionally fine weather, sunny and Northeast wind; so sunny as to conceal how cool it was. When I returned from an early visit to the barbers Paul & Eliz. had already left for a long sail, and with this example of truancy set, Mother & Auntie B. were eager to be off also. So we paddled to Gould's & walked over to the Nantucket Sound beach. There Auntie B. & Mother bathed & I walked off westward. With our new binock[1] I saw Paul & E. off South Chatham & was able to cross-examine as to their movements in coming about. Elizabeth insists that there is no privacy left. Even on the high seas.

Mother bids me tell Jack, that the bunches of grapes were developing a serious blight, and that the two new broome plants (while in a more hopeful state) are still in precarious health. Such are the agonies of farmers.

Auntie B. hasn't had her moonlight paddle yet. Thursday evening we had fires in both dining room & living room; last evening in the latter. Today it is again cold & somewhat less sunny.

Elizabeth walked over yesterday to return Lucy Gregory Henderson's call & got some points given from Marion Maclay on sailing.

It's fine for you to have had so cordial a greeting from Judge Mack, & the reminder of earlier bankruptcy experiences.

Aunt Susie [Goldmark] has written that she will not make the Chatham visit, as she wants to stay with Aunt Do to help cheer Uncle Henry [Goldmark].

Lovingly

You were right in your prophecy about Passaic & the A.F. of L. Com[mit]tee—Botany Mills leave an ominous reminder of Botany Bay.[2]

---

1. Binoculars.

2. Susan Gilbert had been working with the strikers in the bitter Passaic, New Jersey, textile strike throughout the year. It was a classic labor dispute of the 1920s with violence and brutal repression on both sides. The workers claimed intolerable working conditions; the owners charged that the strike was being fomented by Communist agitators. The latest plan for ending the hostilities was to form a new union under the auspices of the American Federation of Labor. On the previous day, however, the vice-president of the Botany Worsted Mills, one of the chief firms resisting unionization, announced that his company would refuse to recognize an AFL union. Botany Bay, of course, was the notorious British penal colony in New South Wales, Australia.

To: Susan Brandeis Gilbert
Date: August 24, 1926
Place: Chatham, Massachusetts
Source: Gilbert MSS

DEAREST SUSAN:

1) Mother bids me say that there is a spare swinging mirror here (like that on my chiffonnier) which Jack may like for shaving & that you should look at when you come.

2) Yesterday was again a day for land expeditions. We introduced Auntie B. to endless stores of blue-berries in the woods behind the Palmers[1] and wandered off ourselves into the region of the swamp behind, rich in cedars and arbor vitae. In the afternoon, we marshalled Mr. Rich, called on aged Mrs. Sears (who was out);—then Mother & Auntie B. called at the Chatham Bars on Mrs. Carne (who was also not in) & later proceeded to North Chatham to see Mrs. Rich & her house.

I meanwhile called at the Carrol [*sic*] Wights.[2] I found him reading Aristophanes. After my call, he escorted me home & talked Kant. I felt that I had been in very good company.   Lovingly

1. Harris Palmer (1861–1934) was a year-round resident of Chatham, living about half a mile from the Brandeises' summer home. He occasionally did work on their property.

2. Carol Van Buren Wight was a summer neighbor of LDB's at Chatham. Besides teaching Greek at Johns Hopkins University, Wight wrote several volumes of poetry.

To: Susan Brandeis Gilbert
Date: September 10, 1926
Place: Boston, Massachusetts
Source: Gilbert MSS

DEAREST SUSAN: Elizabeth & Paul will bring you all news of us.

Mother says, sour cream won't do for the scallop soup & that for recipe see Boston Cook Book which she assumes you have.[1]   Lovingly

1. No doubt the famous Fannie M. Farmer, *The Boston Cooking-School Cook Book,* which was originally published in 1896 and ran through numerous editions.

To: Susan Brandeis Gilbert
Date: September [?], 1926
Place: Washington, D.C.
Source: Gilbert MSS

DEAREST SUSAN: The letter enclosed by [*] was an explanation by Pres[iden]t Harding, [who,] while Senator, voted against my confirmation. His Secretary (Christian)[1] says it was because of my radicalism actual or supposed.[2]

I am sending you some bankruptcy publications which more appropriately should have gone to you.

Lovingly

Mother sends the enclosed to Jack.

Tell Jack I am glad he had so satisfactory a talk with Uncle Henry [Goldmark].

1. George Busby Christian, Jr. (1873–1951), of Marion, Ohio, was the general manager of the White Sulphur Stone Co. when Warren Harding made him his private secretary.
2. Actually, the vote on LDB's confirmation in 1916 was nearly a straight party vote; only three progressive Republicans voted for LDB while twenty-one members of the party, including Senator Harding, voted against.

To: **Alfred Brandeis**
Date: **September 11, 1926**
Place: **Washington, D.C.**
Source: **Brandeis MSS**

DEAR AL: Our trip was carried through per schedule. Reached the [Hotel] Bellevue [Boston], 7:15 Thursday, Miss Grady meeting us at station—and the Frankfurters & Hermann Blumgart for dinner that evening.

Friday A.M. Elizabeth & Paul arrived from their glorious camping (river [*], rapid shooting canoe trip). At luncheon Friday, they, Walter Child, Felix Frankfurter & Miss Grady were with us; and at 6:35 Miss Grady went with us from South Station to Back Bay.

I was at 161 Devonshire[1] all morning where i.a. Herbert White came in & told of his great trip off Labrador to 54° from which he had returned (in Cachil of N[ova] S[cotia]) two days before. He sailed for 400 miles along the iceberg lane, & saw at one time 20. He is his old self.

Walter Child spends his time mainly at E[ast]. Walpole now. With Anna, keeping up his spirits, etc. Charles Bird has been sick for 18 months & probably won't live long.[2]

At the Bellevue, on Thursday evening I had a meeting which should "ring bells" for you. Do you remember Otto Michaels, the handsome soldier boy who was at Uncle Gottlieb's courting Bertha[3] & who showed his strength by tossing me into the air? Was it in 1862 or in 1864? His son George Michaels reminded me of seeing him 30 years ago.

We are in our new apartments,[4] the living apartment No. 505—my study No. 601, above it. We hope you will come & see them soon. The 505 you will like; & the lady would like to see you.

Sadie [Nicholson] came here in August to move to 505 (with Poindexter's help); and the latter moved my office effects into 601; so there is only rearranging for me to do, and Alice too, will not have overmuch to do to get us into rights below.

As you may infer, 505 is on the fifth floor; 601 on the sixth. Eliz. & Paul are spending today in N.Y. with Susan & Jack, and with Paul's sisters & brothers & are to settle for 6 months in Philadelphia, where studies are to be made for their PhD's.[5]   Gruesse

1. LDB's old Boston law office.
2. Charles Bird, Anna Child's husband, died in October 1927.
3. Gottlieb Wehle (1802–81) was related to LDB in several ways. Most directly he was AGB's grandfather. Bertha was one of his ten daughters.
4. The Brandeises had moved to Florence Court West (California St., NW). On 3 September LDB confided to Julian Mack: " 'Improvements' have at last driven us from Stoneleigh [Court]."
5. Elizabeth completed her Ph.D. in November 1927. Her dissertation was entitled "The Wage-Earner and the Common Rule—A Study in the Employer-Employee Relation." The degree was awarded by the University of Wisconsin in 1928. Paul never completed a doctorate.

To: **Alfred Brandeis**
Date: **September 18, 1926**
Place: **Washington, D.C.**
Source: **Brandeis MSS**

DEAR AL: I think you have the steamboat gent nailed to the mast on Great Eastern electric lights. Of course there was an arc-lamp long before the incandescent—but not in the early days of the Great Eastern; & I doubt whether at any time before 1875.

I can't aid you as to date of seeing either Great Eastern or Great Western.

But I am sure were [*sic*] went East in 1861 & 1862 (both at Long Branch)—1864 & 1865, both at Newport. In 1862 we came back over the Erie line (broad guage) [*sic*] with Mr. Tachau & we four children & his feet occupied one seat on the day coach.

Alice bids me enclose this of Edna Ferber's book on River traffic[1]—it was Edna F. who introduced a "Fanny Brandeis" in a book, 10 years or so ago.[2]

Under another cover Alice sends a play of Fulda's which she thinks Jennie may enjoy.[3]

1. *Show Boat* (Garden City, N.Y., 1926). Edna Ferber (1887–1968), the popular American writer, produced numerous plays, novels, and short stories.
2. *Fanny Brandeis* was the steamboat operated by the business of Adolph Brandeis, LDB and Alfred's father.
3. One of the works of the prolific German dramatist and translator Ludwig Fulda (1862–1939).

To: Susan Brandeis Gilbert
Date: September 25, 1926
Place: Washington, D.C.
Source: Gilbert MSS

DEAREST SUSAN: Mother bids me thank you & Jack for the offer of the Trevellyan [*sic*];[1] but we do not care to read this volume. We have his "England in the Nineteenth Century"—which reaches back pretty far into the Eighteenth & also read his "Lord Grey & the Reform Bill".[2] So we are reaching out into other fields.

I personally am trying to see what has been thought (and said) on American governmental problems & have just read Prof. Lindsay Rogers on the "American Senate",[3] which gives some illumination as well as fireworks.

We are glad you & Jack are to lunch at the Nathan Strauses. Mother sends this nice letter to her with enclosure.

What was Bertie's investment in the made-over house?

Elizabeth writes with extraordinary enthusiasm of William P. Hapgood's and Henry S. Denison's Industrial talks.[4]   Lovingly

1. George Macaulay Trevelyan (1876–1962) was the son of the historian George Otto Trevelyan and the great nephew of Thomas B. Macauley. His own researches in the histories of England and modern Italy, together with his sparkling style, made him one of the leading historians of the twentieth century. He taught at Cambridge after 1927. Perhaps Susan and Jack had offered LDB his newest book, a one-volume *History of England* (London, 1926).

2. *British History in the Nineteenth Century, 1772–1901* (London, 1922) and *Lord Grey of the Reform Bill, Being the Life of Charles, Second Earl Grey* (London, 1920).

3. Lindsay Rogers, *The American Senate* (New York, 1926). Rogers (1891–1970) was currently at Harvard teaching political science. He would move to Columbia in 1929. Rogers wrote numerous books and articles on political topics.

4. Both Powers Hapgood and Henry Denison had addressed the meeting of the Congress of American Industry, in Philadelphia, earlier in the week. William Powers Hapgood (1872–1960) was a brother of Norman and Hutchins. He was a manufacturer and the president of the Columbia Conserve Co., a cannery near Indianapolis. Hapgood received national notice for his progressive labor policies, his commitment to industrial democracy, profit-sharing, and medical benefits for his employees.

To: Susan Brandeis Gilbert
Date: September 27, 1926
Place: Washington, D.C.
Source: Gilbert MSS

DEAREST SUSAN: Mother has found—belonging to you—these three silver pieces.

1. The porringer or dish sent you by Mr. Denman Ross—from Florence on learning of your birth.

2. Silver spoon given Mother for you about the same time by Aunt Julia [Wehle Oettinger].
3. A silver lifting fork & spoon which was given to Grandmother Brandeis at her wedding & which has been passed via Mother to you.

Please answer by return mail whether you are now ready to receive these.

Mr. Eastman, his sister, the Boekels [*sic*] & Mary Switzer[1] were in last evening, and Friday Dr. [Leo S.] Rowe dined with us to bring us au fait[2] on Latin-American affairs. Lovingly

1. Mary Elizabeth Switzer (1900–1971) worked with Elizabeth Brandeis on the District of Columbia Wage Board, and the two became good friends. Switzer continued in the federal service in several agencies and departments, becoming one of the highest-ranking women in the federal government.
2. Up to date; proficient in the facts.

To: **Susan Brandeis Gilbert**
Date: **October 1, 1926**
Place: **Washington, D.C.**
Source: **Gilbert MSS**

DEAREST SUSAN: Mother bids me advise you that she procured, as a greeting for Elizabeth, Portia Marries,[1] & that this was accomplished, not by purchase, but from the circulating library opposite at a net cost of 10 cents— for 5 days. Lovingly

1. Jeanette Clarke Gibbs, *Portia Marries* (Boston, 1926).

To: **Susan Brandeis Gilbert**
Date: **October 6, 1926**
Place: **Washington, D.C.**
Source: **Gilbert MSS**

DEAREST SUSAN: Mother bids me say, as to Bliss Perry, that he was sometime editor of the Atlantic, longtime Professor of English at Harvard and a very agreeable person.[1] But she doubts whether Emerson Journals were worth publishing; because Eliot [*sic*] Cabot,[2] Emerson's literary executor, spent 30 years largely on editing Emerson's literary remains & did not see fit to publish the journals.[3]

Thank Jack for the literature. I submitted the [*] article to P[aul].& E[lizabeth]. That on New England I shall send to Uncle Al.

We are sorry Aunt Sue [Goldmark]'s visit had to be deferred.

There was a very crowded courtroom Monday & work has set in. Tell Jack all the Court seem in good form. Judge Holmes a bit younger than last year.   Lovingly

1. Bliss Perry (1860–1954), the prominent editor, teacher, and literary critic, had just produced *The Heart of Emerson's Journals* (Boston, 1926). For Perry's career, see his reminiscence, *And Gladly Teach* (Boston, 1935).

2. James Elliot Cabot (1821–1903) was an architect, a man of letters, and a close friend of Emerson's. He supervised the publication of twelve volumes of Emerson's work as the Riverside Edition.

3. Actually, Cabot refrained from publishing material from the journals because Emerson's death had been so recent and many contemporaries were still alive; by the time of his own death, Cabot was ready to authorize their publication for the Centenary Edition, edited by Edward Waldo Emerson, the philosopher's son.

To: **Susan Brandeis Gilbert**
Date: **October 7, 1926**
Place: **Washington, D.C.**
Source: **Gilbert MSS**

DEAREST SUSAN: Mother sends you this:

Susan for t.t. San Francisco 3.84.

She asked to pay us then.[1]

Mother has paid this.

Tell Jack that I saw his Uncle Jacob of Cincinnati for a moment at Court yesterday. He looks as if he were about Jack's age.

The Edward Keatings, Father Ryan,[2] Eva Kean and Thomas Corcoran,[3] Judge Holmes['s] secretary, are coming in for dinner & later Bob Page.[4]

We started our Victrola concerts yesterday with a Wagner evening. The music comes out much clearer in this apartment.[5]

Why should Siegel have a dinner? Is he being boomed again for the expect[ed] District vacancy?[6]   Lovingly

1. These two lines were in Elizabeth Brandeis Raushenbush's handwriting.

2. John Augustine Ryan, S.J. (1869–1945) was a frequent guest of the Brandeises. A professor of moral theology and industrial ethics at the Catholic University, Ryan was a leader of the liberal wing of the American Catholic Church. He wrote widely on social and moral issues, and in 1933 Pius XI elevated him to the rank of domestic prelate.

3. Thomas Gardiner Corcoran (1900–1981) was one of Felix Frankfurter's favorite students. After clerking for Justice Holmes, he practiced law in New York City. With the coming of the New Deal, "Tommy the Cork" became one of the most influential lawyers in the country—a confidant of President Roosevelt, a highly effective lobbyist, and, with Benjamin V. Cohen, the author of important New Deal legislation. During all of these years LDB remained in close contact with Corcoran and greatly respected his energy and ability. After the Supreme Court's rejection of FDR's legislation and the "Court-packing" scheme of 1937, however, Corcoran and LDB grew apart and saw little of one another.

4. Robert Guthrie Page (1901–70) was LDB's law clerk for the 1926–27 term. LDB and Frankfurter hoped that he would eventually return to teach at Harvard (see LDB to Frankfurter, 30 November 1926, BL), but Page went into private practice in New York City. In 1947 he rose to the presidency of the Phelps Dodge Corporation. See also LDB to Frankfurter, 13 October 1929, BL.

5. See LDB to Alfred Brandeis, 11 September 1926.

6. David Porter Siegel (1895–1958), a New York lawyer, was head of the Criminal Division in District Attorney Emory Buckner's office. Instead of ascending to the district attorney's position, however, Siegel announced his resignation in January 1927. He joined Susan Brandeis's firm as an associate.

To: **Susan Brandeis Gilbert**
Date: **October 9, 1926**
Place: **Washington, D.C.**
Source: **Gilbert MSS**

DEAREST SUSAN: Jack seems to have a good deal of labor through Uncle Henry [Goldmark]'s troubles. It must be a great comfort to Uncle Henry to have this advice & support.

I think Paul Blanshard[1] will have the opportunity of seeing plaintive farmer-cotton planters on his southern excursion. 12½ cent [cotton] will make many weep, and 55 cent silver must be bring[ing] sadness to our hospitable friends in Canada.[2]

At last accounts here, the Daugherty jury was still out.[3] Let me hear the gossip on the trial. I suppose the N.Y. interest is intense. Except when compared with Miss Ederle's triumphal procession.[4]   Lovingly

1. Ordained a Congregationalist minister, Paul Blanshard (1892–1980) developed into a leading social activist and publicist. In 1926 he was the field secretary for the League for Industrial Democracy and, in that connection, was about to embark upon a southern field trip. In the 1940s Blanshard became one of the most vitriolic critics of the Roman Catholic Church, and his book *American Freedom and Catholic Power* (Boston, 1949) achieved considerable popularity and provoked considerable controversy.

2. The largest cotton crop in history had sent prices plummeting disastrously in the fall of 1926. Various schemes were floated for restricting acreage, and later in the month LDB's friend Eugene Meyer got some holding corporations established for the purpose of withholding surplus from the market and extending credit to planters. The price of silver had fallen to fifty-five cents per ounce after the price broke on 29 September. Two causes were given: the dumping of silver onto the market by the Chinese and the schemes of the British to convert India from a gold-based to a silver-based system.

3. After sixty-five hours of deliberation, the jury reported hopeless disagreement in the government's conspiracy case against former attorney general Harry Micajah Daugherty and his co-defendant, Col. Thomas Woodnut Miller. Daugherty (1860–1941), a Columbus, Ohio, attorney, had been forced to resign in March 1924 because of allegations regarding his part in the Harding scandals. His side of the story can be found in his *Inside Story of the Harding Tragedy* (New York, 1932).

4. Gertrude Caroline Ederle (b. 1906) was the first woman to swim the English Channel. On 6 August she swam the 35 miles in 14.5 hours, thereby breaking the existing men's record. When she returned to New York, the city greeted her with tremendous acclaim, including a ticker-tape parade.

To: Susan Brandeis Gilbert
Date: October 11, 1926
Place: Washington, D.C.
Source: Gilbert MSS

DEAREST SUSAN: Note enclosed programs to see what good music we have in W[ashington]—and note particularly that *I* went with mother.

Have you heard Ernest Hutcheson?[1] He is a marvelous pianist.

Lovingly

1. Ernest Hutcheson (1871–1951) was regarded as one of the leading pianists of his time. He was born in Australia and studied in Europe; he arrived in America in 1900 and alternated between touring and teaching. Hutcheson joined the Julliard School at its opening in 1924 and served as its president from 1937 to 1945.

To: **Alfred Brandeis**
Date: **October 18, 1926**
Place: **Washington, D.C.**
Source: **Brandeis MSS**

DEAR AL: Ben & Miss [Mary] Flexner were in this morning & send you greetings. They were in good form. Ben wanted to discuss Palestinian problems, but we talked some on American ones also. He is quite as flabbergasted as we are by the manifestations of business & says that, never in his life, has he felt himself so helpless—so unable to cope with tides about him. And like some others of his generation he doesn't like it at all. Unlike most of his business associates he does not think that the prosperity will last.

He says no one can form a conception of the tearing down of houses & rebuilding now going on in lower New York & that no where except in the devastated regions of France, has he seen such devastation.

He reports Abe [Flexner] in better health than for 2 years & that his book on medical education is having a great reception.[1] It is now being translated into Czech. Simon [Flexner] also is in good health. Was in Edgartown with his family last summer.

1. Abraham Flexner, *Medical Education: A Comparative Study* (New York, 1925).

To: Susan Brandeis Gilbert
Date: October 31, 1926
Place: Washington, D.C.
Source: Gilbert MSS

DEAREST SUSAN: Mother sends the enclosed for Jack.

How fine it is to have these frequent visits from Elizabeth. Even she must succumb to the magnet of the Great Metropolis.

Paul Singer[1] is coming in this afternoon to talk Palestine. And this evening he is to dine with us. The Otto Beyers[2] and Basil Manleys[3] are coming also. From the latter we should learn something of the political prospects. High Republicans here think the Republicans are sure to lose control of the Senate, but that they will retain their control of the House.[4] If Massachusetts slays Butler we may be proud of her again.[5]   Lovingly

1. Perhaps this is Paul Singer the English businessman and economist and vice-president of the Palestine Economic Corporation.

2. Otto Sternoff Beyer (1886–1948) was a construction engineer and an authority on labor relations in the transportation industry. He held various high-ranking positions during the New Deal and World War II.

3. Basil Manley (1886–1950) was a political insider and an old friend of LDB's. An economist who was in and out of government service, Manley advised the Bureau of Labor Statistics, the Federal Trade Commission, the War Industries Board, and other federal and New York state agencies. He occasionally worked as a journalist and wrote a number of books on economic topics.

4. The prediction proved to be correct. As a result of the 2 November voting, the Republicans retained firm control of the House of Representatives, although President Coolidge was to be faced by a hostile Senate for the rest of his administration. There would be forty-eight Republicans, forty-seven Democrats, and one Farmer-Laborite (LDB's friend Henrik Shipstead). But with so many Republican insurgents like Norris, La Follette, Borah, and others, Coolidge would have rough sledding in the upper house.

5. Considerable national attention was given to the senatorial race in Massachusetts to fill the seat caused by the death of Henry Cabot Lodge. David I. Walsh, LDB's friend from Boston days, was challenging William Morgan Butler (1861–1937). Walsh had served in the Senate from 1919 to 1924, when he was defeated for reelection. Butler was both a close friend of Coolidge and the national chair of the Republican Party at the time. His fate was taken to be a measure of the popularity of the administration, and Hoover, Coolidge, and Charles Evans Hughes entered the contest on behalf of Butler. In a rebuke to the Republicans, however, Massachusetts voters elected Walsh by a substantial majority. On the day after this letter LDB wrote his daughter: "If Butler is handsomely beaten we who are not Republican, and indeed progressives of every complexion, may hope to breathe freely again."

To: Alfred Brandeis
Date: November 1, 1926
Place: Washington, D.C.
Source: Brandeis MSS

MY DEAR AL: Enclosed may interest you as showing how live the revived Hebrew language is.

Elizabeth was in New York two days to attend R[ail] R[oad] wage conference meetings. But, like that gent who watched our billiard playing at Silvaplana [in 1872], she writes: "Na, Da Kann man nicht viel lehrnen [sic]."[1]

I feel more interest in politics than for many a year. The Massachusetts situation was made significant by the President's throwing his popularity into the breach; and there seems to be much Mass. opinion that it will prove to be of no effect for Butler & that C[alvin]. C[oolidge]. will come out of the fray badly bruised.[2]

And the [Boston] Transcript of Saturday (which Miss Grady sent me) says it is considered that C.C. "has made his first major political mistake".

Vedremmo.[3] I hope Kentucky will down Ernst.[4]

The C[hief]. J[ustice]. said he thought that would be the result. And Basil Manl[e]y [*] with moot prognostication that the Republicans will lose the Senate.

1. "One can't learn much there." The meetings had begun on 29 October. A newly created board of arbitration was charged with holding hearings to determine the question of higher wages for eastern railway workers. In early December a wage increase was given.
2. See the previous letter, note 5.
3. We shall see.
4. The incumbent, Richard Pretlow Ernst (1859–1934), was narrowly defeated in the Kentucky senatorial contest.

To:	Susan Brandeis Gilbert
Date:	November 4, 1926
Place:	Washington, D.C.
Source:	Gilbert MSS

DEAREST SUSAN: It seems marvellous to have a letter from you, written last evening; and it is a great joy.[1] Perhaps you will be ready soon also for these enclosures.

Mabel's friend Dr. Louise Stanley[2] & others are coming in to dine this evening. Lovingly

1. The Brandeises' first grandchild, Louis Brandeis Gilbert, was born on 4 November 1926. On this date LDB wrote to Frankfurter: "I suppose you and Marion have heard from Auntie B. that Susan's son is a strapping fellow & that all goes well with them" (Urofsky and Levy, *"Half Brother, Half Son,"* 260).
2. Dr. Louise Stanley (1883–1954) was Mabel Willebrandt's housemate and a prominent home economist. After earning a Ph.D. at Yale, she taught until 1923, when she began her lifelong association with the Department of Agriculture. In 1926 she was chief of the Bureau of Home Economics in the department. The next day LDB wrote to his daughter: "Dr. Stanley (whom we liked much) brought Mabel's congratulations."

To:	Susan Brandeis Gilbert
Date:	November 11, 1926
Place:	Washington, D.C.
Source:	Gilbert MSS

DEAREST SUSAN: You seem to be having an unbroken series of royal receptions—with adoration of the crown Prince. Jack will have much to tell us on Saturday.

You certainly had some fine letters.   Lovingly

To: **Hildegarde Nagel**
Date: **November 15, 1926**
Place: **Washington, D.C.**
Source: **H. Nagel**

MY DEAR HILDEGARDE: Your grandmother Brandeis' birthday.

Only your presence could have gladden[ed] the day more than your letter.[1] You would have looked well at dinner with Aunt Do and Elizabeth, Jack, and Paul.

It was a joyous day. And on the next we took our guests, not only to the tow path to which you were trailed, but on that noble Potomac irresistible in its sunny calm. Remember that, while the lure of New York is upon you.

Still I am glad Susan and Jack have you near; and I hope their boy will appreciate the blessing.   With much love

    1. Two days earlier LDB had celebrated his seventieth birthday.

To: **Susan Brandeis Gilbert**
Date: **November 23, 1926**
Place: **Washington, D.C.**
Source: **Gilbert MSS**

DEAREST SUSAN: Auntie B. gives a glowing account of you, Jack & the boy. You certainly are making rapid progress to be walking so much.

Of the Fall-Doheny case I hear little, except that it is expected to last at least 5 or 6 weeks. Some one said today it may last four months.[1]

I guess Auntie B. will stay for Thanksgiving.

I see Walter Pollak in Court. He looks as if we should have an argument from him this week.[2]

I decided a much contested prohibition case for the govt. yesterday. It was argued twice—once by Mabel, once by the Solicitor General.

A companion case was decided the other way today.[3]   Lovingly

    1. Albert Bacon Fall (1861–1944) was a New Mexico lawyer, judge, and senator who was appointed secretary of the interior by President Harding. Deeply implicated in the oil scandals of the Harding administration, Fall resigned his office in March 1923. Edward

Laurence Doheny (1856–1935) was a pioneering California oilman and a good friend of Fall's. The two men stood accused of conspiring to gain leases from the oil rich fields of the Elk Hills naval reserve; their trial before the Supreme Court of the District of Columbia began this week and lasted for twenty-two days. On 16 December the pair was acquitted—much to the surprise and dismay of many who thought the evidence against them was convincing. Fall went on to face similar charges in connection with Harry Sinclair and the reserves at Teapot Dome.

2. Walter Heilprin Pollak (1887–1940) was a Harvard Law School graduate who practiced in New York City. He was one of the leading civil liberties lawyers of the 1920s and defended Anita Whitney and the Scottsboro defendants in two celebrated cases before the Supreme Court. On the day after this letter was written, Pollak argued in *Burns v. U.S.,* 274 U.S. 328, that a conviction obtained under the California Criminal Syndicalist Act was unconstitutional. The Court, following the Whitney case, upheld the act. LDB dissented from the decision.

3. The two cases were *U.S. v. One Ford Coupe,* 272 U.S. 324, and *Port Gardner Investment Co. v. U.S.,* 272 U.S. 564. Both had been argued by Mabel Willebrandt in December 1925 and then reargued by Solicitor General Mitchell in October 1926. The first case originated in Alabama and the second in Washington; but they turned upon the same question. In both cases automobiles concealing illegal liquors had been apprehended by the authorities and the owners of the vehicles claimed that they were unaware of the purposes to which the vehicles were being put. Was the government justified in forfeiting the vehicle? One federal law (Section 3450 of the *Revised Statutes*) held that forfeiture was mandatory, regardless of the interests of innocent persons, when a vehicle was being used for the purpose of defrauding the United States of taxes; but Section 26 of the National Prohibition Act provided protection for the interests of innocent persons. In the Alabama case LDB declared, for a badly divided Court, in favor of the government's right to forfeit the car without protecting the interests of innocent owners; in the Washington case LDB declared, for a unanimous Court (Butler and Stone entering a concurring opinion), that in this instance prosecution was carried out under the National Prohibition Act and the rights of the innocent owners were protected.

To: **Susan Brandeis Gilbert**
Date: **November 24, 1926**
Place: **Washington, D.C.**
Source: **Gilbert MSS**

DEAREST SUSAN: To L.B.G.[1] and his parents our best wishes for Thanksgiving. We shall have in for dinner—

> The Minister for Latvia & wife[2]
> Father Ryan
> Auntie B.
> The Dean Achesons
> Bob Page

& after dinner, Prof. I. L. Sharfman[3] of Ann Arbor, who is here on his survey of the I.C.C., is coming in.   Lovingly

1. The infant Louis Brandeis Gilbert.

440

2. Charles Louis Seya (1885–19[?]) was an experienced Latvian diplomat, serving in the United States since 1925.

3. Isaiah Leo Sharfman (1886–1969), a Russian-born immigrant, was raised in Boston and graduated from the Harvard Law School in 1910. From 1916 to 1955 he taught economics at the University of Michigan, specializing in railroad economics and regulation.

To:	Susan Brandeis Gilbert
Date:	December 8, 1926
Place:	Washington, D.C.
Source:	Gilbert MSS

DEAREST SUSAN: Thanks to Jack for the bunch of clippings.

If you go to the Taylor Society[1] meeting be sure to see Mrs. Gilbreth[2] & other friends of mine. Dr. Person[3] sent me the Society greetings on the 70th.[4]

Mother summoned energy today for a Xmas plunge downtown. Wasn't that heroic. The C.P.'s[5] faculty for sleep has good precedent in earlier generations.   Lovingly

1. The Taylor Society was devoted to furthering the principles of the late Frederick W. Taylor: industrial efficiency, scientific management, and the elimination of waste. LDB had been one of the earliest advocates of the efficiency movement and one of its greatest publicists, particularly in connection with the management of the nation's railroads.

2. Lillian Evelyn Gilbreth (1878–1972) was the widow of LDB's old ally in the efficiency movement, Frank B. Gilbreth, the founder of the Taylor Society. Mrs. Gilbreth was a noted efficiency expert in her own right and a professor of management. She was also the mother of twelve children and the subject, along with her husband, of the popular book and movie *Cheaper by the Dozen*.

3. Harlow Stafford Person (1875–1955) was a teacher of economics and business management and from 1914 to 1933 the president and managing director of the Taylor Society. During the 1930s Person worked as a planner on several New Deal projects, including the Rural Electrification Administration.

4. LDB's seventieth birthday, three weeks earlier.

5. The Brandeises and Gilberts had begun to refer jokingly to the infant Louis Gilbert as "the Crown Prince."

To:	Susan Brandeis Gilbert
Date:	December 17, 1926
Place:	Washington, D.C.
Source:	Gilbert MSS

DEAREST SUSAN: Enclosed may amuse Jack.

You, I suppose, have so trained your memory, that you will never forget Dean Pound's refusal to let you enter the Harvard Law School, & have set apart for him a special compartment of the Inferno.

Norman Hapgood & others were in last evening.   Lovingly

To: Susan Brandeis Gilbert
Date: December 24, 1926
Place: Washington, D.C.
Source: Gilbert MSS

DEAREST SUSAN: Yours of 22d recd late yesterday. Just wired you:

"Hotel Belleclaire satisfactory. We take 11 o'clock Pennsylvania train Monday".

I have also wired Judge Mack that I will lunch with him (& others of the inner circle) at the Esplanade Tuesday; & I wired Mr. deHaas that I will meet with him & some of the old rank & file Tuesday at 5:30.[1] Other than this, I have made no engagements. After I get to N.Y. I shall arrange to call on Mr [Nathan]. Straus and Uncle Felix [Adler] & shall arrange to see Uncle Henry [Goldmark] & a few others—including Hildegarde [Nagel], Louis Wehle & Harry [Brandeis] & wife.

The rest of the time is to be devoted to contemplation of the C.P.—and of the Eternal Verities—accompanied at times by the music of yours & Jack's voices.   Lovingly

1. Zionist activity had picked up in the last few weeks of 1926, because of the visit of Chaim Weizmann, beginning 29 October. He had come in part to make peace between wealthy non-Zionists and the Zionists and openly courted Louis Marshall with a dinner honoring his seventieth birthday (12 December). While Marshall and others were open to Weizmann's proposals—particularly for a new commission to replace the defunct Zionist Commission—LDB and his faction of the Zionist movement remained aloof.

To: Susan Brandeis Gilbert
Date: January 6, 1927
Place: Washington, D.C.
Source: Gilbert MSS

DEAREST SUSAN: Since writing you this A.M. I have yours of yesterday saying that Jack has selected a few letters for framing.[1] Please ask him not to do that. He can, of course, put as many as he wants in an album.

If by any chance such speed has been made in framing that this has already been done, please hang the letters in the privacy of your bedroom where no one else will see them. And please do not show any one except Jack the Nathan Straus letter.

1. LDB had turned over to his daughter, as "the family historian," four large envelopes containing the letters that had come to him on the occasion of his seventieth birthday. These letters were subsequently deposited in the Brandeis collection at the University of Louisville Law School.

To: Susan Brandeis Gilbert
Date: January 13, 1927
Place: Washington, D.C.
Source: Gilbert MSS

DEAREST SUSAN: Very sorry to hear that Jack has lost so good a friend.

Mother thinks enclosed from Mrs. Barton will interest you and Jack.

We are greatly concerned about our country's action re Mexico & Nicaragua[1] & delighted to see the N.Y. Times[2] join the [New York] World in its attack on the President's policy. The Boston Globe & the Herald are taking the same attitude. Cal[vin Coolidge]. will find himself considerably disliked.

Miss Grady sent me the Globe editorial which Senator Bob was so much pleased with that he said he would put it into the Congr. Record.[3]

Lovingly

1. The marines, having been withdrawn from Nicaragua in 1925, were reintroduced in 1926 upon the outbreak of an uprising against the conservative, pro-American Adolfo Díaz administration. The action was needed, Coolidge argued, to protect American lives and property, including the nation's interest in a possible canal. Ultimately the president sent Henry L. Stimson, a personal envoy, who was able to negotiate a settlement (although the marines remained until 1931). In a message to Congress, the president also accused Mexico, under the influence of Bolshevists in its government, of aiding the Nicaraguan rebels. The accusations against Mexico came on the heels of a bitter dispute between the two countries over Mexico's legislation threatening U.S. economic interests, especially oil concessions.

2. The Democratic *New York World* had consistently opposed the president's policy. In editorials of 11 and 13 January the *New York Times* also raised serious questions about the course that the Coolidge administration was pursuing. Calling armed intervention "a doctrine in which a thousand perils lie hidden," the paper urged rationality and caution.

3. The *Boston Globe* editorial of 10 January, criticizing both U.S. actions in Nicaragua and the government's refusal to explain its objectives honestly, was entered into the *Congressional Record* by Senator Robert La Follette, Jr., on 12 January (69th Cong., 2d Sess., 1470). Moreover, in a Senate speech the next day La Follette reviewed extensively and approvingly the widespread editorial attacks on Coolidge's policy, especially his red-baiting of the Mexican government. Saying that "I believe the action of our Government is unjustified and unconscionable," La Follette focused his attack on the allegations of "Bolshevik aims and policies" in Mexico. He also reprinted various editorials from prestigious newspapers critical of the tactics and arguments of the administration. See *Cong. Rec.,* 69th Cong., 2nd sess., pt. 2 (14 January 1927): 1645–53.

To: Jacob H. Gilbert
Date: January 17, 1927
Place: Washington, D.C.
Source: Gilbert MSS

MY DEAR JACK: 10:40 A.M.

Miss Szold[1] & Mrs. Lindheim have just left, after an hour & a half's talk. Miss Szold read me all the recent cables from Palestine & gave the necessary explanatory facts. Mrs. Lindheim added a little. I told them:

1. That I would advise Mr. & Mrs. Straus not to issue any statement.[2]
2. That I advised the Hadassah and its officers to make the Hadassah absolutely autonomous;[3] that Hadassah was committed to the pending U[nited].P[alestine].A[ppeal]. campaign and could not withdraw before its close; but that Hadassah should not hereafter join in any U.P.A. or Zionist (general) appeal, but should make itself financially absolutely independent of the Z.O.; should state that it "will relieve the Z.O. from contributing to the Hadassah expense in the future."
3. That in Palestine the Hadassah should stand resolutely for the highest professional standards and achievement; that Dr. Bluestone[4] must be freed from any control or annoyance other than the supervision and control of the Hadassah Executive; but of course be ever ready to receive the advice of members of an appropriate advisory council.
4. That the course outlined was not only wise, but was demanded by loyalty to truth, to the Zionist cause, to Palestine & to Judaism. That the course to be pursued was clear and simple, a straight line. That the difficulties & problems resulting from adopting it would be many and serious; but in my opinion were not insuperable; that now the need was only for the determination and courage to do the right thing.
5. That in my opinion it was more important now to educate the 39,000 members of the Hadassah as to what loyalty to it and to the Zionist cause and Palestine demands, than to increase its membership; and that the effort of the officers should be devoted so far as possible to carrying forward that education.

I am returning the memo. Perhaps Mr. & Mrs. Straus may like me to keep it among my papers safely.

I wrote you yesterday re Palestinians.

1. Henrietta Szold (1860–1945) was already a legend in the Zionist movement. The daughter of a Baltimore rabbi, she interested herself in Jewish affairs at an early age. After a visit to Palestine in 1909, she founded Hadassah, the women's arm of the Zionist movement, and directed the organization's monumental work in providing health care to the Palestinian settlements. She herself moved to Palestine. When the Nazis began their extermination efforts, Szold established the Youth Aliyah, which rescued many Jewish children by bringing them to Palestine. She was presently in the United States on a visit.

2. Perhaps in connection with the Strauses' approaching trip to Palestine.

3. The Hadassah organization had always been allied with the Brandeis-Mack wing of the Zionist movement—being naturally sympathetic to LDB's plans for Palestine development and his emphasis on financial accountability. In the midst of the Lipsky-Weizmann leadership during the 1920s, Hadassah moved into a more and more independent position with regard to the general Zionist organization.

4. Ephraim Michael Bluestone (1891–1979), like his father, Joseph Isaac Bluestone, was a physician and a committed Zionist. After Columbia Medical School and the army, he became a hospital administrator. In 1926 he went to Palestine as a director of the Hadassah medical organization and chairman of the Nathan and Lina Straus Health Center. Two years later he returned to America to administer the Montefiore Hospital until 1951.

To: **Alfred Brandeis**
Date: **January 30, 1927**
Place: **Washington, D.C.**
Source: **Brandeis MSS**

MY DEAR AL: [William G.] McAdoo's letter, which please return, may interest you. I guess he hasn't a much better chance than Hoover. There is considerable talk here now of Jim Reed.[1] After timid, safe and sane Cal, the country may fly to courageous, emphatic, erratic Jim. Certainly Coolidge is making a pitiable mess of our foreign policy. He was on safe ground when "tun nichts, sag nichts"[2] was his practice. He was of those "That therefore only are reputed wise for saying nothing."[3]   Gruesse

1. James Alexander Reed (1861–1944) had long been interested in making a run for the presidency. He was a Missouri Democrat who served as mayor of Kansas City before beginning a long senatorial career, 1911 to 1929. He denounced LDB in the debate over the Clayton Act in 1914 but came around eventually to voting for his confirmation in 1916—after a meeting with the nominee at Norman Hapgood's home.

2. "Do nothing, say nothing."

3. Shakespeare, *Merchant of Venice,* I, 1:97.

To: **Susan Brandeis Gilbert**
Date: **February 9, 1927**
Place: **Washington, D.C.**
Source: **Gilbert MSS**

DEAREST SUSAN: The C.P.'s first outing is, indeed, news, and his strides in weight are quite astounding.

We had an hour on the tow path in his honor today. The cardinal was gaily flitting about & the song-sparrow singing lustily and the sunshine entrancing.

Lawrence Berenson,[1] your Sam Rosenson[2] and Mr. Lindheim & Dr. Weizmann this afternoon.[3] L.B. left with Dr. W. after the latter had said his say; and then there was a full hour and a half talking over Hadassah and General Jewish Affairs.

Now, Helen Everret M. is coming in with Aunt Belle [La Follette] & the Ottos.[4] Senator Bob can't come. Lovingly

1. Lawrence Berenson (1891–1970) graduated from the Harvard Law School, clerked for Julian Mack, and opened a law practice in New York City. He was an active Zionist.

2. Possibly Samuel Julian Rosensohn (1880–1939), a New York City attorney. He was Felix Frankfurter's roommate at Harvard and worked with Frankfurter in Washington during World War I. During these years Rosensohn was deeply involved in the Zionist movement and held several positions of leadership.

3. Chaim Weizmann had been in America since late October 1926, trying to raise funds for the United Palestine Appeal. LDB met with him on 1 December. Of this second meeting, on this date, LDB reported to Frankfurter (15 February): "Weizmann impressed me more than ever with his ability, resourcefulness & Mephistophelian quality. I rather think M 'was ein Hund dagegen [was a dog by comparison].' When with him, I felt like the good Christians who grasped at the Cross for protection" (Urofsky and Levy, *"Half Brother, Half Son,"* 274).

4. Perhaps the University of Wisconsin professor of philosophy Max Carl Otto (1876–1968) and his family. Otto had been Philip La Follette's teacher at the university and subsequently became friendly with the entire La Follette family. He was the author of several philosophical books on popular topics.

To: **Susan Brandeis Gilbert**
Date: **February 12, 1927**
Place: **Washington, D.C.**
Source: **Gilbert MSS**

MY DEAREST SUSAN: Hand Jack this theatre check as real evidence that Mother & I went to "Every Woman Knows"—a lovely, well-acted play.[1] We stayed through three acts, which was doing pretty well for the likes of us.

In order to prepare, we stole off for the bit of the tow-path in the sun, before noon. All this, although Lincoln's birthday is not a legal holiday in the District of Columbia. Lovingly

1. The four-act sentimental comedy, by James M. Barrie, was first produced in 1908, four years after his better-known Peter Pan. It tells the story of a woman who contrives a successful political career for her mediocre husband.

To: **Susan Brandeis Gilbert**
Date: **February 15, 1927**
Place: **Washington, D.C.**
Source: **Gilbert MSS**

DEAREST SUSAN: Thank Jack for the Ripley book.[1] R. is making quite a stir.

Judd Dewey[2] came in yesterday just as I should have written you. He is aiding Miss Grady in her annual legislative fight—a terrible strain on vitality which generally results in helping along the S[avings].B[ank]. I[nsurance]. movement. Every attack is a puff.

We have had some dull, dreary wet days which have had their reflex on Mother, who has had more pain in her arm & has been much depressed again. The sun is making considerable effort this morning & I hope will conquer rain & Mother's mood.

Elizabeth & Paul should appear in NY tomorrow & you & Jack will have some joyous times with them.

I talked pretty seriously to Norvin Lindheim & I hope he won't be misled by sirens—international or Palestinian.   Lovingly

1. William Zebina Ripley (1867–1941) was a prolific economist and social critic. He taught at Harvard from 1901 until 1933. His newest book, just published, was *Main Street and Wall Street* (Boston, 1927), a collection of essays on various economic topics.

2. Judd Ellsworth Dewey (1884–1961) was a Harvard Law School graduate, who after the war became the legal counsel to the Massachusetts Savings Bank Life Insurance system and therefore Alice Grady's associate and assistant. An active evangelist for SBLI, Dewey eventually became deputy commissioner.

To: **Susan Brandeis Gilbert**
Date: **February 23, 1927**[1]
Place: **Washington, D.C.**
Source: **Gilbert MSS**

DEAREST SUSAN: A.M.

Nothing from you today.

Since Saturday there have been many visitors from the Jewish world. Judge Mack came in Sunday A.M. to see me, & in the afternoon to see Mother. Justine[2] brought in Deputy Gruenbaum,[3] Sunday forenoon. In the afternoon, Rabbi Samuel Sale & two others from St. Louis. Also Saturday, Monday & yesterday still others. And in the forenoon yesterday Mr. deHaas. I think I must be quite au fait[4] in Jewish affairs, national & international.

Yesterday I attended painfully—officially—the President's address. I prefer a work day.[5] Robert Bruere[6] happily came in last evening, and brushed away much of the grimy sordidness of the official performance, by his generous high mindedness.

I hope you & Jack had a good day.

I am writing Prof. Ripley today & am glad that I am able to talk glibly about "Main Street & Wall St."[7]

1. LDB erroneously dated this letter 23 February 1926.

2. Justine Wise Tulin Polier (1903–87), the daughter of LDB's comrade Stephen S. Wise, was a lawyer in New York City. She would soon begin a career as an activist and public

447

servant, specializing in domestic relations and juvenile affairs. From 1935 until 1962 she was justice of the Domestic Relations Court and after that judge of the New York State Family Court.

3. Itzhak Grünbaum (1879–1970) was a deputy in the Polish Sejm (Parliament). He was a zealous advocate of Jewish rights in the diaspora and an active Zionist, for a while serving as president of the Polish Zionist Organization. He was currently visiting the United States. In 1933 he moved to Palestine, where he played an important part in wartime rescue work and in the independence movement.

4. Expert, up-to-date.

5. The previous day President Coolidge had given his Washington's Birthday address, which was widely broadcast by radio. For the text, see the *New York Times,* 23 February 1927. The speech had an unusually jarring affect on LDB, and to other correspondents he was much more graphic. He told Frankfurter: "You cannot conceive how painful, distressful & depressing it was to listen (officially) to Cal's Washington's Birthday address. I think the purpose of those behind (who must have prepared the address) was to confiscate the whole of G.W.'s good will for Big Business, by showing that we owe everything we value to the qualities of business efficiency, commercial courage & vision & thrift & that these were G.W.'s dominating qualities. . . . When I tried to recall the next most depressing & distressful experience of a lifetime, I had to go back to 1894, when in preparing for the Public Institutions Hearings, I went to Long Island (Boston Harbor) Poor-House hospital & passed through the syphilitic ward. I had a like sense of uncleaness [*sic*]" (Urofsky and Levy, *"Half Brother, Half Son,"* 275–76). On 23 February LDB described Coolidge's speech to his brother as "one of the most painful experiences of a lifetime."

6. Robert Walter Bruere (1876–19[?]) was a noted social worker and activist specializing in problems of poverty and labor. He had been the editor of the *Survey* since 1923.

7. See the preceding letter, note 1.

To:	Susan Brandeis Gilbert
Date:	February 26, 1927
Place:	Washington, D.C.
Source:	Gilbert MSS

MY DEAREST SUSAN: Another year has passed, made rich by your steady growth and the development in many lines.[1] Again, I can wish for you nothing more than that this growth, and the happiness which attends it, shall continue.

I am having bound for your law-library a set of my briefs in the Supreme Court of the United States dealing with the Constitutionality of women's labor laws. I thought you would care for them because of the subject matter, as well as because of the authors.[2]

Mother talks much of you, of what you have made of yourself, and the thought gives her much happiness.   Lovingly

1. The next day would be Susan Gilbert's thirty-fourth birthday.
2. LDB's collaborators on those briefs were Felix Frankfurter, Florence Kelley, and Susan's aunt, Josephine Goldmark.

To: **Susan Brandeis Gilbert**
Date: **March 12, 1927**
Place: **Washington, D.C.**
Source: **Gilbert MSS**

DEAREST SUSAN: Mother is delighted with your account of the C.P.'s pranks. I enclose a note from her which deals with other matters.

Now (5 P.M.) we are awaiting Prof. W. S. Holdsworth[1] of Oxford who wrote the 9 volume history of the English Law & with him the Mrs.

I will confess I have not read the 9 vols.   Lovingly

    1. Sir William Searle Holdsworth (1871–1944) was in America to lecture at Northwestern and to receive the Ames medal from the Harvard Law School. He is regarded as second only to William Blackstone among Oxford jurists; his *History of English Law* appeared between 1903 and 1926.

To: **Susan Brandeis Gilbert**
Date: **March 25, 1927**
Place: **Washington, D.C.**
Source: **Gilbert MSS**

DEAREST SUSAN: Mother has telegraphed you; and has written or will write.

It would be great to see the young man's advance. But the time is very inopportune. Mother has been sleeping badly for some little time. The arm is again troubling her more. She is battling nobly. But, unless the longed-for sleep returns, (and even if it does) she will have all she can stand up to—to carry off Sunday evening's dinner and the Monday—At Home—the last, I suppose, of the season.[1]

Sorry to miss the chance of seeing the C.P.   Lovingly

    1. LDB and AGB made it a practice to hold Monday teas for their friends, out-of-town visitors, and cultural and political luminaries. These weekly affairs brought to the Brandeis apartment large numbers of brilliant and powerful "insiders," old hands and young but promising minor civil servants and law clerks. Some of the guests came to get the advice of LDB on particular governmental or economic matters; some LDB pumped for the latest news and gossip. AGB became well known for her skills as a thoughtful and gracious Washington hostess because of her Monday "at homes."

To: **Susan Brandeis Gilbert**
Date: **March 31, 1927**
Place: **Washington, D.C.**
Source: **Gilbert MSS**

DEAREST SUSAN: That's a lovely pen-picture you sent of the C.P.'s new pranks.

Mother & I achieved the Iolanthe this afternoon.[1] A charming show.

Can you recall how Louis Wehle & I used to sing and dance the Chancellor's Song[2] at Petersham for Grandpa?   Lovingly

1. Gilbert and Sullivan's *Iolanthe; or The Peer and the Peri* was first performed in London in November 1882.

2. The Lord Chancellor has several songs in *Iolanthe*, but it is particularly appealing to picture the young LDB singing the Chancellor's opening lines from a song in act 1:

> The Law is the true embodiment
> Of everything that's excellent.
> It has no kind of fault or flaw,
> And I, my Lords, embody the Law.

To:	Susan Brandeis Gilbert
Date:	April 10, 1927
Place:	Washington, D.C.
Source:	Gilbert MSS

DEAREST SUSAN: You seem to have very gay times. Today, if your weather is as fine as ours, you will doubtless be on a hike.

I suppose Elizabeth has informed you that they have accepted the Wisconsin offer. I am glad they had one other offer & the prospect of a second, and that they go back to Madison, thereunto *urged* by those in authority. It may mean much for the future.[1]   Lovingly

1. The Raushenbushes were to spend the rest of their professional careers in Madison, Elizabeth teaching at the university and Paul first teaching and then entering government service.

To:	Susan Brandeis Gilbert
Date:	April 17, 1927
Place:	Washington, D.C.
Source:	Gilbert MSS

Confidential

DEAREST SUSAN: Mother's birthday went off finely,[1] but with much excitement because of the following which Eliz. may not have had time to report to you.

They saw Pres[iden]t. Aydelotte[2] Friday. He urged them strongly to come to Swarthmore (Paul $3500. Eliz. at least $1000—she to work at the same *rate* of pay as Paul for work she does). It was deemed advisable for

P. & E. to leave last night for Madison to talk matters over, with Profs. Kiek.,[3] Meikeljohn,[4] Commons & Pearlman[5] [*sic*] & to determine, with their aid, whether to go to Madison or to Swarthmore.

They had talks here with Mr. [Walton H.] Hamilton & Helen Everett.

In the afternoon P & E and Carl took Mother & Mrs. Rauschenbus[c]h canoeing. In the evening all dined with us.

How did the C.P. celebrate the day?   Lovingly

1. Alice Goldmark Brandeis had just turned sixty-one.
2. Frank Aydelotte (1880–1956) had been president of Swarthmore College since 1921; he would hold the position until 1940.
3. LDB is undoubtedly referring to William Henry Kiekhoefer (1883–1951), an economist and a legendary teacher at the University of Wisconsin from 1914 until his death.
4. Alexander Meikeljohn (1872–1964) was a nationally known educational philosopher and reformer. He left the presidency of Amherst in 1926 to open his Experimental College at the University of Wisconsin.
5. Selig Perlman (1888–1959) was a Polish-born economist and a renowned historian of the American labor movement. He was associated with the University of Wisconsin for fifty years.

To: **Elizabeth Brandeis Raushenbush**
Date: **April 24, 1927**
Place: **Washington, D.C.**
Source: **Brandeis MSS**

DEAREST ELIZABETH: Your and Paul's triumphal march to Madison[1] has laid the foundation for much of the happiness which I wish you two.

Before abdicating the office of Educational Adviser recently assumed I venture to suggest this:

Confine your labor course or courses to American labor. Use your growing knowledge of English labor merely as an enriching background to enable you to understand and elucidate American conditions. Do not profess to teach about English or other foreign labor.   Lovingly

1. See the preceding letter. On 20 April Elizabeth had telegraphed her father: "Wisconsin wins our love." Paul was to work part-time in the Economics Department and part-time in Meikeljohn's new Experimental College, due to open that autumn; Elizabeth was to work entirely in the Economics Department at Wisconsin.

To: **Alfred Brandeis**
Date: **April 27, 1927**
Place: **Washington, D.C.**
Source: **Brandeis MSS**

DEAR AL: Yours of 25th with newspaper matter of the 24th recd.

I am glad you got Callahan,[1] and am not surprised at the abstentions of the likeminded, who abstained from fear & particularly for "business reasons". My own experience with would have been supporters was ample on this line & McAdoo told me much in the same line about present Los Angeles conditions.

I fear "business as usual" is undermining the native courage of Americans. I had rather expected that Kentuckians, who had rather more of courage & manliness than most, would have shown less of the weakness. But I guess Goethe's wisdom is of universal application:

"Nichts ist schwerer zu ertragen
Als ein Reihe von schoenen Tagen."[2]

Gruesse

1. The letter from LDB's brother is lost, but perhaps Alfred reported that he had interested Patrick Henry Callahan (1866–1940) in the effort to improve the University of Louisville. Callahan was a businessman active in philanthropy and city affairs in Louisville.
2. "Nothing is harder to endure / Than a series of beautiful days."

To: **Alfred Brandeis**
Date: **May 26, 1927**
Place: **Washington, D.C.**
Source: **Brandeis MSS**

DEAR AL: You have handled U[niversity]. of L[ouisville]. matters with so much wisdom & skill that I have no suggestions to make except one—on that I have had half-a-century of experience and you none.

Alice's & my plans for the University extend over the next ten years. We don't want to lose our managing partner. It's just 50 years since my eyes gave out.[1] Since then, there has never been a time that I haven't had to bear in mind physical limitations of some sort. The walls curbing activity were always in sight; and I had to adjust my efforts. Your superb constitution relieved you from that necessity. But age is a fact that may not be ignored. It has added to the limitations to which I have been subject, and there is not a day when I am not reminded of it.

Your constitution is better than mine. But you are nearly three years older. Remember that—and Act Accordingly.

Gruesse

Alice thinks enclosed on Educationals Sir Anthony Absolute's Elsewhere may interest you & Jennie.[2]

1. See LDB to Amy Brandeis Wehle, 20 January 1877.
2. Sir Anthony Absolute is a character in Richard Sheridan's *The Rivals* (1775).

DEAREST SUSAN: Tell Jack that his grape-vines are all in place and that we are relieved to think that they are in fair shape for the inspection of Judge [George W.] Anderson, who is to come this week end for his annual visit with Miss Grady.

Also tell him that Mother is tending his fruit trees busily each day (or rather evening) removing the caterpillars which find their luscious leaves most inviting.

Tell him also that yesterday Mother & Auntie B. (with my feeble aid) planted peas and beans, which have been dedicated to you and him.

Yesterday, being barber day, Mother & Auntie B. embraced the opportunity of a free ride, and made as extensive (and expensive) purchases as Jack would have done, had he devoted himself as sedulously to garden truck as to cotton.

Finally, tell him that we have had so far two messes of delicious asparagus & more is promised. The milklady (and boy) is to cut our grass & remove it for hay.   Lovingly

DEAREST SUSAN: Auntie B. has given your house a through overhauling, so that it is now appropriate for the advent of the C.P. Mother is plying the scythe upon the grass—unusually long because of much rain, so as to cut a fair path to the house.

Other activities are proceeding apace. Cold weather is making heavy inroads on our large wood. Auntie B. had to buy yesterday a $1/4$ cord of sawn wood. Mother and I are gradually assembling the ex-grape arbor wood, near the garage so that a supply will be gathered for Jack's strong arm.

Miss Lucy et al are expected for tea, this afternoon.

I suppose N.Y. is over its Lindbergh debauch. But Boston has one in prospect.[1] And I suppose it will be full "two months" before he is forgotten.

I am deep in The Federalist;[2] and of evenings we are reading Beards' latest,[3] which, at Mother's suggestion, Auntie B. has presented to me.

Lovingly

Mother was much disappointed by your decision not to occupy our house for C.P. & yourself. She says my former study (over the kitchen) would be sound proof, so far as she is concerned & would make an admirable nursery for you, as it did for the Hardys. (I am occupying the former guests' room as sleeping room, & the east glass-enclosed porch for my study.) Mother will write you.

1. Upon his return to the United States after his historic solo flight across the Atlantic, Charles Augustus Lindbergh, Jr. (1902–74) was courted by cities across the country. He left Washington, D.C., for New York on 13 June, and the city gave him a momentous greeting: a ticker-tape parade, the key from Mayor Walker, a medal from Governor Al Smith, honors from various civic groups, gala state dinners every night. While in New York he received an invitation from Governor Alvan Fuller to come to Boston; as part of a nationwide tour, the aviator arrived in that city to comparable acclaim on 22 July.

2. Perhaps LDB had acquired the popular new Everyman edition of the classic work by Alexander Hamilton, James Madison, and John Jay: *The Federalist* (New York: Dutton, 1926).

3. In the spring of 1927 the renowned progressive historian Charles Austin Beard (1874–1948) and his wife, Mary Ritter Beard (1876–1958), published their popular and influential work *The Rise of American Civilization* (New York, 1927).

To: Alfred Brandeis
Date: June 19, 1927
Place: Chatham, Massachusetts
Source: Brandeis MSS

DEAR AL: Letter from Walter Child enclosed. His reference to [*] means his annual tramp there in the swamps in search of orchids.

He is one of the men who, opportunities and obstacles considered, made the most of life. He overcame the inherited appetite for drink. He bore & lived down the terrible misfortune inherent in his wife, and he functioned in business despite his lack of business ability. His happiness he earned through pursuit of art & the history which went with it; and the pursuit of orchids & the science which attended it; and took perhaps equal pleasure in the cultivation of a few worthy friends.

There are only a few of our friends who have excelled in the art of living. I count him & Denman Ross, and Prof. [Ephraim] Emerton preeminent among the number.

Gruesse

To: Susan Brandeis Gilbert
Date: September 25, 1927
Place: Washington, D.C.
Source: Gilbert MSS

DEAREST SUSAN: Mother took me for a picnic above Chain-bridge, the first in many years. A gentle paddle on the canal & lunch on the bank amidst wild flowers & a wild duck on the water near.

For luncheon i.a. crackers & olives, as we had them on the expedition with Harry Wehle on the Charles.

This afternoon Mr. & Mrs. Israel Brodie[1] called to bid me goodbye, or rather to let me bid them. They leave in about a month for Palestine, not only with bag & baggage, but with 5 children and all their household belonging[s] to educate their children in Palestine & hoping to remain permanently.

My greeting for the New Year.[2] How will you spend the day.[?]

Lovingly

1. Israel Benjamin Brodie (1884–1965) was a lawyer and an active Zionist from Baltimore. A loyal member of the Brandeis-Mack faction of the movement, he was intimately involved with the Palestine Economic Corporation and participated in a number of ventures designed to develop Palestine economically.

2. This date was Rosh Hashanah, the day welcoming the new year of 5688 by the Jewish calendar.

To: **Susan Brandeis Gilbert**
Date: **October 9, 1927**
Place: **Washington, D.C.**
Source: **Gilbert MSS**

DEAREST SUSAN: I am very sorry for Miss Szold, but don't see how I can congratulate her;[1] or, indeed, say anything to her except to send my good wishes before she sails.[2] She has, of course, made serious mistakes of judgment—from the loftiest of motives.

She will not be so unhappy when she is once in Palestine which she deeply loves. She knows that I have felt for years that her task lies pre-eminently there. The grave difficulty now is that she is assuming burdens, not only too heavy for her years, but for which she lacks the aptitude & experience.

I hope your Hadassah folk are making good progress in their special task.

Lovingly

1. Henrietta Szold, who was visiting the United States, had just been chosen the first woman and the first American to serve on the Palestine Executive of the Jewish Agency. In honor of her election, Zionists planned a gala dinner in her honor at the Hotel Astor. On 7 November eighteen hundred guests gathered to honor her, and tributes were spoken by Louis Lipsky, Stephen S. Wise, Irma Lindheim, Judah Magnes, and others. Susan had evidently reported to her father that Szold was unhappy and asked her father to send a congratulatory message. But LDB believed that the 67-year-old Szold should have confined her energies to her medical work in Palestine and disapproved of her getting involved in the intricacies of Zionist "politics."

2. LDB did send such a letter; see LDB to Henrietta Szold, 10 November 1927, BL.

To: Alfred Brandeis
Date: October 15, 1927
Place: Washington, D.C.
Source: Brandeis MSS

DEAR AL:

1. Enclosed postal, will interest Jennie, Fanny, & Jean. It represents a manuscript recently discovered in Central Europe & secured by the Congressional Library—the earliest, I think, of musical mss., & has been deciphered by Dr. [*] whom Fanny will remember. Tell her to keep it for the homecoming.

2. Charlie N[agel]. made a brief argument in our Court yesterday. He has been in & out of the Court room most of the week. He is in fine form—& in appearance, manner, mannerisms, walk, clothes and attitudes is exactly the C.N. of 50 years ago. There is really little sign of aging except the grayness in hair & moustache. Yetti Hegman would have said: "Er sieht sich selbst lächerlich ähnlich."[1]

3. Have had no time yet to give consideration to the list of historical books submitted by Colvin.[2]

4. In the St. Louis case one Theodore Rassieur, presumably a son of Leo, made an uncommonly good argument. He is a better lawyer than Leo as I remember him.[3]

5. You can tell Otto [Wehle] that his cousin Godfrey Goldmark,[4] also was before our Court yesterday & that he is an uncommonly good lawyer.

1. "He seems ridiculously like himself." See note 3 below.

2. George Colvin (1875–1928) was a lawyer and a state superintendent of education in Kentucky when he became president of the University of Louisville in 1926. His administration was extremely controversial (see LDB to Alfred Brandeis, 2 November 1927, note 1), and the Brandeis family was frustrated for a time in their efforts to build the university. He had at this juncture submitted a list of books that the library badly needed.

3. Leo Rassieur (1844–1929) was born in Russia but set up his law practice in St. Louis. The day before, Theodore Rassieur had argued State of Missouri ex rel. St. Louis Brewing Association v. Public Service Commission of Missouri and Union Electric Light and Power Company. It was one of a set of related cases; in connection with another of them, LDB's brother-in-law Charles Nagel had made his argument. The Court dismissed all of the cases, citing an absence of jurisdiction. See 275 U.S. 489 (1927).

4. Godfrey Goldmark (1880–1968) was a New York lawyer, specializing in corporation law. He was the son of Adolf and Ida Wehle Goldmark.

456

To: Susan Brandeis Gilbert
Date: October 16, 1927
Place: Washington, D.C.
Source: Gilbert MSS

DEAREST SUSAN: That's thrilling news of Louis' essays at walking. It's fortunate he is learning now. By the time he reaches maturity the art may be among the lost—through disuse.

Do you or Jack know Herbert A. Hickman—a man in the thirties who appeared before us for the State Tax Commission?[1] I do not recall in my 11 years of service more than one or two occasions when the State or any of its departments was so well represented.

The day is fine & Mother & I plan some canoeing on the canal from the Chain-bridge boathouse.

Good reports come from Elizabeth. We were in error in assuming that her 10 research students are all graduates. Only 1 is that, the others are seniors.   Lovingly

1. On 13 October Herbert A. Hickman argued *People of the State of New York ex rel. International Bridge Co. v. State Tax Commission,* 275 U.S. 488. The case was decided *per curiam* on 24 October.

To: Susan Brandeis Gilbert
Date: October 17, 1927
Place: Washington, D.C.
Source: Gilbert MSS

DEAREST SUSAN: That must have been a very interesting dinner to Morris Cohen.[1] Judge Holmes has frequently spoken of him as perhaps the best of American minds in thing[s] metaphysical.

Otto & Clara [Goldmark] were in good form.   Lovingly

1. Morris Raphael Cohen (1880–1947) was a Russian immigrant who became a celebrated philosopher and teacher. Cohen was well known for his many popular philosophic books and essays and for the illustrious students that he turned out at the City College of New York. To commemorate his twenty-fifth year at CCNY, a gala dinner was held in his honor on 15 October. A thousand guests came to the Hotel Astor, where Felix Frankfurter presided over the evening. Cohen heard himself praised by Bertrand Russell, John Dewey, Julian Mack, Judah Magnes, and others. Letters of tribute were read, including words from Albert Einstein, Roscoe Pound, and LDB's brother-in-law Felix Adler.

To: Alfred Brandeis
Date: November 2, 1927
Place: Washington, D.C.
Source: Brandeis MSS

457

1. Susan, Jack, Louis and Britta (the nurse) arrive in due time. This is the young man's first birthday.
2. Susie Goldmark left at 11. this morning.
3. Hapgood will be glad to see Barrett's letter.
4. I note that you expect to have meeting with Laurent soon & will send AAUP Report soon.[1]
5. If O'Neal is elected,[2] it will do much toward clearing the University situation.

Gruesse

I assume you thought as much yesterday of our trip to the Husarrenburg as I did.[3] The 55 years make a difference in us as well as in things external.

You and Jennie will be interested in reading this letter of Miss Grady which shows what a rawboned high school girl earning $10 a week 33 years ago has developed into. Wheeler's Point is in Gloucester. Talmage [sic][4] is her brother.

1. The stormy administration of the University of Louisville under President George Colvin culminated in a bitter public controversy that eventually absorbed the entire community. Colvin and ten trustees were charged with anti-Semitism (involving the resignation of historian Louis Gottschalk), favoritism, dishonesty, and trying to abolish tenure. The American Association of University Professors compiled a report that was critical of both Colvin and the trustees, in *AAUP Bulletin* 13 (November 1927): 429–69. The battle interfered with the Brandeis family's efforts on behalf of the university, but those efforts resumed with the death of Colvin in 1928 and the assumption of the presidency by Raymond A. Kent.

2. Joseph Thomas O'Neal (1881–1944), a graduate of the University of Louisville Law School, was running for mayor of the city. He did, in fact, defeat W. B. Harrison.

3. During their sojourn in Europe as boys in 1872 the Brandeis brothers visited the Husaren Temple, near Modling, Austria-Hungary. The monument to officers who had died fighting Napoleon at the battle of Aspen was built in 1813. For some reason, the place made a profound impression on LDB and his brother, and in letters on anniversaries of their stop they often recalled the visit there.

4. Talmadge Grady, the brother of LDB's former secretary, became a field worker for the Savings Bank Insurance system run by his sister.

To: Alfred Brandeis
Date: November 5, 1927
Place: Washington, D.C.
Source: Brandeis MSS

DEAR AL:

1. Re proposed letter to Jouett.[1] I think it unwise to write to him or to talk with him on this subject, unless he initiates the subject. His

term expires, as I recall, in March/28. If O'Neal is elected on Tuesday, it will probably be wise to supplant Jouett when there is an opportunity. He certainly is not a friend of our projects.

2. I hope you are wrong on your Alf. E. Smith guess. I can't believe that Ky or other southern states (except possibly Tenn) will vote against him if he is the Democratic nominee.[2] I "yearn" to live through another Democratic administration.

3. I have recd from Dean Anderson the [*] Com[mit]tee Report. It is comprehensive & complete consideration of G[eorge]. C[olvin]. & his Board.[3]

1. Edward Stockton Jouett (1863–1960) was the attorney for the Louisville & Nashville Railroad. At this time he was the chair of the University of Louisville Board of Trustees.

2. Alfred proved himself a better prophet than LDB. In the presidential election of 1928, Al Smith carried the deep South but lost the border states including Kentucky (59 percent to 41 percent) and Tennessee (55 percent to 45 percent).

3. Probably Dean Warwick Anderson had sent LDB a copy of the AAUP report on the University of Louisville (see the preceding letter, note 1).

To:	Alfred Brandeis
Date:	November 29, 1927
Place:	Washington, D.C.
Source:	Brandeis MSS

DEAR AL: Re yours of 25th

1. I think the decisions on these matters submitted had better be deferred until you & I shall have had full talk on U[niversity]. matters when you come here for Christmas holidays. I suggest, therefore, that you say nothing definitely, either way, to anyone connected with the U.—answering tactfully that you will discuss the matter with me then.

2. I have only this to add: Don't be too discouraged. The future has many good things in store for those who can wait, and have patience and exercise good judgment. There are likely to be fortunate as well as unfortunate accidents. There is nothing more probable than that some improbable things, or even the seeming impossible, will happen. "My faith is great in time, and that which shapes it to its perfect end". And men in a fight should remember that Napoleon's Old Guard "never resigned and seldom died". If Arthur Allen had held his place, we should be in much better fix today.[1]

3. I enclose letter to Charles [Tachau], which please mail after reading & making copies.

As you may not have seen Charles to me of 11/26 I am enclosing same. Please return it.

1. Arthur Dwight Allen (1879–1949) was a Louisville businessman, social activist, and philanthropist. He was also an amateur composer and artist. Allen had been a sympathetic ally of the Brandeis projects at the University of Louisville when he was a member of the Board of Trustees.

To: Susan Brandeis Gilbert
Date: January 12, 1928
Place: Washington, D.C.
Source: Gilbert MSS

DEAREST SUSAN: This evening's Jackson Day Dinner should give us some indication whether the Democrats may hope to elect a President again. Your Governor is certainly gaining much in favor, despite some protests of Democratic Women's organizations.[1]   Lovingly

1. More than 2,000 Democrat loyalists gathered for the gala dinner in Washington, D.C., on this date. Among them were John W. Davis, the party's 1924 nominee, and other potential candidates. The emphasis was on harmony, and the explosive prohibition issue was studiously avoided. A letter from Governor Alfred E. Smith, the only major candidate not present, was greeted with prolonged applause. Even William G. McAdoo, spokesman for the "drys," was conciliatory. On the day before, however, Mrs. Clem Shaver, wife of the chair of the Democratic National Committee, said that Democratic women would regard the nomination of a "wet" with alarm and might even field their own ticket of those who supported the Volstead Act. Governor Smith, of course, was to march triumphantly to the nomination at the Houston, Texas, convention on 26 June.

To: Susan Brandeis Gilbert
Date: January 21, 1928[1]
Place: Washington, D.C.
Source: Gilbert MSS

DEAREST SUSAN: I guess much water will flow under the mill before the Ass[ociatio]n of the Bar of New York changes its Constitution.[2]

Aunt Belle [La Follette] is coming in to see Mother this afternoon. Aren't some of your musician friends planning to review Mother's Karl Goldmark?[3]

Abe Tulin[4] was here Thursday & reports on Weizmann-Lipsky projects. They are becoming ever more brazen in their doings.

We recess Monday for four weeks, with plenty of work on hand to occupy me fully until the sessions are resumed.

Your son seems to be training for some long distance running.

460

At Mr. deHaas' suggestion, I am to see the Palestine Labor representatives tomorrow.[5]

Lovingly

Is Jack pursuing his Zionist studies?
Mother sends these letters of Elizabeth's which please return.

1. LDB erroneously dated this letter 21 January 1927.
2. Probably this remark has to do with Susan Gilbert's attempt to gain membership in the New York Bar Association despite its constitutional provision against women members. She was eventually admitted about ten years later.
3. Alice Brandeis had just published her translation of *Notes from the Life of a Viennese Composer* (New York, 1927), Karl Goldmark's memoir.
4. Abraham Tulin (1882–1973), a Russian immigrant, was a New York lawyer active in Zionist affairs. He was especially interested in technical education in Palestine.
5. In an attempt to ameliorate a severe unemployment crisis among agricultural and factory workers in Palestine, the National Labor Committee for Organized Jewish Workers in Palestine had sent a three-person delegation to the United States to raise $300,000, principally among American-Jewish labor organizations.

To: **Susan Brandeis Gilbert**
Date: **February 26, 1928**
Place: **Washington, D.C.**
Source: **Gilbert MSS**

MY DEAREST SUSAN: The last twelve months have been so good to you and Jack that one cannot wish better for the next than continuation of what is and fulfilment [*sic*] of the beautiful promise which has been made.[1]

Lovingly

1. The next day was Susan's thirty-fifth birthday.

To: **Susan Brandeis Gilbert**
Date: **March 20, 1928**
Place: **Washington, D.C.**
Source: **Gilbert MSS**

DEAREST SUSAN: Jack telephones that he will be in for dinner.[1]

What assurance has Hadassah that it will be repaid the $10,000 loan?[2]

Will it have in its possession later U[nited]. P[alestine]. A[ppeal]. funds from which it can re-imburse itself?

I have just had word from Boston that Miss Grady has won a very nobly contested legislative fight on Savings Bank Insurance. I am a strong believer in Amazons.[3]

Lovingly

1. Jack Gilbert spent most of March 1928 in Washington on business and dined almost every evening with his in-laws.

2. Hadassah apparently had enough cash on hand to advance funds to a UPA project. Since the Lipsky faction controlled the UPA, LDB had doubts about both the probity of the project and the good faith of the UPA to repay the loan.

3. The insurance companies of Massachusetts regularly tried to cripple the Savings Bank Life Insurance scheme. Most often, the attempt was in the form of limiting the amount of policies—in 1927, for example, a bill (ultimately defeated) proposed limiting policies to $2,000 and annuities to $400. In 1928 the Summers bill would have required the SBLI system to reimburse the state for all the money the division spent. As LDB indicates here, it was also defeated. In the midst of the fight, LDB had written Alice Grady: "I know you are a 'bonnie fighter'—& with the right, for which you always battle, on your side—even the legions of the evil ones cannot beat you" (LDB to Alice Harriet Grady, 16 March 1928, BL).

To: **Susan Brandeis Gilbert**
Date: April 4, 1928
Place: Washington, D.C.
Source: Gilbert MSS

MY DEAREST SUSAN: I am sending by Jack—
"For the Right", by Karl Emil Franzos (a translation—1888).[1] The occasion is this: Mrs. Franzos (née Ottilie Benedikt), the widow of Franzos, was my friend & contemporary in Vienna in 1872, and the daughter of [my] Mother's dearest girlhood friend, Bettie Manthner.

Ottilie has written me recently (sending this book) & saying the film producers in Berlin had been greatly interested in the story with a view of purchasing the film rights, but gave it up after much examination, because they found that the cost of production would be too large.

Ottilie has a notion that no costs are too large in America, & no achievement impossible for me. So she suggests that I could find a producer here. Mother suggests that, if any one in the family could do anything with the project, it is you, & that Dave [Podell] might know of possibilities etc. So I am venturing to send this to you, for consideration of the possibilities.

Lovingly

1. Karl Emil Franzos, *For the Right,* trans. Julie Sutter (New York, 1888); originally *Ein Kampf um's Recht* (1882). Franzos (1848–1904) was a Russian-born Jew. After a career in journalism, he turned to writing short stories and novels in German.

To: **Susan Brandeis Gilbert**
Date: April 14, 1928
Place: Washington, D.C.
Source: Gilbert MSS

462

1. Your yesterday's letter has just come & I have wired you: "Must leave Straus matter to your and Jack's discretion. Am writing on other matters."[1]

2. Answering your further enquiry: I think it better that you should not sign the deHaas call. Keep yourself strictly within the Hadassah.[2]

3. It is, of course, imperative that no expense incurred by Hadassah women in connection with the fight against Lipsky be paid out of Hadassah funds, even if the expenses are trifling. A separate campaign fund should be raised; and I shall be glad to contribute through you liberally to that. Of course, the fraction of the whole paid by me must not be so large that it could truthfully be said that I am "financing the Campaign".

4. Don't send me the Wedgewood [*sic*].[3] Mr. de Sola Pool[4] sent me a copy.

5. Note from Mother & letter of E[lizabeth]'s enclosed.

Lovingly

1. As the fight against the Lipsky administration of the ZOA heated in the spring of 1928, it was apparent that Nathan Straus's views would be critical. He had, after all, given more than $1 million dollars to Zionist causes. Three days before this letter, Straus had issued a strong endorsement of Chaim Weizmann's leadership of the World Zionist Organization. However, on 22 April Mrs. Straus, speaking for herself and her husband, read a strong letter of denunciation of the leadership of Louis Lipsky to the Hadassah meeting in New York City and endorsed the efforts of Hadassah to secure a change in the ZOA's leadership.

2. Perhaps it was Jacob deHaas who issued the "call" for a Washington, D.C., conference to discuss ZOA leadership. The meeting of 300 occurred on 29 April and passed very strong resolutions, introduced by Felix Frankfurter, condemning the mismanagement, inefficiency, and general dereliction of the Lipsky regime. Hadassah's earlier vote of "no confidence" was noted at that meeting, but the women's organization played no official part there.

3. Perhaps Josiah Clement Wedgwood, *Palestine: The Fight for Jewish Freedom and Honour* (London, 1926).

4. David de Sola Pool (1885–1970) was the rabbi of the leading Sephardic synagogue in America, Shearith Israel in New York City. He was a prominent Zionist.

To: Jacob H. Gilbert
Date: April 18, 1928
Place: Washington, D.C.
Source: Gilbert MSS

MY DEAR JACK: Both Susan and deHaas have written me of the suggestion that Nathan Straus Junior be urged to allow his name to be proposed for President of the Z.O.A.[1] This would be an admirable solution of a very difficult problem. His personal qualities, his abilities and his devotion to things worthwhile fit him for the post.

I wrote deHaas of your talk on the general situation with Mr. & Mrs. Straus and the Junior last Sunday and asked deHaas to talk with you. Of course, I shall be glad to write to N.S. Junior and to Mr. & Mrs. Straus, also, but you know my views & I think it may be more effective for you to talk with them on this subject.

Tell Susan her Mother & I think your photographer has done an uncommonly good job on the boy's pictures. We are returning them herewith. Those marked first and second choice are the ones the Grandmother desires.

Proofs returned herewith.

1. Nathan Straus, Jr. (1889–1961) graduated from Princeton in 1909, served in the navy during World War I, and was actively engaged in journalism, radio, civic reform, and politics (within a few weeks he was being mentioned as a possible candidate for lieutenant governor as Franklin Roosevelt's running mate). He was interested in Zionist affairs, but nothing came of the proposal to make him president of the Zionist Organization of America. In 1937 President Roosevelt named him head of the federal public housing program.

To: Jacob H. Gilbert
Date: April 18, 1928
Place: Washington, D.C.
Source: Gilbert MSS

MY DEAR JACK: Answering your enquiry re Dr. Wise:[1]

The World War has taught us how "Allied and Associated Powers" may cooperate with success. Exploit to the full the individual initiative but avoid all diversions, physical, intellectual or emotional, which may embarrass the pursuit of the common immediate objective. As stated before, I think that even the slightest reference by Dr. Wise either to Dr. Weizmann, the Jewish Agency, the delinquencies of the World Organization or the Russian agricultural undertakings would be harmful, if made at anytime before the close of the ZOA convention. Let the next two months and a half be devoted to "turning the rascal out" of the American Organization. There is a long future after that.

You will recall what John Morley said of John Stuart Mill:[2] "The only fear he ever knew was fear lest a premature or excessive utterance should harm a good cause. He had measured the prejudices of men, and his desire to arouse this obstructive force in the least degree compatible with effective advocacy of any improvement, set the single limit to his intrepidity."

1. Rabbi Wise was an inveterate and severe critic of the Lipsky administration (his highly public resignation from the ZOA's Administrative Committee at the end of March was perhaps the opening gun in the current campaign to dump Lipsky). But Wise was also a vocal and sometimes unrestrained critic of Chaim Weizmann's administration of the World Organization. LDB thought that Wise's denunciations of Weizmann should be muzzled until the American Zionists got rid of Louis Lipsky.

2. John Morley (1838–1923) was a writer much admired by LDB. He specialized in biographical studies of leading British public figures.

To: **Susan Brandeis Gilbert**
Date: **May 1, 1928**
Place: **Washington, D.C.**
Source: **Gilbert MSS**

DEAREST SUSAN: Mother is delighted to have such good reports from you and sister.[1]

Israel Brodie was in today with most encouraging reports from Palestine which he left April 13. Encouraging except, of course, as to Zionist Organization which is [in] as bad a condition as can be, with poor Miss Szold left to bear the burdens of the triumvirate.[2] He says she is in a terribly hysterical condition & it seems clear that she is not in a state of mind to exercise sound judgment. I am glad she is remaining silent on American affairs.   Lovingly

1. Both of the Brandeis daughters were pregnant—Susan was to deliver in mid-May and Elizabeth in mid-June.

2. Henrietta Szold was a member of the three-person Palestine Executive of the Jewish Agency.

To: **Susan Brandeis Gilbert**
Date: **May 20, 1928**
Place: **Washington, D.C.**
Source: **Gilbert MSS**

DEAREST SUSAN: Mother hopes you are not having such a "pea soup" day as Washington is bathing in. But I am revelling in a temperature that lets even me sit quietly at my desk without coat or vest—and with plenty to occupy the mind. There is even enough work on hand to satisfy my voracious secretary.[1]   Lovingly

1. LDB's secretary for the 1927–28 term was Henry Jacob Friendly (1903–86), one of LDB's favorites. After working with LDB, Friendly practiced law until 1959, when he became a highly respected circuit court judge for the Second Circuit. He served in that position until his death.

To:	Susan Brandeis Gilbert
Date:	May 26, 1928
Place:	Washington, D.C.
Source:	Gilbert MSS

DEAREST SUSAN: Florence Boeckel has just been in bringing a photograph of her children which are being put into competition with yours[1]—of course a vain effort.

Mother is systematically working off her remaining social and other duties so as to be ready for our Hejira June 4.[2] My opinions are making progress, and if all goes well, those remaining will be swung off on that day—with a lyrical intermezzo on Monday next.

Hope you and Jack will have a good Sunday.   Lovingly

1. Susan had given birth to a daughter, the Brandeises' second grandchild and only granddaughter, on 14 May. The child was named after her maternal grandmother. Alice Brandeis Gilbert Popkin was to become a Washington, D.C., attorney.
2. To Chatham.

To:	Charles Gabriel Tachau
Date:	May 27, 1928
Place:	Washington, D.C.
Source:	Brandeis MSS

MY DEAR CHARLES: Replying to yours of 16th, enclosing President Colvin's letter of that date.

1. I had supposed that Miss Lavin was to devote herself to the work of cataloguing the World War Library.[1] If she was competent for the job, I can't quite see why so much remains to be done, and think we should have an accurate knowledge of what has been accomplished in quantity and quality before we commit ourselves to further expenditures.

2. As to the salary for the coming year. I think we had better wait before deciding. As you know, my thought has been to develop the University through the library and not merely to build up a storehouse of books. In this development the individual members of the faculty are essential factors. They, in their several fields, must help individually to build up the library. The library, through that cooperation will develop them. And through them, the students are to be inspired. Moreover, the library is to become dynamic also in respect to the community. Its needs are to awaken interest

466

and make friends for the University. I do not see how this plan of development can be carried out, if the faculty members are to be excluded from active participation in the work of building up the libraries of peculiar value in this work. The ablest librarian, with all available technical knowledge, cannot supply the needs of the situation, unless conditions are such that the cooperation of the faculty members in the manner indicated is not only tolerated, but welcomed; and unless conditions are such that we may feel reasonably sure that it will be given.

1. One of LDB's projects for the building of the University of Louisville's library.

To:	Susan Brandeis Gilbert
Date:	May 31, 1928
Place:	Washington, D.C.
Source:	Gilbert MSS

DEAREST SUSAN:

1. Owing to error of Post Office your letter of 27th went first to Winchester Va., & did not reach me until today.
2. As to the car. Mother bids me say:
   (a) We should have a closed car.
   (b) If it is possible to hire a desirable car for the summer at anything reasonable it will be better to do that than to buy one.
   (c) What car to get Jack will know much better than we could guess.
   (d) We expect Jack (as was discussed with him) to come to Chatham to look over the ground before you & the children come on. When he is there he can talk with Bearse—the Auto Agency of Chatham, who is very anxious to sell or to lease us a car; and perhaps before Jack comes to Chatham he will be able to make some enquiries in N.Y. on the general subject to bring his knowledge up to date.
3. Mrs. Lewis writes that the house[1] will be ready for occupancy June 20—unless she hears that we want it earlier. If we do, she will endeavor to comply with our wishes.
4. I enclose letter & papers from the telephone company which please fill out as to name, as you desire, & mail to the company.
5. Of course, you understand that Mother & I expect to pay not only telephone charges, but all other expenses of your Chatham stay

(including the food bills). You and your family are to be as much our guests as if you were in our own house.

Lovingly

Mr. deHaas and Israel Brodie were in a bit last evening. They are both good fighters.[2]

Morris R. Cohen was in for an hour & a half in the afternoon (He was here for some talks at Brookings) & was most interesting.

Walter Meyer was in on Tuesday. I got him to give $500 to the campaign fund.

Mother & I were on the canal for an hour yesterday A.M. In the afternoon we called on Mrs [Woodrow] Wilson and on Aunt Belle [La Follette].

Answering your enquiry about the Jane Adams [sic] article. I think you had better *not* send it to her. She is safe in your hands.

1. The Gilberts had rented a house in Chatham for the summer. In 1936 they built their own summer home near LDB and AGB's cottage.
2. Preparations were in full swing for the ZOA convention scheduled for 1 July. Both the Lipskyites and their critics were preparing for what promised to be an explosive meeting. In the end Lipsky's group was able to control the convention, and the critics' contentions were brushed aside; Lipsky was reelected to another term as president of the organization.

To: **Susan Brandeis Gilbert**
Date: **June 9, 1928**
Place: **Chatham, Massachusetts**
Source: **Gilbert MSS**

DEAREST SUSAN:

1) We arrived in due time. We had Frank Nickerson meet us at Harwich. He has a new Stearns Knight. Spacious & comfortable. We should have had him meet us at Yarmouth, as unknown to us, the regular train (and Parlor Car) stop now at Yarmouth & we had to change there to the gasoline trolley. I understand that the regular train service will be resumed June 11th.

There you have evidence of the decline of RR passenger traffic under motor competition.

2) Tell Jack I cut this morning a copious supply of large asparagus.
3) It is cold and grey here. But your house is in good order and the canoes have been beautifully painted by Stanley. We have ample need for the copious supply of wood Jack furnished.

Lovingly

To: Susan Brandeis Gilbert
Date: June 13, 1928
Place: Chatham, Massachusetts
Source: Gilbert MSS

DEAREST SUSAN: Mother says I ought to have reported also to Britta on the Cosmos[1] and [*]. And she adds that Stanley has been here & for three hours labored in your and Britta's garden so as to get it into promising condition.

I meanwhile am diligently painting in the sun parlor.

I trust the Hadassah fight goes well. Militancy and eternal vigilance, coupled with the right & such ability as the Newsletters disclose must win.

We await Jack.   Lovingly

    1. A flowering herb.

To: Alfred Brandeis
Date: July 2, 1928
Place: Chatham, Massachusetts
Source: Gilbert MSS

DEAR AL: Tell your "family and friends" that you are entirely right about Smith's chances of election & that they had better get on to the bandwagon quick. There will be such accessions soon that not even standing-room will be available.

Houston selected a winning ticket[1] & the urban vote, so largely increased of late years, will be heard from in November.[2]

We are expecting Miss Grady & Sadie Nicholson for the Fourth.

I have Miss Mason's June report.[3] Suppose you & Mrs. Gross will be going to the U. after the holiday.

    1. The Democratic convention in Houston selected Senator Joseph Taylor Robinson (1872–1937) as Al Smith's running mate. Robinson represented Arkansas in the House from 1903 to 1913. He spent the rest of his life in the Senate.
    2. See LDB to Susan Brandeis Gilbert, 7 November 1928.
    3. On progress at the University of Louisville.

To: Jennie Brandeis
Date: August 8, 1928
Place: Chatham, Massachusetts
Source: Brandeis MSS

MY DEAR JENNIE: In these days Alice and I have talked of Alfred's beautiful, gladsome life.[1] He brought happiness ever to parents, wife, children, grandchildren; help to individuals, the community, his country; joy to all who shared in his activities or with whom he came into contact. From others he received, in large measure, love, friendship, appreciation. Thus he experienced the happiness and satisfaction of a radiant, generous nature.

The long years seem short because each brought so richly of these gifts and youth remained in body, mind, spirit. To all of us there is the comfort that to the end the beauty was unmarred, undimmed.

Frank and Catherine[2] are coming to us tomorrow.

1. On this date Alfred Brandeis, LDB's brother and his oldest and most trusted friend, died in Louisville. He was seventy-four.

2. Catherine Taussig was the daughter of Frank Taussig, Jennie Brandeis's niece.

To: Jennie Brandeis
Date: August 14, 1928
Place: Chatham, Massachusetts
Source: Brandeis MSS

MY DEAR JENNIE: Alfred's will was the natural expression of his confidence in you and his reliance upon you. I do not recall a word of his which could guide your discretion.

Alice and I are very glad that you summoned Louis Wehle. His help in legal and business matters will relieve you much, and no son could have loved more.

I have been reliving early days, aided by a file of old family letters which had escaped destruction. Alfred was always the same—generous, considerate, discerning, wise, joyous, charming. You may care to have these which refer to you in pre-engagement days. The girls and Alfred McCreary will appreciate the one which announces the firm, A. Brandeis & Son. That was a gift of happiness to Father and Mother for the rest of their days.

Please thank Fan and Jean for their letters. Fan's we shall share with Christine and Susie Goldmark.

Alice is much occupied with her grandchildren.[1]

The enclosed from Felix Frankfurter's letter to me shows his discernment.

1. The Brandeises now had three grandchildren. Elizabeth Brandeis Raushenbush had given birth to Walter Brandeis Raushenbush on 13 June 1928. The Raushenbush family was also at Chatham, having arrived on 26 July. Walter Raushenbush was to become a professor of law at the University of Wisconsin.

To:	Susan Brandeis Gilbert
Date:	August 18, 1928
Place:	Washington, D.C.
Source:	Gilbert MSS

DEAREST SUSAN:

1) Mother & I are very glad that you have concluded to make a statement in support of Smith and to campaign for him. I am sure Jack also is pleased.[1]

2) Whalen wants to sell his house, not to rent it. And he wants an unreasonably high price ($8000); and would want an unreasonably high rent, if willing to rent it at all so long in advance, if you asked for a lease now. Moreover, next June is a long time hence. I think it unwise to approach Mr. Snow (or Whalen) now. Mr. Snow offered to sell me the house. I told him we might want to rent it next spring, if it wasn't sold. And my thought is to say & do nothing about it until then. Besides the stockmarket may crumble before then.

Fannie thinks well of your children. It is nice to have Harry and Kate as neighbors.

1. Susan's support for Al Smith was announced by the Democrats on 24 September. See the *New York Times,* 25 September 1928. She was reported as "Miss Susan Brandeis."

To:	Susan Brandeis Gilbert
Date:	September 2, 1928
Place:	Washington, D.C.
Source:	Gilbert MSS

DEAREST SUSAN: Tell Jack that I hope to see much of your Governor[1] after March 4.

It would be inadvisable for me to see him during the campaign except under conditions which would preclude publicity. If he should chance to be in Washington, we should, of course, be glad to see him at the apartment—privately. But I am quite sure he can spend his time to better advantage, as there is no suggestion which I could make which would add to his wise, effective campaign.

Mother says Louis' achievement of Britta's name is quite a feather in his cap—and in celebration of it she bids me enclose this feather.   Lovingly

1. Alfred Smith, the Democratic candidate for the presidency.

To: Susan Brandeis Gilbert
Date: October 14, 1928
Place: Washington, D.C.
Source: Gilbert MSS

DEAREST SUSAN: Glad the speaking went off well. Mother sends you enclosed pignut and bids you tell your son of the expeditions you used to take in search of them in Dedham land. This one was taken along the canal during our walk this morning. It was the first gray day, after more than a week of unbroken sunshine.

We are glad to hear your son is for Al Smith. "Out of the mouths of babes & sucklings"[1] even comes the truth.   Lovingly

  1. Psalms 8:2.

To: Susan Brandeis Gilbert
Date: October 28, 1928
Place: Washington, D.C.
Source: Gilbert MSS

DEAREST SUSAN: Political news is certainly exciting now. Your Mother is deeply concerned.

All Boston observers agree that there was never anything like this outpouring for Smith! Will it mean votes? What will East Side do? Dare it disobey Marshall and Felix Warburg and Otto H. Kahn?[1]   Lovingly

  1. Like Louis Marshall, Felix Moritz Warburg (1871–1937) and Otto Hermann Kahn (1867–1934) were leading German Jews, attached to the American Jewish Committee. Both Warburg and Kahn were partners in the powerful Kuhn, Loeb banking firm, and Warburg was Jacob Schiff's son-in-law. All three men had come out strongly for Herbert Hoover. Here LDB wonders whether the eastern European Jews of the lower east side of New York City would vote for Smith. In the end the Jewish vote was divided, but went predominantly for Smith. Hoover carried New York State, but Smith carried every borough of the city, compiling a plurality of 430,000 votes (1.1 million to 640,000). For a district-by-district breakdown, see the *New York Times,* 7 November 1928.

To: Susan Brandeis Gilbert
Date: November 2, 1928
Place: Washington, D.C.
Source: Gilbert MSS

DEAREST SUSAN:

    1. We are celebrating your son's birthday by having the Carrol [*sic*] Todds,[1] (Ass't to the Atty General under Mr. Gregory), the Dean

Van Vlecks[2] (G.W. Law School) and Frank Tannenbaum[3] in to dine.

2. It was fine to have your report on the Halloween party.

3. Mother bids me say that the Virginians are sad, not to have rec'd your paper until today, as it is now too late to get it into their newspaper.

4. I advise you to keep a complete file of all your published statements and of all public notices about you. Some day the file will prove very useful. And the absence of it might someday prove very embarrassing.

Also a complete file of briefs & the like.

1. George Carroll Todd (1879–1947) specialized in antitrust during his service in the Wilson administration. He left public service in 1919 to resume private practice in Washington, D.C.

2. William Cabell Van Vleck (1885–1956) taught and served as a dean at George Washington University Law School for forty years. He was an authority on the law regarding aliens.

3. Frank Tannenbaum (1893–1969) went from serving a jail term for his role in labor radicalism to earning a doctorate from the Brookings Institution. An expert on labor conditions, especially in Latin America and the United States, he taught at Columbia University from 1935 to 1961.

To: **Susan Brandeis Gilbert**
Date: **November 7, 1928**
Place: **Washington, D.C.**
Source: **Gilbert MSS**

DEAREST SUSAN: This is a smashing defeat.[1] But we live to fight another day. We haven't the afternoon paper, so we are without definite news how N.Y. has gone on Smith & Roosevelt.[2] We shall need very clear explanation why N.Y., N.J., Conn., R.I., Mass, went wrong, so far as they did.[3] Was it the prosperity issue, or the women; liquor, tariff or Tammany;—or religion or all combined.

I am most eager to know what the foreign vote and the labor vote did.[4]

So if you & Jack are wise on these things enlighten us. Your Mother bears up well.   Lovingly

1. Hampered by the general prosperity, his stand on prohibition, and his Catholicism, Smith lost to Herbert Hoover badly on 6 November. He received 15.1 million votes (87 electoral votes) to Herbert Hoover's 21.4 million (444 electoral votes). Hoover carried all but eight states.

2. While Smith lost New York State (see LDB to Susan Brandeis Gilbert, 28 October 1928), Democratic candidate Franklin Delano Roosevelt (1882–1945) won a very narrow victory over Albert Ottinger, a former New York attorney general. Roosevelt garnered about

29,000 more votes (out of around 4 million) than his opponent. Roosevelt's victory immediately sparked speculation about a presidential run in 1932, and from this point onward LDB began to pay close attention to Roosevelt's rise in Democratic and national politics. The two men would eventually be brought into closer contact by Felix Frankfurter.

3. LDB is speculating here on the basis of early returns. Both Massachusetts and Rhode Island ended up in Smith's column. They were the only states outside of the South to do so.

4. Foreign-born citizens (who represented about 17 percent of the total population in 1928) were apparently divided. Scandinavians and Finns went for Hoover; Germans and other central Europeans for Smith. Poles and Italians—despite their Catholicism—were badly divided; for example, eighteen Polish-language newspapers endorsed Hoover and seventeen endorsed Smith; among Italian papers, twenty-two endorsed Smith and eighteen urged readers to vote for Hoover. Labor was also divided but more favorable to Smith, especially the Catholic-dominated unions in the North. Even though most unions endorsed Smith, John L. Lewis of the powerful United Mine Workers endorsed Hoover.

To:	Jacob H. Gilbert
Date:	November 8, 1928
Place:	Washington, D.C.
Source:	Gilbert MSS

MY DEAR JACK: Dr. Holmes'[1] letter and your acceptance of the check sent is a happy solution of the situation presented. What little knowledge I possessed of the art of fee-making is no doubt, obsolete, and never applied to New York conditions. But I found it wise to limit my gratuitous services to public causes and to let private individuals always pay something—limiting the amount to their ability to pay. I think they felt more grateful for my thus enabling them to preserve their self-respect than if I had served them without pay; and they were the more ready to send others as clients whom they felt assured would receive like treatment.

It is a fine relationship which you and Susan have established with a fine man.

Why did Copeland run ahead of Smith in N.Y.C.?[2]

1. The Gilberts had become attached to John Haynes Holmes (1869–1964), a leading liberal clergyman in New York City. Holmes was active in many progressive causes, including the ACLU and the NAACP; he was also sympathetic to the Zionist cause.

2. Royal Samuel Copeland (1868–1938) had been in the Senate since 1923. He won reelection over his opponent, Alanson B. Houghton, by 64,000 votes and ran well ahead of both Roosevelt and Smith in New York State, outpolling Smith by more than 90,000 votes.

To:	Susan Brandeis Gilbert
Date:	November 12, 1928
Place:	Washington, D.C.
Source:	Gilbert MSS

DEAREST SUSAN: No word has come from you in answer to Mother's letter of last week, telling you of the postponement of the Z.O.A. Reorganization Committee scheduled for Thanksgiving and that the special reason for suggestion you coming Thanksgiving instead of for the birthday no longer existed. We are still half-expecting that you will turn up this evening, but I want to make sure that you are not without a greeting from us tomorrow.[1]

We have been hearing from several persons about New York's sad political dereliction.

Ben Flexner has just been in.

Dr. Alfred E. Cohen [*sic*][2] was in for dinner yesterday.

Mr. deHaas was in yesterday afternoon.

It's a sad story—was it primarily the women?

Mother has not lost any of her sorrow over the result, but begins to think of future fights. There will be opportunity enough offered in the next four years for testing the militancy of any opposition.

I am sending you 3 photographs (sent me by Miss Grady who took them) of our First Street house, where we lived 1860–1865.[3] They will interest you & Jack, and someday, I hope Louis and Alice.   Lovingly

1. The next day was to be LDB's seventy-second birthday. It was a family tradition to *send* greetings on birthdays.
2. Probably Dr. Alfred Einstein Cohn (1879–1957), a prominent New York physician who had been connected with the Rockefeller Institute for Medical Research since 1911.
3. The house, in Louisville, was bought by Adolph and Frederika in early 1860. The family lived there until moving to a spacious house on Broadway, in a more affluent neighborhood.

To:	Elizabeth Brandeis Raushenbush
Date:	November 13, 1928
Place:	Washington, D.C.
Source:	Raushenbush MSS

DEAREST ELIZABETH: My thanks to Walter and his parents for their greetings—and the Tamerlane.[1]

I feel almost as if an "Earth Shaker" had been at work on us Smithites during the past week. The experience seems to add to my militancy. There is the opportunity ahead for great fighting.

This pignut, which we picked up on Phelps Place today, is to remind you to tell Walter some years hence of our expeditions in Dedham.

Lovingly

1. For his seventy-second birthday, the Raushenbushes sent LDB a copy of Harold Lamb's popular new biography, *Tamerlane, the Earth Shaker* (Garden City, N.Y., 1928). Tamerlane (1336–1405) was the legendary Asian conqueror and ruler immortalized in Christopher Marlowe's tragic drama of 1587.

To: **Susan Brandeis Gilbert**
Date: December 29, 1928
Place: Washington, D.C.
Source: Gilbert MSS

MY DEAR SUSAN: Miss Malloch will send you with this a check for $9,650.20—calculated as stated in her letter. Hereafter you will receive monthly from the office a check for $125, so as to keep you on even keel with Elizabeth.

To: **Susan Brandeis Gilbert**
Date: January 25, 1929[1]
Place: Washington, D.C.
Source: Gilbert MSS

DEAREST SUSAN: My congratulations on the Doll Receivership fee. That's a good inauguration of the new office and the New Year.

Very glad to hear Louis is out again. Your Mother is much occupied with Mrs. Speck in securing Adie's pantaloons.

We have just had a great thrill in reading again Robert Louis Stevenson's "Treasure of Franchard."[2] Do you recall it?

What you report about Hadassah is very sad.[3] What a wonderful organization it was. Can't Rose Jacobs[4] be induced to return? I notice that the N.Y. Hadassah has not equalled Pearl Franklin's[5] feat of last year. She wrote me that she expects to do at least as well this year.

Did I tell you that I had considerable correspondence with Beulah about the unemployment number, which the Graphic is getting out in March.[6]   Lovingly

1. LDB erroneously dated this letter 25 January 1928.

2. This was a short story by Stevenson published originally in 1888.

3. It is difficult to know what LDB is referring to here. On one level Hadassah was prospering—in 1928 it achieved a record high membership of 37,000, for example. LDB might have been lamenting a new but ultimately unsuccessful attempt by the Lipsky administration of the Zionist Organization to bring the rebellious women of Hadassah into line.

4. Rose Gell Jacobs (1888–1975) was one of the original founders of Hadassah in 1912. LDB admired her leadership of the organization when she became acting president (during Henrietta Szold's absence in Palestine), 1920–23. Jacobs would, in fact, return to the presidency of the organization, but not until 1930.

5. Pearl Franklin (1885–1958) was a lifelong Hadassah activist and for many years the leader of the Chicago chapter. She had set up a friendly competition between her branch and the New York City branch for membership and fund-raising.

6. Actually, the unemployment issue of the *Survey Graphic* did not appear until April 1929. The entire issue was devoted to that subject, and the first page featured a quotation from LDB.

To: **Susan Brandeis Gilbert**
Date: **January 30, 1929**
Place: **Washington, D.C.**
Source: **Gilbert MSS**

DEAREST SUSAN: Our congratulations on the return of Britta & that she was glad to be back.

The New York Receivership evil has happily developed into a scandal.[1] The [New York] World deserves much credit for disclosing the obvious so effectively.

And the Albany News that the project of excluding N.Y. utility receiverships etc. from Federal Courts is being urged is particularly commendable.

The indignation of N.Y.'s Congressmen (including Loring Black)[2] at the discovery of facts which probably all of them knew & many of them furthered has its humorous side. And I see that Charles Evans Hughes has also discovered what everybody knew.[3] Well, a late conversion is better than continued heresy.

I thought you might remember the Solomans. They are the representatives (quite old maids) of the old & most respectable Washington Jewry.

Lovingly

1. A major scandal in the "bankruptcy business" was currently agitating New York. On this date the grand jury handed down its first indictments in the matter. Accusations of bribery, flagrant embezzlement, and corrupt favoritism abounded. Receivers were accused of running bankrupt firms in the interest of themselves, their friends, or even the bankrupt persons themselves. The awarding of receiverships also came under investigation—one lawyer, David Steinhardt, had been granted more than 120 receiverships during the last six years. LDB had long believed that professional receivers, not private lawyers, should be assigned the responsibility for managing bankrupt firms.

2. Loring Milton Black, Jr. (1886–1956), a New York attorney, served in the state's Senate before becoming the Democratic congressman of the 5th District. He served from 1923 to 1935. No doubt LDB singles Black out here because for a time he practiced law with Jacob Gilbert.

3. On 12 January Charles Evans Hughes, at that time the president of the New York Bar Association, pledged full cooperation with the investigation.

To: **Susan Brandeis Gilbert**
Date: **February 3, 1929**
Place: **Washington, D.C.**
Source: **Gilbert MSS**

DEAREST SUSAN: The case from Mabel [Willebrandt]'s firm will help make a good showing for the first month of the New Year.

I don't see that the Receivership publicity can do you other than good.

Your Judge Learned Hand was in yesterday with Judge Hitz, and we had some talk—your Mother would say I lectured—on the New York's lawyers' pursuit of the Golden Fleece.[1]

Poindexter reports it exceedingly cold, but the sun shines bright & we are venturing canalward.

Mother is sending Elizabeth (the deceiver's) picture to her.   Lovingly

1. LDB wrote to Frankfurter the next day that "Learned Hand (with Hitz) called on the afternoon of the day your letter arrived. The talk on the N.Y. receivership scandal gave occasion to discuss the ethics of the bar & generally crime. I aired, with perhaps unseemly vehemence, my views on the leaders—saying i.a., that a single one does more harm etc. than a thousand shysters, & there was considerable discussion of Hughes" (Urofsky and Levy, *"Half Brother, Half Son,"* 357).

To: **Susan Brandeis Gilbert**
Date: **February 17, 1929**
Place: **Washington, D.C.**
Source: **Gilbert MSS**

DEAREST SUSAN: Mabel [Willebrandt] is to dine with us this evening. We had expected to have Gov. & Mrs. Pinchot as good Drys to keep her company. But only Mrs. P. is coming as he is kept busy in New York outfitting his schooner for their trip to the South Seas. The others are Prof. & Mrs. Alexander Wetmore,[1] of the Smithsonian, the bird authority whom Mother has long wanted to meet, Col. Pope Hennessy,[2] the military attaché of the British Embassy and young Swischer [*sic*] of Brookings, who is writing the monograph on Mr. Justice Field[3]—a special compliment to Mabel as Justice Field was California's great contribution to the Court.

Walter Hamilton was in yesterday and told of Prof. Tulin's illness. I am very sorry for Justine.[4]

I hope your son will soon reach the "Streets of New York."

Lovingly

Mrs. Maud Wood Park[5] spoke of Mabel's grief at the way she was treated by her party chiefs, & Senator D. I. Walsh of her hope for a judgeship.[6]

1. Alexander Wetmore (1886–1978) was a biologist and a specialist in western hemisphere bird life. After thirteen years with the Department of Agriculture and a year in charge of the Washington Zoo, he joined the Smithsonian Institution in 1925. He remained there, in various capacities, until his death a half-century later.
2. Major General Ladislaus Herbert Richard Pope-Hennessy (1875–1942) had a long military career in Africa, India, and Europe.
3. The prominent constitutional historian Carl Brent Swisher (1897–1968) was finishing his Ph.D. at the Brookings Institution and would soon move to Columbia University. After six years there and service in the New Deal, he began his long career at Johns Hopkins University in 1937. His biography *Stephen J. Field: Craftsman of the Law* was published

by Brookings in 1930. Field (1816–99) had moved to California during the gold rush of 1849. Lincoln nominated him to the High Court in 1863, and he served until his retirement in 1897.

4. Rabbi Stephen Wise's daughter Justine married Leon Arthur Tulin (1901–32) when she was a law student at Yale in 1926. He was a young professor at the law school. Two years later he moved to the Columbia Law School. He had just been diagnosed with leukemia and was to die in December 1932.

5. Maud Wood Park (1871–1955), a Boston social worker, was a pioneer in the struggle for women's suffrage. She was the first president of the League of Women Voters and served in that position from 1920 to 1924.

6. For at least five years Mabel Willebrandt had waged a frustrating and ultimately unsuccessful campaign to be appointed a federal judge for California. She was unable to overcome the obstacles of her sex (no woman had ever been appointed a federal judge), her staunch position as a dry, and the bitter warfare in the California Republican Party. She resigned her position in the Justice Department in May and returned to California to practice law.

To:	Susan Brandeis Gilbert
Date:	March 4, 1929
Place:	Washington, D.C.
Source:	Gilbert MSS

Our new President looked very fit, and also struck me as looking really significant as he sat among the multitude of Senators & Representatives next to Hon. Calvin Coolidge.[1]   Lovingly

1. On this date Herbert Hoover was inaugurated as the thirty-first president of the United States.

To:	Susan Brandeis Gilbert
Date:	March 5, 1929
Place:	Washington, D.C.
Source:	Gilbert MSS

DEAREST SUSAN: Your Mother was exceedingly patriotic yesterday. She attended the Senate session & some of message reading (until the rain drove her to cover), and in the afternoon went to the White House Reception. In the morning, Poindexter & I conveyed Mother (and Isabel Mahaffie[1]) to the Capitol & back. The afternoon expedition was undertaken with only Poindexter's support, though Mother found at the White House & took Miss Henriques to her home.

I (and Judge Holmes) omitted attendance at the message reading, being thereunto induced by the rain, & I amused myself with your New York papers in the robing-room until Mother was ready to start home.

Your New York Judges seem very nervous about their enquiry into the evil practices of their courts.[2]

Lovingly

Tell Jack that Felix F[rankfurter]. agree[s] with him as to pending N.Y. criminal legislation.[3]

1. Isabel Cooper Mahaffie was the bride of six months of Charles Delahunt Mahaffie (1884–1969), the director of finance for the Interstate Commerce Commission, who was soon to be appointed an ICC commissioner.
2. See LDB to Susan Brandeis Gilbert, 30 January 1929.
3. The Assembly had empanelled a State Crime Commission (the Baumes Commmission) that recommended a large number of laws designed to expedite criminal proceedings. On this date, however, the Assembly summarily killed six of the proposed laws. At the end of the legislative session, the New York Assembly had passed ten of the proposed Baumes laws but had killed fourteen of them, including the most drastic and far-reaching ones.

To:	Susan Brandeis Gilbert
Date:	March 6, 1929
Place:	Washington, D.C.
Source:	Gilbert MSS

DEAREST SUSAN: The new President's social activities have already begun. We are invited for Saturday to an afternoon to hear the Westminster (Dayton) Choir before it leaves for an European tour.

Mother expects to attend.   Lovingly

To:	Susan Brandeis Gilbert
Date:	March 13, 1929
Place:	Washington, D.C.
Source:	Gilbert MSS

DEAREST SUSAN: It was good to see Jack and to hear sweet reports of the family.

That's an interesting undertaking of his & should succeed.

The President made an excellent impression in our brief visit on him yesterday. It is an immense relief to think of Coolidge and Harding in the background of our memories.   Lovingly

To:	Elizabeth Brandeis Raushenbush
Date:	April 22, 1929
Place:	Washington, D.C.
Source:	Raushenbush MSS

DEAREST ELIZABETH: Mother and I were delighted to have the good reports on Walter's Thursday and Friday, and I thought it particularly fortunate that they came today, as Mother was feeling so poorly that she had Dr.

Ecker in. He says it is merely nerves expressing themselves as of old in the stomach, and we hope that tomorrow she will feel quite a bit "menschlich."[1]

Yesterday we had a joyous paddle on the Canal, with nature at its best. Trees and flower and birdsong were all entrancing. And our Mr. & Mrs. [*] charming and happy as becomes their environment.

This should really bring the birthday greetings.[2] Perhaps it will be a day early. We shall wish you Walter's continued progress, and a specially lovely smile from him on the day.

1. Human, civilized.
2. Elizabeth's thirty-third birthday was on 25 April.

To: Susan Brandeis Gilbert
Date: May 3, 1929
Place: Washington, D.C.
Source: Gilbert MSS

DEAREST SUSAN: Thanks for the Hadassah literature.

Mrs. Holmes['] funeral[1] has brought much of Boston here—Felix F[rank-furter]., the Arthur Hills[2] and the John Palfreys have been in today, and yesterday we saw much of Felix also. I think Mrs. Holmes must have been nearly, if not quite, ready to go. The Justice bears himself with his customary heroism.

Good reports come from Elizabeth. Mother sends two of the recent ones. A month from today we should be taking the Federal for Boston.[3]

We are glad to hear that Louis is entertaining and Adee[4] parading in her Paris garb.   Lovingly

1. Fanny Dixwell Holmes, the Justice's wife for sixty years, died on 30 April.
2. Arthur Dehon Hill (1869–1947) was a prominent Boston attorney. He had recently gained notoriety as the chief counsel for Sacco and Vanzetti.
3. On the way to Chatham for the summer.
4. Adee was the family nickname for granddaughter Alice. She received this name because her two-year-old brother Louis was unable to pronounce "Alice."

To: Susan Brandeis Gilbert
Date: May 17, 1929
Place: Washington, D.C.
Source: Gilbert MSS

DEAREST SUSAN: Walter Lippmann has just been in, after three months in Europe, mostly in warmer Italy. He thought England (where it was very cold & where he stayed but 5 days) very depressed. They are certainly having an exhilarating campaign now.[1] I hope the 5000000 newly enfranchised women[2] will not defeat the Laborites. It is fine to have the American press, even the Washington Post, with long daily reports of the English campaign. And the American papers are beginning to realize that, in the American sense, there are no Conservatives in England. As Charles Austère, of Paris, said to me in 1912: "I am a conservative. I have about the views of Senator La Follette."

It sounds quite grown up for Louis to be walking in the Park with Jack.

Lovingly

1. England was in the midst of parliamentary elections at the moment. The results gave no party a clear majority, but the Labour Party won the most seats, and in June Ramsay MacDonald formed a government.

2. In 1918 England had given the vote to women over thirty, but in April 1928 the voting age for women was lowered to twenty-one.

To: Elizabeth Brandeis Raushenbush
Date: June 12, 1929
Place: Chatham, Massachusetts
Source: Raushenbush MSS

DEAREST ELIZABETH: For the article on "The Modern Five Day Week and Short Working Hours" (which some day you will write). I suggest the following motto:

Flavius: "But wherefore art thou not in thy shop today? Why dost thou lead these men about the streets?
Second Citizen: Truly sir, to wear out their shoes, to get myself into more work."

Julius Caesar, Act I. Scene 1.
Ask Walter what he thinks of this.   Lovingly

To: Jacob H. Gilbert
Date: July 20, 1929
Place: Chatham, Massachusetts
Source: Gilbert MSS

MY DEAR JACK: Thanks for Judge Pound's address.[1]

Paul, Elizabeth & Walter have just come. Walter looks very well, as does Elizabeth, but P. has the hang over of a cold which we hope Chatham will quickly dispel.

Susan drove to Harwich to bring them over. Your children & Britta were on hand here as a receiving delegation.

Your son is gaining distinctly in speech and seems happy in his occupation. Your daughter walks about in perfect self-reliance & seems to have equal capacity for self-entertainment when left in her bed. Their Grandmother is filled with admiration.

Susan is vigorous and carries Adee up the hill with the nonchalance of an Alpine guide.

Of course we miss you much.

1. Cuthbert Winfred Pound (1864–1935), a judge whom LDB greatly respected, was elevated to the New York Court of Appeals in 1915. He was to succeed Cardozo as chief justice of the New York court when the latter was named to the Supreme Court. LDB's son-in-law had probably sent a copy of Pound's widely noticed address "Defective Law—Its Cause and Remedy," which was eventually to appear in the September issue of the *New York State Bar Association Bulletin*. See also the editorial discussing Pound's talk in the *New York Times*, 15 September 1929.

To: **Susan Brandeis Gilbert**
Date: **July 31, 1929**
Place: **Chatham, Massachusetts**
Source: **Gilbert MSS**

MY DEAREST SUSAN: Mother and I want to make you and Elizabeth each a gift of eleven thousand ($11,000) Dollars this summer. Miss Malloch will send you with this a check for Five thousand Dollars, dated Aug. 1st, and on September 1 a check for Six thousand Dollars.   Lovingly

To: **Susan Brandeis Gilbert**
Date: **August 31, 1929**
Place: **Chatham, Massachusetts**
Source: **Gilbert MSS**

DEAREST SUSAN: Mother and I are very glad that you purpose devoting much more of your working time to unpaid professional services. In furtherance of that purpose, we have asked Miss Malloch to arrange, before next January, to send you checks aggregating ten thousand (10,000) Dollars and to transfer to you of our registered bonds, bonds aggregating in value nineteen thousand (19,000) dollars.

An equivalent gift will be made to Elizabeth.   Lovingly

To: **Susan Brandeis Gilbert**
Date: **October 10, 1929**
Place: **Washington, D.C.**
Source: **Gilbert MSS**

DEAREST SUSAN: For you and Jack only.[1]

(a) I had the private interview with MacDonald yesterday.[2] Felix had cabled Harold Laski to have Passfield[3] or the P.M. have the British Ambassador request me to meet MacDonald privately. This was done by having us there at what seemed to be the usual afternoon tea at the Embassy & then let me go into another room with Mac-Donald to have my talk. No other than Embassy folk were at the tea except Mother, and Senators Borah and Swanson[4] & wives, & the Senators remained with the other teaers while I was with McDonald [sic].

(b) The private interview was entirely satisfactory, as to the British purposes & I had a chance to put briefly what I thought important.[5]

(c) The last fortnight has been quite active Zionistically because Mr. Warburg came here with Mr. Flexner to see[k] my co-operation.[6] I told him that I stood ready to counsel with him. That has involved conference with our own group (Judge Mack, deHaas, Bob [Szold], Tulin, & Mr. Flexner[)] on the 28th, and on the 3rd & further conference with Mr. deHaas. More of this when I see Jack or you.

Lovingly

That's a charming note from Cousin Rubin.
Mother lunched at the University Women's Club with Ishbel[7] yesterday & heard the P.M. at the House Monday. I declined the public luncheon at the Embassy.

1. A note in AGB's handwriting said "Please let Eliz. see this."
2. Prime Minister James Ramsay MacDonald (1866–1937) rose through labor and socialist organizations to become one of the founders of the British Labour Party in 1900. He served as the first Labour prime minister in 1924 and was returned to power in the elections of May 1929. He was currently visiting the United States—the first British prime minister to do so. Naturally, LDB was anxious to discuss Palestinian affairs and policy with him and had angled for such an opportunity through Felix Frankfurter and Harold Laski.
3. Lord Passfield was the British intellectual and Fabian socialist Sidney Webb (1859–1947), who—with his wife, Beatrice—wrote important and influential studies of the labor movement and socialism. Within a short time LDB would come into conflict with Passfield over his recommendations for the settlement of the Palestine problem; the Passfield White Paper, restricting Jewish immigration to Palestine, was issued on 21 October 1930.
4. Claude Augustus Swanson (1862–1939) was a Virginia governor and congressman. He entered the Senate in 1910 and remained until Franklin Roosevelt named him secretary of the navy. Borah was the chair of the Senate Foreign Relations Committee, and Swanson was the ranking Democrat on the committee.
5. LDB wrote to Frankfurter on this date: "MacDonald was entirely friendly. Said he was glad we had met at last, but I am not sure that much of what I said to him will stick. He tried to listen. We were alone in the front embassy room, seated on the sofa, out of sight even, while we talked, of all others at the tea" (Urofsky and Levy, *"Half Brother, Half Son,"* 393).
6. With the death of Louis Marshall two weeks earlier, Felix M. Warburg assumed leadership of the Jewish Agency and became the leader of the non-Zionist philanthropists who

were willing to contribute money to Palestine projects. When Bernard Flexner proposed a meeting between him and the LDB-Mack wing of American Zionism, Warburg eagerly agreed. At the meeting with LDB, Warburg urged that the Justice leave the Court and take over leadership of American Jewry. LDB instead agreed to break his long silence (one article spoke excitedly about "The Return of the Pilot") and issue a statement at a 5 October meeting arranged by Warburg. The linking of the LDB-Mack faction and the wealthy non-Zionists probably spelled the end of the Lipsky leadership of the movement.

7. Prime Minister MacDonald was traveling with his daughter Ishbel.

To: Jacob H. Gilbert
Date: October 27, 1929
Place: Washington, D.C.
Source: Gilbert MSS

MY DEAR JACK: Thanks for yours of 25th.

Yes, there has been a very severe engagement on Wall St.[1] It will be months before the direct causalities are ascertained & disclosed, and probably six months or more before its effect upon general business becomes apparent.

I am very glad to know that the day at the Tax Department was successful. I am always glad to see your friends or clients.

When you come again without Susan you might enjoy the Cosmos Club more than the Brighton. I shall be glad to put you up there at any time and except in rush seasons a room can usually be had.

1. The stock market was in the process of the most dramatic self-destruction in its history. On Thursday, 24 October (the day before Gilbert wrote to LDB), sell orders flooded the stock exchange and prices plummeted disastrously—until a pool raised by leading New York bankers stemmed the tide. On Friday and Saturday the market was anxious, but generally steady. This letter was written on Sunday amidst optimistic talk about bargain-hunting and sound market conditions. But on Monday and Tuesday, 28 and 29 October, the bottom fell out completely as the "Great Crash" of 1929 marked the start of the general downturn leading to the Great Depression of the 1930s.

To: Susan Brandeis Gilbert
Date: November 8, 1929
Place: Washington, D.C.
Source: Gilbert MSS

DEAREST SUSAN: Re yours of 7th.

The monthly allowance to you and to Elizabeth will end with the Nov. 30th check.

Mother and I concluded, some months ago, that it would be wise for you and Elizabeth to begin now to assume the responsibility of ownership in respect to some of the property which would someday naturally pass to you two. We, therefore, requested Miss Malloch to arrange to have transferred to each of you about $30,000 of our registered bonds, in addition to amounts already transferred. This Miss Malloch is now arranging. It has been, all along, our purpose that when this shall have been done, the monthly allowances shall cease. We, of course, leave wholly to you two the disposition to be made of the income.[1]   Lovingly

1. See LDB to Elizabeth Brandeis Raushenbush, 28 November 1929.

To: **Elizabeth Brandeis Raushenbush**
Date: **November 13, 1929**
Place: **Washington, D.C.**
Source: **EBR**

DEAREST ELIZABETH: My thanks to you all for the birthday greetings, and for the Norman Ware which I am glad to have.[1] From the Susan family comes also a happy letter.

Susan is off today for the Hadassah Convention at Atlantic City, where there will be much of anxiety and talk.[2]

I guess George Young is "slipping".[3] He seemed very wise in the old days of new Europe. Or perhaps it was that we knew so little then that he could impose on us.

I think a general business depression is beginning.[4] The speculation has been so widespread that it affects directly a much larger percentage of the population than any earlier era; and luxuries have formed a much larger percentage of the total expenditures than ever before. Moreover, our productive capacity has never before exceeded so largely our capacity to consume. And the percentage of our exports is bound to shrink with the European recovery and development.   Lovingly

1. For LDB's seventy-third birthday, his daughter sent Norman Joseph Ware, *The Labor Movement in the United States, 1865–1895: A Study in Democracy* (New York, 1929). Ware (1886–1949) was a professor of economics at the University of Louisville until 1926, when he left to devote himself to the writing of labor history and service on various federal and state economic boards.

2. For the meeting, four hundred Hadassah women gathered in Atlantic City's Ambassador Hotel. The "anxiety" was caused by the aftermath of Arab rioting in August that had left more than a hundred Jews dead and put to the test Hadassah's ability to provide medical care. The meeting itself passed uneventfully, and Zip Falk Szold, the wife of Robert Szold, was elected president of the organization.

3. Sir George Young (1872–1952) was an intellectual affiliated with the Labour Party and an authority on middle eastern affairs. LDB's remark was probably occasioned by Young's recent article "The Labour Government and the Near East," *New Republic* 60 (23 October 1929): 260–62, warning that if the Zionists failed to make peace with the Arabs in

Palestine the British government would be tempted to turn the administration over to the League of Nations.

    4. The stock market had reached its nadir two weeks earlier and began a slow rise through early 1930; but by spring it plunged again to new lows.

To:	**Pauline Goldmark**
Date:	**November 15, 1929**
Place:	**Washington, D.C.**
Source:	**Goldmark MSS**

MY DEAR "GESCHWESTER":[1] Your loving birthday greetings came duly—also the Jefferson which we are very glad to have. It will be a great addition to our Chatham collection, and a special joy to me because of the book making. Jefferson has been properly painted for many achievements and qualities—without enough emphasis on the fact that he was the most civilized of our presidents.

    Excellent Mr. Hoover must be having now a very bad time—the stock-market collapse following the tariff law debacle[2] is verily a heaping of Pelion upon Ossa.[3] I rather think that in announcing the proposed tax reduction[4] & the reduction of the Reserve Banks rate,[5] in conjunction with Rockefeller's offer to buy S[tandard]. O[il]. stock,[6] the powers that be have played all their high trumps.

    It looks as if economic laws would again hold away.

    1. "Sister."
    2. The Senate was locked in a fruitless debate over a new tariff law—despite urgings from President Hoover. The usual conflict between agricultural and manufacturing interests prevented a law from being passed. It was not until June 1930 that the controversial high-tariff Smoot-Hawley law was passed.
    3. Two Greek mountains that the giants piled in order to storm Mt. Olympus and dethrone Zeus.
    4. A day before this letter Secretary of the Treasury Mellon had announced a proposed 1 percent cut in income taxes for both individuals and corporations.
    5. The rediscount rate was cut from 6 percent to 5 percent on 1 November. Two weeks later it was cut to 4.5 percent by New York, with other cities quickly following. This was seen as an attempt to encourage borrowing in order to forestall a general business depression.
    6. A day earlier a bid had been made for a million shares of Standard Oil. It was thought that John D. Rockefeller was behind the bid in an attempt to peg the price. See *New York Times*, 14 November 1929.

To:	**Jacob H. Gilbert**
Date:	**November 28, 1929**
Place:	**Washington, D.C.**
Source:	**Gilbert MSS**

Dear Jack: Thanks for the clipping.

It's fine to know that "things seem to be taking a turn for the better at the office". "It's a long lane that has no turning".

I was not eager, as you know, to take a hand in Palestine matters, publicly.[1] But conditions, among others, Magnes' characteristically mistaken action,[2] made it urgent. I suppose you saw the Jewish Daily Bulletin report of Nov. 26 which had a somewhat fuller report, I think, than the Times of 25th.

1. LDB's long anticipated reentrance into the public discussion of Zionism came with his remarks to a meeting of Zionist and non-Zionist Jewish leaders on 24 November. Those remarks are reprinted in the *New York Times*, 25 November 1929. He spoke briefly about the courage and determination of the settlers in Palestine and of the need to persist in following the Zionist ideal.

2. Judah Leon Magnes (1877–1948) was an American-born Reform rabbi who became active in American Zionism in the first years of the century. In 1922 he moved to Palestine and became the chancellor (1925–35) and then the first president (1935–48) of the Hebrew University. Magnes was a pacifist (although he finally advocated war against the Nazis) and, in the face of the devastating Arab riots of August, spoke out for cooperation. In a speech at the university he advocated joint Jewish-Arab cooperation, a parliament for Palestine, and the renunciation of the Zionist insistence on political domination. The Jewish state, he said, should not be founded on "the bayonets of some empire" (*New York Times,* 19 November 1929). The speech was hissed by many in the audience, and, of course, other Jews—from the American Jewish Congress to Louis Lipsky—agreed with LDB that the idea was dangerous and inappropriate at that moment and vigorously denounced Magnes.

To: Elizabeth Brandeis Raushenbush
Date: November 28, 1929
Place: Washington, D.C.
Source: EBR

DEAREST ELIZABETH:

1. Re bonds.[1] It was not Mother's and my purpose to interfere in any manner with you[r] and Paul's purpose to live on your joint income or to influence your expenditures. Our purpose was to impose upon you responsibility for the care of property, which would, in any event, naturally go to you some day, and for the proper disposition of the income, whether by investing or spending it. Judgement in such things, as in others, is aided by experience.

2. Re colds:
   (a) see U.S. Daily Nov 27, p, 1, Column b.
   (b) I agree with you that the cost of V.E.M. is excessive.[2] The cause is subjecting the buyer to the unnecessary expense of a diminutive package—a common evil. Don't you think that being an economist, you have the obligation to write the

proprietor protesting and asking for the opportunity of buying in larger packages?

(c) even so—I, as efficiency expert, declare that V.E.M. is an economy in dollar bills. Our President's Secretary of Commerce[3] will tell you on demand how many millions are wasted annually by not using it twice each day.

Lovingly

1. See LDB to Susan Brandeis Gilbert, 8 November 1929.
2. "V.E.M." was apparently a patent cold remedy that LDB was using and that he recommended to his daughter. See also the next letter.
3. Hoover's secretary of commerce was Robert Patterson Lamont (1867–1948), a former engineer and experienced public official.

To: Jacob H. Gilbert
Date: January 8, 1930
Place: Washington, D.C.
Source: Gilbert MSS

DEAR JACK: Enclosed opinion may interest you.

Sorry to hear that the children have had colds. Being an expert on that subject, I was bold enough to advise Elizabeth and Paul recently; and, at a lesser distance, venture to whisper my recipe into your ears:

(1) avoid drafts
(2) wear rubbers
(3) apply V.E.M. morning and evening; & whenever cold symptoms first make appearance.

It's cheap at the price.

To: Susan Brandeis Gilbert
Date: January 20, 1930
Place: Washington, D.C.
Source: Gilbert MSS

DEAREST SUSAN:

1. I refuse to believe that Hadassah, being now unhampered, will fail to collect the full amount $610,000 assumed at the convention.[1] The times are hard. But times that try men's souls give Hadassah its unique opportunity.

2. As Bill Mack is the Judge's brother,[2] I will send to you the photo for him.

3. Don't you think Jack is getting a pretty thorough education in Zionist personnel?

Lovingly

Our love to your 3.

1. In November 1929.
2. Judge Mack had twelve siblings, and four of the boys (including himself) bore the middle name "William," the same name as their father. Perhaps, however, this is William Jacob Mack, Jr. (1885–19[?]), a younger brother of Julian and a Chicago attorney.

To: Jacob H. Gilbert
Date: February 12, 1930
Place: Washington, D.C.
Source: Gilbert MSS

MY DEAR JACK: Hadassah papers hereturned [*sic*] herewith.

1. I heartily approve of Mrs. [Rose Gell] Jacobs' purpose not to make a new loan for any purpose whatsoever.

2. Also of Susan's recommendation that all salaries in excess of $1400 be cut 10% etc.

3. Also of the proposal that Hadassah relinquish the management of and financial responsibility for the Tiberas [*sic*] hospital.[1]

That hospital should be managed by an independent board of trustees, and maintained by contributions in part (a) from the Hadassah, for a limited period in an annually diminishing amount. (b) from the Government (c) from the local community (d) all the rest from abroad—not only America—raised here by an independent committee of which Mrs. Schweitzer[2] would naturally be the chairman. Hadassah should encourage such independent boards and committees to carry forward parts of its work, as it matures.

4. I favor the suggested separation of Hadassah from Z.O.A.— becoming itself a fraction.[3]

1. In view of the deepening economic collapse, Hadassah, like virtually every other group that relied on private contributions, was forced to consider cutbacks in its activities.
2. Rebecca Schweitzer (1880–1938) was born in Russia to wealthy parents. She married in Russia; she and her husband, Peter (see LDB to AGB, 26 June 1918), came to America and

created an immense fortune based on the manufacture of cigarette papers. They devoted themselves to philanthropic causes and were active Zionists. The hospital in Tiberias was built in 1921 by Hadassah with funds contributed by the Schweitzers and in 1923, after Peter's death, was renamed in his honor. Mrs. Schweitzer was also known for her work on behalf of the blind in both Palestine and the United States.

3. Hadassah did not achieve complete independence from the Zionist Organization of America until 1933; even then it maintained its affiliation with the World Zionist Organization.

To: Jacob H. Gilbert
Date: February 15, 1930
Place: Washington, D.C.
Source: Gilbert MSS

MY DEAR JACK:

1. Enclose[d] letter to P[alestine].E[ndowment].F[und]. with check—which letter please mail after taking copy for my files.
2. I think it will be wiser not to give to Mrs. Jacobs a copy of my letter re Hadassah.[1]
3. I should like to know
   (a) the number of fully paid members in the N.Y. District on the date when Lipsky became President.
   (b) the number of full-paid members added during each week since.

It's fine to know the children are all well. I am about mended but have not been out-of-doors yet.

1. See the preceding letter.

To: Jacob H. Gilbert
Date: June 8, 1930
Place: Chatham, Massachusetts
Source: Gilbert MSS

DEAR JACK:

1) Susan's Mother, Mary Julien and Mr. [Harris] Palmer were in attendance at your cottage to receive your family at 10:15 this morning, and report that the party arrived in good form; also that the cottage is in much improved condition. Painted externally; and internally is with its best bib and tucker on. Rose and the dog are exciting due admiration.

491

2) We have a new supply of timber for your expert handling, and no doubt chores galore will accumulate before the opposing briefs are fully answered. Glad you have so interesting an occupation in your solitude.

3) I note your Ford Problem. In Washington I was told that the best used cars can be had at the buyer's figure.

4) Glad you arranged satisfactorily for extension of the lease at 935.[1] The tales of superfluous real estate and of foreclosed mortgages in Boston and suburbs are impressive. The fall in commodity prices must extend to dwellings; and to business property soon. There is already much woe to the debtor—and there will be more—despite H[erbert].H[oover].'s myths.[2]

1. For ten years the Gilberts lived in an apartment at 935 Park Avenue in New York City.
2. To encourage a business recovery, President Hoover kept insisting in public statements that the fundamentals of the American economy were essentially "sound" and that a restoration of confidence was all that was needed to return prosperity to the nation.

To:	Jacob H. Gilbert
Date:	June 25, 1930
Place:	Chatham, Massachusetts
Source:	Gilbert MSS

MY DEAR JACK: Auntie B., Susan's Mother & I visited your household yesterday via Rich's vehicle, and found the family in great shape on their own domain. Your daughter especially has gained immensely in the 18 days since she left you. Rosy, chubby cheeks with abundant smiles and her resistless energy.

This afternoon, Susan, Evelyn & Louis Gilbert are, we assume, off for tennis.

I suppose you are watching the commodity markets as closely as I am. Your cotton has not fared as badly as grain.[1] Hoover prosperity will long be a by-word, and the "prosperity reserve" an ironic reproach. The whole situation must make a lot of wiseacres feel foolish.

We hope Auntie B. will retain her renewed youth at least until you can have the joy of witnessing her metamorphosis. She literally shed a dozen years.

We expect Josephine, also Charles, Alice Park & Jonathan—on Friday.[2]

1. The downturn was affecting farm income and commodity prices drastically. Cotton fell slightly to eleven cents per pound; decreased production and cooperative marketing cushioned the blow. But wheat production was up (840 million bushels compared to 806

million in 1929) and the 1929 price ($1.09 per bushel) fell to $0.71. The price of corn also dropped (22 percent). Farm incomes were lower in 1930 than in any year since 1921, down 16 percent from 1929. LDB writes "your" cotton because Jacob Gilbert's law practice handled cases from the cotton industry.

    2. The Goldmarks—Alice Park was Charles Goldmark's wife.

To:	Jacob H. Gilbert
Date:	August 8, 1930
Place:	Chatham, Massachusetts
Source:	Gilbert MSS

MY DEAR JACK: Your son asked me yesterday whether I would go with E.B.[1] and him, when they went "in the car" to get you.

He and Adee invited me to play with them on the sand-pile, faute-de-mieux;[2] and we consumed many ice cream cones of sand.

Judge Mack, Felix and Bob Szold were here Sunday for a long conference—prior to the Judge's sailing.[3] I hope he will not be prevented from leaving this P.M., as planned. Dr. Wise is unable to go—because, I am told, of his son-in-law Tulin's serious illness.[4]

Susan tells me that Judge Knox[5] did the expected. Sorry. But there is hope above.[6]

Susan seemed to have emerged from her ivy poisoning in record time.

    1. LDB's daughter Elizabeth was known everywhere as "E. B."
    2. For want of anything better.
    3. Judge Mack was about to sail for Europe to attend the meeting of the Jewish Agency's Administration Committee. He would then proceed to Palestine, returning to America in November.
    4. See LDB to Susan Brandeis Gilbert, 17 February 1929.
    5. John Clark Knox (1881–1966) served as a judge on the U.S. District Court for the Southern District of New York from 1918, when he was nominated by President Wilson, until his retirement.
    6. I.e., there is hope of reversing an unfavorable decision on appeal.

To:	Jacob H. Gilbert
Date:	September 18, 1930
Place:	Washington, D.C.
Source:	Gilbert MSS

MY DEAR JACK: Glad to hear of your Palestine explorations.[1]

    1. If you have not the full minutes of the Permanent Mandate Commission hearings (154 large folio pages, June 1930), be sure to get the document. Every word is interesting and instructive.

2. Have Block Publishing Co. send you a booklet published by it in 1914 entitled "Jewish Questions, Three lectures by Dr. Ignatz Zollschan" 66 pp.[2] You will find the third lecture, "Tendencies of Economic Development among the Jewish People", an usually illuminating paper, showing the inevitableness of Anti-Semitism in the Diaspora.

We are rejoicing over Phil's victory,[3] & were wholly surprised by Bob's marriage.[4]

For you & Susan some enclosures.

1. Gilbert had embarked upon a serious study of Jewish history, Zionism, and Palestine; LDB recommended numerous titles to him.

2. Ignatz Zollschan (1877–1948) was an Austrian physician-turned-anthropologist who became absorbed by theories of race and devoted himself to writing and working in opposition to racism.

3. In a fiercely contested Wisconsin Republican primary, thirty-three-year-old Phil La Follette triumphed decisively over Governor Walter Kohler. The governor was a loyal Hoover man, while La Follette represented the progressive wing of the party. La Follette easily won election to the governorship in November.

4. While the La Follette family was celebrating Phil's victory, his brother Robert quietly married Rachel Wilson Young, a Virginia woman who had worked as a senatorial secretary for both Robert La Follette, Sr., and his son. The wedding took place in Madison the day after the election.

To: Susan Brandeis Gilbert
Date: September 25, 1930
Place: Washington, D.C.
Source: Gilbert MSS

DEAREST SUSAN:

Confidential (1) The P[alestine].E[conomic].C[orporation]. contemplates appointing an Economic Research Com[mit]tee. Mr. Fohs[1] and Isador Lubin[2] will probably be asked to serve; possibly also Walter E. Meyer. Would your friend Warshauer (?), the Comptroller of the National Lead Co.,[3] be desirable for that?

(2) I do not think it desirable that Jack should, at this time, assume any position in Z[ionist].O[rganization of].A[merica].[4]

    (a) I think, at this time, it is of the utmost importance that Jack should not be distracted from building up his practice; and there is so much to do at 111 Fifth Ave[5] now, that he would be completely engulfed if he took hold now.

(b) I don't think it wise for him to take active part there until he has greatly increased by study his knowledge of Zionist and Palestine affairs. That he can do by study evenings & otherwise when not occupied with practice. When he has proceeded a long way in his studies, he will be able to do a man's job.

(3) Jack had omitted to tell me about the $2500 retainer in the Ringling case. That is fine.

(4) I don't know what you refer to, as "confidential memo, giving answers to questions."

(5) [*] has shown that she can do well as President, if she wants to, and I guess she will have tasks enough to keep her fully occupied.

(6) Enclosed correspondence about Marion Calkins book will interest you.[6]

(7) Your Mother sends her love & hopes the children are doing well.

(8) Tell Jack I have had quite a lot of letters from Dr. Wise recently.

Lovingly

1. Ferdinand Julius Fohs (1884–1965) was an oil geologist who had worked in both Kentucky and Texas and was actively involved in various Palestine investigations of natural resources. His work resulted in the creation of some of the area's most important industries.

2. Isador Lubin (1896–1978) was an economist at the Brookings Institution. Franklin Roosevelt was to appoint him commissioner of labor statistics, 1933–46. He was a prolific writer on economic topics.

3. The comptroller of the National Lead Co. was H. T. Warshow.

4. The Brandeis-Mack faction had regained control of the ZOA in June, creating the possibility that Jacob Gilbert would play a part in the organization. The details of the transition from the old Lipsky administration to the returning Brandeis-Mack group were hammered out in difficult negotiations before the Cleveland convention at the end of June. A committee of eighteen "neutrals" was to be formed (six appointed by the Lipsky administration and twelve by the Brandeis-Mack faction) that would attempt to reform the organization, make it more efficient, and in general whip it back into shape in eighteen months. This transfer of leadership accounts for the sudden rise in references to Zionist affairs in these letters—especially to Susan and Jacob Gilbert.

5. ZOA headquarters.

6. Marion Clinch Calkins Merrell (1896–1968) wrote fiction, nonfiction, and poetry under the name Clinch Calkins. She had come up through social settlement house work and during the New Deal worked as a speechwriter for Harry Hopkins. In 1930 she published two books that would have interested LDB: *Some Folks Won't Work,* a study of unemployment that placed much blame on automation, and *Spy Overhead,* an expose of industrial spying against labor unions.

To: Susan Brandeis Gilbert
Date: September 30, 1930
Place: Washington, D.C.
Source: Gilbert MSS

DEAREST SUSAN: When Mother and I made the distribution to you and Elizabeth last year, we assigned to Elizabeth also a claim for money loaned to a friend of hers, but did not treat that as a thing of value. To our great surprise the loan has been repaid.

In order to equal the distribution, I am asking Miss Malloch to send you a check for $1,128.12.   Lovingly

To: Jennie Taussig Brandeis
Date: October 11, 1930
Place: Washington, D.C.
Source: Fannie Brandeis

MY DEAR JENNIE: A glad welcome home.[1] We have followed you joyously through Europe, aided by your and Fannie's messages, richly freighted with precious memories. And already we have from Vienna reports of the pleasure your visit gave others.

The Salzkammergut, Vienna and Florence brought experiences the delight of which remains undimmed and, with your postals and letters, each day there was brought nearer. So I had a veritable voyage autour de ma chambre.[2]

Our summer was entirely uneventful, like those at Ladless which Alfred so loved. But it was a lovely summer as Alice will tell you.

We hope you three travellers are finding all well in Louisville.

1. During the summer of 1930 Alfred Brandeis's widow toured Europe accompanied by her daughters Fannie and Adele and her sister-in-law, Mrs. Walter Taussig.
2. A trip within my room.

To: Jacob H. Gilbert
Date: October 13, 1930
Place: Washington, D.C.
Source: Gilbert MSS

MY DEAR JACK:

1. We are much cheered by the report on your knee.
2. I am enclosing some reports on the Dead Sea project, which will help you to get a realizing sense of what is being done there.

3. If you haven't [read] Viteles'[1] article "Proposals for Organization of the Orange Industry within Palestine" reprinted from July–Aug 30 Hadar, ask the P[alestine]. E[conomic]. C[orporation]. to send it to you.

Vanguard Press will publish Oct. 16, "The Social and Economic Views of Mr. Justice Brandeis" compiled by Alfred Lief, 163 W. 81 St. N.Y. City.[2] I have never seen Lief but have heard that he is connected in some way with the fur trade—whether with the employers' or the workers['] organization, I didn't hear. You may after seeing the book care to make some enquiry about Lief. He would doubtless be pleased with an invitation from you & Susan, and possibly you may find that he could be of service to the Z.O.A. He surely is not averse to intellectual labor.

1. Harry Viteles (1894–1971) was born in Bessarabia and moved to the United States at an early age. After graduating from the University of Pennsylvania and serving in the federal Children's Bureau (1918–20), he grew interested in the cooperative movement. He moved to Palestine in 1925 and became the director of the Central Bank for Cooperative Institutions. He also taught at Hebrew University before returning to America in 1957.
2. Alfred Lief (1901–73) wrote many books on judicial, political, and business topics. In addition to the compilation of LDB's views published by Vanguard in 1930, Lief published a full-length biography of LDB, *Brandeis: The Personal History of an American Ideal* (New York, 1936).

To: Jacob H. Gilbert
Date: October 19, 1930
Place: Washington, D.C.
Source: Gilbert MSS

MY DEAR JACK:

1. Re yours of the 18th. It's fine that you have Tom Warshow[1] fixed for the modified plan. You will have to cultivate him from time to time to make sure that the plant grows.
2. The report of Adm[inistration]. Com[mit]tee of Z.O.A. of Oct. 8 shows that Brodie appointed on his Pal[e]s[tine]. Economic Com[mit]tee, among others, Jonas [*sic*] J. Goldstein[2] and I. D. Morrison.[3] I told Bob Szold today that at Chatham you had suggested talking to both & my objections, but that now, I saw no reason why you should not see what you can do with them. He was content to have you see whether they can be led to help in getting folk interested in (or I.D.M. in putting up money for) Palestine enterprises e.g. Dead Sea Project. I think it might be well for you to

ask Brodie to call on you & have him tell you more about the Dead Sea enterprise etc.

3. I also talked with Bob about your trying to get David Rosenblum[4] to take active part in things economic. He said this would be all right—that D.R. might serve on the Economic as well as on Tulin's Com[mit]tee.

4. I also talked with him about Hortense Levy's brother. He was surprised to hear that Susan thought he was successful in his business, but saw no objection to your trying to interest him. I told Bob that you would not commit him on this or any other person, you would merely expect him to see the prospect and talk over the lines on which aid could be given Z.O.A. by the prospect. Bob is entirely sympathetic.

5. There is much talk that the British Government is contemplating some most objectionable program & that Hope Simpson's report may be made public tomorrow & it will recommended limitation of immigration, suspension of land purchases, parliament & other objectionable features.[5] However bad it may be, the Jews can't be beaten unless they surrender or we refuse active help to our Palestinians. But Jews must be ready to sacrifice their luxuries & comforts, if need be, for the Cause.

Jews determined are unbeatable. And it is not necessary that they be united. If a fair percentage of the Jews lend adequate support, we can beat the British-Arab combination if any. We have a grand case.

1. See LDB to Susan Brandeis Gilbert, 25 September 1930.
2. LDB undoubtedly refers to Jonah J. Goldstein (1886–1967), a prominent New York lawyer active in both Democratic politics in New York (he was Al Smith's secretary) and philanthropic work—especially among families and children. From 1939 to 1956 he served as judge of the Court of General Sessions. His specialty was juvenile and family law. Goldstein was an active Zionist and had just returned from Palestine, where he was the American representative in the inquiry into the recent Arab riots.
3. Isadore D. Morrison (1871–1938) was born in Poland and immigrated to the United States, where he became a leading New York City lawyer. He was a longtime Zionist (serving as secretary to the old Federation of American Zionists from 1899 to 1905) and was especially active in numerous Zionist philanthropic efforts.
4. David Rosenblum (1888–1943) was born in Brooklyn and educated at Harvard. He worked in various business enterprises, but his career culminated as the vice-president and treasurer of the National Broadcasting Company. He was involved with both the American Jewish Committee and various Zionist philanthropies.
5. Sir John Hope-Simpson (1868–1961), an experienced British civil servant living in India, was sent to Palestine to investigate Arab objections to Jewish immigration. After a brief stay, during which—according to his Zionist critics—he listened to only one side, he issued his report on 21 October. The Zionists felt that Hope-Simpson's recommendation for halting immigration into Palestine was based on a radically low estimate of the absorp-

tion capacity of the land. Naturally, both Zionist and non-Zionist Jews were outraged by what seemed to be a renunciation of the Balfour Declaration of 1917. After vigorous criticism, Ramsay MacDonald effectively nullified the Hope-Simpson report and the accompanying Passfield White Paper in 1931.

To: Jacob H. Gilbert
Date: October 24, 1930
Place: Washington, D.C.
Source: Gilbert MSS

MY DEAR JACK: Supplementing mine of yesterday re Walter E. Meyer.

1. In 1918, not long after the Balfour Declaration, Walter was in England; was captivated by Weizmann (who probably saw in him the rich American); and Walter accompanied Weiz., I think as his quasi Honorary Secretary, to Palestine. (Probably Weiz's first visit there, at least after the war.) Weiz. may have tired of Walter or become satisfied that he could not work him. At all events, Walter discovered the yellow streak in Weizmann and his entire lack of economic understanding. When Walter came back to America in Sept. 1918, he came to Washington to tell me in confidence his impression of Weiz., which differed widely from those then current in America.

2. I can't recall whether Walter had done anything for Zionism before he went to Palestine. Eugene [Meyer, Jr.], whom I met in the winter of 1914–1915 had to a very considerable extent—gave me at one time $25,000 as I recall; and lesser sums at other times, but his heart was never in Zionism and he did this largely on my account.

3. Walter has always asserted great devotion to me, spoke of me as his spiritual adviser, but rarely came across with any money for Palestine, except a few small sums. I recall in the old days a $1000 contribution; then (at my request) two or three years ago, $500 to our Reorganization Com[mit]tee which Judge Mack & deHaas were running. He became, not at my request, the Treas. of the P[alestine].E[conomic].C[orporation].; put $10,000 into it; & has never done any work & I guess knows practically nothing of its operations.

4. He has been for many years conducting a fight for minority stockholders of the Kansas City Southern R.R. with Alexander Sachs as his aid (until about a year ago when A.S. went (I think) to the Lehman Corp.). Partly because of my past RR fights, he has

come in, from time to time when in Washington, to have me hold his hand. The fight has been a wholly creditable one; & he has scored some successes & considers the fight as an important public service. He showed stick-to-itness, courage and ability.

5. When he was in Washington early in 1930 (the last time I saw him except yesterday) I put it up hard to him that, having reached fifty (he said not quite, only 49), he should now take up something which would fill his life & I urged his going in to the economic side of Palestine work. E.g. the Dead Sea project. I spoke to him of giving P[alestine]. the benefit of his thinking & experience; did not mention money; but had in mind that this would follow. He then said that he wasn't through with his RR fight; & was otherwise gently resistant. But said he would think it over.

6. A little later when our American Dead Sea Com[mit]tee wanted more subscriptions, I told Bob Szold to try again to get Walter Meyer, and wrote Bob that I thought Walter would subscribe for at least $25,000, as I had agreed to give that amount for the Palestine Endowment Fund for investment in Dead Sea Project. Bob couldn't get a penny out of Walter, nor could anyone else. We had in mind he should become a director in the Potash Limited if he came across largely.

7. Walter is rich—not as rich as Eugene by far, but he inherited considerable & made much in recent years in buying & selling securities; and didn't lose much when the break came. It would be a greater service to Walter to get him thoroughly interested in the Palestine work, putting time & money heavily into it, even than it would be to Palestine. He is really a pathetically lonely, undecided individual, Hamletian in many respects, with constant inhibitions.

8. Among the obstacles to getting him for P. has been his hostility to the Kuhn Loeb outfit, and perhaps specifically to Felix Warburg. Walter doesn't part easily with money, but he is capable of considerable generosity at times.

9. Of course, he should read the Shaw Report[1] and the full Official Permanent Mandates Commission proceedings, & should read also the Palestine & Near East Economic Magazine—all the issues of the year 1930, & should subscribe. I am afraid Davar might frighten his capitalistic sensibilities. You will know what he should read, and in what order.

10. If you can land him, you will do what no human has yet done.

Many, including his dear friend F[elix]F[rankfurter]. have tried in vain. He has given us an opening by his call & enquiries yesterday.

1. In October 1929 the British sent out an inquiry commission to investigate the August riots in Palestine. The Shaw Commission (named after its head, Sir Walter Shaw) issued its findings in March 1930. The majority report blamed the riots on conflicts between Jewish and Arab national aspirations and on unclear British policy. The report recommended slowing Jewish immigration and divorcing administration in Palestine from the Zionist organization. Arabs tended to praise the report, and Jews tended to condemn it as exonerating the rioters.

To: Jacob H. Gilbert
Date: November 4, 1930
Place: Washington, D.C.
Source: Gilbert MSS

MY DEAR JACK:

1.) Re yours of 1st. Enclosures returned herewith. You have been doing effective work.
2. I am glad Sidney Wolf[1] [sic] is coming in.
2.) [sic] Re yours of 3d. I am sending Bob [Szold] your check and J. W. Stephon letter with request to return the letter to you & to talk with you about Stephon.
3. I am glad Podell is prompt in taking the matter up with you.
4. Yes, if we can win [Julius] Rosenwald, it will mean much.
5. I am enclosing for your perusal before mailing a letter to Alexander Sachs; also his card & the articles.

It ought to be possible to make him useful; at least through his bringing to you acquaintances whom you could influence and he cannot. He goes to the City Club every day & can call on you conveniently at the office.

Whether Alex. can give cash I don't know. During the latter part of his employment by Walter Meyer he had a handsome salary, and had accumulated (at least on paper) a considerable sum. He went to the Lehman Corp. & came into receipt then of a much larger salary. It may have been abridged since. And I understand that he lost most or all of his accumulations.

Alexander, while a student (after a short banking experience) became an active worker—in 1914 (I met him at the Emergency Conference Aug. 30, 1914). He served later under deHaas in the N[ew].E[ngland]. Zionist office which I started at 161 Devonshire[2] & was very eager, although not very practical.

I fear he made a bad marriage.³ But I have felt that his soul may still be saved, and I think re-embarking in Zionist work would do it for him. And there should be a net gain to the Z.O.A.

> 6.) I received today a letter from Dr. Wise, enclosing i.a. enclosed carbon of Van Paasin's⁴ [*sic*] letter to McDonald [*sic*] of Oct. 23 which may interest you.

Delighted to hear of Susan's fee and of the birthday party. Weather bad today, & Walter is kept in doors.

Tell Susan that Rudolph [*sic*] Berle⁵ came with his wife to court the other day & asked to see me.

1. Perhaps LDB and his son-in-law were trying to enlist in the Zionist cause Sidney E. Wolff (d. 1951), a New York attorney. Wolff did not become an active Zionist, but he worked in another cause close to LDB's heart: Wolff was the man who introduced a form of Savings Bank Life Insurance in New York.
2. LDB's old law office in Boston.
3. Alexander Sachs's first wife was Jeanne Casselle, a musician.
4. Probably a letter from Pierre Van Paassen (1895–1968) to prime minister Ramsay MacDonald protesting the Hope-Simpson report and the Passfield White Paper. Van Paassen was a noted writer and a Unitarian minister in New York City. He had a deep interest in Palestine and in Judaism and was a close friend of Rabbi Wise's—in 1934 he co-edited a book on Nazism with Wise's son. For his work on behalf of Jewish causes, Van Paassen received an honorary degree from the Jewish Institute of Religion and was made an honorary citizen of Tel Aviv.
5. Rudolf Protas Berle (1901–83) was a New York City lawyer who specialized in banking law. He was the son of LDB's old Boston ally A. A. Berle, the social gospel Congregationalist minister, and the brother (and law partner) of Adolf A. Berle, the brain-truster and advisor to presidents Roosevelt and Kennedy.

To: Jacob H. Gilbert
Date: November 6, 1930
Place: Washington, D.C.
Source: Gilbert MSS

MY DEAR JACK: Re yours of 5th.

> 1. Yes, I hope the task of getting New Yorkers etc. for ZOA will now proceed. Bob [Szold] et al are too much occupied with London communications. I am glad you are on the job of finding & interesting prospects.
> 2. Bear in mind that it is a part of my program to have every American Zionist eventually a stockholder in the P[alestine].E[conomic].C[orporation]. When conditions for a comprehensive move-

ment to this end seem auspicious, Mr. [Bernard] Flexner purposes presenting a plan of action. But I pointed out to him that we had better lose no time in getting anyone to take stock, however little, who can be quietly prevailed upon to do so. And I mentioned to him that you might run across people who could be induced to do so. He said, "All Right, there is stock available." So bear this in mind. There will probably be many among your acquaintances whom we can't make study and work, but may interest to the extent of stockholding.

3. There is another general field where you may have opportunity to help. Two months ago, I presented to Bob a plan for getting our members in the several cities (a) to have the Public Libraries subscribe for Davar and for Palestine & Near East Magazine (b) getting Jewish Centres to do so.

And in respect to N.Y., [I] suggested that these periodicals should go into all branch libraries in districts where there now are many Jews and into all Jewish Centres.

It seemed to me that our members who were short on money might be long on political influence & would be dextrous [sic] in having city money spent.

I have not heard of any progress being made on this program, doubtless because Bob and deHaas were harassed with so many pressing duties. But I deem the proposal of importance (a) in laying a broad foundation here for education (b) for the great encouragement it will give the Palestinians.

Possible [sic] you may have political friends who will effect this in New York City.

I had the Librarian of Congress subscribe; also the Jewish Centre here and the Library of the University of Louisville (these two out of funds which I had contributed for general Jewish publications.)

4. If Brodie is in New York I think it would be profitable to have him call on you sometime to give you his picture of Palestine conditions.
5. It might also be educating to have Miss Jessie E. Sampter[1] (the Zionist poetess—one of the original Hadassah members—who has not only moved to Palestine but has become a Palestinian citizen) call on you. (She is now I think at her sister's Mrs. Washburn? in New Rochelle). She wrote me recently & I told her I need not trouble her to come here at present. She breathes the true spirit; says "Palestinians will hold fast" in any event.

6. I enclose carbon of letter from Judge Mack. Please return.

7. You may keep the Van Passen [*sic*] letter.[2]

1. Jessie Ethel Sampter (1883–1938), Henrietta Szold's disciple and co-worker, overcame childhood polio and a life of pain to write poetry, work in settlement houses, and teach Zionism to countless men and women. She had moved to Palestine in 1919 and eventually gave up her American citizenship. Throughout her life she preached cooperation between Jews and Arabs.

2. See the previous letter.

To:	Jacob H. Gilbert
Date:	November 15, 1930
Place:	Washington, D.C.
Source:	Gilbert MSS

JACK: This man[1] was a client in one matter about 40 years ago & I have seen him but once or twice since. He was a woolen commissioner and quite rich. He is too old to be asked to call, and perhaps too old to be converted to Palestine. But if you ever chance to run across him, remember his past relation to me.

"The long arm of coincidence"[2] is on my mind.

1. This note was written across an incoming birthday greeting to LDB from Adolph Wimpfheimer (1851–1931), who immigrated from Germany and entered the clothing industry in New York City at an early age. He made a fortune in the manufacture of hats.

2. The line comes from act 2 of a once-popular play, *Captain Swift* (1888), by the prolific English playwright Charles Haddon Chambers (1860–1921).

To:	Jacob H. Gilbert
Date:	November 16, 1930
Place:	Washington, D.C.
Source:	Gilbert MSS

MY DEAR JACK:

1. I enclose telegram from & letter to Lewin-Epstein which please read, & supply the address. (I think he is connected with the Rarach(?) business, Brooklyn, in some capacity. Emanuel Neumann[1] told me recently that Lewin-Epstein had induced R. to give $50,000 to Jewish Nat[iona]l Fund within the last year to be used as a revolving fund to help house-building & that R. would probably give more soon. That was the first I had heard of Lewin-Epstein for four years.

504

He was one of the early settlers; came to America as representative of the Wine Growers Association quite long before the World War (I think); became the Treasurer of the Emergency Com[mit]tee & Z.O.A. in my day, and was sent by us to Palestine in 1918, when we first began to function there. He was not a very good treasurer, and not good at his job for us in Palestine (partly because of ill health), but was uncommonly fine in spirit— a man of innate refinement—and I want you to meet him, especially so that he can give you the flavor of the old days & tell you of the struggles and difficulties under Turkish rule. (You will find among the letters sent me for my seventieth birthday one from him which I valued more than most.)

2. I hope the Oct. 29 Davar has reached you. The spirit which it breathes is what American Jews need.
3. Since writing the above I have yours of yesterday with encl. All of your enclosures I return herewith.
    (a) As to N.Y. Libraries,[2] I think several others of the Trustees are dead. But I should think that the way to get the Palestine publications in would be via someone else than the Trustees. Call deHaas on the telephone & see what he knows.
    (b) I am glad you think Boston Hadassah will get [John Haynes] Holmes.
    c. Suggest to Blinken[3] that the remedy for bad Jewish fraternities is to give them a worthy Jewish interest—Palestine.
4. I have written Bob [Szold] today to arrange at once to secure Blinken & to let you know he has done so. If you don't hear from him tomorrow Monday, call him Tuesday A.M.
5. Yes, Morris Ernst[4] would well be worthwhile.
6. Hope you will get Kramer. A man vitally interested in the youth movement is perhaps the most valuable of all assets. It is the youth we must rely upon for the long for the [sic] fight ahead; & it is the great proportion of young in Palestine that gives us the greatest hope.

1. Emanuel Neumann (1893–1980) was one of the central figures in American and World Zionism. Originally siding with Weizmann, he gradually moved closer to the Brandeis-Mack wing of the movement during the late 1920s. Neumann lived in Palestine for most of the 1930s and headed a number of industrial efforts there. He was prominent in the events leading up to the creation of the state of Israel in 1948 and served at that critical time as the president of the Zionist Organization of America.
2. See LDB to Jacob H. Gilbert, 6 November 1930.
3. Maurice Henry Blinken (1900–1986) was born in the Ukraine but came to the United States and became both an attorney and a certified public accountant. He was himself active

in several fraternities and interested in Palestinian business affairs. Two of his sons served as ambassadors in President Bill Clinton's administration.

    4. Morris Leopold Ernst (1888–1976) was a New York attorney active in various reform and civil liberties causes.

To: **Susan Brandeis Gilbert**
Date: December 4, 1930
Place: Washington, D.C.
Source: Gilbert MSS

DEAREST SUSAN: My love and good wishes for you and little brother.[1] How Louis and Alice will rejoice in him.

    Jack['s] telegram following his telephone of yesterday is most reassuring. Mother feels very proud of grandson no. 3.

                                      Lovingly

Mother telephoned Mabel [Willebrandt], but she was out of town.

    1. Frank Brandeis Gilbert, the Brandeises' fourth and final grandchild, had been born in New York City the day before. Frank Gilbert served as the executive director of the New York City Landmarks Preservation Commission and then as an official with the National Trust for Historic Preservation in Washington, D.C.

To: **Jacob H. Gilbert [fragment]**
Date: December 6, 1930
Place: Washington, D.C.
Source: Gilbert MSS

MY DEAR JACK:

    1. We want Sarnoff[1] for director of the P[alestine].E[conomic].C[orporation]. and to have him subscribe for a substantial block of stock. I suppose he could easily take $5000. If he became director & did that, we could build mightily through him.

He was brought in to me by Kirstein last winter (K. is a P.E.C. director, but has, so far as I know done nothing & I fear is not a stockholder. Bernhardt[2] can tell.)

When Sarnoff was in, it seemed inopportune to touch on Palestine. He said then, he would call again soon. But I have not seen either S. or K. since. He impressed me as a man of unusual ability, with a subtle, flexible mind & very engaging qualities. Podell seems a much more appropriate guide than Jonah Goldstein.

2. I have not received any such letter as Nathan Straus speaks of. Possibly the family suppressed it. I did receive several months ago, a letter from the Jr., saying not to mind if his father wrote me an abusive letter as he has to others. I am enclosing[3]

1. David Sarnoff (1891–1971) was born in Russia. He moved to the United States and rose quickly from errand boy to the head of the National Broadcasting Company and the Radio Corporation of America.

2. Joshua Bernhardt (1893–19[?]) was an economist and statistician. At that time he was the secretary of the Palestine Economic Corporation.

3. The second page of this letter appears to be lost.

To: Jacob H. Gilbert
Date: December 18, 1930
Place: Washington, D.C.
Source: Gilbert MSS

MY DEAR JACK:You will recall that at the Cleveland convention, after my message & the willingness of our group to take hold was announced,[1] the various cities agreed to raise in the aggregate $103,000—as a starter.

Up to Dec 9th less than $19,000 was raised. There was evidence of a fall down already before Aug. 1, so I wrote personal letters to the pledgers for the several cities. How little was achieved the above figures shows [sic].

(A little has come in since.)

The worst disappointment has been Dr. Nathan Ratnof [sic].[2] He was on the Com[mit]tee who negotiated with us in the Spring; was thoroughly convinced we were right in our stand; made a very good impression on me & others; and has had a very good record in Palestine work as President of Jewish Physicians society, which raised $100,000 or more I am told for the Jerusalem Hospital or the Medical end of the University.[3] He was made Chairman of the Deficit Committee so I wrote him about Aug. 15th. I enclose his answer dated Aug 15th. Nothing has come to me from him since, and, so far as I know, he has accomplished nothing. If you feel so inclined, ask him to come to your office & see what you can do with him.

1. See LDB to Susan Brandeis Gilbert, 25 September 1930, note 4. The "message" LDB refers to was his letter of 28 June, read to the Cleveland delegates by Robert Szold, pledging his willingness to "advise" the organization on matters of major policy—see LDB to Delegates of the Z.O.A. Convention, 28 June 1930, BL.

2. Nathan Osher Ratnoff (1875–1947) immigrated from the Ukraine at sixteen, earned a medical degree in Baltimore, and became a leading New York City obstetrician and founder of the Jewish Maternity Hospital. He was active in Jewish affairs all his life.

3. Ratnoff's committee raised money for the medical school at Hebrew University—his group contributed one-third and Hadassah the other two-thirds. The medical building at the university was named in his honor.

To: Jacob H. Gilbert
Date: December 26, 1930
Place: Washington, D.C.
Source: Gilbert MSS

MY DEAR JACK: Referring to the thoughtful memo of Samuel Spring[1] and the many other encouraging letters from those who, through you, have promised help to the movement.

Bob Szold and other members of the Administration Com[mit]tee are necessarily engrossed with the fundament[al] political problems growing out of the Passfield White Paper[2] & the occurrences which preceded it; with the preparations for the coming Congress where internal political problems of great perplexity and difficulty must be considered; and with local Palestinian problems of moment, some of long standing, some arising out of the occurrences of the last 17 months.[3]

Unavoidable preoccupation with those problems precludes the officers of the Z.O.A. from giving at present to the building up of the organization, its institutions and allied bodies the attention required; and it is clear that months must elapse before they can possibly do so. But that task is hardly less urgent; and it is indispensable. I suggest that you undertake to do some of that work acting as a sort of Auxiliary Committee, and calling upon the new men with whom you have already conferred & others whom you have it in mind to reach.

The tasks I have specifically in mind are.

1. Bringing into Z.O.A. membership men of ability, experience, standing and influence. Young men of promise; men of any age, position or occupation in whom there lurks a strong Jewish feeling, which can be awakened into active support by knowledge of Palestine achievements & needs.
2. Securing through such men financial support for the various economic undertakings of the P.E.C. and those planned by the Brodie Economic Com[mit]tee—undertakings which underlie the successful handling of problems political and social.

The effective means to those ends are:

A. Private talks, such as you have had with those from whom you have promise of aid. Every man won as an aid in our work should "go and do likewise". Every one of them can, by working privately and independently on those lines, win valuable support from friends and even from chance acquaintances; and each one should, as you do, place this activity among the daily tasks. "Let no Jew escape".

B. Private talks to small groups, acquainting their hearers with Palestine achievements & opportunities. Most of that which is most valuable for Jews is of such recent occurrence, that even well educated and well-informed Jews are usually unacquainted with the facts. The kind of men you have been talking with have the capacity to study, to learn, to think and to impart knowledge. Intimate private discussion by and with them cannot fail to interest the hearers; and when once the hearer is interested, he will almost inevitably become an ally. In this field, as in so many, knowledge is power.

C. There should be developed a Palestine handbook, or handbooks, so as to meet fully the needs of various kinds of people which your associates can use with friends and acquaintances. Many such exist. And there is an immense mass of material already available which is a copious reservoir from which much of the needed handbook could be drawn. Dr. Block[4] [sic] of the N.Y. Public Library, head of the Jewish Division, has the best knowledge of this material and would, I am sure, be glad to cooperate with you and men who, like Samuel Spring, appreciate the need of such instruments for building a strong support in America for Palestine work. But I am sure that the kind of supporters we need most are not an article to be obtained by mass production. Mass meetings won't do. A[nd] mass publications won't do it. And the best of handbooks will be of little service, except as used by, and in support of the personal efforts of those who are good talkers in private to men. Few men will read to good effect for us, unless they are personally converted. The handbook however good is valuable only as an instrument. It won't be automatic. And knowledge must be followed by a motor discharge.

D. Study by our men of ability is essential, and your lawyer friends will recall Coke's[5] advice: "Melius est petere fontes quam sectari rivulous." "It is better to seek the source than look at the river." The best current sources for an understanding of the abundant, constructive life of Palestine are "Davar Weekly English Supplement" and "Palestine Economic Magazine". Your talkers and your writers ought to get into touch with what is happening each day, through such organs. They will instruct and inspire, and they will enable your associates to feel, and make others feel that, although far away, they are part of the great adventure.

E. Most of those you have been talking with, and most of the people with whom they are likely to talk on Palestine, are in a position to have not only an intellectual or spiritual, but an economic stake in Palestine. Some should be glad to take part in the Dead Sea Project, or some other of the enterprises to be fostered by the Brodie Committee. Those who feel that to be impossible should become stockholders in the P.E.C. Every shareholder can feel assured that it is helping on the great work. And the amount of its achievement will be limited only by the cash available to it. The P.E.C. has the unique distinction among Palestinian institutions—*It invests or it lends.* It never borrows. Mohl,[6] Viteles and others who represent it in Palestine have made, by their efficient, business-like administration of its affairs, great contributions to Palestine upbuilding.

1. Samuel Spring (1888–19[?]) was a Harvard Law School graduate (1913), who practiced in California and Boston before moving to New York City in 1920. He was an expert on the entertainment industry and wrote several books on legal and investment topics.
2. See LDB to Jacob H. Gilbert, 19 October 1930, note 5.
3. LDB refers here to the destruction caused by the Arab riots of August 1929.
4. Joshua Bloch (1890–1957) was a Reform rabbi, born in Lithuania, who moved to the United States in 1907. After a decade of teaching at New York University, he began his life work of building the Jewish Division of the New York Public Library into one of the finest Judaica collections in the world. He served as head of the division from 1923 to 1956.
5. Sir Edward Coke (1552–1634) was the preeminent English jurist, compiler of English law, and defender of the authority of the common law.
6. Emanuel N. Mohl (1883–19[?]), a trained engineer, was active in the cause of Palestinian development.

To: Jacob H. Gilbert
Date: January 2, 1931
Place: Washington, D.C.
Source: Gilbert MSS

DEAR JACK: The matter of small loans has become one of national interest, through legislation sought or granted in many states & now being sought in Congress[1] to authorize a rate of interest of 3½ percent a month or 42% a year. The Household Finance Co. is, of the concerns acting, I believe, the largest & most widespread in its operations (as advertised recently in U.S. Daily.) Morris Banks[2] are another variant.

I know of nothing in the practical work being done in Palestine which is more instructive of its social achievements than the operations of the

510

Loan Bank Ltd.,[3] which has supplied the need of the small man, and educated him, at a rate of interest not exceeding nine (9) percent a year. Because of the make up of the Jewish population, conditions prevailing in Palestine, and the high rates of interest there prevailing in ordinary business, this is a remarkable achievement, affording a lesson to Americans which should be widely commented on, thus aiding both America & Palestine.

I think no one would be better qualified to write on this subject than Max Lerner.[4] The New Republic or other desirable (perhaps more desirable) publications should be glad to have such an article. So I am enclosing the Loan Bank Inc.'s report for the five years ending Dec 31/29 and the supplemental report for the financial year ending Sept 30/30.

If Max Lerner will undertake this task, he should, after familiarizing himself with the reports, and generally as to Palestine economic and social conditions, have a talk with Dr. Joshua Ber[n]hardt of the P.E.C. who can tell him much in this connection.[5]

1. The matter of the small loan business reached Congress through its oversight of the District of Columbia, and bills to regulate the industry were introduced in both the House (15982) and the Senate (5629).

2. The Morris Plan was a system of personal loans originated by Arthur J. Morris in 1910. By a series of contrivances, the plan enabled the loaner nearly to double the nominal rate of interest and to evade existing usury law limitations on the interest rate.

3. The Loan Bank Ltd. was one of the institutions through which the Palestine Economic Corporation channeled its funds; it specialized in small loans to farmers, artisans, and small businesses.

4. Max Lerner (1902–92) arrived from Russia in 1907. He studied economics at Yale University and the Brookings Institution but earned his national reputation as a writer, a political commentator, and a teacher. Lerner was to serve as an editor of the *Nation* and was a widely syndicated columnist. For many years he was a professor at Brandeis University.

5. No article on this subject was published over Lerner's signature; nor did the *New Republic* publish such an article.

To:	Jacob H. Gilbert (fragment)
Date:	January 4, 1931
Place:	Washington, D.C.
Source:	Gilbert MSS

MY DEAR JACK:

1. Re your of 31st, 2d, & 3rd. If we had a score of men as devotedly persistent as you are, Zionism would make large strides in N.Y.C.

2. The fact that you are "watching your steps", and have had wide experiences with "the ways and wiles of Tammany" and know "the streets of New York" assures me that you will not be misled

by Lipsky and his ilk. But I know L.L. and his ilk. They not only have not "performed"; they have destroyed. They gradually undermined, by self-seeking and lowered standards, the Z.O.A. which was flourishing in 1920. They bankrupted it financially, morally, intellectually, and depleted its membership. They did worse than deplete its membership. Not only did they drive out practically all worthy folk within it, but they devastated it by preventing new growth. There has not developed in it or through it a single younger man worthy to take a[n] office or leadership. That is the main cause of our present plight. And the paying membership dropped from about 100,000 to a tenth of that number. Moreover, the recent paying members were not financially full members. They came in largely at the tail end of the year for voting purposes for a fraction of the year, paying instead of $5, $3 or even less.

Furthermore, the working force was demoralized & the finances looted by Tammany methods. Political henchmen were put in & kept in, rendering often disservice instead of service—at high salaries.

Lipsky et al. could have helped the New Administration. I know of no instance where they did so. No doubt deHaas, Tulin & especially Rosensohn have faults. Possibly R's more than counterbalance his virtues. But deH is absolutely devoted to Zionism; & Tulin has done considerable service as a speaker. Bob [Szold]'s limitations no one recognizes more than he does. He is literally sacrificing himself. He is a fine character, unfortunately not a leader & not in full vigor. The defects of our group account in large part for the failure of the six months to achieve. But it is due, in part also to the depression & the difficulties inherent in the relations to the [Jewish] Agency. Still in no small part, the failure is due to the depth of the demoralization into which the Zionist organization throughout the country was led by 9 years of Lipsky administration.

Besides all these men by their talks, further demoralize their audiences through slogans and emotions, destroying in large measure our feeble efforts to educate by toilsome study, in order that there should be a following which understands & will be a steady support.

I more than suspect that Lipsky et al want to use me (and you), really to embarrass and ultimately upset our feeble management. But I think their enmities affect them more than they themselves know.[1]

5. But whatever you do, through people sent by Lipsky et al (or Jonah Goldstein) to you, be sure not to let a penny into the N.Y.

district Treasury, or otherwise to be disbursed by them. I have no faith in their handling of funds. Whatever you can raise, let it be expended through the P.E.C. or P.E.F.

1. There is a break in the manuscript at this point.

To: **Jacob H. Gilbert**
Date: **January 4, 1931**
Place: **Washington, D.C.**
Source: **Gilbert MSS**

MY DEAR JACK: No. 2
For your Auxiliary Com[mit]tee.[1]

(1) I suggest that Rabbi Braunstein[2] undertake to form Zionist Study Clubs at Columbia, of students and/or instructors. No club should have more than say 15 or 20 members. It should mean real study. And Braunstein should make it his task to show them how to start & give advice. But study means something very different from listening once a week, or so, to a lecture on Palestine. Let there be as many clubs as he can bring about. N.Y.U. & other Jewish colleges will follow.

(2) For Tom Warshow. I suggest that he write for some periodical an article as follows:

One of the outstanding phenomena in national and international trade with problems for the industrial countries is the fact that many of the less developed countries which used to furnish the great market for manufacturers have been stirred by various causes to strive for self-sufficiency.

With some, the main motive was nationalistic. In most the movement was greatly advanced by the war, when the supply from Europe & America was curtailed. Recently, a great incentive everywhere has been the local unemployment, the need of additional revenues through tariffs and the desire to keep money at home because of adverse trade balances. Thus, throughout the world, there has been a great development of industry in the undeveloped countries.

My impression is, that in none of the undeveloped countries, has the rise of industry (and the growing supply of the home market) made such rapid strides, as in Palestine during the past 8 years.

I suggest that Warshow make a study of the Palestine industrial development & write the appropriate article, which (well done & he can do it)

513

will redound indirectly to the benefit of Palestine, & incidentally give Brodie an instrument which he can use to good effect in his economic strivings.

1. See LDB to Jacob H. Gilbert, 26 December 1930.

2. Lamenting the growing irreligion among his student body, President Nicholas Murray Butler, in February 1929, appointed three religious advisors to the students, a Catholic, a Protestant, and a Jew. The Jewish advisor was Rabbi Baruch Braunstein (b. 1906), a recent graduate of Ohio State University and a rabbi in New York City. Braunstein served at Columbia until 1934. He then headed several congregations in New Jersey and Pennsylvania, lectured, and wrote books and articles.

To: Jacob H. Gilbert
Date: March 15, 1931
Place: Washington, D.C.
Source: Gilbert MSS

DEAR JACK: Re yours of 13th.

Don't let the Zionist affairs interfere with your pressing professional job. There will be plenty to do for Zionists for a generation.

We look forward to Susan & Louis.

To: Elizabeth Brandeis Raushenbush
Date: April 22, 1931
Place: Washington, D.C.
Source: Raushenbush MSS

DEAREST ELIZABETH: May the new year be a happy and useful one.[1]

The year now closing was made beautiful for us by the 3 R[aushenbushe]s.

From Clara[2] come reports of the impression widely made by your public work. The results striven for appear not to have been attained. But I hope the opposition presented will spur you to renewed attacks.

The gloomy years of depression are the only ones in which one may hope for a large crop of legislative hay; and it looks to me as if there would be no Hoover prosperity for some time ahead—despite the recent proclamations of our industrial and financial misleaders. I fear Arthur Woods[3] also is not a good witness.   With very much love

1. Elizabeth Brandeis Raushenbush's thirty-fifth birthday was on 25 April.

2. Clara Mortenson Beyer (1892–1990), the wife of Otto S. Beyer, had a long and illustrious career as a public servant. She worked for the War Labor Board and the Washington, D.C., Minimum Wage Board (where her long friendship with Elizabeth Brandeis began) before starting her service with the Children's Bureau (1928–34). During the 1940s and 1950s Beyer worked at the Bureau of Labor Standards.

3. Arthur Woods (1870–1942) had an extraordinarily diverse career in business, journalism, police work, and government service. He served during World War I in both civilian and military capacities. At the moment he was the chair of the President's Commission for Unemployment and part of the chorus of optimism that characterized the Hoover administration despite the worsening depression.

To: Jacob H. Gilbert
Date: May 11, 1931
Place: Washington, D.C.
Source: Gilbert MSS

DEAR JACK: Re yours of 9th.

1. The Blinken-Weiss report is a very good job; and the informing presentation of the facts justifies the expenditure of $500 for the auditors' services.[1]

2. The recommendations of Blinken & Weiss impress me as wise, with this exception. The $2500 for necessary administrative expenses cannot be supplied by the Z.O.A. because of its own impecuniosity. It should be supplied by those who were directly & indirectly responsible for the financial shortcomings and misfeasances i.e. the directors and officers, primarily Ben Rosenblatt. He and his family should lead the subscription to the $2500 fund. I suggest that Blinken and Weiss undertake to see personally all the persons affiliated with the old management. I feel sure that they (B and W) can put the matter so strongly to each individual as to get from them each something and from all an aggregate of $2500.

3. You are right in assuming that I cannot be induced to pay any part of this $2500, or to take any part in raising the $100,000. In view of this, could you not convince Freiberger[2] and deSalit that they had better not waste money and time in travelling to Washington on the 14th? I don't want to say that I won't see them; but I think it, at least, unnecessary for them to come. They may write me extensively.

1. Upon regaining power in the Zionist Organization of America, the Brandeis-Mack faction demanded a thorough examination of the books. They were not particularly surprised to discover financial discrepancies, mishandling of funds, and very deep indebtedness.

2. David Freiberger (1876–1947) was born in Hungary but was taken at an early age to America. After graduating from the New York University Law School, he practiced in the city. He was active in Zionist affairs (president of the American Zion Commonwealth at the

moment) and was head of a committee to negotiate peace between the Lipskyites and the Brandeis-Mack factions of the ZOA. His task was rendered impossible by LDB's implacable animosity toward Lipsky.

To: **Elizabeth Brandeis Raushenbush**
Date: June 3, 1931
Place: Boston, Massachusetts
Source: Raushenbush MSS

DEAR ELIZABETH: As you know, Mother and I have, for many years, given a large part of our income to public causes in which we took an active part; thus rendering our own work more effective. We think you and Susan may wish to do the like.

With this in view, we have transferred to each of you Ten thousand (10,000) dollars, face value additional bonds. Miss Malloch is having these registered in your names, and will send you herewith a description of the bonds.

There will be no occasion to cut any coupons before late in September so that the firm will hold the bonds for you, upon their return from the registry, until you are back from vacation.[1]   Lovingly

1. LDB sent an identically worded letter to his daughter Susan on this date.

To: **Jacob H. Gilbert**
Date: July 30, 1931
Place: Chatham, Massachusetts
Source: Gilbert MSS

DEAR JACK: Your family is in fine form and seems to have enjoyed much the visit of the Louisville cousins who left this morning.

New York and world news do not lend much support to H[erbert]. H[oover].'s emanations & Julius Klein's.[1]

I think I told you that Miss Grady's brother in law (Joe Cole), for very many years construction engineer of the Mack Motors, was laid off before the summer of 1930 & ever since has been without work. He & his wife have been solving the unemployment problem ever since by living in a solitary camp they built in the Maine woods. They built the camp, get most of their food by fishing & hunting & are having apparently a good time, winter as well as summer. Miss Grady has spent her vacation there; & the Coles' daughter (who is at Radcliffe) also—doubtless because she couldn't get this year employment in one of the children's camps, a job she had last summer.

516

Miss Grady cut her vacation short to make preparations for Bank 21 (Fall River Savings Bk) which has just voted to start an insurance department.

Enclose[d] letter (which please destroy) from Miss Grady will show you how the Coles live at camp; and enclosed "Brief Survey" to the work Miss Grady is returning to.

Letters from Switzerland report [*] of our group sailing for America this week.[2] Judge Mack will stay in Vienna until the fall.

Hope you are not having too bad a time.

1. Dr. Julius Klein (1886–1961) was a longtime official at the Department of Commerce, an expert on international trade, especially with Latin America, and a close friend and advisor of President Hoover. He, like the president, specialized in issuing overly optimistic statements about the economic situation. Three days before this letter, for example, he had announced in a radio speech that the country was obviously emerging from the depression.

2. The group was returning from the Seventeenth World Zionist Congress meeting in Basel, which had begun in late June. The chief business of the Congress was the ousting of Chaim Weizmann from the leadership, and the chief issue was what attitude to take toward the British in view of the Hope-Simpson report and the Passfield White Paper.

To: **Susan Brandeis Gilbert**
Date: **December 28, 1931**
Place: **Washington, D.C.**
Source: **Gilbert MSS**

DEAREST SUSAN: This watch was given me by my parents when I was about thirty. Give it to Louis Gilbert when he reaches that age.   Lovingly

To: **Louis Brandeis Wehle**
Date: **January 19, 1932**
Place: **Washington, D.C.**
Source: **Wehle MSS**

L.B.W.: Kindly attend to the following matter for me:

In 1913, when Norman Hapgood took over (largely with C.R. Crane's money) Harpers Weekly, I wrote for the Weekly the articles later collected and published by Frederick A. Stokes Company under the name "Other People[']s Money" and gave to Norman or the Weekly my copyright rights.

Although Stokes[1] has not advertised this book and few people, even booksellers, know where it can be procured, it has not died; and every once in a while there is a demand by someone (like the Julius Haldeman [sic] concern,[2] or the Upton Sinclair[3] crowd) to print a cheap edition. About two years ago Huston Thompson[4] was eager to have Stokes publish a new

517

edition, and he offered to write a comprehensive introduction to bring the book up to date. Stokes then stated that nothing could be done without the consent of Charles R. Crane, because he was entitled to the royalties. That was the first that I knew of this, and made up my mind that, when Norman returned from Europe and Crane from Asia, I should ask Norman to get Crane to relinquish to me his rights. Norman took the matter up with Crane, and his secretary Brodie, with the result that I received from Crane a letter of which copy is enclosed marked A, dated Jan. 4, 1932. Then I wrote Stokes asking them to send me draft of any copyright assignment which would be satisfactory to them. Under date of Jan. 13/32 they wrote me letter of which copy is enclosed marked B.

What I would like you to do is this: See Stokes, thank them for their courtesy. Arrange to have the copyright assigned to me and royalties paid to me; and that hereafter if there is an application for a cheap reprint (which I suppose would help the sale of Stokes edition), my consent (and theirs if need be) would be all that is required. And if there is a desire for a new edition and Stokes doesn't want to publish it, I can get some other publisher.[5]

There has been in recent years far more of an interest in "Other People's Money" than Stokes is probably aware of. Reviews of the book appear from time to time (about a year ago in Locomotive Engineers Journal). It is extensively discussed occasionally by broadcasting talkers. (Recently by WIBO station in Chicago.) And hardly a month passes without some enquiry coming to me as to where the book can be procured. This month one from [*] came. The present depression, the debunking of the great financial kings, and the losses of those who followed them have made men think, and i.a. realize that "Other People's Money" should have been heeded.

Find out, if you can, what the sales have been.

Of course, Norman will be glad to lend aid in getting Crane's signature or otherwise. Any royalties I get will go to the Savings Bank Ins. League, as do the royalties from my "Business a Profession."

It was worth being disabled[6] to secure four hours talk from you.

---

1. Frederick Abbot Stokes (1857–1939), the chief executive of the publishing house that bore his name, had been with that concern since 1881.

2. Emanuel Haldemann-Julius (1889–1951), whose unusual name was the result of prefixing his wife's maiden name to his own when they wed in 1916, was the publisher of cheap, popular, generally progressive or socialist books in his "Blue Book" series.

3. Upton Beall Sinclair (1878–1968) was the extremely prolific writer whose famous muckraking novel *The Jungle* (1906) is credited with reforming the meat-processing business in the United States.

518

4. Huston Thompson (1875–1966) came to Washington from Colorado and enjoyed a long career in public service. He was assistant attorney general in the Wilson administration and then a commissioner of the Federal Trade Commission until the mid-1920s.

5. Stokes published a new edition of *Other People's Money* in 1932, and the National Home Library Foundation of Washington, D.C., published an edition in 1933. Norman Hapgood wrote the introduction to both of these new editions.

6. LDB was confined to his home with a bad cold.

To:	**Jacob H. Gilbert**
Date:	**January 31, 1932**
Place:	**Washington, D.C.**
Source:	**Gilbert MSS**

DEAR JACK: Hope the family has a clean slate today.

Today I made my first call on Justice Holmes since his retirement.[1] He bears up well.

Mrs. Max Lowenthal[2] was in yesterday & seems amazed at the calm of Washington in contrast to the New York state of mind.

I guess Eugene Meyer has no easy job.[3]

1. After fifty years as a judge, thirty of them on the United States Supreme Court, Oliver Wendell Holmes, Jr., resigned his seat ("I bow to the inevitable") on 12 January 1932.

2. Max Lowenthal (1888–1971) was a New York attorney and a close friend of Felix Frankfurter's. He and his wife, Eleanor, also became close to the Brandeises, particularly in 1930 when Lowenthal was the secretary to President Hoover's (Wickersham) crime commission. Something of a Washington "insider," Lowenthal was roundly denounced by conservatives for his 1950 exposé, *The Federal Bureau of Investigation.*

3. President Hoover had just named LDB's friend Eugene Meyer, Jr., to head the Board of Directors of the new Reconstruction Finance Corporation, the chief depression-fighting device of the Hoover administration. The RFC was designed to prop up the economy by making strategic loans to banks, railroads, and insurance companies. The agency loaned more than a billion dollars in the first six months of its existence. Although there was a "president" of the corporation (former vice-president Charles Dawes), the real power lay with Meyer. See LDB to Frankfurter, 26 January 1932, in Urofsky and Levy, *"Half Brother, Half Son,"* 474.

To:	**Louis Brandeis Wehle**
Date:	**February 10, 1932**
Place:	**Washington, D.C.**
Source:	**Wehle MSS**

L.B.W.: Re yours of 9th.

1. That's a nice letter from Stokes. I think it best to drop the Huston Thompson idea, and to make simply a reprint, with a 1932 Foreword by the publishers in which the publisher will state (aided

by L.B.W.) that more recent events have given added significance to the views expressed by me in 1913–1914.[1] Perhaps you may find in Norman Hapgood's "The Changing Years" published in 1930, in the chapter "Mr. Brandeis," some passage that would be helpful in this connection.[2]

2. I think it would be better not to take up with Ralph Hale the matter of "Business—a Profession" until Stokes have agreed to the reprint of "Other People's Money."[3]

I am returning the R[econstruction].F[inance].C[orporation]. clipping. Krock treated you discreetly and helpfully.[4]

1. See LDB to Louis Brandeis Wehle, 19 January 1932.
2. The thirteenth chapter of Norman Hapgood's autobiography, *The Changing Years* (1930), was devoted to LDB. Ultimately Hapgood wrote the introduction to the new Stokes edition of *Other People's Money.*
3. Ralph Tracy Hale (1880–1951) was head of the publishing house of Hale, Cushman & Flint. In 1914, when he was with Small, Maynard in Boston, he supervised the publication of the collection of eighteen of LDB's speeches and articles known as *Business—a Profession*. That book was reissued in 1925 and would be issued yet again by Hale in 1933.
4. Arthur Krock (1887–1974) worked his way up through Louisville journalism to become a highly influential Washington columnist for the *New York Times*. He was to win the Pulitzer Prize on three different occasions. The clipping LDB refers to here is "New Finance Plan Praised by Wehle," from the 31 January issue of the *New York Times*. LDB's nephew had been the counsel to the War Finance Corporation, and his opinion of Hoover's new Reconstruction Finance Corporation was solicited. Wehle cautiously praised the RFC as a step in the right direction.

To: **Susan Brandeis Gilbert**
Date: **February 18, 1932**
Place: **Washington, D.C.**
Source: **Gilbert MSS**

DEAREST SUSAN: Glad to hear you are planning a joyous outing at Pocono.
Mr. Ratcliffe was in Tuesday, agreeable but not so sparkling as usual.
Yes, the Cardozo nomination is great for Court, country and the Jewish people.[1]
                                                                  Lovingly

1. Although there was already one Jew on the Supreme Court (LDB) and two New Yorkers (Stone and Hughes), Hoover flew in the face of politics and nominated as the replacement for Justice Holmes one of the most respected and influential judges in American history. Benjamin Nathan Cardozo (1870–1938) was born in New York City and educated at Columbia University. In 1914 he was elected to serve on the New York Supreme Court and a year later was appointed to the New York Court of Appeals (in 1927 he became that court's chief justice). Known for his thoughtful opinions, his lucid writing, and his liberal

sentiments, Cardozo already had a sterling reputation. His nomination won wide praise for the beleaguered Hoover and was quickly confirmed by the U.S. Senate.

To:	Susan Brandeis Gilbert
Date:	February 26, 1932
Place:	Washington, D.C.
Source:	Gilbert MSS

DEAREST SUSAN: Frank is making such rapid strides that you will soon have three children at school. So Mother and I think your birthday[1] an appropriate occasion for establishing a school fund, and are transferring to you $10,000 face value of our registered bonds.

Miss Malloch will send you with this letter the data concerning the bonds and will let you know when the bonds are returned from the registry.   Lovingly

1. The next day would be Susan Brandeis Gilbert's thirty-ninth birthday.

To:	Jacob H. Gilbert
Date:	June 14, 1932
Place:	Chatham, Massachusetts
Source:	Gilbert MSS

DEAR JACK: Your family is prospering handsomely. All the children have red cheeks emulating the 1931 record, and Susan carries Frank across the meadows with Herculean ease.

She had doubtless reported on Mr. [Harris] Palmer's new Ford and that he has resumed the functions of mail carrier and choreman, with (for him) joyous spirit.

Mr. Whaley is building a new house near the Grants & wishes to devote his Sundays to that.

Capt. Perry enquired solicitously about your coming & we had report of you from Jack Lazenby.

Capt. Perry says business in Chatham is very bad, mainly because fish has dropped so in price (in N.Y.) that the fishing launches can't earn enough to pay the cost of the gasoline etc. (about $10 a day); also that the clams (hard shell) market also is so low that Gould is not buying or shipping, and that the clammers are doing nothing but planting the young clams on the bed hoping for the future.

I have not been in the village yet.

Our sawn wood supply (and the coal) were apparently stolen. Not a stick of your ample supply remained to greet us.

To: Louis Brandeis Wehle
Date: July 9, 1932
Place: Chatham, Massachusetts
Source: Wehle MSS

L.B.W.: Re yours "Business a Profession" of July 6th with carbons of correspondence with Hale and Norman [Hapgood]; yours of 6th with suggestions for Bonbright's[1] Introduction; and yours of 7th with carbons.

1. As to who will write the introduction:[2] (a) Obviously it should be written in time so that the third edition can be advertised & published with other Fall publications. (b) If Bonbright can't undertake it, will you return to your earlier thought of asking Edwin F. Gay.[3] He is (as you doubtless know) back in Cambridge, 47 Holyoke House; and sent me, under date of July 5th, his article on "The Great Depression," reprint from July "Foreign Affairs," which he begins with a quotation from my Ice opinion.[4]

2. In addition to whatever else goes into the Introduction, there are two subjects which should be stressed:

    (a) The obligation of the employer to provide regularity of employment. This obligation, later formulated in the much quoted statement on p. 385 of "The Social and Economic Views of Mr. Justice B", was first postulated (privately) to William H. McElwain in the spring of 1903 and led to McElwain making the changes in the conduct of his business so as to give absolute regularity of employment discussed in my address "Business a Profession." The subject had been presented by me informally about a month before the Brown [University] commencement at Gay's suggestion one evening to his students. It had been urged by me in talks to and conferences with trade unions between 1903 and 1911; and was afterwards; and I sketched a plan for encouraging regularization.[5] The recent Wisconsin Act for an Unemployment Reserve proceeds, in some respects, on these lines.[6]

    (b) The other subject which should be stressed is Savings Bank Insurance. I enclose leaflets: (1) "Brief Survey 1931 Edition" (2) Miss Grady's Pittsfield address (3) "Twenty three years experience", which are the latest publications. Gay, with Felix

522

Frankfurter and Arthur M. Schlesinger,[7] sent a circular to the Harvard Faculty calling attention to S[avings].B[ank].I[nsurance]. when the Cambridge Savings Bank opened its insurance department in 1930.

3. As to your other pregnant suggestions for the introduction I refrain from saying anything, as I think what the introducer says by way of opinion on my writings had better be uninfluenced by me.

4. As to the compensation to be paid the writer of the introduction, I think publishers would know better than either you or I what would be reasonable compensation. (I guess your figure of $300 is too high.) Obviously, as you suggest, no cash amount should be paid by me or Savings Bank Insurance. A percentage of the royalties should go to the introducer until the amount of agreed compensation has been paid. Books with introductions are numerous, and it should not be difficult to ascertain what may reasonably be accepted as standard.

You will know best how to deal with Hale. He ought to pay his share of the introducer's compensation as Stokes has agreed to do. But if he cannot be induced to do so, I should be willing to have it all taken out of a percentage of the royalties until the agreed sum is liquidated. As to the amount of the introducer's compensation, you might get some light from James [Henle] by finding out what he paid Charles A. Beard for the introduction to "Social & Economic Views of Mr. Justice B." or to [George W.] Kirchwey for the introduction [to] O.W. Holmes' Dissenting Opinions.[8] Henle[9] is a Louisville boy (of the Flexner family), a friend of Charles Tachau.

Since writing the above Elizabeth has received & handed me your telegram about Sliding Scale Gas. The Act's Sliding Scale was predicated upon the price for illuminating gas. The original act (1906 c. 422) was extended from time to time. By 1926 electricity had substantially superseded gas as an illuminant and by Act of 1926 c. 186 the 1906 Act and amendments were repealed.

I don't have any detail as to the adoption & operation of the sliding scale elsewhere. My definite knowledge of its operation in Boston ends with 1916, and I don't know to whom you could be referred for such definite information. Control of the Boston gas interest passed from Boston to Pittsburgh about two or three years ago.

1. James Cummings Bonbright (1891–1985) taught economics at Columbia University for forty years starting in 1920. He wrote scholarly articles on economic subjects and served on several governmental bodies.

2. The new edition of *Business—a Profession* eventually included the original introduction by Ernest Poole and two new introductory essays by Bonbright and Felix Frankfurter.

3. Edwin Francis Gay (1867–1946) had taught economics and economic history at Harvard since 1902. He undertook several important public duties during and shortly after World War I and in the mid-1930s moved to the Huntington Library in California.

4. Edwin F. Gay, "The Great Depression," *Foreign Affairs* 10 (July 1932): 529–40. One of LDB's most notable opinions was his dissent in *New State Ice Co. v. Liebmann,* 285 U.S. 262, 280 (1932). The case involved an Oklahoma law that prevented anyone from entering the ice business without state permission. LDB might have been expected to join the majority, which found the Oklahoma law unconstitutional on the grounds that it stifled competition and prevented individuals from entering into a business. But for LDB the key issue was the state's police power and the right of the state, in the midst of a terrible depression, to confront the emergency. An often-quoted part of the dissent was LDB's contention that the federal system enabled a courageous state to embark upon economic experimentation and his warning to his colleagues "lest we erect our prejudices into legal principles. If we would guide by the light of reason, we must let our minds be bold."

5. See LDB to A. L. Filene, June 1911; see also LDB to J. Franklin McElwain, 18 June 1912, regarding the Brown University commencement speech, both in BL.

6. In January 1932, after a long struggle, the Wisconsin legislature passed and Governor Phil La Follette signed an important unemployment compensation law. Elizabeth Brandeis and her husband, Paul Raushenbush, were active crusaders for the act. The new law made each corporation responsible for building an unemployment reserve for its own workers but rewarded those businesses that provided regularity of employment by reducing the required contribution. See Paul A. Raushenbush, "Starting Unemployment Compensation in Wisconsin," *Unemployment Insurance Review* (April–May 1967): 17–24.

7. Arthur Meier Schlesinger, Sr. (1888–1965) came to Harvard to teach history in 1924. The author of pathbreaking books on many aspects of American history, Schlesinger was among the most distinguished and influential historians of his generation. Of LDB, Schlesinger wrote: "The trait called greatness is an elusive one, but if it comprehends humility, moral majesty, faith in the common folk, deep human compassion, and constancy of purpose—in short, the quality of having made the world better for having lived in it—then Brandeis alone of the men I have known fulfilled the requirements" (Arthur M. Schlesinger, *In Retrospect: The History of a Historian* [New York, 1963], 126).

8. Alfred Lief, ed., *The Dissenting Opinions of Mr. Justice Holmes* (New York, 1929).

9. James Henle (1891–1973) was related to the Flexner family by marriage. He was president of Vanguard Press, which had published the Holmes dissents and Lief's *Social and Economic Views of Mr. Justice Brandeis* (1930).

To:	Fannie Brandeis
Date:	July 11, 1932
Place:	Chatham, Massachusetts
Source:	Fannie Brandeis

DEAR FAN: Our thanks to your mother for the photograph of the bas-relief. I hope your house harbors also the bas-relief of your great-grandfather Dembitz.

Aunt Alice and I think Franklin Roosevelt is much underrated by the Liberals. The opposition of the vested interests, who have opposed him, indicated that they fear him. And the result of the Convention pleases us much.[1] McAdoo, the ablest of the Democrats, is redivivus—that will mean much.[2]

1. The Democrats, meeting in Chicago at the end of June, gave their presidential nomination to New York governor Franklin D. Roosevelt.
2. William G. McAdoo played an important role in the Democratic Convention of 1932, first by breaking a deadlock between Roosevelt and John Nance Garner of Texas by swinging his California delegation behind FDR and then by negotiating the vice-presidential nomination for Garner.

To:	Louis Brandeis Wehle
Date:	August 5, 1932
Place:	Chatham, Massachusetts
Source:	Wehle MSS

L.B.W.:

1. My grief that the Norfolk & Southern [*sic*] had to seek relief in a receivership is somewhat assuaged by the notice that you are counsel for a protection Com[mit]tee. Why didn't the R.F.C. come to the rescue?[1]
2. Sixty years ago tomorrow the family left Louisville for the memorable stay in Europe, sailing on Aug. 10th from N.Y. Aunt Fannie who was in the East with Jessie Cochrane et al. met us in New York.

Yours of 2d re "Business a Profession" recd.

1. The troubled Norfolk Southern railroad had asked for a $325,000 loan from the Reconstruction Finance Corporation. Wehle explained to LDB that the request was refused because the railroad had insufficient security. A large part of its business had consisted of lumbering in regions that were now denuded of forest.

To:	Jacob H. Gilbert
Date:	September 25, 1932
Place:	Washington, D.C.
Source:	Gilbert MSS

DEAR JACK: Our best wishes for the homecoming.

1. The M.D's letter herewith; also one from Susan's Mother.
2. You "done nobly" on the painting. No doubt your services will be requisitioned for further work next summer.
3. There has been considerable Palestine talk. Maurice Hexter[1] and Mrs. Lindheim were here, and a mass of Palestine correspondence have [*sic*] poured in. Certainly something is doing there.

4. In American affairs we learn little that is cheering from the knowing ones here. And the official reports for week ending Sept 17 shows wholesale prices are back to level of Aug 20. And the sainted hog average back to the June low level.

5. Phil's defeat[2] is a severe blow. But I know no one who is better able to bear it, with his youth, vigor and La Follette blood. I guess that the Democratic activity contributed much to the defeat.

1. Maurice Beck Hexter (1891–1990) was active in numerous Jewish philanthropic organizations. He was a director of the Palestine Emergency Fund and a non-Zionist member of the Jewish Agency. Hexter helped with the negotiations with the British after the Passfield White Paper of 1930.

2. Phil La Follette had just lost the Republican primary to his old foe, ex-governor Walter J. Kohler. Kohler was then defeated in the Democratic landslide of 1932 by Albert Schedeman. Two years later, however, La Follette would return to the governorship, this time as head of a new party formed by him and his brother, the Progressive Party of Wisconsin.

To: Louis Brandeis Wehle
Date: September 27, 1932
Place: Washington, D.C.
Source: Wehle MSS

L.B.W.: "Business a Profession" re yours of 26th.

I think it inappropriate that I should write any letter that could be transmitted to Hale.[1] You know that I felt it improper to suggest, in respect to either book, what the introduction should contain & preferred not to see what was written until it had been published. I did not see [Charles A.] Beard's introduction until "The Social & Economic Views" was published; did not know of the Yale Press volume until it appeared;[2] & have consistently refused to look at any of the articles on me prior to publication.

I may say to you that Hale's performance in this respect is quite in keeping with his action and inaction in respect to all other matters relating to the book.

And, I add, as already stated, that I am entirely content with Bonbright's introduction.

No doubt, with your usual tact and resourcefulness, you will put this through as planned.

Bonbright article returned herewith.

1. Ralph Hale considered James Bonbright's introductory chapter too dull. LDB's nephew disagreed and wondered if LDB cared to write a letter that could be transmitted to Hale in which he expressed approval of the piece.

2. LDB refers here to a new book: Felix Frankfurter, ed., *Mr. Justice Brandeis* (New Haven, 1932), a tribute to him with essays by Charles Evans Hughes, Max Lerner, Frankfurter, Donald Richberg, Henry Wolf Biklé, and Walton Hamilton. The volume had an introductory note by Oliver Wendell Holmes.

To:	Jacob H. Gilbert
Date:	October 4, 1932
Place:	Washington, D.C.
Source:	Gilbert MSS

DEAR JACK: We were glad to see the Herald Tribune's featuring of Susan's broadcast.[1] Her Mother spent much of the day in a vain endeavor to arrange for hearing her. But not even the Women's Democratic Club was able to effect the connection.

Meanwhile there is some politics doing in your State. I can't believe that either F.D.R. or Lehman[2] will let themselves be trapped in the Tammany net.[3]

Al's performance in the Outlook article[4] bears out the worst you prognosticated for him. Is drink or Rascob [*sic*][5] the greater demoralizer?

I closed my Zionist season[6] with long sessions Saturday and Sunday with Mohl and Julius Simon.

Hope you and Susan will invite Mr. & Mrs. Mohl for dinner. Their stay in New York will be a short one.

Clara Beyer saw Elizabeth for 2 days & gives a good report.

The carbon of your letter to Dr. Osgood returned herewith.

1. On 3 October Susan made a radio address over Station WOR, under the auspices of the National Federation of Business and Professional Women's Clubs. In her talk she urged women to become involved in politics and to vote in the coming election. She hoped that the total of women's votes would be 40 percent higher than in 1928.

2. Herbert Henry Lehman (1878–1963) spent a few years in his family's banking business before entering politics as a Smith Democrat in New York. He was Roosevelt's running mate for lieutenant governor in 1928. This year he would win the first of his four terms as governor of New York. In 1949 Lehman defeated John Foster Dulles to finish the unexpired term of Senator Robert Wagner, and a year later he was elected to a full term in the Senate.

3. The current leader of Tammany Hall, John F. Curry, was opposed to Lehman for the governorship and tried to block the nomination. The move backfired, however, as Lehman (and his supporters, FDR and Al Smith) refused to knuckle under and the district lieutenants of the Tammany boss rebelled and supported Lehman, who was easily nominated at the Democratic state convention that week.

4. Amid growing rumors of a split between himself and Roosevelt, Alfred Smith contributed an essay in the most recent *New Outlook,* in which he lamented the "forgotten man" theme of the Democratic national ticket as divisive and class-oriented. Although Smith roundly criticized Hoover and endorsed "the Democratic ticket," many close observers of American politics noted that he pointedly declined to mention Franklin Roosevelt by name.

5. John Jakob Raskob (1879–1950) was a businessman and financier. He left General Motors in 1928, at candidate Al Smith's urging, to head the Democratic National Committee.

6. After his faction took leadership of the Zionist Organization of America, LDB warned that his age would prevent his day-to-day involvement, but that he would devote his summers to study and advising the movement. Every year, therefore, as the first week of October came and the Supreme Court began its work, LDB abandoned or greatly reduced his Zionist work.

To:	Susan Goldmark
Date:	October 7, 1932
Place:	Washington, D.C.
Source:	EBR

DEAR SUSIE: Our thanks to the Geschwester[1] for the Nevinson.[2] The volume came most opportunely yesterday early as Alice had set apart the day for resting and enjoyed many hours in the reading.

Whenever one returns to Goethe there are new revelations. I had again the experience in reading "Warheit und Dichtung"[3] this summer. Writing was but an incident of his living.

The Court made its annual call on the President yesterday. He looked very fit after two nights on the train and endless speaking. There is marvellous exhilaration in action—and applause. We are told that a week before, when seen here, he looked like a man of eighty. Perhaps you heard his Des Moines speech.[4] Your radio must have been an added comfort during these trying weeks.

Paul [Raushenbush] is due next Friday for an A.F. of L. conference on unemployment reserve legislation.

1. Sister.
2. Henry Wood Nevinson, *Goethe: Man and Poet* (New York, 1932). The volume was written to mark the centenary of Goethe's death.
3. Goethe's four-volume autobiography, *Aus Meinem Leben: Dichtung und Wahrheit*, was published between 1811 and 1833.
4. In Des Moines Hoover presented his twelve-point farm program to a crowd of 10,000 and a large radio audience. He advocated opening new markets, a St. Lawrence seaway, the maintenance of high tariffs, and the gold standard. He also struck a typically optimistic note about the recovery. For the text of his remarks, see the *New York Times*, 5 October 1932.

To:	Jacob H. Gilbert
Date:	October 9, 1932
Place:	Washington, D.C.
Source:	Gilbert MSS

DEAR JACK: Paul [Raushenbush] is due here Friday and expects to stay until Sunday P.M., for his AF. of L. Unemployment Reserve bill drafting committee meeting.[1] Felix [Frankfurter] will be here also. And the Amer. Bar Ass[ociatio]n functions will do what they can to disturb the ordinary course of occupations. But we shall eschew all Bar activities. The Court's work will give its members adequate employment for the near future.

Mr. Hoover is not making much out of his "business revival"; and his talk at Des Moines[2] about our having been perilously near going off the gold standard was as stupid politics as anything he has been guilty of. If any "adviser" sanctioned that passage, he ought to be quickly despatched.

Hope your Boston trip will prove encouraging.

Tell Susan that a Chicago classmate of hers—Bernard B. Burley called on me this week.

1. See LDB to Louis Brandeis Wehle, 9 July 1932, note 6.
2. See the previous letter, note 4.

To: Josephine Goldmark
Date: October 30, 1932
Place: Washington, D.C.
Source: Brandeis MSS

DEAR JOSEPHINE: Early in November comes the 25th anniversary of our entry upon the Oregon case.[1] I wish to celebrate the day by entering upon another joint enterprise with you, which should be no less interesting and prove equally important.[2]

Alice tells me that you plan to come here for the birthday.[3] Can't you come at least a week earlier and let me talk over the project with you, before the Court resumes its exigent sessions on Monday, the seventh? The sooner, the better?

1. LDB refers, of course, to the landmark case of *Muller v. Oregon*, 208 U.S. 412 (1908). See LDB to AGB, 14 January 1908, note 5.
2. Perhaps LDB hoped to interest his sister-in-law in his own growing fascination with the development of social democracy in Denmark. He would eventually encourage her to write something about the Danish social system, and his urging finally bore fruit. *Democracy in Denmark* (Washington, D.C., 1936) consisted of two parts. The first was a description by Goldmark entitled "Democracy in Action"; the second part, "The Folk High School," was an essay by A. H. Hollman, translated from the German by AGB.
3. LDB's seventy-sixth birthday would be on 13 November.

To: Elizabeth Brandeis Raushenbush
Date: November 2, 1932
Place: Washington, D.C.
Source: EBR

DEAREST ELIZABETH: You and Paul will be interested in the enclosures on Ins[urance]. Reserve. Please return Dean Clark's[1] letter to Felix [Frankfurter].

The clipping will show you how the business curve is turning down.

Thanks for your letter. I am as usual, but the auto men are right. Old machines are unreliable and the maintenance cost high.

1. Charles Edward Clark (1889–1963) was dean of the Yale Law School, 1929–39. Roosevelt then nominated him as judge for the Second Circuit U.S. Court of Appeals, and from 1954 to 1959 he was the chief judge of that court.

To: **Walter Brandeis Raushenbush**
Date: November 25, 1932
Place: Washington, D.C.
Source: Raushenbush MSS

DEAR WALTER: I was very glad to get your letter written in ink. I hope your bird-house is finished. Do you like this one?

I hope the cat won't eat the bird.

To: **Jacob H. Gilbert**
Date: December 9, 1932
Place: Washington, D.C.
Source: Gilbert MSS

DEAR JACK: It's long since I wrote you. Your City affairs are occupying much of the newspaper space.[1] It looks as if misgovernment were being brought home to folks. Apparently it is only by means of the financial nerves that it can be achieved. Here also there are troubles galore. H[erbert].H[oover]. has not done himself very proud in his post-election performances.[2] I guess he is incorrigible.

The cotton reports, with ever increasing crop, must be giving new growing pains.[3]

1. New York City was engulfed in the aftermath of the resignation of Mayor James J. ("Jimmy") Walker on 1 September. The accusations of corruption—both civic and personal—did not end with the colorful and popular Walker's resignation; nor did calls for municipal reform coming from the Samuel Seabury investigation of Walker's financial dealings.

2. On 8 November the American people swept Franklin Roosevelt into the presidency with a resounding majority. He carried 42 states and got 27.8 million votes to Hoover's 15.7, triumphing in the electoral college by 472 to 59.

3. Estimates of the 1932 cotton crop kept rising. The latest guess, two days earlier, had put the total at 12.7 million bales, up considerably from an estimate on 1 November. Although this was much less cotton than was produced in 1931 (17.0 million bales), the price of the commodity was precarious. On 7 December the American Cotton Association called for a "cotton holiday" to prevent the price from falling below $0.10 per pound.

To: Elizabeth Brandeis Raushenbush
Date: April 22, 1933
Place: Washington, D.C.
Source: EBR

DEAREST ELIZABETH: The year just closing[1] has been a beautiful and useful one for you and Paul and Walter. We can wish you nothing better than another such.

It is fine to think that Chatham days are near.

Lovingly

Public affairs are engrossing, and hopeful. But I can't believe in any inflation save through the expenditures on huge public works. Inflation is a question apart from going off gold; that is failing to sustain the dollar abroad.[2]

1. Elizabeth was to celebrate her thirty-seventh birthday on 25 April.
2. This letter was written in the midst of the famous "first hundred days" of Franklin Roosevelt's administration, during which numerous depression-fighting measures were pushed quickly through the Congress. In the National Industrial Recovery Act, which would become law on 16 June, more than $3 billion was included for financing public projects. Roosevelt had moved the nation off the gold standard three days before this letter was written.

To: Jacob H. Gilbert
Date: July 27, 1933
Place: Chatham, Massachusetts
Source: Gilbert MSS

DEAR JACK: I have read the thoughtful letter of your friend, returned herewith. In my opinion, Anti-Semitism can be best combatted, here and elsewhere, by the upbuilding of the Homeland in Palestine; and to that end the efforts of American intellectuals should be directed.

To: Elizabeth Brandeis Raushenbush
Date: September 16, 1933
Place: Washington, D.C.
Source: EBR

DEAR ELIZABETH: This method has occurred to me for dealing with the question of national-state provisions for "unemployment insurance." The Federal Govt should leave the providing wholly to the States; but as a "discourager of hesitancy" should lay an excise tax after a day fixed upon every employer who shall not have made provision thereupon under some adequate state law. The federal tax should go into the U.S. General revenue fund, i.e. not be specifically appropriated to unemployment compensation, lest by so doing we start national provision. But some provision will have to be made for Dist. of Columbia; so we may have to provide for it a system e.g. the Wisconsin scheme.[1]

F.D. [Roosevelt] indicated yesterday to F[elix]. F[rankfurter]. a desire to talk with me generally on matters, before Court convenes. If he carries out his purpose, I want to discuss irregularity of employment with him.[2] Let me have as soon as possible your & Paul's views as to the above; &, if you can, a rough suggestion for a bill.

Note enclosed clipping from AFL news.

1. See LDB to Louis Brandeis Wehle, 9 July 1932, note 6.
2. On 16 November LDB wrote to Frankfurter, who was in England: "I omitted to mention that F.D. did not forget his promise (?) to you to send for me. On 3 November the White House asked Alice & me to lunch with him & Mrs. R. on Sunday the 5th alone. (I suppose he was wiping off his slate in preparation for his leaving for Warm Springs on 17th) It seemed wise to express our regrets. There would have been no fair chance to talk policies with F.D. so I am not sorry we couldn't go." (Urofsky and Levy, *"Half Brother, Half Son,"* 535). See also LDB to Elizabeth Brandeis Raushenbush, 30 September 1933, BL.

To: **Elizabeth Brandeis Raushenbush**
Date: **November 17, 1933**
Place: **Washington, D.C.**
Source: **EBR**

DEAR ELIZABETH: Genl. Johnson[1] came up last Friday, pursuant to our talk over the telephone at Chatham.

I put to him the Wisconsin idea & my project for Federal tax.[2] Yesterday I sent him your article obtained at great expense from N[ew].R[epublic].[3]

When here, the General expressed approval of the general plan; but I guess he didn't understand overmuch. He is, however, definitely for regularization [of employment] & individual reserves paid for by employer.

Lovingly

1. Gen. Hugh Samuel Johnson (1882–1942) was in charge of the draft during World War I, and Roosevelt appointed him to head the National Recovery Administration in 1933. During his year-long control of the agency, Johnson engaged in a spirited public relations campaign, built around the symbol of the "blue eagle," as many American industries devised "codes" to organize their businesses during the depression. Although LDB opposed the idea of the NRA, Johnson consulted with him on a few occasions. In 1934, when his agency came under increasing attack, Johnson claimed in a radio address on 14 September that "I have been in constant touch with that old counselor, Judge Louis Brandeis." There followed a brief flurry of criticism about LDB, a member of the judicial branch, breaching judicial propriety by meddling in the executive and with an institution whose affairs might eventually come before the High Court. Although Johnson's claim was untrue (LDB recounts

meticulously his few encounters with Johnson in a letter to Frankfurter, 22 September 1934; Urofsky and Levy, *"Half Brother, Half Son,"* 554–55), the Justice elected to remain silent. Some attributed Johnson's statement to a growing alcohol problem; others blamed his desperation to save the NRA.

2. See LDB to Louis Brandeis Wehle, 9 July 1932, and the preceding letter.

3. Elizabeth Brandeis, "Employment Reserves vs. Insurance," *New Republic* 76 (27 September 1933): 177–79.

To:	Elizabeth Brandeis Raushenbush
Date:	November 19, 1933
Place:	Washington, D.C.
Source:	EBR

DEAREST ELIZABETH: My thanks to you three for the birthday greetings.[1]

Curb of bigness is indispensable to true Democracy & Liberty. It is the very foundation also of wisdom in things human

"Nothing too much"

I hope you can make your progressives see this truth. If they don't, we may get amelioration, but not a working "New Deal." And we are apt to get Fascist manifestations. Remember, the inevitable ineffectiveness of regulation, i.e. the limits of its efficiency in regulation.

If the Lord had intended things to be big, he would have made man bigger—in brains and character.

My "running waters" suggestion was this. My idea has been that the Depression can be overcome only by extensive public works.

(a) that no public works should be undertaken save those that would be effective in making the America of the future what it should be,

(b) that we should avail [ourselves] of the present emergency to get those public works which Americans would lack the insight & persistence to get for themselves in ordinary times.

These public works are, for every state,

(1.) afforestation
(2) running water control
(3) adult education
(4) appropriate provision for dealing with defectives and delinquents.

By "Running Water Control" I mean this:

In this country, where the rain fall is, in the main, between 35 and 50 inches, and the country largely blessed with hills or mountains, it is absurd to permit either floods or droughts, or waste of waters. We should so control all running waters, by reservoirs, etc., so

(a) as to prevent floods & soil erosion
(b) to make it possible to irrigate practically all land
(c) to utilize the water for power & inland navigation
(d) & for recreation

Every state should have its lakes and ponds galore. Doubtless, you will recall much discourse of mine on this subject.[2]

Lovingly

I am very glad you & Paul are doing so much talking.

1. LDB's seventy-seventh birthday was on 13 November.
2. These remarks may have come in connection with an embryonic movement to organize Wisconsin progressives into a third party, a movement spearheaded by the La Follette brothers and coming to fruition in 1934 with Phil La Follette's reelection as governor on the Progressive ticket. From the beginning Paul and Elizabeth Raushenbush were involved in the effort.

To: Elizabeth Brandeis Raushenbush
Date: November 20, 1933
Place: Washington, D.C.
Source: EBR

DEAREST ELIZABETH: Since writing you yesterday yours of Saturday has come.

1. Phil [La Follette] has given you very bad investment advice. Do not invest in any stock, common or preferred. Changes in the bonds should be made only if you find an opportunity for getting a safer bond. Government bonds, despite the infirmity injected by the New Deal,[1] are probably safer than most investments, if bonds are paid off.
2. If you have more income than you find yourself able to spend wisely, re-invest the surplus so as to make good losses sure to come in some measure, through inflation or otherwise.
3. The underlying objection to investment in common stocks is, that for one with your knowledge & interests, such investment is mere speculation. The dangers of an unlisted stock are obvious. Those of the listed (and others) are not merely the inevitable risks

of business. They arise from the widespread dishonesty, or low ethical standards, prevailing in officers of corporate enterprises.[2]

Lovingly

4. If at any time you have doubt about investments, consult Miss Malloch, as I do.
5. Also, as I said to you last summer—Never endorse or guarantee for anybody. You will know whether your income permits you *to give.*

1. LDB doubtless refers here to the decision by the Roosevelt administration to abandon the gold standard and stop paying government bonds in gold. Eventually the Supreme Court considered the issue and condemned repudiation as both immoral and unconstitutional, but the Court had to uphold the policy so as to avoid chaotic financial results. See *Perry v. U.S.,* 294 U.S. 330 (1935).
2. Compare this to the advice given his brother three decades before; see LDB to Alfred Brandeis, 28 July 1904.

To: **Alice Park Goldmark**
Date: **January 11, 1934**
Place: **Washington, D.C.**
Source: **EBR**

MY DEAR ALICE: It was lovely of you to knit the socks, more beautiful even than their predecessors.

We had a gay Christmas with the Susan family; and Elizabeth came to usher in the New Year. Her time was spent largely on unemployment reserves—spent hopefully; and there may be some results of national significance.[1]

Of course, life in Washington now is stirring, intellectually far more so than I have ever known it. There is much noble thinking and high endeavor; sometimes impatience, sometimes a forgetting that:

"The world's wise are not wise
Claiming more than mortals know."

and that:

"Wenn man der Stein der Weisen hätte
Der Weise mangelte dem Stein."[2]

We are beginning already to think of Chatham, and we hope that nothing will interfere this year with a real visit from you three.

1. Elizabeth Raushenbush came to Washington at the behest of A. Lincoln Filene to meet with a group of policy-makers (including Frances Perkins and Senator Robert Wagner) at the home of Filene's daughter. She tried to persuade those present to push for a federal payroll tax on employers, which would simultaneously award a tax credit for their contributions under approved state unemployment compensation laws like the one she and her husband, Paul Raushenbush, had agitated for in Wisconsin. See LDB to Louis Brandeis Wehle, 9 July 1932, note 6, and to Elizabeth Brandeis Raushenbush, 22 April 1934.

2. "If they had the philosopher's stone, / the stone would lack a philosopher." Goethe, *Faust,* II:5063.

To:	Susan Brandeis Gilbert
Date:	February 1, 1934
Place:	Washington, D.C.
Source:	Gilbert MSS

DEAREST SUSAN: Nathan Straus [Jr.] was in this A.M. Nothing heard yet from Mrs. S.

N.S. thought he might be too busy to see her at all; looked forward to being in conference 10 A.M. to 10 P.M. with only one hour out for luncheon.

The Gilbert family seems to be active in all its branches. Tell Louis, Mozart was my favorite music in the days when as a boy I essayed the violin.

You & Jack seem to have been leading customers for OPM.[1]

1. During these weeks the Gilberts were actively promoting the sale and distribution of the new edition of LDB's book *Other People's Money.*

To:	Jacob H. Gilbert
Date:	March 4, 1934
Place:	Washington, D.C.
Source:	Gilbert MSS

DEAR JACK: Re yours of 2d.

It's fine to hear that the new firm is assured, and that you have secured an arrangement in both partnership and lease matters with which you and Susan are satisfied.[1]

I think your firm name is fine, and we look forward to the developments. A nice letter to me came from Diamond and I am enclosing the acknowledgment which, of course, you and Susan are to read before delivering it.

I am sorry that it seems unwise for me to send the letters of introduction which you suggest. They might be misunderstood by the addressees and prove embarrassing to me.

536

The situation is, of course, very different from that when you went abroad. You were not only my son-in-law for whom I could vouch from personal knowledge, but you were going abroad a stranger to the countries which you were to visit. Diamond is so much at home in England, that I fear any letter would be regarded as an attempt on my part to use influence, in some way, merely because he is the partner of my daughter & son-in-law.

1. The Gilberts were about to enter into partnership with Milton Diamond (1889–1955). Born in Romania, Diamond came to the United States at an early age. He graduated from the New York Law School in 1911. Eventually he specialized in music and entertainment industry law. He was at one time counsel to the American Federation of Musicians and personal counsel to the head of that union, James C. Petrillo. Diamond also went into the business of booking famous singers and entertainers.

To: Jacob H. Gilbert
Date: April 18, 1934
Place: Washington, D.C.
Source: Gilbert MSS

DEAR JACK:

1. I am sending, as requested, 2 autographed photographs.
2. Miss Mullen gave a rapturous account of Louis' qualities & leadership. She must be a very good teacher.
3. [*] is coming in at 3 P.M.
4. Despite reports of increase in dollar value of retail sales, the A & P & other reports showing reduced volume of grocery sales as compared with '33[1] indicate that there is little, if any, real betterment of affairs. Of course, some of the favored are making profits.

1. The Atlantic and Pacific grocery chain had just announced figures for five weeks ending 31 March. While earnings in dollars increased more than 8 percent over the same period in 1933, the figures for the tonnage of sales showed a decline of 3.5 percent (from 495,000 to 477,000).

To: Elizabeth Brandeis Raushenbush
Date: April 22, 1934
Place: Washington, D.C.
Source: EBR

DEAREST ELIZABETH: For you, Paul and Walter, our best wishes for the birthday,[1] wishes for another twelve months as fruitful as those just closing.
It is still believed that the Lewis-Wagner bill will be passed at this session.[2] If it is, even with the tax-rate reduced, a long step forward will be

taken; and you and Paul will have your hands full for the next two years, at least.

As you may have imagined, I see little to be joyous about in the New Deal measures most talked about. N.R.A. and A.A.A seem to be going from bad to worse.[3]

Bob made a good fight on the tax bill, but, even if enacted, as passed by the Senate, the advance will be woefully small.[4]

I am glad Paul is to have Arthur Altmyer's [sic] aid, at least for a while.[5] A.A. would be wise if he stayed at home.   Lovingly

1. On 25 April Elizabeth Raushenbush was to celebrate her thirty-eighth birthday.

2. A proposal for a national system based on the Wisconsin plan for unemployment compensation had been introduced into Congress by Senator Robert Wagner and Maryland representative David J. Lewis. Their proposal embodied LDB's device of a payroll tax on employers that could be deducted by those who were already contributing to approved state plans for unemployment compensation. The bill seemed to be gaining support in Congress, but see the next letter.

3. Both the National Recovery Administration and the Agricultural Adjustment Administration, highlights of Roosevelt's "first hundred days" of depression-fighting legislation, were coming under increasing criticism and were facing impending judicial challenges. LDB detested the NRA because of its emphasis on bigness and consolidation and because it seemed to circumvent the antitrust laws. In 1935 he voted with all of the other Justices to declare it unconstitutional in the important case of *Schechter v. U.S.*, 295 U.S. 553. When the AAA appeared before the High Court and the majority of his brethren declared it also to be unconstitutional, however, LDB and Justice Cardozo joined in Harlan Fiske Stone's powerful dissent. That case was *U.S. v. Butler*, 297 U.S. 1 (1935).

4. Congress was considering an adjustment of the income tax rates. Senator Robert La Follette, Jr., tried to raise the base from 4 to 6 percent, and the surtax increased to 71 percent. In the end Congress compromised at 5 percent and a 59 percent surtax rate. Thus the so-called Wealth Tax bill was not nearly as far-reaching as many progressives had hoped.

5. Arthur Joseph Altmeyer (1891–1972) was a career public servant from Wisconsin. After service in the NRA administration, he took over as chair of the new Social Security Board and held that post from 1937 to 1946. He became a close friend of the Raushenbushes.

To: **Elizabeth Brandeis Raushenbush**
Date: **June 8, 1934**
Place: **Boston, Massachusetts**
Source: **EBR**

Strictly Confidential

DEAR ELIZABETH: Don't be discouraged by the President's message.[1]

He summoned me yesterday & when I reached him at 4:45 P.M. he had in his hand his message & started in to read it to me. When he came to the part on social insurance, I stopped him, told him it was all wrong, & for about 3/4 hours discussed that question & I think convinced him of the error. He said the message had already gone to the Capitol & it was too late to change that; but it would not commit him as to means, etc. I have left some efficient friends in Washington,[2] who are to work for the true faith during the summer.[3]

Trip good & weather fine here.

From small clipping enclosed it looks as if the Walker-Lewis bill has passed in the House.[4]

1. On 8 June Roosevelt asked Congress to delay action on the complicated questions of unemployment compensation and old-age assistance. He recommended combining the two concerns in legislation sometime in the fall. He told Congress that he favored a program of social insurance that would put much of the responsibility on the states while assigning the federal government the tasks of maintaining and safeguarding the reserves. See his message in the *New York Times*, 9 June 1934.

2. LDB wrote this letter from Boston, on his way to Chatham for his annual summer vacation.

3. Three weeks later Roosevelt asked secretary of labor Frances Perkins to chair a new cabinet committee on economic security and to devise a program before Congress reconvened in the fall.

4. The Wagner-Lewis bill did not pass the House of Representatives.

To: Jacob H. Gilbert
Date: June 12, 1934
Place: Chatham, Massachusetts
Source: Gilbert MSS

DEAR JACK: We found your family in excellent form. The children, Louis particularly, have already gained much from the stay here. They, with Susan's supervision, got my books arranged in the study this morning. In another year, they will not need the supervision.

Have had no chance yet for a talk with Susan. She bids me return these opinions and to ask you to supply the address on Mrs. Morgan's letters, also enclosed.

Walter [Raushenbush] is so eager for Chatham, that he announced his willingness to come alone—if his mother "will give him the money for the railroad ticket".

We found Auntie B. [Evans] fairly well, but much older. I think she would appreciate a letter from you, but don't say too much about Chatham. She may not be able to come.

To: Jacob H. Gilbert
Date: July 30, 1934
Place: Chatham, Massachusetts
Source: Gilbert MSS

1. Your family was on full exhibit yesterday and never in better form. In the forenoon, Louis accompanied his grandmother, Elizabeth and Walter on a visit to Mrs. [*]. Alice [*] and gayly attired; her behavior was exemplary. In the afternoon, Susan with your Louis and Frankie came to watch over me while Elizabeth took her Mother for [a] long paddle. And Frankie "had time" to come to my room and alone entertain me & himself.

2. A generation ago (when I was deep in life insurance) I procured a copy of the N.Y. Superin[te]ndent of Insurance's annual report, which contained a full & detailed report for each of the life companies doing business within the State—covering both financial condition, etc. & insurance operations. I assume annual reports of that character are still published; & that you can get one for me (possibly through Aaron Rabinovich [*sic*]¹ or Blinken) for 1933. If the 1933 report is not yet available, I should like to have the 1932. And if there are any interim or supplementary reports (perhaps even running into 1934), let me have those also. I want to learn as much as possible of the present conditions & operations of the companies.

There is a chance that Auntie B. may come today to Chatham for a short stay. She reports herself in fine form.

1. Aaron Rabinowitz (1884–1973) was born in Russia and raised on New York's lower east side. He and his brothers made a fortune in the real estate business, and in the late 1920s Rabinowitz entered into public service. He held many advisory and administrative positions in New York under governors Smith, Roosevelt, and Lehman, and FDR appointed him an advisor to Harold Ickes and the WPA. He was at this moment serving as an advisor to the New York State Insurance Commission.

To: **Jacob H. Gilbert**
Date: **March 14, 1935**
Place: **Washington, D.C.**
Source: **Gilbert MSS**

DEAR JACK: Re yours of 13th and Kanarik & Bohm's courteous letter of March 7th to Susan, returned herewith.

1. I have always recognized the right of any writer to discuss freely my life, acts and public utterances; but never, since I became a

judge, have I "authorized" any such writing and have always refused to examine before publication what was written. In a few instances where permission was expressly asked, I have said "I do not object."

Similarly, since I became a judge, I have refused to sit for any photograph (except the official one or in connection therewith), but have recognized the right of any newspaper photographer to catch a snap of me on the street—when he could. As you know, I have likewise refused to sit for any painter or sculptor since becoming a judge. It seems to me that the rule so long acted on applies also to a motion picture.

    2. I am returning the interesting letters.
    3. We saw Sir Raymond Saturday.

To: **Elizabeth Brandeis Raushenbush**
Date: **March 26, 1935**
Place: **Washington, D.C.**
Source: **EBR**

DEAREST ELIZABETH: Your Mother who is taking a half-day rest bids me send you enclosed picture.[1] Senator Black[2] is more bold & pertinacious than wise.

Things look none too well, here & in the country. The folly of Mr. Wallace's[3] restriction program is being seen now in the cotton price drop[4] & development of growing elsewhere; and the cancelling of spring wheat restrictions for this year is impressive.

"But the world's wise are not wise,
Claiming more than mortals may."

Your Mother is, I think, as well as usual in spring; but constantly impatient of the limitation on the use of legs.

I gauge from Tom C[orcoran]'s report of talk with Witte[5] and with Ray Moley[6] (& other things) that the Social Security legislation is giving much pain; and that Madame Secretary[7] is an obstacle to concessions to lovers of the Wisconsin plan. I shall not be sorry if all unemployment legislation goes over to 1936.[8]

My greetings to your son.

    1. Enclosed with this letter was a clipping from the 26 March issue of the *New York Times,* showing LDB, with Justice Van Devanter and Chief Justice Hughes, testifying against

a bill proposed by Alabama senator Hugo L. Black (see next note) which would have permitted the appeal of injunctions directly to the Supreme Court from lower federal courts.

2. Hugo LaFayette Black (1886–1971) had been Alabama's senator since 1927. In 1937 Roosevelt was to nominate him to the Supreme Court, where he served with distinction for thirty-four years until his death. After his confirmation, revelations of his former membership in the Ku Klux Klan caused a furor, but Black turned out to be one of the most liberal justices in the history of the High Court, particularly in his uncompromising defense of the First Amendment.

3. Henry Agard Wallace (1888–1965) rose through Iowa agricultural journalism and his own studies of agricultural problems to become Roosevelt's secretary of agriculture in 1933. He was currently attempting through the Agricultural Adjustment Administration to reduce crop yields and raise farm prices. In 1940 he joined FDR on the Democratic ticket and served as vice-president during Roosevelt's third term. In 1948, dissatisfied with the conservatism of both parties, particularly in foreign affairs, he broke with the Democrats and started his own Progressive Party, receiving 1.1 million votes for the presidency that year.

4. Two weeks earlier cotton futures had fallen drastically, closing down $6 per bale. Experts blamed growing worries about government crop regulation policies under the Agricultural Adjustment Act and the rumors of ending the price support program.

5. Edwin Emil Witte (1887–1960) was another Wisconsinite actively engaged in labor and unemployment problems; he also taught economics with Elizabeth at the University of Wisconsin. He worked closely with the Raushenbushes in the development of unemployment compensation legislation, and in 1962 his book on the origins of the social security system was published posthumously.

6. Raymond Moley (1886–1975) was a key member of Franklin Roosevelt's "brain trust." He came from Columbia University, where he had taught government and law since 1923. He also wrote an influential column for *Newsweek* magazine for many years. LDB and Moley consulted frequently during the early New Deal years, and Moley was one of the conduits between LDB and the White House. In 1933 Moley resigned abruptly from his government position (assistant secretary of state) and became a private citizen. By 1939 he was a strident critic of the New Deal. He grew more and more conservative, eventually supporting Wendell Willkie, Barry Goldwater, and Richard Nixon for the presidency.

7. The first woman cabinet officer in American history was Frances Perkins (Wilson) (1880–1965). She had been a social activist in New York State (where she was closely connected with the Goldmark sisters) and worked for both Al Smith and Franklin Roosevelt when they were governors. She served as secretary of labor throughout Roosevelt's twelve years as president and recorded her impressions in *The Roosevelt I Knew* (New York, 1946).

8. By late April LDB was persuaded that the Wisconsin system of "experience rating" would survive. In the end the unemployment compensation plan was passed as a part of the Social Security Act, becoming law on 15 August 1935.

To: **Elizabeth Brandeis Raushenbush**
Date: **September 19, 1935**
Place: **Washington, D.C.**
Source: **EBR**

DEAREST ELIZABETH: You and Paul were wise in declining the Washington post.[1] "In die Beschränkung zeigt sich erst der Meister."[2]

I have sent Walter a map of the middle states found among my treasures. Now I am enclosing an envelope of stamps to be given him when you think it time to begin a stamp album. With his love of geography and of numbers it should come soon.

For Paul I am sending the quotation from Collier's of which I spoke. You and he may interested in the enclosed letter of President Eliot.[3]

Yesterday it was a fortnight since we left Chatham. It seems an age. At all events it seems as if we had always been here.

It's good to know that the index is so well advanced.[4] I might send you and Paul Eddie Berman's Bulletin No. 615,[5] but compassionately I refrain.

With love

1. Arthur Altmeyer had offered Paul Raushenbush a job in the capital, coordinating state unemployment compensation legislation. Raushenbush remained in Wisconsin, where he managed the Wisconsin program.

2. "One must first show oneself the master of small things"—one of LDB's favorite quotations. Goethe, *Was Wir Bringen* (1802).

3. Perhaps this was the letter that Harvard's president emeritus sent in May 1916 to endorse LDB's confirmation to the Supreme Court. See LDB to Stephen S. Wise, 18 May 1916, note 1, BL.

4. Elizabeth was working on the third volume of John R. Commons's monumental *History of Labor in the United States;* that volume would be published by Macmillan in 1935.

5. Edward Berman (1897–1938), a University of Illinois economist, had just written *The Massachusetts System of Savings-Bank Life Insurance,* as Bulletin #615 of the Bureau of Labor Statistics. His analysis was later published as *Life Insurance: A Critical Examination* (New York, 1936), which LDB described to Bernard Flexner as "a thrilling book" (LDB to Bernard Flexner, 19 May 1936, BL).

To: **Jacob H. Gilbert**
Date: **November 17, 1935**
Place: **Washington, D.C.**
Source: **Gilbert MSS**

DEAR JACK: Your and family greetings[1] (and the account) should have been acknowledged earlier.

The birthday, and the days since, have passed quietly. We are having great joy in re-reading Young's "The Medici."[2] They were wiser than Il Duce.[3]

1. LDB's seventy-ninth birthday had occurred four days earlier.

2. George Frederick Young's *The Medici* originally appeared in 1909 but went through numerous editions.

3. Italian dictator Benito Mussolini (1883–1945) was in the midst of his campaign to conquer Ethiopia.

To: **Paul Arthur Raushenbush**
Date: **December 2, 1935**
Place: **Washington, D.C.**
Source: **Raushenbush MSS**

DEAR PAUL: My very best to you.[1]

Ernest Draper[2] asked what I thought of the [Social] Security legislation. I spoke of its heresies; and he agreed.

I spoke to Lubin about some compilations desirable to show the delinquencies of the Big Ones, in a way that would enable the ordinary man to appreciate the iniquities perpetuated. Perhaps we shall get the presentation.

Meanwhile, you are making the best possible use of your time in perfecting the Wisconsin implement.

1. Paul Raushenbush's thirty-seventh birthday would be on 5 December.

2. Ernest Gallaudet Draper (1885–1954), after a career as a manufacturer and processor of food products, became assistant secretary of commerce that year. In 1938 Roosevelt named him to the Board of Governors of the Federal Reserve System. As a businessman, Draper pioneered in the adoption of unemployment benefits for his workers.

To:	Fannie Brandeis
Date:	May 27, 1936
Place:	Washington, D.C.
Source:	Brandeis MSS

DEAR FAN:

1. Make sure whether the Library[1] has the reports of the N[ational]. R[ecovery].A[dministration]. "Division of Review." Those are the set of posthumous reports, embodying the results of the work of the N.R.A. & (to some extent) the effects of its discontinuance.[2] These reports are not printed, they come in mimeographed form and are not distributed freely. But, I guess, a beguiling letter from you to Prof. L.C. Marshall[3] who is (or until recently was) "Director, Division of Review" may secure them. I sent one volume to H.B. Doury on the Ice business in the law shipment. And I will send one more, "Restriction of Retail Price Cutting etc" by Mark Merrill (nearly 450 pp) in the supplementary carton, which I plan to send Miss Schneider[4] before we leave for Boston next week. You had better see these two volumes before you write Prof. Marshall; but write him promptly thereafter.

2. When Prentiss Terry was here recently he discussed with me plans for the Centennial celebration[5] & projects for raising funds. I mentioned to him the proposal (discussed from time to time with you) of reaching the several sections of Louisville's population interested in the University by showing, through the Library Collections, the University's interest in them; and to that end

holding on separate days, receptions, at the Library for the different groups. The suggestion appealed to him strongly, and he thought the first reception should be held early in 1937.

As a preparation for them, I think that all bindable material ought to be bound in some form (much inexpensive in boards, etc.); but it ought to be in form to be impressive, where it can be exhibited and its extent expressed in figures.

I suggest that, this summer, the Library force go over all the material to this end. I should be disposed to pay the binding of such of the material as appears ready for binding before the fall term begins.

I hope you had happy times in Michigan.

1. At the University of Louisville.
2. The Supreme Court unanimously declared the NRA to be unconstitutional in *Schechter v. U.S.*, 295 U.S. 553 (1935). The decision came on 27 May 1935, exactly one year before this letter was written.
3. Leon Carroll Marshall (1879–1966), who headed the NRA's internal review program, taught at the University of Chicago and other universities before entering government service.
4. Evelyn Schneider was the librarian at the University of Louisville.
5. The University of Louisville, the oldest municipal university in the United States, was founded in April 1837 and opened its doors to students in the fall of that year.

To: **Susan B. and Jacob H. Gilbert**
Date: **September 23, 1936**
Place: **Washington, D.C.**
Source: **Gilbert MSS**

DEAR SUSAN & JACK: From enclosed of Pennington[1] you will see that Auntie B. is very sick—perhaps near her end.[2]

We hope you two are progressing in your dealings with the landlord, and that the children [are] happily launched on their schooling.

Thanks to Jack for the clipping. David Kahn[3] sent me one from the N.Y. Post, and the one in the Sun came from another source.[4]

This is Uncle Charles Goldmark's birthday & I have from him a beamingly happy letter over his complete recovery.

Over 4000 Jews have entered Palestine this month.

1. J. Pennington Gardiner was the nephew of Elizabeth Glendower Evans.
2. Mrs. Evans suffered illness for more than a year, finally succumbing to pneumonia on 12 December 1937.
3. David Kahn (1893–1968), a friend of the Gilberts, was a New York City businessman. He manufactured fine furniture reproductions to house radios and television sets.
4. The clippings probably were notices and reviews of the new book by Alfred Lief, *Brandeis: The Personal History of an American Ideal.* Stackpole Press in New York had

released the book on 18 September, and it was widely noticed, coming as it did weeks before LDB's extensively observed eightieth birthday.

To: Jacob H. Gilbert
Date: September 27, 1936
Place: Washington, D.C.
Source: Gilbert MSS

MY DEAR JACK: Re yours of 25th.
   I am sorry my letter disturbed you.

1. I wrote you frankly my views, because you have so often asked my advice on your business affairs.
2. With your legal ability, willingness to work hard, devotion to clients' interests, character and capacity to make friends, your practice should give you a reasonable net-income adequate to keep you free from financial worry. That conviction, formed years ago, I am unable to abandon. I have, therefore, given thought to the causes of that worry. My conclusion was, and remains, that it cannot be overcome by adventurous strokes, but by the hum-drum life—remaining at one's post and keeping down fixed charges.
3. I hope nothing I have ever said indicated a desire that you and Susan should adopt in either your professional or personal lives, views or standards on which I act now or acted when of your ages. No one is a stronger believer in the sanctity of each indi-vidual's choice.
4. But I have for 60 years been an observer of the lives of practic-ing lawyers. My conclusions are naturally based on what I have observed. You will recall what Prince Kropotkin[1] said of the ele-phant: "He is not naturally wiser than the lion or the tiger. But he lives longer, and gathers experience."
5. Don't let any past "expense" of mine trouble you. It is the future, not the past, which is of moment. But it is of the essence of wis-dom to remember the past as a guide to future action.
6. You wrote recently that if you secured the short extension the landlord would doubtless require payment of another month's rent. You will, of course, let me know if a check is needed.

Newspaper-folk here say that Landon is not making headway and that the view of the situation commonly held at the Atlantic seaboard, North, is unfounded.[2] Perhaps Frank, with his presidential lore, can give an authoritative opinion also as to future.

    1. Prince Pyotr Alekseyevich Kropotkin (1842–1921) was the famous political theorist and theoretician of modern anarchism.
    2. Roosevelt was cruising smoothly toward his overwhelming victory in the 1936 election. His Republican opponent, Alfred Mossman Landon (1887–1987), the governor of Kansas, was able to carry only the two northeastern states of Maine and Vermont.

To:	Jacob H. Gilbert
Date:	November 13, 1936
Place:	Washington, D.C.
Source:	Gilbert MSS

DEAR JACK: Re yours of 11th.

1. Our best wishes for the new offices. You have laid a good foundation.
2. We shall miss not seeing you today.[1] Elizabeth, who arrived Wednesday, leaves this evening. She plans to meet Susan and the children at the train. Josephine [Goldmark] leaves today at 1 P.M.
3. It is fine that you are getting such relief as to the knee. Be careful not to overdo—the knee carries a heavy weight.
4. A greeting, before sailing, came from your friend Jim Farley.[2]
5. Let me tell you about Baker's argument[3]—when we meet.

You must be very busy these days.
With thanks for your good wishes.
Enclosed opinions may interest you.

    1. LDB's eightieth birthday, celebrated on this date, was marked not only by his family but by many admirers and acquaintances throughout the nation. Letters and tributes poured in to him from famous and humble Americans alike, and many organizations undertook some form of tribute to his career as a reformer and judge. The letters and tributes are deposited in six full folders in the Brandeis MSS at the University of Louisville, Boxes M 9–10.
    2. James Aloysius Farley (1888–1976) was the astute and influential political tactician of the Democratic Party. He rose through New York politics to manage Roosevelt's first two campaigns and was appointed postmaster general from 1933 to 1940; he served simultaneously as head of the Democratic National Committee. He broke with FDR over the third-term issue. On 11 November Farley sailed for Europe, spending time in Ireland, London, and Paris. He returned to the United States in early December.
    3. On 10 November Newton D. Baker had participated in the argument of *Duke Power Co., et al. v. Greenwood County,* 299 U.S. 259. This complicated case began when Greenwood County, South Carolina, wanted to construct and operate a power plant and the federal government agreed to loan money for that purpose. The Duke Power Co. (represented by Baker and other attorneys) sued in district court to prevent the loan and won. Before the appeal could be heard, the federal contract was changed to avoid the difficulties that had

spelled defeat at the district level. When the Circuit Court of Appeals remanded the case back to the district for reargument in view of the new situation, it did not vacate the original order from the district court. This led to an ambiguity over jurisdiction and the nature of the retrial. The Supreme Court condemned the haste and the ambiguity of the circuit court's action, vacated the district court decree, and ordered a new trial.

To: Jacob H. Gilbert
Date: December 26, 1936
Place: Washington, D.C.
Source: Gilbert MSS

DEAR JACK: Your family left this A.M. for Mabel [Willebrandt]'s. Glorious weather, as it has been all these days.

Isaac Don Levine's call on you is cheering.[1] Possibly you and he have not seen the enclosed. I don't recall what papers I gave him.

These data [on Savings Bank Life Insurance] showing progress of the last fiscal year (which ended Oct 31) as compared with the preceding year may interest you and others:

The lapse ratio fell from 2.23 percent to 1.25 percent; the surrender ratio from 2.56 percent to 1.94 percent; the insurance in force rose 11.48 percent; that written during the year 24.65 percent.

Your children can't make a better school record.

I wore one of the green ties yesterday in honor of Xmas.

1. Isaac Don Levine (1892–1981) was a prolific author of books and articles on topics of current interest who was born in Russia and came to the United States in 1911. LDB had been trying to interest him in writing on the Savings Bank Life Insurance system.

To: Elizabeth Brandeis Raushenbush
Date: January 25, 1937
Place: Washington, D.C.
Source: EBR

DEAREST ELIZABETH: Re yours 22d.

1. Lionberger Davis[1] was here 10 days ago. According to schedule, he & his wife must now be on the Atlantic en route to Rio Janeiro.
2. Call on evening telephone Charles Ross[2] of St. Louis Post Despatch [*sic*]. Make him see that the paper should make a great campaign for unemployment reserves. Induce him to come quickly to Madison to investigate Wisconsin results & put him in touch with Wisconsin manufacturers and labor men.

I have reason to know that he is anxious (& his employer Pulitzer is) to boost his paper, after the bad slump that its defection from F.D. [Roosevelt] brought.

At Post Despatch is a younger man, Irving Dilliard,[3] who is also a good friend of Felix & mine & can be relied on if Charles Ross permits.

3. Get in touch with Irving Brant,[4] editor of the St. Louis Times-Star. He is man who wrote "Storm over the Constitution"[5] and put Post Despatch to shame. He is very intelligent, much more to the left & probably ignorant of unemployment reserves but could learn. He has been a strong supporter of me generally.

4. Despite Frances Perkins, A.F. of L. and others (who you would call "dumb") the situation is by no means hopeless. Com[missione]r Miles[6] was in yesterday (postponed a trip to N.Y. in order to do so) was so much impressed with what I told him last year. He said he brought up question with A.F. or L. & ran up against a stone-wall. But I am keeping him thinking & shall send him copy of Wall St. Journal McElwain articles of which I told him.

5. Please send me some more U.B.C. Advisors Circulars.[7]

6. Write articles.

Tell Walter, for me: "Arithmetic is the first of sciences and the mother of safety."[8]

1. Perhaps John Lionberger Davis (1879–1973), a prominent St. Louis attorney, banker, businessman, and philanthropist. He was the chairman of the board of the Security National Bank of St. Louis.

2. Charles Griffith Ross (1885–1950) was Washington correspondent for the *St. Louis Post Dispatch* for more than fifteen years before taking over the editorial page of the newspaper in 1934. In 1932 he won a Pulitzer Prize. Later Ross became the press secretary for President Harry Truman.

3. Irving Dilliard (b. 1904) would stay at the *Post Dispatch* until 1960. He was later to edit *Mr. Justice Brandeis, Great American* (St. Louis, 1941) and books on Learned Hand and Hugo Black.

4. Irving Newton Brant (1885–1976) was a St. Louis journalist for twenty years before beginning a notable career as a historian and biographer. His chief work is the six-volume biography of James Madison (Indianapolis, 1941–61).

5. Irving N. Brant, *Storm over the Constitution* (Indianapolis, 1936). In this book Brant argues that the Founding Fathers had intended more extensive federal powers than the current majority on the Supreme Court was willing to countenance.

6. Vincent Morgan Miles (1885–1947) was an Arkansas lawyer who entered public service and was presently the head of District Six of the Social Security Board. He later worked in the justice department and the post office department.

7. Circulars for the Unemployment Benefits Counselors advisors.

8. One of LDB's favorite quotations, copied into his notebook as a young man. It comes from an 1883 novel by Victor Cherbuliez, *Samuel Brohl and Partner*.

To: Jacob H. Gilbert
Date: March 24, 1937
Place: Washington, D.C.
Source: Gilbert MSS

DEAR JACK: Re yours postmarked 23rd, 4 P.M. We hope all has gone well since you wrote.

It was good of you to write so fully. We are sending your letter to Elizabeth. There must have been days of terrible anxiety for you and Susan, and even if all goes well from now on, the seriousness of the operation will compel anxious care for a long time.[1]

I am glad you went to the DeHaas funeral.[2] He served the Jewish People throughout long years, to the best of his ability.

1. The Gilberts' son Frank suffered from a double mastoid infection. Although that ailment is easily cured by antibiotics today, in the 1930s it required delicate and risky surgery.
2. Jacob deHaas, the man who had done so much to bring LDB to the Zionist movement, died of cancer at Mt. Sinai hospital, New York, on 21 March. He was sixty-five.

To: Elizabeth Brandeis Raushenbush
Date: September 20, 1937
Place: Washington, D.C.
Source: Raushenbush MSS

DEAREST ELIZABETH: The bound volume of 1936 Term opinions goes to you today.

I wish you and Paul had seen Mother during the last 10 days. She has been energetic and joyous, unlike anything at Chatham, and for months before it—quite her old self. You doubtless have felt some of this in her letters which I have not seen.

In her enterprising endeavors she is showing me Washington—the New Washington, which is markedly beautiful. Yesterday we saw the regatta—100 small sailing craft in the Potomac.

To: Jacob H. Gilbert
Date: November 2, 1937
Place: Washington, D.C.
Source: Gilbert MSS

DEAR JACK: Our congratulations to Louis G's parents.[1]

Those are certainly appreciative letters of Susan.

We count on your electing La Guardia by a large majority. If you do, Tammany will go into retirement for some time.[2]

1. This date marked Louis Gilbert's eleventh birthday.

2. Fiorello Henry La Guardia (1882–1947), the colorful and progressive New York Republican, had battled Tammany Hall since the days of the Wilson administration, first winning election to Congress in 1916. After serving in the war, he made a career out of attacking Tammany and especially New York City mayor Jimmy Walker. He won the first of his three terms as mayor in 1933. Fulfilling LDB's hopes, he triumphed on this election day, overwhelming his Democratic opponent, Jeremiah Mahoney, by 454,000 votes, one of the worst defeats ever suffered by the Tammany machine.

To: Jacob H. Gilbert
Date: January 5, 1938
Place: Washington, D.C.
Source: Gilbert MSS

DEAR JACK:

1. Frank's performance is astounding. Don't let him work too much.
2. Justice Sutherland's resignation will be regretted by all the Court despite the views on which we have disagreed.[1] He is a man of unusually high character & of true patriotism, as he considers the public welfare.
3. You may care to see enclosed opinions. No. 208 will cause much pain to many of the patent bar.[2]
4. It must be some comfort to get even a small cash fee in United Cigar.
5. Paul [Raushenbush] was here a few hours today summoned by Congressional Com[mit]tee but had to return without [our] seeing him.
6. He reports Elizabeth & Walter well.

2 encls.

7. I didn't see the N.Y. Post S.B.I. editorial.[3] Hope your Governor recommended S.B.I. in his Inaugural.[4]

1. George Sutherland (1862–1942) was a two-term senator from Utah before President Harding named him to the Supreme Court in 1922. An articulate and gentlemanly conservative, Sutherland was a leader on the Court in the anti–New Deal decisions of the mid-1930s. But despite his disagreements with LDB, the two men liked and respected each other. LDB wrote to Frankfurter on this date: "Sutherland's resignation, at this time, was like all his other acts, animated solely by sense of patriotic duty. He felt that he would soon be unable

to do the work which he thinks he should (In fact, he has done more than his share) and he felt that there should be ample time for F.D. [Roosevelt] & the Senate to consider his successor & get him worked in before the end of the term" (Urofsky and Levy, *"Half Brother, Half Son,"* 606–7). Sutherland left the Court on 17 January.

2. Case #208 was *Leitch Manufacturing Co. v. Barber Co.*, 302 U.S. 458. The Barber Company had patented a process for curing concrete by using a spray made of bituminous emulsion, which was not a patented article of commerce. When the Leitch Company supplied the emulsion to a contractor who used it in the patented process, the Barber Company sued for infringement of patent. LDB for a unanimous Court (Justice Cardozo not taking part in the case) ruled that "the patent did not confer upon The Barber Company the right to be free from competition in supplying unpatented material. . . ."

3. New York was in the midst of a debate about instituting the Savings Bank Life Insurance scheme that LDB had introduced in Massachusetts three decades before. The bill creating the system would be signed by Governor Lehman on 6 April, making New York the second state to adopt the program. The *New York Post* editorial "Mutual Savings Bank Life Insurance" appeared on 3 January 1938. It noted the campaign to establish the system in New York and concluded that, in view of the success in Massachusetts, the proposal merited full examination and discussion.

4. Governor Lehman did, in fact, advocate adoption of the Massachusetts system of Savings Bank Insurance in his inaugural address on this date.

To: **Jennie Taussig Brandeis**
Date: **February 13, 1939**
Place: **Washington, D.C.**
Source: **Mason, *Brandeis*, 634**

DEAR JENNIE: My birthday greeting goes to you a bit early. But I want you to know promptly that I am not retiring from the Court[1] because of ill health.[2] Mine seems to be as good as heretofore. But years have limited the quantity and intensity of work possible, and I think the time has come when a younger man should assume the burden.[3]

It was fine to have the photograph of you and the grandchildren.

1. On this date LDB sent to President Roosevelt a one-sentence notice of his retirement from the United States Supreme Court. On the same day Roosevelt answered: "One must perforce accept the inevitable. . . . The country has needed you through all these years, and I hope you will realize, as all your old friends do, how unanimous the nation has been in its gratitude to you. There is nothing I can do but to accede to your retirement. But with this goes the knowledge that our long association will continue and the hope that you will be spared for many long years to come to render additional services to mankind." Among the dozens of editorials, articles, and praise-filled letters that poured in was one from LDB's daughter Elizabeth: "All the things I want to say sound mawkish—or presumptuous from me to you. I cannot bear to use any words at this time that do not ring true. . . . Measuring my words, I do not see how any one person could have done more than you have done."

2. In fact, LDB's health had been declining at least since 1937. He missed most of the Court sessions in January 1939, first because of a severe case of grippe and then because of a mild heart attack. The number of opinions he produced had decreased by almost half from the years when he had his full energy as a Justice.

3. The "younger man" who replaced LDB was to be William Orville Douglas (1898–1980), a former law professor at Yale and then chair of the Securities and Exchange Commission.

552

Douglas proved to be a staunch liberal on the Court and a highly controversial figure. He was to serve for thirty-six years.

To:	Fannie Brandeis
Date:	April 20, 1939
Place:	Washington, D.C.
Source:	Fannie Brandeis

DEAR FAN: Dr. H. H. Bennett,[1] Chief of the Soil Conservation Service (Dept. of Agriculture) was in today with Morris L. Cooke to tell of the crying need for extending this service; and what is now being done. 15,000 "experts" aided by 80,000 C.C.C. boys[2] are now working in aid of the efforts of 35 states.

I asked him about Kentucky. He said Kentucky is among the states most needing aid, but that, for some unaccountable reason, no substantial interest had developed and that it is not among the 35. I suggested that the [Louisville] Courier-Journal would surely be alive to the need if properly approached, mentioning particularly Barry Bingham.[3] Dr. Bennett said there had been two editorials there, but no campaign.

I am sure you, as a farmer, will feel deeply on this matter; and I hope you will, immediately, talk to Barry Bingham and his associates.

I wonder whether the [University of Louisville] Library has all the conservation documents. Obviously it should have all.

I have two impressive ones. U.S. Dep. Agr. Miscellaneous Publications No. 321 "To Hold the Soil," and "Conservation of the Soil—a Program of Action," which I will send with the next shipment. But make sure promptly that you have all the others. Let me hear from you.

1. Hugh Hammond Bennett (1881–1960) was a leading authority on soil usage. Known as "the father of the soil conservation movement," he was appointed by Roosevelt to lead the Soil Conservation Service.

2. The Civilian Conservation Corps was one of Roosevelt's most successful New Deal programs. Part of the "first hundred days," the program put men aged eighteen to twenty-five to work on reforestation, road-building, and soil conservation projects. By 1935 more than half a million young men were living in special camps, earning federal paychecks of $30 a month—some of which was automatically sent home to their families.

3. George Barry Bingham (1906–88) was the editor and publisher of the *Louisville Courier-Journal* and a friend of the Louisville branch of the Brandeis family.

To:	Jacob H. Gilbert
Date:	May 21, 1939
Place:	Washington, D.C.
Source:	Gilbert MSS

1. Glad to know from yours of 19th of the extraordinarily fine talk Susan made at Town Hall on the work of the Board of Regents.[1]

2. Yes, I am deeply shocked, but not surprised, at British action re Palestine.[2] I am not, however, in any way discouraged. The great work in Palestine will go forward.

Tell Louis Gilbert we are glad to get his of 10th postmarked 16th. Was the Duffus article published?[3]

1. In February 1935 Susan Brandeis Gilbert was nominated by the Democrats and elected by the New York legislature to become the second woman to serve on the New York State Board of Regents, the body charged with supervising all education in the state. She attended her first meeting on 22 February 1935 and served on the board until 1949.

2. On 17 May, under the double pressure of Arab demands and the worsening condition on the continent, the British government issued the MacDonald White Paper. That document, which Zionists angrily denounced as being in direct contradiction to the promises of the Balfour Declaration, contemplated a Palestinian state to be given independence in 1949 and closely tied to Great Britain. It restricted Jewish immigration, even in the face of the mounting dangers to European Jews, to 75,000 over a five-year period and limited land transfers to less than five percent of the area of Palestine.

3. Robert Luther Duffus (1888–1972) was a longtime journalist and a prolific writer of books, articles, and editorials. From 1937 to 1962 he was attached to the editorial staff of the *New York Times*. It is impossible to tell to which of his pieces LDB and his son-in-law were referring.

To:	Elizabeth Brandeis Raushenbush
Date:	October 28, 1939
Place:	Washington, D.C.
Source:	Raushenbush MSS

DEAR ELIZABETH:

1. Mary Switzer (who was in with Josephine Roach [*sic*][1]) yesterday whispered to me as she left that she would be in next week (after her return from Boston) to tell me about her boss—and, as I understood, his talk with me.[2]

2. Josephine Roach is intending to work hard as President of the Consumers League & thinks much can be done. But she looks much older & embittered by her disappointment.[3]

3. Beulah Amidon was in today—is at work on an article on the Wages & Hours mess.[4]

4. Thanks. I shall forego reading Jerome Frank's[5] letter. He never agreed to my views on "Bigness."

5. Tell Walter that yesterday, while motoring, we passed the grounds of the Woodrow Wilson High School, where a match football game was being played; & that his Grandmother was thrilled. Clipping for Walter enclosed.

6. That was a lovely letter Fanny B[randeis]. wrote you.

Please ask Paul to send me some Cooper blades.

1. Josephine Aspinwall Roche (1886–1976) had a career in social work and social reform, including food relief in Belgium, the U.S. Children's Bureau, and the family court in Denver. She had won LDB's approval for her courageous fight against the Rockefeller interests in workers' rights (see LDB to Felix Frankfurter, 13 March 1929, BL). Roosevelt named her assistant secretary of the treasury in 1934.

2. Mary Switzer's boss was Paul McNutt; see LDB to Elizabeth Brandeis Raushenbush, 19 November 1939.

3. As assistant secretary of the treasury, Josephine Roche (starting in 1935) undertook a long and comprehensive study of the nation's health problems. In 1938 she presented her report to the president, calling for decisive governmental action to improve national health. The "disappointment" that LDB mentions here might refer to the swift negative treatment her proposals received both among leaders of the medical profession and in the Congress. Roche was elected president of the National Consumers' League in December 1938.

4. Beulah Amidon's article was "New Floors and Ceilings: The Wage and Hours Administration Reaches a Second Stage," *Survey Graphic* 28 (December 1939): 278ff. As the Federal Wage and Hours Act passed its first anniversary (on 24 October), Amidon reviewed its progress, its administration, and the difficulties that lay ahead. The "mess" that LDB refers to is probably the difficult personnel shakeup of the administrators of the act and the way in which that publicized shakeup diverted attention from both achievements and difficulties.

5. Jerome Frank (1889–1957) was a lawyer and a versatile New Deal bureaucrat. He rose to chair of the Securities and Exchange Commission when former chair William O. Douglas replaced LDB on the Supreme Court. He eventually served as judge of the circuit court of appeals for the Second Circuit. Frank is best known, however, for his writing in the area of legal philosophy and jurisprudential psychology—he became perhaps the chief advocate for the views that became known as "legal realism."

To: Elizabeth Brandeis Raushenbush
Date: November 13, 1939
Place: Washington, D.C.
Source: Raushenbush MSS

DEAR ELIZABETH: My thanks for the lovely letter.[1]

And thanks also to Walter for his—and tell him I had one also from his Grandmother [Pauline Rother] Raus[c]henbus[c]h.

For you and Paul and Walter I am enclosing Felix' opinion on the New Haven, about which the Cape is enthusiastic.[2]

And for you, a memo on Refugees, at Billikopf's[3] request.

We had Susan & the children here from Friday 8 P.M. to Sunday at 11 A.M.—a lovely visit. Frank looks better than I have ever seen him.

Mother has just come in & says she has reported on family affairs, so no more today.

But I must add—if Paul's paper is on his Unemployment Compensation work, let me have it. I am stirring up considerable interest on the question.

Lovingly

1. On the occasion of LDB's eighty-third birthday.

2. *Palmer et al., Trustees v. Massachusetts,* 308 U.S. 79, was argued on 11 October, and Justice Frankfurter delivered his opinion for a unanimous Court (Justice Butler recusing) on 6 November. The New York, New Haven & Hartford Railroad had filed for bankruptcy in October 1935. In December 1937 the bankruptcy trustees petitioned the state of Massachusetts to allow the abandonment of eighty-three of its passenger stations. The railroad's creditors, meanwhile, also petitioned the district court for the same thing. Frankfurter (who cited LDB's 1907 article on the New Haven in his first footnote) ruled that the district court had exceeded its constitutional authority in ruling on this matter and that the power belonged in the state bankruptcy court.

3. Jacob Billikopf (1883–1950), a social worker in the Midwest and later in Philadelphia, had recently turned his interest to the problems of refugees. He was active in numerous causes and organizations.

To: Jacob H. Gilbert
Date: November 16, 1939
Place: Washington, D.C.
Source: Gilbert MSS

DEAR JACK: Yours of 15th recd.

Justice Butler's death[1] will present a difficult problem for the President. A westerner, who is a Catholic and a New Dealer will natural[ly] be his desire.[2] Do you know any such?

What has been the comment on Judge Knox's decision. That disbarment may be even more important in its influence on conduct of the bar than Manton's conviction.[3]

Hope you will have an enjoyable week-end. Weather continues good here, today being almost summerlike.

Give Mrs. Rauschenbusch[4] are [*sic*] warm greetings.

1. Pierce Butler (1866–1939) was appointed to the Supreme Court by President Harding in 1922. During the 1930s he was aligned with the conservative group on the Court and firmly opposed to many of Roosevelt's New Deal initiatives. He died on this date.

2. After waiting until January 1940, Roosevelt nominated Francis ("Frank") William Murphy (1890–1949) to replace Butler. Murphy was mayor of Detroit and governor of Michigan before entering federal service and was currently Roosevelt's attorney general. He was a Democrat and a Roman Catholic.

3. Judge Martin Thomas Manton (1880–1946) was appointed to the bench in 1916. Two years later Wilson elevated him to the Circuit Court of Appeals for the Second Circuit. After the stock market crash, however, with his finances in disarray, Manton began to accept

bribes; in 1939 he was convicted and sent to prison for a year. On this date Judge John Clark Knox disbarred from all federal courts a veteran attorney named Louis Levy. Levy and Manton had been classmates at Columbia Law School, and the lawyer had arranged a $250,000 loan for Manton while the judge was sitting on a case involving a client of Levy's. Knox's disbarment order contained a sharp denunciation of Levy's conduct, specifically his failure to disclose his financial connection with Judge Manton.

4. Pauline E. Rother Rauschenbus[c]h (1864–1949) was the widow of the famous theologian Walter and the mother-in-law of LDB's daughter Elizabeth.

To: **Elizabeth Brandeis Raushenbush**
Date: **November 19, 1939**
Place: **Washington, D.C.**
Source: **Raushenbush MSS**

DEAR ELIZABETH:

1. Mary S[witzer] has been in. I judge the complaints of Social Security folk about McNutt[1] arise from the fact that he is convinced that, contrary to existing law, they are persistently administering the system as if it were—not a state-federal system—but a wholly federal system; and that they are trying to get legislation making it a wholly federal system. Mary thinks that was not Arthur Altmeyer's attitude originally, but that he is falling in line with his bureaucrats. I know from a remark McNutt made when he called that in one matter at least there was unfairness.[2]

2. Paul may receive some inquiry from Wallace Clark,[3] a Scientific Management man who for 20 years has worked mainly abroad from his London and Paris offices; has now returned to America; and says he has some time for public service. I discussed with him irregularity of employment, the Wisconsin system, etc. Gave him a copy of Paul's recent statement: "How Wisconsin Experience Rating Applies etc." I don't know much about Clark.

3. The Karl Putnams were in recently. I found that he (who is of Social Security office) had been working on Paul's memo and Merit Rating.

1. Paul Vories McNutt (1891–1955) was governor of Indiana before coming to Washington on various diplomatic and government assignments. From 1939 to 1945 he headed the Federal Security Administration.
2. For McNutt's visit to LDB, see LDB to Elizabeth B. Raushenbush, 14 October 1939, BL.
3. A consulting engineer formerly associated with LDB's ally in the efficiency movement, H. L. Gantt, Wallace Clark (1880–1948) was a prominent figure in scientific management circles.

To: Jacob H. Gilbert
Date: December 19, 1939
Place: Washington, D.C.
Source: Gilbert MSS

DEAR JACK: Re yours of 19th. We agree with you and Susan that all of my letters should be retained by you two (except so far as you may deem it advisable to destroy them.)

Our best wishes for 99 Wall St.[1]

> 1. The address of the Gilberts' new law offices.

To: Susan B. Gilbert and Elizabeth B. Raushenbush
Date: January 20, 1940
Place: Washington, D.C.
Source: Gilbert MSS

DEAR SUSAN AND ELIZABETH: Uncle Henry [Goldmark] has, for many years, been supported from funds provided partly by Aunt Chris,[1] or her estate, and partly by your mother and me. All arrangements for the support have been made by Pauline and Josephine [Goldmark]. Our contribution has been made monthly by a check to Pauline. The amount, for a long time $100 a month, has recently been only $70, the latter sum being deemed by Pauline and Josephine adequate for the time being.

If Uncle Henry should survive both your mother and me, we hope that you will, throughout his life, continue to make to Pauline and Josephine monthly payment of such sum required, not exceeding $100 a month. Your mother and I had provided by our wills for such payment. We have revoked the provisions in our wills, because we hear that Uncle Henry's wife claims that, under a separation agreement made in 1926, she has some interest in the amount paid under Aunt Chris' will. We wish to avoid the possibility of any such claim in respect to any amount coming directly or indirectly from us.

> 1. Christine Goldmark Openhym was Alice Brandeis's sister.

To: Elizabeth Brandeis Raushenbush
Date: September 9, 1940
Place: Washington, D.C.
Source: Raushenbush MSS

"Home again, home again, dancing the jig."

558

Arrived on time (11:05) after a good trip—and some fine weather at Chatham.

At 4:45 P.M. we drove to our beloved Montrose Park and found it as lovely as ever—thanks to the long-continued copious rains. We have not seen anyone here except Jackson & Susie.

Hope Walter enjoyed his first day in the Senior High.

To:	Elizabeth Brandeis Raushenbush
Date:	October 3, 1940
Place:	Washington, D.C.
Source:	Raushenbush MSS

DEAR ELIZABETH:

1. Bob's coming out for F.D. is significant.[1] Tell us what you know about it.
2. Mother sends you these clippings.
3. Lincoln Filene was in this week & was rewarded by a copy of "Steadier Jobs"[2]—But he was in poor shape physically and cheerless, so that I don't expect much from him.
4. Justice Stone, a good reader and talker, was also rewarded for his visit.
5. Have you or Paul seen Abraham Flexner's autobiography?[3] It has a special interest for me. But you also may find it very interesting.

1. Senator Robert M. La Follette, Jr., had become an increasingly vocal critic of Roosevelt's interventionist foreign policy (echoing his father's attitude in the Wilson administration). He had also led the Senate in opposing a third term for Coolidge in 1927 and 1928. Thus although he had supported FDR in 1932 and 1936, his attitude this time was by no means certain. After much soul-searching, however, and partly because he could not see much difference between the foreign policies of Roosevelt and Wendell Willkie, La Follette endorsed FDR on 30 September.

2. Elizabeth and Paul Raushenbush had organized a "Steadier Jobs" conference in Milwaukee in June. Paul was the final speaker. The proceedings were published, and this is what LDB was evidently handing out to visitors.

3. Abraham Flexner, *I Remember* (New York, 1940). The book was updated and revised in 1960, with an introduction by Allan Nevins.

To:	Walter Brandeis Raushenbush
Date:	November 20, 1940
Place:	Washington, D.C.
Source:	Raushenbush MSS

MY DEAR WALTER: It was good to get your informing birthday greeting; to learn that you are having a happy time, of the fun at football and of the expected report on the school work. Some day, I shall hope to hear more about the report.

You must have been greatly pleased by the electoral vote[1] and the re-election of Senator Bob.[2] There was much relief here—but also great concern as to many difficulties ahead.   With much love

1. On 5 November the American people returned Franklin Roosevelt for an unprecedented third term as president. Roosevelt received 449 electoral votes (from 38 states) and his Republican opponent, Wendell Willkie, received 82 (from 10 states).

2. To the satisfaction of the Wisconsin Raushenbush family, their friend Robert M. La Follette, Jr., was reelected to the Senate, running as a Progressive (as he had in 1934). He was even more controversial than before because of chairing the so-called La Follette Civil Liberties Committee from 1936 to 1940, investigating anti-labor activities in the United States. Nevertheless, he handily defeated his Democrat opponent, Fred H. Clausen, 605,609 to 553,692.

To: Elizabeth Brandeis Raushenbush
Date: December 5, 1940
Place: Washington, D.C.
Source: Raushenbush MSS

DEAR ELIZABETH: Re yours of 3rd.

1. It would not do any harm for the [Wisconsin] Progressives to start an S[avings]. B[ank]. I[nsurance]. movement at the next session. But it must be said that there is less reason for it in Wisconsin than elsewhere. The Northwestern Mutual is the best company in the United States, and I should be slow to believe that it had resorted to the practices of the other companies in attempting to beat FDR.

Irving Dilliard of the St Louis Post Dispatch writes me that determined effort to get S.B.I. will be made in Mo. And an effort will be made in Connecticut, with not only the old [*] League which came pretty near winning two years ago, but probably also Alfred M. Bingham,[1] editor of Common Sense, pushing it. In Pennsylvania, also, the S.B.I. bill may be pushed with an important bank urging it.

2. Enclose[d] carbon of letter of Morris Cooke to Golden has just come from the Advisory Commission of the Council of National Defense. That looks as if Cooke had talked to Phil Murray.[2] Please return the carbon.

560

1. Alfred M. Bingham (1905–98) was a Connecticut editor and writer who authored several popular books on political and economic affairs. In 1935 he published *Insurgent America: Revolt of the Middle Classes*.

2. Philip Murray (1886–1952) was one of organized labor's most influential figures. Born in Scotland, he arrived in America in 1902 and went to work in the coal mines of Pennsylvania. Soon he was prominent in the United Mine Workers. With the formation of the CIO in 1936, Murray was given the responsibility of organizing the steel workers. He headed that union after 1942; a month before this letter was written he replaced his friend John L. Lewis as head of the CIO.

To:	Walter Brandeis Raushenbush
Date:	December 5, 1940
Place:	Washington, D.C.
Source:	Raushenbush MSS

DEAR WALTER: Re. yours of 3rd.

Obedient to your order, I reply by return mail:

The horseshoe crab skeleton was brought us by Mr. & Mrs. Robert Bruère. They found the crab on our beach at Chatham where they lunched in October, at a fire they built.

They are good friends, who visited us in Chatham about two years ago, after Mr. Bruère was appointed chairman of the Maritime Labor Board. He had served with me, nearly thirty years ago on an arbitration board on the Garment Trade. Your Mother can doubtless tell you about them. They had a fortnight in October for a vacation and determined to spend the time on Cape Cod.

The Saturday Evening Post article will be returned to you later.

We were glad to hear from your Mother of your school record.

Lovingly

To:	Elizabeth Brandeis Raushenbush
Date:	March 7, 1941
Place:	Washington, D.C.
Source:	Raushenbush MSS

DEAR ELIZABETH: Re yours of 2d

Yes. It is a pity you didn't get Uncle Al to tell the grain story. And a much greater pity that I did not get Father to dictate to Miss Bakewell[1] the whole story of his life. The only consecutive tale I heard from him was on a long walk we took in Blankenburg in 1875. He possessed the art of story-telling.

When we meet, I will tell you what I can piece together from the bits I had from Father and Uncle Al on the grain trade.

Fanny [Brandeis] will know whether there are any books or papers that would help.

561

It will be fine if the S[ocial].S[ecurity]. Board ceases to harass Wisconsin. As Mother will have told you, we have had much beautiful weather. The S[avings].B[ank].I[insurance]. bill recommended by the Gov. of Conn. & the Legislative Com[mit]tee is now before the house.[2]

1. Bakewell was a Louisville native who probably attended Adolph Brandeis at the end of his life. See LDB to Alfred Brandeis, 3 March, 1906, BL.

2. See LDB to Elizabeth Brandeis Raushenbush, 5 December 1940. Connecticut adopted the Savings Bank Life Insurance scheme, which went into operation on 9 September 1941.

To:	Jacob H. Gilbert
Date:	March 25, 1941
Place:	Washington, D.C.
Source:	Gilbert MSS

DEAR JACK: It was lovely of you to send the footstool,[1] and much appreciated.

All the enclosures are returned herewith. The letters from your family were fine; and will be duly acknowledged.

The weather was perfect, so we had our usual drive. In the afternoon, President Kent,[2] a son and a daughter were in. Also Mittell[3] and Claytor.[4] No one else.

The day passed without anyone here or elsewhere knowing of the Fiftieth, except the immediate family and two former clients—clients of more than fifty years ago—one at Los Angeles and one in New York. The latter sent 50 roses, so we had flowers galore.

1. The footstool was a gift; on 23 March 1941 the Brandeises quietly celebrated their fiftieth wedding anniversary.

2. Dr. Raymond Asa Kent (1883–1943) succeeded George Colvin as president of the University of Louisville in 1928. He had previously taught school and been a superintendent and a dean at Northwestern University. He remained as Louisville's president until his death.

3. Sherman Fabian Mittell (1904–42) founded the National Home Library Foundation, which republished cheap editions of notable books. In 1933 Mittell's outfit had offered an inexpensive edition of LDB's *Other People's Money*.

4. One of LDB's last law clerks—serving during the October 1937 term—was William Graham Claytor, Jr. (1912–94), who had previously clerked for Learned Hand. After working for LDB, Claytor joined the prestigious Washington firm of Covington & Burling. He became an expert in railway administration, served as secretary of the navy, acting secretary of transportation, and deputy secretary of defense in the Carter administration, and ended his career as head of the Amtrak system.

To:	Pauline Goldmark
Date:	April 25, 1941
Place:	Washington, D.C.
Source:	EBR

DEAR PAULINE: It is too bad we could not have you and Do here with Elizabeth, but grand to hear from Jack [Gilbert] that you two were at (or after) the Consumers' League dinner.[1] We shall hope to see you two here in May.

La Guardia's willingness to run again is fine.[2] Also C[harles].C.B[urlingham]'s activities.[3] Thanks also for the Metropolitan bulletin.

1. On 23 April the Consumers' League of New York State celebrated its fiftieth anniversary with a gala dinner at the Roosevelt Hotel in New York City. Secretary Frances Perkins, a veteran of the organization, was present as speakers praised the record of the league in gaining legislation benefiting women workers and resolved to seek better enforcement of the existing laws.

2. There had been rumors that Fiorello La Guardia wanted a national office, possibly even as Roosevelt's running mate. He easily won reelection for a third term as New York City's mayor.

3. Charles C. Burlingham was an active supporter of La Guardia. A few days before the election he announced that LDB (who had since died) favored La Guardia, buttressing his assertion by producing a note from LDB indicating support for the mayor. Burlingham took this step because La Guardia's opponents were claiming that LDB was not in favor of his reelection. They based their allegation on the fact that Susan Brandeis had made several speeches for William O'Dwyer, La Guardia's opponent.

To: Jacob H. Gilbert
Date: April 27, 1941
Place: Washington, D.C.
Source: Gilbert MSS

DEAR JACK: It was a great relief to us to hear through your letter that Pauline & Josephine [Goldmark] were at the Consumers' League dinner,[1] although only for a short time. We had feared that they might be unable to attend.

Elizabeth celebrated her birthday with us,[2] returning to Madison on yesterday's train. She reports Paul and Walter in good form.

If you have such delightful weather as Washington has been getting, the longing for Chatham must be great indeed. That here makes me feel that I should like to be in a canoe.

1. See the previous letter.
2. Elizabeth Brandeis Raushenbush's forty-fifth birthday was on 26 April.

To: Jacob H. Gilbert
Date: May 7, 1941
Place: Washington, D.C.
Source: Gilbert MSS

DEAR JACK: Re yours of 2d & of 6th.

1. We have treated you no better than you deserved. We appreciate the fine qualities you have exhibited; the difficulties with which you have been confronted in practice; and the efforts you have made to overcome them.
2. Frank must feel quite grown up—with the long pants and his long walk alone from the school.
3. We are glad you had the Judge Richards[1] in and plan to see more of them. He is certainly an exceptionally fine man, one who enhances one's faith in our fellow men.

Our summer weather continues, with *promise* of rain.

1. Edward A. Richards (1879–1956) was a judge of the municipal court from 1907 to 1919. He left the bench to go into banking, however, and became a leader in the Savings Bank movement. He was active in getting the New York act passed that enabled savings banks to open insurance departments and became president of the Savings Bank Life Insurance Fund in New York state. He was also an active supporter of the Boy Scouts and the YMCA.

To: Elizabeth Brandeis Raushenbush
Date: July 8, 1941
Place: Chatham, Massachusetts
Source: Raushenbush MSS

DEAR ELIZABETH: It will be fine if you are leaving for Chatham today, as you thought possible. Especially so as Mother had an accident—slipping on her steps, which bruised her right arm and, as we find from an x ray, broke a little bone. All goes well, but it will be a few weeks before she has the use of the arm, and your presence here will add cheer to the company.

Happily Miss Kara is here.

Perhaps we shall see you before this reaches Madison.   Lovingly

To: Elizabeth Brandeis Raushenbush
Date: September 23, 1941
Place: Washington, D.C.
Source: Raushenbush MSS

DEAR ELIZABETH:

1. You send much good news—that Willard Hurst[1] has a fine wife; that Lloyd Garrison's[2] work on the Allis-Chalmers[3] appears to have been effective; and that Walter is enjoying his Latin.

2. Felix wants to know about the Mrs. Salter of Madison, who has been writing fine letters to the Herald-Tribune about the Lindberg [*sic*] speech.[4]

3. You may not have seen enclosed Herald-Tribune editorial.

4. I guess Lindberg has rendered the Jews a good service by his attack.

5. He certainly has put the America First crowd into a very embarrassing situation. Do you hear anything on the subject in Madison?

6. It seems a long time since your camping; but I want you to know how glad I am that it was entirely successful, and that all went well with Mother during the period.

More today.

1. James Willard Hurst (1910–97) graduated from Harvard Law School in 1935 and clerked for LDB in 1936–37. From there he went on to a long, distinguished career at the University of Wisconsin Law School, where he became a valued colleague first of Elizabeth Brandeis and then of her son, Walter Brandeis Raushenbush. He wrote numerous books and articles on the history of American law, but is perhaps best known for *The Growth of American Law* (Boston, 1950).

2. Lloyd Kirkham Garrison (1897–1991) practiced law in New York City for ten years after his graduation from Harvard Law School in 1922. From 1932 to 1945 he was the dean of the University of Wisconsin Law School. After World War II, however, he returned to New York City.

3. At its convention in Buffalo in early August, the United Auto Workers Union refused to seat the delegates from the local at the Allis-Chalmers manufacturing plant in Milwaukee. The UAW's investigating committee alleged undemocratic practices, unfair election procedures, and even the use of goons to intimidate the opponents of the local's leadership. A new election was ordered. Evidently Dean Garrison, who was experienced in labor relations and was to play a prominent role in that field during World War II, was involved in the negotiations following the controversy.

4. On 11 September the famous aviator Charles Lindbergh, who had become a leader of the isolationist America First Committee, made a speech in Des Moines under the auspices of the committee. In that speech he charged that "the administration, the Jews and the American-British are the three major agitators for American entry into war. They knew the people had no intention of going to war, so they planned first to prepare the United States for foreign war under the guise of American defense; second to involve us in the war step by step, without our realization; third to create a series of incidents which would force us into the actual conflict. If any one of these groups—the British, the Jewish, or the administration—stops agitating for war, I believe there will be little danger of our involvement." The speech is quoted extensively in the *New York Times,* 12 September 1941.

To:	**Elizabeth Brandeis Raushenbush**
Date:	**September 24, 1941**
Place:	**Washington, D.C.**
Source:	**Raushenbush MSS**

DEAR ELIZABETH: Pauline or Do has doubtless reported to you Aunt Susie [Goldmark]'s sudden illness and death.[1] We know no more than what appears from Pauline [Goldmark]'s letter and telegrams enclosed.

To me it seems a merciful ending after sixty-three years of suffering—an end come after Aunt Susie had achieved her great desire to see mountains again, and had, with marvelous courage overcome all difficulties and borne the attendant discomforts. Her cheerfulness as evidenced by the letters to Mother was remarkable; and she had gotten pleasure from being with members of the family as to whom she had long been only critical. She had lived life at its best.

Mother has borne Aunt Susie's passing with great calmness—wholly controlled.

I am enclosing John Collier's speech to his staff[2] which Mother thought you and others might care to see.

Mother had today a letter from Willard [Hurst] in which he expressed deep appreciation of you and Paul in Madison.[3]

1. Susan Goldmark had died in New York City the day before. She was seventy-nine.

2. John Collier (1884–1968) was the former social worker and activist who rose to the position of commissioner of Indian affairs in the Roosevelt administration. Serving from 1933 to 1945, Collier was the architect and tireless crusader for the so-called Indian New Deal that restored some measure of tribal sovereignty to Native Americans.

3. Shortly after this letter was written, LDB's health began to fail rapidly. On 1 October, after he and his wife returned from a ride through Rock Creek Park, he had another heart attack. On Saturday, 4 October, he sank into a coma and died at 7:15 P.M. on Sunday, 5 October. He was cremated, and on the first anniversary of his death his ashes were placed in the entranceway of the University of Louisville Law School (now the Louis D. Brandeis School of Law). When Alice Brandeis died four years later, her ashes were placed next to his.

Index

Numbers in italics indicate letters addressed to the person named.
Asterisks (*) indicate page on which a person identified in a footnote is mentioned.

Hayden, Dr., 405
Haynes, Lynn, 211, 226
Hearst, William R., 181*
Heber, Reginald, 376
Hebrew University, 318, 507
Hecht, Louis, 60*
Hecht, Mrs. Jacob, 60*
Hegman, Yetti, 456
Heine, Heinrich, 259, 399
Henderson, Gerard C., 354*
Henderson, Lucy G., 428
Heney, Francis J., 129*, 132, 163, 164, 192, 256, 280
Henle, James, 523*
Henriques, Miss, 479
Henry, Charles L., 188*
Hermann, Henry, 4
Herzl, Theodor, 424
Hewitt, Mrs., 108
Hexter, Maurice B., 525*
Heyse, Paul J. L., 13
Hickman, Herbert, 457*
Higginson, Henry Lee, 261*
Hill, Arthur D., 481*
Hill, David B., 81*
Hill, James J., 110*
Hill v. Wallace, 379
Hilles, Florence, 405*
Hilles, William S., 405*
Hillman, Sidney, 421*
Hillquit, Morris, 189*
Hills, Elsie, 404*
Hines, Walker D., 425*
Hirsch, Emil G., 270*, 271
Hirst, Francis W., 351*, 417
Hitchcock, Gilbert M., 221*
Hitz, William, 259*, 283, 311, 478
Hoars, Mrs., 147
Hobson, John A., 351*
Hodder, Mrs., 407*, 428
Hoffman, Frederick L., 233*
Holdsworth, Sir William, 449*
Holland, Rush L., 404*
Hollis, Henry F., 221*, 252
Holman, William A., 312*
Holmes, Fannie D., 481*
Holmes, John H., 474*, 505
Holmes, Oliver W., Jr., 23*, 115, 144, 171, 316, 326, 328, 353, 411, 417, 426, 434, 457, 479, 481, 519, 523
Holt, Hamilton, 191*
Holt, Miss, 54
Holt, Mrs., 58
Homer, 61

Hoover, Herbert, 306*, 309, 311, 316, 329, 336, 337, 350, 355, 359, 361–66, 371–72, 376, 445, 479, 480, 487, 492, 514, 516, 528–30
Hope-Simpson, Sir John, 498*, 502, 517
Hopkins, Mary D., 330
Horses, 39, 41, 47, 48, 53, 56, 60, 68, 70, 85, 86, 96, 98, 107–109, 126, 305–309, 312, 314
Houghton, Henry O., 33*
Hourwich, Isaac A., 233*
House, Edward M., 201*, 247, 280, 323, 337, 350, 355, 356
Houser, Walter L., 177*
Houston, David F., 217*, 367
Houston, Helen B., 367*
Howe, Frederik C., 188*
Howells, William Dean, 234*
Hoyt, Henry M., 141*
Hughes, Charles E., 117*, 120, 149, 362, 378, 379, 477
Hugo, Victor, 74
Hull, G. G., 235
Hunt, William M., 10*
Hurley, Edward N., 310*, 311
Hurst, James Willard, 564*, 566
Hutcheson, Ernest, 436*

"Incorporation of Trades Unions," 233–34
India, 83, 379
Industrial Relations Commission, 186–87
"Inefficiency of the Oligarchs," 213
International News Service v. Associated Press, 320
Interstate Commerce Commission, 114, 116, 145, 160, 175, 195, 201, 211–14, 219, 226, 230–43, 250, 252, 262, 266–68, 272, 274, 298, 310, 420, 440
Israels, Louis, 242
Italy, 10, 83
Ives, David O., 133*, 160, 162, 200, 221, 222–24, 225–26, 240
Ives, Mrs., 226, 370

Jacobs, Rose G., 476*, 490, 491
Jacobson, Blanche, 332*
James, Ollie M., 141*, 149, 152, 176, 210
James, William, 223*
Japan, 90, 95, 98, 130, 379
Jewish Agency, 464, 484, 512
Jewish National Fund, 504
Johnson, Alvin S., 414*
Johnson, Hugh S., 532*
Johnson, Mr., 66

582